ENCYCLOPEDIA OF

THE ANCIENT WORLD

ENCYCLOPEDIA OF
THE ANCIENT WORLD

Volume 1
Overviews
ʿAbd al-Malik–Corinthian War

Editor
Thomas J. Sienkewicz
Monmouth College, Illinois

——————— *Editorial Board* ———————

Lawrence Allan Conrad
North America
Western Illinois University

Geoffrey W. Conrad
South America
Indiana University

Christopher Ehret
Africa
University of California, Los Angeles

David A. Crain
Mesoamerica
South Dakota State University

Katherine Anne Harper
South and Southeast Asia
Loyola Marymount University

Robert D. Haak
Egypt, Mesopotamia, Near East
Augustana College

Chenyang Li
East Asia
Central Washington University

Thomas H. Watkins
Greece, Rome, Europe
Western Illinois University

Managing Editor, **Christina J. Moose**

SALEM PRESS, INC.

Pasadena, California   Hackensack, New Jersey

1-8-02

Editor in Chief: Dawn P. Dawson

Managing Editor: Christina J. Moose   *Research Supervisor:* Jeffry Jensen
Project Editor: Rowena Wildin   *Research Assistant:* Jeff Stephens
Acquisitions Editor: Mark Rehn   *Production Editor:* Joyce I. Buchea
Assistant Editor: Andrea E. Miller   *Graphics and Design:* James Hutson
Photograph Editor: Philip Bader   *Layout:* William Zimmerman
Administrative Assistant: Dana Garey   *Additional Layout:* Eddie Murillo

Maps by: Electronic Illustrators Group, Morgan Hill, Calif.
Cover Design: Moritz Design, Los Angeles, Calif.

Library of Congress Cataloging-in-Publication Data

Encyclopedia of the ancient world / editor, Thomas J. Sienkewicz.
   p. cm.
Includes bibliographical references and index.
   ISBN 0-89356-038-3 (set) — ISBN 0-89356-039-1 (v. 1) — ISBN 0-89356-040-5 (v. 2) — ISBN 0-89356-041-3 (v. 3)
   1. Civilization, Ancient—Encyclopedias. I. Sienkewicz, Thomas J.

CB311 .E54 2001
930′.03—dc21

                  2001049896

First Printing

CONTENTS

Publisher's Note ix
Contributors xiii
Key to Pronunciation xxi

List of Maps xxiii
Complete List of Contents xxv

OVERVIEWS

Agriculture and animal husbandry 1
Art and architecture: The Americas 6
Art and architecture: East Asia 9
Art and architecture: Europe and the
    Mediterranean region 13
Art and architecture: India 20
Art and architecture: Southeast Asia 25
Art and architecture: West and
    South Africa 28
Calendars and chronology 31
Daily life and customs 40
Death and burial 46
Education and training 51
Government and law 57

Languages and literature 64
Medicine and health 74
Navigation and transportation 86
Performing arts 92
Philosophy 100
Religion and ritual 106
Science 114
Settlements and social structure 124
Sports and entertainment 130
Technology 138
Trade and commerce 144
War and weapons 151
Women's life 160
Writing systems 166

ENCYCLOPEDIA

ʿAbd al-Malik 177
ʿAbd Allāh ibn al-ʿAbbās 178
ʿAbd Allāh ibn az-Zubayr 179
ʿAbd Allāh ibn Saʿd ibn Abī Sarḥ 179
Abipón 180
Abraha 181
Abū Bakr 181
Accius, Lucius 182
Achaean League 182
Achaean War 183
Achaemenian Dynasty 183
Achilles Painter 185
Achilles Tatius 185
Acte, Claudia 186
Actium, Battle of 187
Adena culture 187

Adrianople, Battle of 188
Advaita 188
Aegospotami, Battle of 189
Ælle 190
Aemilius Paullus, Lucius 191
Aeneas 191
Aeschines 192
Aeschylus 193
Aesop 194
Æthelbert 195
Aetolian League 196
Afanasievo culture 196
Afrasans 197
Africa, East and South 198
Africa, North 201
Africa, West 203

African rock art, southern and eastern 206
Agapetus, Saint 207
Agariste 207
Agathias 208
Agathon 209
Agaw 209
Agesilaus II of Sparta 210
Agricola, Gnaeus Julius 211
Agrippa, Marcus Vipsanius 211
Agrippina the Elder 212
Agrippina the Younger 213
Ahab 213
Aidan, Saint 214
Aiñkurunūru 215
Ainu 215
ʿĀʾishah bint Abī Bakr 216
Ājīvikas 217
Akanānūru 218
Akapana pyramid 218
Akhenaton 219
Akiba ben Joseph 220
Akkadians 220
Alani 221
Alaric I 222
Alaric II 223
Alboin 223
Alcaeus of Lesbos 224
Alcibiades of Athens 225
Alcman 225
Alesia, Battle of 226
Aleutian tradition 227
Alexander Polyhistor, Lucius Cornelius 228
Alexander the Great 228
Alexandrian library 230
Alexandrian patriarchs 231
ʿAlī ibn Abī Ṭālib 231
Allemanni 232
Altar de Sacrificios 232
Alwa 233
Amaravātī school 233
Amaru 234
Amasis Painter 235
Amazonia 235
Ambrose 237
American Paleo-Arctic tradition 237
Ammianus Marcellinus 238
Amos 239
ʿAmr ibn al-ʿĀṣ Mosque 239
Anacreon 240
Ānanda 240

Anasazi 241
Anastasius I 242
Anatolia 243
Andes, central 244
Andes, south 246
Andhradesha school 248
Andocides 248
Andronovo culture 249
Aneirin 250
Angles, Saxons, Jutes 250
Ankhesenamen 251
Antae 252
Anthemius of Tralles 253
Anthony of Egypt, Saint 253
Antigonid Dynasty 254
Antiochus the Great 255
Antipater 255
Antipater of Idumaea 256
Antiphon 257
Antonia the Elder 257
Antonia the Younger 258
Antoninus Pius 258
Antony, Marc 259
Anyte of Tegea 260
Apedemak 260
Apollodorus of Athens (artist) 261
Apollodorus of Athens (scholar) 261
Apollodorus the Architect 262
Apollonius of Perga 263
Apollonius of Tyana 263
Apollonius Rhodius 264
Appar 265
Appian 265
Appian Way 266
Apuleius, Lucius 266
Aqhat epic 267
Ara Pacis 268
Arabia 268
Arakanese 270
Arameans 271
Āraṇyakas 272
Aratus 273
Arausio, Battle of 273
Arawak 274
Archaic North American culture 275
Archaic South American culture 275
Archaic tradition, northern 276
Archidamian War 277
Archidamus II of Sparta 278
Archidamus III of Sparta 278

Archilochus of Paros	279
Archimedes	279
Archytas of Tarentum	280
Arctic Small Tool tradition	281
Ardashīr I	281
Aretaeus of Cappadocia	282
Argead Dynasty	283
Argishti I	283
Arianism	284
Aristarchus of Samos	285
Aristarchus of Samothrace	286
Aristides	286
Aristides of Athens	287
Aristides of Miletus	287
Aristophanes	288
Aristotle	289
Arkamani	290
Armenia	291
Arminius	292
Arria the Elder	293
Arrian	294
Arsacid Dynasty	294
Artabanus I-V	295
Artavasdes II of Armenia	296
Artemis, temple of, at Ephesus	296
Artemisia I	297
Artemisia II	298
Arthur	298
Āryabhaṭa	299
Asaṅga	299
Ashurbanipal	300
Ashvaghosa	301
Aśoka	301
Aspasia of Miletus	302
Assyria	303
Astyages	306
Āśvalāyana	307
Athanasius of Alexandria, Saint	307
Athens	308
Atlatl	311
Atossa	311
Atrahasis epic	312
Attalid Dynasty	312
Atticus, Titus Pomponius	313
Attila	314
Augustine, Saint	315
Augustine of Canterbury, Saint	316
Augustus	317
Aurelianus, Lucius Domitius	318
Ausonius, Decimus Magnus	318
Australia, Tasmania, New Zealand	319
Avesta	322
Avitus, Eparchius	322
Axum	323
Babylonia	325
Bacchylides	328
Bactria	329
Ball game, Mesoamerican	330
Ban Gu	331
Bāṇa	331
Banpocun culture	332
Bantu, Congo Basin	333
Bantu, Mashariki	334
Bar Kokhba	335
Basil of Cappadocia, Saint	335
Bathsheba	336
BaTwa	337
Beaker people	338
Beja	338
Belisarius	339
Ben-Hadad I	340
Benedict Biscop, Saint	340
Benedict of Nursia, Saint	341
Berbers	342
Bhagavadgītā	343
Bharata Muni	344
Bhāravi	344
Bhartṛhari	345
Bhāsa	345
Bhavabhūti	346
Bible: Jewish	347
Bible: New Testament	348
Black Pottery culture	349
Bodhidharma	350
Boethius	350
Book of the Dead	351
Boudicca	352
Boylston Street weir	353
Brāhmaṇas	354
Brahmanism	354
Brasidas of Sparta	355
Brazil, eastern	356
Britain	357
Brutus	360
Buddha	360
Buddhism	362
Buddhist cave temples	364
Budhasvāmin	364
Byzantine Empire	365

Caesar, Julius 369
Cai Lun 370
Cajamarca pottery 370
California peoples 371
Caligula 372
Callicrates 373
Callimachus of Cyrene 374
Calpurnius Siculus, Titus 374
Camillus, Marcus Furius 375
Campantar 375
Canaanites 376
Caṅkam 377
Cannae, Battle of 377
Cao Cao 378
Cao Zhi 379
Capella, Martianus 379
Caracalla 380
Caratacus 380
Caribbean 381
Carrhae, Battle of 382
Carthage 382
Cartimandua 385
Cassander 386
Cassian 387
Cassiodorus 387
Cassius 388
Cassivellaunus 389
Cātanār 389
Catiline 390
Cato the Censor 390
Cato the Younger 391
Catullus 392
Celsus 393
Celsus, Aulus Cornelius 393
Celts 394
Chadic peoples 398
Chaeronea, Battle of 399
Chalcedon, Council of 399
Châlons, Battle of 400
Chandragupta Maurya 401
Chavín de Huántar 402

Chichén Itzá 402
Chifumbaze culture 403
China 404
Chinchorro mummies 409
Chlotar I 410
Cholula 410
Christianity 411
Chunqiu 414
Cicero 414
Cimmerians 416
Cimon 416
Cincinnatus, Lucius Quinctius 417
Claudian 418
Claudius 418
Claudius Caecus, Appius 419
Cleisthenes of Athens 420
Cleisthenes of Sicyon 420
Clement of Alexandria 421
Clement I 421
Cleon of Athens 422
Cleopatra VII 423
Clodia 424
Clodius Pulcher, Publius 425
Clovis 425
Clovis technological complex 426
Cobá 427
Cochise culture 428
Colossus of Rhodes 429
Columba, Saint 430
Columella 430
Commius 431
Confucianism 431
Confucius 434
Constans I 435
Constantine the Great 435
Constantinople 436
Constantius I-III 437
Copán 438
Copper Belt 439
Corbulo, Gnaeus Domitius 439
Corinthian War 440

PUBLISHER'S NOTE

Salem Press's three-volume *Encyclopedia of the Ancient World* presents a survey of the cultures and civilizations of the world from prehistory through about 700 C.E. In addition to providing comprehensive coverage of the ancient Greeks and Romans, often regarded as the foundation of Western civilization, the encyclopedia examines the civilizations, cultures, traditions, monuments and artifacts, significant wars and battles, and important personages of the rest of the world: Europe (outside Greece and Rome), Africa, the Americas, Asia, and Oceania. The set also provides descriptions of important documents of antiquity, definitions of selected terms, and overviews of general topics that provide cross-cultural views of the ancient world. The 1,195 articles consist of 26 overviews and 1,169 alphabetically arranged encyclopedic articles that range from 250-word biographies of important figures such as Marc Antony and Xunzi to 2,500-word essays on major subjects such as Imperial Rome and Classical Greece.

The time span covered in this encyclopedia ranges from prehistory to about 700 C.E., and the date given for each essay reflects this emphasis, although the civilization or group might have existed beyond this date. Occasionally, coverage has been extended a few hundred years to complete coverage of a topic (such as a civilization) that naturally ends at that later date.

To enable readers accurately to identify literature or ancient documents mentioned within essays, references to these works contain the original title (when available) in its original language and the date of first publication as well as the title and date of any English translation in publication. For a number of the untranslated works, an English rendering of the title appears in lower case and in quotation marks.

The overviews are presented in alphabetical order, with subheads to guide the reader to specific geographical areas or topics of interest within them. The encyclopedic entries are presented in alphabetical order, in ready-reference format with top matter highlighting pertinent information such as date, location, and significance of cultures and civilizations and birth and death dates, associated civilizations, and major role or position of important military and cultural leaders. For the essays on traditions, monuments or artifacts, documents, and places or sites, the top matter includes the date, location, associated civilizations, and significance. The essays on wars and battles, in addition to providing the date, locale, associated civilizations, and significance, contain boldfaced subheads such as "Background," "Action," and "Consequences" to make them easy to understand and absorb. Pronunciations for most of the less familiar names and places used in essay titles appear at first mention of the name or place in the text for the essays. The guide to pronunciation that appears in the front matter of each volume provides a key to the pronunciation system used in this encyclopedia.

Ample cross-references guide readers to entries that may further their understanding of each topic. Each essay contains a short list of resources—appropriate and up-to-date books and articles—for further study. This set features 25 maps of selected areas within the ancient world, about 25 sidebars and short time lines, and about 300 informative illustrations and photographs. For easy reference, a list of maps, complete with page numbers, is located in the front matter to every volume.

To enable users to easily understand how the ancient world developed over time, the encyclopedia features a chronological listing of its 1,169 entries as well as a general time line that places significant events of the ancient world in chronological order. In order for readers to access articles by geographical locale, the set provides a list that categorizes the essays by 22 geographical regions, with some essays falling into more than one region. The largest number of articles are on Rome (288), followed by Greece (212), India and South Asia (105), China and Tibet (91), Africa (68), Near East (57), Europe (54), North America (41), South America (33), Egypt (33), Persia (31), Mesopotamia (28), British Isles and the Celts (27), Armenia and Anatolia (25), Arabia and Muslim Near East (21), Japan and Korea (21), Mesoamerica (20), worldwide (26), Central Asia (16), Alexandria (15), Southeast Asia (9), and Oceania (8).

A separate categorized list of all entries makes it easy for the reader to find all the essays that address a particular subject area. The essays are grouped into 40 categories. The more than 550 personages are classified into 300 rulers and military/political leaders, 110 religious figures, 109 poets, playwrights, and performers, 55 philosophers, 56 writers and scribes, 50 women, 32 historians, 21 scientists, inventors, and mathematicians, 12 orators, 12 medical practitioners, 9 lawgivers (along with laws and edicts), 9 geographers, 7 grammarians, 7 sculptors, 7 architects, 6 painters, and 3 biographers (some are in duplicate categories). Some 108 civilizations, 77 cultures, 30 dynasties and empires, 18 cities, and 3 leagues appear, as well as places and sites in Africa (14), Anatolia and Armenia (10), Central Asia (4), East Asia (16), Egypt (5), Europe (27), Mesoamerica (13), Middle East (11), Near East (4), Oceania (6), South America (7), and South and Southeast Asia (16). Other major categories are art, architecture, and monuments (62), documents (54), religion (66), and wars, battles, and treaties (43).

The set also contains a glossary defining more than 160 words found within the text. For further research, the set includes a list of about 120 Web sites and a categorized bibliography. Finding information on a particular topic is made easy by the inclusion of a comprehensive general index as well as a personages index.

Due to the wide scope of *Encyclopedia of the Ancient World*, it includes many names and words that must be transliterated from languages that do not use the Roman alphabet, and in some cases, there is more than one transliterated form in use. In most cases, transliterated words in this set follow the American Library Association and Library of Congress (ALA-LC) transliteration format for that language. These include Arabic, Greek, Hebrew, Japanese, Khmer, Korean, Lao, Sanskrit, Thai, and Tibetan. Chinese is transliterated using the Pinyin system as detailed below. See below for more about the ALA-LC transliteration of Arabic and Sanskrit. In some cases, a topic heading is a form of a name or word that is judged to be the most common and useful, though it does not fit the ALA-LC transliteration format for that language. In all cases, topic headings include the common variants of names or words, and these alternate forms are cross-referenced in the index.

Chinese: The Pinyin transliteration is used for Chinese topics. The Wade-Giles transliteration, as well as older or traditional spellings, are included as variants. For example, "Gu Kaizhi," "Also known as: *Wade-Giles* Ku K'ai-chih; Changkang." In a few cases, a Chinese topic will be listed by a common name that is not a Pinyin transliteration. For example, the topic heading for the philosopher Confucius is "Confucius," and variants are listed as follows: "Kong Qui; *Wade-Giles* K'ung Ch'iu."

Arabic: Words in Arabic are transliterated using the ALA-LC format except in cases in which a well-known figure has a common English name that would be obscured by the use of the ALA-LC format. When there is a common form, the ALA-LC name is included as a variant. To provide pronunciation information, the ALA-LC transliteration of Arabic uses diacritical marks that are likely to be unfamiliar to many readers. The following is a simple explanation of the most common diacritical marks used in the ALA-LC transliteration of Arabic, but these rules are not exhaustive or definitive: Macrons such as $\bar{a}$ or $\bar{\imath}$ indicate a long vowel. Subdots indicate an emphatic pronunciation of that letter: h strongly aspirated *h*, s like *ts*, z like *dh*. An ayn (ʿ) indicates a throaty guttural, and a hamza (ʾ) is close to a glottal catch.

The American Library Association and Library of Congress (ALA-LC) transliteration has been used for most of the Sanskrit words in the set. As with Arabic, a variety of transliteration methods are in use, and in some cases, a more common form of a word has been used. When possible, the ALA-LC form of the word is provided as a variant of the more common form. The following is a simple explanation of the most common diacritical marks used in the ALA-LC transliteration of Sanskrit, but these rules are not exhaustive or definitive: Some long vowels are indicated by a macron ($\bar{a}$, $\bar{\imath}$, and $\bar{u}$); other vowels (*e*, *ai*, *o*, and *au*) are regularly long and are not modified with a macron. The letter r indicates a vocalic *r* like a purring sound. The letter *h* indicates aspiration including in *th* and *ph* (pronounced as in *coathook* and *uphill*). The letters *t*, *d*, and *n* are dentals as in English pronounced with the tongue against the teeth; when used with a subdot (*t*, *d*, and *n*), they indicate retroflex consonants pronounced with the tongue far back in the mouth. The letter s and $ś$ indicate slightly differing sounds, both close to *sh*.

Latin: Latin nomenclature uses three names: *praenomen*, *nomen* or family name, and *cognomen*. In this set, most individuals are listed by their *nomen*, but some individuals are listed by their common English name. For example, Marcus (*praenomen*) Tullius (*nomen*) Cicero (*cognomen*), commonly known as Cicero, is listed as "Cicero" in the topic heading, with the variants listed as follows: "Also known as: Marcus Tullius Cicero." In addition, Marcus Tullius Cicero is cross-referenced in the index as Tullius Cicero, Marcus.

Many Roman men had at least two names, a *prae-*

nomen and the family name or *nomen*. Roman women are given the grammatically feminine form of their father's *nomen*. Marcus Tullius Cicero's daughter is Tullia. If there are two daughters they are called Major and Minor for elder and younger. In addition to the *praenomen* and *nomen*, some Roman men had a *cognomen*. In some cases, this is the common English name of famous Romans such as Caesar, Cicero, and Scipio. A name may have more than one *cognomen*, and these are typically nicknames or titles given for military success. Marcus Porcius Cato is commonly known as Cato the Censor, or in Latin, Marcus Porcius Cato Censorius. For his military victories over Carthage (an area called Africa by the Romans), Publius Cornelius Scipio became Publius Cornelius Scipio Africanus.

Notable exceptions to these basic rules are Augustus and the emperors following him. Augustus was born Gaius Octavius and by adoption became Gaius Julius Caesar Octavianus. In 27 B.C.E., he was given a very honorable and quasi-religious name, Augustus. This is one reason that he is called the first Roman emperor. All subsequent emperors took the name Caesar Augustus followed by their *praenomen*, *nomen*, and *cognomen*.

Creating an encyclopedia of the ancient world requires the expertise of many scholars. Salem Press would like to thank the many academicians—historians, archaeologists/anthropologists, literature specialists, and others—who have contributed to *Encyclopedia of the Ancient World*. Salem would also like to thank Thomas J. Sienkewicz, Minnie Billings Capron Professor of Classics and Departmental Chair at Monmouth College in Monmouth, Illinois, for his expertise, advice, and enthusiasm as the project's Editor and for working with a group of colleagues—Lawrence Allan Conrad of Western Illinois University (North America), Geoffrey W. Conrad of Indiana University (South America); Christopher Ehret of the University of California, Los Angeles (Africa), David A. Crain of South Dakota State University (Mesoamerica), Katherine Anne Harper of Loyola Marymount University (South and Southeast Asia), Robert D. Haak of Augustana College (Egypt, Mesopotamia, Near East), Chenyang Li of Central Washington University (East Asia), Thomas H. Watkins of Western Illinois University (Greece, Rome, Europe)—and creating the list of topics that fill this encyclopedia.

CONTRIBUTORS

Amy Ackerberg-Hastings
Iowa State University

Andrew Adams
North Central College

Patrick Adcock
Henderson State University

Neil Adkin
University of Nebraska—Lincoln

Richard Adler
University of Michigan—Dearborn

J. M. Adovasio
Mercyhurst Archaeological Institute

Mark Aldenderfer
*University of California,
    Santa Barbara*

Emily Alward
Henderson, Nevada, District Libraries

Roger W. Anderson, Jr.
North Central College

Stephen J. Andrews
*Midwestern Baptist Theological
    Seminary*

James A. Arieti
Hampden-Sydney College

Jerome S. Arkenberg
California State University, Fullerton

O. Kimball Armayor
University of Alabama

Robert J. Ball
University of Hawaii at Manoa

Barry L. Bandstra
Hope College

Carl L. Bankston III
Tulane University

Bernard F. Barcio
Butler University

David Barratt
Independent Scholar

Thomas F. Barry
Himeji Dokkyo University

Rozmeri Basic
University of Oklahoma

Emily E. Batinski
Louisiana State University

Barbara C. Beattie
Independent Scholar

Patricia A. Behlar
Pittsburg State University

Albert A. Bell, Jr.
Hope College

Evelyn E. Bell
San Jose State University

Alvin K. Benson
Brigham Young University

Milton Berman
University of Rochester

Robert L. Berner
*University of Wisconsin—
    Oshkosh*

Richard M. Berthold
Independent Scholar

Margaret Boe Birns
New York University

Nicholas Birns
New School University

Robert Black
Southern Wesleyan University

Walter C. Bouzard, Jr.
Wartburg College

Denvy A. Bowman
Coastal Carolina University

Thomas Vester Brisco
*Southwestern Baptist Theological
    Seminary*

Norbert Brockman
St. Mary's University of San Antonio

E. Bruce Brooks
*University of Massachusetts at
    Amherst*

David L. Browman
Washington University

Daniel C. Browning, Jr.
William Carey College

Alexander M. Bruce
Florida Southern College

Fred Buchstein
John Carroll University/Dix & Eaton

John Buckler
University of Illinois

John M. Bullard
Wofford College

Kenneth L. Burres
Central Methodist College

Joan B. Burton
Trinity University

Joseph P. Byrne
Belmont University

Kenneth R. Calvert
Hillsdale College

Edmund J. Campion
University of Tennessee

Byron D. Cannon
University of Utah

Robert W. Cape, Jr.
Austin College

Roy L. Carlson
Simon Fraser University

Richard C. Carrier
Columbia University

Donald E. Cellini
Adrian College

Paul John Chara, Jr.
Northwestern College

Frederick B. Chary
Indiana University Northwest

Mark W. Chavalas
University of Wisconsin—La Crosse

Dennis C. Chowenhill
Chabot Community College

Stefan G. Chrissanthos
California State University, Fullerton

Thomas Clarkin
San Antonio College

Douglas Clouatre
Kennesaw State University

Weston F. Cook, Jr.
*University of North Carolina
   at Pembroke*

J. S. Costa
Independent Scholar

David A. Crain
South Dakota State University

Thomas I. Crimando
SUNY College at Brockport

Robert D. Cromey
Virginia Commonwealth University

Edward R. Crowther
Adams State College

Robert I. Curtis
University of Georgia

Touraj Daryaee
California State University, Fullerton

Janet B. Davis
Truman State University

Paul K. Davis
University of Texas at San Antonio

Rene M. Descartes
SUNY, Cobleskill

M. Casey Diana
*University of Illinois at Urbana-
   Champaign*

Jeffrey Dippmann
Central Washington University

T. Keith Dix
University of Georgia

Sviatoslav Dmitriev
Harvard University

Stephen B. Dobrow
Fairleigh Dickinson University

Margaret A. Dodson
Independent Scholar

William J. Dominik
University of Natal

John P. Doohen
Morningside College

Steven L. Driever
University of Missouri, Kansas City

Laura Rinaldi Dufresne
Winthrop University

Ronald J. Duncan
Oklahoma Baptist University

William E. Dunstan
North Carolina State University

Tammy Jo Eckhart
Indiana University, Bloomington

Wilton Eckley
Colorado School of Mines

Christopher Ehret
University of California, Los Angeles

Victoria Erhart
The Catholic University of America

Roger S. Evans
Payne Theological Seminary

Todd William Ewing
William Baptist College

Carol C. Fan
University of Hawaii at Manoa

Stephen Felder
University of California, Irvine

Jonathan Fenno
College of Charleston

Lester L. Field, Jr.
University of Mississippi

Michael S. Fitzgerald
Pikeville College

Richard D. Fitzgerald
Onondaga Community College

Dale L. Flesher
University of Mississippi

E. P. Flores-Meiser
Ball State University

Edwin D. Floyd
University of Pittsburgh

Michael J. Fontenot
Southern University at Baton Rouge

Robert J. Forman
St. John's University, New York

Catherine Cymone Fourshey
University of California, Los Angeles

R. M. Frakes
Clarion University

Donald R. Franceschetti
University of Memphis

C. George Fry
University of Findlay

Richard N. Frye
Harvard University

G-Young Gang
Yeungnam University

Elizabeth A. Gardiner
Independent Scholar

Keith Garebian
Independent Scholar

Abigail J. Gertner
Independent Scholar

Jon L. Gibson
University of Southwestern Louisiana

Kristin L. Gleeson
Independent Scholar

Marc Goldstein
Independent Scholar

Nancy M. Gordon
Independent Scholar

Margaret Bozenna Goscilo
University of Pittsburgh

Karen K. Gould
Independent Scholar

Johnpeter Horst Grill
Mississippi State University

Mark Gustafson
Calvin College

Robert D. Haak
Augustana College

Michael Haas
Independent Scholar

Irwin Halfond
McKendree College

Brian Hancock
Rutgers University Libraries

Craig L. Hanson
Muskingum College

Robin G. Hanson
Muskingum College

Kenneth W. Harl
Tulane University

Katherine Anne Harper
Loyola Marymount University

Atsuko Hattori
University of Pennsylvania Museum

Darlene L. Brooks Hedstrom
Miami University

Noelle Heenan
Bronx High School of Science

Brigitte Hees
California State University, Hayward

Arthur W. Helweg
Western Michigan University

Diane Andrews Henningfeld
Adrian College

Ceferina Gayo Hess
Lander University

Anna Dunlap Higgins
Gordon College

John R. Holmes
Franciscan University of Steubenville

James P. Holoka
Eastern Michigan University

William L. Hommel
University of Central Oklahoma

Leslie J. Hoppe
Catholic Theological Union

Michael B. Hornum
*R. Christopher Goodwin &
 Assoc., Inc.*

Melissa Hovsepian
University of St. Thomas

Randall S. Howarth
Mercyhurst College

George J. Hoynacki
Merrimack College

Patrick Norman Hunt
Stanford University

Mary Hurd
East Tennessee State University

Raymond Pierre Hylton
Virginia Union University

M. Mehdi Ilhan
Middle East Technical University

Robert Jacobs
Central Washington University

Ian Janssen
University of Miami

Martha G. Jenks
Illinois Wesleyan University

Edward Johnson
University of New Orleans

Hiroko Johnson
*California State University,
 San Diego*

Leah Johnson
Wayne State University

Linda L. Johnson
Concordia College

Sheila Golburgh Johnson
Independent Scholar

Robert R. Jones
Granite School District

Sondra Jones
Brigham Young University

Charles L. Kammer III
The College of Wooster

Sugwon Kang
Hartwick College

John W. Killigrew
SUNY, College at Brockport

Leigh Husband Kimmel
Independent Scholar

Grove Koger
Boise (Idaho) Public Library

J. Kenneth Kuntz
University of Iowa

David J. Ladouceur
University of Notre Dame

Philip E. Lampe
University of the Incarnate Word

David H. J. Larmour
Texas Tech University

Erik W. Larson
Florida International University

Eugene Larson
Pierce College

George F. Lau
Yale University

Melinda Leach
University of North Dakota

Thomas T. Lewis
Mount Senario College

Charles Xingzhong Li
Central Washington University

Chenyang Li
Central Washington University

Patricia Lin
*California State Polytechnic
    University, Pomona*

Victor Lindsey
East Central University

Sherwin D. Little
Indian Hill High School

Lihua Liu
People's University of China

Craig E. Lloyd
College of Mount St. Joseph

Lloyd Michael Lohr
Independent Scholar

Ronald W. Long
*West Virginia University Institute
    of Technology*

Scott Lowe
University of North Dakota

Zhaolu Lu
Tiffin University

Eric v.d. Luft
SUNY, Upstate Medical University

Herbert Luft
Pepperdine University

Jeremiah B. McCall
Ohio State University

Joseph M. McCarthy
Suffolk University

T. Davina McClain
Loyola University, New Orleans

Sara MacDonald
St. Thomas University

William P. McDonald
Tennesee Wesleyan College

Thomas McGeary
Illinois State Geological Survey

Michael J. McGrath
Georgia Southern University

Heather I. McKillop
Louisiana State University

Michelle C. K. McKowen
Independent Scholar

John M. McMahon
Le Moyne College

Emerson Thomas McMullen
Georgia Southern University

Wilfred E. Major
Loyola University, New Orleans

Mark J. Mangano
Minnesota Bible College

Nancy Farm Mannikko
Michigan Technological University

Hubert M. Martin, Jr.
University of Kentucky

Marc Mastrangelo
Dickinson College

Jennifer P. Mathews
Trinity University

Ralph W. Mathisen
University of South Carolina

Frederick C. Matusiak
University of Southern Colorado

Ruben G. Mendoza
*California State University,
    Monterey Bay*

Elizabeth L. Meyers
Onondaga Community College

Martin C. J. Miller
Metropolitan State College of Denver

Diana H. Minsky
Bard College

R. Scott Moore
University of Dayton

William V. Moore
College of Charleston

Terry R. Morris
Shorter College

Hans-Friedrich Mueller
Florida State University

B. Keith Murphy
Fort Valley State University

Alex L. Mwakikoti
University of Texas at Arlington

Alice Myers
Simon's Rock of Bard College

John E. Myers
Simon's Rock of Bard College

Byron J. Nakamura
University of Washington

Christopher Nappa
University of Minnesota

Kari Naso
*The Cleveland Museum of Natural
    History*

William Nelles
*University of Massachusetts at
    Dartmouth*

David Langdon Nelson
Dallastown Area Schools

Edwin L. Neville, Jr.
Canisius College

Ann M. Nicgorski
Willamette University

John A. Nichols
Slippery Rock University

Eric Niderost
Chabot College

Joanne Mannell Noel
Montana State University

James B. North
*Cincinnati Bible College and
Seminary*

Bradley P. Nystrom
*California State University,
Sacramento*

John Maxwell O'Brien
Queens College

Steve O'Bryan
Metropolitan State College of Denver

Shawn O'Bryhim
Southern Illinois University

Charles M. Odahl
Boise State University

Sara E. Orel
Truman State University

Sandra L. Orellana
*California State University,
Dominguez Hills*

James H. Pace
Elon College

Catherine Pagani
University of Alabama

Ranee K. L. Panjabi
*Memorial University of
Newfoundland*

Sophia Papaioannou
University of Tennessee

Zoe A. Pappas
Columbia University

Robert J. Paradowski
Rochester Institute of Technology

Robert L. Patterson
Armstrong Atlantic State University

Michael C. Paul
University of Miami

Mary L. B. Pendergraft
Wake Forest University

John Pepple
Kenyon College

James L. Persoon
Grand Valley State University

George E. Pesely
Austin Peay State University

Nis Petersen
New Jersey City University

Alan P. Peterson
Gordon College

David B. Pettinari
American Classical League

John R. Phillips
Purdue University—Calumet

Christopher Sean Planeaux
*Indiana University—Purdue
University at Indianapolis*

Thomas C. Pleger
University of Wisconsin—Fox Valley

George R. Plitnik
Frostburg State University

Oliver B. Pollak
University of Nebraska at Omaha

John Grady Powell
Independent Scholar

Luke A. Powers
Tennessee State University

Frances Skoczylas Pownall
University of Alberta

William H. Race
University of North Carolina

Kokila Ravi
Morehouse College

Michaela Crawford Reaves
California Lutheran University

Paul L. Redditt
Georgetown College

Rosemary M. Canfield Reisman
Charleston Southern University

Ralf Erik Remshardt
University of Florida

Thomas Renna
Saginaw Valley State University

Burnam W. Reynolds
Asbury College

Edward A. Riedinger
Ohio State University Libraries

Edward J. Rielly
Saint Joseph's College

Andrew M. Riggsby
University of Texas at Austin

Duane W. Roller
Ohio State University

F. E. Romer
University of Arizona

Michele Valerie Ronnick
Wayne State University

Shawn A. Ross
University of Washington

Jonathan P. Roth
San Jose State University

Robert Rousselle
Independent Scholar

Adriane Ruggiero
Independent Scholar

Scott M. Rusch
University of Pennsylvania

Irene Struthers Rush
Independent Scholar

Brian Rutishauser
Fresno City College

Ronald H. Sack
North Carolina State University

Christina A. Salowey
Hollins University

D. Brent Sandy
Grace College

Reinhold Schumann
Boston University

Stephen Scully
Boston University

Judith Lynn Sebesta
University of South Dakota

Nancy Serwint
Arizona State University

Susan O. Shapiro
Xavier University

Jo-Ann Shelton
University of California, Santa Barbara

Kenneth R. Shepherd
Henry Ford Community College

R. Baird Shuman
University of Illinois at Urbana-Champaign

James P. Sickinger
Florida State University

Thomas J. Sienkewicz
Monmouth College

Jeffrey Sikkenga
Ashland University

Narasingha P. Sil
Western Oregon University

Michael J. Siler
California State University, Los Angeles

Michael Bland Simmons
Auburn University at Montgomery

Michael W. Simpson
Chimanade University

Andrew C. Skinner
Brigham Young University

Svetla Slaveva-Griffin
Florida State University

James O. Smith
Moberly Area Community College

Roger Smith
Independent Scholar

Larry Smolucha
Benedictine University

Sonia Sorrell
Pepperdine University

Oguz Soysal
University of Chicago

Carl P. E. Springer
Illinois State University

James Stanlaw
Illinois State University

Kelli E. Stanley
San Francisco State University

Steven M. Stannish
Miami University

August W. Staub
University of Georgia

Barry M. Stentiford
Grambling State University

Stephen A. Stertz
Mercy College

Joan C. Stevenson
Western Washington University

Fred Strickert
Wartburg College

Sally A. Struthers
Sinclair Community College

Lealan N. Swanson
Jackson State University

Patricia E. Sweeney
Independent Scholar

Glenn L. Swygart
Tennessee Temple University

Guillaume de Syon
Albright College

Kumiko Takahara
University of Colorado

Robert D. Talbott
University of Northern Iowa

Andrius Tamulis
Cardinal Stritch University

Kenneth B. Tankersley
Kent State University

Daniel J. Taravella
Western New England College

Alison Taufer
California State University, Los Angeles

Donathan Taylor
Hardin-Simmons University

Gregory S. Taylor
Grambling State University

Jeremiah R. Taylor
Independent Scholar

Timothy M. Teeter
Georgia Southern University

Cassandra Lee Tellier
Capital University

Carol G. Thomas
University of Washington

Burt Thorp
University of North Dakota

Mary G. Tindle
Independent Scholar

A. G. Traver
Southeastern Louisiana University

David Treviño
Texas A&M University, Kingsville

C. Wayne Tucker
Hampden-Sydney College

Lee Ann Turner
Boise State University

Kriston J. Udd
Michigan Theological Seminary

Jiu-Hwa Lo Upshur
Eastern Michigan University

Salli Vargis
Georgia Perimeter College

Renee Beauchamp Walker
Skidmore College

Allen M. Ward
University of Connecticut

Annita Marie Ward
Salem-Teikyo University

Albert T. Watanabe
Louisiana State University

Thomas H. Watkins
Western Illinois University

William E. Watson
Immaculata College

Ronald J. Weber
University of Texas at El Paso

Marcia J. Weiss
Point Park College

Richard Westall
Stanford University

Thomas Willard
University of Arizona

Leland Edward Wilshire
Biola University

Joseph P. Wilson
University of Scranton

Richard L. Wilson
University of Tennessee, Chattanooga

John D. Windhausen
Saint Anselm College

Shelley Amiste Wolbrink
Drury University

Andrew Wolpert
University of Wisconsin, Madison

Michelle R. Woodward
University of Colorado

Ian Worthington
University of Missouri—Columbia

Lisa A. Wroble
Redford Twp. District Library

Hong Xiao
Central Washington University

Edwin Yamauchi
Miami University

Juliana Y. Yuan
University of Missouri—St. Louis

Yiwei Zheng
St. Cloud State University

Jonathon R. Ziskind
University of Louisville

KEY TO PRONUNCIATION

Many of the topics covered in the encyclopedia may be unfamiliar to students and general readers. For most of the more unfamiliar topics covered in these volumes, the editors have attempted to provide some guidelines to pronunciation upon first mention of the topic in text. These guidelines do not purport to achieve the subtleties of the languages in question but will offer readers a rough equivalent of how English speakers may approximate the proper pronunciation.

Symbols	Pronounced As In	Spelled Phonetically As
a	answer, laugh, sample, that	AN-sihr, laf, SAM-pul, that
ah	father, hospital	FAH-thur, HAHS-pih-tul
aw	awful, caught	AW-ful, kawt
ay	blaze, fade, waiter, weigh	blayz, fayd, WAYT-ur, way
ch	beach, chimp	beech, chihmp
eh	bed, head, said	behd, hehd, sehd
ee	believe, cedar, leader, liter	bee-LEEV, SEE-dur, LEED-ur, LEE-tur
ew	boot, lose	bewt, lews
g	beg, disguise, get	behg, dihs-GIZ, geht
i	buy, height, lie, surprise	bi, hit, li, sur-PRIZ
ih	bitter, pill	BIH-tur, pihl
j	digit, edge, jet	DIH-jiht, ehj, jeht
k	cat, kitten, hex	kat, KIH-tehn, hehks
o	cotton, hot	CO-tuhn, hot
oh	below, coat, note, wholesome	bee-LOH, coht, noht, HOHL-suhm
oo	good, look	good, look
ow	couch, how	kowch, how
oy	boy, coin	boy, koyn
s	cellar, save, scent	SEL-ur, sayv, sehnt
sh	champagne, issue, shop	sham-PAYN, IH-shew, shop
uh	about, butter, enough, other	uh-BOWT, BUH-tur, ee-NUHF, UH-thur
ur	birth, disturb, earth, letter	burth, dihs-TURB, urth, LEH-tur
y	useful, young	YEWS-ful, yuhng
z	business, zest	BIHZ-ness, zest
zh	vision	VIH-zhuhn

MAPS

Ancient World, The, 200-500 C.E. I–125

Assyria and Babylonia, 600-500 B.C.E.. . . . . . I–304

Australia and the South Pacific. I–320

Byzantine Empire, circa 565 C.E.. . . . . I–366

Carthage, circa 800-146 B.C.E. I–383

Celtic Europe, 60 B.C.E.. . . . . I–395

Chavín Culture and the Central Andes,
　　Selected Sites in the I–245

China During the Han Dynasty II–599

China During the Warring States
　　Period I–408

Eastern and Southern Africa,
　　Selected Sites in Ancient I–199

Egypt, Eighteenth Dynasty,
　　circa 1550-1352 B.C.E. II–490

Egypt, Old Kingdom,
　　circa 2700-2200 B.C.E. II–495

Greece, Classical, Fifth Century B.C.E. II–574

Hellenistic World, The, 185 B.C.E. III–996

Indian Kingdoms and Empires,
　　400 B.C.E.-500 C.E. II–644

Israel and Judah II–663

Mesoamerican Cities and Areas,
　　Ancient II–772

North American Sites and Areas,
　　Ancient II–487

Persian Empire, 500 B.C.E.. . . . . II–883

Rome, Imperial, circa 200 C.E. III–960

Sāsānian Empire, Sixth Century C.E.. . . . . . III–986

Southeast Asia, Centers of Power
　　in Ancient. II–544

Sumer and Akkad III–1047

Western and Northern Africa,
　　Selected Sites in Ancient I–204

Western Europe, circa 500 C.E. II–562

Complete List of Contents

Volume 1

Overviews

Agriculture and animal husbandry 1
Art and architecture: The Americas 6
Art and architecture: East Asia 9
Art and architecture: Europe and the
    Mediterranean region 13
Art and architecture: India 20
Art and architecture: Southeast Asia 25
Art and architecture: West and
    South Africa 28
Calendars and chronology 31
Daily life and customs 40
Death and burial 46
Education and training 51
Government and law 57

Languages and literature 64
Medicine and health 74
Navigation and transportation 86
Performing arts 92
Philosophy 100
Religion and ritual 106
Science 114
Settlements and social structure 124
Sports and entertainment 130
Technology 138
Trade and commerce 144
War and weapons 151
Women's life 160
Writing systems 166

Encyclopedia

ʿAbd al-Malik 177
ʿAbd Allāh ibn al-ʿAbbās 178
ʿAbd Allāh ibn az-Zubayr 179
ʿAbd Allāh ibn Saʿd ibn Abī Sarḥ 179
Abipón 180
Abraha 181
Abū Bakr 181
Accius, Lucius 182
Achaean League 182
Achaean War 183
Achaemenian Dynasty 183
Achilles Painter 185
Achilles Tatius 185
Acte, Claudia 186
Actium, Battle of 187
Adena culture 187
Adrianople, Battle of 188
Advaita 188
Aegospotami, Battle of 189
Ælle 190

Aemilius Paullus, Lucius 191
Aeneas 191
Aeschines 192
Aeschylus 193
Aesop 194
Æthelbert 195
Aetolian League 196
Afanasievo culture 196
Afrasans 197
Africa, East and South 198
Africa, North 201
Africa, West 203
African rock art, southern and eastern 206
Agapetus, Saint 207
Agariste 207
Agathias 208
Agathon 209
Agaw 209
Agesilaus II of Sparta 210
Agricola, Gnaeus Julius 211

Agrippa, Marcus Vipsanius 211
Agrippina the Elder 212
Agrippina the Younger 213
Ahab 213
Aidan, Saint 214
Aiñkururnūru 215
Ainu 215
ʿĀʾishah bint Abī Bakr 216
Ājīvikas 217
Akanāṉūṟu 218
Akapana pyramid 218
Akhenaton 219
Akiba ben Joseph 220
Akkadians 220
Alani 221
Alaric I 222
Alaric II 223
Alboin 223
Alcaeus of Lesbos 224
Alcibiades of Athens 225
Alcman 225
Alesia, Battle of 226
Aleutian tradition 227
Alexander Polyhistor, Lucius Cornelius 228
Alexander the Great 228
Alexandrian library 230
Alexandrian patriarchs 231
ʿAlī ibn Abī Ṭālib 231
Allemanni 232
Altar de Sacrificios 232
Alwa 233
Amaravātī school 233
Amaru 234
Amasis Painter 235
Amazonia 235
Ambrose 237
American Paleo-Arctic tradition 237
Ammianus Marcellinus 238
Amos 239
ʿAmr ibn al-ʿĀṣ Mosque 239
Anacreon 240
Ānanda 240
Anasazi 241
Anastasius I 242
Anatolia 243
Andes, central 244
Andes, south 246
Andhradesha school 248
Andocides 248
Andronovo culture 249

Aneirin 250
Angles, Saxons, Jutes 250
Ankhesenamen 251
Antae 252
Anthemius of Tralles 253
Anthony of Egypt, Saint 253
Antigonid Dynasty 254
Antiochus the Great 255
Antipater 255
Antipater of Idumaea 256
Antiphon 257
Antonia the Elder 257
Antonia the Younger 258
Antoninus Pius 258
Antony, Marc 259
Anyte of Tegea 260
Apedemak 260
Apollodorus of Athens (artist) 261
Apollodorus of Athens (scholar) 261
Apollodorus the Architect 262
Apollonius of Perga 263
Apollonius of Tyana 263
Apollonius Rhodius 264
Appar 265
Appian 265
Appian Way 266
Apuleius, Lucius 266
Aqhat epic 267
Ara Pacis 268
Arabia 268
Arakanese 270
Arameans 271
Āraṇyakas 272
Aratus 273
Arausio, Battle of 273
Arawak 274
Archaic North American culture 275
Archaic South American culture 275
Archaic tradition, northern 276
Archidamian War 277
Archidamus II of Sparta 278
Archidamus III of Sparta 278
Archilochus of Paros 279
Archimedes 279
Archytas of Tarentum 280
Arctic Small Tool tradition 281
Ardashīr I 281
Aretaeus of Cappadocia 282
Argead Dynasty 283
Argishti I 283

Arianism 284
Aristarchus of Samos 285
Aristarchus of Samothrace 286
Aristides 286
Aristides of Athens 287
Aristides of Miletus 287
Aristophanes 288
Aristotle 289
Arkamani 290
Armenia 291
Arminius 292
Arria the Elder 293
Arrian 294
Arsacid Dynasty 294
Artabanus I-V 295
Artavasdes II of Armenia 296
Artemis, temple of, at Ephesus 296
Artemisia I 297
Artemisia II 298
Arthur 298
Āryabhaṭa 299
Asaṅga 299
Ashurbanipal 300
Ashvaghosa 301
Aśoka 301
Aspasia of Miletus 302
Assyria 303
Astyages 306
Āśvalāyana 307
Athanasius of Alexandria, Saint 307
Athens 308
Atlatl 311
Atossa 311
Atrahasis epic 312
Attalid Dynasty 312
Atticus, Titus Pomponius 313
Attila 314
Augustine, Saint 315
Augustine of Canterbury, Saint 316
Augustus 317
Aurelianus, Lucius Domitius 318
Ausonius, Decimus Magnus 318
Australia, Tasmania, New Zealand 319
Avesta 322
Avitus, Eparchius 322
Axum 323

Babylonia 325
Bacchylides 328
Bactria 329

Ball game, Mesoamerican 330
Ban Gu 331
Bāṇa 331
Banpocun culture 332
Bantu, Congo Basin 333
Bantu, Mashariki 334
Bar Kokhba 335
Basil of Cappadocia, Saint 335
Bathsheba 336
BaTwa 337
Beaker people 338
Beja 338
Belisarius 339
Ben-Hadad I 340
Benedict Biscop, Saint 340
Benedict of Nursia, Saint 341
Berbers 342
Bhagavadgītā 343
Bharata Muni 344
Bhāravi 344
Bhartṛhari 345
Bhāsa 345
Bhavabhūti 346
Bible: Jewish 347
Bible: New Testament 348
Black Pottery culture 349
Bodhidharma 350
Boethius 350
Book of the Dead 351
Boudicca 352
Boylston Street weir 353
Brāhmaṇas 354
Brahmanism 354
Brasidas of Sparta 355
Brazil, eastern 356
Britain 357
Brutus 360
Buddha 360
Buddhism 362
Buddhist cave temples 364
Budhasvāmin 364
Byzantine Empire 365

Caesar, Julius 369
Cai Lun 370
Cajamarca pottery 370
California peoples 371
Caligula 372
Callicrates 373
Callimachus of Cyrene 374

Calpurnius Siculus, Titus 374
Camillus, Marcus Furius 375
Campantar 375
Canaanites 376
Caṅkam 377
Cannae, Battle of 377
Cao Cao 378
Cao Zhi 379
Capella, Martianus 379
Caracalla 380
Caratacus 380
Caribbean 381
Carrhae, Battle of 382
Carthage 382
Cartimandua 385
Cassander 386
Cassian 387
Cassiodorus 387
Cassius 388
Cassivellaunus 389
Cātaṇār 389
Catiline 390
Cato the Censor 390
Cato the Younger 391
Catullus 392
Celsus 393
Celsus, Aulus Cornelius 393
Celts 394
Chadic peoples 398
Chaeronea, Battle of 399
Chalcedon, Council of 399
Châlons, Battle of 400
Chandragupta Maurya 401
Chavín de Huántar 402
Chichén Itzá 402
Chifumbaze culture 403
China 404
Chinchorro mummies 409

Chlotar I 410
Cholula 410
Christianity 411
Chunqiu 414
Cicero 414
Cimmerians 416
Cimon 416
Cincinnatus, Lucius Quinctius 417
Claudian 418
Claudius 418
Claudius Caecus, Appius 419
Cleisthenes of Athens 420
Cleisthenes of Sicyon 420
Clement of Alexandria 421
Clement I 421
Cleon of Athens 422
Cleopatra VII 423
Clodia 424
Clodius Pulcher, Publius 425
Clovis 425
Clovis technological complex 426
Cobá 427
Cochise culture 428
Colossus of Rhodes 429
Columba, Saint 430
Columella 430
Commius 431
Confucianism 431
Confucius 434
Constans I 435
Constantine the Great 435
Constantinople 436
Constantius I-III 437
Copán 438
Copper Belt 439
Corbulo, Gnaeus Domitius 439
Corinthian War 440

Volume 2

Coriolanus, Gnaeus Marcius 441
Cornelia 441
Crassus, Marcus Licinius 442
Crates of Athens 442

Cratinus 443
Crete 443
Critias of Athens 447
Croesus 448

Cunaxa, Battle of 449
Cunobelinus 449
Curtius Rufus, Quintus 450
Cushites 451
Cyaxares 452
Cyclades 452
Cynoscephalae, Battle of 453
Cyprian of Carthage, Saint 454
Cyprus 455
Cypselus of Corinth 457
Cyril of Alexandria, Saint 457
Cyrus the Great 458

Dallán Forgaill 460
Dalton tradition 460
Damascus document 461
Daṇḍin 461
Daoism 462
Darius the Great 463
Darius III 464
David 465
Dead Sea Scrolls 465
Delphi 466
Demetrius Phalereus 467
Demetrius Poliorcetes 468
Democritus 468
Demosthenes 469
Denis, Saint 470
Deptford culture 470
Dhammapada 471
Diadochi 472
Dido 473
Dio Cassius 474
Dio Chrysostom 475
Diocles of Carystus 475
Diocletian 476
Diogenes of Sinope 476
Dionysius I the Elder of Syracuse 478
Dionysius the Younger 478
Divinity 479
Djanggawul cycle 479
Domitian 480
Donatism 480
Donatus, Aelius 481
Dong Zhongshu 482
Dorset phase 482
Draco 483
Dreaming 483
Dzibilchaltún 484

Eastern African Microlithic/
    Khoisan peoples 485
Eastern peoples 485
Edwin 488
Egypt, Pharaonic 488
Egypt, Prepharaonic 494
Egypt, Ptolemaic and Roman 496
El Tajín 499
Eleusinian mysteries 499
Elijah 500
Ennius, Quintus 501
Epaminondas 501
Ephialtes of Athens 502
Epictetus 503
Epicurus 503
Erasistratus 504
Eratosthenes of Cyrene 505
Erinna 506
Esarhaddon 506
Essenes 507
Ethiopia 508
Etruscans 510
Euclid 513
Eudocia 514
Eudoxia, Aelia 514
Eudoxus 515
Eumenes II 516
Eupalinus of Megara 516
Eupolis 517
Euripides 517
Eusebius of Caesarea 518
Eutropius 519
Exodus 520
Ezana 521
Ezekiel 521
Ezra 522

Fabius 523
Fabius Maximus, Quintus 523
Fabius Pictor, Quintus 524
Faustina I 525
Faustina II 525
Faxian 526
Fertile Crescent 526
Figulus, Publius Nigidius 528
Finnic peoples 528
Flamininus, Titus Quinctius 529
Flavian Amphitheater 530
Folsom technological complex 531
Fortunatus, Venantius 532

Four Emperors, Year of the 532
Four Hundred 533
France. 534
Franks. 537
Fremont culture 539
Frontinus, Sextus Julius. 539
Fronto, Marcus Cornelius. 540
Frumentius, Saint 541
Fu Hao's tomb 541
Fulgentius, Fabius Planciades 542
Fulvia 542
Funan 543

Galen 545
Galerius Valerius Maximianus, Gaius 546
Gallic Wars 546
Gallienus 547
Gandhāra art 548
Garamantes 548
Gash civilization 549
Gaudapāda 550
Gaugamela, Battle of 550
Gauls 551
Ge Hong 553
Gellius, Aulus. 553
Gelon of Syracuse 554
Germany 554
Ghana 556
Gigaku 557
Gilgamesh epic 557
Gnosticism 558
Gorgias 559
Gortyn, law code of. 559
Gosāla Maskarīputra 560
Goths 561
Gracchus, Tiberius Sempronius, and
    Gracchus, Gaius Sempronius 563
Granicus, Battle of 564
Gratian 565
Great Basin peoples. 566
Great Wall of China. 567
Greco-Persian Wars. 568
Greece, Archaic. 569
Greece, Classical 572
Greece, Hellenistic and Roman 578
Greece, Mycenaean 583
Gregory of Nazianzus. 586
Gregory the Great. 587
Gu Kaizhi 587
Guang Wudi. 588

Guṇāḍhya 589
Gupta emperors 589
Gyges 590

Hadrian 592
Hadrian's villa 593
Haghia Sophia 593
Halafian culture 595
Halicarnassus mausoleum 595
Hallstatt culture 596
Hammurabi's code 597
Han Dynasty 599
Han Feizi 600
Haniwa 600
Hannibal 601
Harivaṃśa 602
Harkhuf 602
Harmodius and Aristogiton 603
Harṣa 603
Hatshepsut 604
Hattusilis I 605
Hawaii 606
He Yan 606
Hecataeus of Miletus 607
Helena, Saint 608
Heliodorus of Emesa 608
Helton phase 609
Henotheism 609
Herodas 610
Herodian 610
Herodian Dynasty. 611
Herodotus 611
Heron 613
Herophilus 613
Hesiod. 614
Hesychius of Alexandria 614
Hezekiah 615
Hieron I of Syracuse 616
Hieron II of Syracuse. 617
Hilary of Poitiers, Saint. 617
Himiko 618
Hinduism 618
Hipparchus 620
Hippias of Athens. 621
Hippocrates 622
Histiaeus of Miletus 622
Hittites 623
Hohokam culture 625
Homer. 626
Horace 627

Hortensia 628
Hosea 629
Huaca de la Luna 629
Huaca del Sol 630
Huainanzi 630
Huangdi 631
Hui Shi 632
Huiyuan 632
Huns 633
Hurrians 634
Ḥusayn 635
Hydaspes, Battle of 635
Hyginus 637
Hyginus, Gaius Julius 637
Hyksos 638
Hypatia 639

Iamblichus of Syria 640
Ibycus 640
Ictinus 641
Ignatius of Antioch 641
Iḷaṅkō Aṭikaḷ 642
Imhotep 642
India 643
Indian temple architecture 648
Indus Valley civilization 650
Ion of Chios 651
Ionian Revolt 652
Ipiutak 652
Ireland 653
Irenaeus, Saint 655
Isaeus 656
Isaiah 657
Isidore of Seville, Saint 658
Isis, cult of 658
Islam 659
Isocrates 661
Israel 662
Issus, Battle of 666

Jainism 668
James the Apostle 669
Japan 669
Jātakas 673
Java 674
Jehu 675
Jeremiah 675
Jeroboam I 676
Jerome, Saint 676
Jerusalem, temple of 677

Jesus Christ 678
Jewish diaspora 679
Jimmu Tennō 680
Jingū 680
Johanan ben Zakkai 681
John Chrysostom, Saint 682
John the Baptist, Saint 682
John the Evangelist, Saint 683
Jōmon 684
Jordanes 684
Josephus, Flavius 685
Josiah 686
Juba I of Numidia 687
Juba II of Mauretania 687
Judaism 688
Jugurtha 690
Julia (daughter of Augustus) 690
Julia (daughter of Julius Caesar) 691
Julia Domna 692
Julia Mamaea 692
Julian the Apostate 693
Junius Brutus, Lucius 693
Justin Martyr, Saint 694
Justinian I 695
Justinian's codes 695
Juvenal 696

Kachemak tradition 697
Kadesh, Battle of 697
Kaleb 698
Kālidāsa 698
Kalittokai 699
Kaniṣka 700
Karaikkal Ammaiyar 701
Karasuk culture 701
Kaska 702
Kassites 702
Kauṭilya 703
Kelteminar culture 703
Kerma 704
Khoikhoi 706
Khoisan 707
King's Peace 708
Kitoi culture 708
Kofun period 709
Koguryŏ style 710
Korea 710
Kuruntokai 713
Kushān Dynasty 714

La Florida pyramid 715
La Tène culture 715
Labarnas I. 716
Lactantius, Lucius Caelius Firmianus 716
Langobards 717
Laos 718
Laozi 719
Latin League and War 720
Laurel culture 720
Legalists 721
Leo I (emperor) 722
Leo I, Saint 722
Leonidas 723
Leucippus 724
Leuctra, Battle of 724
Leyden plate 725
Liangzhu culture 725
Licinius, Valerius Licinianus 726
Licinius Lucullus, Lucius 726
Lima culture 727
Linear B 727
Ling Lun 728
Liu Xie 729
Liu Yiqing 729
Livia Drusilla 730
Livius Andronicus, Lucius 730
Livy 731
Locarno Beach 731
Longinus 732
Longshan culture 732
Longus 733
Lü Buwei 733
Lu Ji 734
Lucan 735
Lucian 735
Lucilius, Gaius (poet) 736
Lucilius, Gaius (satirist) 737
Lucretia 737
Lucretius 738
Luwians 738
Lycia 739
Lycurgus of Sparta 740
Lydia 741
Lysander of Sparta 742
Lysias 743
Lysimachus 743
Lysippus 744

Maccabees 745
Macedonia 745

Macrobius, Aurelius Theodosius 748
Madagascar 749
Maecenas, Gaius 750
Magna Graecia 751
Magnesia ad Sipylum, Battle of 753
Mahābhārata 753
Mahābodhi temple 754
Mahendravarman I 755
Makouria 756
Malalas, John 757
Malay 757
Mande 758
Manichaeanism 759
Manilius, Marcus 760
Mantinea, Battles of 760
Mao Shan revelations 761
Marathon, Battle of 762
Marcus Aurelius 763
Marcus Aurelius's column 764
Maritime Archaic 764
Marius, Gaius 765
Maroboduus 765
Marpole phase 766
Martial 766
Mary 767
Masada, Battle of 768
Mauryan Dynasty 769
Mausolus 769
Maxentius 770
Maximian 770
Maya 771
Mela, Pomponius 775
Melanesia 775
Meleager of Gadara 777
Menander (Greco-Bactrian king) 778
Menander (playwright) 779
Mencius 780
Menelaus of Alexandria 780
Menippus of Gadara 781
Merenptah 781
Merovingian Dynasty 782
Messallina, Valeria 783
Messenian Wars 784
Microblade tradition, Northwest 784
Micronesia 785
Midas 787
Middle Woodland tradition 787
Milan, Edict of 789
Milinda-pañha 790
Miltiades the Younger 790

Milvian Bridge, Battle of 791
Mimaji 792
Mimnermus 792
Minucius Felix, Marcus 793
Mitanni 794
Mithradates I 795
Mithradates II 795
Mithradates VI Eupator 796
Mithrism 797
Mixtecs 798
Moabites 800
Moche culture 801
Mogollon culture 802
Mon-Khmer 803
Mongolia 804
Monophysitism 806
Montanism 807
Monte Albán 807
Montuhotep I 809
Moschus of Syracuse 809
Moses 810
Mozi 811
Mu'allaqāt, Al- 811
Muḥammad 812
Mulanshi 813
Mummius, Lucius 814
Muwatallis 814
Mycenae, palace of 815
Myron 817

Naevius, Gnaeus 818
Napata and Meroe 818
Nārāyaṇa 821
Narriṇai 822
Narses (Byzantine military leader) 822
Narses (Sāsānian emperor) 823
Nasca culture 824
Natufian culture 825
Nāṭya-śāstra 825
Nebuchadnezzar II 826
Nefertiti 827
Nemesianus 828
Neolithic Age Europe 828
Neoplatonism 830
Nepos, Cornelius 831
Nero 831
Nerva, Marcus Cocceius 832
Nestorius 833
Nicaea, Council of 833
Nicander of Colophon 834

Nicias of Athens 835
Nicolaus of Damascus 835
Nicomachus of Gerasa 836
Niger-Congo 836
Nihon shoki 838
Nilo-Saharans 839
Nilotes 840
Nine Saints 841
Nintoku 842
Nobatae 842
Nok culture 843
Nonnus of Panopolis 844
Northern Wei Dynasty 844
Norton tradition 845
Nubia 846

Octavia 849
Odoacer 849
Ōjin Tennō 850
Old Copper complex 851
Olmecs 851
Olympias 854
Olympic Games 855
Omotic peoples 856
Oribasius 856
Origen 857
Orphism 857
Ovid 858

Pachomius, Saint 860
Pacuvius, Marcus 860
Paeonius 861
Pak Hyŏkkŏse 861
Palenque 862
Paleo-Indians in North America 863
Paleo-Indians in South America 864
Palermo stone 865
Palladius, Rutilius Taurus Aemilianus 865
Pallava Dynasty 866
Panaetius of Rhodes 867
Pāṇini 867
Pantheon 868
Paripāṭal 869
Parmenides 869
Parthenon 870
Parthia 871
Pārvatī Devī temple 873
Patiṉeṇkīlkkaṇakku 873
Patirruppattu 874
Patrick, Saint 875

Paul, Saint. 875
Paulinus, Saint 877
Paulinus of Nola, Saint 877
Pausanias of Sparta 878
Pausanias the Traveler 878
Pelagianism. 879
Peloponnesian War 880
Periander of Corinth 881
Pericles 881

Persia 882
Persius Flaccus, Aulus 886
Peruṅkatai. 887
Peter, Saint 887
Petronius Arbiter 889
Peyar 890
Phaedrus 890
Pharos of Alexandria 891
Pharsalus, Battle of 892

Volume 3

Phidias 893
Philip II 893
Philip V 894
Philippi, Battle of 895
Philistines 895
Philo of Alexandria 896
Philochorus 897
Philodemus 897
Philostratus, Flavius 898
Phineas 898
Phoenicia 899
Phrygia 902
Picts 903
Pindar 904
Pisistratus 905
Pittacus of Mytilene 905
Piye 906
Plains peoples. 906
Plataea, Battle of 908
Plateau peoples 909
Plato. 910
Plautus 911
Plebeian secession 912
Pliny the Elder 912
Pliny the Younger. 913
Plotinus 914
Plutarch 914
Polybius. 915
Polyclitus 916
Polycrates of Samos 916
Polygnotus 917
Polynesia 918
Pompeii and Herculaneum 920

Pompey the Great. 921
Poppaea Sabina 922
Porphyry 923
Posidonius 923
Poverty Point 924
Poykai. 925
Praxiteles 926
Pre-Socratic philosophers. 926
Priscian 928
Priscillian 928
Procopius 929
Propertius 929
Protagoras. 930
Prudentius, Aurelius Clemens 931
Ptolemaic Dynasty 931
Ptolemy 933
Publilius Syrus 933
Punic Wars 934
Puranāṉūṟu 935
Purāṇas 936
Pūtāṉ 937
Pyramid of the Moon 937
Pyramids and the Sphinx 938
Pyrrhon of Elis 939
Pythagoras 940
Pytheas 941
Pyu 942

Qijia culture. 943
Qin Dynasty. 943
Qin tomb 944
Qu Yuan. 945
Quinctilius Varus, Publius 946

Quintilian 946
Quintus Smyrnaeus 947
Qur'ān 947

Radegunda, Saint 949
Raimondi stone 949
Rāmāyaṇa 950
Rameses II 951
Rameses III 952
Recuay 953
Res Gestae Divi Augusti 953
Rift Valley system 954
Roman arch 955
Roman Forum 955
Rome, Imperial 957
Rome, Prerepublican 962
Rome, Republican 964
Romulus and Remus 969
Romulus Augustulus 970
Rosetta stone 971
Rutilius Claudius Namatianus 972

Sabina, Vibia 973
Sacred Wars 973
Saharan rock art 974
Saint Mungo phase 975
Saite Dynasty 975
Salamis, Battle of 976
Sallust 977
Salvianus 978
Samarran culture 978
Sammu-ramat 979
Samson 980
Samuel 981
Sappho 982
Saracen conquest 982
Sarduri I 983
Sarduri II 983
Sarduri III 984
Sargon of Akkad 984
Sargon II 984
Sarmatians 985
Sāsānian Empire 986
Sātavāhana Dynasty 987
Saul 988
Scaevola, Quintus Mucius (Auger) 988
Scaevola, Quintus Mucius (Pontifex) 989
Scipio Aemilianus 989
Scipio Africanus 990
Scopas 991

Scribonia 991
Scylax of Caryanda 992
Scythia 993
Sea Peoples 994
Second Sophistic 995
Seleucid Dynasty 995
Seleucus I 997
Semonides 998
Sempronia 998
Seneca the Elder 999
Seneca the Younger 999
Sennacherib 1000
Septuagint 1001
Sesostris III 1002
Seti I 1002
Severus, Lucius Septimius 1003
Severus, Sulpicius 1004
Shabaka 1004
Shang Dynasty 1005
Shang Yang 1006
Shāpūr I 1007
Shāpūr II 1007
Sheba, Queen of 1008
Shi Huangdi 1009
Shintō 1010
Shōtoku Taishi 1011
Shulgi 1012
Sibylline Books 1012
Sidonius Apollinaris 1013
Silk Road 1014
Sima Qian 1015
Sima Xiangru 1015
Simon Magus 1016
Simonides 1017
Six Dynasties 1017
Slavs 1018
Snefru 1020
Social War 1020
Socrates 1021
Solomon 1021
Solon 1022
Sonota culture 1023
Sophocles 1024
Sophonisba of Numidia 1025
Soranus of Ephesus 1025
South America, southern 1026
South American Intermediate Area 1027
Southwest peoples 1029
Spain 1030
Spartacus 1033

Speusippus. 1034
Sri Lanka 1034
Srong-brtsan-sgam-po. 1036
Statius, Publius Papinius 1037
Stesichorus 1037
Stilicho, Flavius 1038
Stonehenge 1038
Strabo 1040
Subarctic peoples 1041
Śūdraka 1042
Suebi. 1043
Suetonius 1044
Sui Dynasty 1044
Sulla, Lucius Cornelius 1045
Sulpicia 1045
Sumerians 1046
Śuṅga Dynasty. 1047
Suppululiumas I 1048
Sūtras 1048
Sūttanipāta. 1049
Sutton Hoo. 1050
Śyāmilaka 1050
Sylvester I, Saint. 1051
Symmachus, Quintus Aurelius 1052

Ta-Seti 1053
Tacitus 1053
Taharqa 1054
Tai 1055
Taizong 1056
Tale of the Two Brothers, The 1057
Taliesin 1057
Talmud. 1058
Tang Dynasty 1059
Tantras 1060
Tao Hongjing 1060
Tao Qian 1061
Tarquins 1062
Telipinus 1062
Teotihuacán 1063
Terence 1065
Terpander of Lesbos 1066
Tertullian 1066
Teutoburg Forest, Battle of 1067
Thapsus, Battle of 1067
Themistius 1068
Themistocles. 1068
Theocritus of Syracuse 1069
Theoderic the Great 1070
Theodora. 1070

Theodoret of Cyrrhus 1071
Theodosius of Alexandria 1071
Theodosius the Great 1072
Theodosius II 1073
Theognis 1074
Theophrastus 1074
Thera. 1075
Thermopylae, Battle of 1077
Theron of Acragas 1077
Thespis 1078
Thirty Tyrants 1079
Thom's Creek 1079
Three Kingdoms 1080
Thucydides 1080
Thutmose III 1081
Tiberius 1082
Tibet 1083
Tibu 1085
Tibullus, Albius 1085
Tiglath-pileser III 1086
Tigranes the Great 1087
Tikal 1087
Timoleon of Corinth 1088
Tipiṭaka 1089
Tiruttakkatevar. 1090
Tiruvaḷḷuvar 1090
Tissa, Dēvānaṃpiya 1091
Titus 1091
Tiwanaku 1092
Tōlāmoḷittēvar 1093
Tolkāppiyam 1094
Totila. 1095
Trajan 1095
Trajan's column 1096
Triumvirate 1097
Troy 1098
Tullius Tiro, Marcus. 1100
Tutankhamen 1101
Twelve Tables, The 1102
Tyrtaeus 1102

Ubaid culture 1104
Ulpian 1104
ʿUmar ibn al-Khaṭṭāb 1105
Umayyad Dynasty. 1106
Upaniṣads 1106
Ur-Namma. 1107
Urartu 1108
ʿUthmān ibn ʿAffān 1109
Uxmal 1109

Vākāṭaka Dynasty 1111
Valens 1111
Valentinian I 1112
Valentinian III 1112
Valerian 1113
Valerius Flaccus, Gaius 1114
Valerius Maximus 1114
Valerius Probus, Marcus 1115
Vālmīki 1115
Vandals 1116
Vardhamāna 1117
Varro, Marcus Terentius 1118
Vasubandhu 1118
Vātsyāyana 1119
Vaṭṭagāmaṇi 1120
Vedas 1120
Vedism 1121
Vegetius Renatus, Flavius 1123
Velleius Paterculus, Marcus 1123
Vendae 1124
Vercingetorix 1124
Vergil 1125
Verginia 1127
Vespasian 1127
Vietnam 1128
Villanovan culture 1129
Vindolanda tablets 1130
Viśākhadatta 1130
Vitruvius Pollio, Marcus 1131

Wallia 1132
Wang Bi 1132
Wang Chong 1133
Wang Xizhi 1133
Wawat 1134
Weiyang palace 1135
Wendi 1135
Wu Hou 1136
Wudi 1136
Wujing 1137

Xenophanes 1139
Xenophon 1139
Xerxes I 1140
Xia Dynasty 1141
Xiaowen Di 1142
Xie He 1142
Xie Lingyun 1143
Xin Zhui's tomb 1144
Xiongnu 1144

Xuanzang 1145
Xunzi 1146
Xushen 1146

Yam 1148
Yamato court 1148
Yan Liben 1149
Yang Di 1150
Yang Xiong 1150
Yangshao culture 1151
Yannai 1151
Yayoi culture 1152
Yose ben Yose 1153
Yue 1153
Yue ware 1154
Yuezhi culture 1155

Zama, Battle of 1156
Zapotecs 1156
Zealots 1160
Zengzi 1160
Zeno of Citium 1161
Zeno of Elea 1162
Zenobia 1162
Zeus at Pergamum, Great Altar of 1163
Zeuxis of Heraclea 1163
Zhangdi 1164
Zhiyi 1164
Zhou Dynasty 1165
Zhou style 1166
Zhuangzi 1166
Zhuge Liang 1167
Zi Si 1168
Znaga 1168
Zoroaster 1169
Zoroastrianism 1170
Zoskales 1171
Zurvanism 1171

Time Line 1173
Glossary 1193
Geographical Guide to the Ancient World . . . 1199
Chronological List of Entries 1208
Web Sites 1223
Bibliography 1229

Categorized List of Entries III
Personages Index XV
Subject Index XXXI

OVERVIEWS

AGRICULTURE AND ANIMAL HUSBANDRY

Plant cultivation and controlled stock breeding increased human population density and resulted in the emergence of urbanism, occupational specialization, social stratification, writing, and long-distance trade. Agriculture also necessitated the development of metallurgy, engineering, astronomy, and mathematics and transformed both religious and political systems as humans altered the environment through deforestation, terracing, and irrigation.

Archaeological evidence that attends humankind's great transformation from hunter-gatherer to agriculturalist includes pollen samples, vegetal remains, and animal bones. Art, writing, agricultural artifacts, and topographical modifications provide information on early farming systems.

Although the precise mechanism that led to domestication remains unknown, models proposed to explain the transition from hunting and foraging to incipient agriculture emphasize climatic change, population growth, and accidental domestication. The domestication process began independently in the Near East, Mexico, sub-Saharan Africa, eastern North America, South America, and eastern Asia. From these regions, techniques, cultigens, and animals diffused throughout the world.

THE NEAR EAST AND EGYPT

Domestication began in an environmentally diverse region, the Fertile Crescent, a rugged, naturally rich habitat. Distribution of wild cereals, such as emmer and einkorn wheat and barley, and wild legumes, such as peas and lentils, paralleled the areas of earliest cultivation. Farming began in the Jordan Valley and spread into adjacent lands. By the eighth millennium B.C.E., autonomous villages had been established in areas occupied by modern Israel, Jordan, Syria, and Turkey.

By 8000 B.C.E., at Zawi Chemi Shanidar in modern Iraq, goats and sheep had been domesticated, and at Aswad in Syria and Cayonu in Tur-key, wheat and barley had been cultivated. Peas and lentils may have been grown as early as the ninth millennium B.C.E. at Aswad. At Cayonu, pigs had been domesticated by 7000 B.C.E. Evidence of domesticated cattle has been secured from sites in Turkey and in southwestern Europe dating to 6500 B.C.E. Initially, cattle were used for meat and draft purposes. Agriculture was a powerful subsistence strategy within the Fertile Crescent by 7000 B.C.E. Gradually, knowledge and the artifacts of agriculture diffused into Crete, Thessaly, Egypt, and lowland Mesopotamia.

Early tools were simple. The digging stick, which has been used in hunting and foraging communities from time immemorial, was a primary tool. Sickles for harvesting cereals were constructed of chipped flint. Food-processing tools such as mortars and pestles were made of ground stone.

The Tigris and Euphrates floodplains were farmed after 6000 B.C.E. By 5500 B.C.E., irrigation canals had been constructed to move water from the rivers to field systems and to facilitate field drainage following spring inundations. Construction and maintenance of large irrigation works required a centralized political authority for effectively coordinating labor.

Intensive irrigation, along with the plow, allowed population to increase in the developing urban centers on the Mesopotamian plains. The plow, or ard, probably evolved from a digging stick into a wooden device harnessed to oxen and designed to scratch the surface of the soil. Such plows were in use by the late fourth millennium B.C.E. Figs, olives, and grapes were grown in the eastern Mediterranean lands during the fourth millennium B.C.E. The date palm was cultivated for fruit and wood on the Mesopotamian floodplains.

Farming variations emerged by 3000 B.C.E. in the Near East and eastern Mediterranean. One pattern emphasized dependence on rainfall for cereal

Egyptians draw water from the Nile River for irrigation in this frieze from about 2000 B.C.E. (Hulton Archive)

cultivation and livestock raising. Another variant, centered in the river valleys, relied on irrigation. By the end of the first millennium B.C.E., canalization was accompanied by lifting devices such as the waterwheel. Such devices and practices persisted into the twentieth century C.E.

Egyptian food production practices were derived from the cereal and livestock economies of the Mesopotamian floodplains. Early farming communities were evident in Egypt by the sixth millennium B.C.E., and by 4000 B.C.E., agricultural practices had spread across the Nile Valley. In contrast with Mesopotamian irrigation techniques, Egyptian farmers employed a system of basins and sluices to regulate and divert floodwater to growing crops. The annual deposits of silt that remained after the floodwaters receded in the Nile and Mesopotamian floodplains enhanced the soil's fertility. However, the Mesopotamian hydraulic system carried an overabundance of salts, ultimately retarding the soil's fertility there. In contrast, in Egypt, the receding floodwaters cleansed

the system, creating and maintaining high fertility levels for millennia.

EUROPE

The crops, animals, and culture of early farming diffused from the Near East into Anatolia and the Aegean region. By the mid-seventh millennium B.C.E., cattle had been domesticated in Greece. Between 6000 and 4500 B.C.E., permanent farming villages were located over wide areas in the Balkans. By 6000 B.C.E., the cereal and livestock complex of southeastern Europe had spread up the Danube and into central Europe.

Agricultural technology changed and adapted as it spread and moved into the European forests. The diffusion of agriculture along the Mediterranean and Atlantic coasts, as well as the penetration of northern Europe, required varied subsistence and technological strategies. Climate and altitude were crucial considerations. In some locales, hunting, fishing, and shellfish collecting remained important.

Cultivation within the forest zones required fire and stone adzes to clear dense wooded tracts. After an area was burned, seeds were sown in the nutrient-rich ash using simple tools. Slash-and-burn farming was a key technique in the evolution of European agriculture. By the fourth millennium B.C.E., people had harnessed the power of oxen, which combined with the simple ard (plow) to enhance efficiency. Early European farmers planted barley, wheat, vetch, flax, peas, beans, and lentils. Oats and rye were probably domesticated in Europe.

By 4500 B.C.E., the rising productivity of agriculture, coupled with the evolving social organization of populations, had resulted in the construction of elaborate tombs in Western Europe. The most enduring achievement of these agrarian societies, however, was their megalithic edifices, the greatest of which was Stonehenge (3100-1550 B.C.E.), located on Salisbury Plain, England.

Agriculture shaped economic foundations long before the appearance of the classical world. In Greece, implements remained simple and the general complex of cereals, fruits, and vine crops were cultivated. By the late fifth century B.C.E., mills had been constructed for pressing olives, and animals treaded stone floors to thresh grain. The Greeks wrote little on agriculture, but the Romans produced a broad literature on agricultural topics, covering topics such as soil fertility, farm management, and field procedures. To feed its great urban centers, Rome used slave power in tandem with numerous simple and mechanical wooden and iron tools. Cereals, olives, grapes, fruits, and vegetables moved from diverse environments along Roman roads and seaways.

European society in the early Middle Ages rested on an agrarian base. Manorialism evolved following the collapse of Roman administration in the Western Empire (476 C.E.). Feudalism, the larger political and military framework that included manorialism, was based on a system of personal loyalties and territorial arrangements. Local landlords allowed peasants, or serfs, to reside in manorial villages and perform agricultural and other tasks in exchange for various services. Peas-ant agriculture in the post-Roman world was labor intensive, and physical mobility was circumscribed. Peasant life and work revolved around a religious and agricultural calendar.

Plowing and general hauling was accomplished with oxen. Northern European soils demanded a plow that would cut through the heavy soil and turn it over to facilitate drying. During the sixth century C.E., German and Slavic populations developed such a plow. Conservation concerns were manifested in the two-field system, which allowed one of a pair of fields to lie fallow and replenish its fertility. The two-field system, which by the mid-eighth century C.E. had become the three-field system, was based on growing winter cereals while allotting equal fallow ground. It was used in southern Mediterranean Europe, where inadequate moisture meant poor spring seedings.

In contrast to the market-oriented large Roman estates, the manors during the early Middle Ages strived for self-sufficiency. Perhaps 90 percent of the European population was directly involved with agriculture and manorial labor.

AFRICA

In contrast to other regions of the Old World, the evidence for the development and spread of agricultural practices in Africa is poor. Before the Saharan region was largely abandoned because of desiccation (c. 2500-1000 B.C.E.), millet and sorghum may have been domesticated between 4000 and 2000 B.C.E.

Vegeculture (the cultivation of multiple species within a single field) may have been practiced in West Africa by the fifth millennium B.C.E. Coffee was domesticated in Ethiopia, and millet, yams, sorghum, okra, African rice, and groundnuts were all cultivated in West Africa with stone tool technology. Plow agriculture was unknown until the nineteenth century C.E. Sub-Saharan Africa posed many ecological obstacles including diseases and poor soils, and tropical cultivators adapted in numerous ways over the millennia.

The general cereal crop complex diffused into North Africa from the Middle East. In the forest zones, slash-and-burn was the foremost technique before tillage. As soil fertility ebbed, populations shifted and opened new forest tracts. Indigenous domesticated animals were few: guinea fowls, cattle, and perhaps donkeys. Evidence suggests cattle were domesticated in the Sahara region, perhaps by 4500 B.C.E. East African cattle culture is ancient, and pastoralism remained a major subsistence pursuit among tribes into the twentieth century C.E.

SOUTH AND EAST ASIA

Early food production in India is linked to the Near Eastern and East Asian patterns of domestication. The site of Mehrgarh (c. 7000 B.C.E.) in modern Pakistan revealed evidence of the cultivation of wheat and barley. By 5500 B.C.E., the population in India and other parts of South Asia was extensively exploiting wild cattle, sheep, and goats, suggesting a predomestication period similar to that of the Near East. By the end of the third millennium B.C.E., domesticated water buffalo, pigs, cattle, goats, and sheep were mainstays of village life. A millennium later, donkeys, camels, and horses, used in transport, were to be found over much of South Asia.

Few crops and animals were domesticated independently in India. The exceptions are chickens and cotton, which date from as far back as 5000 B.C.E. Dates, grapes, and seed plants such as sesame were probably grown by the third millennium B.C.E. Agricultural hand tools, like the adze and ax, were simple and constructed of stone.

The dense urban populations of Harappā and Mohenjo-Daro, cities of the Indus civilization (c. 2500-2000 B.C.E.), were supported through farming. The supporting technology included engineering projects to control flooding of the Indus River. The plow is believed to have been introduced into India following the collapse of the Indus civilization. The livestock, crops, and technological complex of village India has persisted into the modern world.

Early northern Chinese agriculture focused on the cultivation of millet, whereas in southern regions, rice became a staple. By 6000 B.C.E., foxtail and broomcorn millet as well as Chinese cabbage had been cultivated at the northern site of Peiligang, and rice had been cultivated in southern China at Pengtoushan. Additional plants included fruit trees (peach, pear, and apricot), soybeans, and the bottle gourd. The mulberry tree was grown for silkworm raising. At Hemudu (c. 5000 B.C.E.) in the Yangtze Valley, rice was cultivated, and stone, bone, and wooden agricultural tools were discovered. Livestock included pigs, chickens, cattle, goats, and sheep. Cattle were used for traction and probably pulled wooden plows for rice cultivation. The principal tools remained the hoe and spade. Fishing provided an important supplement for agricultural communities.

From these peasant villages evolved monumental Chinese civilizations. During the third millennium B.C.E., the Longshan culture in north China began to shift from extensive to intensive cultivation. Social differentiation, copper metallurgy, and specialized labor intensified, increasing the social complexity. In the second millennium B.C.E., the traditional agricultural economy enabled the Shang Dynasty (1600-1066 B.C.E.) to emerge, and people began to use the water buffalo. During the first millennium B.C.E., higher levels of efficiency were introduced into Chinese agriculture through the use of extensive irrigation works and iron implements, including the plow.

OCEANIA

Kuk swamp, Papua, in the New Guinea highlands provides the earliest evidence for agricultural activity: drainage systems, perhaps for sugarcane and taro cultivation, dating to 7000 B.C.E. This date suggests the possibility of another independent center for plant domestication. By 4000 B.C.E., tree foods, coconut and perhaps sago, were used in the lowland Sepik Basin. Independently of these precocious developments, migrations from Southeast Asia, beginning about 1500 B.C.E., initiated colonization through the remainder of Melanesia, as well as Micronesia and ultimately Polynesia, including New Zealand. These migrations diffused the primary domesticated fauna, dogs, pigs, and chickens, in addition to the greater yam, sugarcane, and new varieties of bananas throughout Oceania.

Successful settlement of the Pacific Basin was based on continuous adaptation to environmental diversity. The mainstay of life, vegeculture, persisted into the historic period, accompanied by the tree crops of breadfruit, coconuts, and bananas. Ecological variability caused prehistoric populations to evolve varied exploitative systems: raised bed cultivation in swampy locales for yams; sunken fields for taro, designed to benefit from subsurface moisture; and hillside terracing and irrigation. Swidden, or slash-and-burn technology, remained the premier cultivation technique into historic times. Tools were simple: the digging stick, a mainstay of tuber horticulture, and adzes of shell and stone. In contrast to mainland Asia, Melanesian chiefdoms and the Polynesian civilizations followed a different evolutionary course based on sophisticated vegeculture, tree food cultivation, and the resources of the sea.

NORTH AMERICA

The Native Americans lacked the technology of the Old World civilizations, which included large animals for traction, metallurgy, and the wheel. A powerful energy base and a formidable subsistence technology evolved, however, permitting sophisticated adaptations, and in some environments, spectacular urban civilizations.

In the woodland regions of eastern North America, native populations domesticated a number of seed plants: lamb's quarter, goosefoot, and the sunflower. Sunflowers and squash were domesticated by the mid-third millennium B.C.E. Hunting, fishing, and shellfish collecting supplemented wild food gathering and cultivation. Digging sticks and stone hoes were used in seed-bed preparation. Plants of ritual and economic importance diffused from Mexico: Tobacco and maize arrived in the Midwest by the second century C.E. Maize was a minor cultigen until the ninth century C.E.

An entirely different pattern evolved in the Salt and Gila River Valleys in the American Southwest. Rooted in the Mesoamerican tradition, the Hohokam (1-1400 C.E.) irrigated their fields in the hot Sonoran desert. Canalization, dated circa 300-200 B.C.E., included segments more than 15 miles (24 kilometers) long and irrigated thousands of acres. Hohokam agriculture included floodwater farming: These techniques allowed population expansion and political evolution. Large hydraulic works at the Snaketown site implied labor coordination, not only for construction but also for annual maintenance.

MESOAMERICA

In the regions of modern Mexico, Guatemala, and adjacent Central America, independent domestication took place. Plant species were numerous, the foremost being maize, beans, squash, and chili peppers. Animal domesticates were few, consisting of the turkey and hairless dog. At Tehuacán in Mexico, maize was cultivated by 5000 B.C.E., chili peppers by 4000 B.C.E., and beans during the late first millennium B.C.E. Evidence of squash from Guila Naquitz in Oaxaca may date to 6000 B.C.E. By the fourth millennium B.C.E., villages in the Tehuacán Valley employed small-scale canalization. The shift to complete reliance on domesticates encompassed five millennia, a period in which hunting and foraging remained important. In the lowlands, the slash-and-burn technique was used to clear heavy vegetation; in the highlands, the digging stick remained the primary tool. Ground stone tools (the mano-metate) processed corn into meal.

Domesticates (particularly the triad of maize, beans, and squash) provided the nutritional base for Mesoamerican civilizations. The Olmec (c. 1200-400 B.C.E.) of the humid Gulf Coast farmed the rich soils adjacent to the lowland rivers. Teotihuacán (1-750 C.E.) in the central Mexican plateau became an urban center boasting a population estimated between 125,000 and 200,000 people. Irrigation was used selectively, as was *chinampas*, a form of raised field farming in which decomposing materials and mud are piled in a watercourse and secured by stakes and branches. After taking root, the branches and saplings held the "floating garden" firm.

In lowland Central America, a variant of shifting cultivation, *conuco*, was developed to grow such crops as sweet potatoes and manioc. The primary tool remained the digging stick, or *coa*.

SOUTH AMERICA

In pre-Columbian lowland and highland South America, regions with extreme ecological variability, emphasis was placed on root crops. Potatoes, manioc, quinoa, beans, peanuts, cotton, and oca are among the many plants that facilitated the growth of civilization. Domesticated fauna were limited: the duck, alpaca, llama, and guinea pig. Llamas and guinea pigs were domesticated by the fourth millennium B.C.E. Domestication enjoyed a significant time span in Andean South America: Potatoes, for example, were domesticated by the late third millennium B.C.E., cotton between 4000 and 1200 B.C.E., and beans by 5800 B.C.E.

Irrigation was widely used. In the Moche Valley of north coastal Peru (first to seventh centuries C.E.), water was diverted for cotton, peanuts, beans, and other crops. Cultivation was by hand. Canals were constructed of mud and earth: Engineering was sophisticated to ensure the correct gradient of water flow down hillsides. Soil fertility was replenished through guano gathered from offshore islands. Moche intensive agriculture may have supported a population of 50,000. The Moche state was a heavily stratified, politically complex society, as evidenced by monumental building projects and an elaborate mortuary ritual. An equally complex agricultural infrastructure supported the sociopolitical hierarchy.

ADDITIONAL RESOURCES

Cowan, C. Wesley, and Patty Jo Watson, eds. *The Origins of Agriculture: An International Perspective*. Washington, D.C.: Smithsonian Institution Press, 1992.

Grigg, D. B. *The Agricultural Systems of the World: An Evolutionary Approach*. New York: Cambridge University Press, 1974.

Harris, David R., ed. *The Origins and Spread of Agriculture and Pastoralism in Eurasia*. Washington, D.C.: Smithsonian Institution Press, 1996.

Isager, Signe, and Jens Erik Skydsgaard. *Ancient Greek Agriculture: An Introduction*. New York: Routledge, 1995.

SEE ALSO: Africa, East and South; Africa, North; Africa, West; Andes, south; Archaic South American culture; Australia, Tasmania, New Zealand; Egypt, Prepharaonic; Fertile Crescent; Greece, Archaic; Hohokam culture; India; Longshan culture; Melanesia; Micronesia; Middle Woodland traditions; Moche culture; Nilo-Saharans; Nilotes; Omotic peoples; Polynesia; Rome, Prerepublican; Shang Dynasty; South America, southern; South American Intermediate Area; Southwest peoples; Stonehenge; Teotihuacán.

—*Rene M. Descartes*

ART AND ARCHITECTURE: THE AMERICAS

NORTH AMERICA

During the Ice Age, a frozen land bridge known as Beringa stretched across the Bering Strait from Asia to Alaska. From about 50,000-11,000 B.C.E., intermittent waves of Asian and Siberian peoples migrated across Beringa, down into North America and, eventually, into Central and South America. These early peoples brought with them a Stone Age technology, giving the era its name, the Lithic (Stone) period.

By 9000 B.C.E., specific groups can be identified by their spearpoint-making technologies and territories. Two of these groups are the Old Cordilleran culture in the Cascade region of the Columbia River and the Desert culture in the Great Basin area of the American Southwest. The Desert culture developed the first-known woven basketry in the Americas. As the weather warmed and game disappeared, gathering activities intensified. This period is known as the Archaic (Foraging) Age (8000-1000 B.C.E.), a time of advancements in tool making and basket weaving. During the Archaic Age, peoples developed into three principal cultures: the Cochise, Old Copper, and Red Paint. The Cochise culture (8000-1 B.C.E.) of Arizona and New Mexico was the first to cultivate corn, perhaps learned from contact with peoples in Mexico. The Cochise, who lived in pit houses covered with brush roofs, fashioned figurines of clay. The Old Copper complex (4000-1000 B.C.E.) in the Great Lakes area learned to heat and hammer copper into tools and jewelry. The Red Paint culture (3000-500 B.C.E.) of New England and Eastern Canada were a people named for their practice of lining their graves with powdered red hematite, perhaps as an offering representing life-giving blood. They also placed tools and sculptures in the graves, presumably for use by the deceased in the afterlife.

The Southwest cultures (9500 B.C.E.-700 C.E.), named for the southwest region of America in which they lived, are divided into three main cultures. The Mogollon culture, or Mountain People (200 B.C.E.-1200 C.E.), are named for the mountains that lie along the southern borders of New Mexico and Arizona and are thought to be the earliest culture in the Southwest to pursue agriculture, a practice that allowed the Mogollon to settle in one place, build houses, and create pottery for storage of food and other items. The ingenious Mogollon pit houses, dug deep into the earth and covered with branches, maintained a relatively constant temperature compared with the exterior environment. Very large pit houses were probably used as *kivas* (ritual spaces). The early Mogollon made simple brown clay pottery and wove blankets and baskets. The Hohokam culture, or Vanished Ones (1-1400 C.E.), was a desert-dwelling culture that practiced agriculture, complex irrigation, pit house construction, and advanced decorative pottery and textile making. The Anasazi culture, or the Ancient Ones (100-1300 C.E.), resided

on the high plateaus of the Four Corners region (Colorado, Utah, New Mexico, and Arizona). The Anasazi lived in pit houses like their contemporaries (the famed Anasazi pueblo-style structures were constructed after 750 C.E.). The early phase of the Anasazi culture is referred to as Basketmaker II because of their sophisticated basketweaving skills.

In the midwestern and eastern areas of North America, Woodland cultures (1400 B.C.E.-1500 C.E.) and Mound Builders (1000 B.C.E.-700 C.E.) developed. The earliest of these, the Adena culture (1000 B.C.E.-100 C.E.), originated in the Ohio River Valley. This agricultural society constructed round wattle-and-daub houses, with wide overhanging roofs supported by four interior poles. The Adena practiced an elaborate type of mound burial that involved the inclusion of grave goods, with quality and quantity based on the deceased's social position. Burial mounds were typically circular, but effigy mounds took many forms, including that of a huge coiled serpent in Ohio. Another mound-building culture, located in Ohio, Illinois, and parts of the Mississippi River Valley, was the Hopewell culture (300 B.C.E.-700 C.E.). The Hopewell elaborated on the Adena practices of mound building and the inclusion of burial goods in tombs. Unlike the Adena, the Hopewell lived in circular, domed wigwams.

MESOAMERICA

The term Mesoamerica (Middle America) refers to the geographical area of southern Mexico and Central America. The chronology of Mesoamerica is divided into four phases: the Prehistoric period (about 12,000-2000 B.C.E.), a time of migrations south through Mexico and down into the Yucatán and Central America; the Pre-Classic or Formative period (2000 B.C.E.-250 C.E.), during which agriculture and cities developed; the Classic period (250-900 C.E.), the apex of Mesoamerican cultures; and the Post-Classic period (900-1519 C.E.), a period of diffusion, decline, and invasion by Europeans.

During the Pre-Classic phase, the Olmec culture (c. 1200-400 B.C.E.) arose along the Mexican coast of the Gulf of Mexico. The Olmec culture is often referred to as a "mother" culture because it was the source of many Mesoamerican cultural traits, such as highly stratified societies, hereditary kingship, elaborate ceremonial centers, pyramid temples, and strong central control over highly organized workforces. Unique to the Olmec are the creation of basalt stone heads ranging in height from 6 to 8 feet (1.8 to 2.4 meters), which probably represented kings. Contemporary with the Olmec was the Colima culture of western Mexico, noted for its elaborate shaft graves that housed multiple tombs and a wide array of ceramic grave figurines representing everyday life in Pre-Classical Mexico.

The Maya of the Yucatán Peninsula left many stone carvings of their gods, including this of Chac Mool in Cancún. (Corbis)

The transition from the Pre-Classic to the Classic phase is exemplified in the major ceremonial center established at Teotihuacán (1-750 C.E.), northeast of Mexico City. Teotihuacán was divided into quadrants with wards based on ethnicity and social status. During massive building programs, older temples were left intact and covered over with new temples, leaving an excellent record for archaeologists. The Maya culture, originating as early as 1000 B.C.E., reached its height in the Classic period, during which the Maya constructed their great ceremonial centers in Guatemala, Honduras, Belize, and southern Mexico. Once believed to be a society of peaceful priests and time-keepers, the Maya were, in fact, an aggressive culture based on kingship, ritual bloodletting, warfare, and human sacrifice. The Maya developed an elaborate cosmology and recorded it in complex hieroglyphics and detailed calendars. Central to every Maya center were temple pyramids, which housed tombs of the kings; observatories for tracking movements of celestial bodies; and ball courts, in which ritual games were played.

SOUTH AMERICA

In South America, ancient Andean cultures developed along the Andes Mountains, with urban centers in the coastal deserts, rural centers in the mountains, and forest peoples in the eastern Amazon region. During the Preceramic period (before pottery), a Stone Age culture of nomadic hunters and gatherers sought shelter in Panaulauca cave in central Peru (8000-1800 B.C.E.). Burials testify to a respect for the dead, possibly indicating a belief in the afterlife or the practice of ancestor worship. Cave paintings from the region depict camelids (vicuna, llama, and alpaca), which would have provided fiber for textiles, leather for sandals and ropes, bone for tools, and meat for food. The camelids also served as pack animals for the ancient Andean cultures, which never developed the wheel.

Between 2500 and 1800 B.C.E., hunting and gathering was replaced by agriculture. The first cities in South America arose along the dry western coasts, where elaborate irrigation systems were constructed to bring water from the mountains. The Chavín culture (1000-200 B.C.E.), named for its central location at Chavín de Huántar in the Peruvian Andes, constructed religious centers composed of U-shaped platforms opening up to the mountains from which came their life-giving water. Stone relief sculptures and stirrup spouted vessels reveal the Chavín interest in animals and nature. The Chavín wrapped their dead in patterned textiles that denoted the deceased's family and clan.

Between 50 and 800 C.E., the Moche culture dominated the coastal regions of Peru. The Moche constructed adobe houses on raised platform mounds, as well as temple mounds and pyramids. Without the aid of the potter's wheel, the Moche created an abundance of skillful ceramics, most notably naturalistic portrait vessels, which were placed in tombs alongside other items for use in the afterlife.

Roughly contemporary with the Moche was the Nasca culture (c. 100 B.C.E.-600 C.E.). The Nasca lived in the southern desert of Peru, where they developed an elaborate religion based on water and irrigation. Nasca homes were constructed of tied canes plastered over with mud; their ceremonial centers included temples and pyramids. Like other Andean cultures, the Nasca excelled at ceramics and textiles. They are most noted, however, for their giant geoglyphs (earth writing). By removing the top layer of dark, oxidized desert surface to expose the lighter sediments below, the Nasca created huge designs on the desert floor, from abstract geometric forms to gigantic monkeys, birds, fish, spiders, and even a 450-foot-long (137-meter-long) hummingbird. The exact purpose of the Nasca lines is unknown, but archaeologists speculate that they were part of a religious ritual to ensure the fertility of the earth.

ADDITIONAL RESOURCES

Coates, Anthony G., ed. *central America: A Natural and Cultural History.* New Haven, Conn.: Yale University Press, 1997.

Josephy, Alvin M., Jr., et al. *The Native Americans: An Illustrated History.* Atlanta, Ga.: Turner, 1993.

Kauffmann-Doig, Federico. *Ancestors of the Inca: The Lost Civilizations of Peru.* Memphis, Tenn.: Lithograph, 1998.

Von Hagen, Adriana, and Craig Morris. *Cities of the Ancient Andes.* London: Thames and Hudson, 1998.

SEE ALSO: Adena culture; Amazonia; Anasazi; Andes, south; Andes, central; Ball game, Mesoamerican; Chavín de Huántar; Cochise culture; Hohokam culture; Maritime Archaic; Maya; Middle Woodland traditions; Moche culture; Mogollon culture; Nasca culture; Old Copper; Olmecs; Southwest peoples; Teotihuacán.

—*Sonia Sorrell*

ART AND ARCHITECTURE: EAST ASIA

CHINA

In the second half of the twentieth century, Chinese archaeology entered its golden age. Although China is arguably the oldest continuous civilization in human history, serious archaeological research into its ancient past did not occur until after the establishment of the People's Republic. The literal translation for the traditional Chinese name for the country is "the middle kingdom," meaning the center of Earth. Chinese religion was animistic in its earliest form, leading to Daoism, a kind of natural mysticism first expressed by Laozi (born 604 B.C.E.). Ancient China was eventually dominated by the ethical teachings of Confucius (551-479 B.C.E.), who prescribed a conservative philosophy founded on ritual, decorum, and social order. Buddhism arrived in China in the early first century C.E. and by the sixth century became the most popular religion.

Neolithic. Significant finds from China's Neolithic period (6000-2200 B.C.E.) include pottery, jade congs, and religious complexes decorated with murals and clay statues of female figures. One clay bowl, made by the Yangshao people from Banpo, near Xi'an, Shaanxi, has decorative marks along the rim resembling an early form of Chinese writing. Congs are jade tubes encased in rectangular blocks carved with reliefs of abstract masks representing animals, deities, or ancestors. The earliest congs are found in Neolithic burials from Fan Shan, Yuyao, in southeastern coastal China. Two large stone buildings containing altars, graves, pottery, jade, murals and statues built by the Hongshan people were found in the modern Liaoning province of northeastern China. These three examples demonstrate that evidence of China's earliest civilizations can be found at multiple sites, not only in the area surrounding the Yellow River as once believed.

Shang Dynasty. The finest works from the Shang Dynasty (1600-1066 B.C.E.) are the hundreds of bronze vessels found in the royal tombs near Yinxu, or present-day Anyang. The tombs are a tribute to the great wealth, power, and ruthlessness of their leaders, for in addition to objects of great artistry, they contain many human and animal sacrifices. Shang Dynasty bronzes are found in thirty different shapes and contained food, wine, and other offerings to the ancestors. They were created using the complex piece-mold technique for bronze casting, and many weighed more than 240 pounds (109 kilograms). The most compelling feature of these bronzes is their complex surface decoration inspired by woodcarving. Stylized geometric shapes suggesting animals make up most of the designs. The bronzes were found in

tombs containing chariots, bells, knives, mirrors, weapons, jade, and oracle bones. Shamans used bones or shells to predict the future by inscribing their surface with questions and heating them until cracks formed. The shaman interpreted the cracks to make a prediction. The questions scratched onto the bones constitute one of the earliest extant forms of Chinese writing.

Zhou Dynasty. The Zhou Dynasty (1066-256 B.C.E.) was home to two of China's greatest philosophers, Confucius and Laozi. The supreme deity, Tian, dwelled in heaven, and the Zhou kings were called the Sons of Heaven. Traditional large-scale burials were created to commemorate deceased kings and their families. One of the most magnificent was the tomb of Marquis Yi of Zeng, discovered in 1994. More than 7,000 artifacts were found in his tomb, including six bronze warrior figures, each weighing 660 pounds (299 kilograms). The Marquis was buried with twenty-one women, thirteen of whom were musicians. Musical instruments including sixty-five bronze bells mounted on a wooden frame surrounded their remains. The bells were precisely calibrated to sound two tones, depending on where they were struck.

Qin Dynasty. Shi Huangdi, king of the Qin state (dynasty, 221-206 B.C.E.), became the first emperor of a united China, built the predecessor of the present Great Wall, numerous palaces, a magnificent tomb, and a network of roads connecting his new kingdom. The Great Wall of China is one of Shi Huangdi's most renowned accomplishments. Using a huge workforce of convicts and outcasts, he built a 6,000-mile (9,654-kilometer) wall creating a continuous line of defense from the deserts of Central Asia to the eastern coast. The wall was intended to separate the Mongolian grasslands from the settled farmlands of China. It was made of molded clay bricks, fired, and then stacked on top of one another to a height of 15 to 30 feet (4.6-9.1 meters). Research by scholar Arthur Waldron, however, indicates that what is now known as the Great Wall was actually built in the Ming Dynasty in the sixteenth century, and that the wall built by Shi Huangdi was probably destroyed.

The actual burial chamber of Shi Huangdi's 600-foot-high (183-meter-high) burial mound has not been excavated, although outer areas have been. In 1974, archaeologists excavating three outside chambers of the emperor's tomb found more than 7,000 life-sized terra-cotta soldiers and two thousand horses. The soldiers and horses were placed in military formation, guarding the approach of the tomb. Ironically, these monumental terra-cotta figures survive only because later Han invaders tried to destroy the tomb. They set fire to the wooden portions of the tomb, causing its walls to collapse, unintentionally burying and preserving the figures. The statues are each painted and individualized by costume, rank, and elaborate hairstyles. Scholars believe many represent portraits of specific individuals in Shi Huangdi's army. There are archers, cavalry, foot soldiers, even warriors in martial arts positions. Literary sources describe the unexplored chamber as decorated with representations of the stars, rivers, and mountains of Qin.

Han Dynasty. The era of Han Dynasty (206 B.C.E.-220 C.E.) rule ushers in an unparalleled period of peace and prosperity for ancient China. The Silk Road was established, linking China to Rome with a 5,000-mile (8,000-kilometer) trade route. The ancient Romans paid dearly to obtain silk from China, as the technology of silk production was unknown to them. A beautiful painted silk was found covering the innermost coffin of Xin Zhui, the Marquise of Dai, in her tomb (c. 150 C.E.) at Mawangdui, near modern Changsha. This 6-foot-8-inch-long (2-meter-long) T-shaped silk banner is decorated with paintings portraying the three levels of the universe: heaven, Earth, and the underworld. A crow resides in the Sun, a toad in the Moon, which are on either side of the great ancestor of the Han, depicted as a dragon. Beneath this scene lie two intertwined dragons looping through a painted representation of the *bi*, a circular symbol of heaven usually made of jade. Here, at the gate of heaven, begins the middle zone of Earth, occupied by four women and two men offering gifts. One of these figures is a portrait of the Marquise of Dai leaning on a cane. Fish and other fantastic creatures occupy the underworld represented below.

Although many Han Dynasty tombs contained small pottery figures of soldiers to protect the deceased in the next world, the less powerful substituted objects made of jade, with its magical protective properties, for such miniature funerary armies. In the tomb of the prince of Zhongshan, at Mancheng, Hebei, members of the royal family are encased in magnificent suits made of thousands of jade plates joined together with wires made of gold and silver. Knowledge of the architecture of ancient China is acquired from ceramic house models found in such tombs. One 4-foot-high (1.2-meter-high) clay house model, covered in white slip and decorated with red pigment, survives in excellent condition. It portrays a four-storied home crowned with a watchtower, surrounded on one side by a courtyard. Decorative painting on the walls illustrates posts, beams, foliage, and birds. Literary sources from the Han Dynasty describe palaces from this period decorated with precious stones and metals. This model also shows the elaborate bracketing system supporting broad eves and the tiled roof so characteristic of traditional Chinese architecture.

Six Dynasties. The Six Dynasties period (220-588 C.E.; consisting of the Three Kingdoms, Western and Eastern Jin, and Southern and Northern Dynasties) is described by historians as one of chaos, war, and migration. During the Tartar invasions of the third century C.E., the royal court of China was forced to flee south. Aesthetic theories as well as names of artists appear in the written record for the first time during the Six Dynasties era. Written sources show that the Chinese judged the quality of a painting by its brushstrokes; each line had to express the spirit or *qi*, representing breath or energy. Painted silk hand scrolls appear at this time and provide some of the finest examples of ancient Chinese painting. One attributed to the great painter Gu Kaizhi (c. 345-c. 406 C.E.) illustrates a Confucian epic entitled *Nushi Zhen* (third century C.E.; "the admonitions of the instructress to the court ladies"). This hand scroll delineates in word and image edifying examples of wifely virtue. The first illustration portrays Lady Feng protecting her cowering husband from an attacking bear. Another illustration shows two beautifully dressed young women, their robes forming rounded pools of fabric about their feet, floating across the space toward their teacher, to watch her paint just such a hand scroll. Collectors' seals of later owners on the scroll clutter the otherwise empty setting.

Buddhism reached China with the opening of the Silk Road and was strengthened by the invading Buddhist Tartars. It flourished during the Six Dynasties period, particularly under the patronage of emperor Wudi of Liang (502-577 C.E.), who built many monasteries and temples during his rule, although few survive. The most monumental Buddhist art from ancient China is found among the hundreds of caves cut into the rocks surrounding the Silk Road in the north. The caves and carvings at Yungang in Shanxi are cut from the surrounding rock. Cave 20 contains a 45-foot-high (14-meter-high) sculpture of the Seated Buddha created in 460 C.E. Once protected inside the cave, this severe, massive figure is now exposed to the elements as the front part of the cave has crumbled away. This Buddha has the long earlobes, topknot of wisdom (*ushnisha*), and the shallow, stylized drapery typical of the artistic tradition of Central Asia.

Sui and Tang Dynasties. Buddhism continued through the Sui Dynasty (581-618 C.E.). During the Tang Dynasty (618-907 C.E.), all classes of Chinese society adopted Buddhism. The Big Wild Goose pagoda in Xi'an is a rare example of ancient Chinese architecture. The architects merged this multistoried variation of the Indian stupa, a burial mound containing Buddhist relics, with the Chinese watchtower structure to create the well-known pagoda form. Although built of masonry, the Big Wild Goose pagoda imitates its wooden predecessors through its relief carvings on the walls, which resemble the bays and brackets of wooden architecture. The pagoda, with its simplicity, symmetry, and projecting roofs for each

A Jōmon earthenware bowl. (© Sakamoto Photo Research Laboratory/Corbis)

story, establishes the most enduring form of Chinese architecture imitated throughout East Asia.

JAPAN

Japanese art and architecture benefited from waves of Chinese and Korean immigrants bringing with them their own distinct art, technology, and religious practices. Shintō, which involves the veneration of nature, is the indigenous religion of Japan. Buddhism, however, arrived on the shores of Japan in 552 C.E. from Korea and was eventually adopted by the Japanese court after a period of clan warfare.

Jōmon period. Neolithic peoples in Japan created remarkable pottery and clay figurines during the Jōmon period (c. 8000-300 B.C.E.), which takes its name from the original cord-marked patterns found on its pottery (*jōmon* means "cord markings"). These vessels, made in imitation of reed baskets, often have pointed bases. Most have burn marks indicating they were used for cooking. Later, a flat-bottomed storage vessel was developed. The pots were decorated by pressing cords into the damp clay, creating scratchy relief patterns. With time, the rims of Jōmon pots were decorated with elaborate flamelike shapes. Artists also fashioned small human figures called *dōgu*, usually about 10 inches (25 centimeters) in height. *Dōgu* have slit or goggle-shaped eyes, heart-shaped faces, and incised tattoo patterns on their bodies. Although their function is unknown, scholars speculate that they act as effigies manifesting a powerful sympathetic magic.

Yayoi and Kofun periods. During the Yayoi period (c. 300 B.C.E.-c. 300 C.E.), the Japanese learned to cast bronze, using it in artistic and more practical objects. During the Kofun period (c. 300-710 C.E.), a large number of keyhole-shaped mound tombs called *kofun* were built for members of the imperial family, giving the period its name. Rows of clay cylinders and sculptures called *haniwa* were placed on these tombs. The *haniwa* come in a variety of forms, most commonly that of warriors or horses, but sometimes they portray shamans, houses, boats, deer, dogs, and monkeys. Unlike Chinese tomb ceramics, *haniwa* are unglazed, rarely symmetrical and always expressive. It is theorized that they served as a link between the world of the living and the dead. The ancient Shintō shrine at Ise, southwest of Tokyo, was built in the first century C.E. and survives to this day be-cause it is systematically rebuilt every twenty years. The shrine is built entirely from unpainted wood; it has a sharply pitched roof and is supported by wooden posts. A high wooden fence encloses the buildings, punctuated by a *torii*, or sacred gateway. It is hoped that by passing through the *torii*, the worshipper will experience rebirth.

ADDITIONAL RESOURCES

Fong, Wen. *The Great Bronze Age of China: An Exhibition from the People's Republic*. New York: Metropolitan Museum, 1980.

Hutt, Julia. *Understanding Far Eastern Art*. New York: E. P. Dutton, 1987.

Pearson, Richard. *Ancient Japan*. Washington, D.C.: Sackler Gallery, 1992.

Rogers, Howard, ed. *China, Five Thousand Years: Innovation and Transformation in the Arts*. New York: Guggenheim Museum, 1998.

Sullivan, Michael. *The Arts of China*. 4th ed. Berkeley: University of California Press, 1999.

SEE ALSO: Buddhism; Buddhist cave temples; China; Confucianism; Daoism; Fu Hao's tomb; Great Wall of China; Gu Kaizhi; Han Dynasty; *Haniwa*; Jōmon; Kofun period; Qin Dynasty; Qin tomb; Shang Dynasty; Shi Huangdi; Shintō; Silk Road; Six Dynasties; Sui Dynasty; Tang Dynasty; Three Kingdoms; Weiyang palace; Xin Zhui's tomb; Yangshao culture; Yayoi culture; Yue ware; Zhou Dynasty; Zhou style.

—*Laura Rinaldi Dufresne*

ART AND ARCHITECTURE: EUROPE AND THE MEDITERRANEAN REGION

Neolithic art (c. 8000-6000 B.C.E.) marks the rise of permanent agricultural settlements in Europe and the Mediterranean. In Europe, colossal stone megaliths were erected in alignment with the Sun at the solstices and equinoxes, attesting the rising importance of agriculture. Examples include Stonehenge (3100-1550 B.C.E.) on the Salisbury Plain, England, and long parallel ranks of stone monoliths (menhirs) found at Carnac (c. 4000 B.C.E.) in southern Brittany. Menhirs occasionally bear simple relief carvings of the *horror vacuii* (leaving no spot untouched) type. Other megalithic monuments include "table stones," or dolmen, believed to be the remains of passage graves; cromlechs, or stone grave circles; and cairns, or stone mounds marking a gravesite.

In the Near East, Neolithic fortifications at Jericho (c. 8000-7000 B.C.E.) included a 5-foot-thick (1.5-meter-thick) brick wall more than 12 feet (3.7 meters) in height and a tower 30 feet (9 meters) in height and diameter. "Spirit traps" made from decorated human skulls found at Jericho (c. 7000-6000 B.C.E.) indicate cults of ancestor worship. Excavations at Hacilar and Çatalhüyük, in Anatolia (c. 6000 B.C.E.), reveal a Neolithic culture spanning eight hundred years. The settlement at Çatalhüyük consists of rectangular mud-brick chambers interconnected via common walls for easy defense. Interior decorations include wall murals depicting silhouettelike images of hunters as well as numerous shrines to an unknown bull deity. Clay statuettes from Çatalhüyük resemble earlier Paleolithic fetish objects, such as the *"Venus" of Willendorf* (c. 30,000-25,000 B.C.E.), and may represent homeopathic magic-making images.

ANCIENT MESOPOTAMIA

This region encompassed the alluvial plain north of the Persian Gulf corresponding to modern-day Iraq. From circa 3000 to 300 B.C.E., several kingdoms rose successively to prominence in this semi-arid region. The culture of Sumer (c. 3500-2300 B.C.E.), a group of cities near the convergence of the Tigris and Euphrates Rivers, emerged as the first of the great Mesopotamian civilizations and therefore served as a paradigm for later development in this region. The Sumerian representational style, roughly contemporaneous with ancient Egypt, was widely emulated, especially its use of the simultaneous profile, which combines profile and frontal views of the figure. Artworks celebrate the power and prestige of the local gods and the ruler-king, whose power was usually absolute.

Sumerian images often incorporate sequential narrative, a pictorial device linked to the Sumerian

invention of linear texts, as in the Standard of Ur (c. 2600 B.C.E.). Votive figures of carved marble are distinguished by their rigid frontal quality: For example, statuettes from Tel Asmar, Iraq (c. 2700-2500 B.C.E.), have their arms folded across the chest in solemn prayer with eyes wide and staring, outlined in black. A bearded bull, perhaps representing a legendary god-hero, appears as a design motif on a harp from Ur (c. 2600 B.C.E.).

Temples took the form of enormous step-pyramids called ziggurats, an example of which, the ziggurat of the Moon god Nanna, Ur (c. 2250-2233 B.C.E.), has been partly reconstructed. Built of mud brick and bitumen, ziggurats were topped by a shrine to which, it was believed, the god descended for earthly visits.

Principal Mesopotamian civilizations include Akkad (c. 2300-2100 B.C.E.), especially under the semilegendary Semitic ruler Sargon of Akkad (r. c. 2334 to 2279 B.C.E.) and his grandson Naram-Sin (r. c. 2200 B.C.E.), remembered in a victory stela; Babylonia (1900-1500 B.C.E.), especially during the reign of the famed lawmaker Hammurabi (r. 1792-1750 B.C.E.), remembered in a stela; Assyria (c. 2300-612 B.C.E.), especially under Sargon II (r. 721-705 B.C.E.), notable for his palace complex at Dur Sharrukin (later Khorsabad); and Persia (c. 1000 B.C.E.-334 B.C.E.), especially under the Achaemenian kings Darius the Great (r. 522-486 B.C.E.) and Xerxes I (r. 486-465 B.C.E.), whose palace complex at Persepolis blends elements from earlier epochs: colossal Assyrian *lamasu* figures of winged bull-men, Egyptian ornamental details, and Ionian volutes and columns.

ANCIENT EGYPT

Ancient Egypt (c. 3100-300 B.C.E.) occupied the fertile river valleys bordering the Nile River. About 3100 B.C.E., the Lower Kingdom surrounding the Nile Delta and the Upper Kingdom extending south of Memphis were united by King Menes (also known as Narmer), who established his capital at Memphis, thus beginning the dynastic period. The first artist known by name is the Egyptian Imhotep (fl. twenty-seventh century B.C.E.), a figure mentioned in period writings as the "father of medicine." Imhotep served as architect of the step pyramid tomb of King Djoser (r. c. 2687-2668 B.C.E.) at Saqqara.

Egyptian art revolved around the ruling pharaoh and his preparations for the afterlife. Preservation of the body through mummification provided a dwelling place for the *ka*, or vitalizing force. Sculptural *ka* portraits, such as the *Khafre*, from Giza (c. 2570-2544), served a purpose similar to that of spirit traps. Spare body parts were provided as well as small modeled servants (*ushabti*) for pharaoh to command.

Old Kingdom tombs (before c. 2200 B.C.E.) evolved from squat rectangular *mastabas* into the massive pyramids at Giza, whose form is thought to derive from the *ben-ben*, a fetish representing the beneficent rays of the Sun god Amun-Re. The Egyptian necropolis (city of the dead) included pyramid tombs, temples, and guardian statues such as the Great Sphinx at Giza (c. 2550 B.C.E.), carved from a spur of living rock elaborated with brickwork. Middle Kingdom rock-cut tombs, such as those at Beni-Hasan (c. 2000-1500 B.C.E.), consist of horizontal chambers cut into the rocky hillsides and fronted by column-and-entablature facades. New Kingdom mortuary temples (after c. 1570 B.C.E.) were located some distance from the burial site to confound tomb robbers. A notable example is the elaborate terraced temple complex dedicated to the female pharaoh Hatshepsut (r. c. 1502-1483 B.C.E.).

Pharaonic tombs included painted reliefs depicting scenes of earthly pleasures as well as rites of passage into the afterlife drawn from the Egyptian *Book of the Dead* (also known as *Book of Going Forth by Day, Coming Into Day*, compiled and edited in the sixteenth century B.C.E.). Among these is a cycle of paintings known as the psychostasis (soul-balancing), in which the deceased's heart is tested against the feather of truth while a hybrid demon, the lesser god Ammit, stands ready to devour the unjust; an example of this type of painting is *Last Judgment Before Osiris*, Thebes (c. 1310 B.C.E.).

The Egyptian figural style derives from the seminal *Palette of Narmer* (c. 3150 B.C.E.). Rela-tive size of the figures indicates relative importance; the king was always largest. Egyptian art is highly formalized, carved in accordance with mathematical canons of proportion to ensure conformity. Persons of lesser prestige and animals are represented in a more realistic manner, while persons of prestige are idealized. Relatively few stylistic changes occurred until the reign of the pharaoh Akhenaton (c. 1390-c. 1360 B.C.E.), whose courtly Amarna style is distinguished by its relaxed naturalistic compositions. A religious as well as an artistic reformer, Akhenaton embraced the cult of Aton, a solitary solar deity (*Akhenaton* means "he is pleasing to Aton"). Following Akhenaton's death, however, the old gods and rigid artistic conventions were soon reasserted. The last Pharaonic dynasty (the Thirty-first) ended in 305 B.C.E., after Alexander the Great's death, when one of his generals established a Greek-speaking dynasty in Egypt.

PRECLASSICAL HELLADIC CIVILIZATIONS

These civilizations, from circa 2500 to 1000 B.C.E., arose on the Peloponnese and the islands of the Aegean Sea. Principal among these was the Minoan civilization (c. 2500-1200 B.C.E.) on the island of Crete, a center of maritime traffic and cultural exchange. King Minos's palace at Knossos (c. 1500 B.C.E.) is among the largest of the unfortified Minoan palaces; its rambling, mazelike plan may have inspired the myth of the Minotaur. Among the remarkable fresco fragments from Knossos is a portrait of a pretty green-eyed brunette nicknamed *La Parisienne* (c. 1500 B.C.E.) because of the subject's uncanny resemblance to the young women of Paris. Also represented are frescoes (such as the *Toreador fresco*, also known as *The Bull-Games*, c. 1500 B.C.E.) of bull vaulting, a ritual that involved grasping the horns of a charging bull and somersaulting over, or perhaps onto, the animal's back.

Minoan Kamares ware ceramic vessels such as the *Octopus Jar*, Gournia (c. 1600 B.C.E.), recovered near Phaestus, bear painted images of sea life, decorative whorls, and other sea-inspired patterns. Glazed statuettes of an unknown Minoan goddess or priestess, including the *Snake Goddess*, Knossos (c. 1600 B.C.E.), standing bare-breasted with open bodice and grasping a writhing snake in each hand, are also common.

In contrast, Mycenaean art (c. 1500-1200 B.C.E.) exhibits the warlike character of the Mycenaean kings inhabiting the Greek Peloponnese. Important citadel palaces at Tiryns and nearby Mycenae were protected by massive stone walls pierced by long corbeled galleries. Beehive tombs, such as the misnamed Treasury of Atreus at Mycenae (c. 1250 B.C.E.), employ corbeling to generate high ogival domes, some more than 40 feet (12 meters) in height and diameter. Relief carving above the lintel of the lion gate at Mycenae (c. 1250 B.C.E.) depicts two imposing heraldic lions, now partially ruined, flanking a column of the "inverted" Minoan type, evidence that such columns were revered as cult objects. Ancient Mycenae bore the Homeric epithet "rich in gold," and the Mycenaean taste for metal craft is evident in artifacts recovered from shaft graves, including bronze dagger blades inlaid with gold and silver and gold repoussé work made by hammering a relief image from thin sheet metal. One example of this metalwork is the Vaphio cup (c. 1650-1450). Mycenaean repoussé funerary masks, such as the *Mask of "Agamemnon"* (c. 1550-1500 B.C.E.), bore a stylized likeness of the deceased.

Cycladic art (c. 2500-2000 B.C.E.) encompasses the Bronze Age cultures of the Cyclades Islands, which, because of their physical insularity, lagged somewhat behind the more developed cultural centers at Crete and the mainland. Marble plank idols ranging in size from several inches (five or six centimeters) to more than four feet (slightly over a meter) in length often accompany burials and most probably represent a goddess of rebirth. Seated male musicians holding lyrelike instruments made up a later three-dimensional variant in the *Harp Player* from Keros (c. 2500-2200 B.C.E.). Similar clay figures found on Crete and the Greek mainland suggest that these cultures enjoyed some contact, though not intensive enough to inspire a significant intermingling of traditions.

CLASSICAL GREECE

The Hellenic Age (fifth and fourth centuries B.C.E.) marks the rise of the Greek city-states following the Persian armada's defeat at the Battle of Salamis (480 B.C.E.). The art of Classical Greece, with Athens as its cultural epicenter, existed in service of philosophical ideals expressed through reasoned aesthetic principles. Its development can be traced through several evolutionary phases and substyles; in ceramics, simple repetitive geometric style designs, as in the Dipylon Vase (eighth century B.C.E.), evolve into increasingly complex representational images in black figure style, such as the François Vase (c. 570 B.C.E.), and a later red figure style represented by Euphronius's Death of Sarpedon (c. 515 B.C.E.).

Sculpture was the favored art form of the ancient Greeks. Sculpted marble figures of the Archaic period (800-500 B.C.E.) manifest an "Egyptian stride," especially evident in the nude male *kouros* figures, grave memorials formerly thought to represent the god Apollo (female counterparts are called *kore*). Earlier Archaic figures such as *Kouros from Tenea* (c. 570 B.C.E.) appear stylized and tentative. Faces present a generic type stamped with a distinctive "archaic smile" whose very ubiquity suggests a meaning other than happiness—perhaps the facial rigor of the deceased as a funerary marker. In just over one hundred years, however, the Greek *kouroi* sculptors mastered the subtleties of anatomical representation, including the elegant counterpoise of hip and shoulder when body weight is shifted onto one leg, called ponderation, as can be seen in *Kritios Boy*, Athens (c. 480 B.C.E.).

In Greek philosophy, as in Greek art, perfection of form was thought to go hand in hand with perfection of concept: For a thing to be perfect, it had to look perfect as well. Therefore, later classical sculptors (c. fifth century B.C.E.) developed canons of proportion thought to yield an ideal figure, as in Polyclitus's *Doryphorus* (c. 440 B.C.E.). Most Greek marble carvings were painted, especially facial details and drapery, to enhance their verisimilitude; the pristine appearance of classical sculpture is entirely an accident of time.

Classical Greek architecture used mortarless post-and-lintel construction techniques. Temple forms are varied, but most incorporate a rectangular *naos* (or cella) fronted or surrounded by columns supporting a spanning entablature and gabled roof. The pediment, or triangular area beneath the roof gables, was frequently adorned with sculpture. Three classical orders are readily identified by their distinctive column capitals: the Doric Order with its plain cushionlike capitals; the Ionic Order with its elegant scroll-shaped volutes; and the Corinthian Order, originating from Asia Minor, with its bundled acanthus leaves.

The most famous examples of classical architecture are the temples on the Athenian Acropolis (literally, "hill city"), built in gratitude to the protector goddess Athena Parthenos. The Parthenon, a Doric temple with Ionic features (built by archi-tects Ictinus and Callicrates in 447-432 B.C.E.), originally housed a 40-foot (12-meter) gold and ivory statue of Athena (now lost) by the sculptor Phidias, as well as the treasury of the Delian League. The Parthenon's original relief carvings and pediment statues (by the workshop of Phidias) are now in the British Museum. The Erechtheum, a rambling Ionic structure built by Mnesicles (fl. fifth century B.C.E.) to commemorate a contest between Athena and Poseidon, contains within its compass several cult items: a sacred olive grove, a stone marked by Poseidon's trident, a saltwater spring, and the tomb of the semi-legendary hero Erechtheus; therefore, the Erechtheum is asymmetric and built on two different levels. The south Porch of Maidens is famous for its caryatids, female figures used as supporting columns. The Propylaea built by Mnesicles, gateway to the Acropo-

The Erechtheum in Athens, built by Mnesicles, is known for its Porch of Maidens with caryatids, female figures used as columns. (PhotoDisc)

lis, contained a picture gallery-museum in its north wing.

The later period following the death of Alexander the Great of Macedonia (r. 336-323) was regarded as a decadent epoch by Roman scholars such as Pliny the Elder, who called it Hellenistic (meaning "Greek-like"); it has since come to be appreciated in its own right, however, for its distinctive emphasis on realism, movement, and emotion. Among the many Hellenistic masterpieces are the *Nike of Samothrace* (c. 190? B.C.E.) and *Laocoön* by Agesander, Polydorus, and Athenodorus of Rhodes (c. 100 B.C.E.), a work much admired by Michelangelo. Many surviving classical sculptures are actually Roman marble copies of lost Greek originals.

ROMAN ART

In the two centuries following the birth of Christ, the Roman Republic expanded from a small Etruscan settlement to an Empire encircling the Mediterranean Sea and extending, at its zenith, well into Britain, North Africa, and Asia Minor—the entire known world. From an artistic standpoint, the Romans especially admired Greek culture and emulated it, employing Greek slaves as artisans; thus, Roman art continues the Classical Age begun in Greece in the fifth century B.C.E.

The Romans excelled at civic architecture, employing the round arch and its variants, the barrel vault, the intersecting groin vault, and the dome, in combination with decorative elements borrowed from Classical Greece, as in the Flavian Amphitheater in Rome (c. 80 C.E.). Roman architecture used concrete poured over stone rubble and faced with slabs of marble veneer. The Pantheon, a temple dedicated to the planetary gods (c. 125), incorporates most of the distinctive Roman architectural elements. Roman triumphal arches, such as the arch of Titus (c. 81), and columnar monuments, such as the column of Trajan (dedicated 113), feature reliefs commemorating significant military campaigns. Roman public monuments often bear the inscription SPQR, an abbreviation for *Senatus Populusque Romanus* ("the senate and people of Rome").

Especially popular were the numerous Roman baths, the "people's palaces," which featured warm, hot, and cold pools, hence their Latin name *thermae* ("hot springs"). Notable examples are found in the city of Bath (Aquae Salis) in southwestern England and the ruined Baths of Caracalla in Rome (c. 215). Lavishly decorated, the baths provided the plebeian class with a taste of patrician comfort and splendor. A system of sloped watercourses called aqueducts, some more than 20 miles (32 kilometers) long, brought fresh water from distant mountain streams.

The ancient Romans worshiped ancestral gods (*lars*); therefore, portrait busts are plentiful. Sculptors offered stock figures for sale, carved "in the Greek style," with blank or missing faces to be carved to order. Portraits of the emperors are idealized, dressed in military cuirass, and gesturing as if delivering a proclamation. The larger-than-life marble *Augustus of Prima Porta* (early first century C.E.) is a work of this type; the cupid astride a dolphin may allude to Augustus's imagined link to the line of Aeneas, son of Venus and the founder of Roman civilization.

In the later Imperial era (after mid-second century C.E.), the realism of the Republican period gives way to a more stylized, doll-like figural type influenced by the art of Asia Minor. This later "decadent" type established the paradigm for most early Christian art.

EARLY CHRISTIAN ART

From about the second to third centuries C.E., the early Christians eschewed the worldly cultures of Greece and Rome for a higher didactic purpose: to teach the way to salvation by spreading the Christian faith. Physical beauty became a secondary concern. Early Christians were bitterly persecuted for suspected ideological sedition until the Roman emperor Constantine the Great (r. 306-337 C.E.) converted to the new religion after a battlefield vision. Constantine legalized Christianity through his promulgation of the Edict of Milan (313 C.E.) and later established Christianity as the favored religion of the Roman Empire (324 C.E.).

Stylistically speaking, early Christian art is a continuation of the late Roman decadent style; only the subject matter differs. Ironically, the old gods were occasionally pressed into Christian service as a ready link to the mythic past, for example, in *Christ Depicted as Apollo Driving the Sun Chariot*, vault mosaic detail, Mausoleum of the Julii, Rome (c. 250-275).

During the Great Persecution (303-313 C.E.), Christian rituals were secretly enacted in private homes. Hastily painted catacomb frescoes appeared in the mazelike burial passageways beneath the city of Rome. In the Recognition period (after 313 C.E.), the emphasis shifted to architecture. Churches emulated Roman meeting halls (*basilicas*) following either a central plan after the Greek cross, as at San Vitale, Ravenna (526-547 C.E.), or a longitudinal plan after the Latin crucifix, as at San Apollinaire Nuovo, Ravenna (c. 500). Church exteriors are unadorned, and interiors are ornate, reflecting the Christian dichotomy between body (debased matter) and soul (transcendent, immortal). Mosaics of coarse stone or glass incorporate denaturalized figures to avoid idolatry; sculpture was not favored, for obvious reasons.

BYZANTINE ART

Following the collapse of the Western Roman Empire in 476 C.E., the city of Ravenna, on Italy's Adriatic coast, enjoyed a period of cultural ascendancy under Emperor Justinian I (r. 527-565 C.E.). A second capital had been established in 329 C.E. by Constantine at Constantinople (Istanbul, formerly called Byzantium) to serve the sprawling Eastern Empire. Byzantine art is characterized by Islamic influences filtering westward from the Eastern half of the empire, as evident in Haghia Sophia, a church in Constantinople (consecrated in 537 C.E.).

The Byzantine style continued the denaturalized forms of late Roman art but with a greater feeling for visual design. Images incorporated arabesque motifs borrowed from Islamic wall reliefs and the pages of the Qur'ān. Figures became flatter and more stylized and took on a weightless

quality. Mosaic remained the dominant medium for architectural decoration with gold backgrounds indicating that a scene took place outside of normal space and time, as in the apse mosaic *The Second Coming*, San Vitale (c. 547). The sanctuary mosaic at San Vitale of *Emperor Justinian and His Retinue* (c. 547) indicates relative importance of the personages by placement and overlapping (an ambiguity is evident in the placement of Justinian relative to Bishop Maximianus).

ART OF THE MIGRATION PERIOD

A great migratory wave of Germanic Visigoths, Ostrogoths, Slavs, and Asiatic peoples among others swept across Western Europe and into southern Britain from about the fifth to ninth centuries C.E. Prominent among these were the Norsemen or Vikings. The ferocity of the Viking raids is evidenced in an Old English prayer that ends with a supplication for protection against "the fury of the Northmen." The characterization of the migration cultures as ruthless "barbarians," however, is not entirely accurate; such cultures were highly developed within their own limits, reflecting complex adaptations to their environments.

Norse and Germanic artifacts and nomad gear are generally associated with practical ends: wrought-edged weapons, carrying satchels and purses, jeweled brooches for fastening capes, utensils, and horse tack. Wood and metalwork designs suggest plaited strips of leather and exhibit the *horror vacuii* found in primitive art. Common motifs include stylized heraldic animals in mirror-reverse poses, as in the Purse Lid, Sutton Hoo cache (c. 655-656). Forged and cast implements predominate with little or no repoussé work in evidence. Jewelry was chiefly cloisonné (colored glass or enamel set between thin strips of soldered metal). Ceremonial weapons were decorated with inlay of ductile wire (copper, silver, or gold) hammered into the grooves of a chiseled design.

Intact Viking ships have been recovered from burial sites at Sutton Hoo, England (early seventh century) and Oseberg, Norway (c. ninth century), the latter found buried with its hawser tied to a nearby boulder. All feature shallow draft hulls that allowed the ships to be rowed in close to shore. Removable wooden figureheads of stylized beasts were believed to ward off spirits. A single sail, embroidered and trimmed in fur, hung from a removable mast slotted into the ship's keel. Norse migration period dwellings take the form of long halls whose roof lines, interestingly enough, resemble inverted ships' hulls.

HIBERNO-SAXON ART

Hiberno-Saxon art (sixth to seventh centuries C.E.) reflects the culture of Christianized Ireland in the period following the pagan conquest of Britain. Gospel books were hand-copied from older manuscripts by monks working in the monastic scriptoria. The *Lindisfarne Gospels* (c. late seventh century C.E.) is noteworthy for its serpentine designs influenced by Celtic cordwaining. Illuminations of the figure are highly denaturalized because medieval copyists, unaccustomed to drawing from life, resorted to constructing figures from calligraphic marks.

Once referred to disparagingly as the Dark Ages, the thousand-year span from the fall of Rome (fifth century C.E.) to the rebirth of Greco-Roman culture in the Italian Renaissance (c. 1400 C.E.) has since come to be appreciated as a rich cultural epoch dominated intellectually, spiritually, and artistically by the Catholic Church and, to a lesser degree, the secular nobility of continental Europe and Britain.

ADDITIONAL RESOURCES
Boardman, John. *Greek Art*. 1964. Reprint. London: Thames and Hudson, 1985.
Bonnefoy, Yves. *Mythologies*. Translated by Wendy Doniger. Chicago: University of Chicago Press, 1991.
Osborne, Harold, ed. *The Oxford Companion to Art*. Oxford, England: Oxford University Press, 1970.
Pritchard, James B., ed. *The Ancient Near East: An Anthology in Texts and Pictures*. 2 vols. 1958. Reprint. Princeton, N.J.: Princeton University Press, 1973.

SEE ALSO: Achaemenian Dynasty; Aeneas; Akhenaton; Akkadians; Alexander the Great; Angles, Saxons, Jutes; Augustus; Babylonia; *Book of the Dead*; Britain; Byzantine Empire; Callicrates; Celts; Christianity; Constantine the Great; Cyclades; Darius the Great; Egypt, Pharaonic; Flavian Amphitheater; Goths; Greece, Archaic; Greece, Mycenaean; Hadrian's villa; Haghia Sophia; Hatshepsut; Ictinus; Imhotep; Islam; Justinian I; Milan, Edict of; Neolithic Age, Europe; Phidias; Pliny the Elder; Polybius; Polyclitus; Pyramids and the Sphinx; Roman Arch; Roman Forum; Rome, Imperial; Salamis, Battle of; Sargon of Akkad; Sargon II; Slavs; Stonehenge; Sumerians; Sutton Hoo; Trajan's column; Xerxes I.

—*Larry Smolucha*

ART AND ARCHITECTURE: INDIA

Evidence of notable artistic and architectural accomplishments in India can be traced as far back as the Indus Valley civilization (c. 3500-1700 B.C.E.), which is best known by its two largest cities, Mohenjo-Daro, beside the Indus River in Sind, and Harappā, beside the former course of the tributary Ravi, nearly 400 miles (644 kilometers) northeast in the Punjab.

MOHENJO-DARO AND HARAPPĀ

Mohenjo-Daro seems to have been a well-planned city. The many dwelling houses vary in size from small buildings with two rooms to a palatial structure having a frontage of 85 feet (26 meters) and depth of 97 feet (30 meters), with outerwalls 4 to 5 feet (1.2-1.5 meters) thick and made of high-quality burnt bricks. Evidence suggests the use of large bricks measuring 20.25 inches (51 centimeters) long, 10.5 inches (27 centimeters) broad, and 3.5 inches (9 centimeters) thick. The big houses have two or more stories and are furnished with paved floors and courtyards, doors, windows, and narrow stairways. A bathroom, drain, and walls are features of every house, and large pillared halls, some measuring 80 feet (24 meters) square, of elaborate structure and design, are commonly found in spacious buildings.

The roads cut each other at right angles, an arrangement that helped the prevailing winds work as a sort of suction pump, automatically cleaning the atmosphere. A sophisticated drainage system used brick-laid channels that varied from 9 to 12 inches (23-30 centimeters) deep to double that size flowing through every street. The channels were covered with loose bricks that could be removed when necessary. Brick-lined cesspits allowed the flow of rainwater and sewage from the houses. Long drains were provided with sumps at intervals to facilitate easy cleaning of the channels. Large brick culverts were constructed on the outskirts of the city to carry storm water. The Great Bath, 180 feet (55 meters) long and 180 feet (55 meters) wide, consisting of a large open quadrangle in the center with galleries and rooms on all sides, is the most imposing structure in the city. In the center of the quadrangle is a large swimming enclosure 39 feet (12 meters) long, 23 feet (7 meters) wide, and 8 feet (2.4 meters) deep. It has a flight of steps at either end and is fed by a well in one of the adjoining rooms. The water is discharged by a huge drain with a corbeled roof more than 6 feet (1.8 meters) in height.

Harappā reveals the oldest example yet known of systematic town planning. The citadel mound was fortified by a mud-brick rampart tapering upward from a 40-foot (12-meter) base, with a similarly tapering external revetment of baked brick. The 300 yards (274 meters) between the mound and the river enclosed barracklike blocks of workmen's quarters, serried lines of circular brick floors with central wooden mortars for pounding

grain, and two rows of ventilated granaries, twelve in all, marshaled on a podium. The total floorspace of the granaries was greater than 9,000 square feet (837 square meters). To the south of the citadel was an extensive cemetery.

The people of the Indus Valley had a large variety of pottery, both decorated and plain. All the ornamented wares are coated with an opaque red slip, on which various designs and motifs are painted with a thick black pigment. The paint appears to have come from the adjacent river and is tempered with sand that contains a large percentage of mica, or lime. The regular striations inside practically every vessel suggest the use of a potter's wheel. The pottery made in Mohenjo-Daro differs very little in shape and mode of decoration from that of Harappā. The slip used for most pottery is red ochre, and designs were painted with brush on this red surface before firing. A common motif resembles a large comb with solar signs or chessboard patterns, and another design features a series of intersecting circles or tree patterns placed in metopes or panels alternating with other motifs. Figures of animals are juxtaposed with natural objects such as grass or leaves. Beautifully carved beads, seals, and seal amulets made of stealite, as well as some bronze and copper ware, have been identified as belonging to the Indus Valley civilization.

Evidence of notable post-Indus Valley civilizations is found in the legendary city of Hastināpura, dating back to about 1000-800 to 500 B.C.E., in the upper Ganges Valley, where remains of mud or mud-brick walls of unascertainable plan and distinctive gray painted pottery with black linear patterns have been found. Iron seems to have been widely used, and in later periods, a hard and distinctive glossy black ware emerged, which imitated polished iron with its steel-like quality. Hastināpura was the epic capital of the Kaurava kings and Ahicchattrā, near Ramnagar in Uttar Pradesh, is the capital of North Panchala; the splendor of both cities is richly described in the epic *Mahābhārata* (400 B.C.E.-400 C.E., present form by c. 400 C.E.; *The Mahabharata of Krishna-Dwaipayana Vyasa*, 1887-1896).

MAURYAN EMPIRE

After the Greek invasion of Persia in the early fifth century B.C.E., the convergence of need and opportunity brought to the Mauryan Empire trained artisans from Persia who, in collaboration with native artisans, ushered in a revolution in masonry architecture in India. The defenses of Old Rājgīr in the hills of southern Bihar, 25 miles (40 kilometers) in length, are dry-built of unshapen stones, with square bastions at frequent intervals, and enclose the city of Magadha, which achieved distinction in the sixth century B.C.E. with the association of Buddha and Vardhamāna.

In the fifth century B.C.E., the rulers of Magadha built a fortress on the plain beside the rivers Ganges and Son, where the town of Patna now stands. About 320 B.C.E., the first Mauryan emperor enlarged this fortress of Pāṭali into the splendid capital city of Pāṭaliputra. From the accounts of Megasthenes, the envoy of Seleucus I at the Mauryan court about 302 B.C.E., and archaeological excavations, it has been determined that Pāṭaliputra formed an oblong beside the river more than 9 miles (14.5 kilometers) long and more than 1 mile (1.6 kilometers) wide. Fortified by a ditch 200 yards (183 meters) across and a timber palisade with towers and loopholes for archers, the city was beautified by several parks, fish tanks, shady groves, and pastures planted with trees. The sophistication of the architectural endeavors is confirmed by the lengths of imposing timber framework and masonry that have been unearthed, particularly a column-capital with stepped impost, side volutes, and central palmettes of Persian and bead-and-reel patterns. Religion plays an integral part in the artistic and architectural attainments of a culture, and the influence of Buddhism and Jainism along with Hinduism is evident in the art and architecture of the Mauryan Empire.

The art of sculpture or rock cutting reached its zenith during Aśoka's reign (r. c. 265-238 B.C.E.), when Buddhist edicts were engraved on highly polished monolithic pillars. The capital of the famous Sārnāth pillar consists of four lions that originally supported the wheel of law resting on the abacus bearing in relief an elephant, a horse, a bull, and a lion. Sudama cave, an excavated hall of the Aśokan period found at Barabar Hills, consists of a circular chamber and an antechamber with side

These stupas from the Mauryan period were discovered near Sanchi in the 1990's. (AP/Wide World Photos)

entrances. The remains of Aśoka's palace at Pāṭaliputra resemble the pillared halls of the Achaemenian kings of Persepolis.

Sanchi in Bhopal contains the most remarkable group of early Buddhist shrines, or stupas, belonging to Mauryan, Sungan, and the Sātavāhana periods (72-25 B.C.E.). The reliefs of the great gateway, whose principal themes are drawn from the life of the Buddha and from the *Jātakas*, are marvels of decorative storytelling. There are three main stupas and several smaller ones, on average measuring about 120 feet (37 meters) in diameter and 54 feet (16 meters) in height and all originally plastered. The balustrade and gateways are carved with numerous details from Buddhist legends and carry fascinating details—processions and battles and sieges; walled townships, temples and holy trees; kings and warriors, fairies, dwarfs, and snake-gods; elephants and chariots, lions, goats, camels, bulls, griffins and peacocks—all depicting everyday life. Another interesting relic of Aśoka's age is the Bharhut stupa (located near Allahabad), which is covered with a coat of plaster and in which hundreds of triangular shaped recesses had been made to hold lights for the illumination of the monument. It was common Buddhist practice to decorate the stupas with flowers, garlands, banners, and lights.

Taxila, an ancient city mentioned extensively in Alexander the Great's campaign records, has several temples and shrines contained within 12 square miles (31 square kilometers). The north gate in the town wall, about 15 to 20 feet (4.6 to 6 meters) thick, is the main entrance to the city and leads on to the main blocks of buildings, each with a frontage of 110 to 120 feet (34 to 37 meters), divided off by streets at right angles on each side. The building foundations that remain date to the first centuries before and after the common era and for the most part formed the basis of private houses and shops. Found on the east side are exceptional examples of Buddhist or Jain stupas that combine classical Hellenistic design with Corinthian plasters but also include niches in purely Indian modes. Important Buddhist religious shrines include Mohrā Morādu, Pipalīya, Jaulian southeast

of Sirsukh, and those that grew up in the vicinity of the famous Dharmarājika Stupa, which was itself refaced at this time. During the Kushān Dynasty (second century B.C.E. to c. 300 C.E.), the Dharmarājika Stupa area was a focus for architectural and artistic activity.

In addition to their architectural splendor, these sites have a wealth of sculpture in clay and plaster belonging to the Gandhāra School (named after the ancient name for the region), which is a northern Kushān art style complementary to the southern Mathurā school of Muttra. Its outstanding characteristic is the admixture of late Hellenistic conventions with native Indian styles. At the Jaulian site, on a hilltop 300 feet (91 meters) above the plain, is the finest collection of late Gandhāra stucco work, most of it dating from the fifth century C.E.

Significant architectural accomplishments after the Aśokan period include the Great Stupa of Amaravātī, which originally was built in the late second century B.C.E. and was provided with sculptured casing slabs and railings in the first, second, and third centuries C.E. On the drum of the stupa are four projecting offsets facing each of the entrances and each displaying five pillars called Āryaka Khambhas. Surrounded by a rail, the stupa was decorated with rosettes, stories from the *Jātakas*, walled and moated cities, palace buildings, and stupas. The old *vihāra* (monastery) at Bhaja near Poona, datable to the second century C.E., contains unique reliefs. Bedsa and other caves of the same period near Poona consist of a nave, apse, and aisle; the apse contains a solid stupa, and the aisle continues round the apse, thus providing a path for circumambulation. The *caitya* (hall of worship) at Karle, which may be dated to the first century B.C.E., has magnificent horseshoe windows, great pillars, and finely carved reliefs.

THE GUPTA PERIOD

Indian architecture and sculpture attained their zenith in the Gupta period (fourth to sixth century C.E.) and are best represented in temple architecture, a notable example of which is the famous

Dhamekh stupa, with exquisitely carved geometrical and floral ornaments, at Sārnāth near Banaras, datable to the sixth century C.E.

The Cālukyan Dynasty (c. 550-642) used the river gorge of Ajanta, with its almost sheer rock sides at an impressive horseshoe bend in the stream, to build a series of rock-cut structures, which fall into two classes: *caityas* (halls of worship) and *vihāras* (monasteries), having a central court, cells for monks, and a shrine. All caves are long-aisled structures with colonnades forming an apse around a stupa, which, in the later *caityas* belonging to the Mahāyāna sect of Buddhism, are fronted by an image of the Buddha. The *vihāras* essentially have a square central court with a veranda and, in the later examples, pillars within the court with surrounding cells and a shrine at the rear. The rock-hewn structures reproduced, underground and in solid stone, the features of the monasteries, shrines, and assembly halls previously built in wood above. On some pillars are found striking figures of bodhisattvas, which in their pose and details of drapery resemble the semi-Hellenistic Gandhāra tradition of northwest India, and the pictorial scenes consist mainly of *Jātakas*, legends of the former existences of the Buddha. The most famous one is the great bodhisattva with the lotus (Padmapani) on the left of the entrance to the shrine.

The Deccan area, with fine-grained homogenous volcanic formations that eroded into almost vertical rock faces, was conducive for elaborate subterranean architectural sculpture and gave rise to the paintings of Ellora. The best preserved of the group depicts a large figure of the Buddha on a lion throne flanked on the sidewall by great standing figures of bodhisattvas. Tin Thal, a *vihāra* dating from the early eighth century C.E., has a large Buddha on the ground floor with attendant figures and an open veranda and pillared hall on the first floor with a shrine in the back wall and numerous other sculptures. The top story, with its forty-two plain square columns in accurate alignment, is very impressive. Two finely sculptured deer bear the Buddha on a throne below. The main group of rock temples, consisting of seventeen constructions,

belongs to the Brahmanical or Hindu religious tradition, and the temples range in date from the eighth to the ninth centuries C.E.

The Kailāsa, probably begun by the Rāshtrakūta Dynasty in 760 C.E., is an exemplary piece with the temple carved by digging out a great rectangular quarry 154 by 276 feet (47 by 84 meters), more than 100 feet (30 meters) deep, around a central block of stone. The northernmost group consists of double-storied temples of the Jain faith built from around the second half of the eighth century C.E. Dilwāra, Vimala, and Tejapāla are Jain temples that contain elaborately conceived stonework and ingenious craftsmanship in marble. Between 950 and 1050 C.E., the beautiful temples at Khajuraho were erected. Exquisitely hewn floral and human sculptures add considerably to its beauty.

The Pallavas

The Pallavas were a great power in southern India and on the east coast between circa 500 and 800 C.E. and contributed significantly to the artistic and architectural growth in south India. The five *rathas* (chariots) at Mahabalipuram are all monoliths datable to the first half of the seventh century C.E. The great *gopurams* (temple towers) of the Pāṇḍya period are found at Srirangam, Madurai, and Kumbakonam. The examples of the great pillared *mandapa* (temple prayer hall) of the Vijayanagar period are found at Kanchi, Vijayanagar, and Vellore.

Additional resources

Coomaraswamy, Ananda K. *Essays in Architectural Theory.* Delhi, India: Oxford University Press, 1995.

Majumdar, R. C. *Ancient India.* Delhi, India: Motilal Banarsidass, 1968.

Piggott, Stuart. *Some Ancient Cities of India.* London: Oxford University Press, 1945.

Puri, B. N. *Cities of Ancient India.* Delhi, India: Meenakshi Prakashan, 1966.

Smith, Vincent. *Asoka: The Buddhist Emperor of India.* Oxford, England: Clarendon Press, 1901.

Wheeler, Mortimer. *Civilizations of the Indus Valley and Beyond*. New York: McGraw-Hill, 1966.
_____. *My Archaeological Mission to India and Pakistan*. London: Thames and Hudson, 1976.

SEE ALSO: Amaravātī school; Andhradesha school; Aśoka; Buddha; Buddhism; Buddhist cave temples; Gandhāra art; Gupta emperors; Hinduism; India; Indian temple architecture; Indus Valley civilization; Jainism; *Jākatas*; Kushān Dynasty; *Mahābhārata*; Mahabodhi temple; Mauryan Dynasty; Pallava Dynasty; Pārvatī Devi temple; Selecus I.

—*Kokila Ravi*

ART AND ARCHITECTURE: SOUTHEAST ASIA

The art and architecture of Southeast Asia reveal a complex process of blending the indigenous with the foreign, particularly the arts and architecture of its powerful neighbors China and India, and the transformation of utilitarian artifacts into artistic traditions. For much of the late Neolithic and the Bronze Age periods, no cultural borders existed between southern China and Southeast Asia. In addition to the difficulty in determining exactly what art and architecture can be termed indigenous to Southeast Asia, the chronology of civilization in that area is somewhat difficult to determine. Despite extensive archaeological research, no site has been found that has a comprehensive archaeological sequence connecting the prehistorical and historical periods of Southeast Asia. Early Southeast Asian history may be divided into two periods, the Prehistoric (2500-150 B.C.E.) and Indianized (100 B.C.E.-1300 C.E.).

The earliest but isolated evidence of Southeast Asian metallurgy was found in Thailand in 3000 B.C.E. However, the use of metal was not widespread until 1500 B.C.E. Soon after this time, the typical Neolithic assemblages in the region included cattle, pigs, dogs, fowls, cultivated rice, flooded fields, incised pottery, and metalworks. Unbaked clay figurines of animals and humans from this period are often found together, especially in burial sites. Metalworkers employed the lost-wax method as well as bivalve molds of clay strengthened by rice chaff; however, the most influential metalworks did not develop in the region until around 600 B.C.E.

DONG SON CULTURE AND DONG SON STYLE

Skilled artisans centered around the Red River in northern Vietnam fashioned unique and beautiful bronze drums by which this culture, Dong Son, became identified. Researcher Peter Bellwood draws a distinction between Dong Son culture and Dong Son style, saying that the former refers only to the north Vietnamese area in which these drums most likely were manufactured and traded and that Dong Son style refers to the "classic expression of prehistoric and protohistoric bronze metallurgy in Southeast Asia." Dong Son drums reveal amazing expertise and provide a great degree of documentation for social and ritual activities in the prehistoric period. These drums stood on splayed feet, had rounded upper sides, and a flat tympanum. To an anthropologist, the utilitarian significance of these objects is paramount; to the artist, their decorative embellishment is primary.

Among the earliest drums, known as the Heger type, the most famous has a flat top, a bulbous rim, and straight sides and is footed. Cast in one piece and measuring 26 inches (65 centimeters) in diameter, the top has concentric circles decorated with bands of incised geometric designs or friezes illustrating armed humans with bird-feather headdresses, animal figures such as birds, deer, lizards, and fish, and what look like houses raised on platforms. This type of house, regarded as indigenous Southeast Asian architecture, has been attributed to Austronesian-speaking (Malayo-Polynesian-speaking) seafaring people who had invaded much of insular and parts of mainland Southeast Asia by

2500 B.C.E. The sides of some of the finest drums are decorated with friezes of boats, with prows shaped like the heads of birds and sterns shaped like tail feathers, and sometimes with boat cabins containing drums. Of the two hundred or so Dong Son drums found in Vietnam, Cambodia, Thailand, the Malay Peninsula, and Indonesia, more than half were believed to have originated in Vietnam. None has been found in Borneo or the Philippines. Often they are found in burial sites accompanying lacquered coffins suggestive of stratified communities. Other bronze pieces associated with Dong Son include bracelets, belt hooks, buckles, plaques, axes, and dagger handles, again usually decorated with animal and human figures.

The lost-wax method believed to be the main technique used in the production of the Dong Son vessels was not known in China before 300 B.C.E., an argument that lends authenticity to the Southeast Asian origins of the culture and its extensions. However, a theory of direct migration of the technique from Europe and western Asia to Yunnan (northern Vietnam) is also seriously entertained by some scholars. The Dong Son drums were manufactured and used in Southeast Asia for many centuries.

BURIAL JARS AND RELATED ARTIFACTS

A few metal-age sites in Laos and south Vietnam have gained publicity because of their association with jar burial, most likely a secondary burial of cremated or previously macerated bones. Pottery jar burials at Sa Huynh in south Vietnam, which date to about 500 B.C.E., are the earliest evidence of this practice in mainland Southeast Asia, although this tradition goes back much earlier in the Philippines and Borneo to at least 1000 B.C.E. Found buried in clusters, the jars at Sa Huynh are round based or footed, stand about 31 inches (80 centimeters) high, and are plain or cord-marked. Decorated by horizontal bands of incised triangles and lozenges or stamped geometric patterns of dots, circles, and rectilinear figures as found in other ceramic artifacts, these mainland jars bear closest affinity to a Philippine pottery culture, Kalanay, rather than to pottery of other islands in the region. Considered local innovations from Indonesia and the Philippines, burial pottery jars in later years were colored and more polished. One example is an elegant, long-necked flask from Melolo of Sumba Island decorated in incised geometric and anthropomorphic designs with white lime infills. A humanlike figure stands on top of the bulbous, rounded urn, with a spout on one side. The figure can very easily serve as a handle while pouring.

Other burial jars were not ceramic but cast iron or stone. Stone jars were a localized development in Laos discovered by French archaeologist Madeline Colani in 1935. Colani describes two types of stone structures in Laos: megaliths and tombs in the northeast and stone jars in north-central Laos. In the Plain of Jars at the Ban Ang site in Tranh Ninh province, there are 250 stone vessels fashioned out of soft local stones. Bulbous and cylindrical with thick bases, these stone jars measure between 5 and 10 feet (1.5 and 3.0 meters) in height and diameter. Some have mushroomlike forms, others are decorated with relief quadrupeds, perhaps tigers or monkeys, or simply with relief concentric circles. All types of burial jars were found with or without lids and often containing beads.

MEGALITHIC STRUCTURES

Before Indianization occurred in Southeast Asia, megalithic records for the mainland were virtually nonexistent except in Laos, where besides the stone burial jars, there were megalithic tombs equipped with underground burial chambers and large sitting stones reminiscent of the "dolmens" of Sumatra Island. However, the prehistoric megaliths of insular Southeast Asia are more varied, including slab graves in Malaya and huge human statues carved on large stone blocks depicting men astride a buffalo or flanking an elephant. One Sumatran relief carving depicts a man pulling a sitting elephant by its ear while carrying a sword at his side and a small Dong Son drum on his back. Other artifacts from Sumatra include stone blocks with hollowed-out mortars, troughs, avenues of upright stones, and terraced graves.

Found at Sulawesi, Indonesia, were a number of circular stone vats, some of which were decorated with human faces on their sides and some of which had lids with animal motifs. One such vat was decorated by a series of horizontal lines that look like ribs. A Laos-Sulawesi parallel and connection have been suggested; however, these vats did not contain anything to indicate funerary usage, and the two regions are separated by 3,000 miles (4,830 kilometers).

INDIAN INFLUENCE IN SOUTHEAST ASIA

The introduction of Hinduism and Buddhism into Southeast Asia has been attributed to all sorts of people: Brahmin priests, monks, adventurers, traders, and even princely politicians. Although the two religious traditions were separated by about seven hundred years in India, in Southeast Asia, both arrived almost simultaneously. The architectural legacy produced by this cultural invasion has been impressive and often compared to the monuments of India. The most well known are the Hinduized Angkor Wat on the mainland and Māhāyana Buddhist Borabodur in Java. Built long after 700 C.E., their realization took many centuries. Records for these times remain spotty throughout the region.

Southeast Asians used as their base the Indian notion of *nagara*, a town or sacred city modeled after the legendary Mount Meru, which would have its highest point (peak) protruding from the center, the base of which would consist of a series of descending layers of terraces and palisades. At the heart of this town was the temple. Scholar Carol Brown Heinz noted that although Hindu and Buddhist monuments both tended to have a central raised part, Hinduized leaders such as those at Angkor Wat viewed the temple as housing the lingam of Śiva, Śiva's phallic icon, and Buddhist monarchs viewed these temples as stupas housing relics of the Buddha. Both the Buddhist and Hindu leaders regarded these temples as places where the royal and divine mixed.

A monk examines a doorway of Angkor Wat, a temple built in the twelfth century C.E. This structure reflects the influence of India and Hinduism on Southeast Asia. (Hulton Archive)

The Indian architectural blueprint would be replicated over and over again as *nagaras* rose and fell, often leaving abandoned palaces and temples as new leaders built more buildings and tried to recapture the lost cosmological powers. Funan, Chenla, Angkor, Srivijaya, Ava, Ayutthia, and Borabodur had similar fates. Relief decorations in every nook and corner of temples bore cultic devotions to Hindu gods and their adventures or depictions of the Buddha's life history and demeanor. Many of these reliefs require major restoration; some have been recovered only in fragments.

Until the early eighth century C.E., the finest masterpieces of pre-Angkor art were created in the region of Sambor Prei Kuk and the Mekong River in Cambodia. In Cambodia, home of the Khmers, history started with legendary Funan, noted in Chinese annals as early as 192 C.E., then replaced by Chenla to the north in the sixth century and later to be reconstituted in the glory of the Angkor period between the ninth and thirteenth centuries. Art records for pre-Angkor remain sparse: A group of sixth century C.E. statues, probably Funanese, was discovered carved in rock caves then shielded by a brick wall at Phnom Da, Angkor Borei. Archaeological excavations at Oc Eo, the ancient Funanese maritime capital, yielded several images of the Buddha, one of which was probably a fourth century C.E. creation.

The earliest architectural brick buildings on record were built in Chenla during the seventh century C.E. Stone masterpieces of the sixth and seventh centuries include a statue of Krishna holding up the mountain with his left arm, 63 inches (161 centimeters) tall; standing Buddha in the pagoda of Tuol Lean, 22 inches (56 centimeters) tall; Buddha seated in meditation, 35 inches (90 centimeters) tall, from Phum Thmei; the head of Vishnu at the national museum at Phnom Penh, 7 inches (18 centimeters) tall; the torso of Durga from Sambor Prei Kuk, 23 inches (59 centimeters) tall; and a reclining Vishnu relief at Battambang, 62 inches (158 centimeters) long and 25 inches (63 centimeters) high. Contemporary of Chenla and earlier Funan were the state of Dvarati and the kingdoms of the Pyus and Mons, which would lay the foundations for later Siam and Burma, whose artistic production would involve more use of wood, shell inlay, ivory gold leaf and textiles. The Pyus are believed to be the highest users of gold among the ancient states of Southeast Asia. Chenla was also in part contemporary to the island kingdoms of Sumatra and Java.

ADDITIONAL RESOUCES

Bellwood, Peter. *Man's Conquest of the Pacific*. New York: Oxford University Press, 1979.

Giteau, Madeleine. *Khmer Sculpture and the Angkor Civilization*. London: Thames and Hudson, 1965.

Heinz, Carol Brown. *Asian Cultural Traditions*. Prospect Heights, Ill.: Waveland Press, 1999.

Pal, Pratapaditya. *A Collecting Odyssey: Indian, Himalayan and Southeast Asian Art*. Chicago: Art Institute of Chicago, 1997.

SEE ALSO: Buddhism; China; Funan; India; Java; Laos; Malay; Mon-Khmer; Sea peoples; Tai; Vietnam.

—E. P. Flores-Meiser

ART AND ARCHITECTURE: WEST AND SOUTH AFRICA

ROCK ART: SOUTH AFRICAN

The earliest known art in Africa was found in a cave located in the Huns Mountains of Namibia in southern Africa. In the cave known as Apollo II, archaeologists unearthed seven small pieces of stone, each no more than 6 inches (15 centimeters) long, on which images of animals were painted. Using radiocarbon dating, scientists have estimated that these small, stylized artworks were created between 25,000 and 23,000 B.C.E. The paintings of animals reflect the early Africans' dependence on animals to provide food, bones to make tools, and skins for clothing. Paintings on rock are typically subject to greater deterioration than are engravings on rock; therefore, early rock paintings, particularly of the early date of the Apollo II examples, are exceptionally rare.

South of the Zambezi River, other early artworks are found on rock-shelter walls located in areas as widespread as Namibia, Lesotho, Bot-

A watercolor copy of a San peoples cave painting hangs on the wall above a South African researcher retracing preliminary copies of other paintings. (Hulton Archive)

swana, and Zimbabwe, indicating that the rock art tradition was introduced into these areas by the migrating groups of nomadic hunters and gatherers such as the San peoples (formerly known as Bushmen). The artists used sharpened bone implements and animal-hair brushes to apply the black, white, and red pigments. These early paintings depict animals and humans, subjects of interest to the San hunters and gatherers. The earliest of these rock-shelter wall paintings has been dated to 2500 B.C.E.

ROCK ART: THE SAHARA REGION

Bubaline period. The oldest-known examples of African rock wall engravings in the Sahara region are those located in the Tassili and Fezzan regions, the earliest of which may date to 8000 B.C.E., at which point in time the Sahara was not yet a desert. This period is named for the now extinct buffalo, the *Bubalus antiquus*. In addition to the *Bubalus antiquus*, rock engravings from this period depict the rhinoceros, hippopotamus, ostrich, elephant, and giraffe. The animals are depicted in a detailed and naturalistic manner. Unique to the Bubaline period is the very large scale of some of the engravings. Human figures are depicted up to 11 feet (3.3 meters) tall and one rhinoceros is more than 26 feet (7.9 meters) long. The presence of extinct *Bubalus antiquus* in the artworks, plus the fact that the humans carry clubs and axes, lead archaeologists to assign a very early date to the Bubaline period. For most of the Bubaline period, humans appear to have led a hunting and gathering existence, following herds of wild game and collecting plants, seeds, and berries along the way. Art may have been a means to cope with the challenging environment by calling on spirits for assistance or favor.

Cattle period. The line between stylistic periods in art is never clear-cut, and typically there is a period of overlap or transition between two periods. Toward the end of the Bubalus period, the Sahara began to dry up, and in art, domesticated cattle began to be depicted alongside the *Bubalus antiquus*. When, at last, the *Bubalus antiquus* ceased to appear in rock art, sometime about 5000 B.C.E., the Cattle period is said to have begun. During this period, rock engravings were replaced by rock paintings in which cattle were depicted alongside the earlier repertoire of wild animals. Human figures during this period were depicted using the newer technology of bows and arrows. Cattle period renderings are more generalized, less naturalistic, and much smaller in scale, typically no more than 4 feet (1.2 meters) high. The domestication of cattle was one step away from hunting and gathering and toward the development of a pastoral lifestyle.

Horse period. The tendency toward increasing abstractionism, generalization, and smaller scale continued during the Horse period, commencing about 1500 B.C.E. The Horse period is divided into three subperiods, each based on the horse and its use by humans. The Chariot subperiod, as its name implies, is the period in which the horse-drawn chariot was introduced. Rock paintings depict single-shaft chariots drawn by two horses and driven by triangular-shaped human figures. The humans were armed with shields, spears, and daggers. Both the chariot and the weaponry show contact with Egypt and the eastern Mediterranean, perhaps through trade or warfare. Elephants appear in several Chariot subperiod paintings, as do domesticated cattle and dogs. During the Horseman subperiod, humans are shown riding on horseback as well as driving in chariots. The ability to ride horses would have permitted greater mobility over rugged terrain than riding in chariots. The small triangular human forms are adorned with elaborate feathered headdresses, perhaps indicative of their status within their group. In the Horse and Camel subperiod, increasingly cruder and smaller scale paintings show camels alongside horses.

Camel period. The last of the Sahara prehistoric rock art periods, which started about 600 B.C.E., is known as the Camel period because of the predominance of the camel in the rock paintings.

As the Sahara became dryer, the camel became the animal of choice for those who stayed in the region. The other groups who migrated southward took their artistic traditions to regions from Senegal to Nigeria and eventually into southern Africa. Saharan rock paintings during the early Camel period depict tiny humans, often no more than stick drawings several inches high, carrying spears. It appears that the spiritual role of rock art lessened as humans gained greater control over their environment.

SCULPTURE: SOUTH AFRICAN

At the beginning of the first millennium C.E., agrarian peoples from the north moved southward into San territories, bringing new technologies of agriculture, pottery, and ironworking into southern Africa. At Lydenburg in the Transvaal, archaeologists discovered seven sculpted terra-cotta human heads buried in a pit. Created sometime between 500 and 700 C.E., these hollow heads are between 9 and 15 inches (23 and 38 centimeters) high and were formed by adding separate clay features that were then blended into an abstract human face. The faces were adorned with ridges, perhaps representing ritual scarification. Decorative notched herringbone patterns about the necks may represent beaded collars. Because the terra-cotta heads were found buried in a pit, archaeologists speculate that the heads were brought out only on ceremonial occasions, then reburied for protection.

SCULPTURE: WEST AFRICAN

About the same time as the Camel period of wall painting in the Sahara region, a new sculptural tradition was developing near the village of Nok in Nigeria, West Africa. Radiocarbon dates for Nigerian sites place the Nok culture between 500 B.C.E. and 200 C.E. The sculptural medium of choice for the Nok was terra-cotta (baked or fired clay). Creating a sculpture from clay is an additive, modeling process, in which the sculptor adds clay and then models the forms. Woodcarving, on the other hand, is a reductive, carving technique, in which the sculptor cuts away the material, revealing the final form. The flat, abstracted areas of the Nok terra-cotta figures appear more like carved wood than modeled clay, thereby leading art historians to believe that Nok terra-cotta sculptures were based on an earlier and a contemporary woodcarving tradition. Because none of the perishable early wood sculptures remain, the Nok terra-cotta sculptures are the only extant evidence of the early wood sculpture tradition in Africa.

Nok sculptures depict large human heads in a stylized form, with the face composed of hollow pupils set into bow-shaped eyes placed above a protruding nose and mouth. These large heads dominate their smaller proportioned bodies, whose long torsos are supported by short, sturdy legs. Although Nok sculptures have seldom been found intact, it is estimated that the typical size of a sculpted human figure was about 4 feet (1.2 meters) tall, with the head making up one-quarter to one-third of the entire height of the figure. The anatomical forms are rendered in broad, generalized, cylindrical shapes, articulated with strings of beads, bracelets, anklets, and elaborately arranged hair. The high degree of body ornamentation may indicate that the figures represent kings or priests, indicative of a highly stratified society. Some archaeologists believe the figures represent deceased ancestors, whom the living believed could help or harm them from the afterlife. Human forms in Nok art were represented in an abstract manner, whereas animals were represented naturalistically. The Nok sculptors may, like their later counterparts, have purposefully refrained from rendering humans in too lifelike a manner for fear of capturing human spirits or offending human ancestors. Alongside the Nok terra-cottas, archaeologists have found examples of pottery and ironwork indicating that these arts were present at this early date in Nigeria. Many of the Nok stylistic traits were assimilated by their successors, the Ife, during the late first millennium C.E.

ADDITIONAL RESOURCES

Perani, Judith, and Fred T. Smith. *The Visual Arts of Africa: Gender, Power, and Life Cycle Rituals.* Upper Saddle River, N.J.: Prentice Hall, 1998.

Reader, John. *Africa: A Biography of a Continent.* New York: Alfred A. Knopf, 1998.

Willett, Frank. *African Art: An Introduction.* London: Thames and Hudson, 1993.

SEE ALSO: Africa, East and South; Africa, North; Africa, West; African rock art, southern and eastern; Nok culture; Saharan rock art.

—*Sonia Sorrell*

CALENDARS AND CHRONOLOGY

Calendars are devices used to track the passage of time. Even in cultures in which there are no "clocks" of any kind (whether mechanical or simpler devices such as sundials), the passing of days can be noted to monitor natural phenomenon and religious and civic activities. How days are grouped and organized is the basis of all calendrical activity. The kind of calendar a society uses is the basis for its sense of chronology—the sequence of dates and arrangements of events that are important to cultural continuity. Just as individuals cannot really know themselves without remembering the events of their lives, a society cannot really endure without knowing where it came from, how long it has been in existence, and what is coming next. In other words, a calendar is vital to a culture's sense of history and identity; indeed, it could not exist without one.

Obviously, calendars help people keep track of what day it is, but they do much more than that. The first use is agriculture. It was necessary for ancient societies—especially those with little or no writing—to know when to plant, when to harvest, when the rivers would rise or fall, when the rainy season would come, and when to expect other changes in the environment. Indeed, complex farming, supporting large-scale societies, could not have existed without such knowledge.

Likewise, calendars are necessary for politics and complex governments. Taxes and other financial transactions are measured in time. Elections must occur periodically. Kings need to document the lengths of their reign. Judges must pass sanctions such as prison sentences, and calendars and units of time are required for all this.

Calendars are also necessary for economics. It would be impossible, say, to develop a modern capitalist economy—based on the time-dependent exchange of money—without a calendar. Loans and interest, for example, could not be calculated unless there was a simple and public means to know just how long the money was held.

Finally, there are religious and spiritual aspects to calendars, these being perhaps the most obvious uses of all. Days must be set for spiritual observances. Decisions must be made on whether to base these determinations on the motions of the Sun or the Moon. That is, should a celebration occur after a definite number of days into the year (such as Christmas in the West)? Or should it occur after a certain number of lunar months, falling on, or next to, a seasonal moment such as an equinox (such as Jewish Passover)? Questions such as these have always reinforced the close connections between astronomy and religion in the ancient world.

FIRST OBSERVATIONS OF THE HEAVENS

No one knows exactly when the first devices to measure time or motion in the heavens were developed. However, there are remnants of instruments that many think were probably at least incipient calendars. For example, the scratches and notches on bones of the Ishango culture —a Neolithic fishing society living near Lake Edward in Africa about 10,000 B.C.E.—appear to track lunar months (from the appearance of one full Moon to the next). Also, all over the world there are hundreds of pictures or petrogylphs (images or diagrams chiseled in stone) that show astronomical phenom-

ena and calendarlike images. Astronomers (and now even amateurs with readily available software packages) can use computers to show how the sky appeared hundreds or thousands of years ago. Much research shows that early rock art or cave paintings were actually depictions of astronomical events. One of the most famous cases is of the supernova explosion in the Crab Nebula on July 5, 1054 C.E. Japanese and Chinese written records describe the event in exact detail, but much evidence suggests that many Native American cultures in the American Southwest, for example, noted this incident with rock drawings and carvings showing what the sky would have looked like on this date. All this demonstrates that ancient cultures were astute observers of the sky and could make accurate calculations based on these observations.

MOTION OF THE SUN AND MOON

Although calendars are present in every culture, they are by no means simple devices to construct nor simple devices to use. The are several reasons for this, as is evident by examining what goes into the construction of a calendar. All calendar makers face the same questions as they begin: when to start; what named cycles of what length into which to group days (though Westerners feel that seven-day weeks are natural, other cultures present many other possibilities, often cycles longer than a single year); how the named cycles articulate with the solstices (the longest and shortest day of the solar year) and the equinoxes (the two days in each solar year that are of equal length); and whether to add any intercalations. The calendar maker must decide whether to periodically add a unit of time—such as a day every four years during leap year in the Western Gregorian calendar, or a whole extra month after several years in some other system—to fix time lost (or gained) during the year. The Gregorian calendar rounds up or down to a whole number of days to deal with the fact that a year is about 365.25 days. Intercalation also has the advantage of keeping solar time and lunar time synchronized.

This last question on intercalations involves

what the natural units of a calendar should be. It is commonly assumed that a "day" is defined as one rotation of the earth about its axis (from one sunrise to another); a "year" is one orbit of the earth about the Sun; and a "month" is one orbit of the Moon about the earth. However, none of these lengths of time are integral multiples of each other. That is, a lunar month is about 29.5 days rather than a simple number such as 30. As mentioned above, a year is really about 365.25 days long rather than 365 days; this is why there is an additional leap day every four years. Another problem is, if "day" is defined as successive appearances of the Sun, this unit will vary from season to season: As everyone knows, days in summer are longer than days in winter. Add to this the lack of a writing system for many ancient cultures, and it is apparent that great human ingenuity was required to make the first calendars several millennia ago.

CALENDRICAL SYSTEMS

Depending on the starting point and assumptions, many different kinds of calendars are possible. Some of the calendars listed in the table of calendrical systems on the following page are representative of other systems related geographically or culturally (for example, systems similar to the Maya calendar were found throughout much of Mesoamerica). Even within the same culture area, such as Rome, different calendars were invented for varying purposes. Many are solar calendars, based on the motion of the Sun, but others are lunar, based on the orbit of the Moon. Some are combinations of both (lunisolar), and a few are based on the motions of the stars or constellations (stellar). The length of year under each system, given in the right column of the table, often reflects the desired unit of measure rather than any scientific accuracy. The following are descriptions of some of the ancient world's calendars.

Classical Middle East. The earliest calendars of classical antiquity were lunar. The Sumerians as far back as 2000 B.C.E. used a hypothetical year of twelve months of 30 days (giving a year of 360 days). In 1800 B.C.E., the Babylonian Empire adopted the Sumerian calendar (and the Persians

later adopted the Babylonian calendar). The Babylonians added leap months periodically to make the solar and lunar years coincide.

Early on, however, the Egyptians, as far back as 2000 B.C.E., discovered the solar calendar of 365 days. It is likely that the extreme predictability of the Nile floods—and the repeated measuring of their high-water marks—helped them to establish these dates. Also, the Egyptians discovered that Sirius (the Dog Star) rises once a year in direct line with the Sun (which also coincided with the Nile floods). By timing Sirius's appearance from year to year, the Egyptians calculated that the solar year was actually a quarter-day longer than 365 days (though this was not often incorporated into their calendrical calculations). This was almost two thousand years before Julius Caesar established his Julian calendar in Rome.

Greek and Roman calendars. The most famous calendars in the West are those developed by the Greeks and Romans. Originally, the ancient Greek and Roman calendars were lunar, based on twelve months of about 29.5 days (giving a year of 354 days). However, these soon proved inadequate, being 11 days short of the solar year. For example, using this shorter lunar calendar, within a mere sixteen years, the summer and winter solstices would switch, causing this lunar calendar to be totally out of synchrony with the seasons (and making it completely useless for agricultural planning).

Julius Caesar, after dallying with Cleopatra VII in Egypt, returned to Rome in 47 B.C.E. with knowledge he had gained of Egyptian mathematics and astronomy. One of his first decrees was to reform the calendar throughout the whole of the vast Roman Empire. As one writer argues, such action was not just a practical convenience but a demonstration that the empire and the emperor had the authority and symbolic power to reorder time. Caesar called the best minds of the era together, from as far away as Alexandria, to fix the inadequacies of the old calendar. Basically, Caesar adopted the system proposed almost two hundred years earlier by Ptolemy III: Assume the year is 365.25 days long, count each year as 365 days, and

SELECTED IMPORTANT CALENDRICAL SYSTEMS

Culture	Approx. Time	Type	Length of Year
Hindu	c. 3000 B.C.E.	solar	360 days
Sumerian	c. 2100 B.C.E.	lunisolar	360 days
Egyptian	c. 2000 B.C.E.	lunar	365.25, 365.5 days
Megalith (Stonehenge, etc.)	c. 1500 B.C.E.	lunisolar	365 days
Chinese	c. 1400 B.C.E.	solar	364.25 days
Greek	c. 1300 B.C.E.	lunar	354 days
Roman	c. 800 B.C.E.	lunar	305 days
Roman	c. 700 B.C.E.	lunar	355 days
Jewish	c. 600 B.C.E.	lunar	≈354 days
Roman	c. 555 B.C.E.	solar	366.26 days
Persian	c. 538 B.C.E.	lunisolar	366 days
Greek	c. 500 B.C.E.	solar	360 days
Babylonian	c. 432 B.C.E.	lunisolar	≈365 days
Chinese	c. 300 B.C.E.	lunar	354 days
Roman (Julian)	c. 45 B.C.E.	solar	365.25 days
Hopi	c. 100 C.E.	solar	≈365 days
Mayan	c. 200 C.E.	solar	365 days
Hindu	c. 500 C.E.	solar	365.35 days
Muslim, Arabic	c. 634 C.E.	lunar	354 days
Polynesian (Hawaii)	c. 700 C.E.	stellar, lunar	360 days
African (Yoruba)	c. 800 C.E.	stellar	≈365 days
African (Swahili)	c. 900 C.E.	solar	≈365 days
Pan-Pueblo	c. 900 C.E.	solar	≈365 days
Navaho	c. 1000 C.E.	stellar	≈365 days
Native American (general)	c. 1000 C.E.	lunar	12 moons
African (San)	c. 1000 C.E.	stellar	seasonal
Inca	c. 1100 C.E.	lunar	370, 329 days
Cahokia	c. 1150 C.E.	solar	≈365 days
Aztec	c. 1300 C.E.	solar	365 days
Roman (Gregorian)	c. 1600 C.E.	solar	365.2422 days
approximate lunar year			354 days
approximate solar year			365 days
Western average leap year			365.2425 days
exact solar year	c. 2000 C.E.		365.242199 days, or 365 days, 5 hours, 48 minutes, 45 seconds
exact lunar month	c. 2000 C.E.		29.53059 days, or 29 days, 12 hours, 44 minutes, 29 seconds
exact lunar year	c. 2000 C.E.		354.36707 days

have a leap year of 366 days every four years. Certain adjustments had to be made—such as where the leap day should go and how to get the current year back in alignment with the equinox—but the so-called Julian calendar was proclaimed on January 1, 45 B.C.E. The word *kalendus*—the first day of the month of March (New Year) in the Roman calendar—is the origin of the English word "calendar."

However, the new system was not without its flaws nor was it immune to meddling from later pontiffs and emperors, well-intended or merely vain. For example, the Roman senate decided to honor the emperor Augustus by renaming a month after him. To prevent his month having fewer days than the month named after Julius Caesar (July), the senate voted to give the month of "August" 31 days. Days, then, had to be borrowed from someplace else (February). Later emperors tried similar modifications. However, the biggest problem was that the Julian calendar was still slightly too long (about eleven minutes per year, meaning it would gain about a week every millennium). Pope Gregory XIII in 1582 C.E. issued a papal bull correcting these problems with a more accurate value of the solar year, declaring that three out of every four

THE SYSTEMS OF MONTHS IN SELECTED CALENDRICAL SYSTEMS

(number of days are in parentheses; leaps and exceptions are ignored)

Gregorian	Hindu	Babylonian	Jewish	Muslim
January (30)	Caitra (30) (March-April)	Nisanu (30) (March-April)	Nisan (30) (March-April)	Muharram (30)
February (28)	Vaisakha (30) (April-May)	Ayaru (30) (April-May)	Iyar (29) (April-May)	Safar (29)
March (31)	Jyaistha (30) (May-June)	Simanu (30) (May-June)	Sivan (30) (May-June)	Rabi' I (30)
April (30)	Asadha (30) (June-July)	Du'uzu (30) (June-July)	Tammuz (29) (June-July)	Rabi' (29)
May (31)	Sravana (30) (July-August)	Abu (30) (July-August)	Av (30) (July-August)	Jumada I (30)
June (30)	Bhadrapada (30) (August-September)	Ululu (30) (August-September)	Elul (29) (August-September)	Jumada II (29)
July (31)	Asvina (30) (September-October)	Tashritu (30) (September-October)	Tishri (30) (September-October)	Rajab (30)
August (31)	Karttika (30) (October-November)	Arakhsamna (30) (October-November)	Heshvan (29) (October-November)	Sha'ban (29)
September (30)	Margasira (30) (November-December)	Kislimu (30) (November-December)	Kislev (29) (November-December)	Ramadan (30)
October (31)	Pausa (30) (December-January)	Tebetu (30) (December-January)	Tevet (29) (December-January)	Shawwal (29)
November (30)	Magha (30) (January-February)	Shabatu (30) (January-February)	Shevet (30) (January-February)	Dhu al-Qa dah (30)
December (31)	Phalguna (30) (February-March)	Ardu (30) (February-March)	Adar (29) (February-March)	Dhu al-Hijja (29)

centennial years would not be leap years (for example, 1700, 1800, and 1900 would not be leap years but the year 2000 was). A complex formula for calculating Easter was also established. These reforms became known as the Gregorian calendar, which is the one used in most Western countries today (and is the de facto universal calendar throughout the world). The traditional Julian calendar continues to be used in many rites of the Eastern Orthodox Church, especially for calculating Easter. It currently runs 13 days behind the Gregorian calendar.

By the first century C.E., the seven-day week had become commonplace throughout the Roman world (perhaps being taken from Jewish custom). The origins of the seven-day week in the West are obscure; other cultures have weeks of varying lengths (four days in Africa, five days in Central Asia, six days in ancient Assyria, or ten days in ancient Egypt, to name only a few). It is likely that the approximately four seven-day phases of the Moon in each month gave rise to this division. Each of the days was named after a Roman or Scandinavian god ("Thor's Day" becoming "Thursday," "Saturn" becoming "Saturday," and so on).

The Jewish calendar. The first Jewish calendars may have been written as early as in the time of Solomon around 1000 B.C.E. They are similar to older Roman and Middle Eastern calendars in that the year is solar and the month is lunar. However, Jewish months do not necessary coincide with full moons, and the number of days in the year varies. The supposed date of creation is 3761 B.C.E. Because of the importance of the Sabbath, a seven-day week and the divisions of the day were important to early calendar makers. Part of the complexity of the Jewish calendar is caused by the way of creating cycles to make the solar year and lunar year line up. This is crucial, as most of the important Jewish observances, such as Rosh Hashana (New Year), Yom Kippur (Day of Atonement), and Passover, are month-dependent.

Hijrah Muslim calendar. Most countries in the Muslim ancient world used the *hijrah* calendar. *Hijrah*, or "flight," refers to the Prophet Mu-

hammad's exodus from Mecca to begin teaching in Medina on July 16, 622 C.E. (hence the day the calendar begins). This was the time when Muḥammad began his public preaching. The Islamic year is 354 days long, consisting of twelve lunar months of usually 29 or 30 days. Because of the shortness of the lunar year of 354 days compared with the 365 days of the solar year—and because no intercalations are added—the months make a complete cycle every thirty years. Ramadan, the ninth month (of 30 days), is the most important time in the Islamic year, and devout Muslims abstain from all food and drink from dawn until dark. As with all Islamic months, Ramadan moves through the seasons.

Today, most Muslim countries still use the *Hijrah* calendar, though some countries, such as Turkey in 1677 C.E., have adopted the solar Western calendar. As the calendar is consistently lunar, it is relatively easy to convert dates to the Gregorian calendar: Take the *Hijrah* year and multiply it by 0.97, then add 625.5. To get a *Hijrah* date from a Gregorian date, subtract 625.5 from the Western date, multiply by 1.0307, and add 0.46 (rounding up).

Calendars of sub-Saharan Africa. Compared with Muslim, Egyptian, and North African astronomical and calendrical systems, much less is known about those in ancient sub-Saharan Africa. Many, however, as with the dynasties of the west African Yoruba kings, were quite complex. Apparently most were seasonal and often depended on stellar observations as much as those of the Moon or the Sun. Among hunting and gathering foraging bands such as the San (formerly Bushmen), for example, the Moon is the epitome of the cycle of life and death. Even the curved draw of the hunting bow is associated with the crescent Moon.

In many places, calendar systems of other areas are incorporated into the local practices. For example, the Swahili cultures on the east coast of Africa also use the Muslim calendar for many important Islamic religious activities. However, the older Swahili calendar is used for spirit festivals and many agricultural events. Also, New Year's in the traditional Swahili calendar was supposed to coincide with the Persian New Year.

Maya calendars. Many of the Native American cultures of Latin America were accomplished observers of the heavens. The Aztecs of Mexico and the Inca of Peru all had very complex astronomical and calendrical systems. However, it was the Maya of Mesoamerica who had the most evolved and accurate calendars, and for their time, they were one of the most advanced cultures of the ancient world. They were probably better astronomers than their European contemporaries, and their measurements even rival those of modern times. For example, Maya values for the lunar month varied from 29.5302 to 29.53086 days (compared with the value of 29.53059 days as reckoned in modern times).

The Maya actually used two calendars: the Tzolkin (count of days) religious calendar and the Haab civil calendar. The Tzolkin had a 260-day cycle derived from repeating thirteen numbered "weeks" with 20 named days (that is, 13 times 20, or 260 days). Any given day in the cycle, then, would be called by its name and the number: 12 Kan, 4 Ahau, and so on. Each of these 260 days had astrological and religious significance.

The Haab civil calendar was solar and had eighteen *uinal* "months" consisting of 20 days each. Five days were added at the end to give a year of 365 days (18 times 20, or 360 days, plus the 5 extra). In general, these days named occurrences of more secular significance (such as agricultural events).

The Maya used both systems simultaneously, with both cycles repeating within each other to produce fifty-two "civil" years. If the 365-day system (18 times 20, plus 5) and the 260-day lunar year (13 times 20) were started at the same point, it took fifty-two years to get back to the exact same spot in both cycles. This sacred cycle of fifty-two years was called the Calendar Round, and the end of each Calendar Round was thought to have auspicious, usually catastrophic, significance.

However, a fifty-two-year cycle would not allow the Maya to make the important connections to the past that they, as expert genealogists and historians, desired; therefore, another system also was developed. This Long Count began on August 12, 3113 B.C.E., apparently the date the Maya believed the world began. The Long Count, however, was neither solar or lunar but purely mathematical, based on nine cycles. A *uinal* "month" consisted of 20 days; eighteen *uinal* months was one *tun*, or "year"; twenty *tun* years gave one *katun* cycle; twenty *katun* gave one *baktun*, twenty *baktun* gave one *pictun*, and so on in multiples of twenty. This gave cycles of more than 63,000,000 (Western) years.

North America. Although much is known about the famous Maya and Aztec calendars, knowledge of other Native American systems is rather sparse. However, though the precise details are not known, ample evidence exists that at least various Pueblo cultures in the American Southwest—the Hopi, Zuni, the ancient Anasazi, and also the Navajo—were students of the heavens. Some based their calendars on the motions of the stars (which, in some ways, are simpler to follow than the motions of the Sun or Moon). For instance, according to traditional Navajo mythology, when the constellation Revolving Male (similar to part of the Big Dipper in the West) lies parallel to the horizon in early evening, it is time to plant. Its position also indicates when different animals will be mating or when winter has arrived. When the constellation known in the West as the Pleiades appears, this means it is too late to plant and still be able to harvest before the first frost.

However, there is also evidence that Eastern woodland Native Americans probably had complex calendrical systems. One of the most famous examples is from the Cahokia site, just across from St. Louis on the Illinois side of the Mississippi River. At this site stand more than a hundred mounds, including Monk's Mound, a giant earthen pyramid that is the largest pre-Columbian artificial structure in the New World north of Mexico. The Cahokia civilization may have had as many as thirty thousand to forty thousand people living in a complex urban society when the culture reached its peak population about 1200 C.E. Most striking, however, is the presence of the huge Woodhenge circles—named analogously with the famous Stonehenge structure in England—which many feel were used for calendrical observations. Numerous holes containing remains of cedar posts were first discovered in the 1960's, though road construction crews obliterated some of them. Regardless, enough evidence still exists to lead many astronomers and archaeologists to conclude that the 200-foot (61-meter) diameter circles of Woodhenge—and there are at least four—were giant observatories. For example, the Sun rises behind the same poles on three overlapping circles on both the spring and autumn equinoxes. Likewise, the winter and summer solstices, which apparently can be predicted within a day or two, can also be readily observed by standing in the center of one of the circles. Such a solar calendar would make for a year of about 365 days, although, interestingly, it appears that the Cahokia astronomers had little interest in lunar activity. There is also ample evidence of other mathematical abilities: The city itself is well-planned, and the mounds appeared to be deliberately aligned along certain axes, oriented in nonrandom directions.

South and Southeast Asia. The early Hindu calendar of around 1000 B.C.E. divided the solar year into twelve months of 28 or 30 days each, adding a leap month every five years. By 400 C.E., outside influences, especially Greek and Mesopotamian, brought a new fascination with astrology and, hence, increased interest in the Sun, the constellations, and the Zodiac. Dates in this classical calendar were given as lunar month, fortnight (depending on the waxing or waning of the Moon), day (a thirtieth part of a lunar month), and solar year of the era.

In 78 C.E., the Shaka (or Shakakāla) calendar was supposedly started by the legendary king Shālivāhana. This is the standard Hindu calendar that many places in India and Southeast Asia still follow. Almost all Hindu festivals follow the Shaka calendar. As it is generally a solar calendar, little more needs to done to obtain the Western Gregorian year than subtract seventy-eight.

Around 500 to 600 C.E., Indian astronomy underwent two transformations. First, technical observational knowledge increased, and this had impact on the scientific calendrical systems. For example, precise measurements of Jupiter showed that it had a twelve-year cyclical period with certain background stars, and new calendars were made with new months incorporating places in this twelve-year cycle. However, partly prompted by this increase in technical skill, people began to take a more intense interest in astrology and divination. This prompted the development of the Kaliyuga calendar, or Chronology of Fictitious Times. It begins on February 18, 3101 B.C.E., the supposed starting point of all celestial revolutions when the Sun, Moon, and all the planets were aligned in perfect conjunction. From this starting point, another such conjunction was predicted to occur 4,320,000 years later. Much of Indian philosophy of ancient times was an attempt to uncover what the meanings of these cycles might be.

China and East Asia. There is little doubt that the Chinese were also excellent astronomers; many say they were the most precise in the world until about 1200 C.E. They also built some of the world's first observatories. The Chinese bureaucracy realized that calendrical knowledge not only represented royal authority but also political control: That is, knowledge of calendars allowed for control of knowledge about agricultural and water cycles; controlling the water system allowed the government to regulate the economy and the people.

The earliest Chinese written ideographic characters appear on Shang oracle bones from around 1400 B.C.E.; there is also evidence that the Chinese knew of a solar year of 365.24 days and a lunar month of 29.5 days. They also realized, a century or two before the Greeks, the necessity for intercalations—adding extra days to adjust for the differences between a real solar year and an assumed one of just 365 days. In the third century B.C.E., a meteorologically based calendar also became popular.

The basic Chinese lunar calendar had months of 29 or 30 days (giving a year of only 354 days), requiring extra months be added seven times during a twelve-year cycle. Each of these years in this cycle are named after one of the well-known twelve animals in the Chinese zodiac: rat, ox, tiger, rabbit, dragon, snake, horse, ram, monkey, rooster, dog, and pig (for example, the year 2001 is the year of the snake). Each of these signs has a personality, as do people born in those years.

Ancient Chinese calendars were closely tied to Chinese divination practices, and classical writings such as the *Yijing* (eighth to third century B.C.E.; English translation, 1876; also known as *Book of Changes*, 1986). However, the Chinese were great almanac compilers as well. In a lunar calendar, every month begins with a new Moon; therefore, it is always possible to tell what day of the month it is from the phases of the Moon. As most Chinese festive occasions are lunar, such a calendar is convenient. However, solar calendars are more beneficial for farmers, so the ancient Chinese put their (quite substantial) knowledge of the subject in various almanacs. Besides giving astronomical information, these almanacs also gave readers personal advice (much like newspaper horoscopes in the West). Some of these are still used today by traditional Chinese.

Stonehenge and other megalith calendars. Probably no discussion of ancient calendars could be complete without mentioning Stonehenge, the famous Druid Neolithic observatory built between 2000 to 1500 B.C.E. Hundreds of other such structures have been found throughout the British Isles. The stone archways set in a large circle could predict eclipses and summer and winter solstices; the rising and setting of the Sun and Moon could also be tracked and the lunar months observed.

Techniques for keeping track of time arose at many times and in many places. This is in stark contrast to other intellectual achievements over the course of history. For example, the invention of the alphabet or the number zero appear to have been discovered only a few times. Anthropologists and archaeologists, then, believe that calendars, or some way of keeping track of time, are something that all cultures, past and present, possess. In that sense, then, calendars take their place along with notions of family, marriage, and a belief in the supernatural as human universals.

ADDITIONAL RESOURCES

Aveni, Anthony. *Empires of Time: Calendars, Clocks, and Cultures*. New York: Basic Books, 1989.

Bretcher, Kenneth, and Michael Feirtag, eds. *Astronomy of the Ancients*. Cambridge, Mass.: MIT Press, 1979.

Duncan, David Ewing. *Calendar: Humanity's Struggle to Determine a True and Accurate Year*. New York: Avon Books, 1998.

Hawkins, Gerald. *Stonehenge Decoded*. New York: Delta, 1965.

Ifrah, Georges. *The Universal History of Numbers*. New York: John Wiley & Sons, 2000.

Krupp, E. C. *Echoes of the Ancient Skies: The Astronomy of Lost Civilizations*. New York: Oxford University Press, 1994.

————. *Skywatchers, Shamans, and Kings: Astronomy and the Archaeology of Power*. New York: John Wiley & Sons, 1997.

Malville, J. McKimm, and Claudia Putnam. *Prehistoric Astronomy in the Southwest*. Rev. ed. Boulder, Colo.: Johnson Books, 1993.

Marshack, Alexander. *The Roots of Civilization*. New York: McGraw-Hill, 1972.

Williamson, Ray A. *Living the Sky: The Cosmos of the American Indian*. Norman: University of Oklahoma Press, 1987.

SEE ALSO: Africa, East and South; Agriculture and animal husbandry; Anasazi; Augustus; Babylonia; Caesar, Julius; China; Egypt, Prepharaonic; Greece, Archaic; Hinduism; Islam; Judaism; Maya; Middle Woodland traditions; Muḥammad; Persia; Religion and ritual; Rome, Imperial; Rome, Republican; Southwest peoples; Stonehenge; Sumerians.

—James Stanlaw

DAILY LIFE AND CUSTOMS

The daily lives of most ancient people were set to the rhythms of nature: day and night, the seasons, sowing and reaping, pregnancy, birth, sickness, and death. For the vast majority, their routines revolved around survival, and the tasks and customs that each culture required or evolved to ensure it for each member and for the society as a whole. Though people in many cultures no doubt struggled at achieving simple survival and safety, ancient civilizations in Africa, the Americas, and Eurasia provided the framework of social, material, and intellectual conditions and resources that allowed many in their populations to thrive well beyond basic needs.

FAMILY LIFE

Mesopotamia. In Mesopotamia, families tended to be nuclear, with older female or younger male relatives attached. Fathers ruled their wives and children with absolute authority, so much so that children could even be legally sold into slavery for debt. Sons were expected to support their aged parents, and the eldest inherited the social position and identity of the family. Children lived at home until able to form their own families or until they were called to military or civil service. Parenthood seems to have been revered by the society and children well cared for. The fact that adoption was common supports the idea that children and child rearing were important aspects of Mesopotamian culture. Legal documents, letters, and even myths shed light on familial relations, and the legal codes, like that of Hammurabi, are often quite explicit about social expectations.

Greece. Ancient Greeks lacked a specific term for family but like the Mesopotamians used a term (*oikos*) that denoted a household arrangement. Older men tended to marry young women, and the norm was for monogamous marriages arranged through the family of the woman. Marriage was a means of uniting resources rather than hearts.

Married women ruled domestic life as their husbands ruled the political life of the city-state. They emerged from the confines of their homes under strict circumstances, generally related to religious cults, and always in the company of servants, slaves, or other family members: The society's fear of adultery was nearly obsessive. Although the society practiced abortion and left children (especially girls) to die by exposure, the Greeks valued their children, and the urban child, at least, went through a succession of ceremonies marking stages in its life. Children's grave markers often express tender sentiments. Nonetheless, fathers tended to ignore their offspring until they reached a politically useful age, so that most were raised by their mothers, servants, and slaves. In Sparta, mothers served the fathers' role, even in inculcating the sense of military duty and honor that marked their extreme machismo.

Egypt. Egyptian society emphasized the contractual nature of the marriage relationship, though the contract was between the man and the woman's family. These contractual arrangements included the gifts exchanged at the time of coupling and even stipulations about property sharing in the (uncommon) event of divorce. Despite having an unusually high level of freedom for ancient women, those in Egypt generally fell into domestic work and life, with work of any status outside the home reserved to men. Children were raised in large part by the society's women, though depictions of parents and children hunting or otherwise enjoying recreation together do exist in tombs.

India. In India, the family, or *kula*, was culturally constructed and controlled very carefully. It was recognized as the most important social unit and the means by which the ethical standards that held the society together were passed to each succeeding generation. The *kula* was generally an extended affair, with several generations and relations of varying degrees, along with servants and dependents living together under the authority of the father as household head. The family head, or *grhastha*, lived as a kind of king in his family: sternly rewarding and punishing, enforcing and living by the culture's rules and ethics, and garnering the profound and obsequious respect of family members. Polygamy was openly practiced as a means of ensuring male heirs. The hearth was the center of the household, and the fire the symbol of its unity. Daily life was filled with rituals that bonded generation to generation and invested the children with the values that had formed the family's adults. As among the Greeks, the mistress of the household avoided the public sphere and rarely left the family compound alone. She controlled the domestic sphere, challenged in authority only by a live-in mother-in-law.

China. The Confucian ethic established a very firm basis of family life and structure in China. Homes were virtual temples, and fathers were revered ancestors in training, to be treated by their sons as honored elders and sources of wisdom. The fathers were expected, however, to act in ways to merit the reverence that stemmed from filial piety. Ancestral altars in the homes reminded all of the importance of these entities. Women and girls were subordinated to the males, and trays were used to serve the father, lest female hands inadvertently touch his. The father of the household had the power of life and death over his offspring, though this was constrained in practice. The mistress of the house was subject to both her husband and, more directly, her mother-in-law, especially when the husband was young. Concubinage further complicated life in the wealthy home, though the concubines were clearly subordinated to the principal wife.

Rome. Roman families echoed the Chinese in their insistence on nearly unfettered domination by the father (*paterfamilias*) and by worship of the male ancestors' spirits (geniuses). Romans recognized a basic unit of a three-generation family. In its ideal form, all sons and grandsons of a common sire lived together until his death dissolved that unit, then each son would establish his own domicile. Household gods and the rituals attached to

them anchored the members of the family to the domestic space. Women who married into such a situation did so under clearly articulated contracts that essentially provided her husband with the rights to her children by him. Her infertility was a matter of personal shame for her and gave her husband the right of repudiation, which sent her back to her father or other authoritative male relative with her dowry. However, marriages also created and represented other types of familial alliances, especially among the political class in Rome, and were thus often carefully crafted.

DINING AND DRINKING

Before the agricultural revolution and domestication of animals, much of the human's day was spent hunting or gathering, and living quarters had to be located near fresh water sources. As cultures developed through specialization, settlement, and trade, provision and preparation of food became more sophisticated and diets more varied. Food came to be seen by ancient societies as a determinant and symbol of status, often expressed by wealth and the prices of foods. The disparity between rich and poor was generally a matter of variety, quality, and caloric value. In most cultures, it seems that people feasted at special times in the collective calendar or for personal or familial reasons, and the provision of unusually large quantities, types, or varieties of food marked the occasion as special. For many ancient peoples, provision of one's best comestibles was incumbent on the proper host, whether of friends or strangers. On the other hand, what one did not eat could also be socially important: The Indian caste of Brahmans avoided meats, Egyptian priests shunned pork, and Hebrews defined their very culture—in part—by the foods they refused to consume. For Romans, one was what one ate, and they would avoid uncooked foods or those that grew wild, lest they grow crude or savage in nature. Food and drink were no less important as symbolic social or economic elements than as biological nourishment.

Daily life for people was punctuated by two meals. The earliest might be a breakfast at dawn, as among the Inca, or a later lunch, as with the

This wall painting from a fifth century B.C.E. tomb depicts Etruscans enjoying a banquet. (North Wind Picture Archives)

Greek *ariston*. Simple, nourishing foods that required little fuss characterized a family's preparation for or pause in the working day in most cultures. More elaborate dining took place when the day was over.

Among Indians, the evening meal was highly ritualized, with washings preceding the meal, and a strict order kept among diners: the father and guests, then the mother, and lastly the children. Indian cooking was characterized by a heavy reliance on rice (as gruel, flour, or simply boiled), soups, beans, barley, and a wide variety of spices. Water, milk and whey were supplemented by various beers and fruit liquors or fermented sap of palmyra or coconut.

In Mesopotamia, barley and wheat were transformed into beer or breads, and cuneiform records tell us of a wide variety of both. In cities, specialty taverns served beer, but wines were rare for common people. Meat was expensive, but wealthier folk could dine on beef, mutton, goat, pork, fowl, horse, and fish, cooked in hot embers, pots, or ovens. The less well-off made do with starchy soups or stews, heavy on the vegetables and spices (thanks to trade). Many fruits and their juices and syrups provided for those possessed of a sweet tooth.

Among the Andean peoples, vegetable soups thickened with tuber starch and meal and spiced with hot peppers were common fare. They ate no dairy and no eggs and relied on limited fish and game, llama, dog, and guinea pig for animal proteins. These were cooked over fires or boiled, but they did not have a spit on which to hang the flesh. Juices of fruits such as passion fruit and pineapple and a lightly alcoholic beer made from chewed corn sufficed for beverages.

With its huge empire and extensive trade system beyond its boundaries, Rome provided its better-off citizens with a plethora of foodstuffs. Self-conscious culinary artistry was probably imported from Greece, but the huge range of foods available made for terrific rivalries among cooks and patrons alike. The only real meal for the Romans was the *cena* at the close of the day, which could range from bread, wine, and a few vegetables drizzled with olive oil, to hot dishes prepared in cook shops, to multicourse banquets with carefully calculated excess that ensured conspicuous waste. Romans claimed a hierarchy of foods, which ranged from the produce of the soil, which was most robust, to the quickly putrefying shellfish, whose quick spoilage was considered an aid to digestion. Putrefaction was in fact a characteristic of higher foods, and *garum*, a sauce made from rotting fish, was considered a delicacy. The Mediterranean world provided Romans with a variety of wines, which they often consumed to excess, not least in the upper classes' convivium, in which alcohol, social conversation, music, and other entertainment—sometimes sexual—blended into an occasion somewhere between a mere meal and an orgy. The symposium (from "to drink together") was a similar feature of Greek society, and it also served the political and social needs of the higher classes.

For the northern Chinese, millet was the staple grain, and rice was cultivated in the south. Grains were made into cakes, and a meal might be fleshed out with beans, root crops, fruits, and spices or garnishes such as ginger, basil, and onions. Southern agriculture expanded the offerings with citrus fruits, bananas, and coconuts. By the Han Dynasty (206 B.C.E.-220 C.E.), tastes had broadened to include a greater variety and use of spices, pickling, and sauces. Trade brought in new types of spicy fare from the Indian Ocean that appealed to the Chinese elite and replaced for them the simple, traditional peasant foods. Initially, tea drinking was for barbarians alone, but by the end of the ancient period, it became common, and even ceremonial, as among traditionally minded modern Japanese. Millet and rice provided the stuff for beers, which were consumed by all classes, while various wines, including grape, found favor regionally and among particular status groups.

CLOTHING

Across the ancient world, clothing provided protection from the elements, a degree of personal modesty and, in many societies, a ready indication of one's social status or class. Earliest human clothing was most certainly animal skins, later supplemented and then replaced by woven fabrics of plant or animal fibers. In the Andes, men wore a simple loincloth of wool or cotton and a more formal long tunic, which was the common dress for women. Women also wore long skirts with short jackets, while both men and women donned woolen cloaks and caps in colder or rainy places and times. Simple rawhide sandals and a pouched

belt for food, tools, and perhaps an amulet filled out a typical ensemble. Women wore their hair long, held in braids or by combs, while men might wear theirs long or cut with obsidian knives.

In Mesopotamia, textile manufacture was an industry, with wool cloth most common and flaxen linen reserved for finer garments and higher classes. About 700 B.C.E., cotton was introduced and silk somewhat later. The warm climate allowed men to go about bare chested with kilts or loincloths. Fringed tunics served both men and women of all classes, though cloaks signified higher status. Leather sandals served for workers, but the elite could afford felt sandals or shoes. In the Persian era, trousers became fashionable. Although men often shaved their heads, head coverings tended to be reserved for ceremonial use.

Similarly, Egyptians avoided hats but did use clearly artificial wigs and protected their feet with sandals of rushes or of leather. Men wore more or less simply folded short kilts of linen or wool (in winter), and cotton during the Roman period. These were accessorized with longer overskirts, stoles, or shirts for formal occasions. Egyptian women wore cloth sheaths with or without sleeves in a wide variety of drapery fold patterns or simply hung by straps from the shoulders.

Like the Egyptians, Greeks made their cloth at home and fit it to their bodies loosely and with little stitching. For women, both the early *peplos* and later *chiton* hung from the shoulders and were tacked with pins. The *chiton* hugged the female form more tightly, as depicted clearly in Greek art. Men donned the *chiton* as formal attire but generally wore short tunics held in place with brooches, pins, or knots at the shoulder. Undergarments consisted of a loincloth for the male and a strip of cloth to cover a woman's breasts. Spartan simplicity in fashion seems to have dominated over time, at least during the classical period. Women might wear a veil over their heads in public, and men wore a broad, flat hat of felt or straw to protect them from the sun. Leather sandals were worn unless travel called for laced boots.

As Rome developed, it accepted many of the clothing types of the people with whom it had contact, from Egyptian kilts to Jewish robes and Germanic trousers. The single most characteristic piece of Roman clothing was the toga: the public garment of the Roman citizen. Made of a single piece of cloth up to nineteen feet (six meters) in diameter, it was draped loosely around the body and had to be held in place by the left hand, leaving only the right free (for handshaking, saluting, or oath taking). In its impracticality, it was the antithesis to the soldier's or laborer's closely fitted garb. Normally an earthy, unbleached tone, if pure white (*candidus*), it signified a candidate for office; if purple, one who was sacrosanct, and if edged in gold, one of the highest social rank.

Among the people of India and China, clothing also denoted class. The Indian peasant man wore simple loincloths and turbans and peasant women traditional saris, with their long hair twisted in a coil on their necks. Brahmans went about bare chested in characteristic sandals and with their hair top-knotted; while Buddhist monks wore distinctive robes of saffron or red when in public. In China, silk was reserved for the elite, and commoners wore fabrics woven of hemp, ramie, or even kudzu or banana. The classical Chinese outfit was of two pieces: a longer tunic topped by a jacket whose materials and ornamentation signaled the wearer's status. To go barefoot was to act as a barbarian, so peasants wore straw sandals, and the upper classes wore slippers of damask or brocade. Foreign influences often affected Chinese fashion, such as the use of undergarments or leather trousers like the barbarians or hairstyles in the manner of the Persians or Turks. Commoners wore simple kerchiefs or hats of straw, and headgear for the more elite followed changing fashions.

WORK AND LEISURE

Even in the most advanced ancient civilization, the vast majority of people labored in the fields. In less-developed cultures, these people also took care of most of their other needs, perhaps exchanging surplus food or crafts for other needed or desired items. With settled agriculture and then cities, a small percent of the population could spe-

cialize in tasks other than farming or herding, and specialization of labor began to emerge. This is the hallmark of a civilization: The many in the fields support the few in the city who defend the society, placate the gods, rule and administer the state, craft the tools and baubles, travel for trade and diplomacy, build and record, and serve. Little clear evidence exists concerning the everyday life of the farmers and herders, but what exists suggests monotony and a low level of material culture. Tasks were dictated by season, and in some regions, the year passed marked by long bouts of tedium interspersed with frenetic activity.

In the more artificial atmosphere of cities, life's rhythms moved rather differently. Craftspeople and local merchants probably experienced a relatively regular pattern of activity, working while the light allowed. In most societies, the priests and other servants of the divine cults determined the festal and sacrifice days on which workers were most active and on some of which the people were allowed to rest. For the Hebrews, this was the weekly Sabbath, as well as annual festivals such as Passover that memorialized important events in their ethnic history. The Indian year was punctuated with numerous rites and festivals that blended the agricultural and natural cycles with deeply significant religious elements and general carousal. In Egypt, government workers received a free day for every nine worked, and general religious festivals occurred when the Nile was in flood and agricultural work was impossible. Work in Mesopotamian cities was interrupted during temple festivals, when people could watch the cult idols wend their way through the streets, followed by the prayers of the needy.

In all civilized societies, class and occupation went hand in hand and dictated to a great extent one's daily activities, material wealth, and potential for social mobility. In China, a clear distinction was made between the people: The peasantry, which made up the vast bulk of the Chinese population, supported the warrior elite by their labor. However, peasant work was not confined to agricultural toiling: For men, it could unexpectedly turn into military service, which was often a life sentence. The Han Dynasty's great conquests and their defense were on the backs of countless conscripts ripped from the soil.

Defeat in battle led to slavery, an institution common to all ancient societies. The lives of slaves in the ancient world differed so widely—by circumstance of enslavement (for example, capture in battle or war, by piracy, for debt) and culture and needs of the society—that no generalities, beyond general lack of freedom, can be posited. Military prisoners were usually relegated to the worst situations: rowing in Roman galleys or working the lead mines in Greek Syracuse (Sicily). At the other end of the spectrum, many cultures, including the Romans and Greeks, recognized the value of well-educated servants. Women might serve as unfree courtesans and men as tutors, scribes, and even business agents. While captive, their lives could be nearly as gracious and materially rich as those of their owners; once emancipated (often upon death of the owner), they could take their place in free society.

Free persons of ordinary rank enjoyed the opportunity to fail as well as succeed. Little is known of the daily lives of these denizens of the countryside and cities, for they captured few writers' interest and wrote virtually nothing themselves. Archaeology, however, has captured some aspects of their material culture. Markets and bazaars as well as individual shops served as outlets for crafts as well as foodstuffs and prepared foods. Where coinage existed, as in the eastern Mediterranean Basin after the sixth century B.C.E., for example, it is possible to envision the nature of the daily exchanges. However, in the absence of an abstract medium of exchange, purchases must have been subject to a far greater level of haggling. Success for seller and purchaser alike must have been a matter of great patience as well as pride, and specialization far less typical than in the modern world.

For aristocrats throughout the world, their class or status ensured them of the highest material life the culture could provide. Within the class, there certainly could be distinctions, especially where powerful rulers such as the Roman or Chinese emperors held sway and commanded large shares of the society's economy, especially that of luxury goods. In the countryside or the provinces, life was also best among the owners or administrators of the land. High-quality food, shelter, clothing, and freedom from menial tasks all made life at the top far more bearable. The presence of servants and, where personal ownership was recognized, slaves, allowed a life of relative leisure that allowed the creation and support of all manner of creative expression that lower-class folks could hardly afford.

ADDITIONAL RESOURCES

Auboyer, Jeanine. *Daily Life in Ancient India: From Approximately 200 B.C. to A.D. 700.* Westport, Conn.: Greenwood, 1994.

Brier, Bob, and Hoyt Hobbs. *Daily Life of the Ancient Egyptians.* Westport, Conn.: Greenwood, 2000.

Disselhoff, Hans Dietrich. *Daily Life in Ancient Peru.* New York: McGraw-Hill, 1967.

Dupont, Florence. *Daily Life in Ancient Rome.* Cambridge, Mass.: Blackwell, 1994.

Garland, Robert. *Daily Life of the Ancient Greeks.* Westport, Conn.: Greenwood, 1998.

Malpass, Michael A. *Daily Life in the Inca Empire.* Westport, Conn.: Greenwood, 1996.

Matz, David, *Daily Life of the Ancient Romans.* Westport, Conn.: Greenwood, 2001.

Nemet-Nejat, Karen. *Daily Life in Ancient Mesopotamia.* Westport, Conn.: Greenwood, 1998.

Sharer, Robert. *Daily Life in Maya Civilization.* Westport, Conn.: Greenwood, 1996.

Shaughnessy, Edward. *China: Empire and Civilization.* New York: Oxford University Press, 2000.

Time-Life Books. *What Life Was Like Among Druids and High Kings: Celtic Ireland A.D. 400-1200.* Alexandria, Va.: Author, 1998.

_____. *What Life Was Like at the Dawn of Democracy.* Alexandria, Va.: Author, 1997.

_____. *What Life Was Like on the Banks of the Nile.* Alexandria, Va.: Author, 1997.

_____. *What Life Was Like When Rome Ruled the World.* Alexandria, Va.: Author, 1997.

Vamosh, Miriam F. *Daily Life at the Time of Jesus.* Nashville, Tenn.: Abingdon Press, 2001.

SEE ALSO: Agriculture and animal husbandry; Babylonia; China; Confucianism; Egypt, Phar- aonic; Egypt, Prepharaonic; Greece, Archaic; Greece, Classical; Han Dynasty; India; Religion and ritual; Rome, Imperial; Rome, Republican; Women's life.

—*Joseph P. Byrne*

DEATH AND BURIAL

Death, the final rite of passage experienced by all, has been held in awe and fear since humans first became conscious of their mortality in Paleolithic times. Death came to be regarded as a major "rite of passage" that many religious systems addressed in great depth. Mortality, death, and the unknown were ritualized out of a mixture of affection for the deceased, awe of death's mysteries, and the obligation to prepare for an afterlife. It is likely that death and the afterlife generated a fear that haunted people more than any other experience or reality. Everything possible was done to prepare the departed for the unknown world they would enter. A change in status from life to death could not be taken lightly. Fear and awe concerning death were present since prehistoric times as was a belief that the deceased were a source of blessings and beneficence, especially if the rite of passage was properly ritualized.

Such sentiments evolved into a cult of the dead in many early societies, and many prehistoric people developed some form of religion and perhaps a belief in some type of afterlife. Various primitive societies throughout sub-Saharan Africa, Asia, Oceania, and Latin America are mirrors of Stone Age views concerning the soul, the hereafter, and corpse disposal. Death, if not caused by violence, is generally ascribed to actions of supernatural spirits or to witchcraft. In the cult of the dead, attitudes toward the deceased and their afterlife generally revolved around fear of the power of the spirit and diligence in performance of death rituals. Full burial ensured proper dispatch to the next life; partial performance resulted in the dead becoming unsanctified ghosts that haunted the living in an attempt to get grievances rectified. Hence the dead were treated in different ways not only for reasons of status, but also as a sanction on those who remained behind. Because the spirit of a dead person was often viewed as a dangerous source of harm, sickness, and death, the corpse had to be removed as soon as possible to minimize "catching death."

This fear explains in part why bodies were buried in various ways, burned, or removed from sight in some manner. The need to control the spirit influenced what people did with the dead. Inhumation, cremation, exposure, and abandonment of the corpse have their origin in beliefs about death, the power of the spirit, and the afterlife. The variety of burial receptacles as resting places for the body, the meticulous preparation of the body for its journey to the next existence, and the awe, fear, and belief in the power of the dead all contributed to attitudes regarding death as the great *mysterium tremendum* addressed in countless myths and a variety of religious rituals to remove pollution and other evil consequences, to propitiate the deity, and to obtain the favor of the deceased spirit.

INHUMATION

Burial was the most prevalent practice among ancient peoples and appears to have been an earlier practice than cremation. There were no fixed rules governing the treatment of the dead. Burial involved placement in the ground, in a mound or tumuli, or in a grotto and marking the spot for future ritual practices. The most elaborate and imposing resting places involved entombment or erection of immense mansions of the dead seen in several places in the world.

Together with burial evolved grand myths that controlled treatment of the dead, the spirit world, nature of the final resting place, and preparation for rebirth in a new life. The deliberate burial of the dead, first associated with Paleolithic people some 25,000 years ago, represents one of humankind's earliest cultural achievements. *Homo sapiens*, who seems to have shared most of the psychological characteristics of modern humans, deliberately buried their dead, covered the body with red ochre to give it a blood-red color of renewed vitality, and provided food, flowers, and useful paraphernalia near the body, all of which suggests a human concern for the welfare of the deceased and perhaps a "belief" in some sort of survival after death. The corpse was not separated from the living but was placed in a grotto where all lived. The dead may have been viewed as in a state of "sleep" from which they might awaken. In various regions of Southern Europe, the Middle East, and Central and South Asia, Neanderthal caves revealed ample evidence of respect for the dead. The same inhumation practice was followed among Cro-Magnon people some 10,000 year ago, with bodies interred in a flexed position, covered with animal shoulder blades, and smeared with red ochre amidst shells, bone necklaces, tools, and other items.

There also is evidence that cremation or cannibalism may have occurred because only skulls were found in some grottoes. This may suggest a type of ancestor worship with a possible belief the spirit rested in the head and the consumption of the brain absorbed the "soul essence." Cannibalism, more widely practiced than previously believed, has persisted from prehistoric times down into the twenty-first century. There is every indication that many peoples, at one time or another, passed through a cannibalistic stage, and the custom has survived in various degrees among certain Australian aborigines, sub-Saharan African primitives, societies of Oceania, and New Guinea. Various reasons underlie the custom of anthropophagy, or cannibalism, such as hunger, acquisition of a victim's strength or soul, magic, revenge, religious sacrifice, or honor of the dead. The dead's essence and qualities were also regarded as present in the skull or bones worn by tribal members for protection.

Grotto burial progressed and took a huge step forward among the ancient Egyptians, whose elaborate tombs and mummification techniques were developed in preparation for an afterlife. Mummification is associated with the cult of the dead and ancestor worship and was designed to preserve the body as a permanent residence for the soul. Among various African and Oceanic so-

The majority of ancient societies buried their dead. This archaeological excavation along Farthing Down in Surrey, England, uncovered the grave of a Saxon. (Hulton Archive)

cieties, mummification is practiced to the present day to preserve the corpse until funeral and burial occurs, sometimes months or years after death.

Tombs or *mastabas*, pyramids, and elaborate funerary rites emerged to lessen the malevolent and increase the beneficent influences of the dead. The corpse was provided with numerous items he or she loved in life and could enjoy again in the land of the dead. The pyramids were erected for the pharaohs and *mastabas* for servants and royal aids near the ruler's tomb. These pyramids evolved gradually from a series of *mastabas* placed one on top of the other. They were elaborately decorated inside with murals of daily Egyptian life and filled with treasures. The pyramid represented a staircase to heaven for the mummified body of the ruler, who was believed to become one with Osiris, the god of death. Because the ancient Egyptians believed that the soul needed a lasting body in which to dwell, rules and rituals of mummification were observed meticulously so that the soul would proceed properly to the Underworld. The pharaoh then became a divine intermediary between the people and their gods.

Such elaborate burial practices were also followed in the Middle East, where royal tombs or chambers of brick and limestone were erected by Mesopotamian cultures around 3000 B.C.E. Again the corpse was buried with personal property, soldiers, courtiers, and servants, all to serve their master in the afterlife. In the Helladic Mycenaean culture area around 1400 B.C.E., magnificent rectangular chamber tombs were cut in rock and encircled by upright stone slabs for the Royal House, and in China during the Shang Dynasty (1600-1066 B.C.E.), royal chambers lined with heavy timbers were built at the bottom of a shaft 40 or more feet (12 meters) deep with a ramp for access. As in Egypt, the inner walls were elaborately decorated, and ritual bronze vessels, stone and jade objects, food, garments, and human attendants were interred to serve the emperor in the next life.

With the death ritual developed the cult of ancestor worship, which served as a unifying bond and communication between the living and the dead. Because the living were under the watchful eyes of the spirits, rituals were absolutely necessary to placate the spirits by providing for their needs in the afterlife. To forget the ancestors would merit the return of the soul and its wrath. If treated properly, the ancestors were a source of great benevolence. Ancestor worship in China developed into a religion and affected all aspects of family life.

In Europe around 3500 to 1500 B.C.E., hunting-gathering cultures along the Atlantic seaboard built massive megalithic tombs of standing rocks with a slab placed atop as a roof where the dead were placed, covered with rocks. Many were communal burial places for family members who were provided with food and other items. The tomb was walled up to prevent the spirit from leaving. With each burial, the seal was broken, offerings made to the spirit of the first occupant, and skeletons of previous bodies were piled up to one side. A *menhir* or single upright stone marked the head of the tomb as a resting place for the soul and a marker to indicate the way back to the tomb. It is surmised that the megaliths represented the womb of the earth where the dead would be reborn. Death was viewed like winter, a time of darkness and cold. The earth goddess, representations of which were found in burial spots in Europe and elsewhere, would rescue people from death as she revitalized the earth each spring with living plants.

Around 500 B.C.E., various cultures accepted inhumation as a custom. The Etruscans of Italy built houselike tombs on the outskirts of cities where bathed, oil-scented, and richly arrayed bodies were placed in sarcophagi. It was believed that the dead lived in such "houses."

The Druids of the British Isles, on the other hand, believed in metempsychosis. Souls were immortal and lived again for a number of years in another body. The Huns (c. 300 C.E.) included valuables with the body but no mound over the grave nor any mourning ritual. In Bronze Age Scandinavia around 500 B.C.E., huge boulders were set around a grave in the outline of a ship to carry the soul to Valhalla, the palace of the god Odin. By the seventh and eighth centuries C.E., actual ships were used for warriors and buried on the shore. Ordinary women, children, the old, and the sick were given a poor burial or cremated. Their situation in the next world would match their station in earthly life. Occasionally slaves were buried with the warrior, which was a privilege since they would enter Valhalla with the warrior they served. This avoided the usual dreary afterlife reserved for slaves. Ship graves have been discovered throughout Europe.

In Mesoamerica between 2000 B.C.E. and 700 C.E., Olmec and Maya civilizations flourished in Mexico and Central America. The Olmecs, an enigmatic people of uncertain origin and the mother culture for later Mexican civilizations, also buried their distinguished dead in tombs. This practice was followed by the Maya, a civilization preoccupied with death, the fate of the soul, reincarnation, and an elaborate concept of hells, paradises, and mythical lands. They buried the dead in caves believed to be gates to paradise. Souls then passed through various mythical realms. The good were rewarded with one of three paradises, depending on their spiritual status and behavior in life. The evil were condemned to an inferno at the center of the earth, a place of colorless existence rather than suffering. Reincarnation also was part of Maya theology. Souls of warriors became birds, aristocracy higher animals, and plebeians a variety of lower animals.

Cave burial was an archaic and widely distributed mode of burial still practiced in the Moluccas, the Philippines, Australia, Melanesia, Polynesia, Madagascar, and throughout Africa, where bodies or desiccated bones are placed in cliffs of rock. Such burial chambers became forerunners of grandiose sepulchres characteristic of ancient cultures.

Among the Hebrews and Christians of the Middle East, the mortal body was sacred and was interred with love, dignity, and care. Some Hebrews, such as the Sadducees, denied any conscious existence after death or bodily resurrection; the Pharisees, however, believed in bodily resurrection on earth. Christianity interpreted resurrection in the sense of a higher spiritual body in an eternity of love, peace, and happiness with God. The soul was an individual who was subject to final judgment that determined the nature of eternal life.

CREMATION

Cremation, as an alternate method of body disposal, was practiced by only a few cultures. Among them were Australian, Tasmanian, Siberian, Melanesian, and African groups. There is some evidence that it may have been used by Paleolithic people because traces of burning were found on some skeletal bones. During the Bronze and Iron Ages in Europe circa 6000 B.C.E., agricultural communities practiced both cremation and inhumation. As the second millennium B.C.E. approached, cremation was accepted as the primary method, and by the late Bronze Age, bodies were cremated in urn fields or cremation cemeteries.

Germanic tribes and the Etruscans, circa 800-600 B.C.E., consistently cremated the dead and buried the ashes in urns or ossuaries either secured with a cap or buried under small mounds. The Greco-Romans likewise practiced cremation and inhumation. Bodies were usually carried out at night, and purification rites were completed nine days after the funeral. Although relatively common among European societies, cremation was not the custom in the Middle East. The Far East did not practice the custom until it was introduced by Buddhism between 400-700 C.E. Only in Ancient Persia was cremation present in the early Parsi or Zoroastrian tradition where an ancient text, the *Avestan Vidēvdāt*, alludes to "cooking of corpses."

Crematory practice was, and still is, the custom par excellence in Vedic and Brahmanical India. Apparently Neolithic India did not practice the custom, but it was introduced in Vedic India because burial urns with bone fragments and ashes have been found at Mohenjo-Daro, a Harappā city of the third millennium B.C.E. Originally bones were collected, which implied a bodily resurrection, but cremation quickly converted this belief into the subtle body concept. Harappān Aryans, who developed the present Indian crematory rituals, burned corpses in a burning ground, or *śmaśāna*, where the reading of sacred texts, circumambulation of the pyre, and purification bathing in a river, tank, or lake accompanied the ritual. The charred bones were gathered on the third day and immersed in a river, preferably the Ganges. Water, milk libations, and rice-ball offerings, or *piṇḍa*, were offered to the manes at *śrāddha* ceremonies linking the living with the dead. The entire ritual was presided over by Agni, the fire deity, who restored the dead, determined the good and evil of the individual, and prepared the path to eternity in Yama's kingdom. Such *śrāddha* ceremonies were vital for the well-being of the ancestors and provided the dead with a type of corporeal substance, a new body. Otherwise the soul would have to resume the course of rebirth. Around 300 B.C.E., the ritual of *satī* was introduced, which required a widow to join her husband on the funeral pyre in a practice of ritual suicide. Such ritual immolation was not only a custom in ancient India but also among early Indo-Europeans, Israelites, Japanese, and Scythians, who introduced the custom to India. In earliest India, horses were also sacrificed to carry the souls into the afterlife.

EXPOSURE

Only a few cultures of the ancient world practiced exposure of a corpse to decay or consumption by animals. In early Egypt, disposal in desert regions was practiced but quickly was replaced by embalming. The Harappān Aryans often abandoned bodies in the cremation ground to be devoured by dogs and birds of prey. Scythians in Central Asia suspended bodies in a tree for birds to consume, and the bones were collected and buried. Because the body was considered an empty shell whose spirit would be reborn in a new life no matter what happened to the body, Tibetans abandoned corpses to the vultures.

However, it was the Parsis of ancient Persia who ritualized exposure of bodies. Bodies of the deceased were washed, cleanly arrayed, and then removed to decay and be consumed by birds of prey. Exposure served to purify the remains by contact with the rays of the Sun, which was the great visible emblem of the invisible godhead. Their sacred texts, the *Zend-Avesta* (*The Zend-Avesta*, 1880-1887), *Bundahisn* (*Zand-Akasih: Iranian or Greater Bundahism*, 1956) and *Dinkard* (*The Dinkard*, 1874-1900) of the sixth century B.C.E., present a clear picture of death and afterlife that has been the basis of Zoroastrian religious philosophy. Earth, water, and flame were considered sacred elements. Because contact with death was the source of the greatest defilement, burial was forbidden, contact with water would render it unfit, and cremation would defile the sacred flame. Ablution with water or cattle urine was necessary if contact with a corpse was made. Hence the dead body was placed on a bed of stones or lime or placed in trees or on scaffolds to decay and be consumed by birds of prey or other animals. Defilement of the natural elements was avoided at all costs.

Suspension from tree branches, placement on scaffolds or summits of cliffs, placement on beds of vegetation in forests, abandonment to the elements, preying dogs, and wild beasts, or immersion in the sea were various methods practiced by coastal societies of Australia, Andaman Islands, Irian Jaya, Ceylon, Siberia, Oceania, and Africa from earliest times.

ADDITIONAL RESOURCES

Bendann, E. *Death Customs*. 1930. Reprint. Detroit: Gale Research, 1974.

Goody, Jack. *Death, Property and the Ancestors*. Stanford, Calif.: Stanford University Press, 1962.

Jones, Barbara. *Design for Death*. Indianapolis: Bobbs-Merrill, 1967.

Maringer, J. *The Gods of Prehistoric Man*. New York: Alfred A. Knopf, 1960.

SEE ALSO: Africa, East and South; Australia, Tasmania, New Zealand; Britain; Buddhism; China; Christianity; Egypt, Pharaonic; Etruscans; Germany; Greece, Mycenaean; Huns; India; Judaism; Maya; Neolithic Age Europe; Oceania; Olmecs; Persia; Shang Dynasty; Zoroastrianism.

—*George J. Hoynacki*

EDUCATION AND TRAINING

PRELITERATE SOCIETIES

In the ancient world, the majority of communities were preliterate. Structurally primitive, they were organized by family, clan, and tribe, contending constantly with their environment and other social groups in a harsh struggle for existence in which passing on social knowledge, religious knowledge, and physical and technical skills to the young was vital for survival. Informal education within the family, usually conducted by imitation of adult behaviors, was enough to pass on basic skills such as food gathering, cooking, and production of clothing. Sex differentiation of tasks was strict in most of these societies: There was women's work and men's work. Girls learned to perform work such as the gathering and preparing of food and the making of clothing. Boys learned to make weapons, hunt, and become warriors. Advanced technical skills, such as stone carving or blacksmithing, were passed down within families. A boy from outside a skilled family who wanted to learn a particular skill would have to leave his own family and go live with a knowledgeable family for a lengthy apprenticeship. Such formal schooling as existed focused on inculcation of the group's religious beliefs and its history.

Oceania/Pacific Islands. For island dwellers, the sea and its ways conditioned enculturation of the young. Children had to understand not only the fire and the house but also the canoe and the sea. This made for an almost exaggerated concern for physical training, especially in swimming and prudent boat handling. Beyond that and training in respect for private property, children enjoyed a great latitude in behavior until puberty. At that point, girls lived among the adult women and learned the intricacies of adult behavior by observation. The boys became warriors until their mid-twenties and concerned themselves with raiding other villages. They then entered adult society and learned adult roles in the process of acquiring property and honor.

Australian Aboriginal groups kept children of both sexes among the women. There they could learn about nature and how to gather food. At age thirteen, girls were initiated into adult society by circumcision and marriage. At the same age, the boys began going on hunting trips and underwent the first of four initiation ceremonies that would span the period from age fifteen to thirty. Relationships, taboos, behavioral norms, and sex roles were taught and learned through daily life. The ceremonies surrounding puberty demonstrated the sacred significance of sex roles and set the whole experience of the community in the context of its specific religious beliefs.

Sub-Saharan Africa. Most preliterate groups educate their children by having the whole society teach the experiences of the tribe through example. Variations on the pattern are most often observable in the initiation rites and relate to the developmental stage of the group, the nature of its territory, or its historical experience.

In sub-Saharan Africa, for example, hunting tribes made initiation a straightforward ceremony celebrating the boy's first kill. Having proven his competence in killing his own food, whatever his age, the boy received the congratulations of his elders, took on special dress, tattoos, or tribal scars, then married and took his place among the men. Among farming tribes, however, the process was much more elaborate and involved initiation schools that took all of the boys of the clan who were nine years old and spent a year teaching them morality, discipline, and tribal secrets. The process began and ended with ceremonies acting out a symbolic death to childhood and rebirth as an adult, involved circumcision and endurance of ordeals, and gave the child a thorough grounding in tribal law, custom, and religion. Through the initiation, the young man became fit to take his place as a responsible adult attuned to pleasing the harvest gods. Semi-nomadic tribes that herded animals needed to defend themselves against raiders, so their initiation training emphasized warlike behaviors and the hunting and killing of predators that would menace their animals.

The Americas. The numerous Native American tribes in North America displayed many interesting variations on the common practices of tribal education. Among the Indians of the Pacific Northwest, for example, the importance of family and genealogy, visible in the practice of erecting totem poles, meant that family history was too important to be left until puberty. Therefore, very young children would be constantly and repetitively told the story of the great deeds of the family, the relationships of family members for generations back, and the events of the larger world as they had affected the family. By the time children were ready to take on adult responsibility and start a family, they themselves would be ready to instruct a new generation in these vital matters. The Native Americans of the Southwest lived in desert areas and had to exercise great care in the conservation of water. The children had to be taught from infancy to use water wisely. Part of early childhood education was conditioning children to take responsibility for their younger siblings and spend time grinding corn, thereby freeing adults to make water containers and to carry water back to the settlement from distant places.

The Olmec civilization of Mesoamerica achieved a high degree of technological sophistication, expressed not only in great stone temples and artwork but also in rigid social stratification. A preliterate culture for most of its existence, the Olmec developed a rudimentary writing system even as it came to an end. This society developed military and priestly schools so that the children of its aristocrats would be prepared to inherit leadership. Lengthy and demanding apprenticeships fitted young men for careers as engineers and artisans. At the very end of the ancient period, the Maya emerged in Central America as a theocratic civilization in which hereditary priests ruled society. This culture evolved a writing system and a complex calendar, the knowledge of which, along with history, medicine, and religious ritual,

formed the curriculum of the schools that prepared priests. As part of the training for leadership, the school required candidates to abstain from sex and the use of intoxicants and engage in group work projects.

The Celts. From their origins in central Europe, the Celts spread throughout Western Europe and by the end of the ancient era were particularly well-established in Brittany, Ireland, Wales, and Scotland. Their priestly class, or Druids, were rigorously trained for years not only in theology but also in intricate liturgical formulas that had to be perfectly memorized. Even when they made the transition to literacy, it was forbidden to write down the prayers and rituals, preserving their priestly training methods intact. The Celtic lawyers and judges, *brehons*, were similarly trained, having to memorize an entire corpus of law and legal tradition. Unlike the religious formulas, the *brehon* laws were recorded in writing when Celtic society became literate, leaving *brehon* education to concentrate its rigor on the exploration of legal casuistry.

LITERATE SOCIETIES

Schools emerge when a culture is large enough to need public reinforcement of private training in civic virtue. Another important factor in the emergence of schools is the introduction of basic accounting and the keeping of written records, for those require precision and consistency that are best produced by group instruction. It is safe to say that once a society and its schools become literate, the arts of literacy (and numeracy) dominate the curriculum even to the point of altering the ways in which moral and religious knowledge is communicated. Ancient Egypt and Babylonia, both literate societies, simultaneously developed the earliest school systems in recorded history.

Egypt and Babylon. As early as in the second millennium B.C.E., Egypt had produced a coherent system of schools for children of priests and of the wealthy. These were attached to temples and taught by the priests. By copying texts and taking dictation, boys age four to fourteen learned the skills necessary to become scribes who would carry on state business. Though they were constantly exhorted to love ideas and practice virtue, the real emphasis was on acquiring writing skills by rote memorization and practice. At the outset, boys transcribed moral maxims, laboriously learning proficiency in calligraphy and orthography, then moved on to lengthier moral writings. They also learned simple arithmetic and used it to solve set problems. The nature of discipline in these schools is summed up in a teacher's saying: "The ears of a boy are upon his back, and if you beat him, he will listen." Those who performed best at writing could go on to a school of government run by the state treasury and upon graduation be apprenticed to a public official to begin a distinguished career in the state bureaucracy.

Of course, schools such as these were not the only available mode of training for every person or every occupation. For very low-level positions in the government bureaucracy, a certain amount of training by a parent or relative might be enough when combined with an apprenticeship, especially in a department headed by a family member. Even in the case of more important positions, an apprenticeship of indeterminate length in which a candidate both learned and demonstrated the requisite skills might be enough to enable a candidate to take the place of an official who died or retired, providing he was not ambitious to go higher. Those who were to enter their father's business or profession usually learned it by apprenticeship because most professions in ancient Egypt maintained a cloak of secrecy around their specialized knowledge.

The Babylonian school was also oriented to the production of scribes and relied heavily on memorization but also taught mathematics, grammar, literature, and religious ideas inherited from the Sumerians. "Elder brothers," or older students, did a great deal of the teaching of younger students, and among the teachers was one known as the "man in charge of the whip." As in Egypt, scribes might be simply copyists or public secretaries but might also rise to be military planners, royal counselors, or government department heads. Therefore, school examinations covered music, land

measurement and allocation, weights and measures, drawing, and other subjects. Two universities, at Nippur and Babylon, provided advanced training. The only women to acquire an education were those who would learn to be priestesses in the cults of some goddesses.

Israel. From the time Israel established itself in Canaan to the onset of the Babylonian captivity (c. 1000-587 B.C.E.), Jewish parents conducted in their homes the crucial task of giving their children a moral and religious education based on the doctrinal heritage of their Exodus from Egypt and the wisdom of judges and prophets. This heritage saw the origins of the community in a contract with God: The community would prosper by adhering to the contract (that is, obeying God's laws) and suffer by straying from it. The obligation for instructing children was primarily the family's, and schools could only be adjuncts to their work. In fact, only a few schools existed in the larger towns. Apprenticeship supplied training in practical arts. The emergence of a class of scribes—not government officials but preservers and interpreters of the Jewish scriptures and religious traditions—resulted in the love of learning as a form of worship becoming one of the highest ideals of the community.

After the return from exile (c. 538 B.C.E.), the Jews became more urbanized, and schools became common after 200 B.C.E. Their curriculum and methods were shaped by the scribal class's custodianship of religious ideas. Elementary schools taught the basics of reading, writing, and arithmetic but also instructed children in social and religious doctrine by close reading of the scriptural writings richest in lore about the law and religious rituals. Such secondary schools as existed delved more deeply into religious law and the methods of understanding and interpreting it. Emphasis was always on preservation of the letter and spirit of the law by both knowledge and careful observance. Teachers were seen as responsible for perpetuating the community's highest ideals and teaching pupils to fear and love God.

China and India. Ancient Chinese education was a sorting machine that produced an intellec-

These ruins are what remain of Nalanda, a Buddhist school in northern India founded in the fourth century B.C.E.
(Hulton Archive)

tual elite for high positions in government service, ensuring that the public business would be in the hands of scholars and making intellectual power the most highly prized achievement in society. This was done by subjecting candidates to three stages of progressively more difficult examinations that focused not only on writing, mathematics, music, and knowledge of rituals but also on archery and charioteering. Because the examinations were open to anyone who could pass preliminary screening, some social mobility was possible even though it was unlikely that poor children could attain enough education to compete successfully. Schools were available throughout the land, culminating in a national university that enrolled about thirty thousand students by the sec-

ond century C.E. This national university and other Chinese universities were magnets for scholars from other parts of Asia. Over time, the examination system became more and more rigid and backward-looking, centered on literary and philosophical classics to the exclusion of all else.

In India, the educational system emphasized the development of character and discipline through the study of the Vedas, the Hindu scriptures. Children attended a village school from age five to eight. Those fortunate enough to continue their education then studied with their own personal teacher, or guru, until they were twenty, concentrating on mastery of grammar, logic, philosophy, practical arts, and medicine. Ancient India produced six great universities, the greatest of which, Nalanda, founded in the fourth century B.C.E., was the capstone of the Buddhist schools that sprang up as an alternative to Hindu education. Its students undertook a twelve-year course of study, during which they had to remain celibate.

The Spartan ideal. Sparta was a totalitarian garrison state in which the citizens were constantly endangered by rebellions among the more numerous population of slaves (helots). Supported by the labor of slaves they despised and feared, citizens were expected to serve the military needs of the community and were trained accordingly. Newborn male children were judged by a council; ill-formed and weak ones were abandoned to die of exposure. Those accepted spent from ages seven to eighteen organized in packs learning to live off the land by foraging and stealing, learning endurance by physical hardship, and learning to kill by ambushing stray helots. At age eighteen, they became ephebes, took an oath of allegiance to the state, and were recruited into private armed bands that competed with one another constantly in gymnastics, hunting, and pitched battles using real weapons. At age twenty, those who had proven themselves worthy were allowed to join Sparta's army and spend ten years on active service. At age thirty, they left active service as full citizens who were part of a military reserve for life.

The Athenian ideal. The Athenians led the other Greek states in elaborating a notion of citizenship that found its models in the mythic figures of Achilles and Odysseus. Achilles epitomized the strong, skilled, and single-minded warrior, and Odysseus added to the strength of the warrior a clever and supple strategic mind and a taste for experience and new knowledge. Thus, Athenian education would produce military prowess but add to it development of a broad culture rooted in the study of literature and philosophy.

Until about 500 B.C.E., Athens was a kingdom whose aristocrats were educated almost exclusively in physical skills and heroic ideals. As Athens developed into a democracy and nonaristocrats began asserting themselves in public life, a school system emerged for those who could not af-

ford to employ private teachers. After home training until age seven, during which the child had a master or pedagogue to guide his basic moral development, the child went to primary school to learn the basics of reading, writing, counting, and drawing. During primary schooling or just after it, the Athenian boys undertook physical education under the direction of a private teacher known as a paidotribe. The boy then went to a music school until age fifteen to learn not only singing and playing the lyre but also poetry and mythology. The capstone of the Athenian education was study at the gymnasium, an institution for advanced physical training. The five gymnasia in Athens each included a stadium, practice fields, baths, wrestling pits, meeting rooms, and gardens.

By the fifth century B.C.E., ephebic training had become the culmination of Athenian education. At age eighteen, boys could petition to become ephebes. If accepted, they received military training, and those successful could take an oath of allegiance and complete two years of military service as a gateway to citizenship. In time, ephebic training was extended to embrace advanced intellectual training.

As society continued to democratize, the practical study of oratory became more and more important. Citizens were expected to carry out the public business in assemblies, and the ability to express oneself with clarity and power came to be highly prized. Teachers able to produce effective orators did very well for themselves.

The Hellenistic world. When Alexander the Great followed the conquest of Greece by leading Macedonian and Greek armies in the conquest of Egypt and the Persian Empire, Greek educational ideas and forms were exported to the new kingdoms that emerged. The cities of the new kingdoms were not free and autonomous as the Greek city-states had been and lacked the driving civic spirit that fostered organization and community in those cities. Education was vital to promote the interests of the conquerors by inculcating the ideals of the heroic past of the Greeks. Yet the core ideas of freedom, responsibility, and civic virtue that were central in Athenian education rang hollow in the Hellenistic cities. The practice of oratory was now directed to display and exhibition rather than to decision making.

Cultural transmission of a vanished past became the task of the schools. Elementary schools were mandated for all free children in the Hellenistic world. They concentrated on reading, writing, and counting, gradually moving away from drawing and music. Unfortunately, children were treated very harshly and learned almost nothing. Students who persevered could go on to secondary school when they were about twelve. There they studied the literary techniques of the classic authors, especially Homer, grammar, geometry, arithmetic, astronomy, and music. In addition, most cities had higher education in the form of advanced schools of rhetoric and philosophy. In some places there were ephebic schools, no longer concerned with military arts but with broad literary culture. A few medical schools existed, and advanced scientific training was obtainable at museums. The beginnings of the specialization of education institutions into elementary, secondary, and higher education took place in the Hellenistic world.

Rome. For the first five centuries of its existence, Roman education aimed at preparing the youth for public life in the service of the community. This meant a family education that implanted civic virtue by constant repetition of the stories of the gods and Roman heroes, proceeded to memorization of the Twelve Tables of the Roman law, and concluded with a public apprenticeship. After 272 B.C.E., Rome annexed Greece and parts of Asia, becoming a bilingual empire. Greek culture became popular in Rome, and Greek teachers were welcomed. A dual system of schools, one committed to classic Roman culture and the other to classic Greek culture, emerged. Elementary schools took children of both sexes from ages seven to twelve. They taught reading, writing, arithmetic, and moral virtue. The children of the upper classes could then go on to a secondary school for about three years to study literature and grammar, whether in Greek or of Greek authors translated into Latin (or worthy Latin authors after

the first century B.C.E.). Of course, purely Greek schools were the norm throughout Greece and Asia, the Latin schools being common only in Italy, Spain, Gaul, and North Africa.

Higher education institutions and curriculum throughout the Roman Empire were those of the Hellenistic world. The core of the experience was the study of oratory. As had been the case in the Greek experience, oratory became an important study at about the time public deliberative oratory became superfluous, when the free political institutions of the Roman Republic gave way to the dictatorship and the emergence of the Roman Empire. The only truly distinctive feature of Roman education lay is the development of law schools, organized when the law and its interpretation became so complex as to be beyond the skill of individual teachers.

Christianity. The earliest Christians, convinced that the world would end at any moment, had little use for schools that taught classic culture. Families provided religious formation for their own children, and catechetical schools taught basic doctrines to persons seeking to become Christians. Those who wanted a classical education had plenty of schools available but had to wrestle with the problem of how to acquire classical learning without imbibing paganism along with it. Some catechetical schools emerged in which Christian teachers taught the classics to other Christians. These gave rise to other catechetical schools that were devoted entirely to exploring Christian doctrine more deeply and extensively than the catechumenal schools. Still another type of catechetical school prepared candidates for clergy positions. These faded away as bishops formed cathedral schools to train boys for the priesthood.

THE END OF THE ANCIENT WORLD

With the collapse of the Western Roman Empire in the fifth century C.E., the old Roman schools largely disappeared in Western Europe and North Africa, apart from some secondary schools in northern Italy that remained in existence until the Great Renaissance. The Visigoths in Spain maintained a vigorous intellectual culture, including vibrant schools, for three more centuries. However, the transition from the world of Rome to barbarian successor states was a calamity for education, and the most numerous and visible schools in Western Europe from the sixth to the eighth centuries C.E. would be the cathedral schools. In the Eastern Empire, Hellenistic and Christian educational institutions continued to evolve until the fall of the Eastern Empire in 1453 C.E.

ADDITIONAL RESOURCES

Bonner, Stanley F. *Education in Ancient Rome from the Elder Cato to the Younger Pliny.* Berkeley: University of California Press, 1977.

Chaube, S. P. *Education in Ancient and Medieval India: A Survey of the Main Features and a Critical Evaluation of Major Trends.* New Delhi, India: Vikas Publishing House, 1999.

Crenshaw, James L. *Education in Ancient Israel: Across the Deadening Silence.* New York: Doubleday, 1998.

Kennell, Nigel M. *The Gymnasium of Virtue: Education and Culture in Ancient Sparta.* Chapel Hill: University of North Carolina Press, 1995.

Marrou, H. I. *Education in Antiquity.* New York: Sheed and Ward, 1956.

Morgan, Theresa. *Literate Education in the Hellenistic and Roman Worlds.* New York: Cambridge University Press, 1998.

Robson, Eleanor. *Mesopotamian Mathematics, 2100-1600 B.C.: Technical Constraints in Bureaucracy and Education.* New York: Clarendon Press, 1998.

Too, Yun Lee. *The Pedagogical Contracts: The Economics of Teaching and Learning in the Ancient World.* Ann Arbor: University of Michigan Press, 2000.

SEE ALSO: Africa, East and South; Archaic North American culture; Athens; Babylonia; Celts; China; Christianity; Egypt, Pharaonic; Egypt, Prepharaonic; Greece, Archaic; Greece, Classical; Greece, Hellenistic and Roman; Homer; India; Israel; Judaism; Maya; Oceania; Olmecs; Persia; Rome, Imperial; Rome, Republican; Southwest peoples; Twelve Tables, The.

—*Joseph M. McCarthy*

GOVERNMENT AND LAW

Ancient law and legal tradition containing the rudiments of the modern civil legal system relate to the nature and structure of society of the times in which they developed and in which they operated. The nature of law in the ancient world is understood by looking to Roman law and legal custom. Customary law operated among wandering small groups, settled tribes, and small communities. It flourished in circumstances in which law was practical rather than theoretical. Unwritten law developed out of custom when it was known to be accepted as law and practiced as law by the persons who shared it. Legal rules and legal tradition were separate from yet related to societal ideas and practices. Feudal and canon law also paralleled the development of Roman law.

MESOPOTAMIA

Located between the Tigris and Euphrates Rivers, Semitic people including the Sumerians, the Akkadians, the Chaldeans, the Hittites, the Babylonians, the Israelites, the Phoenicians, the Lydians, the Assyrians, and the Persians settled in the Fertile Crescent about 2000 B.C.E. Civilizations of that area developed writing, schools, libraries, and written law codes, moving civilization from prehistory to history. Their contributions included the wheel, glass, iron, bronze, the sail, coinage, mathematics, the alphabet, calendars, and farming and irrigation.

One of the remarkable rulers of history was the famous lawgiver Hammurabi (r. 1792-1750 B.C.E.), an autocrat who ruled with the blessing of the gods. He unified southern Mesopotamia, and his capital was at Babylon. The most important achievement of the Babylonians was the creation of written law, which governed people's relations with one another and with the state. The earliest existing written laws are found in the law code of Hammurabi. Although it showed a high sense of justice, like most early legal systems, this code was based on the dominant religion of the culture and dealt harshly with those who broke its rules of behavior. For example, adultery was punishable by death, and the law of retaliation dictated that if a defective building collapsed and the owner was killed, the building architect was put to death. The civil and criminal laws of Hammurabi regulated practically everything in life, applying to personal property, real estate, business, trade, agriculture, inheritances, and adoption; they controlled the price of labor and animals, purchases, sales, contacts, leases, the rights of women, children, and slaves. There were penalties for injuries to property and to the body; in general, the law made a distinction between the three classes of society, so that a poor person injuring a noble received a more severe penalty than in the reverse case. The basis of the law was retaliation ("an eye for an eye"). Cases were tried in their local communities, but appeals to the king were permitted.

The concept of retaliation was also found in the Hebrew system, which borrowed heavily from the Babylonian code. Both the Babylonian and Hebrew systems relied on capital punishment and slavery as punishment for breaking civil and criminal law. Like the Babylonians, the Hebrews believed the law was of divine origin. The basis for Hebrew law, however, was the first five books of the Old Testament and the Talmud (the written traditions governing Jewish life). Many early Hebrew laws were solutions to practical problems. For example, dietary restrictions on eating certain foods such as pork reflected the dangers presented by lack of refrigeration and sanitation. The king was surrounded by a large bureaucracy: ministers, judges, and various officials for the collection of taxes, and tribune, for the maintenance and control of canals, and for the regulation of business matters. Busi-

ness agreements of every kind had to be in writing to be valid. Another group surrounding the king consisted of both citizen soldiers and professionals; the latter received land lots from the king, which they could bequeath to their sons on condition that the sons also render military service—a practice followed by certain other ancient peoples.

The king and his civil and military officials, the priests, and landed proprietors, the rich merchants, and the manufacturers formed one of the three classes recognized by Babylonian law. The second class consisted of laborers and farmers; many of the latter were tenants who paid a share of their produce to the owner. The lowest class in Babylonian society was made up of slaves, persons who had been captured in war or who had lost their freedom through debt. The law protected them carefully. Although the slaves were chattel, they could own property and eventually buy their freedom; a male slave was also allowed to marry a free woman. Their offspring were free. The courts recognized women as free individuals who could own property, marry, and even obtain divorce. In contrast, women in the United States could not own property in their own name until the early twentieth century.

GREECE

The significance of the Greek or Hellenic civilization is that they were the first people in history to establish the institution of democracy. The Greek polis, or city-state, has been characterized as Western civilization in miniature. That form of government expressed a set of political values that remained fundamental throughout Western history. The political and military strengths inherent in the organization permitted the Greeks to expand abroad, while local patriotism and mutual suspicion divided the homeland into many tiny sovereign units. Although these states were banded together by a common culture and could occasionally cooperate against an outside enemy, their continuing rivalry eventually was to destroy Greek freedom. Class rivalry and search for individual gain produced economic growth in all Western civilization.

Greek philosopher Plato (shown here), along with Aristotle, sought to determine the ideal political unit. (North Wind Picture Archives)

The great political theorists Plato and Aristotle discussed the nature of an ideal political unit. The city-state was a small sovereign political unit in which all important activity was conducted and where communal bonds were supreme. Citizens assembled periodically to vote on major issues and to elect officials. A steering committee or council was created in Sparta and Athens by 600 B.C.E. Elsewhere, the council represented the developing aristocracy and ran the government; its members were chosen for life. Membership was limited to landholders. The single office of king was replaced by a number of officials. All citizens were equal members of the polis, and all possessed fundamental private rights. Slaves existed, as did serfs. Women were considered politically incompetent. The polis was based on principles of justice, embodying basic equality, even-handed justice, participation in public activities, and government by law.

DEVELOPMENT OF ROMAN LAW

Roman law has been the most innovative and most copied system in the West. As the Roman Empire developed, so did a complex system of laws geared toward governing an increasingly urban population. Many types of law existed as a result of the diverse backgrounds of the people in the empire. In Celtic communities and among the nomad tribes on the Syrian frontier, the custom of the ancestors was an unwritten code. The Greek cities relied on the more advanced principles of Hellenic law. Rhodian sea law, a special field of Greek law, was standard over most of the empire.

When modern legal historians speak of Roman law, they are referring to private or civil law. Cicero, the Roman philosopher and trial lawyer, defined three elements of law, which predominated in all legal systems: legislation, administrative edicts, and judicial reasoning. Roman law spread throughout Europe, and after the fall of the Roman Empire, Constantinople continued to develop the concepts of Roman law. The first major surviving book on Roman law, the *Institutiones* (c. 160 C.E.; republished by Justinian I as part of *Corpus Juris Civilis*, 533 C.E.; *Justinian's Institutes*, 1915), was a textbook written in the reign of Marcus Aurelius. In 528 C.E., Emperor Justinian I collected these laws and published them as the code of Justinian, or *Corpus Juris Civilis*. This code is the cornerstone of modern civil law systems dominant throughout Europe, South America, Scotland, and Quebec. In the United States, only Louisiana bases its legal system on civil law, reflecting its heritage as a French colony. The other states base their laws on the common law derived from England.

Julius Caesar recognized the need for codification of Roman law, not only because of conflicting laws passed by the assemblies though the centuries but also because of the need to bring order to the principles that had developed. Caesar, however, died before fulfilling the planned codification, which was done at periodic stages after his death. During the early Republic, the civil law (*jus civile*) received its first movement forward with the adoption of the Twelve Tables in 449 B.C.E. They continued to be the foundation of justice for centuries; as part of their education, Roman boys committed them to memory, and in the late Republic, the jurist Servius Sulpicius Rufus wrote a commentary on them.

Until the adoption of the Twelve Tables, the laws had been unwritten. The patricians, who alone were acquainted with them, handed them down orally from father to son, an exclusive knowledge that they used for the oppression of the plebeians. The patrician judge decided cases in favor of men of his own class, and no plebeian could quote the law as proof of injustice. The tribunes, therefore, began to urge the codification of the laws in the interest of the common people. The senate yielded, and a committee went to some of the Greek states of southern Italy to study their codes of law. When they returned, ten men were elected for one year for the purpose of drawing up the laws. The task was completed the following year (449 B.C.E.).

The new laws were set up in the forum on twelve wooden tablets and became known as the Twelve Tables. They were simple and harsh, but they codified the law of the time. Intermarriage between patricians and plebeians was prohibited; fathers were given the power of life and death over sons. Nothing was mentioned about legal procedure. The wealthy plebeians resented the law of the Twelve Tables that forbade marriage between classes, viewing it as a social stigma. They also viewed intermarriage as a stepping-stone to office. Because patricians themselves came to favor intermarriage because of their decreasing numbers and diminishing wealth, the prohibition was removed about 445 B.C.E. by the Canuleian Marriage Law.

From about 200 B.C.E. begins the "classical" period of Roman law. Freed of the rigidity of the Twelve Tables, the jurists accepted a "formula" for each case coming before them. This contained the essence of the legal issues involved and defined the penalty to be assessed by those who heard the evidence and pronounced judgment. Although the plaintiff drew up the formula (amended by the defendant), he turned for its preparation to a specialized consultant. The Praetor's Edict, issued each year, was a steadily growing body of these formulas. Beside the praetors stood the other skilled aristocrats who gave "responses" or advice on specific points at issue and developed a more professional body of legal commentary.

When the Romans acquired land in war, they leased a small part of it or granted it to settlers. The larger part was added to the public domain. Anyone who wished to do so could occupy it by paying the government a percentage of the animals grazing or of the produce. In theory, this practice seemed equitable, but in reality, only the patricians and the wealthy plebeians were able to exercise the privilege. They bought, sold, and bequeathed the land, until eventually they came to regard it as their own. The plebeians were determined to end this injustice and at the same time win admission to all the offices in the state. The Struggle Between the Orders occurred in 367 B.C.E., when two tribunes, Licinius and Sextius, proposed a series of laws. The Licinian-Sextian laws provided that the custom of electing military officers instead of consuls should cease, and that two consuls should be regularly elected, one of whom could be a plebeian. It was further stipulated that no one could occupy more than 300 acres (122 hectares) of the public land or permit more than one hundred cattle or five hundred sheep to graze on it.

With the Hortensian law in 287 B.C.E., it was decreed that all plebiscites were to be binding on the entire populace as laws, thereby making the plebeian council a sovereign body freed from the senate. The government was a democracy in form but actually an oligarchy, for the senate exercised more actual power than ever. Patrician aristocracy gave way to a hybrid oligarchy composed of old and blue blood families intermarried with newly rich plebeians. Factions and manipulation of votes in the assemblies were rampant. The criminal law was developing along with the civil law, but criminal law was often arbitrary and penalties for crimes began by the second century C.E. to be different for members of the upper classes and lower classes, and the latter were regularly subjected to judicial torture to gain the truth. During the first century C.E., the Roman jurists began to devise remedies to fill gaps in the contractual system. A favored remedy was barter. Remedies for extortion and fraud were also introduced at that time.

EGYPT

The ancient Egyptians made their own genuine unprecedented laws, legislation, and administrative regulations, which continually progressed over time. Legal and legislative texts were found on the walls of palaces and temples on papyri written in hieroglyphics, Greek, Latin, Hebrew, Aramaic, and Arabic. About 3200 B.C.E., King Menes laid down the oldest legislative systems in human history when he issued the law of Tehut, god of wisdom, as the only law applicable throughout Egypt. He also made Memphis the capital of the first unified and centralized state in history, with an organized system of government, administration, judiciary, education, police, and armed forces.

The Egyptian pharaoh or king was a living god, an autocrat with almost unlimited power. His primary duty was to preserve the right order of things and ensure justice, a duty expressed in the Egyptian word *ma'at* (untranslatable). That concept confirmed the stability and unchanging continuity of the pharaoh's rule. Also included was the concept of the good. The Egyptians regarded their pharaoh as an ideal leader, composed of power and graciousness. The king controlled executive and judicial powers and exercised his executive power with the assistance of many civil servants. Officials could dispense his law, but the king was able to exercise discretion to guard his people and to act as deputy of the gods on earth. The king was the chief priest of all the gods, as well as the commander of the army, administrator of justice, and controller of economic life of the country. He theoretically owned all the land in Egypt and directed the planting of crops and every major activity. The

kings had a bureaucracy that gradually grew in size. Large-scale corruption resulted. The higher officials formed nobility, which was largely hereditary. The officials were educated so that they could help the king administer justice and supervise the erection and care of public works.

Members of the royal family, officials, nobles, and priests formed the upper class of Egyptian society, which had a highly stratified structure. Peasants made up the largest class; slaves were at the lowest level of society. Throughout ancient Egyptian history, most of the people were poor, living in mud huts. Agriculture was the basis of economic life, and the small landowner paid taxes on his farm and possessions. Prisoners and criminals were subject to forced labor in the mines and quarries. It was the duty of the peasant and the government to maintain the irrigation ditches and canals.

The imperial law in Egypt was embodied in edicts, codes, and imperial constitutions as well as so-called laws of the land, which were the remnants of the laws of the Ptolemaic Dynasty (323-30 B.C.E.) and a series of special legal arrangements affecting particular groups. Roman law was promulgated to the people of Egypt through the edicts of the prefect, who was the provincial governor and representative of the emperor and also the supreme judicial, fiscal, administrative, and military authority of the country during his term in office. The edicts were widely circulated to every community in Egypt. They were written in Greek, however, so even though they may have been posted everywhere, only those literate in Greek could actually read them. The subject matter of the edicts varied widely, ranging from the particular to the general, but the surviving fragments indicate that the texts dealt with areas such as fiscal administration, religious practices, criminal and civil law, and government abuses.

INDIA

India's caste system divided society into functional classes: Brahmans, the highest caste who had magical powers and priestly duties; Kṣatriya, who were the rulers and warriors; Vaiśya, who were the cultivators; and Śūdras, who were the peasants and the lowest caste. The Panchamas, or untouchables, who fell below the peasants, lacked inherited status or caste. Moral law, or dharma, depended on the observance of these divisions, and the king was the guarantor of dharma, particularly the privileges of the Brahmans. Ancient Indian society was a monarchy. Set against the monarchy, however, was the concept of self-rule by members of a guild, a village, or an extended kin-group with a common set of interests. This cooperative self-government often produced republicanism and even democracy.

Republican polities were most common and vigorous during the peak of the Buddhist period (sixth or fifth century B.C.E.-c. 200 C.E.). At that time, India was in the midst of urbanization; cities were full of traffic and noise. Trading caravans moved between cities, stopping for many months in a single village. Wandering priests and self-proclaimed teachers brought religious teachings that threatened the Brahmans. Warlords sought to control this society; nonmonarchical forms of government existed. New vocabulary developed, and by the sixth century B.C.E., words translated as "republic," in which decisions were made by group members working together, entered public parlance. Indian republics, however, differed greatly from Western democracy partly because of the clan basis and the exclusivity of the ruling class. Republican polities were based on the settlement or conquest of a given area by an identifiable warrior people who dominated the political life of that area. Some were subject to a king; in others, the citizens themselves ran their affairs in a republican manner. In both types of states, the government was dominated by Kṣatriyas, people of the warrior caste.

In most states, however, political participation was restricted to members of a specific royal clan, the Rajanya. It is likely that political power was restricted to the heads of a limited number of royal families among the ruling clans. The heads of these families were consecrated as kings and participated in deliberations of state. Power, therefore, was concentrated in the hands of a few patriarchs representing the leading lineages of sections

of the warrior caste. Indian kings were seldom as powerful as they wished to be and, therefore, were not in a position to restructure society or create states. They were generally content to gain the submission of their neighbors. These defeated rivals were often left to control their own affairs, required only to pay tribute and provide troops for the conquerors. The existence of warlords was not fatal to the republican tradition.

The sense of political "community" was slowly abandoned, and by the third and fourth centuries C.E., states known earlier as "republics" were subject to hereditary heads of government, and eventually became monarchies. "Government by discussion" continued, but the idea of hierarchy and inequality and caste became increasingly dominant.

CHINA

The early emperors of China claimed to be the sons of heaven, with authority to govern all the earth. The main business of government, however, was performed by officials who had been selected through a civil service examination. These officials were responsible for collecting taxes, directing building projects, deciding on punishments for various crimes, and compiling the calendar. The emperor was responsible for leading various ceremonies. There were no ancient laws in China under which the republic was governed. Whoever succeeded in gaining possession of the throne, regardless of his ancestry, made new laws according to his way of thinking. His successors on the throne were obliged to enforce the laws that he promulgated as founder of the dynasty, and these laws could not be changed without good reason. The Chinese government was a monarchy and, to some extent, an aristocracy. All legal statutes inaugurated by magistrates required written confirmation by the king on the petition presented to him, but he himself made no final decision on important matters of state without consulting the magistrates.

There were two orders or grades of magistrates: those who governed the various courts of the royal palace (considered to be a model for the rule of the entire realm) and all provincial magistrates or governors who ruled a province or city. Other orders of magistrates served the king's business and were entrusted by him with the responsibility of keeping the public conscience; that is, informing the king as they saw fit as to any infraction of the law in any part of the entire kingdom. This scheme appears similar to the equity courts in common law countries.

The Shang Dynasty (1600-1066 B.C.E.) is the earliest Chinese dynasty for which written evidence exists. During this dynasty, the emperor and his court relied on soothsayers to predict the future and make decisions through oracle bones. Shang civilization was a series of towns united under the king. The Zhou Dynasty replaced the Shang in about 1066 B.C.E. and ruled until 256 B.C.E. Under the Zhou, China made many technological advances and began to experience steady population growth. To control their holdings, Zhou kings set up an agricultural system in which nobles owned the land and serfs worked it. They appointed their relatives to govern, giving each a city-state. Each local lord had total authority on his own land and built his own army.

In 221 B.C.E., the first emperor of the Qin Dynasty unified the land on a new imperial basis. The Qin ruler conquered all the other states in northern China and created the first true Chinese empire, calling himself Shi Huangdi, or the first emperor. He adopted many new techniques for unifying China, including standardizing coins, creating a uniform system of weights and measures, and adopting a single writing system. One of the most significant building projects of the Qin was the Great Wall of China (although the present-day Great Wall of China is probably not the same wall). The Han Dynasty overthrew the Qin in 206 B.C.E., governing until 220 C.E. Under the Han, China enjoyed a four-hundred-year period of peace and the expansion of trade routes that became known as the Silk Road, one of the most-used trade routes in the world.

MESOAMERICA

Civilizations developed in Mexico and upper Central America after about 1400 B.C.E. Meso-america is distinguished from all other parts of the Americas by the presence of a well-developed writing system. One important use was the recording of history. States were stratified into a series of classes headed by a highly centralized, hierarchical government. The most powerful member of the elite class was the ruler or king. Power was based on economic or religious considerations, and the belief that their supernatural origins gave the king and his family the divine right to rule. Leaders were seen, both in their lifetimes and after, as the incarnations of deities.

Mexico's greatest pre-Hispanic civilization, the Maya, was agriculturally based. The Maya had a complex and elaborate writing system. The classical form of political organization had no standing armies and emphasized the qualities of the individual leader. Primogeniture was the most recognized principle of succession. Although there were no standing armies, warfare was important, and wars were initially fought to obtain tribute and captives for sacrifice. The prevailing mode of warfare was ritualized conflict or raiding without intent to gain territory, a practice common in Meso-american societies. The aim later expanded to include territorial and resource acquisition, prestige, and increased power. The form of government changed over time, from egalitarianism to elitist, then to a system of shared power.

BRITAIN

The breakdown of Roman law and civilization in Britain occurred rather swiftly after the departure of the Roman army in 410 C.E. Raids from continental pirates and Vikings brought mercenary soldiers from Europe to defend against attack. These mercenaries were the Angles and Saxons from northern Germany. These invaders were not centrally organized as the Romans had been or as the Normans would be. Roman Britain was replaced by Anglo-Saxon Britain, with the Celts remaining in Cornwall, Wales, and Scotland.

The English tribes that came from the Continent possessed an elaborate and developed legal system, containing three branches: legislative or lawmaking; executive, which ensured the observation of laws; and judicial, which determined whether laws had been broken and dictated necessary sanctions. The legislative functions were carried out by the king and his council. Legal codes were produced at regular intervals. There was no law enforcement body to perform the executive function. It was up to victims or their family to seek justice. The judicial role was performed by a court called the hundred court, which met every four weeks at a prominent local landmark. The king's reeve usually presided over the court, which performed many functions, including parish council business, planning, and magistrates court.

ADDITIONAL RESOURCES

Halpern, Baruch, and Deborah W. Hobson, eds. *Law, Politics, and Society in the Ancient Mediterranean World*. Sheffield, England: Sheffield Academic Press, 1993.

Raaflaub, Kurt, and Nathan Rosenstein, eds. *War and Society in the Ancient and Medieval Worlds: Asia, the Mediterranean, Europe, and Mesoamerica*. Washington, D.C.: Center for Hellenic Studies, 1999.

Sinnigen, William G., and Charles Alexander Robinson, Jr. *Ancient History from Prehistoric Times to the Death of Justinian*. 3d ed. New York: Macmillan, 1981.

Starr, Chester G. *A History of the Ancient World*. 4th ed. New York: Oxford University Press, 1991.

Watson, Alan. *The Evolution of Law*. Baltimore, Md.: Johns Hopkins University Press, 1985.

SEE ALSO: Angles, Saxons, Jutes; Aristotle; Britain; Caesar, Julius; Celts; China; Cicero; Constantinople; Egypt, Pharaonic; Egypt, Prepharaonic; Greece, Classical; Greece, Hellenistic and Roman; Hammurabi's code; Han Dynasty; India; Israel; Judaism; Justinian I; Justinian's code; Maya; Plato; Ptolemaic Dynasty; Qin Dynasty; Rome, Imperial; Rome, Republican; Shang Dynasty; Shi Huangdi; Twelve Tables, The; Zhou Dynasty.

—*Marcia J. Weiss*

LANGUAGES AND LITERATURE

Language is a defining capability of *Homo sapiens*. It and human culture evolved together, a process that began, most scientists believe, 100,000 to 200,000 years ago. The prehistoric world saw the development of complex language and its ability to transmit information from one generation to the next. These oral traditions long preserved the knowledge of bands of primitive humans and, later, tribes, chiefdoms, and nations. The beginnings of writing about 5,500 years ago and its triumphant dissemination through much of the world before 700 C.E. freed human culture from dependency on fragile oral transmission. Literature, which could safeguard information long beyond a single generation's or even a nation's existence, inaugurated an entirely new, fundamental feature of culture: history.

THE ORIGIN OF LANGUAGE AND LANGUAGE FAMILIES

There are two basic theories about the origin of language. The first, monogenesis, holds that language began only once. Groups speaking the original "proto-World" language became separated as primitive humans migrated into new territories. The tendency for pronunciations to change and for new words to appear among the isolated groups eventually made their speech unintelligible to one another. The second theory, multigenesis, finds that the incredible variety among modern languages, of which about 3,500 are still spoken, indicates that language was invented more than once. Both theories recognize that languages constantly change and that modern languages belong to a small number of language families, many of which have left written records from ancient times. These form the literature of regions and nations in the broadest sense—any information recorded in the form of carved, inked, engraved, chiseled, or molded letters or characters: deeds and wills, genealogies, administrative accounts and censuses, laws, the tenets and traditions of religions, manuals, histories, songs, and stories.

Whatever their ultimate origin, ancient languages either died out entirely or mutated into one or more modern languages. The group of languages descended from a single forebear constitutes a language family. Linguists generally agree that twenty-nine families exist, along with a few language isolates, such as Basque, whose affiliation is unclear: Afro-Asiatic, Algonquian, Altaic, Andean-Equatorial, Australian Aboriginal, Austro-Asiatic, Austronesian, Aztec-Tanoan, Caucasian, Dravidian, Eskimo-Aleut, Ge-Pano-Carib, Hokan, Indo-European, Indo-Pacific, Japanese, Khoisan, Korean, Macro-Chibchan, Macro-Siouan, Na-Dené, Niger-Congo, Nilo-Saharan, Oto-Manguean, Paleosiberian, Penutian, Sino-Tibetan, Tai, and Uralic. Some scholars distinguish even larger groupings—superfamilies, or macrophyla: Nostratic (including Afro-Asiatic, Dravidian, Indo-European, Altaic, Uralic, Korean), Dené-Caucasian (including Na-Dené, Sino-Tibetan, Eskimo-Aleut, Caucasian), Amerind (most native American Indian languages), and Austric (including Austronesian, Tai, Austro-Asiatic).

In most cases, the original parent language speakers remained more or less in their ancestral lands; most languages and literatures were regional. However, Indo-European and Sino-Tibetan peoples traveled and conquered so extensively that a few ancestor languages, particularly Latin, Greek, and Chinese, became international languages of commerce and learning.

MESOPOTAMIA

Mesopotamia (*Greek*, "between rivers") refers to the early city-states lying between the Euphrates and Tigris Rivers, now in modern Iraq. The Sumerians built the first of these city-states about 3500 B.C.E. and within five hundred years had turned an accounting system for crops and property into the first writing system, cuneiform. Although some scholars find correspondence between the Sumerian language and Indo-European, most consider it unrelated to any other language. Sumer was conquered by the Akkadians in 2350 B.C.E., and by 2000 B.C.E., Sumerian had died as a spoken tongue, but the Akkadians and closely related Babylonians and Assyrians used it as a liturgical and scholarly language. The Akkadians, whose language belonged to the Semitic branch of the Afro-Asiatic family, adopted cuneiform and shared many of Sumer's literary genres and myths. Mesopotamia lost its cultural autonomy after the Persians conquered it in 539 B.C.E.

Thousands of cuneiform tablets in Sumer and Akkad miraculously escaped destruction during Mesopotamia's long, war-torn history. Much of the literature remains untranslated, but what has been deciphered reveals literary riches. There were narratives unfolding creation myths and the origin of Sumerian gods, such as the *Enuma Elish* (c. 2000 B.C.E.; English translation, 1902), treatises on astronomy and mathematics, hymns, poems praising royalty, wisdom literature, manuals for training scribes, dictionaries, collections of fables and riddles, catalogs of literary works, and cult songs.

However, the period is best known for two works. The first is the Gilgamesh epic (2000 B.C.E.; translated into English as *Gilgamesh Epic*, 1917), the greatest of the Mesopotamian epics—in fact, among the most poignant and tragically powerful epics ever created. Stories about Gilgamesh, a Sumerian king of Uruk (c. 2700 B.C.E.), were written down in Sumerian no later than 2000 B.C.E., but the version that came down to modern readers dates from a seventh century B.C.E. Akkadian text attributed to the poet Shin-eqi-unninni. It tells of friendship between the partly divine Gilgamesh and the animal-like Enkidu, battles, a quest to the underworld for eternal life, and a massive flood, similar to the biblical story of the flood. The second famous work is Hammurabi's code, which was inscribed on a pillar about 1770 B.C.E. in the name of a Babylonian king. It contains 282 laws and a prologue explaining the king's mandate to rule.

AFRICA

Along with the Middle East, northern Africa is home to the Afro-Asiatic language family. Once known as Hamito-Semitic, the parent tongue was spoken about nine thousand years ago. Among the most important of its Hamitic branch of languages in early historical times were Egyptian, Coptic (the name used for Egyptian early in the Christian era), and Numidian, all of which left literary records. Egyptian dates back to the third millennium B.C.E., and an extensive variety of literature survives in hieroglyphic inscriptions. Much of it is funereal and mythological: incantations, brief biographies or genealogies, or invocations intended to commemorate the dead and send their souls on to the afterlife. The surviving records from the Old Kingdom (c. 2700-2200 B.C.E.) are almost entirely mortuary hymns, ritual incantations, and autobiographies, most frequently for the tombs of royalty. The First Intermediate period (c. 2200-c. 2050 B.C.E.) brings the beginnings of odic poetry. In the Middle Kingdom (c. 2050-c. 1790 B.C.E.) appear hymns, autobiographies, memorials of events, instructional texts for royalty, and fiction, as well as tales about giants and monsters, such as *Story of the Shipwrecked Sailor* (c. 2000 B.C.E.; English translation, 1914), and philosophical discourse, as in *The Dialogue of a Man with His Soul* (c. 1975 B.C.E.; English translation, 1968). The New Kingdom (c. 1570-c. 1085 B.C.E.) produced the *Book of the Dead* (also known as *Book of Going Forth by Day, Coming Into Day*, compiled and edited in the sixteenth century B.C.E.), a collection of mortuary texts, as well as hymns, poetry, and inscriptions in celebration of military exploits, epics (such as *The Battle of Kadesh*, c. 1178 B.C.E.; English translation, 1960), and instructional texts for the bureaucracy. After 332 B.C.E. (the Late Period), Egyptian literature was influenced by Greece and Rome and included magical texts, works of science, collections of maxims, histories, and fables. Coptic was the language of the Egyp-

tian Christian church, used in its liturgy and in such devotional works as accounts of saints' lives. About 700 C.E., Christian works also began to appear in Old Numidian, a Nilo-Saharan language.

None of the remaining language families in Africa—Niger-Congo (such as Bantu and Swahili), and Khoisan (a small group of languages spoken in the Kalahari Desert area)—produced a literature in ancient times. If writing systems existed, they were the jealously guarded tools of priesthoods or secret societies and reserved for ritual. However, Africa nurtured a singular oral literature, and the stories recorded by modern folklorists preserve tales and poetry that in some cases hark back to ancient times. These suggest widespread traditions of epics, which were acted as they were recited, religious poetry, incantations and chants, dirges, praise poetry, songs, epigrams, and tales about gods and legendary heroes.

INDIA

The Indian subcontinent was home to two major language families in ancient times. In central and northern India, Sanskrit was the literary language of the Indo-Iranian branch of Indo-European. Languages of the Dravidic family were spoken to the south, of which Tamil produced the earliest literary records.

Sanskrit is the language of the oldest sacred literary texts of all Indo-European languages: four Vedas, each containing traditional hymns to the gods to be chanted during ritual sacrifice. Beginning with the *Rigveda* (also known as Ṛgveda, c. 1500-1000 B.C.E.; English translation, 1896-1897), they were written down between 1500 and 500 B.C.E. Associated with them are three kinds of prose works: *Brāhmaṇas*, with illustrative examples as commentary; *Āraṇyakas*, with magical interpretations; and *Upaniṣads*, philosophical discussions. With the Vedas, two epic poems form the source for the social and religious doctrines of Hinduism. The *Mahābhārata* (400 B.C.E.-400 C.E., present form by c. 400 C.E.; *The Mahabharata of Krishna-Dwaipayana Vyasa*, 1887-1896), among the longest poetical compositions in any language, consists of ninety thousand couplets of narrative poetry. Attributed to the ancient sage Vyāsa, it was probably a compilation by several poets and priests between 400 and 300 B.C.E., and it recounts the war-torn history of the king of Kurukshetra; its best known section, the *Bhagavadgītā* (c. 200 B.C.E.-200 C.E.; *The Bhagavad Gita*, 1785), is a dialogue unfolding the teachings of the god Krishna. The *Rāmāyaṇa* (c. 500 B.C.E, some material added later; English translation, 1870-1889), the second major epic, was written by the poet Vālmīki. Its twenty-four thousand couplets depict the campaign of the hero-king Rama, aided by the armies of monkey-kings, to rescue his wife from a demoniac foe.

Although almost wholly a literary rather than a spoken language, Sanskrit was the medium for an outpouring of literature in the fifth, sixth, and seventh centuries C.E. as writers attempted to collect and codify all knowledge. In addition to anthologies of lyric poetry and works on law and government, there were shastras, treatises on the arts and sciences. Particularly valuable to modern scholars is a Sanskrit grammar, the first concerning any Indo-European language called *Aṣṭādhyāyī* (c. 500 B.C.E.; *Astakam Paniniyam: Panini's Eight Books of Grammatical Sutras*, 1887) by Pāṇini. After the second century C.E., vernacular dialects, called Prākrits, appeared in popular literature, especially in drama. They later became the languages for Buddhist and Jainist religious texts. In the courts of southern Indian kingdoms, poets wrote lyric and mystical verse in Tamil as early as the first century B.C.E.

CHINA

Chinese belongs to the Sino-Tibetan language family, which developed in the western and coastal regions of modern China, Tibet, and parts of Southeast Asia. The Chinese branch started with a language that grew distinct from the Tibetan branch sometime in the third millennium B.C.E., Set down in pictographs and then logographic characters, Chinese literature grew to be among the most extensive, sophisticated, and aesthetically cohesive of the ancient world. Inscriptions on bone and bronze date from early in the second millennium B.C.E.,

and around 1500 B.C.E. Wenyan, a literary language, developed. Its specialized vocabulary and spare style was the standard for literature in all the Chinese languages thereafter.

At the heart of ancient Chinese literature are the five classics, the *Wujing*, attributed to the philosopher Confucius (551-479 B.C.E.), although he did not write them all. These books served as the basis for formal education for the upper classes. The first, *Shijing* (traditionally fifth century B.C.E.; *The Book of Songs*, 1937), collected 305 ballads composed between 1000 and 700 B.C.E. Originally meant to be sung, the ballads bespeak the universal themes of young love and courtship, failed marriage, separation, the glory and carnage of war, mourning for dead loved ones, and the protests of the poor against the rich. The *Yijing* (eighth to third century B.C.E.; English translation, 1876; also known as *Book of Changes*, 1986) was a manual of divination, explaining how to interpret the meaning revealed in the positions of special sticks cast by the diviner, but in so doing, the book lays out a metaphysical view of nature and its relation to humans. The *Shujing* (compiled after first century B.C.E.; English translation in *The Chinese Classics*, Vol. 5, Parts 1 and 2, 1872; commonly known as *Classic of History*) contains documents from early dynasties, which were regarded as examples of good government and political wisdom. The *Liji* (compiled first century B.C.E.; *The Liki*, 1885; commonly known as *Classic of Rituals*) guides readers in both religious and daily behavior. The *Chunqiu* (fifth century B.C.E.; *The Ch'un Ts'ew with the Tso Chuen*, 1872; commonly known as *Spring and Autumn Annals*) recounts two hundred years of history in the province in which Confucius lived. Confucius also wrote several works about his moral philosophy, the most important of which was the *Lunyu* (later sixth-early fifth centuries B.C.E.; *The Analects*, 1861).

Other philosophers wrote influential books at about the same time. The foremost among them was the *Dao De Jing* (possibly sixth century B.C.E., probably compiled late third century B.C.E.; *The Speculations on Metaphysics, Polity, and Morality of "the Old Philosopher, Lau-Tsze,"* 1868; better known as the *Dao De Jing*), attributed to Laozi. Its brief, poetical maxims promoted the goal of naturalness and harmony that formed the underlying principles of Daoism, the chief rival of Confucianism. The turbulent era following 200 C.E. produced a wealth of nature poetry and ballads, along with works in rhyming, rhythmical prose. By the end of the seventh century, the influence of Indian poetry, conveyed by Buddhist monks, brought new prosodic discipline to Chinese poetry. At the same time the first prose fiction, novel-like accounts of heroes, appeared. The era also produced scientific, political, and military treatises, most notably *Sunzi Bingfa* (probably 475-221 B.C.E.; *Sun Tzu: On the Art of War*, 1910), a Daoism-influenced book about strategy by Sunzi, a contemporary of Confucius.

MIDDLE EAST

The Middle East includes the Arabian Peninsula and Iran. Languages from the Semitic branch of Afro-Asiatic were spoken on the peninsula from the beginning of historic times. Of them Phoenician, Hebrew, Old Aramaic, and, more recently, Arabic produced important literatures. In the area of modern Iran, people spoke Persian, an Indo-European language closely related to Sanskrit, and developed a literary language, Avestan.

The Phoenician language dates from about 3000 B.C.E., and according to Greek and Roman authors, Phoenician writers of the first millennium B.C.E. from the area of modern Palestine and such North African colonies as Carthage wrote chronicles, epic poetry, and books of history, geography, and agriculture. However, only a few short inscriptions survive in Phoenician, and almost everything else is lost, except for poetry translated into Greek.

Hebrew poetry written down in cuneiform exists from the fourteenth century B.C.E., and records in old Hebrew characters date from as early as the ninth century B.C.E. It was at this time that writers and editors, often working from multiple sources, compiled the present version of the Old Testament of the Bible, one of the monuments of world literature. In its twenty-four books are examples of history, heroic saga, love poetry, prophetic poetry,

wisdom literature, and short stories. The first five books especially, collectively called the Pentateuch or Torah, contain the creation story of Adam and Eve, racial history, and laws, including the Ten Commandments, which together underlie much of Western culture and are sacred to Judaism and Christianity. Jewish writers continued producing narrative works in Hebrew or Aramaic between 300 B.C.E. and 200 C.E., such as the books known as the Apocrypha, as well as commentaries on the Bible, such as the Mishnah (second century B.C.E.) and Talmud, a compendious work completed in the fifth century B.C.E. that discusses every aspect of Jewish life.

Cuneiform inscriptions in Old Persian date from as early as the sixth century B.C.E. At about the same time, oral versions of hymns, laws, stories of the gods, and devotional guides were composed. They were written down sometime during the fourth through sixth centuries C.E. Some of the hymns written by Zoroaster were collected in the *Avesta* (1000-600 B.C.E.), the sacred text of the Zoroastrian religion. The refined form of Old Persian used for the book is called Avestan after it.

Pre-Islamic Arabic literature appeared with suddenness and considerable sophistication as early as the sixth century C.E. as orally transmitted proverbs, legends, and poetry. The poetry, not transcribed until the eighth century C.E., includes both short rhyming poems, called *rajaz*, and long odes in praise of Arabic customs, of which the most celebrated are the *Mu'allaqat* (hanging odes). The glory of Arabic literature, however, is the Qur'ān, the sacred book of Islam. An editor probably compiled the standard text about 650 C.E. from passages that the prophet Muḥammad (c. 570-632 C.E.) wrote following his revelatory vision in 610 C.E. In the courts of the rulers who embraced Islam, poets composed lyrics dedicated to love, wine, and hunting before 700 C.E.; the chief prose works were grammatical treatises and commentaries on the Qur'ān.

ANATOLIA

Anatolia, or Asia Minor, is the area of modern Turkey south of the Bosporus. In the second millennium B.C.E. the Hittites, a confederation of city-states, most speaking an Indo-European language, constituted the major culture. In hieroglyphs and cuneiform, the Hittites produced historical texts, such as annals, accounts of military campaigns, edicts, letters, and treaties; legal texts; administrative records; literary works, such as hymns, lyrics, proverbs, and mythological tales; ritual texts; prayers; oracular sayings; and vows. In the eighth century B.C.E., the Hittites were displaced by the Phrygians, whose language was related to Greek. About one hundred Phrygian inscriptions survive from the seventh through fourth centuries B.C.E. The Phrygians in turn were eclipsed by the Lydians, whose language was a descendant of Hittite. A small number of funerary inscriptions, verses, and sacral texts survive from the sixth through fourth centuries B.C.E. in the Lydian alphabet. In 546 B.C.E., the Persian Empire conquered the Lydians, and Anatolian literature subsequently became extensions of Persian, Greek, or Roman literature.

GREECE

The mysterious peoples who migrated into Greece and the eastern Mediterranean islands in prehistoric times spoke an Indo-European language with many non-Indo-European words. By the fourteenth century B.C.E. the Mycenaeans of Crete were using a script, now called Linear B, to record administrative business in an early form of Greek. However, this wealthy Minoan culture (named after the mythic King Minos) fell into decline, and with it, the art of writing lapsed for centuries.

At the beginning of the eighth century B.C.E., there was a rebirth of learning and the arts, among them the use of an alphabet borrowed from the Phoenicians. It was then that the poet Homer, drawing on stories about the twelfth century B.C.E. Trojan War, composed the two most influential epics of the Western literary tradition. Preserving elements of the oral-formulaic style of their sources, the *Iliad* (c. 800 B.C.E.; English translation, 1616) recounts the fall of Troy to a confederation of Greek armies, and the *Odyssey* (c. 800 B.C.E.; En-

glish translation, 1616) follows the ten-year struggle of one band of warriors to return home to Greece. The Homeric epics, like the epics of India, became the basis for aristocratic education, teaching a code of conduct as well as presenting stories about the relations between humans and gods.

Philosophic discourse and scientific enquiry spread throughout the Hellenic world. Natural philosophers wrote treatises on physics (such as Archimedes, c. 287-212 B.C.E.), medicine (Hippocrates, c. 460-c. 370 B.C.E.), mathematics (Euclid, c. 330-c. 270 B.C.E.), and astronomy (Aristarchus of Samos, c. 310-c. 230 B.C.E.). The pre-Socratic philosophers, such as Protagoras (c. 485-c. 410 B.C.E.), not only speculated about the nature of the universe; some of them, known as the Sophists, taught young men the practical art of rhetoric and wrote manuals systematizing their methods. Such education was needed in the city-states of Greece, above all in Athens, during the fifth and fourth centuries B.C.E. Athens was a democracy and depended upon public debates to set policy and settle disputes; accordingly, Athenians were litigious, contentious, and fond of ideas. The twenty-nine dialogues and *Apologia Sōkratous* (399-390 B.C.E.; *Apology*, 1675) of the poet-philosopher Plato (c. 427-347 B.C.E.) re-create this atmosphere of debate in recounting how Socrates (c. 470-399 B.C.E.) guided the thinking of fellow citizens with penetrating questions designed to lead them to greater insight; the dialogues, taken together, are a philosophical saga, among the world's finest prose works, and one of the two most influential philosophic oeuvres in the Western world. The other is the work of Plato's younger contemporary, Aristotle (384-322 B.C.E.), who produced treatises on the sciences, politics, the arts, and ethics.

Greek philosophical discourse tended to grow abstract and unworldly, while in a contrary manner, the manuals on rhetoric tended to dwell on specific cases to the exclusion of general principles. To the classical Greek mind, literature complemented philosophy and rhetoric by occupying a middle ground, enabling writers to present concrete stories in order to illustrate such important abstract concepts as the relation of the people to their society or to gods. The three great tragic dramatists, Aeschylus (525/524-456/455 B.C.E.), Sophocles (c. 496-c. 406 B.C.E.), and Euripides (c. 485-406 B.C.E.), as well as the comic dramatist Aristophanes (c. 450-c. 385 B.C.E.), created plays to be staged at public festivals for communal consideration. For private entertainment and edification, poets such as Sappho of Lesbos (c. 630-c. 568 B.C.E.) and Pindar (c. 518-c. 438 B.C.E.) wrote lyric and odic poetry. The Hellenic age also produced the first Western attempts to record and interpret the past on a large scale, particularly in the histories of Herodotus (c. 484-c. 425 B.C.E.), Thucydides (c. 459-c. 402 B.C.E.), and Xenophon (c. 431-c. 354 B.C.E.).

Greek became the language of learning and commerce in the eastern Mediterranean and Middle East. In addition to the philosophers and historians at north African centers such as Alexandria,

Euripides is a fifth century B.C.E. Greek dramatist whose tragedies influenced many later playwrights. (Library of Congress)

writers of the new Christian religion usually wrote in Greek. The twenty-seven books and four gospels of the New Testament of the Bible were written in koiné, or common, Greek in the first century C.E. The books incorporate letters, sermons, histories, and prophetic writing.

THE AMERICAS

At least three great migrations of peoples from Asia populated the North and South American continents, and in 1987, historical linguist Joseph H. Greenberg argued that all New World languages belong to three families: Amerind, which includes most languages of the two continents; Na-Dené, languages of Canada and Alaska; and Eskimo-Aleut, spoken in the circum-polar regions of North America. However, most Americanists group New World languages into at least thirteen families, the largest of which for North America were Algonquian and Aztec-Tanoan and for South America Andean-Equatorial and Ge-Pano-Carib.

Many cultures left pictographic inscriptions that record events or religious beliefs, and the Olmec culture (c. 1200-400 B.C.E.) of Central America developed a system of hieroglyphs; however, only the Maya of the Classic Period (300-900 C.E.) produced a large body of literature. Maya hieroglyphic, logographic, and phonetic-syllabic inscriptions concerned myths, history, and rituals. Additionally, three books and a fragment of a fourth survive. Intended as almanacs, they cover topics such as agriculture, weather, disease, hunting, and astronomy. A Maya book written with the Roman alphabet, the *Popul Vuh* (n.d.; *Popul Vuh: The Sacred Book of the Ancient Quiché Maya*, 1950), preserves oral traditions concerning the classical Maya story of creation.

ROME

Latin, an Indo-European language, was spoken in a variety of dialects in Italy during the first millennium B.C.E. By the middle of the third century B.C.E., Rome emerged as the dominant power of the region. Its dialect of Latin became the literary standard.

The Romans inherited much of Greek culture and consciously modeled their literature on the works of Greek authors. Nevertheless, the Romans, of a more conservative, practical mentality than the Greeks, produced a distinctive literature, and in great abundance. The greatest Roman epic poet, Vergil (70-19 B.C.E.), for example, borrowed from Homer for the structure and narrative style of his *Aeneid* (c. 29-19 B.C.E.; English translation, 1553)., but he shaped it for a distinctively Roman purpose: to legitimize Roman power through a mythical history of Rome's founding. The most vibrant classical Latin drama was comedy, especially that of Plautus (c. 254-184 B.C.E.) and Terence (c. 190-159 B.C.E.), although tragedies were written, most ably by the Stoic philosopher Seneca the Younger (c. 4 B.C.E.-65 C.E.). Lyric poets such as Catullus (c. 84-c. 54 B.C.E.) and Ovid (43 B.C.E.-17 C.E.) composed not only love poems but also dramatic dialogues and narrative poetry about both historical and legendary figures, often with a satirical intent. Likewise, the magisterial discursive poet Horace (65-8 B.C.E.) wrote both philosophical poems and satires about Roman manners and politics, as did Juvenal (c. 60-c. 130 C.E.). The *Satyricon* (c. 60 C.E.; *The Satyricon*, 1694) of Petronius Arbiter (died c. 66 C.E.), a medley of ribald poetry and slangy prose, brought a degree of gritty, rollicking humor to satire seldom equaled since. More in line with the Roman virtue of intellectual gravity, Lucretius (c. 98-55 B.C.E.) used poetry to encapsulate the science and philosophy of the era in *De rerum natura* (c. 60 B.C.E.; *On the Nature of Things*, 1682).

Roman prose was as diverse and prolific as the poetry. The histories by Julius Caesar (100-44 B.C.E.), Sallust (c. 86-35 B.C.E.), and Tacitus (c. 56-c. 120 C.E.) describe the political and military struggles of Rome while introducing many of the peoples of northern Europe into history. The philosopher-politician Cicero (106-43 B.C.E.) brought Latin prose to a level of supple eloquence equal to that of the best Greek writers in his essays about

politics, oratory, and manners. Many writers sought to compile exhaustive textbooks about a field of knowledge, notably the physician Galen (129-c. 199 C.E.), the natural history scholar Pliny the Elder (23-79 C.E.), and the rhetorician Quintilian (c. 35-after 96 C.E.).

EUROPE

Two general waves of migration took Indo-European-speaking tribes across the continent of Europe during the first millennium B.C.E. First came the Celts, who were eventually displaced to the borders of the mainland and into the British Isles by invading Germanic tribes. Inscriptions in continental Celtic date from the second century B.C.E., and the Irish left inscriptions in their singular script, Ogam, as early as the fifth century C.E. The Germanic parent language split into three branches during the migrations. Northern Germanic, source of the Scandinavian languages, was used for runic inscriptions on stone and bone beginning in the third century C.E., some of which were in verse. In about 350 C.E., Bishop Ulfilas (c. 311-c. 382 C.E.) translated parts of the Bible into Gothic, an eastern Germanic language; a commentary on the gospel of John was also written.

It was in the western branch that the first indigenous European literature began. Tacitus and Alcuin, an eighth century churchman, both refer to the oral heroic poems that Germanic peoples recited about legendary heroes. In the seventh century C.E., *Widsith*, the earliest literary example of the heroic tradition, was written down, and around the same time, Christian poets borrowed the heroic alliterative style for religious subjects, as in the *Dream of the Rood* (eighth century C.E.) and "Cædmon's Hymn" (c. 658 C.E.).

In France, Italy, England, and Ireland, poets and writers, using Latin, had already produced histories, didactic poems, sermons, encyclopedias, riddles, chronicles, prayers, accounts of pilgrimages, saints' lives, and philosophical works. Most of these works were Christian. Among the most celebrated were the sermons and philosophical works of Saint Augustine (354-430 C.E.) and *De consolatione philosophiae* (523; *The Consola-*

tion of Philosophy, late ninth century) by Boethius (c. 480-c. 524), a dialogue in prose and verse. This late Latin literature guided the education and intellectual life of Europeans for a millennium after Rome's fall.

JAPAN AND KOREA

Some linguists believe that Korean, and possibly Japanese, belong to the Altaic family of languages, but the attribution is controversial. Both show the influence of languages of other families, Chinese above all. The earliest literature of Japan dates from the seventh century, although recorded later. Two prose books, the *Kojiki* (712 C.E.; *Records of Ancient Matters*, 1883) and the *Nihon shoki* (compiled 720 C.E.; *Nihongi: Chronicles of Japan from the Earliest Times to A.D. 697*, 1896), lay out the nation's history, beginning with its mythological founding by gods. That the first is written in a mixture of Chinese and Japanese in Chinese characters and the second is wholly in Chinese underscores the dominant role the mainland had in Japanese culture. Confucianism, Daoism, and, to a lesser extent, Buddhism provided the intellectual milieu for the Japanese aristocracy. Early Japanese poetry was also written in Chinese at times. The earliest Japanese language poems, from the late seventh century, exist only in later collections, of which the most famous is the *Manyoshu* (late eighth century C.E.; *The Manyōshū*, 1929-1964; better known as *The Manyoshu*, 1967). Imitating the Chinese metrical style, Japanese poets alternated lines of five and seven syllables both in short poems, such as the five-line *waka*, and the *choka*, which could run to 150 lines. The poetry of Kakinomoto Hitomaro (fl. 689-710 C.E.) epitomizes the tone and thematic thrust of the ancient style: A poem expresses the deepest feelings by communicating the poet's own experience with complete sincerity.

Korean literature followed a similar course. After political unification in 668 C.E., the nation's culture blossomed. Students left to study in China, and Buddhist monks were welcomed for their learning. In the long tradition of the nation's beloved folk songs, poets composed lyric poetry to be accompanied by music. A small number of these early poems appear in later collections, written in Chinese characters adapted to the Korean language.

OCEANIA

Waves of migration gradually peopled the scattered lands in the Pacific Ocean, settling the continent of Australia as early as 65,000 years ago and the archipelago of Hawaii, Easter Island, and the Society Islands by 600 C.E. Three language families correspond to the migrations: the settlers of modern Madagascar, Indonesia, and most of the Pacific Islands spoke Austronesian; in New Guinea and the islands immediately to the west, Indo-Pacific; and in Australia, aboriginal languages.

None of these peoples developed a writing system in ancient times, but the Australians, at least, recorded events and religious symbols in pictographs of great antiquity. Moreover, Oceania possessed a rich, diverse body of oral literature. In Australia, storytellers preserved events in story form and had a large repertoire of story cycles about legendary figures. Additionally, aboriginal tribes had origin myths explaining not only their existence but also their relation to a region's land and animals. These traditions concern the "dreamtime" of a vanished epoch in which the land was created. Aborigines still have a connection to it through specific sacred sites. These sacred sites, perhaps augmented by a form of record keeping called tally marks or story lines, amount to a literature of landscape.

Polynesians in the Pacific Islands also used oral literature to organize and validate their culture. However, although the Polynesians had creation myths and tales of gods and legendary heroes, much of their oral tradition had practical social ends. Pedigree was central to establishing a person's place in society, and to this purpose, genealogies, which sometimes could take days to recite, were jealously preserved. Historical traditions often contained detailed information about the voyages that brought islanders to their homes in the distant past. The rituals of the priesthood and nobility entailed recitation of prose pieces, which were spoken, and poetry, which was chanted or sung in a highly artificial, archaic diction. In disputes about land or custom, Polynesians often cited information from poetry, as well as genealogies and historical sagas, to support claims.

SOUTHEAST ASIA

The ancestor of Burmese, a Sino-Tibetan language, was spoken during ancient times in the area of modern Myanmar, Tai languages in the area of modern Thailand, and Austro-Asiatic languages in the region of modern Cambodia, Laos, Vietnam, and Malaysia. China to the north and India to the west supplied models for the literature of Burma and Thailand. In addition to Buddhist and Hindu texts, the Indian *Rāmāyaṇa* was particularly popular in ancient times and, called the *Ramakian* in Thai, was adapted to local dialects. In the area of modern Vietnam, songs were part of the oral tradition. However, the region did not produce indigenous literatures in local languages until after 700 C.E.

ADDITIONAL RESOURCES

Asher, R. E., and E. F. Koerner, eds. *Concise History of the Language Sciences: From the Sumerians to the Cognitivists*. New York: Pergamon, 1995.

Auroux, Sylvain, et al., eds. *History of the Language Sciences: An International Handbook on the Evolution of the Study of Language from the Beginnings to the Present*. New York: Walter de Gruyter, 2000.

Bakalla, M. H. *Arabic Culture Through Its Language and Literature*. London: Kegan Paul International, 1984.

Burnley, J. D. *The History of the English Language: A Source Book*. New York: Longman, 2000.

Chadwick, H. Munro, and N. Kershaw Chadwick. *The Growth of Literature*. New York: Cambridge University Press, 1986.

Crystal, David. *The Cambridge Encyclopedia of Language*. 2d ed. Cambridge, England: Cambridge University Press, 1997.

Diamond, Jared. *Guns, Germs, and Steel: The Fates of Human Societies*. New York: W. W. Norton, 1997.

Evans, Robert John Weston. *The Language of History and the History of Language*. New York: Oxford University Press, 1998.

Fischer, Steven R. *A History of Language*. London: Reaktion Books, 1999.

Green, Dennis Howard. *Language and History in the Early Germanic World*. New York: Cambridge University Press, 1998.

Hock, Hans Henrich, and Brian D. Joseph. *Language History, Language Change, and Language Relationship: An Introduction to Historical and Comparative Linguistics*. New York: Walter de Gruyter, 1996.

Horrocks, Geoffrey C. *Greek: A History of the Language and Its Speakers*. New York: Longman, 1998.

Jackson, Kenneth Hurlstone. *Language and History in Early Britain: A Chronological Survey of the Brittonic Languages, First to Twelfth Centuries A.D.* Dublin, Ireland: Four Courts Press, 1994.

Keene, Donald. *Seeds in the Heart: Japanese Literature from Earliest Times to the Late Sixteenth Century*. New York: Columbia University Press, 1999.

Khanlari, P. N. *A History of the Persian Language*. Translated by N. H. Ansari. New Delhi, India: Sterling, 1979.

Maddieson, Ian, and Thomas J. Hinnebusch, eds. *Language History and Linguistic Description in Africa*. Trenton, N.J.: Africa World Press, 1998.

Pountain, Christopher J. *A History of the Spanish Language Through Texts*. New York: Routledge, 2001.

Saenz-Badillos, Ángel. *A History of the Hebrew Language*. Translated by John Elwoldle. New York: Cambridge University Press, 1996.

Schütz, Albert J. *The Voices of Eden: A History of Hawaiian Language Studies*. Honolulu: University of Hawaii Press, 1994.

Sihler, Andrew L. *Language History: An Introduction*. Philadelphia: J. Benjamins, 2000.

Stevenson, Victor, ed. *A World of Words: An Illustrated History of Western Languages*. Rev. ed. New York: Sterling, 2000.

Trask, R. L., ed. *The Dictionary of Historical and Comparative Linguistics*. Chicago: Fitzroy Dearborn, 2000.

Trimpi, Wesley. *Muses of One Mind: The Literary Analysis of Experience and Its Continuity*. Princeton, N.J.: Princeton University Press, 1983.

Vogel, Joseph O., and Jean Vogel, eds. *The Encyclopedia of Precolonial Africa: Archaeology, History, Languages, Cultures, and Environments*. Walnut Creek, Calif.: Sage Publications/AltaMira Press, 1997.

SEE ALSO: Aeschylus; Africa, East and South; Africa, North; Africa, West; Akkadians; Arabia; *Āraṇyakas*; Archimedes; Aristarchus of Samos; Aristophanes; Aristotle; Augustine, Saint; Australia, Tasmania, New Zealand; *Avesta*; *Bhagavadgītā*; Bible: Jewish; Bible: New Testament; Boethius; *Book of the Dead*; *Brāhmaṇas*; Buddhism; Caesar, Julius; Catullus; Celts; China; Christianity; *Chunqiu*; Cicero; Confucianism; Confucius; Daoism; Djanggawul cycle; Dreaming; Egypt, Pharaonic; Egypt, Prepharaonic; Euclid; Euripides; Galen; Gilgamesh epic; Greece, Classical; Greece, Hellenistic and Roman; Greece, Mycenaean; Hammurabi's code; Herodotus; Hippocrates; Hittites; Homer; Horace; India; Islam; Japan; Judaism; Juvenal; Korea; Laozi; Linear B; Lucretius; Lydia; *Mahābhārata*; Maya; Muḥammad; *Nihon shoki*; Olmecs; Ovid; Pāṇini; Performing arts; Petronius Arbiter; Philosophy; Phoenicia; Phrygia; Pindar; Plato; Plautus; Pliny the Elder; Polynesia; Pre-Socratic philosophers; Protagoras; Quintilian; Qur'ān; *Rāmāyaṇa*; Religion and ritual; Rome, Imperial; Rome, Republican; Sallust; Sappho; Seneca the Younger; Socrates; Sophocles; Sumerians; Tacitus; Talmud; Terence; Thucydides; *Upaniṣads*; Vālmīki; Vedas; Vergil; Writing systems; *Wujing*; Xenophon; Zoroastrianism.

—Roger Smith

MEDICINE AND HEALTH

To reconstruct ancient medicine and health, scholars depend primarily on three sources: human remains, artistic representations, and texts. For example, a spongelike porosity in a skeletal eye orbit may imply an anemia to the paleopathologist who specializes in ancient disease. On pre-Columbian human-shaped jars from Peru, furrowed areas around the mouths may suggest leishmaniasis, a disfiguring parasitic condition still found in the Andean highlands. A vague expression such as "jaguar-macaw seizure" in a curative incantation requires a Maya expert to find a modern equivalent.

In determining ancient medical and health practices, archaeology plays an important role, as does oral tradition, especially in conservative areas such as the Yucatán. In rare cases, surgical instruments survive, such as the scalpels, forceps, and needles of a physician who died in the eruption of Mount Vesuvius in 79 C.E. In Pompeii, archaeologists discovered a shop for the practice of medicine with residues of medicaments. Another source of information is fossilized excrement (coprolites), which, when analyzed, reveals much about parasitic infection and diet in an ancient population.

From a scientific perspective, disease is caused by living organisms, physical factors, chemicals, psychic factors, physiological changes, genetics, and nutritional deficiencies or excesses. A nonscientific model of disease locates causes in the individual, the natural world, social context, or the supernatural world. Many people and cultures attribute disease to both scientific and nonscientific factors, without sharply differentiating the two. For example, Mesopotamian medicine, often characterized as strictly supernatural, has at least a naturalistic side, if not a scientific aspect.

To ask who first practiced medicine and where is pointless. Primates in captivity have been observed practicing simple therapeutic procedures such as extracting splinters. One case, however, stands out. About 46,000 years ago, in the Shanidar cave in northern Iraq, there lived a Neanderthal whose skeleton reveals numerous problems including arthritis, trauma to the face and skull, and blindness in his left eye. His right arm, by one interpretation, had been amputated. Yet he had survived and been cared for by his group until he died at about age forty. In a nearby grave, the remains of flowers today recognized as medicinal have been hailed, prematurely, as evidence for proto-pharmacology.

NEOLITHIC MEDICINE

Beginning about 12,000 years ago, the Neolithic revolution ushered in fundamental changes that, contrary to the name, occurred gradually and irregularly at different rates in different locations. Ground and polished tools replaced tools formerly produced by chipping and flaking. Cultures that had once been hunter-gatherers now turned to agriculture and began to domesticate animals and make pottery.

The adoption of a sedentary lifestyle had profound health implications. Diseases of high infectivity and latency—arbovirus, chickenpox, rabies, tuberculosis, and herpes simplex—had probably already affected hunter-gatherers. As population densities increased as well as human-animal contacts, however, opportunities arose for other viruses and bacterial infections, especially in areas where sanitation and hygiene were minimal. For example, the use of unglazed pottery for storage would have easily led to outbreaks of food poisoning. Permanent structures would have quickly attracted vermin and insects carrying yellow and dengue fevers. As the landscape was cleared, stagnant irrigation pools would have become homes to snails that harbor schistosomiasis and malarial mosqui-

toes. Because the measles virus requires at least twenty-five to fifty new hosts annually, hunter-gatherer groups of less than one hundred would have suffered little if any exposure. By mathematical simulation, as densities increased to over 300,000, it would have become problematic. Although subject to individual variation and further analysis of skeletal evidence, studies of many different Neolithic locales suggest that, at least initially, there were some increases in physiological stress and mortality because of infectious diseases and diets lower in protein, vitamins, and minerals. Stature diminished from Upper Paleolithic and Mesolithic norms in the eastern Mediterranean. In South Asia, the adoption of vegetable food sources is associated with porotic hyperostosis, caries, abscess, rickets, and scurvy.

The Neolithic Age presents some of the earliest evidence for surgical intervention. In trepanation, holes were bored and sawed, scraped, or grooved into skulls of living people. In the absence of anaesthesia, antisepsis, and asepsis, the fact that many survived is extraordinary. The motivation is still debated: relief of fracture or headache, epilepsy, mental illness, demoniac possession, or some unrecoverable ritual because it was also practiced post-mortem. Sinicipital cauterization of the scalp, which leaves a characteristic T-shaped lesion on the skull, was practiced primarily on females and may have been a form of ritual branding rather than therapy.

EGYPTIAN MEDICINE

Later generations who venerated the wise men of the Pyramid age regarded the Egyptian Imhotep not only as their premier physician but also as a veritable god of healing. Even the conquering Greeks came to equate him with their god of medicine and continued to build temples in his honor. A Renaissance man, Imhotep may well have been the chief architect of the step pyramid built by King Djoser (r. c. 2687-2668 B.C.E.) at Saqqara, but no third millennium B.C.E. evidence exists to link him to the art of healing.

From the dynastic period, however, the names of some 150 physicians have been gathered from such sources as tombs, texts, and even mines and quarries where they plied their trade. In status, they range from high court physicians to commoners, and some were perhaps trained in a literate temple context. Hierarchal titles are often appended (for example, chief of physicians or inspector of physicians), but without context, their significance remains opaque. Two women physicians are attested, Peshet from the Old Kingdom and Tawe from the Ptolemaic period. The etymology of *swnw* ("physician") is still debated. Drawn with an arrow, a pot, and the determinative for man, it sometimes is thought to represent an "arrow man," one who extracts arrows in a military context, but this view is conjectural.

In the fifth century B.C.E., the Greek historian Herodotus described an unusual degree of medical specialization among the ancient Egyptians. To what extent this evidence may be extrapolated to the third millennium B.C.E. is unclear. Titles such as "physician of the eyes," "shepherd of the anus," "chief of dentists" are subject to interpretation. The semantic range of the word translated "anus" is wide and may include both small and large intestines. Also, given the common Egyptian notion that disease could arise from autointoxication brought on by intestinal stasis, the label may refer to someone who prepared and administered enemas. The translation "proctologist" would be too precise as well as anachronistic; equally inappropriate is the label of "ophthalmologist" for someone who may have treated eye infections with ointments. Even much of the evidence once adduced to prove dental intervention is now rejected. Holes, supposedly drilled in a mandible to relieve an abscess, today are interpreted as channels created by the abscess itself. A golden prosthesis could never have sustained its two teeth in a living, masticating mouth but was perhaps inserted postmortem. Surgical therapies did include circumcision, trepanation, sutures, and treatment of fractures.

Although some diseases were attributed to naturalistic causes such as autointoxication, many were ascribed to magical and supernatural causes. Disease, it was believed, could arise from gods,

demons, and ghosts and therefore could be combated with incantations, amulets, knotted hair, and even the eating of excrement (coprotherapy) to create an intolerable environment for an indwelling spirit. Troublesome cases might require the services of physician, magician, and priest of Sekhmet, the goddess of disease.

An essential source of information is the seventeen extant medical papyri. The earliest, the Kahun papyrus (1820 B.C.E.), deals in part with gynecology and ascribes many afflictions to a wandering uterus. The Edwin Smith papyrus, though extant only in a copy from about 1550 B.C.E., may date to the Old Kingdom. It sets out forty-eight cases, mostly of trauma, generally in a pattern of title, examination, diagnosis and prognosis, and treatment. Treatment often uses honey, which, from a biomedical point of view, would have antibacterial properties, and there is scarcely any resort to magic. The Ebers papyrus of 1500 B.C.E. is a compendium of different sources and focuses on internal medicine. It alludes to a basic notion of the circulatory system with the heart connected to different organs by channels. The notion of intestinal waste products as a cause of disease is mentioned here.

Another critical source of information are the mummified remains of the Egyptians themselves. Sophisticated CAT (computerized axial tomography) scans allow noninvasive examination, and DNA (deoxyribonucleic acid) analysis has added new information. Among some of the diseases that have been detected are schistosomiasis, tapeworm, tuberculosis, atherosclerosis, sand pneumoconiosis, joint disease, and possibly smallpox.

MESOPOTAMIAN MEDICINE

Of the successive civilizations that controlled the land between the Tigris and Euphrates Rivers, two are especially important in the history of medicine: the Sumerians and the Akkadians. By the third millennium B.C.E., the Sumerians, who spoke a language unrelated to any known linguistic group, had established complex bureaucratic city-states in an area of 10,000 square miles (26,000 square kilometers) along the rivers and canals. By the end of the millennium, Semitic speakers, among whom were the Akkadians from Iraq, had assumed a rule that would last for fifteen hundred years. Just as Greek culture prevailed over the conquering Romans, so too did the high Sumerian culture overpower the Akkadians, who worshiped its gods and zealously studied its literature.

Drawing a picture of Mesopotamian medicine presents sometimes challenging difficulties. In contrast to Egypt, human remains are few, apart from skulls. Medical texts, though numerous, contain vague terminology translatable in various ways. A word rendered "leprosy" by one scholar, to another may mean "scurvy" or "diphtheria." The orientation of the texts is not theoretical but pragmatic. Reconstructing the culture's general notion of disease is therefore hard, and often what modern physicians would call a symptom, such as a cough, is treated more like an individual affliction. Behind a simple description like "the evil cough," on the other hand, may lurk a condition as serious as pulmonary tuberculosis.

The earliest reference to a physician (Sumerian *azu*; Akkadian *asu,* from the Sumerian) occurs about 2500 B.C.E. A false etymology of this term as "he who knows the waters" led many scholars to assume physicians were originally priestly diviners. Mesopotamian disease causation was therefore largely characterized as magical and supernatural (stemming from witches, demoniac possession, and divine displeasure). In fact, complementary magical and naturalistic therapeutic traditions existed throughout Mesopotamia. Natural agents of disease included heat, cold, dryness, indigestion, and even love. One text seems to imply some idea of contagion.

The priestly *ashipu* ("conjurer") employed magical incantations and rituals and, on occasion, herbal remedies, and the *asu* focused primarily on an elaborate pharmacopoeia specified in detailed herbal texts. In intractable cases, the services of both might be retained as well as the diagnostic skills of a seer (*baru*). The status of the physician is uncertain. In the code of Hammurabi (r. 1792-1750 B.C.E.), a physician is treated as a craftsperson subject to monetary fines or even retaliatory capi-

tal punishment in the case of a noble patient's death.

The world's earliest medical text is Sumerian and comes from Nippur (c. 2000 B.C.E.). A fragmentary list of fifteen prescriptions, it probably draws on a long folk herbalistic tradition. The *materia medica* is based on plants, animals, and minerals. Instructions are given to pulverize and compound these in a mixture with beer to create poultices and internal remedies. Exactly what diseases are being treated is unclear.

A fundamental Akkadian text that survives in a late form is the *Sakkiku* (*All Diseases*). Originally written on forty tablets with some three thousand entries, it contains some rudimentary diagnosis of symptoms. A yellow complexion is traced to the yellow disease, jaundice. Elsewhere, however, it often parallels omen texts. If on the way to a patient's house, the conjurer sees a black dog or pig, the patient will die; if white, he will live.

The texts are almost silent about surgery, and to what extent it was practiced is controversial. The code of Hammurabi alludes to an eye operation. Cesarean section, probably post-mortem, was practiced but apparently only on slaves. Simple scalp abscesses were treated with pressure, incision, and scraping. Another text may refer to removal of a liver abscess.

One promising approach is to treat Mesopotamia as a chapter in the history of tropical medicine. Current Iraqi medical journals are quarried as much as ancient texts to set disease parameters. Some ancient conditions that continue to afflict the modern population are deficiency disorders (scurvy), helminthic disorders (worms), cutaneous leishmaniasis (a skin condition), typhoid, and pneumonia.

GREEK MEDICINE

The word "physician" (*i-ja-te*) first occurs in a second millennium B.C.E. Linear B tablet from Pylos. Elsewhere there are references to an unguent boiler, female bath keeper, and medicinal plants. No specific diseases are mentioned. Skeletal evidence presents at least five cases of trepanation. A Mycenaean example on an aristocrat's skull is sophisticated, but the patient appears to have died shortly afterward. Among diseases detected in bone is spinal osteoarthritis. In the classical period, malaria, tuberculosis, and chronic deficiency diseases are common.

The Homeric epics supply the earliest literary evidence. Disease arises from divine displeasure. In the *Iliad* (c. 800 B.C.E.; English translation, 1616), Apollo, sometimes a god of healing, shoots arrows at the Greek camp to avenge Agamemnon's insulting treatment of his priest. A plague ensues, striking the mules and dogs first, then humans. Apollo's epithet here, Smintheus ("Mouser"), has been taken too readily as evidence that Homer recognized rodents as carriers. Description of 147 war wounds reveals a knowledge of anatomy that is at times precise and practical (for killing purposes) and at times fanciful.

The sources of this knowledge were probably the battlefield and analogous inferences drawn from animal slaughter in cooking or sacrifice. Systematic dissection was not practiced until the third century B.C.E., primarily in Alexandria. Wounds are sometimes treated with a bitter root probably related to onion, an astringent. Some are dressed, others left open. Sucking is mentioned but whether therapeutically (to remove pus or poison) is unclear. In the *Odyssey* (c. 800 B.C.E.; English translation, 1616), Odysseus's flow of blood is stanched by a magical incantation, an ancient Indo-European practice.

Hesiod's slightly later *Erga kai Emerai* (c. 700 B.C.E.; *Works and Days*, 1618) suggests that the countless plagues that escaped from Pandora's jar attack humans "spontaneously." Some have seen this passage as a movement to a more naturalistic

This Greek bas-relief from about 350 B.C.E. shows the famous physician Hippocrates looking on as a doctor examines a young patient. (Hulton Archive)

explanation of disease, but the jar still did come from Zeus, to avenge Prometheus's theft of fire.

By the fifth century B.C.E., the shift had occurred, catalyzed in part by the natural philosophers of the Ionian revolution who sought rational explanations for phenomena. To trace the change in detail is impossible because no pre-Hippocratic medical texts survive. One pivotal figure was Alcmaeon of Croton in southern Italy, a major medical center. Born about 510 B.C.E., Alcmaeon believed that disease arose in the blood, marrow, or brain from a lack of equilibrium (*isonomia*) of certain bodily qualities (wet, dry, cold, hot, bitter, sweet).

Combined with Empedocles' theory of the four elements (fire, air, earth, water), Alcmaeon's ideas proved instrumental in the development of Hippocratic medicine. The *Corpus Hippocraticum* (fifth to third century B.C.E.; "Hippocratic collection") is a heterogeneous assemblage of more than sixty treatises, none of which predates the fifth century B.C.E. Which essays, if any, were actually composed by Hippocrates of Cos, the father of medicine, has been vainly debated since antiquity. Internal inconsistencies imply that it is not the work of one person or dogmatic group. The first essay in the Hippocratic corpus, *Peri archaies ietrikes* (fifth or fourth century B.C.E.; *Ancient Medicine*), stresses that medicine must depend on observation and not philosophical speculations. *Peri ieres noysoy* (fifth or fourth century B.C.E.; *On the Sacred Disease*, 1849) argues that epilepsy is not a divine affliction but may be naturally explained; phlegm blocking the veins that lead to the brain causes paralysis and seizure. *Peri physios anthropou* (fifth or fourth century B.C.E.; *On the Nature of Man*, 1968) contains the fundamental humoral theory that would prevail in Western medicine for more than two thousand years. In the human body, four fluid substances (blood, phlegm, yellow bile, and black bile) occur, an imbalance of which causes illness. In general, therapy is conservative and depends on dietetics, which stresses proper food, lifestyle, and environment. Commonly prescribed diets for the sick include barley soup as well as honey and water. Surgical intervention in-

cluded trepanation and nephrotomy for kidney stones and bleeding.

Physicians initially were on the level of craftspeople and traveled from place to place to earn a living and gain experience. In contrast to modern practice, patients were often diagnosed and treated in a public context. A system of apprenticeship existed, and some of the duties of an apprentice to his master are specified in the Hippocratic Oath. How generally applicable the oath was is debatable.

Remarkable advances in anatomy occurred in the third century B.C.E. in Alexandria under the authoritarian Ptolemies who allowed physicians such as Herophilus to engage in vivisection on condemned criminals. The voluminous works of Galen (129-c. 199 C.E.) codify and refine earlier medical concepts. Stoic mixture theory is applied to the humoral system, and in this influential form, Hippocratic concepts are transmitted down to the nineteenth century.

Together with this rational medicine there persisted a temple medicine connected with the cult of Asclepius, the son of Apollo. It involved incubation, sleeping at a temple to receive a cure or dream instruction. Evidence survives in actual temple accounts and in the literary narratives of Aristides.

ROMAN MEDICINE

Roman medicine was a complex amalgam of Greek, Hellenistic, Etruscan, and native traditions. Unlike the Greek, the native tradition was nontheoretical and little concerned with diagnosis and prognosis. Instead, it was pragmatic and rooted in an agrarian lifestyle that espoused the view that the *paterfamilias* (head of the household) should possess sufficient medical knowledge to ensure the well-being of his family, slaves, and livestock.

In his treatise *De agricultura* (c. 160 B.C.E.; *On Agriculture*, 1913), Cato the Censor (234-149 B.C.E.) offers such knowledge to owners of middle-sized estates. Though well acquainted with things Greek, he poses as a skeptical xenophobe in his phihellenic environment and orders his son Marcus to have no dealings with physicians. His panacea was cabbage, administered internally or externally, for afflictions as diverse as sinusitis and cancer. Any slave whose condition did not respond to cabbage, he believed, should be disposed of promptly as an economic liability. Wool and honey figure prominently among his remedies. Washed ram's wool soaked in oil is recommended for uterine inflammation. In the case of fracture, a magical incantation combining archaic Latin and gibberish is offered.

In general, the native healing tradition fell under the influence of magic and religion. Divine displeasure was the fundamental cause of disease. Major deities like Mars might be invoked to stave off pestilence, but there was also a multitude of minor deities linked to specific morbidities and physiological changes. Bone growth was the province of the goddess Ossipaga, and Carna protected organs made of flesh (*caro*). Fever, to the Romans, was not a symptom but an illness in its own right and was personified by a goddess Febris who could be invoked in temples. Among some of the common diseases suffered were tuberculosis, eye infections, osteoarthritis, and gout. Numerous epidemics have been debatably identified as bubonic plague, typhus, and smallpox.

Despite mistrust of foreign physicians, Greek medicine continuously made inroads into Roman culture. When a devastating plague stuck in 293 B.C.E., the cult of Aesculapius (Asclepius), the healing god and son of Apollo, was introduced. After the epidemic ceased, a temple was erected in his honor. In 219 B.C.E., the Greek physician Archagatus established a publicly funded practice in Rome. At first a popular wound healer, in time, because of his severity with the knife and cautery, he became known as the "butcher." Far more illustrious was Asclepiades (first century B.C.E.), who subordinated Hippocratic humoral theory to a corpuscular theory. Disease, in his view, resulted from the clogging of interatomic spaces in the body, which inhibited the free movement of bodily substances. The major Hellenistic medical sects persisted, with the Dogmatists emphasizing philosophical speculation, the Empiricists, experience with individual patients, and the Methodists,

nonhumoral dietetics. In this intellectual ferment, other sects developed, and dividing lines were always shifting.

In the early Republic and into the imperial period, many physicians were slaves or freedman of low social status. In 46 B.C.E., however, Julius Caesar granted citizenship to Greek physicians who had established practices in Rome. Like craftspeople, physicians could form their own collegia or guilds. Women were allowed to enter the profession. Although ordinary patients might be treated in the doctor's own house or a streetside shop, the wealthy were usually seen in their own houses. Particularly skillful practitioners rose quickly into the upper echelons of society. Antonius Musa with his hydrotherapy counted the emperor Augustus among his patients. Galen progressed to become court physician to Marcus Aurelius. Medical training began under Asclepiades in the form of apprenticeships. Vespasian was the first emperor to establish a public salary for medical teachers. Civic posts with tax immunity were established in cities and towns.

In addition to Pliny the Elder (23-79 C.E.), a fundamental early imperial source is the encyclopedist, Aulus Cornelius Celsus, an aristocrat grounded in Greek medicine who divided medicine up into dietetics, pharmacology, and surgery. His regimen included a balanced diet without too many honeyed sweets, exercise, baths, and massage. His description of inflammation remained standard into the twentieth century (redness, swelling, heat, and pain). Surgeries included cataracts, bladder calculi, hip reduction, and cosmetic repairs. The surgical instruments found at Pompeii reveal the technological advances since the Hippocratics.

The Romans refined military medicine by *valetudinaria* (hospitals of a sort), though for the common soldier, there was little organized medical care. In hygiene, public sanitation, and waste disposal, the Romans showed their characteristic genius in the aqueducts and the draining of marshes. Under the Christians, in the sixth century C.E., doctor-saints were invoked in churches built over the temple of Asclepius.

CHINESE MEDICINE

Of the legendary cultural heroes and emperors of the third millennium B.C.E., tradition linked three to the healing arts. Fuxi established the eight diagrams of the *Yijing* (eighth to third century B.C.E.; English translation, 1876; also known as *Book of Changes*, 1986) and thus laid the foundations of medical philosophy. Shennong supposedly first taught people to cultivate the five grains and amassed knowledge of curative plant properties. Huangdi, the Yellow Emperor, acquired his remarkable therapeutic skills directly from the gods. Later generations would erroneously ascribe to these last two figures two of the fundamental works of Chinese medicine: *Shennong bencao jin jizhu* (c. 500 C.E.; *The Divine Farmer's Materia Medica*, 1998, also known as *Classic of Shennong* or *Divine Husbandman's Materia Medica*), an annotation or commentary on an earlier, lost work, *Shennong bencao jing* (late first or early second century C.E) and *Neijing* (also known as *Huangdi beijing*, c. 300 B.C.E.; *Huang Ti nei ching su wên: The Yellow Emperor's Classic of Internal Medicine*, 1949).

Archaeological evidence for medical activities occurs first in the Shang Dynasty (1600-1066 B.C.E.). To the Shang elite, any misfortune, including illness, originated in the displeasure of ancestors who advised Di, the supreme ancestor. To communicate with the spiritual world, cattle bones and tortoise shells were perforated, inscribed with questions, and subjected to heat, which caused cracking. The king or his diviner "read" the cracks to resolve a question (for example, "Tooth illness. Is there a curse? Perhaps from father?"). Snow, wind, and possibly sorcery were also recognized as causes of disease. Wine jars depicted on the bones and found in the tombs are often assumed to have contained therapeutic concoctions but may simply have been sacrificial; tomb evidence does exist for medicinal herbs.

In the Zhou Dynasty (1066-256 B.C.E.), demons replaced ancestors as the primary agents of disease. The secretive therapies of this period are nearly impossible to reconstruct. Talismans and raucous parades in which weapons were thrust

into the air were thought to aid in their expulsion. The notion of physician as demoniac exorcist persisted even after a naturalistic paradigm appeared. In the Mawangdui graves of 168 B.C.E., straightforward prescriptions appear as well as a magical incantation to stanch blood flow.

From the end of the Zhou Dynasty through the Han Dynasty (206 B.C.E.-220 C.E.), a new biological paradigm evolved under the influence of various natural philosophical conceptions as well as Confucianism and Daoism. One impetus for its holistic nature may have been the political unification of the empire itself. Inconsistent ideas, applied medically, are syncretized in the *Classic of Internal Medicine*, not the work of Huangdi, but originally a heterogeneous assemblage of eighty-one essays, the earliest of which may date to the second century B.C.E.

These foundational conceptions are complex and can be set forth here only in a drastically simplified way. The doctrine of systematic correspondences claims that everything in the universe, concrete and abstract, is interconnected. All phenomena exist in dualistic and complementary relationships (yin-yang). Everything can be reduced, symbolically speaking, to five elements or phases (fire, air, earth, water, and metal). To maintain health, the body must maintain a balance of yin and yang. Imbalance alters the interaction of the body's five elements and impedes the movement of vital energy (*qi*). Outside causes of disease include weather, seasons, temperature, and wind. The seven emotions and dietary irregularity may also be causative.

Given this holistic paradigm, not surprisingly the Chinese made little progress in surgery. There exist fanciful accounts of removal of a portion of necrotic spleen and development of anesthesia. Hard evidence exists for opening of abscesses, castration, and removal of cataracts. Other therapeutic practices included moxibustion (localized burning) and acupuncture, which, despite claims of antiquity, is first mentioned in a text of about 100 B.C.E. Needles were inserted to restore the movement of *qi* through the body's channels or meridians. In dietetics, balance could be achieved by the five types of grain, fruits, vegetables, domesticated animals, and flavors.

In the first millennium C.E., the major achievement was the development of an elaborate drug therapy as exemplified in the *Shennong bencao jin jizhu* (c. 500 C.E.; *The Divine Farmer's Materia Medica*, 1998, also known as *Classic of Shennong* or *Divine Husbandman's Materia Medica*), an annotation or commentary on an earlier, lost work, *Shennong bencao jing* (late first or early second century C.E). Its *materia medica* was based on plants, animals, and minerals and included substances still used in traditional herbal medicine.

SOUTH ASIAN MEDICINE

As early as the third millennium B.C.E., a concern for public hygiene manifests itself in the cities of the Indus Valley civilization. At Mohenjo-Daro, the town planners provided fresh water tanks and connected bathrooms in individual houses to drains that ran beneath the city's streets. Removable brick covers allowed the main drains to be cleared periodically. In its sophistication, the system was unequalled until early Roman imperial times. The Great Bath west of the main street has sometimes been described as hydropathic, that is, designed for the treatment of diseases by means of water. In the absence of deciphered texts, uncertainty prevails, and it may instead be a prototype of the Pushkar, the ritual tank of a Hindu temple. In general, this emphasis on cleanliness probably arose more out of a concern with ritual rather than with hygiene.

For obscure reasons (perhaps partly a climate change), the Indus Valley civilization declined. By 1500 B.C.E., Aryans had emigrated eastward out of the passes of Afghanistan and hastened decline and subjugation with their powerful two-wheeled chariots. Their sacred oral literature, the Vedas, were collected and arranged shortly after 1000 B.C.E. Of these, the *Atharvaveda* (c. 1500-1100 B.C.E.; *The Hymns of the Atharva-veda*, 1895-1896) is a major source for their medical practices. The general perspective of these hymns, some virtually medicinal charms, is magico-religious, though trauma (for example, fracture) could be explained naturally.

Dropsy to the modern physician is a morbid accumulation of serous fluid in tissue that may be caused by kidney or heart problems. In the hymns, "water-belly" comes from the god Varuna as a punishment for perjurers who swear falsely by the divine waters. In jaundice, a demon is conjured to move to the yellow Sun, and water is sprinkled over the patient and over yellow parrots to transfer the visible symptom of yellowness into the birds. Certain other actions accompanied the incantations. In one case, primitive catheterization with a reed corrects blocked urine flow.

Despite apparent crudeness, already in this Vedic period there are advances that presage classical Hindu medicine. Intermittent fevers suggestive of malaria are carefully observed, plants are used in ways not simply magical, anatomy is being investigated, and a pneumatic notion of physiology is evolving.

By about the fifth century B.C.E., a confluence of Vedic practices, other forms of folk medicine, and above all Buddhism and Yoga lead to the development of Ayurveda, the science of longevity. Two classic texts are the compendia of the semilegendary physicians Caraka and Susruta. The first stresses general medicine, the second, surgery. The compendia of Susruta suggest some remarkable surgical feats: removal of urinary calculi, cataract operations, treatment of inflammation, suturing with ant mandibles, and plastic surgery to repair ears and noses. Systemization occurs from this point to the tenth century C.E., and the Ayurvedic tradition remains vital to this day.

Ayurveda is a holistic approach that is both preventive and therapeutic. It encouraged physicians, private and state, to follow an ethic ensuring the patient's privacy, much as the Hippocratic Oath does. Treatment emphasizes equally diet, lifestyle, medicines, and certain therapeutic purification procedures. Palpation and auscultation were two diagnostic tools. To simplify complex theory, the body is a microcosm of the universe and, like it, composed of five elements. These elements occur in the body as the three *doshas*, akin to the humors of Hippocratic medicine: wind (air and space) associated with the colon, bile (fire and water), with the stomach, and phlegm (earth and water), with the lungs. Improperly digested food and drink block the body's channels with a sludgelike substance, *ama*. An imbalance of the *doshas* results, which causes disease. An elaborate pharmacopoeia was based primarily on plants but also on animals and metals. Magical elements persisted right through the seventeenth century. A testimony to Ayurveda is its vitality in modern India as well as Western medicine's current interest in it as an alternative therapy.

MESOAMERICAN MEDICINE

When the Spanish entered Central America in the sixteenth century C.E., they encountered a remarkable civilization that had been in decline for at least six hundred years. The Maya (1000 B.C.E.-900 C.E.) at their peak had numbered as many as perhaps 10 million people in an area with twelve major centers controlled by shamanistic kings. The complex society was highly stratified, and the division of labor was elaborate.

Near the end of the Classic period (300-900 C.E.), the civilization mysteriously collapsed. In less than 150 years, the population may have fallen to 1.8 million, and the great palaces and temples were abandoned. The exact reasons are elusive, though scholars have suggested such factors as internal strife, outside military intervention, and climate changes. One theory, directly related to health and medicine, surmises that the population carried within it a kind of biological time bomb. Skeletal and other evidence indicates that the pre-Columbian Maya were subject to such endemic diseases as yellow fever, malaria, nutritional diseases like scurvy, and Chagas' disease, which can cause cardiomyopathy in children. When combined with some other stress such as agricultural crisis, what was endemic perhaps turned explosively epidemic.

The medical practices of the pre-Conquest Maya, to a certain extent, may be reconstructed from colonial sources, given the conservatism of the Yucatán natives. An example is the narrative of the Franciscan Diego de Landa. Also, though written in European script, some extant Maya texts of

the seventeenth and eighteenth centuries may contain material based on hieroglyphic texts destroyed by the Spanish. Ethnobotanical medical texts present a wealth of information on plant remedies for respiratory diseases; gynecological problems; bites and stings; bowel, ear, and eye complaints; inflammation; and many other problems.

The mythological text *Popul Vuh* (n.d.; *Popul Vuh: The Sacred Book of the Ancient Quiché Maya*, 1950) presents supernatural notions of disease that may be pre-Conquest. Among the lords of Xibalba, the terrifying underworld, One Death and Seven Death assign the others rulers specific commissions. Scab Stripper and Blood Gatherer draw blood from people. Demon of Pus and Demon of Jaundice make people swell up, leak pus from their legs, and turn yellow from jaundice. Bone Scepter and Skull Scepter bring on edema and emaciation. Perhaps a survival of this notion is the practice of contemporary Maya shamans who magically (and maliciously) place dry or moist bones within someone's body. The dry bones induce emaciation, the moist, fluid accumulation, dropsy. A worm, according to the text, causes toothache, and bonesetters also treat diseases of the eye, a combination still attested today, as in the Quiché dialect eyes are classified as bones.

The *Rituals of the Bacabs* (n.d.; English translation, 1965), perhaps likewise traceable to hieroglyphic texts, sets out magical incantations against various diseases, which are treated as personalized entities. In chanting, the shaman insultingly relates the personal history and lineage of the disease as if thus to assert his power over it. Threatening it with his fan and staff, he often seeks to consign it to Metnal, an odiferous region of the underworld. The modern Maya concept that disease arises from evil winds is also hinted at in the text. Elsewhere both natural and supernatural concepts occur, but whether they were sharply demarcated is uncertain. Sexual excess is mentioned as bringing on disease and required confession and penance to restore harmony with the gods. Sorcery and witchcraft play a role as well.

The Spanish distinguished three classes of healers: physicians, herbalists, and sorcerers, but there seems to have been some crossover in their functions. If the patient were lower class, a physician might conduct his own diagnostic divination. The profession, it seems, was hereditary.

Dental filing and inlay reached high levels but were essentially ornamental and not therapeutic. In general, surgery appears to have been primitive, but phlebotomy was practiced with special lancets and possibly circumcision.

NORTH AMERICAN MEDICINE

One of the earliest sources for Native American medicine is an illustrated Latin narrative by Jacques LeMoyne, an artist who recorded the French attempt to establish a Huguenot base in Florida in 1564-1565. A captioned plate reveals how the Temacua tribe treated their sick. One patient lying on a bench has his forehead cut with a shell and then has his blood sucked out and spit into a jar. Another lies face down on a bench as seeds are thrown over burning coals below him. The smoke induces vomiting and thus supposedly expels the cause of the illness. A third inhales a plant called "tobaco" to draw out morbid fluids. Finally, the text alludes to natural remedies for venereal disease.

Subject to ethnological evaluation, there is much here that parallels techniques common to many North American tribes and possibly predates contact with Europeans. Sucking a wound is well attested geographically and temporally. The Kansas Potawatamis in the 1930's and the Wisconsin Ojibwas in the 1940's were still employing this technique. Its purpose is variable: simple therapy to remove pus or venom; providing blood from a brave warrior to nursing women so that their own male infants might be empowered; and allowing the shaman, the intermediary between the human and spirit world, to extract the etiological agent, sometimes conceived as an object or animal. Bloodletting itself was probably learned from Europeans. Much evidence also exists for fumigation, especially in the treatment of respiratory or rheumatic diseases. Well documented also is the use of tobacco to cure disease, assist in exorcism, and, among the Seminoles, even ward off natural elements such as lightning.

Another common therapy was moxibustion (localized burning) in which reeds were placed on the skin and kindled, especially in cases of gout or sciatica. Trepanation occurs, but there is no evidence for elaborate surgery. Scarification was practiced over a pain site as a form of counterirritant and to create an exit point for the pain. Amputation was sometimes employed but ritually and punitively. Treatment of fractures and dislocations was highly skilled with the use of form-fitting splints molded with clay or rawhide. The treatment of wounds with boiling water has sometimes been interpreted as primitive asepsis. Perhaps the greatest achievement was the use of plants in the treatment of various illnessses. Sassafras and prickly pear were used in diuretic remedies, jimsonweed, a bronchodilator, for asthma. Unlike Europeans, the Native Americans knew how to treat scurvy.

Not merely an assemblage of therapies, medicine implied mystery and drew on religion and often rituals and incantations. Disease, viewed as a disruption in balance between the sick person and the surrounding natural environment, might arise from witchcraft, sorcery, spirit intrusion, soul loss, taboo violation, and intrusion by a foreign object or animal. To outsiders, a shamanistic medicine-man (sometimes woman) appeared as the stereotypical healer. In fact, in some tribes, naturally and supernaturally caused diseases were distinguished. In one case, the medicine-man, as a religious leader and communicator with the spirit world, might be employed, in another, a healer possessed of straightforward remedies. The Lakota, for example, made use of both the *wakan witshaska* "mystery man" and the *pejihuta witshaska* "grassroots man." Medicine societies also occurred, dedicated to animal spirits whom they could invoke to cure disease, repel withcraft, and ward off natural disasters.

European colonization with its dense-population diseases such as smallpox, measles, typhus, and scarlet fever exacted a devastating toll on the Native American populace. By one estimate, a population of 18 million was reduced to only 500,000 by 1900. The notion that precontact Native Americans were paragons of health, however, has been slowly disproved by paleopathological evidence. Amoebic dysentery, influenza, and pneumonia, complicated by overpopulation and competition for resources, were major problems before the arrival of Europeans. Skeletal studies of Archaic and Woodland populations in the Northern Plains do, however, reveal a generally healthy population apart from arthritis and dental disease.

SUB-SAHARAN AFRICAN MEDICINE

Historical study of African therapeutics is a recent phenomenon. In the absence of native written sources, reconstruction depends largely on oral tradition and, to a limited extent, archaeology. Fundamental is the notion that many modern therapies, especially herbalism, are traceable back over three millennia to the practices of ancient hunter-gatherers. Historical linguistics by comparative analysis of vocabulary in Bantu-speaking areas provides some insight into earlier phases of the languages and so also into ancient culturally shared ideas of medicine and disease. Examples of reconstructed roots in proto-Bantu are *gidu*, referring to taboos, the violation of which may lead to disease, and *dok*, also an etiological concept related to angry words, blows, or poisons. Traditionally, the three major diseases have been sleeping sickness, malaria, and smallpox, in cases of which the Yoruba made sacrifices to the god Ipoona.

Complicating the picture are the various foreign influences that over the centuries have acted on local traditions, whether directly or indirectly: Egyptian, Greek, Christian, and Islamic. Medical pluralism remains characteristic of African healing and, in a modern context, has created problems for governments struggling to impose Western concepts of licensing.

Also, scholars have begun to recognize economic, environmental, and social structural factors generating diverse approaches even within certain tribes or among speakers of the same language. As elsewhere, disease conditions and responses to them would have altered with the historical context. The health problems of hunter-gatherers would have been less complex than sedentary agriculturists of the first millennium B.C.E. In addition, even more infectious diseases and viruses must have developed in the urban centers of the first and second millennia C.E. as trade grew with the Mediterranean and Europe. A more specific example are the two distinctive West and East-Central African lifestyles and medicines dictated by the presence or absence of the tsetse fly, the vector of sleeping sickness: agriculturalism versus pastoralism.

Despite these cautions about overgeneralizing, studies have revealed certain common ideas about health and disease. These include notions of purity; balance with one's environment and social context; ideal bodily structure, which includes color coding ideas (white = health, black = chaos, red = perilous transition); coolness versus heat, which is associated with disease; flow and blockage; and contagion. In the past, pus from smallpox victims was introduced into scratches of the uninfected, but the modern conception of immunization was not operative here.

The causes of disease may be personal (deities, spirits, ancestors, sorcerers, witches), in which case, the services of a diviner are required to determine the agent's identity. In other instances, especially where the cause is clear, as in accidental trauma, the problem may be naturalistically explained. Among the physical agents of disease are heat, cold, and dampness. In some cases, both forms of explanation may be invoked.

One form of traditional ritualized therapy found throughout Central and South Africa is *ngoma*, named after the long drum used in its practice. Reputedly at least two millennia old, it is often a final resort in cases of debilitating chronic disease. The patient is initiated into a sort of corporation of fellow sufferers and is then treated psychotherapeutically by a range of activities that include drumming, dancing, dream visions, and the establishment of a new identity. A cured patient may progress from initiate to healer within the corporation. Perhaps the most striking aspect of traditional therapy is the extraordinary variety of medicinal plants. Their use runs the gamut from markers to determine if an illness is spiritually induced to biomedically efficacious medicaments for diarrhea and diabetes.

One area where archaeological excavation has revealed historical evidence about disease is lower Nubia, especially during the times of intensive agriculture, the Meroitic, Ballana, and Christian periods (350 B.C.E.-1300 C.E.). Skeletons show signifcant decline in stature from earlier periods, nutritional deficiencies, developmental stress, dental caries, and premature osteoporosis. Too much reliance on a single crop, millet, probably caused much of the deficiencies. Surprisingly low rates of infectious disease are perhaps explained by the ingestion of tetracycline, an antibiotic produced by a bacterium that might have flourished in the mud bins used to store grain.

ADDITIONAL RESOURCES

Jackson, Ralph. *Doctors and Diseases in the Roman Empire*. Norman: University of Oklahoma Press, 1988.

Longrigg, James. *Greek Rational Medicine*. London: Routledge, 1993.

Majno, Guido. *The Healing Hand*. Cambridge, Mass.: Harvard University Press, 1975.

Nunn, John F. *Ancient Egyptian Medicine*. Norman: University of Oklahoma Press, 1996.

Prioreschi, Plinio. *A History of Medicine*. 3 vols. Omaha, Neb.: Horatius Press, 1996-1998.

Unschuld, Paul U. *Medicine in China*. Berkeley: University of California Press, 1985.

Vogel, Virgil J. *American Indian Medicine*. Norman: University of Oklahoma Press, 1970.

SEE ALSO: Africa, East and South; Akkadians; Aristides; Augustus; Caesar, Julius; Cato the Censor; China; Confucianism; Daoism; Eastern peoples; Egypt, Pharaonic; Egypt, Prepharaonic; Galen; Great Basin peoples; Greece, Archaic; Greece, Classical; Hammurabi's code; Han Dynasty; Herodotus; Herophilus; Hesiod; Hippocrates; Homer; Imhotep; India; Indus Valley civilization; Maya; Middle Woodland traditions; Nubia; Pliny the Elder; Rome, Imperial; Rome, Republican; Shang Dynasty; Sumerians; Vedas; Zhou Dynasty.

—*David J. Ladouceur*

NAVIGATION AND TRANSPORTATION

Transportation, the methods used by people to move themselves and their goods, is strongly dependent on technology. Starting with human locomotion and animal power, it evolved into the use of wheeled vehicles, ships, and, later, mechanically powered vehicles. In the infancy of new transportation systems, military applications often come first, followed by commercial adaptations. For example, the vessels that started as fighting galleys were also used as trading ships in early Mediterranean civilizations, and the war chariot was the fastest land vehicle in the days of Julius Caesar. Because of the need to communicate rapidly with garrisons and outposts, the Romans, among others, built roads of extremely high quality. As each means of transportation matures, military and commercial needs diverge. By 2000 B.C.E., many parts of the world contained relatively advanced civilizations in terms of technology and commerce.

BEGINNINGS

The first pathways to cross the countryside were created by animals pushing aside vegetation and pounding the earth with their feet. Although animals could trample, they, unlike people, could not actively construct pathways other than by wearing down the vegetation; people, however, need both incentive and organizational support to create paths. The built path was a result of increased social and economic pressures exerted by a growing civilization. The first human pathways led to campsites, to food, and to water. As travel needs extended beyond the local area and trade increased, these "highways" became more sophisticated and included fords, passes, and planned routes through unsafe areas. Some existing routes can be traced back to 5000 B.C.E.

When the ground surface permits the use of some contrivance for hauling, people can drag more than they can carry. Human porterage, whether on head or back, survived for a very long time on the African continent because of endemic diseases affecting grass-eating animals such as the horse or mule.

The first new technology applied to transport was not the wheel but the provision of power. After the use of footpaths became widespread, the next innovation was the use of animals, initially as beasts of burden and subsequently for pulling sleds, carts, wagons, and carriages. For most of its history, the world's roadway system has operated with domesticated animals as its sole source of power, beginning with the domestication of large animals in about 7000 B.C.E. until about a century ago. Cattle, donkeys, asses, dogs, goats, horses, mules, camels, elephants, buffaloes, llamas, reindeer, and yaks are some of the species used for transport. For example, the Asiatic elephant—as opposed to the African elephant—has long been captured and domesticated and used as transport in India and surrounding areas; its ability to handle enormous loads comes at the expense of an enormous appetite. The llama is confined to the sierras of South America and does not do well at low altitudes. Dogs are useful for transport in Arctic regions because their low weight enables them to run in packs over snow-covered ground pulling a load. The camel with its thirst-defying stomach, its capacity for thriving on semi-desert herbage, and its flat feet are ideal for desert sands. The ox was the most widely distributed of transport animals.

Fleet-footed runners were a favored way to deliver messages quickly. The Greeks were able to send messages 120 miles (193 kilometers) in a single day by using runners in a relay system. Similar speeds were reached by North American Indians running along the Iroquois Trail. The Incas, by running stages day and night—and six-minute miles—were able to double that.

Horse riding probably began in Russia in about 3000 B.C.E. and was introduced into Mesopotamia in 2000 B.C.E. It gained popularity at a slow pace and only began to appear frequently after 1000 B.C.E. The horse was initially used primarily for war rather than for transport. Throughout this period, the horse remained an expensive animal, and most riders used the much cheaper donkey and mule. The next developments in horse riding were the stirrup (India, about 200 B.C.E.), and the saddle, allowing the horse and rider to act as one. Saddles arrived in Europe in about 200 C.E. and stirrups in about 700 C.E. Horseshoes, uncommon in Roman times, became widespread by then. Just as the horse was important in Europe, the camel played a crucial role in trade in Arabia and Central Asia, being ideally suited for grasslands, steppes, and deserts. Humans have also been used as teams of bearers to carry other humans such as with the Roman litter.

A single horse and rider could routinely manage 35 to 50 miles (56 to 80 kilometers) a day. By periodically changing horses in a multistage system, the Persians under King Cyrus the Great in about 550 B.C.E. achieved 150 miles (241 kilometers) per day on their exclusive royal roadway. The Romans and Chinese were able to beat this. The Chinese record was about 250 miles (402 kilometers) per day.

When freight has to be moved, many parts of the human anatomy were gainfully employed and augmented with sticks, slings, and poles. Loads of 55 pounds (25 kilograms) per bearer over distances were feasible. When the loads to be carried demanded greater strength or power than could be supplied by humans, innovation resulted in the use of domesticated feed animals as beasts of burden. Wicker baskets were transferred from human shoulders to the backs of cattle, producing the first pack animals. Pack transport took a step forward in about 3500 B.C.E., when the domesticated donkey came out of Africa. There are records from 2000 B.C.E. of organized pack convoys operating in the Middle East. Horses could carry about one-third of their body weight in freight. Compared with horses, camels could carry much more and donkeys much less.

From remote antiquity, there has been a contrast between the working animals used in different countries, often related to climatic and ecological factors. A pair of oxen could be fed much more cheaply on inferior fodder of a kind available in areas of Greece and Italy where the pasture was not adequate to support horses. The oxen could pull a heavier load than horses of comparable size, but their progress was slower, not a key issue in ancient transportation. The speed and mobility of horses was more important in cavalry battle tactics. The oxen could serve as food when their working life was over.

Sleighs on snow and ice require very little haulage force and therefore need a simpler technology and less power, as reflected in the common use of dog teams in northern countries. There is evidence of sleighs (on snow and ice) in use in 6000 B.C.E. and sleds (on dry land) in 5000 B.C.E.

EARLY VEHICLES AND ROADS

The wheel was invented in Mesopotamia in about 5000 B.C.E., probably as an adjunct to the sled. The next important stage was the use of an axle to join two wheels together and thereby provide increased stability and load capacity. By about 3000 B.C.E., a variety of vehicles in ancient Mesopotamia and northern Iran had begun to make practical use of the solid wheel. The first were two-wheeled A-frame carts. The two-wheeled chariot with a single harness pole, pulled by donkeylike onagers, was developed in Sumer in about 2800 B.C.E. Cumbersome four-wheeled wagons, requiring oxen for haulage power, followed in about 2500 B.C.E. The wooden running surfaces of the heavy wheels had a short life; to solve this, leather tire coverings were introduced in about 2500 B.C.E. and protruding copper nails in about 2000 B.C.E. By this time, wheeled vehicles had become common throughout the Middle East and had arrived in Europe.

The Chinese developed the wheelbarrow, a convenient device for moving goods and even people relatively short distances, in the first century B.C.E. This concept did not occur in Europe until well into the Middle Ages.

The Celts invented the spoked wheel with curved wooden rims, substantially reducing the weight to allow lighter, faster vehicles. Primitive hauling harnesses appeared, and the horse became established as an animal for hauling as well as for riding. The horse and light chariot provided a popular but expensive 20-mile-per-hour (32-kilometer-per-hour) military vehicle. In a major advance, the Celts developed the shrink fitting of iron tires in about 400 B.C.E. Steerable wagon axles were achieved in about 500 B.C.E. Harnessing animals in file became common by about 100 B.C.E. and dramatically increased payload size. The use of wheeled vehicles gave rise to a whole new set of roadway needs because the vehicles were wider and heavier than a human or ridden horse or a beast of burden.

The horse, the mainstay of all transport in medieval and later times, played an insignificant part in Greek and Roman transport. Its place was taken for light transport by the mule and for heavy transport by oxen. More common than wheeled vehicles were the human porter or the donkey or mule with a pair of baskets affixed. The Greeks and Romans did not make any very important advances in vehicle design; however, Celtic wagonmakers in France and Germany in the early centuries C.E. developed their designs to a highly sophisticated level. Almost every type of wagon in the classical world was originally designed to be drawn by two animals, attached by yoke and pole; there is evidence that the ox-drawn vehicle came well before the horse-drawn.

Before 1000 B.C.E., the people of north China were making use of two-wheeled carts and war chariots on land. Carts pulled by people or animals were the dominant form of local transportation in addition to wheelbarrows. Large carts using three or four animals became common throughout China. For more distant transportation, caravans of animals came into general use in the first and second centuries C.E.

The Americas were different. Before the arrival of the Europeans, the Indians lacked horses, oxen, and most other beasts of burden used in other parts of the world. Andean Indians did use alpacas and llamas for light loads, however. The Plains tribes used dogs. The wheel was never developed. Trails were for walking, running, carrying, and dragging.

Towns and cities arose to meet social needs, for joint defense, to minimize travel, and to facilitate trade and manufacture. Given the above general factors, towns were typically sited at river crossings, defensible locations, ports, crossroads, the navigable limits of rivers, and other sites with geographic advantages. When trade was more dominant than defense issues, the economics of transport strongly favored the movement of freight on water rather than on land, so productive development occurred adjacent to harbors and rivers.

The earliest cities had a web of narrow streets, all less than 8 feet (2.4 meters) in width and barely permitting passage of a pack animal, let alone a wheeled vehicle. Cities were typically an irregular entanglement of streets, houses, and blocks. The randomness of the network was a useful tool in defending the city against invaders who had penetrated the outside wall. Some cities had ordered arrangements of streets, such as the ancient Middle Eastern cities of Ashur and Nineveh; King Nabopolassar in Babylonia built a long, straight processional avenue. Hippodamus of Miletus, the first recognized town planner, introduced Greek cities to the use of wide, straight streets. The Greeks and Romans built walled cities with a rectangular street grid. The Chinese also used a rectangular pattern.

SHIPS

Transport by water usually requires less effort than travel by land. The earliest type of boat was the raft, made of grass, logs, bundles of reeds, or light materials held together that float even when burdened with a load. Rafts were used by people ranging from the early Egyptians on the Nile to the Incas on Lake Titicaca. Other early boats were made of skins on a frame, shaped bark, or hollowed-out logs. Native Indians in Brazil used both dugout canoes and sailing craft called jangadas.

The birchbark canoe, birchbark pieces joined together on a wooden frame, common among the American Indians and Inuit, seems flimsy. However, per pound of its own weight, it can safely carry a much greater weight than any other craft and survive rougher water. It enabled people to reach places impossible to access by other means.

People of the Pacific Islands developed a number of remarkable dugout canoes, some of which can carry as many as sixty people. Although the basic boat was a canoe, addition of a prow, stern, side planks, and a log outrigger increased its capacity and stability. Double hulls were joined by decking to create a seagoing transport. The Polynesians, for example, crossed great expanses of ocean with this type of vessel. In about 400 C.E., their navigators had made the 2,300-mile (3,700-kilometer) trip across the open Pacific from the Marquesas Islands to Hawaii. The inhabitants of the Society Islands made extremely sophisticated canoes with elevated prows and sterns and with sails as well as paddles.

Many city sites of trading peoples were chosen because a good anchorage was available nearby. Much import and export trade was carried by sea, overland transport being slow and costly. Rowed galley-style shipping required a nightly landfall for rest; longer nonstop journeys required the development of sails.

For example, naval supremacy in the Aegean was what enabled Athens to dominate that area for the greater part of the fifth century B.C.E. The Greeks had a preoccupation with the sea and ships, while the Romans were not really a seafaring people until forced into that role. Ostia, Rome's port, was insignificant until major harborworks were completed in the mid-first century C.E., by which time Rome had become dependent on overseas grain. Only at the start of the Punic Wars (264-146 B.C.E.), when the Romans had to face a major sea power, did they build their first fleet of warships.

Greek and Roman merchant ships, except for quite small ones, were normally under sail. Warships used sails on long voyages or while cruising on patrol, but in battle conditions or during a battle alert, they cut down the weight by leaving mast and sail ashore and relied entirely on rowers.

The shape and size of the hull varied greatly, according to the function to be served by the boat; two basic types can be described as long ship and round ship. The long ship was essentially a warship or pirate vessel, designed for rowing at high speed in action, though sails could be carried for cruising or long voyages. The round ship was a merchant vessel for sailing only, apart from the smallest ones that were rowed on rivers or in harbors. Design issues involved placement of rowers and placement of sails. The most striking contrast between ancient and modern sailing boats is the sail itself. Until late antiquity (fourth century C.E.), almost every vessel in the Greek and Roman world had a square sail set at right angles to the hull, unlike the fore-and-aft rig, in line with the keel, today's more effective arrangement. Ropes controlled the sails. An ordinary, smallish merchantman had a cargo capacity of 120 to 150 tons (108-136 metric tons) with 60-foot (18-meter) length; ships capable of carrying 400 to 500 tons (362-453 metric tons) were by no means uncommon.

The center figure holds an astrolabe, a disc-shaped instrument used to calculate the altitude of a heavenly body, thus allowing ships to navigate better. (Hulton Archive)

The Phoenicians, Greeks, and Romans were able to navigate the oceans in vessels equipped with sails and with one to three banks of oars; and it was by means of these crafts that they established and maintained their colonies.

China, with its vastness, looked to water for its transportation needs. The Chinese joined two canoes with planking to form a raft and then built up the sides. This developed into the junk, a flat-bottomed sailing vessel with a high stern and four-cornered sails used in the China Seas. The design provided seaworthiness and structural rigidity, plus the ability to be beached in shallow water. Chinese shipbuilders contrived a watertight box extending through to the deck, allowing a controllable rudder

to be placed on the centerline for convenient sailing. The rudder was developed in China in the first century C.E. or earlier, yet the idea did not make it to the West until the Middle Ages.

By 1500 B.C.E., peninsular India was engaging in extensive maritime trade with Africa and Arabia. The discovery of regular winds allowed a straight course across the Arabian Sea. Sanskrit documents talk of ship design. One surviving piece talks about suitability of various woods for shipbuilding and classification of ships based on their size, length, and even cabin position. One type of ship for sea voyages had a long and narrow hull, while a second type had a higher hull. Sextant and compass were used.

In ancient times, navigation was based on observing landmarks along the coast and the position of the Sun and the stars. In the absence of a well-developed system of celestial navigation, long voyages out of sight of land were not very feasible. For many centuries, practical navigators oriented themselves based on meteorological clues such as wind direction. With the reliance on winds to get to the destination, narrow seas afforded intermediate stops for refuge as well as ease in navigation. The Baltic, the Mediterranean, the Persian Gulf, the Bay of Bengal, and the South China Sea are among those fitting this category. Skilled mariners used astrolabes, which measured altitudes of celestial bodies and determined their position and motions, to find latitude, longitude, and time of day.

Traditional navigators of the Central Caroline Islands developed a sizable body of lore for voyaging up to several hundred miles among the tiny islands and atolls of Micronesia. They had to commit to memory knowledge of stars, sailing directions, landmarks, and reading the waves and clouds to find currents and predict weather. The stars were used as a reference system for determining direction.

By comparison to sea transport, land transport was less important in the classical world. Any large community that could not support itself through foodstuffs grown locally or raw materials produced locally depended on importation by sea, particularly in the Mediterranean area, although Western Europe was less sea-dependent. Elsewhere, geography determined which was transport method was best.

ROADS

The basic roadmaking dilemma is that natural material soft enough to be formed into a smooth surface is rarely strong enough to bear the weight of a loaded vehicle. Some of the earliest roads were stone-paved streets in Ur in about 4000 B.C.E., corduroy roads in England in 4000 B.C.E., and brick paving in India in 3000 B.C.E. Flagstones for paving local streets became feasible by 2000 B.C.E. In 670 B.C.E., Assyrian king Esarhaddon or-

dered that roads should be laid out throughout his kingdom to facilitate trade and commerce. In the centuries just before the common era, the Assyrian, Persian, Indian, and Chinese road systems expanded so that by 100 B.C.E., the Silk Road and its connections had become an active trade route between China and the Mediterranean.

With the possible exception of the Chinese, all ancient roadmaking efforts pale into insignificance beside the roads, bridges, and tunnels of the Romans. These were a remarkable achievement, providing travel times across Europe, Asia Minor, and northern Africa that were not to be appreciably exceeded until the coming of the train two millennia later. As were the Persians before them, the Romans were very conscious of the military, economic, and administrative advantages of a good road system. The Romans brought together the lime-cement and masonry of the Greeks, the cement of the Etruscans, the pavements of the Carthaginians, and the surveying techniques of the Egyptians and developed the innovation of adding gravel to the mortar to make concrete. Beginning in 312 B.C.E., Rome built the first of its major roads, the Appian Way, a gravel road wide enough for two carriages abreast or a legion of soldiers to march in their customary six-abreast pattern. At its peak in 200 C.E., the network involved 50,000 miles (about 80,500 kilometers) of first-class roads—completely ringing the Mediterranean and running from Britain to Asia Minor. The Romans built a magnificent road structure but had relatively poor vehicles and riding equipment; in contrast, some of the barbarians had no road infrastructure, but good vehicles and riding equipment.

The use of wheeled vehicles gave rise to a whole new set of needs because the vehicles were wider and heavier than a human, a ridden horse, or a beast of burden. Many countries set standards. The Chinese emperor Shi Huangdi in 221 B.C.E. standardized the gauge of chariot wheels at a "double pace" (about 5 feet, or 1.5 meters) and determined standard road widths from that. Some places even had load limits; the earliest recorded value dates from the Romans in 50 B.C.E.

An extensive road system existed in ancient China, including a few paved roads and some major early bridges. The system was created in the Western Zhou Dynasty (1066-771 B.C.E.); traces are still visible. Chinese road development occurred mainly after 220 B.C.E., particularly during the reign of Emperor Shi Huangdi, who built post roads all over the empire. The Chinese road system peaked during the Tang Dynasty (618-907 C.E.) and then declined.

Indian road construction was quite advanced by 2000 B.C.E. with growing use of brick-paved streets, subsurface drainage, and bitumen as mortar for the better sections. Literature from 1500 B.C.E. made reference to "great roads." However, other parts were of inferior quality. Goods were transported mainly in caravans of oxen and donkeys, but only in the dry seasons as the rains created impossible travel conditions. Coastal and river shipping were clearly cheaper than overland transport.

The collapse of the Roman Empire meant the decline of Europe's transportation system. After the Romans, only small pockets of wagon technology continued to flourish; carts were largely restricted to farm and local travel and were only occasionally used for long-distance travel. During the days of the empire, a journey from Italy to Britain took several days through a settled country over good roads. By the late sixth century C.E., the journey took weeks through territories full of unmaintained roads, thick with thieves, marauders, and abandoned lands.

ADDITIONAL RESOURCES

Georgano, G. N. *Transportation Through the Ages*. New York: McGraw-Hill, 1972.
Landels, J. G. *Engineering in the Ancient World*. Berkeley: University of California Press, 1978.
Lay, M.G. *Ways of the World*. New Brunswick, N.J.: Rutgers University Press, 1992.

SEE ALSO: Africa, North; Agriculture and animal husbandry; Andes, central; Andes, south; Appian Way; Arabia; Assyria; Athens; Brazil, eastern; Britain; Caesar, Julius; Carthaginians; Celts; China; Cyrus the Great; Egypt, Prepharaonic; Esarhaddon; Etruscans; Greece, Classical; India; Micronesia; Persia; Phoenicia; Polynesia; Punic Wars; Rome, Imperial; Rome, Republican; Sea peoples; Shi Huangdi; Silk Road; Tang Dynasty; War and weapons; Zhou Dynasty.

—*Stephen B. Dobrow*

PERFORMING ARTS

Artifacts from 30,000 years ago indicate that Ice Age people may have been performing religious rituals, and it is likely that the performing arts of music, theater, and dance formed the crucial elements of that ritual. Some 10,000 years later, drawings in caves in France, Spain, and Africa show performers in costumes representing various animals. Some of these performers are also carrying musical percussion and string instruments.

The earliest historical records of performing arts come from Egyptian pyramids circa 2,800 to 2400 B.C.E. These so-called pyramid texts consist of hieroglyphics and scenes depicting trials through which a spirit must pass before being admitted into a happier place. Some scholars believe that these texts were actually dramas, danced and enacted with accompanying music by performer-priests to ensure the well-being of the dead pharaoh and to demonstrate the continuity of life. Other scholars cite the Ikhernofret stone (c. 1868 B.C.E.), which contains the primary evidence about the Abydos passion play, said to be the first recorded text of a performance presented in ancient Egypt. The annual play, which concerns the life, death, and rebirth of the god Osiris, probably contained elements of all the performing arts. In addition to such passion plays, the Egyptian pharaoh was expected to demonstrate publicly his mastery of several sports, including archery, throwing, and chariot racing. It is from these Egyptian spectator events that most scholars date the beginnings of the performing arts in ancient civilizations.

DANCE

The most fundamental of the performing arts is dance, for in its most simple manifestations, dance requires only the human body in motion. The basic dance is that of wild and vigorous jumping and leaping in rhythm, the so-called ecstatic dance. Used in religious ceremonies from sub-Saharan Africa to ancient Israel to Classical Greece and Rome, the ecstatic dance usually begins with restraint but becomes so wild that the dancers often fall unconscious from exertion. It was believed that during such a dance the god being worshiped actually took possession of the performer's body. The Greeks called this phenomenon *enthousiasmos* (literally "possessed by the god"), from which is derived the English word "enthusiasm." Such a dance was practiced by the Hebrew prophets when attempting to get in touch with the word of God. A similar dance seems to have been performed by the ancient inhabitants of Crete where priestesses danced in worship of the great mother goddess. Young Cretan men performed a kind of bull dancing, a very dangerous artform akin to modern Hispanic bullfighting, in which young male dancers executed such maneuvers as somersaulting between the horns of the raging animal. Those that failed to execute these moves were often gored to their death, in effect being sacrificed to the divinity.

Throughout the ancient world, dance was associated with the most basic of human needs and activities. Members of the Tarahumara tribe in Mesoamerica use the same word for dance and work. Fertility of the soil, animals, and people was invoked and celebrated in ancient dance. A painting by English painter John White in 1585 records a Virginia Indian ritual of ancient origin in which seminude young men are seen dancing in a circle around the three most beautiful virgins of the tribe.

A similar painting by American artist George Catlin (1832) depicts a Mandan Indian traditional buffalo dance in which the people wearing animal heads dance to ensure abundance of the valuable bison. Other animal dances are practiced by primitive peoples who mask themselves as an animal, such as a lion, in order to acquire the desired characteristics of that animal. An interesting cave painting from North Africa depicts dancers costumed as the praying mantis insect.

The Talmud of the ancient Hebrews describes dances of Hebrew maidens that seem related to fertility dances of primitive peoples. Perhaps the most famous of the Jewish women's dances are those mentioned in the Christian Bible when Salome, daughter of Herodias, "danced before him and his guests and pleased Herod." Also famous is King David's dance before the Ark of Covenant. Muslim dances of Turkey and the Mideast are famous for the ecstatic, spinning movements of the holy men known as whirling dervishes, a dance that is now outlawed. A more playful form of Hindu-Arabic dance is the famous *singki* of the Muslim princesses. The dance tests the performer's grace and skill as she dances between two pair of bamboo poles clapped together in syncopated and ever-accelerating rhythm.

Ancient Egypt and sub-Saharan Africa are alike in that their dances often involved death and journeys into the world of the spirit. The Yoruba people of southern Africa have elaborate dances associated with ritual journeys of the spirit, as well as elaborate dance-dramas devoted to the mother goddess. These latter dances have been well documented in film. The most significant spirit dance of all comes from the Hindus of India. According to Hindu theology, the god Śiva actually danced the world into existence. To this day, young women, following a tradition of many hundreds of years, start training at the age of five or six in the intricate steps and gestures that make up Indian temple dance. These dancers are in some way "married" to the deity in whose temples they are found. Known as *kathakali*, the dance-dramas of northern India have survived to the present. Also surviving from a tradition more than a thousand years old are the dances of India's neighbors: Ceylon, Cambodia, Bali, and Siam. Each of these dance forms is unique to its region but all are based on the radical flexing of hands, wrists, ankles, and feet, as opposed to the more fluid use of these body parts by Western cultures.

Island peoples from around the globe have distinct dances. In New Guinea, the Dani, whose customs and living conditions are still Stone Age, have various ritual dances, including a ritual dance-battle between warring villages in which actual violence and death may take place. Filipino dance draws its background from the various invaders of the islands, including Hindu, Muslim, and Chinese, the latter of whom are most famous for the dance-drama known as Beijing opera.

The Chinese, as well as the Koreans, contributed to the famous Japanese classical music *gagaku* and its accompanying dance-drama known as *bugaku*. The performers of *bugaku* were known as dancers of the right, who performed dances drawn from Korea, and dancers of the left, who performed dances that originated in China or South Asia. Right dancers are dressed predominantly in green and dance to music produced on percussion instruments. Left dancers are dressed mostly in red and perform to woodwinds. *Bugaku* is still danced today and is clearly the basis for the classic Japanese theatrical forms of Noh and Kabuki, which date from the eleventh century C.E.

Just as the Japanese borrowed dance forms from China and Korea, the ancient Greeks borrowed dance from Crete. Therefore, as in Crete, the ecstatic dance in archaic Greece (before 600 B.C.E.) was done by women, the maenads, in honor of Dionysus, the god of fertility. Many visual depictions of the maenads exist. They carry a sacred staff, the thyrsus. Their heads are thrown back, and their clothes twist wildly about them. The name maenad is the source of the English word "maniac," and indeed the women became so wild and maddened in their dancing that they are said to have had seizures. The chorus of dancing maenads were later replaced by men who performed a more sedate, controlled, military dance in honor of the god Dionysus, known as the dithyramb. Groups of young men were organized into dithyrambic choruses, and in the name of Dionysus, they competed against one another at spring fertility festivals.

Other dances were also practiced by the ancient Greeks, including the *geranos*, or snake dance, and various other animal dances depicting lions, bears, foxes, and even birds. Numerous vase paintings and other visuals show dancers wearing animal masks and headdresses, as well as full animal costumes. The great comic playwright Aristophanes wrote an entire play, *Ornithes* (414 B.C.E.; *The Birds*, 1824), which featured a dancing chorus of avian creatures. Of course, the satyrs, or male goat-dancers, were a standard feature of dramatic choruses. Satyr dancers, wearing horns, hooflike foot gear, and short furry pants, are depicted in many vase paintings. Because the satyr dancers are sacred to Dionysus, god of wine, vegetation, and fertility, they often wear vine leaves in their hair and display large, false genitals.

All young male citizens in Classical Greece were trained in dance because, like modern-day military marching, it was considered good preparation for group discipline in battle. Like modern marching bands, Greek dance groups were trained to form shapes or *schemata* that had particular meaning for the spectators. Dance also taught communication skills as each dancer learned the effective and graceful use of meaningful gesture known as *cheironomia*. Moreover, dance was considered the most sacred of arts, having been associated with the saving of the life of the great god Zeus. According to legend, the Titan Rhea had taught the art of dance to the Curetes, sons of earth who dwelled in Crete. When Rhea gave birth to Zeus, she fled to Crete to avoid Cronus, the father Titan who devoured all of his children immediately after they were born. She gave the baby to the Curetes. When Cronus came looking for the infant, the Curetes performed the dance taught them by Rhea, filled with wild, leaping, noisy, and ecstatic choreography. The vigorous visual and vocal activity diverted the attention of Cronus so that he did not see the baby nor hear it crying. Zeus survived to overthrow Cronus and become king of all the gods. Because of its sacred nature, dance was assigned a special muse, Terpsichore, one of the nine great muses of ancient culture. In the fifth century B.C.E., the greatest honor that could come to a young Greek man was to be selected a member of one of the dancing choruses that performed in the sacred dramas given at the major theatrical festival, the city Dionysia.

Dancers not only appeared in festivals and theatrical performances but also were considered an important part of private entertainments in both Greece and Rome. Although neither culture encouraged couples dancing as a social activity, dancers did appear at lavish all-male Greek dinners known as *symposia* and at Roman banquets of various types. Dancers at these events were often accompanied by related kinetic artists such as acrobats and contortionists. In Classical Greece, most dancers were amateurs, but later professional actors and dancers banded together into a quasi-religious group known as the Artists of Dionysus.

In Rome, most entertainers were professionals or even slaves. Performers from the Roman animal shows or circuses were part-time dancers and part-time contortionists and acrobats. An unusual and significant Roman dance form was the pantomime, a dance-theater presenting narratives entirely without words. Invented in 22 B.C.E., the pantomime became the most popular of Roman entertainments, aside from such violent forms as the gladiatorial games, staged animal hunts, staged naval battles, and chariot races. In later Roman times, professional dancers from Africa and other exotic areas of the empire and various curiosities such as dwarf dancers were introduced. Christians were especially offended by a Roman dance of increasing popularity known as the *kordax*, a dance originating in theatrical comedies that featured rolling and swaying of the hips and other movements that the early church fathers considered sinful and lewd. The Christian ban on the *kordax* led to a general ban by the Church on all forms of dance in the ancient world.

THEATER

Dance was an intricate part of theater in the ancient world, and the cultures of India, China, Ja-
pan, Greece, and Rome drew little distinction between the actor and the dancer. The plays of the Greek theater, known as *dramenon*, or happenings, featured dancing choruses as a major element of all productions. The word "theater" is drawn from the Greek *theatron*, or seeing place. The relation between theater and dance is nowhere better illustrated than in the fact that the large performing circle found in most Greek theaters is called the *orchestra*, or dancing circle. Although theatrical presentations are as old as humankind, modern Western theater seems to be a product of ancient Greece. Its origins were in the funeral rituals of Egypt, the sacred dance-drama of India, and the fertility rituals of Crete.

The Greek city-states had developed public religious festivals around two important seasons: spring and fall. The spring festival was devoted to Dionysus and was called the Dionysia, at which a number of rituals and dramas were performed. The Dorian Greeks claimed to have invented drama, but it was the Athenians who brought it to its classic form. In 534 B.C.E., Pisistratus, the ruler of Athens, made the Dionysia a legal state function. Thereafter, all male citizens of Athens were required to attend the plays each year. Thespis, the famous leader of a dithyrambic chorus, was named the first archon (producer) of Athens's city Dionysia. Thespis is credited with formalizing dialogue in theater in that he would call out to his dancing chorus and they would answer him in a call-response pattern. Such performers were called answerers, or *hypokritoi*, which became the Greek word for actor and the English word "hypocrite." At first only two types of *dramenon* were performed at the Dionysia, tragedies, or plays about the death of a hero and his replacement by another hero, and satyr plays, or comedies about the sexual escapades of the gods. It was the satyr plays that featured a chorus of singing and dancing goat-men or satyrs. Tragedies also featured a singing-dancing chorus, thought to be as large as fifty persons. All performers in Greek theater were men, although they frequently played women's roles. The plays themselves were composed of two types of narrative elements: choral odes and the scenes between characters, known as the episodes. Choral performers were amateurs, young men chosen for their dancing ability. The actors were professional priest-performers. Costuming was very elaborate, and actors and chorus wore masks that completely covered the head.

The playwrights were known as poets (or makers) of *dramenon*. Three playmakers were selected each year, and each was responsible for one day of plays, which consisted of three tragedies and a satyr play. At the end of three days, a jury of twelve tribal leaders voted on the winner of the Dionysia, and that poet received a large sum of money. The vote was supposed to be directed by the hand of the god. Each day of plays was paid for by one of the three wealthiest men of Athens of that particular year, and one of those men, known as the *choregus*, or choral leader, was given the honor of

being named the winner of the *agon*, or dramatic contest. Usually, the winner would put up a monument commemorating his victory and listing the names of the playwright and the *hypokritoi*, so that considerable information survives about the Dionysia. The most famous playwrights of fifth century Athens were Aeschylus, Sophocles, and Euripides. Their most famous plays are *Agamemnōn* (458 B.C.E.; *Agamemnon*, 1777), *Oidipous Tyrannos* (c. 429 B.C.E.; *Oedipus Tyrannus*, 1715), and *Mēdeia* (431 B.C.E.; *Medea*, 1781), respectively.

Never as highly respected as tragedies or even satyr plays, comedies were not admitted into the Dionysia until 587 B.C.E. Only the comedies of Aristophanes survive in written form, of which the most famous is *Lysistratē* (411 B.C.E.; *Lysistratē*, 1837). No satyr plays survive.

As early as the sixth century B.C.E., Greeks gathered for festivals in large outdoor theaters built into hillsides such as this one, honoring Dionysus (Bacchus) in Athens. (Hulton Archive)

After Sparta defeated Athens in the Peloponnesian War (431-404 B.C.E.), the performing arts declined in Athens and throughout Greece. A special form known as New Comedy, or comedy of manners or character type, developed, of which Menander was considered the master. The Romans took up new comedy and produced two playwrights of comic genius, Plautus and Terence. Roman theater can be said to have begun officially in 240 B.C.E., when the Iudi Romani (Roman games) were established. However, Romans preferred the pantomime to spoken drama, and spectacles such as the circus, gladiatorial and wild animal fights, or even Christians being devoured by lions. These spectacles were presented in circular arenas such as the famed colosseum. Chariot races were held at the Circus Maximus, and sea battles were presented in special water theaters known as *numachia*. When Rome converted to Christianity, most of these shows were banned. Although some theater continued in the Byzantine Empire, and an actress, Theodora, even became the wife of an emperor, it may be said that with her conversion to Christianity in 527 C.E., the ancient Western performing arts, at least symbolically, drew to an end.

In the East, the sacred dance dramas of India continue to this day, as do the Noh and Kabuki theaters of Japan (descendants of the *bugaku* dancers) and the shadow puppet theater of Malaysia. In China and Korea, ancient theater forms, which included dance and acrobatic skills, are recalled by the present popularity of the modern Bejing opera. Indian drama began as dance narratives performed in temples. It was codified in a book compiled in the second century C.E. This work contained sections on theater architecture, dramatic technique, musical accompaniment, speech, choreography, and characterization. Specific gestures of the hand, head, eyes, cheek, neck, eyes, and even six gestures for the nose were listed. The temple performances of India, at first supported mainly by the aristocracy, gradually moved into popular culture where they embraced the other aspect of Indian theatrical performance, the storytellers and clowns of village theater, as well as the more ancient form of puppet theater known as the shadow puppet theater in which intricate two-dimensional forms are used to create shadow images on a white screen. The temple dance gave Indian theater its serious drama; the clowns and storytellers contributed comedy and farce. The strict division of dramatic forms that was typical of Greece and Rome was combined into a single narrative in Indian theater. The oldest surviving Indian play scripts are known as Sanskrit dramas, the most famous of which is Śūdraka's *Mṛcchakaṭikā* (c. 300-c. 600 C.E.; *Mrchhakatika*, 1898).

As in India, Chinese theater was a product of the temples, where eighth century B.C.E. records show that performers were part of holy worship, and even as early as 1500 B.C.E., there is evidence that members of the ruling class maintained theatrical entertainers. By 210 B.C.E., China came under the control of the Han Dynasty. The Han emperors maintained so large a group of entertainers—from tight-rope walkers to actors, mimes, dancers, and musicians—that the nights were known as "the hundred plays." The actual performance space of ancient Chinese theater very much resembles an English Elizabethan playhouse. A large structure housing the backstage area had a raised stage before it. As in Elizabethan England, the stage was open on three sides so that the audience stood on the ground around the stage. A balcony with seating for more important personages was also provided. Theater became so popular with the Chinese rulers that in 714 C.E., an imperial acting school known as the Pear Garden was established. Chinese actors are still known as "students of the Pear Garden." What now remains of the early Chinese theater is a contemporary form known as Beijing opera, whose highly acrobatic and richly costumed actors, performing in a stylized tradition, are reminiscent of the glories of "the hundred plays." The Chinese also borrowed from India the shadow puppet theater, which became widely popular by 260 B.C.E.

Indeed, throughout Southeast Asia, the theater of the shadow puppet is perhaps the dominant form of indigenous entertainment. Although the shadow puppet play is known to have started in India, the details of its origins are lost in antiquity.

The Malaysian puppet, like most others, is an intricately carved leather figure between 6 inches (15 centimeters) and 3 feet (nearly 1 meter) in length. Performances are at night so that a light can be placed behind the figure whose shadow is then projected on a white silken screen. A single manipulator performs the whole show, which can last throughout the night. Most narratives are adventures of heroes fighting giants or dragons.

MUSIC

Of all the performing arts, music in the ancient world is the least known because little evidence remains. The first musical instruments would most likely have been the human voice and body, with the voice providing melodic statement and the body creating basic percussion in the form of clapping and stamping. One only has to think of modern tap dancing to realize that to have a body and to be human means that music is immediately possible. However, undoubtedly, musical instruments were present from early times, and considerable visual evidence of instruments exists in Egypt and other parts of Africa, India and China, the Near East, and all about the Mediterranean Sea. Flutes, lyres, drums, and stringed instruments akin to the guitar, such as the Indian sitar, are abundantly pictured in archaeological remains.

In southern France, in the cave of Trois Fères in Ariège, there is a crude painting of a dancing man dressed in a bison skin. In his mouth, he holds a musical bow. With his left hand, he supports the instrument, which he twangs with his right hand. This painting is at least seventeen thousand years old. Yet this same instrument, a one-string "guitar" using the mouth and skull as a sounding board and called the okongo, can still be heard in areas of sub-Saharan Africa. A version was also used by Native American peoples. It is clearly the ancestor of all stringed instruments, and its acoustical principles are virtually identical with other chordophone instruments that can still be heard around the world in the form of gourds strung with gut strings, turtle shells strung with fiber chords, or silken strings mounted on wooden bowls. A more sophisticated version, in

which the sounding box is a large, hollow ball, is still used by the Baule tribesmen of Africa's Ivory Coast. The rhythms created with this instrument and with the drums of these and other African tribes go back millennia but are still heard today in modern jazz, spirituals, and other forms of contemporary music.

The simple drums and resonating chambers of Neolithic times were replaced in the ancient world by stringed instruments of various types. The original single-string instrument evolved into the Abyssinian lyre, the Arabian rebab, the Indian sarangi carved from a single piece of wood, and finally the Indian sitar, an instrument so ancient that its name predates any known visual representation of the musical object.

The sitar has a documented history of some four thousand years. It developed from an earlier stringed instrument, the veena, sacred to Sarawarthi, the Hindu goddess of art and learning. The sitar is a very elaborate instrument with six or seven main playing strings and a dozen or so sympathetic strings that echo the main musical mode. It is an extremely demanding instrument to play, and yet it has become the queen instrument of Indian music to the present day. Only about 10 percent of the music practiced on the sitar is written down. The vital 90 percent consists of improvisation within a strict range of ragas, or melodic patterns. In this sense, the music of the Indian tradition is not unlike modern American jazz. The rhythm and melodic patterns of Indian music are passed from master to student, from generation to generation in a pattern of listening and playing known as *guruparampara*. This tradition of master-to-pupil learning is not uncommon in musical practice throughout the ancient world. From Japanese koto players to Nigerian drummers, music has traditionally been learned by hearing someone play it.

Another widely used musical instrument of ancient times was the harp, which was a dominant instrument of the ancient Egyptians. In the eastern Mediterranean, art depicts people playing guitars and recorders. In Greece, the double flute was also very popular.

However, no written musical literature is available until Classical Greece, and then only a few fragments of compositions survive. Many musicologists believe that Greek music was oriental in sound, but more is known about the names of musical types than about the quality. Plato in his *Nomoi* (360-347 B.C.E.; *Laws*, 1804) reports that there are various classes and types of Greek music, including hymns, dirges, paeans (songs of joy and praise), and dithyrambs (songs and dances to the god Dionysus used in public festivals and theatrical performances). Pictorial evidence reveals that the dithyrambs and choral odes of tragedy and probably even the solo speeches were accompanied by two basic musical instruments: the lyre and the aulos, or double-pipe flute. The lyre is a stringed instrument used for the less raucous and vigorous chorus speeches, hence the English term "lyrical." It was the instrument sacred to the Greek god Apollo, the divinity of light, healing, and music, who is usually depicted carrying the lyre. The aulos, however, seems to have produced a sound that was a cross between an oboe and a bagpipe and was used with the more tumultuous odes and episodes in the theater. Percussion instruments, the most fundamental of all musical devices, were used throughout Greek performances. Tambourines were special favorites of Roman musicians, as were flutes and wind instruments made of brass or, following a more ancient Hebrew tradition, of animal horns.

Greek music is known to have used various modes or scales. The music was written down in two systems, one for vocal music and one for instrumental, both of which were unlike modern Western systems for transcribing music. Both consisted of indicating notes by using letters of the alphabet above the song word, but neither is clear in application, and only a few fragments survive. Also surviving is a treatise, *De musica* (probably third century C.E.; *Aristides Quintilianus: On Music*, 1983) by Aristides Quintilianus, dealing with musical harmony and rhythm; the moral, educational, and therapeutic values of music; and music's scientific and mathematical aspects. Part of the education of every Greek youth was training in

music, as much for its mathematical as for its aesthetic value.

The ancient Romans generally seemed to have valued music less than classical Greeks; however, it was used extensively in ceremonies and in theatrical performances. Apparently up to two-thirds of the lines in Plautus's plays were accompanied by music. Roman pantomimes required a sizable orchestra of flutes, pipes, cymbals, and other percussion instruments. Although almost nothing is known of Roman musical modes, something of their quality can be surmised from the plain song used by early Christian churches and taken directly from Roman ceremonial chants, as well as from Hebrew religious chants.

Music was very important in the religious services of the Hebrew peoples. Every synagogue had its song leader, or cantor, who led the worshipers in "lifting a joyful noise unto the Lord" and in making "song in the house of the Lord with cymbals, psalteries, and harps." The First Corinthians mentions a total of 225 skilled musicians in the service of Solomon's temple. Portions of the Jewish sacred service—especially the "Hallelujah" and the "Holy, Holy, Holy"—were taken directly into the Christian liturgy. Many other traditional synagogue chants were altered to suit Latin texts. The antiphonal singing of certain Jewish sects—in which a chorus of men and a chorus of women both sing in unison and also sing in call-and-response patterns—became the basis for most of the great body of so-called plain-song music of the early Christian church.

There was apparently little difference between early Church music and the music of everyday life, for Saint John Chrysostom of Constantinople (400 C.E.) comments on the similarities of church psalms to the lullabies sung by mothers to put their children to sleep. Indeed this similarity between sacred music and that of the people would follow the Hebrew tradition, for Saint John Chrysostom observed that God aided people in understanding the scriptures by giving them the music of the Psalms and the words of King David, "For nothing so uplifts the mind, giving it wings and freeing it from the earth . . . as the modulated melody and the divine chant." In the sixth century C.E., Pope Gregory the Great collected almost four thousand plain-song compositions, which would henceforth be known as the Gregorian chants, still in use in Christian liturgy. Most of the instruments used in church services as well as in everyday European life were, like the Hebrew chants, imported from the Near East. When the Arabs invaded southern Spain, they brought with them the musical achievements of the ancient civilization of Persia. The Spanish took up the Arabian music and its varied instruments and spread their use into all of Europe. However, it would take more than four centuries for the Spanish to invent the five-line stave that would become the basis for modern musical notation and literature.

ADDITIONAL RESOURCES

Brockett, Oscar G. *History of the Theater.* Boston: Allyn and Bacon, 1995.

Drewal, Henry John, and Margaret Thompson Drewal. *Gelede: Art and Female Power Among the Yoruba.* Bloomington: Indiana University Press, 1990.

Drewal, Margaret Thompson. *Yoruba Ritual: Performance, Play, Agency.* Bloomington: University of Indiana Press, 1992.

Gardner, Robert, and Karl G. Heider, *Gardens of War: Life and Death in the New Guinea Stone Age.* New York: Random House, 1968.

Grunfeld, Frederic V. *Music.* New York: Newsweek Books, 1974.

Main, William P. *Music Cultures of the Pacific, Near East, and Asia.* Englewood Cliffs, N.J.: Prentice-Hall, 1967.

Meserve, Walter I., and Mollie Ann Meserve. *A Chronological Outline of World Theater.* New York: Feedback Theater Books, 1992.

Sachs, Curt. *The Rise of Music in the Ancient World.* New York: W. W. Norton, 1943.

————. *World History of the Dance.* New York: W. W. Norton, 1937.

Sorrell, Waiter. *The Dance Through the Ages.* New York: Grosset and Dunlap, 1967.

Wyckham, Glynne. *A History of the Theater.* Cambridge, England: Cambridge University Press, 1992.

SEE ALSO: Aeschylus; Africa, East and South; Agathon; Arabia; Aristophanes; Athens; Bacchylides; Byzantine Empire; China; Christianity; Crates of Athens; Cratinus; Crete; Egypt, Prepharaonic; Eupolis; Euripides; *Gigaku*; Greece, Classical; Gregory the Great; Han Dynasty; Hinduism; India; Israel; Japan; John Chrysostom, Saint; Judaism; Korea; Malay; Menander (playwright); Peloponnesian Wars; Persia; Pisistratus; Plato; Plautus; Rome, Imperial; Sophocles; Śūdraka; Terence; Theodora; Thespis.

—August W. Staub

PHILOSOPHY

Philosophy of the ancient world covers a broad range of subjects. It was usually not separate from religion, mythology, and other aspects of culture. The following are major schools of these philosophies.

GREEK PHILOSOPHY

Western philosophy can be traced back to ancient Greek philosophy. It started in Greece and the Greek-speaking parts of the Mediterranean, which now includes parts of Italy, western Asia, and Egypt. "Philosophy" in Greek means "love of wisdom," and those engaged in philosophy were considered wisdom-lovers. It is conventionally believed that Greek philosophy started in the mid-sixth century B.C.E. with Thales of Miletus, who conjectured that the origin of the world is water. Early Greek philosophers were mostly concerned with the nature of reality. Parmenides, in the early fifth century B.C.E., argued that reality

Athenian philosopher Socrates drinks poisonous hemlock after being sentenced to death for impious behavior and corrupting the young. (Library of Congress)

is one and unchanging, whereas Heraclitus of Ephesus (c. 540-c. 480 B.C.E.) argued that change is the nature of the world. According to Heraclitus, everything is flux, and one cannot step into the same river twice. Greek philosophy culminated in the works of Plato and Aristotle.

Socrates and Plato. Socrates (c. 470-399 B.C.E.) is considered the first philosopher in the West to shift the focus of philosophy from the natural world to human values. He did not write for fear that written words would dogmatize philosophical thinking. What is known about Socrates comes from the writings of his student Plato (c. 427-347 B.C.E.). Plato's works are mostly in the form of dialogues; Socrates is usually the main interlocutor in these dialogues. Socrates believed that philosophy aims to know truth, but he believed that true knowledge comes not from experience of the physical world but from the soul of the individual. Pursuit of knowledge is taking care of the soul, which is immortal and hence more important than the physical body. The function of the philosopher is that of the midwife in helping individuals "recollect" their own knowledge from their souls. Socrates was charged before an Athenian popular court of being "impious" toward the Olympian gods and corrupting the youth through his critical conversations with them and was sentenced to death. After refusing friends' help to escape, he died from drinking hemlock at age seventy. He was probably the first person who died for the sake of free thinking and free speech.

After Socrates' death, Plato established the Academy in Athens to teach philosophy. Plato developed the theory of forms to account for reality. He argued that because the physical world is imperfect and changing, it cannot be the object of true knowledge. The real therefore has to be beyond this physical world. Plato believed that reality consists of what he called "forms," a kind of nonphysical existence that is perfect and eternal. Physical objects, which are objects of opinions, are merely copies of their respective pure forms. Like his teacher Socrates, Plato believed that reason is the most important principle in humans and is the foundation of knowledge and morality. If people follow reason they will become not only knowledgeable but also virtuous. In his *Politeia* (388-368 B.C.E.; *Republic*, 1701), Plato developed a theory of ideal society that consists of three classes: the ruling, executive, and economic. The ruling class, which he called philosopher-kings, are decision-makers for the society. The executive class, or auxiliaries, enforce the laws made by philosopher-kings. The third class is the economic, consisting of people who produce and provide for the society. He argued that the existence of classes is justified and necessary because people have different aptitudes and society has different needs.

Aristotle. Although Aristotle (384-322 B.C.E.) was a student of Plato's, he disagreed profoundly with his teacher. Aristotle outrightly rejected Plato's theory of forms. Instead, he believed in the reality of the physical world. Aristotle is known for his theory of substance, believing that the world consists of various independent entities that he called "substances," which in turn are made up of form and matter. Aristotle's view of the soul is different from that of Socrates because Aristotle believed it is a living force that exists not only in humans but also in other living organisms. The human soul is, however, different from the rest because it possesses intellect, enabling human beings to engage in rational thinking. Aristotle advocated an ethics of virtue, in which humans are to develop various virtues in order to achieve their teleological goals. Politics as a science aims to describe a society that embodies these virtues in individual and social life. In logic, Aristotle is best known for his formulation of the deductive theory of syllogism.

Stoicism. Founded by Zeno of Citium (c. 336-334 to c. 265-261 B.C.E.) and later developed by Roman philosophers, Stoicism was once the most influential philosophy of the Hellenistic age. Stoicism views the universe as a rational harmonious organism planned by God and governed by its own rational soul. Among all creatures, the ones that most closely approximate the total universe are rational beings, which include humans and gods. Stoic ethics prescribes the doctrine of living according to the benevolence and orderliness of the universe. The means to achieve such a life is virtue.

INDIA

Ancient Indian culture was a product of the integration of the Aryan culture and the indigenous culture after the Aryan people moved into the Indus Valley around 1500 B.C.E. One major characteristic of Indian philosophy is that philosophy and religion are closely connected.

Hindu philosophy. Hindu philosophy, an important part of Hinduism, began with speculations and argumentation in such Hindu scriptures as the Vedas, the *Upaniṣads*, and the *Bhagavadgītā*. The issues discussed included the origin and nature of the universe, gods, and human life. One central issue was the relation between the self (*ātman*) and the ultimate reality (*brahman*). The Vedic scriptures assert that the two are identical. Hindu philosophers generally viewed the Vedic scriptures as revelation and accepted the identity of *ātman* and *brahman*. However, this does not mean that everyone realizes this identity. Often the individual confuses the real self, which is identical to *brahman*, with the empirical self, which is full of earthly desires. Studying philosophy is a way to achieve this final realization of *ātman-brahman*.

Hindu philosophy was later divided into numerous schools. The Sāṁkhya school advocated a dualistic theory of reality. It held that there are two kinds of reality: the spiritual principle *purusha*, which is the ultimate self, and nature or *prakriti*, which is the material that constitutes the empirical self. Sāṁkhya developed an evolutionary theory of the universe in terms of these two principles. The Yoga school accepted most of Sāṁkhya's theories, including the evolution theory, but added that the evolution process started because of a god's intervention. Yoga primarily focused on the practical aspect of the realization of *ātman-brahman*. Its goal was to liberate people from various forces of bondage that prevent them from attaining spiritual liberation or *mokṣa*, and its practice incorporates spiritual, moral, and physical disciplines.

The Nyāya school is most known for its five-step syllogism of inference. It includes the proposition ("Yonder hill has fire"), the reason ("Because it has smoke"), the example ("Whatever has smoke has fire, for example, a stove"), the application ("Yonder hill has smoke such as is always accompanied by fire"), and the conclusion ("Therefore yonder hill has fire"). The Vaiśeṣika school believed the universe had a pluralistic realism, fitting the world into seven categories: substance, quality, motion, generality, particularity, inherence, and nonexistence. The Vedānta school focused on the issue of the ultimate reality and developed different theories of the relation between reality and appearance.

Jaina philosophy. Jainism took shape in the sixth century B.C.E. Like Hindus, Jains believed that suffering in the world is caused by individuals' karmic matter, which pollutes the soul, namely the negative effect generated by one's previous deeds. The goal in life is to purify the soul in order to gain spiritual liberation. Jaina philosophers divided the world into two fundamentally different kinds of substances, *jiva*, the soul, and *ajiva*, matter. The two are mixed in the world; every instance of *ajiva* has *jiva* in it. In the case of human beings, the goal is to separate the soul from *ajiva*. The Jain's way to liberation includes fourteen stages of purification. They are most known for their moral principle of *ahiṁsā* or "nonhurting/nonviolence." Jaina philosophy maintained that reality is many-sided and that one's knowledge is necessarily limited by one's perspective, and therefore knowledge of reality is always imperfect perspective (*naya*) knowledge.

Buddhist philosophy. Buddhism originated in the sixth or fifth century B.C.E. with Siddhārtha Gautama (c. 566-c. 486 B.C.E.), who was later known as the Buddha. Its central teaching is the Four Noble Truths : That there is suffering, that the cause of suffering is desire, that the extinction of suffering is by the extinction of desire, and that

the way to the extinction of desire is the Eightfold Path. The Eightfold Path, as directed by the Buddha, consists of right view, right determination, right speech, right conduct, right livelihood, right effort, right mindfulness, and right concentration. Like later Buddhists, early Buddhists did not believe in an independent self even though they accepted the doctrine of reincarnation as the Hindus and Jains did. Buddhist philosophers argued that one's self passed to later lives in a way similar to the way a flame passes from one candle to another. They also developed a theory of interdependent arising. They maintained that things in the world always exist conditionally; because anything's existence depends on other things, nothing has its own reality. This view was later further developed by such schools as that of Pure Consciousness.

PHILOSOPHY OF CHINA

Since its beginning, Chinese philosophy has been concentrating on human values. This concentration is probably the result of philosophy's arising in the sixth century B.C.E. when the society fell into chaos and solutions were being sought to restore social order. Numerous philosophical schools vied for dominance: The Legalist school advocated harsh punishment as a cure to disorder in society, and the Moist school prescribed universal love. In the end, only two schools survived and maintained their influence, Confucianism and Daoism. Along with Buddhism, which was brought to China at the beginning of the first century C.E., these two philosophical schools have provided the backbones of Chinese civilization.

Confucian philosophy. This school of philosophy was founded by Confucius (551-479 B.C.E.) and developed and revised later by various individuals including Mencius (c. 372-c. 289 B.C.E.) and Xunzi (c. 298-c. 230 B.C.E.), the naturalist Confucian. Confucian classics include the *Lunyu* (later sixth to early fifth centuries B.C.E.; *The Analects*, 1861), *Menzi* (first transcribed in the early third century B.C.E.; English translation in *The Confucian Classics*, 1861; commonly known as *Mencius*), *Liji* (compiled first century B.C.E.; *The Liki*, 1885; commonly known as *Classic of*

Rituals), *Yijing* (eighth to third century B.C.E.; English translation, 1876; also known as *Book of Changes*, 1986), *Shujing* (compiled after first century B.C.E.; English translation in *The Chinese Classics*, Vol. 5, Parts 1 and 2, 1872; commonly known as *Classic of History*), and *Chunqiu* (fifth century B.C.E.; *The Ch'un Ts'ew with the Tso Chuen*, 1872; commonly known as *Spring and Autumn Annals*). Confucianism was made the state official philosophy in the second century B.C.E. during the Han Dynasty, and that status lasted, with a few interruptions, until the 1911 nationalist revolution.

After Confucius died, his successors took his ideas in two different directions. Mencius, who represented the optimistic branch of Confucianism, developed an idealist version of Confucianism, believing that human nature is good and human beings need to cultivate their original moral tendency. Xunzi, however, argued that human beings have a tendency to do evil and have to be cultivated toward the good. Confucian philosophy, rather than being the philosophy of a single person, encompasses a complete tradition.

Confucian philosophy centers on the concept of *ren*, which was articulated first by Confucius.

Laozi, traditionally regarded as the founder of Daoism, rides an ox. One of the main concepts of Daoism is noncontention, a flexible approach to life. (Hulton Archive)

The term—rendered in English as humanity, benevolence, goodness, kindness, virtue, and love—is about good human relationships. Confucian philosophers advocated that human beings foster a positive relationship with fellow human beings in which people love and care about one another. This type of relationship is to be first of all manifested in family relations between parents and children, siblings, and husband and wife; it is also manifested in relationships between good friends and between superiors and the subordinate. In achieving this goal, Confucian philosophers believed that it is crucial that everyone follows *li*, appropriate behavioral guidelines that are usually crystallized in everyday rituals. A vitally important doctrine in Confucianism is *xiao* (filial piety); children must obey and revere their parents. Another notion important to Confucianism is *yi*, righteousness, the idea that people must be guided by what is right rather than what is profitable. Confucian political philosophy advocated government ruling by moral virtue instead of punishment.

Daoist philosophy. The two most important Daoist philosophical canons are the *Dao De Jing* (possibly sixth century B.C.E., probably compiled late third century B.C.E.; *The Speculations on Metaphysics, Polity, and Morality of "the Old Philosopher, Lau-Tsze,"* 1868; better known as the *Dao De Jing*) and the *Zhuangzi* (traditionally c. 300 B.C.E., compiled c. 285-160 B.C.E.; *The Divine Classic of Nan-hua*, 1881; also known as *The Complete Works of Chuang Tzu*, 1968; commonly known as *Zhuangzi*, 1991). The word *dao* literally means "road" or "way." In Daoism, it means the source and principle of everything in the universe. It is not anything concrete, tangible, or fixed, although it is at work in everything. The *Dao De Jing* describes it using such words as "soft," "quiet," and "empty." Between yin and yang, Daoism is usually taken as emphasizing the yin. Its doctrine of reversal states that, if pressed hard, everything will turn to its opposite.

The Daoist attitude toward life and the world is best summarized in the doctrine of *wuwei*, or the principle of "noncontention." According to the *Dao De Jing*, *wuwei* is to be "waterlike," to follow the flow of nature and not to oppose it. A waterlike person is reserved, flexible, and willing to go to low places but at the same time always finds ways to demonstrate his or her strength and accomplishes his or her goals. Daoism embraces a laissez-faire political philosophy. It promotes a small state and discourages the use of force. Its moral philosophy is directly opposed to that of Confucianism.

Although Confucianism believes in rebuilding social order by strengthening moral code, Daoism minimizes the role of moral code. Instead it encourages a low-key approach by reducing people's desires. A similar opposition can be found in Confucian and Daoist attitudes toward knowledge. While Confucian philosophy takes learning and increasing one's knowledge as an important aspect of self-realization, the Daoist "low-desire" approach extends to learning and knowledge as well. Daoists seem to believe that Daoist wisdom does not need knowledge and that becoming sophisticated in learning can be harmful to the individual. Daoism advocates the unity and harmony between humanity and nature and discourages the human tendency to separate from nature. It is arguably one of the most original environment-friendly philosophies. Usually taken as a complement to Confucianism, Daoism was second only to Confucian philosophy in influence in Chinese history.

PHILOSOPHY OF AFRICA

There are few written records on philosophy in sub-Saharan Africa in ancient times. Philosophical thought, however, may be inferred from religious practices and beliefs as evidenced in archaeological discoveries.

In sub-Saharan Africa, many peoples shared a belief in an afterlife. Human existence included two stages, one on earth and the other an eternal existence. Individual souls were connected through a lineage to a founding ancestor's soul. The ancestral souls would not be extinguished as long as lineage groups on earth continued to perform rituals in their names. This belief obviously played an important role in ancient African societies.

PHILOSOPHY IN MESOAMERICA

Popul Vuh (n.d.; *Popul Vuh: The Sacred Book of the Ancient Quiché Maya*, 1950), a sacred work of the ancient Maya in Mesoamerica, indicates philosophical reflections in the early times. It describes the beginning of the world as empty sky and calm water, without humans, animals, birds, fishes, trees, or stones. There was no motion or sound but pure darkness and quietude. The gods created the human beings and other things.

ADDITIONAL RESOURCES

Chan, Wing-tsit, trans. and ed. *A Sourcebook in Chinese Philosophy.* Princeton, N.J.: Princeton University Press, 1957.

Coplestone, Frederick. *Greece and Rome.* Vol. 1 in *A History of Philosophy.* New York: Doubleday, 1993.

Graham, A. C. *Disputers of the Tao: Philosophical Argument in Ancient China.* La Salle, Ill.: Open Court, 1989.

Jones, W. T. *A History of Western Philosophy: The Classical Mind.* 2d ed. New York: Harcourt Brace Jovanovich, 1970.

Monanty, J. N. *Classical Indian Philosophy.* New York: Rowman & Littlefield, 2000.

Radhakrishnan, Sarvepalli, and Charles Moore, eds. *A Sourcebook in Indian Philosophy.* Princeton, N.J.: Princeton University Press, 1957.

SEE ALSO: Africa, East and South; Aristotle; *Bhagavadgītā*; Buddha; Buddhism; China; Confucianism; Confucius; Daoism; Greece, Classical; Hinduism; India; Jainism; Legalists; Maya; Mencius; Parmenides; Plato; Socrates; Stoicism; *Upaniṣads*; Vedas; Xunzi; Zeno of Citium; *Zhuangzi*.

—Chenyang Li

RELIGION AND RITUAL

Religious beliefs in antiquity were characterized by major deities (most but not all were polytheistic), festivals, shrines, and in some cases theology. Archaeological evidence indicates that many prehistoric societies had animistic religious beliefs involving the worship of spirits inherent in forces of nature. Fertility images such as the Venus of Willendorf (Germany) depict women with exaggerated breasts; similar images, as well as rituals involving stone axes, appeared as late as Classical Greek times. The absence of written records makes other information, except for the belief in magic and the existence in some cases of elaborate burials of the dead, problematical.

MESOPOTAMIA

In the cradle of civilization, the lands centering on modern Iraq, religious beliefs were generally polytheistic. Many of the later Mesopotamian civilizations adopted belief systems that differed from that of the earliest known civilization, Sumer, primarily in the names of the gods. An was the highest god, representing the vault of heaven; Enlil was the active force of nature, Nin-khursag the earth goddess, and Enki the god of waters. All four created the universe, an event commemorated in the Babylonian new year festival, when the priests recited an account of the creation myth beginning with the words *enuma elish*, "when on high." A Hebrew version of this phrase, usually translated "in the beginning," begins the Book of Genesis. More than fifty other gods were worshiped.

Mesopotamia's gods, like those of Egypt, Greece, and Rome, were generally human in form, drinking, fighting, and debating like human beings, although they were immortal. Only occasionally did they pay attention to human beings. After death, people went to a dark, dreary place regardless of their merits; however, on one occasion, the gods did send a great flood (depicted from a different viewpoint in the Bible) to punish human sins. Perhaps of other origin was the belief in a fertility goddess and god who died and were reborn annually. There were priests and nuns, and the worship of the fertility goddess in some areas included cult prostitution.

EGYPT

Like the Mesopotamians, the Egyptians were polytheists. The king was worshipped as a god, unlike in Mesopotamia, and many of the gods were depicted in animal form. The Egyptian priesthood was powerful and frequently involved in politics. The sky-god Horus was depicted both as a falcon and as the son of the mother-goddess Isis. Osiris, a god of agriculture and the afterlife, was the husband of Isis; he was, according to a myth arising in the Old Kingdom (c. 2700-c. 2200 B.C.E.), cut to pieces and thrown into the Nile by his evil brother Seth but was resurrected in order to beget Horus. In later years, the cult of Re, later called Amun-Re, the Sun god, whose cult was centered at Memphis, near the modern Cairo, assumed great importance.

Egyptian concepts of the afterlife differed substantially from those of the Mesopotamians. Egyptians believed that human beings had two souls, the *ka*, to which funeral offerings were made, and the *ba*, which could separate from the corpse. Egyptians were buried with various objects that they could continue to enjoy in the afterlife; elaborate embalming was necessary to preserve the spirit, which was judged on the basis of morality by Osiris. Various magical spells and charms were also believed to be necessary to conduct the dead to the afterlife. In the Old Kingdom, the Egyptians apparently believed that admittance to the afterlife was reserved to kings and other high-ranking personages; the pyramids are in fact royal tombs, as are the later colossal rock tombs of Abu Simbel in Upper (south) Egypt. The so-called pyramid texts describe these beliefs.

In later times, it came to be believed that the afterlife was open to ordinary people, provided they followed the moral and magical practices described in the *Book of the Dead* (also known as *Book of Going Forth by Day, Coming Into Day,*

compiled and edited in the sixteenth century B.C.E.) dating from the New Kingdom (c. 1570-c. 1085 B.C.E.). Akhenaton, king from 1379 to 1362 B.C.E., attempted to introduce a solar monotheism, but after his death, the old religion was restored. The old religion continued to be practiced while Egypt was under foreign rule, until well into the common era. The Egyptians adopted Christianity in the fourth century C.E. and, for the most part, Islam after the Arab conquest in the seventh century.

THE HEBREWS

According to the Book of Genesis, Hebrew religion began when the first prophet, Abraham, destroyed idols at Ur in Chaldaea (Mesopotamia; modern Iraq), after becoming convinced that there is one God (monotheism). This made the Hebrews unique (except perhaps for Akhenaton's short-lived solar monotheism) among ancient peoples before the beginnings of Christianity. This event may have occurred in about 1900 B.C.E. Perhaps five hundred years later, the Hebrews, according to the Book of Exodus, were led out of Egyptian captivity by Moses, who received the Ten Commandments from God on Mount Sinai. These commandments form the primary document of Hebrew ethical monotheism.

In later years, the Hebrews conquered the Promised Land of Israel, where between 966 and 959 B.C.E., King Solomon built the temple of Jerusalem. Access to parts of the temple was severely restricted, and animal sacrifice took place. In 587 or 586 B.C.E., the Babylonians destroyed the temple, sending the Jews, now so called from Judaea, the area around Jerusalem, into captivity. During this period, synagogue worship seems to have begun. The temple was rebuilt, and the captivity ended under Persian rule beginning in 531 B.C.E.

By then, the writings of the prophets, further emphasizing ethical monotheism, were added to the Torah (five books of Moses). Together with other writings, they form the Hebrew scriptures, the reading of which is a major feature of synagogue worship. The Second Hebrew Commonwealth began after the Maccabees revolted from the Seleucid Empire in the second century B.C.E.,

In the garden of Eden, Eve (the first woman) offers Adam (the first man) the fruit that contains the knowledge of good and evil. Christianity and Judaism share this story of how people began the cycle of birth, life, and death. (Library of Congress)

worship under the rabbi, "teacher," replaced temple worship.

Beginning in the second century C.E., Jewish laws and traditions were codified in the Talmud, of which there are Palestinian and Babylonian versions. The Jews were and are distinctive for their dietary laws, observance of the Sabbath on Saturday, and holidays such as Passsover, in the spring, commemmorating the Exodus, and the High Holidays, Rosh Hashanah (New Year) and Yom Kippur (Day of Atonement, a day of fasting and prayer), in the early fall.

THE GREEKS

The Greeks were polytheistic, although in the Mycenaean period (2100-1000 B.C.E.), some gods were depicted as snakes and other animals.

After the Greek Dark Ages (c. 1000-800 B.C.E.), Greek myths began to be written down and to be depicted in art. The poet Hesiod, who lived about 700 B.C.E., in the *Theogonia* (c. 700 B.C.E.; *Theogony*, 1728) supplements the earlier *Iliad* and *Odyssey* (both c. 800 B.C.E.; English translation, 1616) ascribed to Homer in depicting twelve major gods who inhabited Mount Olympus in northern Greece and consumed substances called nectar and ambrosia, which gave them immortality. These deities, like those of Mesopotamia, were human in form, drank, argued, caroused, and sometimes mated with human beings, the resulting offspring being such heroes as Heracles and Achilles. Numerous myths depict the gods as actively intervening in human affairs. They had acquired their powers by defeating earlier beings called Titans, who were now shut up in chains because they could not be killed. The twelve major Olympian gods included Zeus, their king (married to Hera); Athena, goddess of craftsmanship and patroness of the city of Athens, her main temple having been the Parthenon; Poseidon, god of

and the temple was rebuilt by King Herod between 20 and 18 B.C.E. By the following century, Judaism was divided into factions, including the Sadducees, closely connected with the temple, the Pharisees, the priesthood in general, and the ascetic Essenes. Later Judaism was primarily influenced by the ideas of the Pharisees. Under Roman rule, the temple was destroyed after the revolt of 70 C.E., and the majority of Jews dispersed around the civilized world after the revolt of 132-135. The office of patriarch lasted until 425 C.E., but synagogue the sea; Apollo, god of the arts and culture; Ares, the war god; Aphrodite, the goddess of love; Hephaestus, the lame smith of the gods; Demeter, the earth goddess; and Hermes, messenger of the gods. Much of early Greek literature and art dealt with the extensive body of myths involving these and other gods.

The Greek priesthood was often hereditary and included women, who were priestesses of goddesses and women's cults. Although all major gods were worshiped throughout the Greek world, particular gods were patrons of individual city-states. Temples were the most architecturally impressive buildings in the Greek world, being solidly built and displaying the orders of architecture. Unlike modern churches, they did not have extensive seating arrangements for a congregation. Inside the temple, a large image of the god or goddess filled up much of the space; individual devotions, often involving the burning of incense or the dropping of wine or oil as a sacrifice, were the main activities. Animal sacrifices took place at an altar outside the temple.

Some religious festivals, such as the Olympic Games, involved all Greeks. Other such panhellenic religious institutions included the Delphic oracle, in which questions were put to a priestess, often on important occasions such as the foundation of a city (the answers were usually deliberately vague), and the Eleusinian mysteries, centered on a temple at Eleusis, near Athens. Although the details of this initiation rite were closely guarded secrets, any worthy person, even foreigners and slaves, could become a *mystes* (initiate). The mysteries generally involved agricultural fertility, and initiates enjoyed a good afterlife (the Greeks generally believed that most of the dead went to a dark, gloomy place called Hades, although belief in reincarnation also existed). Local initiation rites, oracles, games (including women's games), and festivals also existed. The most important local festival in Athens, the Greek city of which the most is known, was the Panathenaica, involving a great procession followed by the presentation of an elaborate robe to the image of the goddess, followed by games. The frieze of the Par-

thenon depicts scenes from this procession. In the 1990's, one scholar postulated that human sacrifice was involved in this festival.

In the Hellenistic period, following the death of Alexander the Great in 323 B.C.E., religious beliefs from Asia, Egypt, and elsewhere spread to Greece and influenced Greek religion. Earlier rationalism and even atheism had spread among an intellectual elite. Under Roman rule, following 146 B.C.E., massive temples were built. Later Christianity spread, replacing Greek polytheism after the conversion of the emperor Constantine the Great in 313 C.E.

THE ROMANS

The Romans were polytheistic but at first did not make images of their gods; early Roman temples seem to have been wooden. The neighboring Etruscans had some influence on early Roman religion; gladiatorial games originated as a form of Etruscan human sacrifice. The Romans, like the Etruscans, had a gloomy view of the afterlife. The personal cults of families were a major factor in Roman religion; each family had its *lares* and *penates*, household gods. Ancestor worship also existed. Characteristic Roman gods included Janus, who had two faces, one looking forward to the future and the other backward to the past. His temple was open only during wartime.

There were special priests, *fetiales*, who performed ancient rituals relating to war. Numerous priesthoods, some with substantial political influence, existed; the highest priest was the *pontifex maximus*, the "greatest bridge-builder," a title later held by the emperor and still later by the pope.

Bridges as well as arches had significance in Roman religion, and were connected with elections in ways not fully determined. Divination from livers or thunder, the Etruscan discipline, was practiced by *haruspices*. There were six Vestal Virgins, girls chosen at the age of six by the *pontifex maximus* from noble families, who had to keep the fire of the hearth-goddess burning at all times and who could leave the service of the shrine of Vesta only after thirty years. They had substantial political influence and had reserved front seats at the games. At an early date, the major Roman gods were considered equivalent to Greek gods; therefore, Iove or Jupiter was identified with Zeus, Neptune with Poseidon, Vulcan with Hephaestus, Venus with Aphrodite, Mars with Ares, and Minerva with Athena.

By the third century B.C.E., Greek-influenced images and temples had appeared. Worship of the gods was based on the concept *do ut des*, "I give so that you may give," mutual benefit to people and gods. Animal sacrifice was an important part of ritual. Major festivals included the Lupercalia, a fertility festival held in February, and the Saturnalia, coinciding with the winter solstice, combining elements of modern popular celebrations of Christmas and Mardi Gras. After about 200 B.C.E., Greek, Egyptian, and Asiatic influence increased; the *genius* (soul, conscience) of the emperor was worshiped in later years. In 3213 C.E., under Constantine, Christianity was legalized throughout the Roman Empire.

TEUTONIC PEOPLES

The Germanic peoples to the north of the Western Roman Empire, including Scandinavia, were polytheists, worshiping among their main gods Woden (Odin), the one-eyed father of Thor, the god of thunder and the sky, and the fertility-goddess Freya, wife of Thor. There were numerous minor gods. There were no permanent temples in ancient Germany, groves having been the center of worship, which included tree-worship. Sacrifices included humans; priests practiced divination using runes, a system of writing based ultimately on the Roman alphabet. There seem to have been both good and bad sides of the afterlife, the former, called Valhalla by the Scandinavians, being for warriors killed in battle. The world, it was believed, would end in the future. How prevalent some of these beliefs were in Germany before the fall of the Roman Empire is debatable; most of the information comes from later Scandinavian sources. Conversion of the Germans to Christianity began before the barbarian invasions of the fifth century C.E., that of the Scandinavians much later.

CHRISTIANS

Christianity began in Judaea as a Jewish sect. The Christian scriptures, known as the New Testament, are, however, written in Greek. Before the beginning of the second century C.E., non-Jews converted to Christianity, and even earlier, Peter introduced the faith to Rome. Christians believed that Christianity fulfilled the prophecies in the Hebrew scriptures, which they called the Old Testament, and an apologetic literature in Greek and then Latin began toward the end of the first century C.E. Various forms of Christianity, called heresies by those calling themselves orthodox Christians, arose, and persecution began in the time of the Roman emperor Nero (r. 54-68 C.E.), if not earlier, because the Christians refused emperor-worship and, unlike the Jews, actively proselytized people of all nationalities. After the emperor Constantine the Great was converted in 313 C.E., the Council of Nicaea worked out the Nicene Creed, which remains the basis of Christian belief. During the fourth and early fifth centuries C.E., the church fathers, such as Saint John Chrysostom and Gregory of Nazianzus writing in Greek and Saints Jerome and Augustine in Latin, continued to build the foundations of Christian theology. In later centuries, parts of northern Europe, north of the former Western Roman Empire, were Christianized, while in the seventh century C.E., the Arab conquest brought Islam to the majority of the population of the Middle East.

AFRICA

Because of the absence of writing in antiquity in the majority of regions in Africa other than Egypt and Ethiopia, information on ancient religion is largely conjectural and dependent on archaeology. In Carthage (in modern Tunisia), inhabited by settlers from Phoenicia (modern Lebanon), religion was polytheistic. Until the Roman defeat of Carthage in 146 B.C.E., firstborn infants were sacrificed in ovens to the god Moloch. Farther west, among the Berbers of modern Algeria and Morocco, images of gods with names similar to those of the pre-Islamic gods of Arabia were venerated.

In Ethiopia, an advanced civilization existed in or before the second millennium B.C.E. Early religion was polytheistic with both Egyptian and Sabaean (Arabian peninsula, modern Yemen) influence. Jews (Falashas) settled in Ethiopia at a very early but undetermined date, introducing monotheistic beliefs. Ethiopians claim descent from the Queen of Sheba, who visited Solomon, and Solomon himself. In 330 C.E., Saint Frumentius introduced Christianity as the state religion and was consecrated a bishop by Saint Athanasius of Alexandria. Ethiopian Christianity resembles that of the Copts of Egypt, forming part of what is known as Eastern or Oriental (not the same as Eastern Orthodox) Christianity. About three hundred years later, Ethiopia, fighting to spread Christianity, conquered and temporarily ruled Yemen. Later Islam was introduced into the region.

Farther south, in East and South Africa, the Bantu peoples, like the peoples of India, accorded a religious significance to cattle. Ancestor worship was prevalent; in some areas, chiefs were regarded as divine. Belief in magic and witchcraft was also frequent. A supreme deity was usually located in the sky.

In West Africa, families often had their own religious rites. Initiation schools, in which youths were taken to the forests at puberty and taught secret rites, were frequently found in this region, as was belief in witchcraft. Elaborate images and masks of gods were carved in wood. As far south as the equator, by the beginning of the common era and probably much earlier, Abraham and Moses were reputed to have been great magicians, but other aspects of Judaism do not seem to have been widespread in antiquity.

MESOAMERICA

In antiquity, the most advanced civilizations in the Western Hemisphere were found in the region of Mesoamerica, consisting of modern central and southern Mexico as well as Central America. The Maya of the Yucatán Peninsula in Mexico and some related peoples seem to have had a writing system. The Maya, like other Meso-american peoples, were polytheistic, worshiping the creator-god Kukulcan, "queztal-bird-snake" (which later became the Aztec Queztalcoatl), pictured as a feathered serpent, representing life, as well as the sky god Itzamna, the rain god Chac, and numerous other deities personifying forces of nature. These and other gods are frequently depicted in stone carvings. Relatively little is known about rituals. What little is known about the earlier inhabitants (Olmecs) seems to indicate a belief in magic and the use of ecstacy-inducing drugs.

NORTH AMERICA

The earliest peoples of North America arrived from Asia long before the invention of writing. Religion was shamanistic ("medicine men") and totemistic. In many areas, there was vague belief in a great spirit, as well as in agricultural spirits, and in a few, there was human sacrifice. Ancestor worship existed in some areas. Initiation rituals were found in many areas; religious artifacts included masks and, in the Pacific Northwest, totem poles. Among the Pueblo tribes of the American Southwest, there were small religious statues (*kachinas*) and underground rooms used for rituals (*kivas*). Elaborate ceremonies involving self-torture, including swinging from poles, found in the Great Plains, have analogies in India.

SOUTH AMERICA

The earliest cultures in Peru, generally considered to be the site of the most advanced indigenous civilizations in South America, flourished at Tiwanaku and nearby regions in the four centuries following 200 B.C.E. Among the earliest cultures, the rain god Uiracocha was associated with fertility; other gods existed; totemism was practiced by neighboring peoples. Ancestor worship and mummification were widespread. Elsewhere in South America, culture was less advanced. Shamanism and the use of ritual dances were widespread, as were initiation rituals. Temples were built only in the northwest of the continent. In many areas, elaborate images and masks, often of precious metals, were used.

CHINA

From about 1600 B.C.E., early Chinese civilization, the Shang Dynasty, was localized along the Yellow River. Oracle bones, tortoise shells, and ox shoulder bones, inscribed with syllabic characters, were heated and the resulting cracks read to predict the weather and tell fortunes. The Chinese were polytheistic, worshiping Shang Di, "ruler above," and many other gods as well as their own ancestors. Rulers were buried in elaborate graves, not unlike those of Egyptian kings, with weapons, valuable objects, and sacrificed servants.

Confucius (551-479 B.C.E.) was a philosopher during a period of national disunity. His teaching, that right relationships between different types of people, such as father and son and king and subject, are essential, stated in the *Lunyu* (later sixth-early fifth centuries B.C.E.; *The Analects*, 1861), gave rise to the religious philosophy of Confucianism, which received official sanction and is still a major factor in Chinese life. Such later Confucians as Mencius (c. 372-c. 289 B.C.E.), who thought people were naturally good and therefore could be easily taught wisdom, and Xunzi (c. 298-c. 230 B.C.E.), who believed that people, although naturally bad, were still capable of correction, were also influential. Earlier Laozi (604-sixth century B.C.E.) introduced the mystical philosophy of Daoism, which in succeeding centuries attached itself to polytheistic and magical beliefs. Early in the common era, Buddhism, originating in India, gained great popularity in China, and before long, many or even most Chinese practiced all three religions simultaneously, as is still the case, because, unlike Western religions, their beliefs are not thought of as mutually contradictory.

JAPAN

According to tradition, the first emperor of Japan ascended the throne in 660 B.C.E.; however, the Japanese state of Yamato probably appeared in the Kofun period (c. 300 C.E.-710 C.E.). Until the end of World War II in 1945, the emperor was considered divine under Shintō ("the way of the gods"), the indigenous, polytheistic religion of Japan. Buddhism was introduced from China in 552 C.E. and became an official religion in 587 C.E. From an early date, most Japanese combined Shintō and Buddhist beliefs and rituals.

KOREA

Early Korean beliefs were shamanistic; many of the shamans were (and are) women. Later Confucianism, Daoism, and still later Buddhism, were introduced from China. As in China and Japan, Koreans combined the beliefs and rituals of these three religions.

TIBET

Earliest Tibetan religion, known as Bon, was polytheistic and shamanistic. It has been overlaid and combined with a form of Buddhism that emphasizes the emotions and assigns great authority to monks, known as lamas, to the extent that it has been called (by Western scholars) lamaism. Belief in reincarnation is particularly important.

INDIA

Early Indo-Aryan civilization was polytheistic, worshiping gods, some of whom corresponded to those of the Greeks; images were venerated at a very early date. The earliest works dealing with religious thought and custom are the Vedas, consisting of hymns, chants, and ritual phrases, of which the *Rigveda* (also known as Ṛgveda, c. 1500-1000 B.C.E.; English translation, 1896-1897), consisting of more than a thousand hymns to various gods, is best known. In the second half of the first millennium B.C.E., proto-Hinduism became more mystical; the priests wrote the *Brāhmaṇas*, prose commentaries on the Vedas, and the more famous *Upaniṣads* (a large group of documents compiled and composed c. 1000-c. 200 B.C.E.), mystical works on seeking after truth written by ascetics or monks circa 700-500 B.C.E.

The message of the *Upaniṣads* is that the individual soul, the *ātman*, is identical with the soul of the world, the *brahman*, and it is the chief goal of people to fully realize this identity through prayer and meditation, the alternative being repeated reincarnation, the nature of which depends on acts in the previous incarnation (*karma*), which has to be "burned up" through meditation, the physical world being a mere illusion (*māyā*).

Siddhārtha Gautama (c. 566-c. 486 B.C.E.), known as the Buddha, or Enlightened One, founded a new religion, Buddhism, from Hindu roots. According to tradition, the Buddha, brought up in luxury as a king's son in northern India, first encountered death, disease, and old age as a young man. As a result, he became an ascetic, later turning in disappointment with asceticism to the Middle Way, emphasizing practical morality over extreme self-denial. To Buddhists, desire (attachment) causes the suffering of life, which leads to an endless cycle of reincarnation; however, a cessation of desire is possible if one follows the Eightfold Path, which leads to Nirvana, the cessation of desire and attachment. In Buddhism, each individual can attain Buddahood; therefore, there is no central god figure.

Buddhism, usually in combination with other beliefs (syncretism), became the dominant religion in eastern and southeastern Asia but had little long-term impact in India, which remained predominantly Hindu. Vardhamāna, said to have lived in India at about the same time as the Buddha, was, according to tradition, the founder of Jainism, which has some features in common with Buddhism but places far greater emphasis on asceticism. A few million Jains still live in modern India.

IRAN

The Persians are Indo-European in language and culture. They were originally polytheistic, with priests called magi, from which the word "magic" derives. In what later became Iran, the priest Zoroaster, in the sixth century B.C.E., preached an ethical faith, in which the good force, Ahura Mazda, opposed the personification of evil, Angra Mainyu (Ahriman). The *Avesta* (1000-600 B.C.E.), early Zoroastrian writings, preach truth telling and self-denial. The elements, especially fire, played a major part in Zoroastrian rituals. Much later, in the third century C.E., the Sāsānian Dynasty encouraged the priest Mani to develop Zoroastrianism into a more ascetic form known in later centuries as Manichaeanism, which teaches that an evil force created material things; Manichaeanism had some influence in Europe in later centuries in the form of heresies; later Zoroastrianism remains the religion of a small minority in Iran and of the Parsees of Bombay.

CELTS

Early Celts, inhabiting central Europe, including the Gauls in what is now France, were polytheistic, worshiped fertility gods, had priests called Druids, and practiced human sacrifice, especially in wartime. They built stone and earth places of worship, which may have had astronomical significance. The well-known Stonehenge (3100-1550 B.C.E.) in England is believed by archaeologists to have been built in an earlier period, before the Celts' arrival on that island. Evidence is limited because of a lack of written records.

PACIFIC AND OCEANIC PEOPLES

The Polynesians, Melanesians, and Micronesians of the Pacific Islands generally practiced sprit worship and polytheism. The first group believed that certain objects have *mana*, "sacredness" or "power," while others are taboo, forbidden to be touched by most people. All three had elaborate creation myths but none had written records. The full significance of the stone heads of Easter Island is a matter of dispute.

ADDITIONAL RESOURCES

Cerny, J. *Ancient Egyptian Religion*. New York: Greenwood Press, 1979.

Finegan, Jack. *The Archaeology of World Religions*. Princeton, N.J.: Princeton University Press, 1952.

Frend, W. H. C. *The Rise of Christianity*. London: Darnton, 1984.

Jacobsen, Thorkild. *The Treasures of Darkness*. New Haven, Conn.: Yale University Press, 1976.

Nilsson, Martin P. *History of Greek Religion*. 2d ed. New York: W. W. Norton, 1964.

Orlinsky, Harry M. *Ancient Israel*. 2d ed. Ithaca, N.Y.: Cornell University Press, 1960.

Rose, H. J. *Ancient Roman Religion*. New York: Harper Torchbooks, 1959.

SEE ALSO: Akhenaton; Andes, central; Andes, south; Athanasius of Alexandria, Saint; Athens; Augustine, Saint; Bantu, Congo Basin; Bantu, Mashariki; Berbers; Bible: Hebrew; Bible: New Testament; *Book of the Dead*; *Brāhmaṇas*; Buddha; Buddhism; Carthage; Celts; China; Christianity; Confucianism; Confucius; Constantine the Great; Delphi; Egypt, Pharaonic; Egypt, Prepharaonic; Eleusinian mysteries; Ethiopia; Exodus; Frumentius, Saint; Germany; Greece, Classical; Gregory of Nazianzus; Hinduism; Henotheism; Hesiod; Islam; Jainism; Jerome, Saint; Jerusalem, temple of; John Chrysostom, Saint; Judaism; Korea; Laozi; Maya; Melanesia; Mencius; Micronesia; Milan, Edict of; Moses; Nicaea, Council of; Olmecs; Olympic Games; Polynesia; Rome, Imperial; Shang Dynasty; Sheba, Queen of; Shintō; Solomon; Southwest peoples; Sumerians; Tibet; Tiwanaku; *Upaniṣads*; Vedas; Xunzi; Zoroaster; Zoroastrianism.

—*Stephen A. Stertz*

SCIENCE

Mathematics and prescience appeared in many of the world's ancient civilizations but evolved only in Greece. In other cultures, proto-scientific endeavors either remained stillborn curiosities or became hopelessly mired in superstition.

Natural science may be defined as a systematic body of knowledge obtained by careful observation, critical experimentation, and skeptical analysis of objective data. Science attempts to construct logically consistent abstract principles, called theories, to explain experimentally obtained facts. To be accepted as valid, a theory must be internally consistent and a consensus of competent researchers must agree that it is at least useful, if not true. Science by its very nature must be a social activity in which mathematics, experimentation, and rational, objective dialogue provide the means scientists employ to convince and persuade.

THE ORIGIN OF SCIENCE

Scientific thinking probably evolved parallel to the development of language over the past two million years as the human brain, growing in size and complexity, conferred a selective advantage to the hunter-gatherer ancestors of humans. During the New Stone Age (18,000 to 5000 B.C.E.), the invention of agriculture and animal husbandry marked the beginning of human civilization as well as the emergence and rapid development of mathematics and technology. However, it was the invention of writing about five thousand years ago that provided the means to store a permanent body of knowledge.

Written knowledge is an absolute prerequisite to the development of science. A culture with stored knowledge may have records of tangible causes and effects to explain nature, the essence of proto-science, whereas nonliterate societies tend to rely on supernatural explanations. However, simple knowledge of cause and effect is not sufficient to transform supernaturalism into science. What is required are demonstrations that controlled effects can be produced by manipulating their causes. It is then that explanations move from the realm of religion to the realm of science. As more facts become scientifically known and the law of controlled causation covers more cases, the need to seek supernatural interpretations shrinks proportionately.

The transformation of primitive humans from Neolithic hunter-gatherers to urban dwellers occurred in three primary locales in the West: Mesopotamia, Egypt, and the Indus Valley. An important trait of this revolution was the creation of mathematics (arithmetic and geometry) and proto-astronomy as well as the complete absence of natural science. Geometry, as its name (literally "earth measure") indicates, originated with land measurements. Astronomy began with observations of the stars in order to determine the optimum time for planting and harvesting, but an obsession with predicting the future convoluted astronomy into astrology.

Celestial observations, preserved as magical knowledge and transmitted as part of a clerical heritage, produced a privileged priestly class in charge of religious rituals and arcane knowledge. Religion, arising from an innate sense of wonder and a fear of the powerful forces of nature, was used by priests for their own benefit. By monopolizing knowledge and encouraging superstition, priests acquired power over the weak and uneducated. Not surprisingly, the spirit of rational inquiry, the precursor of natural science, was actively discouraged, while the more practical concerns of agricultural and construction advanced mathematics and technology.

Arithmetic, geometry, and proto-astronomy evolved in the earliest cities because they were essential to the development of the urban revolution itself. Arithmetic was essential to keep the inventories and account books of the merchants and traders under the guardianship of the priests who ruled the cities. Geometry was required by architects and engineers for the construction of the monumental structures that characterized these civilizations. Astronomical observation was indispensable to the development of an accurate calendar for agriculture, for without sufficient food, the growing city-states would have collapsed. These sciences, which conformed to the prevailing belief system of officially sanctified superstition, provided the infrastructure necessary to support the urban revolution. City residents willingly submitted to the priests who maintained power by their monopoly on astronomical and mathematical knowledge. Performing simple arithmetic was an act of religious ritual, and geometrical diagrams appeared as mysterious hieroglyphics decipherable only by the priests. As long as astronomy remained embedded in religion and was the sole domain of priests, it could never progress from the realm of embryonic proto-science to a natural science based on objective rational inquiry.

Natural science develops only when the circumstances are right, and the right circumstances occurred in ancient Greece. Some of the key components necessary for science and mathematics, open debate and objective thinking, are already evident in the oldest Greek literature (Homer's *Iliad* and *Odyssey*, both c. 800 B.C.E.; English translation, 1616). In these works, despite the gods' manipulations of their lives, humans control their own destinies and arrange their own affairs. Because Greek society was stable for about one thousand years, there was ample time for these prescientific attitudes to develop into Greek proto-science.

For a variety of reasons, science did not develop in the other great civilizations of the ancient world. China produced many technological innovations and took tentative steps toward science, yet science did not develop. Indian science was a diluted version of Greek science; it had the substance but not the form. The Arabs originally learned Greek science from India and later directly from translations of the Classical Greek texts, but this knowledge was not brought to fruition. These failures show that even proto-science can arise only under a very precise set of cultural circumstances. Even then, the highly rational Greek science, by relying exclusively on the intellectual with little recourse to experiment, tended to be somewhat subjective. It was not until the Renaissance that Europe, under another set of somewhat unlikely circumstances, extended the limits and limitations of Greek science and propelled the advance of modern science. Greek science began in the human mind and remained there; modern science begins outside the human mind—with nature.

MESOPOTAMIA (4000 B.C.E. TO 539 B.C.E.)

From its beginnings in Sumer before the mid-third millennium B.C.E., Mesopotamian science was characterized by tedious enumeration attempting to order all things in the world into columns and series but without any desire to synthesize and reduce these data into a system. Although they knew the essence of Pythagoras's theorem one thousand years before Pythagoras, it was never formulated as a law nor was any attempt made to derive it. Although great strides in astronomic observation, mathematics, and time reckoning were made before 3000 B.C.E., no laws of nature were derived over the long history of this civilization.

Babylonian priests studied the stars not only for practical reasons, but to divine the future. For this they needed precise astronomical data obtained by accurate observation. Their timetables of celestial events eventually became the calendars that were employed to regulate all organized social activities, from the growing of crops to religious ceremonies. By 2000 B.C.E., the observations could accurately predict astronomical events such as planetary conjunctions and eclipses. Although the theoretical foundation of Babylonian science was based on mythological assumptions, the theories worked.

By 1000 B.C.E., the astronomer-priests had plotted the paths of the Sun and Moon through the fixed stars and determined the dates of the solstices and equinoxes. They divided the yearly path of the Sun through the fixed stars into the twelve signs of the Zodiac and divided this circular path into 360 degrees, the supposed number of days in a year. The degrees of a circle were subdivided into sixty minutes, and a minute into sixty seconds of arc. Their obsession with accurately measuring time by the movements of the heavenly bodies led to the invention of the sundial and the clepsydra, or water clock. The division of the month into four seven-day weeks, the clock into twelve hours, the hour into sixty minutes, and one minute into sixty seconds are all vestiges of Babylonian astronomy.

To the Babylonian priests, the most interesting objects in the celestial dome were the planets (wanderers through the fixed stars) consisting of the Sun, the Moon, Mercury, Venus, Mars, Jupiter, and Saturn. The motion of the planets through the constellations of the Zodiac had a double significance; it provided accurate data for the priest's records, and it conveyed symbolic astrological messages predicting the future and the fate of humans. In this way, precise celestial observation remained inextricably intertwined with the pseudo-science of astrology, and true science stagnated.

Being merchants, the Babylonians needed simple mathematics to facilitate recording monetary transactions. Early in their civilization, they developed a place-value notation in their number system, the place of a digit indicating its value. By 2000 B.C.E., the familiar arithmetic operations of addition, subtraction, multiplication, division, squaring, cubing, and extracting roots were being performed. Because a number system based on place values encounters the problem of an empty space when that position is null, the concept and symbol for zero was incorporated. Eventually, the Babylonians even developed a numerical algebra capable of solving certain fourth-order equations, and they were able to solve several complex geometrical problems using the concept of similarity. They advanced geometry sufficiently to compute the area of irregular surfaces, but their computation of pi as equal to 3.0 was a surprisingly crude approximation. They knew that the diagonal of a square is the square root of two (1.414) times the length of a side, but they never discovered that the square root of two is an irrational number.

Babylonian mathematics was concerned exclusively with solving specific problems. No proofs or explanation of a general method was ever provided, and despite the algebraic skill employed, mathematics remained quite elementary. It reached its zenith in the time of Hammurabi (r. 1792-1750 B.C.E.) and continued for another three thousand years without further development.

EGYPT (3000-332 B.C.E.)

In Egypt, as in Babylonia, the scholars were the priests who, dwelling in the comfort and security of the great temples, had the time and the interest to observe nature and study mathematics. It was these priests who, despite their superstitious worldview, advanced mathematics and established Egyptian technology. At the beginning of Egyptian recorded history, mathematics was already fairly well developed and priests were engaged in careful astronomical observations. Although areas and volumes could be accurately computed, the lack of decimals and a concept of zero made Egyptian math somewhat cumbersome. The dependence of Egyptian life on the fluctuation of the Nile River led to the development of accurate surveying techniques and careful land measurement. Accurately predicting the annual flooding to determine the best time to plant crops necessitated precise astronomical observations. The scrupulous records of planetary motions, accumulated over thousands of years, enabled the astronomer-priests to construct a calendar accurate enough to include leap years.

Although they did not develop physical science, over the centuries, the Egyptians' mathematics and measurement techniques became sophisticated enough to permit the construction of complicated architectural and engineering projects such as gigantic pyramids and the intricate colonnaded temples that still adorn the land. The Egyptians sought mathematical knowledge not for its own sake but for its practical applications. Their mathematics was very elementary (arithmetic) and was surrounded by an aura of magic; arithmetic problems were occult secrets. The Egyptians knew that a triangle with sides in the ratio of 3:4:5 was a right triangle, but they knew nothing of the Pythagorean theorem.

Pharaoh Akhenaton, who ruled during the fourteenth century B.C.E., developed the quasi-scientific penchant of considering the Sun as a light-emitting disc rather than as a god. Although this view jeopardized the priest's power, nothing could be done while the pharaoh was alive because he ruled with absolute authority. After his death, however, his name was struck from the calendar of kings, and he was vilified as a criminal when he was mentioned at all. The priests could not tolerate any threat to their power over the people, and the people were more than relieved to restore their old Sun god back to his rightful place in the pantheon. Even this small deviation toward scientific objectivity could not be sanctioned; such is the strength and tenacity of myth. If even the all-powerful pharaoh could not interfere with religious beliefs, it is not difficult to imagine the formidable odds preventing celestial observations from developing into a true science.

INDIA (2500-329 B.C.E.)

The history of Indian science is one of the longest and most amply documented. It begins in prehistory and ends with Alexander the Great's conquest of India. Indirect evidence suggests that mathematics and astronomy developed in the Indus Valley (present-day Pakistan) at the third great center of early Western civilization. The evidence is indirect because the ancient scripts containing the relevant information have yet to be deciphered. Nevertheless, oblique evidence suggests that astronomic observations were being made before 2000 B.C.E.. After 1750 B.C.E., this civilization declined and was followed by a one-thousand-year dark age of preliterate peasant communities. In the seventh century B.C.E., a new age of urbanization began in the Ganga Valley. Although rational natural science was not present in the earlier civilization, science did surface briefly during the second urbanization when the forces tending to suppress science had weakened somewhat.

During this time, Uddālaka Āruni took the first profound and important steps from prescience to science. The prevailing Vedic culture was not only uninterested in science but also actively disparaged it, direct perceptions of nature being considered anathema to the ruling deities. Nevertheless, Uddālaka was able to formulate and practice scientific methodology using experimental verification of hypotheses by simply ignoring the mythological belief system of the Vedic scriptures. Although some of his explanations seem naïve, one must remember that his experimental method was confined to the unaided human senses applied to incompletely controlled variables. Uddālaka was the first to attempt a comprehensive and unified naturalistic explanation of the evolution of the world, the origin of life, the making of humans, and the generation of mind. He postulated a universal cosmology without gods and moved away from ubiquitous animism to a separation of matter and life. His secularization of nature foreshadowed natural science, and his methodology of experimental demonstration was a precursor of the scientific method. His ideas, however, being ensconced in the Hindu tradition and at variance with Brahman orthodoxy, were doomed from the beginning. No school to promulgate his ideas was ever established, and with time, his ideas suffered progressive distortion to make them more amenable to the prevailing dogmatism of Hinduism.

Indian mathematics influenced the development of Arabic algebra, as well as providing the Arabic numerals and the concept of zero. However, the main characteristic of the Indian civilization was a turning inward to strive toward higher consciousness. At its most profound level, Indian philosophy completely denied existence and encouraged religious doctrine to be accepted without question. Despite a long tradition of philosophical discourse, even proto-science cannot develop in a milieu in which rational objective inquiry is denigrated.

GREECE (600 B.C.E.-140 C.E.)

Egyptian technology and mathematics, which made their impressive feats of engineering possible, were greatly admired and copied by the early Greeks, while early Greek cosmology was borrowed from the Babylonians. However, in the sixth century B.C.E., a new development swept the Ionian culture: Rational thought emerged as the hallmark of philosophy, and Greek ideas came to be dominated by the love and pursuit of reason. Mythological explanations of nature were discarded and replaced by natural causes, and the universe became a rational, ordered system capable of being comprehended. Perhaps as new ideas and diverse philosophies clashed at the crossroads of trade, superstitions canceled each other and reason prevailed. Increased trade also created a wealthy leisure class with time to think and contemplate new thoughts, unrestrained by ancient texts or powerful priests with a vested interest in preserving the status quo.

Although the roots of Greek science were Babylonian, the Greek religion itself paved the way for the secularization of human thought as a rational

and consistent understanding of nature was sought through reason unconstrained by myth. The Greek pantheon contained a plethora of gods, but ruling both gods and humans was Moira, or Fate, an impersonal higher law to which even the gods were subject. It is then but a short step to replace Moira by incalculable, but comprehensible, laws of nature; order and regularity replace chaos and chance, and mythology begets science as philosophers search for natural causes.

Thales of Miletus (c. 624-c. 548 B.C.E.), who imported geometry to Greece, and knew enough Babylonian astronomy to predict an eclipse of the Sun, asked fundamental questions on the origin of the universe and would not accept mythological answers. By searching nature for answers, he liberated proto-science from the spell of superstition. His answers may have been incorrect, but by the questions asked and by searching nature for answers, he employed a new process for understanding the universe and took the first decisive step toward science.

Another Ionian philosopher, Anaximander (c. 610-c. 547 B.C.E.), postulated that the stars are pinpricks in a rotating celestial dome revealing the cosmic fires beyond, and the Sun is a hole in the rim of a huge wheel turning about Earth. This is the first approach to a mechanical model of the universe; the Sun god's chariot of the Babylonians and Egyptians having been replaced by a rotating wheel in an automated universe.

However, it was Pythagoras of Samos (c. 580-c. 500 B.C.E.), skilled mathematician and the originator of a mystical religious philosophy, who could be considered the true founder of both mathematics and natural science. Pythagoras and his disciples believed that numbers were the ultimate reality and imbued these with magical qualities. Their concentration on orderliness and number founded mathematics, and their careful observations of nature spawned science. As a case in point, Pythagoras was able to relate musical intervals to simple arithmetic ratios of the lengths of a vibrating string. He also observed that the simpler the ratio, the more consonant the sound of two simultaneously plucked strings, an embryonic theory of music.

Pythagoras is best known as the father of the Pythagorean theorem, although it was known for special cases by the Egyptians and the Chinese hundreds of years before he was born. The Egyptians may have discovered formulas for geometrical calculations, but the Greeks proved these formulas and introduced the concept of generality; they developed abstract methods of proof not restricted to particular cases. It was not the discovery of the Pythagorean theorem that marked the Greek contribution to mathematics, but the proof of the theorem.

The mathematization of the universe by Pythagoras may not have been valid, but mathematical equations still remain the most utilitarian method for delineating physical laws. In other civilizations, no one even imagined that mathematical relationships might be the key to unlocking the secrets of nature. Today this concept is so ingrained into science that without mathematics, modern physics could not exist. Starting with the Pythagoreans, Greek mathematics made the leap from concrete to abstract thinking. Geometry became a rational science of theorems proved by logical deduction from postulates and axioms, which Euclid later organized into a comprehensive whole. This invention probably occurred only in Greece because of the Greek public assemblies where great prestige was attached to debating skills based on rules of argumentation developed over centuries. In the process of developing strong arguments, the early Greek mathematicians discovered formal logic and thereby transformed Eastern numerology into true mathematics.

Although later Greek philosophers such as Aristotle (384-322 B.C.E.) concocted bizarre physical theories, no supernatural agents were involved. The apparent whims of nature were still explained by natural causes operating in certain sequences with predictable regularities. Although Aristotle paid insufficient attention to physical data, his science, though erroneous, was important because it was constructed on logical reasoning and rational deduction. The literary religion of Greece was not dominated by priests with a vested interest in preserving their power, and even the gods were not exempt from physical law. Greek culture with its penchant for reason and objective thinking smashed the barrier of egocentric superstition. Logic, deductive reasoning, and science can originate only in a mind that has freed itself from belief in its own omnipotence.

Greek mathematician and philosopher Pythagoras used numbers to explain much of the natural world, including music. (North Wind Picture Archives)

ROME (400 B.C.E.-410 C.E.)

By the start of the common era, Rome had come to dominate the entire Mediterranean region. The sophisticated and progressive Roman civilization, with access to the entire corpus of Greek science, produced not a single scientist. Except for arithmetic and the rudimentary knowledge of geometry necessary to plan a temple or survey a farm, science was not part of the education of Roman citizens. Roman technicians used Greek geometry for building their vast engineering projects but added not a single theorem. As for the science of astronomy, in the Roman Empire, it stagnated; Romans citizens were more interested in astrology than in understanding the cosmos.

How can the Romans' complete lack of interest in science be explained? Perhaps slavery, by stifling the drive for industrial innovation, was the cause, but this seems somewhat simplistic. Perhaps Rome's social structure, which considered science as fit only for casual speculation or practical techniques, left no place for the appreciation of science. Or perhaps arcane scientific knowledge was considered magic, and Rome had a long history of aversion to gross forms of magic. Although the reasons may never be known, there is perhaps a warning here that a civilization that uses the fruits of science without understanding or practicing science will stagnate and eventually decline.

THE MIDDLE EAST

The ancient Israelites were essentially indifferent to science; the little science they did possess was borrowed from their Babylonian and Egyptian neighbors. Hebrew geometry was rudimentary and used exclusively for practical applications and empirical procedures. Hebrew cosmology was derived entirely from Babylonian myths, but with Yahweh replacing the Babylonian gods. It is instructive to compare the two fundamentally different ways Israel and ancient Greece acquired knowledge. In the oldest Greek literature (*Iliad*), there is a strong preexisting tradition of noncontradictory debate, indicating the Greek penchant for acquiring knowledge through rational argument. This is a major step toward the separation of the internal and external worlds essential to the subsequent development of science. The pervasive tradition of the Old Testament is of prophets communicating directly with God to ac-

quire knowledge of his will, which they exhort the people to obey. Prophets do not attempt to persuade by reasoned arguments but proclaim revealed truth. In this egocentric environment, scientific thinking could not and did not arise.

There has been a long history of active cultural contact between Arabic-speaking lands, India, and Europe; therefore, it is not too surprising that the earliest Arabian science was imported exclusively from Greece. Arab philosophers tended to believe that the important knowledge had already been discovered, and they need only concentrate their efforts on gathering this wisdom and translating it into Arabic. This search for truth through extant wisdom did give them a taste for methodical investigation; they eventually realized that experimentation was a necessary stepping stone to scientific truth. Considering science as an active effort helped it evolve away from metaphysical speculation toward the modern concept of science as experimentally imbued knowledge. Their concern with observation, accurate description, and precise measurement did much to develop an objective scientific attitude that was later covertly transmitted back to the West with the ancient Greek science they so carefully preserved.

Despite the Arabic love of knowledge, in the theocratic society spawned by Islam, all foreign ideas except medicine were suspect and no social foundation for science existed. The centers of scientific culture were few and far between, and little information was shared, rendering any sustained development virtually impossible. The Arabian style of scholarship was for one savant to attempt to master all secular knowledge. This individual might advance science to some degree, but the lack of cooperative scholarship rendered this approach ineffectual. But the coup de grâce that prevented science from developing in the Arab world was the four-hundred-year ban on printing in Muslim countries, instituted by imams for religious reasons. Thus, although the Arabs saved Greek knowledge and kept it alive until it was reintroduced to the West, Islam was cut off from the European scientific revolution of the Renaissance that it had helped initiate.

MESOAMERICA AND SOUTH AMERICA

The ancient cultures of the Americas, particularly the Maya, developed a complex civilization that rivaled that of Egypt. Since an interest in mathematics and astronomy seems to be an adjunct of civilization, it is not surprising that they accomplished sophisticated astronomical observations and developed arithmetic. Although they had taken the first steps toward proto-science, it would be misleading to label the religious systems and technical achievements of these people "science" because of their preoccupation with divination and mystical problems.

The Maya used pictographs to record information, a decimal counting system, and a highly sophisticated ritualistic calendar to reckon time. The calibration of the calendar was left to an elite group, the priest-astronomers who exerted great intellectual effort into contriving this elaborate system. They were aware of the cycles of solar and lunar eclipses and could predict these fairly accurately, which helped maintain their stranglehold on power. Ancient Maya mathematics enabled the priests to count with very large numbers, but only numbers related to their calendar were recorded. Maya culture was a pervasive theocracy: The gods ruled, the intellectual and religious life was dictated by priests who interceded with the gods, and the people obeyed. Time was an emotional fetish for the Maya, and the calendar was the foundation of all their actions. In order to preserve human existence, the priests had to calculate each ritual according to their convoluted methods to coordinate each god's sacrifice to the calendar. Every moment of their lives was preoccupied with knowing the position of the planets, for if the gods were not propitiated by having their prayers and sacrifices at exactly the right moment, the world would end. The Maya priests dominated the people by fear and superstition; lacking any motivation to move away from supernatural explanations, there was no incentive for the appearance of science.

CHINA

The Chinese empire existed as a stable society for most of the past four thousand years, ending in the early 1900's. Thousands of years ago, China developed remarkable inventions and brilliant technology and took tentative steps toward astronomy, physics, chemistry, and seismology. The scientific creativity of the Chinese people, however, was severely handicapped by the very culture creating the enduring stable environment indispensable to the parturition of science.

Because Chinese scholars preferred continuity over discontinuity, their worldview was organic, rather than mechanistic: Every phenomenon was connected to every other according to a hierarchical order. Chinese astronomers, disinclined to trust theory, proposed no explanations of planetary motions, although they could predict eclipses. Their careful experimentation enabled them to discover magnetic declination and to register the exact chemical conditions required in kilns to accurately reproduce extraordinary ceramic pieces. Mechanical properties of matter were being studied as early as the fifth century B.C.E. Treatises on the atmosphere and the geometrical forms of crystals were written during the Han Dynasty (206 B.C.E.-220 C.E.). Han scholars also determined that snowflakes are composed of hexagonal crystals, a fact not discovered in the West for another fifteen hundred years.

The ancient Chinese proposed a wave theory to explain sound propagation, studied musical scales, and designed musical instruments based on scientific observation. They understood resonance and how to eliminate it when it became problematic centuries before the West. Besides inventing the magnetic compass in 1100 B.C.E., the Chinese also studied the magnetic properties of magnetite. The science, unfortunately, stopped after the observations; magnetic attraction was explained in terms of an internal *qi* that necessitated that magnetite and iron attract each other so that the yin of one complements the yang of the other.

By the fifth century B.C.E., elaborate studies on image formation by mirrors were carried out by Mozi (fl. fifth century B.C.E.). He also used a pinhole to project an inverted image in a dark room, investigated the linear propagation of light, and studied the motion of the shadows of flying birds.

By the fourth century B.C.E., Chinese astronomers knew that moonlight is actually sunlight reflected from the Moon. Zhang Hua, experimenting during the Western Jin Dynasty (265-316 C.E.), discovered that a piece of ice cut into a sphere will focus light, the basic principle of the convex lens. Yet despite a myriad of scientific observations and the invention of many technological marvels, Chinese physics descended into the occultism of feng shui and the metaphysics of yin-yang.

A mathematical treatise produced during the early Han Dynasty contains the first known mention of a negative quantity, and Zu Chongzhi calculated the correct value of pi to six decimal places in the fifth century C.E. However, because Chinese mathematicians were more concerned with the moral order of society than with mathematical proofs, they never developed Euclidean geometry with its concurrent geometrical way of visualizing nature. Chinese mathematics consisted of reckoning rules that, despite their great sophistication, could only be applied to the detailed calculations for which they had been designed. Although these methods gave a false sense of understanding nature, they did not lead to any rational conception of a cosmos controlled by discoverable laws.

Chinese culture amalgamated two disparate philosophies: the Confucian, concerned with the individual's duty to family and society, and the Daoist striving to transcend everyday life and achieve a mystical union with the universe. The Confucian ideal was a society of tradition, social etiquette, moral standards, and scholarship. In a culture in which social harmony is regarded as more important than abstract principles, individualism tends to be smothered and the disquieting spirit of scientific inquiry tends to be anathema. The Daoists, on the other hand, observed nature only as a means of intuiting characteristics of the Dao (the way of liberation from this world) by eschewing all logical thought. Although Daoists may have had a basic disposition toward scientific observation, their deep mistrust of the analytic method prevented them from developing laws or constructing scientific theories.

Although the three great inventions (magnetic compass, gunpowder, printing press) that transformed Europe after the Renaissance all came from China, it was Europe that achieved the breakthrough to modern science. The Chinese philosophy of nature, based on organic analogies, could not accommodate the picture of dead matter moving in accordance with rigid mathematical laws. Western science was conceived on the method of reductionism, whereby the properties of a complicated system could be understood by studying the behavior of its component parts. Because their religious philosophy emphasized the interconnectedness of all nature, the Chinese approach was primarily holistic. However, holism without the accompanying reductionism is not amenable to scientific progress.

The Greeks believed in the absolute invariance of the laws of nature. From the inevitable relationship between cause and effect they created the worldview that the universe was predictable and knowable, as well as the incentive to reveal that order. In China, there was no confidence that such a code existed, and even if it did, no one was sure that it could be comprehended by mere mortals.

CURRENT VIEWS

There are two prevailing views on how science was acquired by humans. The traditional view maintains that the true beginnings of science occurred only once—in ancient Greece. Only the Greeks developed the concepts of objectivity and deductive reasoning that are the hallmarks of science. By severing the human inclination toward the supernatural connection and differentiating internal thought from external reality, the Greeks promoted the unique set of cultural circumstances which spawned science.

As twentieth century scholars unearthed evidence of proto-science in India and China, the second theory of the birth of science emerged. This view is that the human brain is predisposed toward scientific thought, and therefore, every culture eventually develops science. If science had not arisen from the Hellenistic world it would have, sooner or later, appeared in other cultures. The main problem with this idea is that it cannot explain why, if the human brain evolved to its present form 150,000 years ago, real scientific knowledge has only been achieved in the past three hundred years.

The twentieth century viewpoint was given further impetus in 1991 with the appearance of Martin Bernal's *Black Athena*, which hypothesized that ancient Greek philosophy and technology originated in Africa and migrated to the West through Egypt. Those scientific traditions that never left their traces in modern Western science were purposely suppressed by first, denying that non-Western achievements were really science; second, rewriting the history of the origins of European civilization to make it self-generating; and third, appropriating non-Western knowledge through conquest, recycling it as Western, and suppressing knowledge of its origins.

The consensus of modern scholars, however, seems to be that the Bernal hypothesis is a melange of poor research and fabrication masquerading as a scholarly investigation. This pseudoscholarly propaganda is not a serious contender to the traditional view that Greek civilization arose autonomously and that the contributions from its North African neighbors, while important, were not substantial. Not only was Greece the undisputed fountainhead of science, but also no other civilization seemed able to abolish irrationality and completely separate internal thought from external reality. Other cultures may have played important roles in the preservation and subsequent development of science, but none was able to develop the objectivity necessary for science to liberate itself from the shackles of superstition.

Though the roots of modern science lie deep in many ancient civilizations, these civilizations, despite highly developed technologies, mathematical systems, and accurate planetary data, functioned with a complete absence of natural science. The Babylonians, Chinese, and Maya kept extensive accurate records of astronomical observations but never attempted to discover a mechanism to explain their observations. The ancient Chinese believed the unpredictable irregularities of nature

were important signs from heaven; consequently, regular patterns tended to be ignored. Egypt and Rome were content to use elementary mathematics for practical matters and the applications of science to engineering endeavors. Although India protected Greek knowledge in the centuries between the fall of Rome and the rise of Islam, and the Arabs subsequently maintained the Greek interest in science for many ensuing centuries, they too eventually succumbed to the allure of the supernatural. Most early civilizations never graduated from superstition and thaumaturgy (the performance of magic) to a general curiosity about nature. Only the ancient Greeks, through the development of rational debate, took the definitive step toward the separation of the internal and external worlds essential to the subsequent development of science. The Greeks did not excel in developing technology; rather, they originated the novel concept that the world is governed not by capricious gods but by the natural laws amenable to systematic investigation.

ADDITIONAL RESOURCES

Chattopadhyaya, D. *History of Science and Technology in Ancient India*. Calcutta, India: Firma KLM, 1991.

Chinese Academy of Science. *Ancient China's Technology and Science*. Beijing: Foreign Languages Press, 1986.

Cromer, Alan. *Uncommon Sense: The Heretical Nature of Science*. New York: Oxford University Press, 1993.

Durant, Will. *Our Oriental Heritage*. New York: Simon & Schuster, 1954.

Finley, M. I. *The Ancient Greeks*. London: Penguin Books, 1977.

Koestler, Arthur. *The Sleepwalkers*. New York: Grosslet & Dunlap, 1963.

Needham, Joseph. *The Grand Titration: Science and Society in East and West*. Toronto: University of Toronto Press, 1969.

Newman, James. *The World of Mathematics*. Vol. 1. New York: Simon & Schuster, 1956.

Sarton, George. *Ancient Science Through the Golden Age of Greece*. New York: Dover, 1993.

Schneer, Cecil. *The Evolution of Physical Science.* New York: Grove Press, 1960.

SEE ALSO: Akhenaton; Arabia; Aristotle; Babylonia; Calendars and chronology; China; Confucianism; Daoism; Egypt, Pharaonic; Greece, Hellenistic and Roman; Han Dynasty; Homer; India; Indus Valley civilization; Islam; Israel; Maya; Palestine; Pythagoras; Pre-Socratic philosophers; Religion and ritual; Rome, Imperial; Sumerians; Writing systems.

—George R. Plitnik

SETTLEMENTS AND SOCIAL STRUCTURE

Human settlements and societies varied greatly in antiquity. They ranged from small groups moving from place to place to large nations living in cities of stone or brick. In some settlements, all members were relatively equal, while in others, power was concentrated in the hands of rulers who were revered as gods. These differences did not come from biological differences among people but from adaptations to varying environments, from contacts with other societies, and, most important, from economic strategies. Generally, people in small, mobile groups were relatively equal and showed little occupational specialization. Large societies, especially those dependent on agriculture, tended to show relatively high degrees of social inequality and specialization. Religious beliefs provided justifications for social structures and ethical principles for guiding social relations. The societies described below illustrate many of the variations in ancient social structures.

MESOPOTAMIA

The word "Mesopotamia" comes from the Greek language and means "in the middle of rivers." It refers to the area between the Tigris and Euphrates Rivers in Western Asia. In the area surrounding Mesopotamia, people in the hills of what are now Turkey, Iraq, and Iran learned to domesticate wild sheep and other herd animals, to spin and weave wool, and to cultivate grains. Because they produced more than they needed, they began to engage in trade and to establish villages and cities as trade centers. One of the most prominent early trade centers was the oasis city of Jeri-

cho, near the Mediterranean Sea at the northern edge of the Arabian peninsula, on the route between Asia and Egypt. Jericho, which was founded about 8,000 years ago, was a walled city with rectangular buildings that were at first made with reed and mud, then with baked clay, and finally of bricks.

About 3300 B.C.E., large cities grew up on the fertile plains between the Tigris and Euphrates in a land that was called Sumer. The harvests that supported such cities as Kish, Lagash, Eridu, and Uruk were made possible by extensive networks of irrigation canals. Creating and maintaining these canals required a large labor force and a high degree of social organization, and this tended to concentrate power in the hands of priest-kings, who ruled over the cities. The surplus food, in addition, produced varied classes of people for administration, trade, crafts, and other occupations. Religion supported the entire social structure. Great temples erected on terraces of bricks were the physical and spiritual centers of these cities.

The Sumerians were conquered by the Akkadians under Sargon of Akkad in approximately 2334 B.C.E. Under the Akkadians, the ruler became regarded as a god, and society became even more centralized around the person of the ruler. Powerful rulers also characterized the Assyrian and Babylonian states that followed the Akkadians. As social organization became more complex, however, it became necessary to create rules for living beyond the spoken commands of kings and their officials. Several rulers attempted to establish systems of laws. The best known of these systems was the code of the Babylonian king Hammurabi (r. 1792-1750 B.C.E.).

Hammurabi's code gives us some insight into the social classes of Babylonian society because the laws differed depending on whether the person in a legal case was an *awilum*, a *muskenum*, or a *wardum*, suggesting that ancient Mesopotamian society, at least at this time, was divided into three categories. It is clear that the *wardum* was a slave, a person who could be bought or sold. *Muskenum* seem to have been people employed by the royal palace, who used property but did not own it. *Awilum* were apparently independent owners of property.

PROTO-INDO-EUROPEAN SOCIETY

Most of the languages of Europe and India and some other languages such as Iranian (Persian) and Armenian are related. This means that they all descend from a common language, known as Proto-Indo-European. Although there is debate about the original homeland of the Proto-Indo-Europeans, they probably lived in the far eastern part of Europe and the western part of Central Asia.

The society of the early Indo-European peoples appears to have been divided into three classes: priests, warriors, and herder-cultivators. This social division may have been the basis of the self-classifications of later Indo-European speakers. The Proto-Indo-Europeans sacrificed horses, which were important animals in their culture, and engaged in war raids to steal cattle.

The linguistic evidence suggests that the Proto-Indo-Europeans were patrilineal; they traced their families through the fathers. Analyses of common words in Indo-European languages also indicate that their economy was based on the breeding of animals and that they lived in clusters of houses in extended families or clans. A warlike people, they also had fortifications consisting of high walls.

SOUTH ASIA

The earliest civilization in the region now occupied by India and Pakistan is known as the Harappā civilization, after the ancient city of Harappā. The people of this society lived along the river Indus in cities of brick houses and canals laid out in checkerboard grids. They carried out extensive trade along the river and may have been in contact with the ancient Sumerians.

THE ANCIENT WORLD, 200-500 C.E.

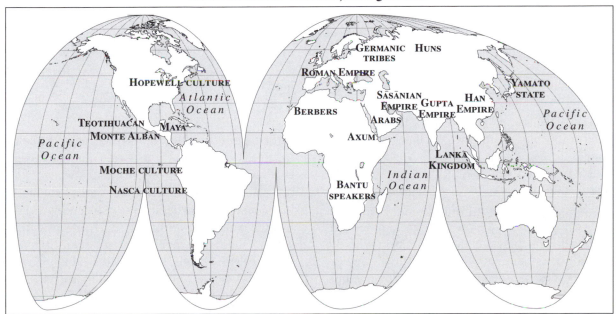

About 1500 B.C.E., according to most historians, an Indo-European people known as the Aryans began migrating from the northwest through the lands of the Harappā civilization and into the Ganges Valley. The Aryans had war chariots, which gave them military superiority, and they gradually came to control much of India. The caste system of India probably emerged as a result of the combination of the three Indo-European classes—Brahmans (priests), Kṣatriya (warriors), and Vaiśya (peasants)—with the conquered people, who were known as Śūdra, or people of the lowest class. The pariahs were people without a caste and came to be considered below even the lowest caste. In addition to these major castes, India gradually developed numerous subcastes, known as *jatis*, that defined occupational groups. By about 600 B.C.E., kingdoms and republics, based on towns, had emerged throughout northern India, and the economy had become increasingly complex, with growing numbers of artisans and merchants.

New religious teachings appeared in the changing social environment of South Asia, including the Buddhist religion (sixth or fifth century B.C.E.). Much of India was united under the rulers of the Mauryan Dynasty in the fourth century B.C.E., and the Mauryan emperor Aśoka (r. 269-238 B.C.E.), took up the Buddhist faith and supported Buddhist missionaries to other countries. When South Asian political and religious ideas spread into many parts of Asia, Buddhism became part of many Asian social systems.

IRAN

The place name "Iran" comes from "Aryan." After 1500 B.C.E., Iran, which lies between the Punjab in South Asia and Iraq in West Asia, was invaded by two waves of Indo-Europeans. The first wave was made up of groups known as the Sogdians and Bactrians and the second by groups known as the Medes and the Persians. These Indo-European newcomers came into contact with the earlier Mesopotamian societies, and by conquering these societies and adopting some of their cultural practices, the Indo-Europeans began to change into empires on the Mesopotamian mod-

els. The empire of the Medes appeared at about 715 B.C.E. One hundred and fifty years later, the Persians defeated the Medes and established the Persian Empire.

Mesopotamian ideas of kingship became deeply rooted among the Persians. Elaborate ceremonies were practiced at court, subjects of the Persian king were regarded as his slaves, and subjects were expected to prostrate themselves before the king. The empire was administered in a highly systematic fashion. It was divided into twenty districts, known as satrapies, which were taxed in fixed amounts. Royal roads connected the central administration, based in Persepolis, with outlying provinces.

GREECE

One of the earliest complex societies in the area of Greece developed about 2600 B.C.E. on the island of Crete, in the Mediterranean across from the southern tip of mainland Greece. The Cretan society, known as Minoan, was based on seagoing and trading activities and established cities at harbors. Many archaeologists believe that women held influential positions among the Cretans.

During roughly the same period that some Indo-European groups invaded India, others filtered down through mainland Greece to Crete, where the newcomers established their rule by 1425 B.C.E. Throughout the Greek world, a social order dominated by aristocratic charioteers living in large fortresses began to emerge about 1600 B.C.E. Known as the Mycenaean era, this warrior society lasted until roughly 1100 B.C.E., and the society described in the Homeric poems is based on traditions and legends from this time.

Settlements around the Mycenaean fortresses led to the growth of city-states. City-states were small independent powers. Although virtually all city-states were ruled by kings and aristocrats early in the histories, during the seventh century B.C.E., many developed into oligarchies (rule of a few, wealthy men) or democracies (rule of all citizens). Even in democracies, such as Athens in its classical period, the citizens made up only a small portion of the residents in a city-state because there were also many slaves and resident foreigners.

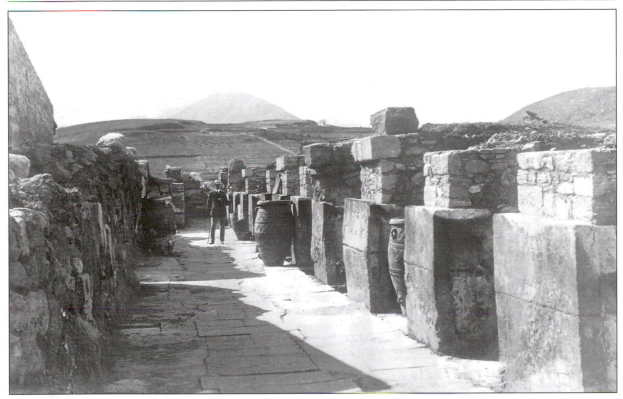

Early settlements ranged from small, temporary encampments with easily dismantled shelters to cities (and states) anchored by massive structures such as the palace of Minos at Knossos on Crete. (Hulton Archive)

Sparta, another celebrated city-state, became a military society after conquering the neighboring Messenians in wars in the eighth and seventh centuries B.C.E. As a result of the war, Sparta became organized into the *spartiates*, or full citizens who were in permanent military training; the *perioeci*, or inhabitants of the countryside who had few rights and had to give military service on demand; and the helots, or slavelike peasants who were required to give half their harvests to the *spartiates*.

ROME

Rome is believed to have been established about 750 B.C.E. through the joining of the Latins and Sabines under the influence of the Etruscans. The Etruscans were a nationality believed to have arrived in Italy from West Asia. The early population of the area around Rome consisted of shepherds, peasants, and landowners, with some artisans in the city itself.

The main social classes that emerged in Roman society were known as patricians, or aristocrats, and plebeians, or common people. The patricians were supported by their clientela, or dependents. After the Romans did away with their monarchy and became a republic, about 500 B.C.E., the economic and legal disadvantages of the plebeians led to a series of class struggles, until about 300 B.C.E. These class struggles were solved partly by allowing plebeians to hold high political office and partly by Rome's military expansion, which benefitted members of both groups.

Rome extended its power throughout the Mediterranean world, but Roman soldiers alone would not have been able to hold such an enormous expanse of territory. Gradually, the ruling classes of all areas within Roman control came to identify themselves and their interests with Rome. Rome itself changed from a republic to an empire, and its social and political structure came to resemble the absolute monarchies of Mesopotamia and Persia. Under the emperor Diocletian (r. 284-305 C.E.), the citizens of the empire became subjects. The class system of the empire had also changed by Diocletian's time, as peasants became serfs, known as *coloni*, who were permanently tied to the land on large estates of powerful landholders.

The Roman emperor Constantine the Great (r. 306-337 C.E.) converted to Christianity, and gradually Christianity became the religion of the Roman Empire. Christian beliefs and the Christian Church hierarchy became an important part of social and political life in and around the empire.

Egypt

The best-known early settlements and societies on the African continent were established in the northeastern corner, along the fertile banks of the Nile River. The periodic floods of the Nile brought rich mud and silt to its shores, bringing concentrations of people who established villages. With the growth of population and increased harvests, kingdoms emerged in Upper and Lower Egypt about 3000 B.C.E. When these two kingdoms were united, a single ruler, known as the pharaoh, took control of Egypt.

Most of the people of Egypt were peasants. However, there were also powerful nobles, feudal lords of the provinces of Egypt. There was therefore a continual tension between the centralizing force of the pharaoh and the competing forces of the feudal lords. When the pharaoh was weak, the lords struggled with each other to dominate Egypt. The pharaohs succeeded in concentrating the control of Egyptian society, however, and Egypt continued to be a highly centralized civilization with a peasant population after it fell under the political dominance of Persia (525-332 B.C.E.), the Greeks (332-30 B.C.E.), and the Roman Empire (30 B.C.E.-642 C.E.).

Sub-Saharan Africa

Above the Sahara Desert, Egypt and the northern coast of West Africa were part of the Mediterranean world and became parts of the Roman Empire. Below the Sahara, though, stretches an enormous continent. Until about 10,000 B.C.E., the Sahara was a grassy plain. As the climate changed, this plain became a desert, and people moved southward into the area of what is now Nigeria in sub-Saharan West Africa. About 2000 B.C.E., early West Africans, probably living around the Niger River, discovered agriculture. This promoted an increase in population and led to further southward movement. From roughly 200 B.C.E. to the beginning of the common era, people speaking related languages known as Bantu languages spread out through most parts of the continent. These Bantu speakers often displaced the ancestors of those today known as Khoisan and Mbuti (formerly known as Pygmy). About 200 B.C.E., the use of iron was probably introduced into sub-Saharan Africa from Egyptian culture through the Meroe civilization on the Nile River, and this helped the Bantu speakers in their settlement of the continent.

African societies were divided into many ethnic groups, and they did not have any single social pattern or economic activity. Nevertheless, some social structures were apparently common among these ethnic groups. Extended family was generally seen as the basis of social life, and marriages were thought of as unions between extended families. Lineages, groups of related families who could trace descent from common ancestors, created larger social organizations. The eldest male of the most senior family was frequently the chief or headman of a village.

East Asia

The most influential society of East Asia developed in China. About 6000 B.C.E., people in what is now China began to cultivate millet and rice and to use stone tools for clearing land. From 3000 to 2000 B.C.E., the surplus food production led to complex settlements, warfare, and elaborate systems of social status. In about 1600 B.C.E., the Shang Dynasty, the first historical kingdom of China, made its appearance. The people of the Shang made use of bronze tools and weapons. After 1200 B.C.E., they also made use of war chariots, which they may have adopted as a result of contact with Indo-Europeans in the West.

The Shang Dynasty possessed a hierarchy of priests, political officials, artisans, and peasants, all under a hereditary king. The king's position was supported by the worship of royal ancestors, suggesting the importance of extended family and kinship in Shang society. The Shang Dynasty was succeeded in Chinese history by the Western Zhou Dynasty (1066-771 B.C.E.) and the Eastern Zhou Dynasty (770-256 B.C.E.). The centuries of the Western and Eastern Zhou were times of conflict, during which the kings lost power to local lords, much as the pharaohs had lost power to local elites during troubled times in ancient Egypt. During the Eastern Zhou Dynasty, however, the philosopher-teacher Confucius (551-479 B.C.E.) devised an ethical system based on social obligations and respect for family relations that became a fundamental part of Chinese social structure in the following centuries. The Zhou Dynasties were followed by the Qin (221-206 B.C.E.), the Western Han (206 B.C.E.-23 C.E.), and the Eastern Han (25-220 C.E.). During these centuries, power was once again centralized under Chinese emperors, and the Chinese state developed an elaborate bureaucracy involved in guiding and regulating the society.

Chinese social patterns greatly influenced other areas of East Asia. After apparent settlement by waves of immigrants from Korea, Japan established the Yamato state in the Kofun period (c. 300 C.E.-710 C.E.). The Yamato state was culturally dominated by China, and by about 700 C.E., a bureaucratic state modeled on that of China was established in Japan. Many elements of Chinese social structure also entered Vietnam, which came under direct Chinese rule in 43 C.E., and Korea.

THE AMERICAS

According to most scholars, the Americas were settled some time during the Ice Age when the ancestors of Native Americans crossed from Asia by means of a land bridge between Siberia and North America. As these early settlers spread out through North and South America, they developed an enormous variety of social structures, from small, nomadic groups to large civilizations with sophisticated architecture and varied social classes.

A number of the ancient Native American societies were primarily hunters and gatherers. Others became settled societies, concentrating on agriculture. The cultivation of maize (corn) spurred the development of the Hopewell culture, which lasted from about 200 B.C.E. to about 200 C.E., in the Ohio and Illinois River Valleys. The surplus produced by the corn economy led to the creation of a privileged, wealthy class.

Some of the most complex social structures of ancient America developed in Mesoamerica (modern Mexico and Central America). As in Mesopotamia, the development of agriculture in this region provided the basis for permanent villages and cities. Between 6500 and 1500 B.C.E., people in Mesoamerica learned to cultivate maize (corn), beans, and squash. About 1500 B.C.E., villages began to appear, and soon after, the Olmec civilization appeared in what is now Mexico. Contact with the Olmecs may have influenced the development of Maya civilization in Guatemala and the Yucatán Peninsula of Mexico. Maya society was apparently highly unequal, characterized by a vast gap between the common people and the rulers and hereditary nobles. Warfare for obtaining slaves and human sacrifices appears to have been one of the main preoccupations of the nobles. Maya settlements are best known for their large stone buildings, particularly for their large ceremonial pyramids. Most common people, though, probably lived in wooden structures around the stone pyramids, palaces, and courts that remain today.

In South America, complex societies began to develop in the region of the Andes Mountains, along the Pacific Coast, about 2300 B.C.E. Little is known about the early complex societies of the Andes, but these influenced later societies, such as the Chimu, the Tiahuanoco, and the Inca.

OCEANIA

The area containing the islands of the Pacific Ocean is often referred to as Oceania. It covers an enormous expanse of territory, from Australia to Hawaii to Easter Island. New Guinea and Australia and some of the other islands of Oceania were settled 30,000 to 40,000 years ago by dark-skinned ancestors of the Melanesians and Australian Aborigines. The Polynesian inhabitants of Oceania are believed to have moved from mainland Southeast Asia into the islands of Indonesia. They began traveling into the Pacific Ocean in canoes about 2000 B.C.E., and by 500 C.E., they had settled much of the vast region of Oceania.

Irving Goldman, in his book *Ancient Polynesian Society*, divided the social structure of much of Oceania into three categories. In New Zealand, Tikopia, Manihiki, and Rakahang, there were continual gradations of social status, without clear class divisions. In a second category, including Easter Island, Mangaia, and Niue, political power was in the hands of skilled war leaders, although hereditary chiefs had some traditional, religious influence. In the highly stratified societies of Tahiti, Tonga, Mangareua, and Hawaii, clearly delineated noble and common classes were present, and marriage between the two classes was forbidden. The chiefs or kings were not only powerful, but also sacred and their persons were surrounded by rituals and rules known as tabu (taboos).

ADDITIONAL RESOURCES

Bellwood, Peter S. *The Polynesians: Prehistory of an Island People*. New York: Thames and Hudson, 1987.

Hanson, Victor Davis. *The Other Greeks: The Family Farm and the Agrarian Roots of Western Civilization*. New York: Free Press, 1995.

Johnson, Allen W., and Timothy Earle. *The Evolution of Human Societies: From Foraging Group to Agrarian State*. Stanford, Calif.: Stanford University Press, 2000.

Mallory, J. P. *In Search of the Indo-Europeans: Language, Archaeology, and Myth*. New York: Thames and Hudson, 1989.

Roberts, J. A. G. *A History of China*. New York: St. Martin's Press, 1996.

Schele, Linda, and David Freidel. *Forest of Kings: The Untold Story of the Ancient Maya*. New York: Morrow, 1990.

Van de Mieroop, Marc. *The Ancient Mesopotamian City*. New York: Oxford University Press, 1997.

SEE ALSO: Adena culture; Africa, East and South; Africa, West; Akkadians; Andes, central; Andes, south; Australia, Tasmania, New Zealand; Babylonia; Bantu, Congo Basin; Bantu, Mashariki; China; Christianity; Confucius; Constantine the Great; Crete; Diocletian; Egypt, Pharaonic; Egypt, Prepharaonic; Greece, Mycenaean; Hammurabi's code; Han Dynasty; Hawaii; India; Indus Valley civilization; Japan; Khoisan; Korea; Maya; Mbuti; Melanesia; Meroe; Olmecs; Persia; Polynesia; Qin Dynasty; Rome, Imperial; Rome, Prerepublican; Rome, Republican; Shang Dynasty; Sumerians; Yamato court; Zhou Dynasty.

—*Carl L. Bankston III*

SPORTS AND ENTERTAINMENT

The first detailed description of sport in the Western world is found in Book 23 of Homer's *Iliad* (c. 800 B.C.E.; English translation, 1616). About two centuries later, drama began to develop in Athens and elsewhere in Greece, as the festivals honoring the god Dionysus became as much public entertainment as religious observance. During the next five hundred years, as Hellenistic ideas spread over the Mediterranean area, the Romans were deeply influenced by Greek concepts of sport and entertainment. Vergil (70-19 B.C.E.), in Book 5 of his *Aeneid* (c. 29-19 B.C.E.; English translation, 1553), reproduces the funerary games described in the *Iliad*. Roman playwrights used Greek models, adapting them to suit their own ethnic temperament.

The crowd looks on and cheers as these shield-bearing Greeks run during an event at the Olympic Games. (Hulton Archive)

GREEK OLYMPICS

In the *Iliad*, the hero Achilles honors the slain Patroclus, his dearest friend, with a lavish funeral. Athletic games are a part of the funeral celebration, and Achilles awards prizes to the winners. Chariot races, foot races, spear throwing, and wrestling matches are among the contests described. It is possible that games such as Homer describes date from the Mycenaean period because he is recounting events that supposedly preceded his own time by several centuries. However, he may have been projecting backward in time a portrait of Olympic Games with which he was familiar in his day. It is believed that Homer composed the *Iliad* in about 800 B.C.E., the beginning of the century in which information about the Olympic Games is officially recorded for the first time.

The chronographer Eusebius of Caesarea (c. 260-c. 399 C.E.) recorded the winners of each Olympic festival from 776 B.C.E. until 217 C.E. However, the games may well have begun earlier than the former date. The four Panhellenic athletic competitions were the Olympic Games and the Nemean Games honoring Zeus, the Pythian Games honoring Apollo, and the Isthmian Games dedicated to Poseidon at Corinth. Of these, the Olympic Games were the most prestigious and were held once every four years at the first full moon following the summer solstice. The four-year period between Olympic festivals was known as an Olympiad. The various Greek city-states set aside their political disputes during the athletic competitions.

No barbarian (one whose native language was not Greek) was allowed to compete, and initially, only free men could compete. After 632 B.C.E., however, boys were accepted as competitors, and eventually, during the Roman period, the Greek language restriction was waived for the Romans

---

Pankration

The ancient Greek sport of *pankration* (pancratium), particularly popular among Spartans, was introduced to the Olympic Games in 688 B.C.E. It combined wrestling and boxing and permitted strangling, twisting, kicking, hitting, and struggling on the ground. Although bouts were quite rough and dangerous, biting and gouging were not allowed. The contest was judged to be over when one opponent conceded.

---

themselves. The earliest Olympian events were foot races, wrestling, and throwing events. By the seventh century B.C.E., chariot racing was featured, and from 472 B.C.E. onward, the games were expanded to include horse racing (the prize was awarded to the horse's owner, not its rider), the discus throw, the javelin throw, boxing, the pentathlon, and the *pankration*. Pentathlon, which means "five contests," consisted of jumping, wrestling, the javelin, the discus, and running. The *pankration* was a "no-holds-barred" form of wrestling.

The athletic games, like the Greek drama that would develop somewhat later, were acts of worship as well as entertainment. The poet Pindar (c. 518-c. 438 B.C.E.) often emphasizes the religious or mythological aspects of the athlete's striving in his works. So sacred was the area where the games took place that no slaves or women, excepting the local priestess of Demeter, were permitted to enter. Any transgressor was hurled to his or her death from the Typaeon Rock.

Athletes were required to train for a minimum of ten months before they competed. During the final thirty days before the festival, they resided in a special gymnasium at Olympia itself. There, under the supervision of the Hellenodicae, a board of ten men who also served as referees during the games, the athletes ran and threw the javelin or the discus. The victory prize was a wreath of olive leaves, but the competing city-states often supplemented the official prize with a monetary award. Ironically, considering the heavy emphasis placed upon the amateurism of the Olympian during most

of the twentieth century, the winning athletes of ancient times often received awards that made them rich for life.

During the reign of Augustus (r. 27 B.C.E.-14 C.E.), the emperor wished to revive old Roman values that had waned during the years of civil war and disorder. In this effort, he recruited Vergil and other poets. In Vergil's patriotic *Aeneid*, he imitates Homer by harkening back to the genesis of the Olympic Games. He has his Trojan hero, Aeneas, organize funeral games in honor of his father, Anchises, who had died in Sicily during the Trojans' first visit there. Thus, the Greek and Roman traditions are merged. However, in 393 C.E., the Roman emperor Theodosius the Great, a Christian, terminated all athletic games in Greece, deeming them to be pagan practices.

GREEK DRAMA

In the sixth century B.C.E. or earlier, the Greeks established an annual festival to honor Dionysus (also known as Bacchus and Iacchos), god of fecundity, wine, and bounty. The City, or Great, Dionysia was celebrated in March and featured a chorus of fifty singers and dancers whose performance of the dithyramb, a wildly emotional tribute to Dionysus, was a key part of the religious rites. Eventually, to the cosmopolitan City Dionysia was added a second, domestic festival, the Lenaea ("wine press"), held in January. The site of each festival was a large outdoor theater built into a hillside. The spectators-worshipers would enter from above, ranging down the incline, with the priest of Dionysus and city dignitaries seated closest to the performers.

The first evolution of the chorus produced a leader who, presumably, would take occasional solo turns during the performance. However, until a performer existed apart from the chorus to ask its members questions, to be questioned by them, and to perhaps challenge assertions made in their lyrics, no absolute dramatic form was possible. Sometime during the last one-third of the sixth century B.C.E., Thespis, an Athenian of whom little is known historically, is said to have invented this character, the first actor. Thus, the performances were changed from a pageant of song and dance into drama.

The traditional date for the appearance of tragedy as a part of the City Dionysia is 534 B.C.E., and tragedies appear to have been acted as a part of the festival every year thereafter. No comedy is mentioned as having been performed at the City Dionysia until 486 B.C.E. The dramas at the Lenaea were solely comic in 442 B.C.E., and although tragedy was added in 432 B.C.E., comedy continued to dominate.

The third, fourth, and fifth days of the City Dionysia were given over to tragic and comic contests. During the Peloponnesian War (431-404 B.C.E.), tragedies were performed in the mornings, comedies in the afternoons. At the Lenaea, the number of comedies was reduced to three for the duration of the Peloponnesian War. Before and after the war, however, five comic poets and two tragic poets regularly competed.

GREEK AND ROMAN TRAGEDY

According to tradition, Thespis won the first dramatic prize awarded at a Dionysian festival in 534 B.C.E. Some classical scholars have speculated that this prize was a goat, a not insignificant award in ancient Greece. Further, the prize may have been appropriate because the etymology of the word "tragedy" can be traced to a word meaning "song of goats," and Thespis's performances were perhaps rather crude representations of the doings of satyrs, lustful, mischievous goat-men. Eventually, the winning dramatist received a monetary prize donated by a prominent Athenian. Each donor was chosen by the city government before the competition began.

The evolution of the tragic form was rapid. The first great Athenian tragedian, Aeschylus (525/524-456/455 B.C.E.), added a second actor and, in his later plays, seems to have reduced the size of the chorus to twelve. Seven of the ninety plays he produced have survived. Aeschylus was succeeded by Sophocles (c. 496-c. 406 B.C.E.), who, at age twenty-eight, competed successfully with him and won the first prize with his tragedy. In his long career, Sophocles wrote more than 123 plays.

Twenty-four gained the first prize and none fell below second. Only seven of Sophocles' plays have survived. He added a third actor to his dramatic scenes and fixed the number of the chorus at fifteen. The last great tragedian of the golden age of Athens was Euripides (c. 485-406 B.C.E.). He further expanded dramatic potential by adding a fourth actor. He was less popular than his predecessors—although far more of his ninety-two plays, eighteen, survive—because his frankness in criticizing Athenian conventions angered his audiences. He was awarded first prize only four times in his life.

In the competitions, each playwright produced three tragedies and a satyr play, a burlesque on a mythic theme. The three plays could form a trilogy, portraying successive stages of one extended action, or they could tell quite separate stories. Aeschylus appears to have favored the former method of organization, Sophocles the latter. The tragedies were composed as poetry, the meters of which were prescribed according to strict rules. The subject matter was limited to Greek history and mythology, but playwrights were allowed wide latitude in handling the material so as to develop the desired theme. The gods of the Greeks were willful, inconstant in their sympathies, frequently the source of disorder and strife. To the playwrights fell the lot of supplying a moral dimension to the worship of Dionysus and the other gods. As a result, during the fifth century B.C.E., the great Athenian tragedians dramatized the deepest and subtlest moral conflicts of humankind.

The audiences for these plays, including both men and women, were huge—the open-air theater of Dionysus in Athens could seat seventeen thousand spectators. Closest to the audience was the orchestra, a semicircular dancing place for the chorus. Immediately beyond the orchestra was the acting area behind which was the skene, a tall façade indicating the setting of the play. Still further to the rear was an altar where the priest of Dionysus performed some type of ritual. The actors, all male, wore elaborate costumes and large masks, reflecting the dominant emotion of the character. The *kothornos* (cothurnus), a high, thick-soled boot or buskin, was worn by each actor to make him appear taller to the audience, many of whom were very far away. The actors entered and exited through openings in the skene. Aristotle (384-322 B.C.E.) discusses the various conventions of tragedy in his *De poetica* (c. 335-323 B.C.E.; *Poetics*, 1705), which has survived only in part.

Only one satyr play has survived, but it is known that these short plays were bawdy farces, the exact opposite of the three tragedies that preceded them. Aeschylus was known for the exalted language, high-mindedness, and deep seriousness of his tragedies. So it is fascinating, even puzzling, that Aeschylus was acknowledged by his contemporaries to be the finest writer of satyr plays.

Seneca the Younger (c. 4 B.C.E.-65 C.E.), a Roman statesman, author, and Stoic philosopher, was also the leading tragedian of the Augustan age (the latter part of the first century B.C.E. and the early years of the first century C.E.). Seneca wrote nine tragedies adapting subjects used by the Greek playwrights. However, although the tone of Greek tragedy is elevated and restrained, Seneca's tragedies are intense, violent melodramas full of rhetorical language. As a Stoic, Seneca believed that catastrophe results when passion destroys reason, and his tragedies dramatize this idea. His plays influenced tragic drama in Italy, France, and Elizabethan England more than did those of the great Greek tragedians. The emperor Nero forced Seneca to commit suicide because he believed the playwright had plotted against him.

GREEK AND ROMAN COMEDY

The greatest comic writer in the last half of the fifth century B.C.E. was Aristophanes (c. 450-c. 385 B.C.E.). Unlike the tragedians, the Greek comedians entered only one play in each contest and were not restricted in their subject matter. They could deal with contemporary affairs, and Aristophanes mercilessly ridiculed his fellow Athenians. Among his victims were the statesman Cleon of Athens, the philosopher Socrates (c. 470-399 B.C.E.), and the playwright Euripides. Cleon is portrayed as a demagogue, Socrates as a Sophist

and a fraud, and Euripides as a misogynist. His plays are a combination of crude clowning, obscenity, sparkling wit, wonderful lyrical writing, masterful language, and originality. Aristophanes' comedies were unlike any written before or after his day. They featured multiple choruses, outrageous—often lewd—costumes, and slapstick scenes. Forty or more plays are ascribed to Aristophanes. Eleven have survived, of which *Lysistratē* (411 B.C.E.; English translation, 1837) is the best known. It is the hilarious account of a sex strike by the women of Athens and Sparta designed to end the Peloponnesian War.

Aristophanes is the only writer of Old Comedy whose work has survived. The term was coined merely to distinguish it from the comedy that developed later (New Comedy). The later playwrights eschewed the violent attacks on living persons and wrote more of a comedy of situation. This New Comedy of the Greeks (such as the plays of Menander, c. 342-c. 292 B.C.E.) served as a model for the Latin comedies that eventually flourished in the Roman world. Plautus (c. 254-184 B.C.E.) and Terence (c. 190-159 B.C.E.) were the great Roman writers of comedy. They strove to attract the audience's attention immediately, because at the festivals where their plays were staged, they competed with gladiatorial shows, rope dancing, and boxing matches. They adapted Greek plays but abandoned fantasy, politics, and the chorus as integral parts of the drama, concentrating instead upon the misadventures of stock characters.

OTHER ROMAN ENTERTAINMENTS

During the Augustan age, great poets flourished in Rome. Writing during this general period were, in addition to Vergil, Catullus (c. 84-c. 54 B.C.E.), Horace (65-8 B.C.E.), Ovid (43 B.C.E.-17 C.E.), and somewhat later, Petronius Arbiter (d. c. 66 C.E.). Vergil and Horace were directly employed by the emperor to aid in his campaign of public relations. These poets were widely published and must also have read in public. In his writings, the satirist Horace records his amusement at how pompously or ill some poets read their works in the marketplace.

However, many Romans sought entertainments offering coarser pleasures than those afforded by tragic or comic drama and poetry recitations. Gladiators were trained warriors—usually prisoners of war, slaves, or criminals—who fought bloody battles to entertain the people of Rome. The first gladiator games were held in a cattle market in 364 B.C.E. at the funeral of an aristocrat. Gladiators used a variety of weapons: a stabbing sword about two feet long, a scimitar (a short, curved sword), or a trident (a three-pronged spear used with a net). Some freemen, and even women, fought for money and fame. One emperor, Lucius Aurelius Commodus, also fought in the arena. Perhaps the most famous of all gladiators was Spartacus (late second century-71 B.C.E.), a Thracian slave who led an unsuccessful rebellion of gladiators and slaves.

At the Colosseum, the great amphitheater at Rome, wild beasts fought in the morning, and the gladiators fought in the afternoon. Many Greek theaters were converted into gladiatorial arenas. Battles were usually fought to the death, but the spectators could spare the loser's life by signaling mercy. The justification offered for these contests was that Roman citizens would be hardened to the demands of war by watching blood being shed in the arena. The emperor Honorius finally banned the battles about 404 C.E. Interestingly, in modern times, professional boxers, wrestlers, and football players in America have often been called "gladiators."

NORTH AMERICA AND MESOAMERICA

For centuries before Europeans established a presence in North America, Native Americans played many games and pursued many recreational activities that happened to be much like those of peoples elsewhere. Children mimicked the behavior of adults, playing with dolls, miniature figures, and miniature implements. Almost all adults played games. The women played as much as the men, but played different games separately. Most games probably had some religious significance in earliest times, though this significance was often lost as the years passed. Some tribes

used games as a means of training warriors and winning honors.

Children played tag. The child who was "it" might pretend to be a fierce beast, such as a jaguar. They also played with tops and swings. They amused themselves with cat's cradle, wherein a symbolic string figure was constructed on the player's fingers. Both youths and adults played games with balls made of hide or fiber. In almost all these games, the players were not permitted to touch the ball with their hands. In the eastern region of North America, a kind of racket ball was popular and developed into the game of lacrosse. A favorite in the North American Midwest was chunkey, a sort of bowling employing a stone disk rather than a ball. Hoop-and-pole was played throughout most of the Americas. In this game, participants threw spears or sticks at a hoop rolling along the ground. Shinny, or shinty, a kind of field hockey usually played by women only, was common in North America. In snow snake, each player attempted to slide a smooth stick farthest along a course of snow or ice. Also, competitions in foot racing, wrestling, and archery were staple entertainments of the ancient Native Americans. Various guessing games and games of chance were long popular.

In Mesoamerica, games were played with rubber balls. The Mesoamerican ball game called *tlatchtli* was like an incredibly difficult variety of basketball. It was played on a rectangular court, and the object was to bounce a large, hard rubber ball through a stone hoop high on the court wall. Players could use all parts of their bodies except their hands. Scoring was so difficult that when either team scored the game was over. In Mesoamerica, these games were seen as rituals of such cosmic significance that the captain of the losing team was sometimes sacrificed to the gods.

AFRICA AND EGYPT

Scholars studying "sport" in ancient African societies are faced with two daunting difficulties. First, there is a critical lack of information about what is to be termed play, games, and sport. Second, it is unclear whether African sport is a transformation of institutions and patterns of action existing in ancient horticultural and hunter-gatherer societies or is a comparatively modern invention. Were games, music, and dance recreational, or did they serve some societal function for which this descriptive term is inappropriate? For example, wrestling was a traditional sport in ancient Egypt and became common in Black Africa at some unknown time. However, whereas Olympic wrestling was clearly a "sport," the context and purposes of Nuba wrestling (establishing the dominance of one tribe or village over another) were so different that it cannot automatically be included in the same classification.

In Egypt, on the other hand, there are many excellent sources of information about sports from very ancient times. Some of this information exists in the form of visual representations—on temple and tomb walls, stelae (upright stone slabs or pillars used as monuments or grave markers), sculptures, and miniatures—and in written accounts also found in inscriptions on temple and tomb walls and stelae, or preserved on papyri and ostraka. Good records exist from the earliest period (c. 2950 B.C.E.) right up through the time of Roman rule (30 B.C.E.-385 C.E.).

Egyptians, both royalty and private persons, participated in a variety of documented sports: running, target archery, driving chariots and training horses, jumping, wrestling, stick fighting, boxing, swimming, rowing, fishermen's (or boat) jousting, ball games, acrobatics (originating as a part of the dance), and hunting (big game for the pharaoh, mostly birds for others). A variety of nonathletic games, such as board games and children's games, are also recorded.

A tradition strongly associated with Egyptian sport was that of the athletic king. The pharaoh was idealized as a warrior because in the minds of his subjects, nothing less than the order of the world rested upon his shoulders. His subjects endowed him with overwhelming physical strength, and he was, in truth, constantly training for potential military engagements. In the ancient world, the martial and the athletic skills were the same, so, naturally, the greatest warrior became logically the greatest athlete. This aspect of ancient Egyptian sport parallels ancient Greek sport. As noted above, in Book 23 of the *Iliad*, Homer's heroic warriors during the funerary games show themselves to be superb athletes as well.

EAST ASIA

In antiquity, games in which two teams, or sides, attempted to kick, push, or in some way propel a ball in opposite directions toward the opponents' goal existed in China and Japan. The ball varied in shape from round to oval. As early as 206 B.C.E., a football game was being played in China, and by 500 C.E., round footballs stuffed with hair were being used. By the seventh century C.E., a football game was being played in Japan.

Like people in other ancient cultures, the Chinese enjoyed board games. Mah Jongg, still played in the modern era, was invented in China. It features four players using 136 or 144 pieces marked in suits and called tiles. A player wins by building combinations or sets through drawing, discarding, and exchanging tiles. Some suggest that chess also originated in Asia and spread westward to Persia during the 500's C.E. The game eventually spread to Arabia and Spain, then throughout Europe. Chinese checkers, a game played with marbles on a board, developed from another game called halma. Interestingly, Chinese checkers did not come from China.

The martial arts originated in East Asia. They are various systems of self-defense (some peculiar to China, some to Japan, and still others to Korea) that were, and still are, also engaged in as sports. Kung fu is a Chinese system of self-defense that emphasizes circular rather than linear movements. Karate, a Japanese martial art, is characterized chiefly by chopping blows delivered with the side of the open hand. Judo, from *ju* (soft) and *do* (art), a Japanese sport similar to wrestling, was once called *jujitsu*. It was practiced by the samurai, the military class in ancient Japan. The athlete attempts to get his opponent off balance so that he can throw, trip, choke, or hold him. Judo developed as a complex system of skills intended to produce both physical and mental fitness.

INDIA

The *Rigveda* (also known as *Ṛgveda*, c. 1500-1000 B.C.E.; English translation, 1896-1897) is the earliest Indian literary source. It was produced by the Aryans, a people who ranged from Eastern Europe to Central Asia before invading India circa 2000 B.C.E. The Aryans delighted in gambling, as shown by the dice found in the remains of the Indus cities and in the "Gamester's Lament," one of the few predominantly secular poems in the *Rigveda*. In the Kauṭilya's *Arthaśāstra* (dates vary, third century B.C.E.-third century C.E.; *Treatise on the Good*, 1961), kings are often referred to as gambling with their courtiers, as well as hunting, a recreation in which only the kings and nobles could participate. The plot of the *Mahābhārata* (400 B.C.E.-400 C.E., present form by c. 400 C.E.; *The Mahabharata of Krishna-Dwaipayana Vyasa*, 1887-1896), one of the two great Indian epic poems, hinges around a great gambling tournament.

Dice were also used in board games similar to modern children's games. By the early centuries of the common era, a game played on a board of sixty-four squares (*aṣṭapāda*) had become a game of some complexity called *caturaṅga*. Indian scholars accept it as the forerunner of chess. These scholars believe it was learned by the Persians in the sixth century C.E. and by the Arabs who later conquered the Persians. Along the way, the use of dice to determine the moves was given up, probably by the Persians. The crusaders learned the game from the Muslims and took it back to Europe with them. By the late Middle Ages, it had almost attained its modern form as chess.

In general, ancient India did not put much stress on athletics. Organized outdoor games were common only among children and young women, who are sometimes referred to as playing ball. Chariot racing is mentioned as early as the *Rigveda*. Ancient documents refer often to boxing and wrestling but generally as the province of low-caste professional pugilists, who performed as entertainment for an audience. A kind of hockey was also played. Classical sources mention gladiatorial displays at the court of Chandragupta Maurya,

who reigned c. 321 to 297 B.C.E. Polo, for which India has become famous, was not introduced from Central Asia until the Middle Ages. However, archery contests were a much-loved amusement of the warrior class. Vivid descriptions of such contests occur in both the *Mahābhārata* and the *Rāmāyaṇa* (English translation, 1870-1889), the other great Indian epic poem.

EUROPE

Games played with a ball appeared in England and throughout Europe at an early date. The game of harpastum, brought from Greece to Rome by the second century B.C.E., may have been introduced into England by Roman legions during the Roman occupation (43-410 C.E.). The game began with a ball being tossed in the air between the two teams. Each team then attempted to push it beyond the opponents' goal line. One report suggested that the Irish were kicking a stuffed ball even before the Roman occupation. In later centuries, Shrove Tuesday became a traditional day for playing football in England and Scotland. At Chester, the game commemorated the day in 217 C.E. when a powerful flying wedge drove the Romans out. At Kingston-on-Thames, a game similarly celebrated the driving out of the Danes during the 700's C.E.

In early medieval Europe (c. 400-c. 900 C.E.), mob games, called melees, or mellays, originated. The game was played with a ball that was usually an inflated animal bladder. As many as one hundred players from two competing towns or parishes would start at a midpoint, using their localities' limits as goals. They then attempted to advance the ball by kicking or carrying it, while punching their opponents along the way.

Wrestling and archery were popular sports during the period of Roman rule and the centuries immediately following. In fact, it was not until the fourteenth century C.E. that the melees were finally banned in England by royal decree, and it was because King Richard II felt they interfered with archery practice. Other European monarchs issued similar decrees into the next century, but so popular was the rowdy sport that these proscriptions had little effect.

ADDITIONAL RESOURCES

Auguet, Roland. *Cruelty and Civilization: The Roman Games*. London: Routledge, 1994.

Baker, William J., and James A. Mangan, eds. *Sport in Africa: Essays in Social History*. New York: Africana-Holmes & Meier, 1987.

Basham, A. L. *The Wonder That Was India: A Study of the History and Culture of the Indian Sub-Continent Before the Coming of the Muslims*. Rev. ed. New York: Hawthorn, 1963.

Casson, Lionel. *Masters of Ancient Comedy: Selections from Aristophanes, Menander, Plautus, Terence*. New York: Macmillan, 1960.

Decker, Wolfgang. *Sports and Games of Ancient Egypt*. Translated by Allen Guttmann. New Haven, Conn.: Yale University Press, 1992.

Drees, Ludwig. *Olympia: Gods, Artists, and Athletes*. New York: Praeger, 1968.

Gernet, Jacques. *A History of Chinese Civilization*. Translated by J. R. Foster. Cambridge, England: Cambridge University Press, 1982.

Golden, Mark. *Sport and Society in Ancient Greece*. New York: Cambridge University Press, 1998.

Lot, Ferdinand. *The End of the Ancient World and the Beginnings of the Middle Ages*. Translated by Philip and Mariette Leon. New York: Barnes & Noble, 1966.

Spencer, Robert F., Jesse D. Jennings, et al. *The Native Americans: Ethnology and Backgrounds of the North American Indians*. New York: Harper & Row, 1977.

Thomson, George. *Aeschylus and Athens: A Study in the Social Origins of Drama*. London: Lawrence and Wishart, 1973.

Tiedemann, Arthur E. *An Introduction to Japanese Civilization*. New York: Columbia University Press, 1974.

Woodman, Tony, and David West, eds. *Poetry and Politics in the Age of Augustus*. New York: Cambridge University Press, 1984.

SEE ALSO: Aeschylus; Aristophanes; Aristotle; Augustus; Ball game, Mesoamerican; Britain; Catullus; Chandragupta Maurya; China; Cleon of Athens; Egypt, Pharaonic; Euripides; Eusebius of Caesarea; Greece, Classical; Greece, Hellenistic and Roman; Homer; Horace; India; Japan; *Mahābhārata*; Menander (playwright); Olympic Games; Ovid; Peloponnesian War; Persia; Petronius Arbiter; Pindar; Plautus; *Rāmāyaṇa*; Rome, Imperial; Seneca the Younger; Socrates; Sophocles; Spartacus; Terence; Theodosius the Great; Thespis; Vergil.

—*Patrick Adcock*

TECHNOLOGY

Technology is knowledge applied to achieve a goal. Technology consists both of tools and the use of tools, from the smallest devices such as tweezers to enormous construction cranes. Technology encompasses every facet of human existence: How people feed, clothe, house, and protect themselves all depend on the use of technology. Technologies reflect the resources available and the problems people confront in the environment in which they live. For example, in ancient times, cultures such as the Chavín de Huántar of South America that developed in areas where ores such as copper or gold were readily available became skilled at working with metals, while cultures with other resources may have become skilled at woodworking, pottery, or weaving. The Chinese had access to a fine quality kaolin, a type of clay, and developed porcelain; the Harappāns of the Indus River region lived where cotton grew naturally and became proficient weavers.

Although the first uses of technology undoubtedly involved basic survival—tools used for hunting, for example, or digging sticks and irrigation systems for farming—as civilizations evolved, ancient engineers began to use technology to make life easier for humanity. City sewer systems, public baths and water supply systems, central heating in houses, and other mundane aspects of urban infrastructure were common in many parts of the ancient world. At the same time, many of the earliest examples of engineering (applied technology) involved sacred spaces and religious practices: tombs and temples. Before people established permanent settlements and made the transition from hunting and gathering to farming, they began burying their dead and building religious structures. Architects also developed public spaces for recreation, entertainment, and trade: the ball courts of the Olmecs of Central America, the theaters of the Greeks and Romans, and the central market spaces found in towns and cities around the world.

TOOLS AND APPLICATIONS

Ancient peoples used the tools they devised to construct an impressive variety of temples, palaces, cities, roads, irrigation systems, dams, and bridges even before they developed systems of written language and permanent records. Although the hand tools they employed seem simple by modern standards—axes, rollers, levers, chisels, and so on—artisans had both time and their societies' support for their efforts. The origins of the block and tackle, a device that allows a person to easily lift and move objects weighing more than his or her own body weight, is lost in antiquity, but its use was known in a wide variety of cultures: The Egyptians, Sumerians, Romans, and others all used it. Similarly, although early engineers may not have been able to articulate the laws of physics that would explain how a lever works, they nonetheless understood how to use levers effectively to move blocks of stone weighing 30 tons (27 metric tons) or more. In a few cases, such as with the Egyptians who left highly detailed paintings in tombs, there are actual illustrations that show precisely how the engineering work was completed.

The levels of technological complexity varied widely throughout the ancient world, as well as within individual societies. Not all cultures developed the same tools, nor did they always recognize the full potential of devices they did possess. The Greek engineer Heron reportedly invented complex water clocks, rudimentary steam engines, and other devices in the third century B.C.E. but never turned them into anything other than clever novelties. The one exception was a portable water pump used for fire fighting, a design that remained in use until replaced by steam pumps in the nineteenth century C.E.

Some scholars have suggested that one reason many technological devices never became widely disseminated was the lack of machine tools and the ability to make parts to standard specifications. More likely, in a time when labor was cheap and slavery was universal, most people saw no need to mechanize what could be done just as cheaply using human labor. The Romans, for example, did use some highly complex devices in specific settings. An odometer, for example, that had a complicated set of gears was developed for use in measuring distance. Roman engineers used it in laying out military encampments, designing roads and aqueducts, and in other settings in which a precise measurement of distance was necessary.

WARFARE AND TECHNOLOGY

At the same time, many cultures designed and used highly complex machines for use in warfare. Beginning with the Sumerians during the second millennia B.C.E., armies built large siege towers and catapults to use in attacking enemy fortifications. Others, such as the Scythians, a nomadic people who lived in what is now Ukraine during the first millennia B.C.E., perfected small weapons suitable for use by a light, highly mobile cavalry. The Scythians' reputation as skilled bowmen spread across the ancient world. They used compound bows formed from laminates of wood, horn, and metal. The bows were small but powerful, allowing the Scythians to shoot bronze-tipped arrows with deadly accuracy.

THE WHEEL AND TRANSPORT

Peoples native to the Americas constructed elaborate stone pyramids and buildings, had record-keeping systems and sophisticated calendars, but apparently never used the wheel as anything other than an amusing toy despite being linked by a trade network that connected much of the Americas. Wheeled toys have been found in Mesoamerican archaeological digs, but no evidence exists of full-size wheeled vehicles. Trade goods were moved by human porters or, in South America, on the backs of pack animals such as llamas.

Other cultures invented carts and wagons to transport materials, which in turn may have encouraged the development of roads and highways to connect cities, although it is impossible to say which came first. Long before the Romans built the roads that linked their empire, the Persians constructed the Royal Road, 1,700 miles (2,735 kilometers) of highway linking Sardis in what is today western Turkey to Susa in the center of the Persian Empire. Transport between different regions of the ancient world was slow by modern standards, with caravans often being limited to the average distance a person could walk in one day, but goods did move thousands of miles. By the first century C.E., for example, Roman merchants sold silk fabric woven in China.

Even with communication and trade occurring across vast distances, innovations in one region did not always move quickly to another. The Chinese, for example, are credited with inventing the wheelbarrow well before the year 1 C.E., yet this commonsense device did not appear in Europe until a thousand years later. In the case of the wheelbarrow, the merchants who saw it probably considered it not worth mentioning. In other cases, such as weaving silk or manufacturing fine porcelain or jewelry, governments guarded the knowledge behind the technology as state secrets in an attempt to protect a trade monopoly.

IRRIGATION

In agriculture, farmers in Asia, Africa, and the Americas developed sophisticated irrigation systems. The ancient Egyptians' diversion of water from the Nile River is well known, but Maya in Mesoamerica, the Chinese in Asia, and other peoples also built canals and dams for irrigating their crops. As irrigation allowed more land to be culti-

vated, populations grew, and cities evolved. Irrigation systems may have begun as simple ditches, but by 1000 B.C.E., elaborate canal networks existed in Mesopotamia, China, South America, and elsewhere. In South America, China, and Southeast Asia, farmers also terraced mountainous hillsides to increase the amount of arable land.

BUILDINGS

As populations grew, massive engineering projects were undertaken in Africa, Asia, Asia Minor, Europe, and the Americas. Materials used for construction ranged from sun-dried brick, as in the ziggurats of Sumer in Asia Minor, to the massive stones found in the megaliths of Europe and the pyramids and temples of Egypt and Mesoamerica. Many of the engineering works constructed by the ancients remain marvels today, including Stonehenge in Great Britain and the pyramids at Giza in Egypt.

There is little mystery as to how ancient civilizations completed these large building projects. Bronze Age builders did not need mechanized equipment, nor did the Greeks and Romans of the Iron Age, because they enjoyed an abundant supply of both labor and time. In some cases, labor may have been supplied by slaves or prisoners. In others, the work was done by free citizens who provided labor as a form of taxes or out of a sense of religious obligation. This may have been especially true for structures such as Stonehenge, a megalithic circle of standing stones located in southern England. Although its precise significance to its builders is unknown, scholars agree construction took place over hundreds of years beginning about 3100 B.C.E. Moving stones weighing 30 tons (27 metric tons) or more over 100 miles (161 kilometers) using only hand tools and human muscle remains an impressive feat, but more for the organizational abilities of the builders than for the actual physical work when progress is measured in decades or centuries. Scientists and engineers have demonstrated that it is actually a comparatively simple matter to position massive stones using simple tools such as levers and wood cribbing.

Megaliths similar to Stonehenge—circles and lines of standing stones—are found throughout Europe. Their origins remain shrouded in mystery. The builders left no written records, and artifacts found with the megaliths have yielded few clues. Although traces of villages have been found relatively close to European megaliths, the archaeological record provides little information on the lifestyles or religious beliefs of the people during the time period in which the megaliths were raised. Based on the mortise and tenon joints connecting the capstones with the uprights, archaeologists have concluded that the builders of Stonehenge were people used to working with wood. The builders of Stonehenge were not the only early engineers to transfer principles of wood construction to building with stone: An examination of Greek temples built a thousand years after Stonehenge, for example, reveals that the Greeks also applied wood construction techniques to stone.

INDUS RIVER AND SUMERIAN CITIES

In contrast with the enigmas surrounding Europe's standing stones, archaeological sites in Asia and the Americas have provided a great deal of information about ancient civilizations and their technologies. In the Indus River Valley of what is modern-day Pakistan, for example, scientists have been able to trace the evolution of the Harappān culture from its origins as small farming villages in approximately 2500 B.C.E. to an empire with cities of 40,000 persons or more five hundred years later. Harappān engineers designed cities built of both fired and sun-dried brick on mounds elevated well above flood levels of the Indus and its tributaries. For the city of Harappā, from which the culture takes its name, builders protected the base of the city with a 45-foot-thick (14-meter-thick) brick embankment. Although Harappān cities included large public buildings, they did not indulge in the public ornamentation or elaborate statuary characteristic of the Sumerian cities of the same time period along the Tigris and Euphrates Rivers of Asia Minor in what is now the country of Iraq. Building facades were austere, and the interiors simple.

Sumerians embellished the facades of buildings in the city of Ur and elsewhere with colorful mosaics and other decorative elements. Builders constructed the structures from sun-dried brick but pressed cone-shaped glazed tiles into the exterior bricks while they were still soft. The tiles both presented a colorful appearance and protected the sun-dried brick from the occasional rains that fell in the Fertile Crescent. The region's climate is naturally arid; only the extensive irrigation systems that directed the rivers' waters into farmers' fields made agriculture possible.

Sumerian cities apparently grew unplanned as maps of the ancient city of Ur and other archaeological sites present a bewildering maze of streets and alleys. The same was not true of Harappān cities, in which streets formed neat grids. In addition, one particularly intriguing aspect of Harappān cities is the municipal infrastructure: The Harappān people apparently placed a high value on cleanliness. Individual homes had bathrooms that often included toilets that drained into a city sewer system, an impressive feat of city planning that predated Roman engineering by two thousand years. The Harappāns also designed a system for city trash collection, an innovation unknown in many other societies.

CHAVÍN CULTURE

At the same time that Harappān society began to decline, new civilizations emerged in the Americas. In South America, in what is now Peru, farmers began constructing irrigation canals to expand the area of cultivated land near rivers. Villages grew into cities. Temple mounds appeared, topped first by simple buildings constructed of adobe brick and later by more elaborate stone structures. About 1500 B.C.E., architectural styles changed to reflect the spread of a new religious cult. Just as in Europe where construction of megaliths stretched over centuries, archaeologists believe the 50-foot-high (15-meter-high) temple at Chavín de Huántar in Peru took several hundred years to complete. The building, constructed from massive stone blocks, was embellished with relief carvings portraying battle scenes as well as colossal statues of supernatural beings. Just as the builders of Stonehenge used methods developed for use with wood, so did the builders at Chavín de Huántar. Ceilings are flat, with stone being used as beams. The stone work is cantilevered over hallways, and ventilation shafts are chiseled through the stone walls.

Although the Chavín culture eventually declined, it had a lasting impact on the South and Central American societies that followed, such as the Olmecs. Olmec temples also used massive stone blocks, and, like the Chavín, relied on cantilevering to form passageways. Neither society ever perfected a building technique now taken for granted: the arch.

THE ARCH AND CONCRETE

Before the discovery of the true arch, builders relied on corbeling to create passageways or rooms with rounded ceilings. In corbeling, each layer of stone is cantilevered over the edge of the layer below until the final layer of stones meets at the top. Compared to arches, corbels are unstable and require more building materials. In a true arch, the stones are carefully fitted to push against each other so that the force of the weight of the material above the arch is directed through the arch and into the piers supporting it. In a corbel, the weight of the material above each stone is pushing straight down on it. In an arch, the forces are directed to the sides.

The combination of the arch and the discovery of concrete allowed the Romans to build on a massive scale. Many cultures developed mortar to help secure stone work. The Olmecs, for example, used an adobe (clay) mortar to join the large stone blocks in temple pyramids, but the Romans were the first to fully exploit cement and concrete. They went beyond using mortar to join masonry blocks and clay bricks to using cement as a building medium in itself. Cement is a mixture of sand, lime, and water. The Romans were fortunate to have an abundant supply of a volcanic sand that yielded a

An aqueduct built by the Romans still stands in Segovia, Spain. (Digital Stock)

superb cement. When aggregate (small rocks, or gravel) is added to cement, the result is concrete. The Romans' use of arches and cast concrete made possible construction of numerous public works projects, particularly aqueducts and sewer systems, as well as domed buildings such as the Pantheon, which still stand today.

GREAT WALL OF CHINA

The Great Wall of China provides one exception to the general rule that many massive construction projects took decades to complete. Sections of the Great Wall had been completed under previous Chinese rulers when Shi Huangdi ordered construction that would tie the wall into one continuous structure 2,600 miles (4,183 kilometers) long. The Great Wall consists of two parallel rock walls faced with brick with the space between filled with clay and dirt. Forty-foot-high (12-meter-high) guard towers are spaced several hundred yards apart, allegedly at a distance that ensured that no attacker would ever be out of range of archers stationed in the towers. Completion of the Great Wall reportedly took only seven years, although no written records remain to either verify that claim or to explain how the emperor's engineers organized the work. However, some recent scholars believe that the Great Wall created by Shi Huangdi is not the Great Wall that is still standing. The first emperor's wall probably was destroyed, and the extant wall was created during the Ming Dynasty. In addition to the Great Wall, Shi Huangdi's reign was characterized by massive construction projects. During this same time period, a 20-mile (32-kilometer) barge canal linking two rivers in the Yangzte Valley was completed. The canal is still in use more than two thousand years later.

METALLURGY

Ancient civilizations did not confine their use of technology to building projects. Significant innovations occurred in ceramics, weaving, metallurgy, and other fields. Many different cultures learned to work with metals. As with many technological innovations, metalworking appeared in many different regions of the world at about the same time. Often the presence of float copper (pure copper in a malleable form) may have encouraged artisans to work with the metal.

In North America, for example, archaeologists have traced copper artifacts found as far south as the Yucatán Peninsula to copper ore originating in the Lake Superior region. The ore was so pure that it did not require smelting. Pure float copper is comparatively rare, however. More commonly copper is found in ore with other elements. In some cases, the secret to extracting copper from ore may have been found by accident. In ancient Egypt, for example, copper was usually found as an element in semiprecious stones such as malachite. Historians of technology speculate that the Egyptians may have learned to extract copper from ore accidentally while attempting to glaze jewelry. Malachite, a green carbonate of copper, was widely used for beads and other jewelry, and ground malachite was a common cosmetic.

Copper is one of the two metals that can make up bronze. The other most commonly used ore is tin, although some metalsmiths used arsenic. By 4500 B.C.E., cultures in the Balkans, Armenia, Thailand, and China had learned to smelt bronze. Metalsmiths in the Americas discovered bronze slightly later than their counterparts in Asia, Europe, and Africa, but by 1500 B.C.E., the Chavín metalsmiths were also working with bronze. As with many new materials, bronze was initially seen as a luxury item and used primarily in decorative ornaments—brooches, earrings, and so on—but as it became more common, it began to be used for weapons, dishes, and other utilitarian items. Glass was also used to make jewelry and other ornaments before being formed into drinking cups or plates, just as iron would appear first as jewelry and later as more practical objects.

Still, bronze never became a material that every person could possess. Many common people went straight from having flint knives to owning iron. Float copper was rare, mining and smelting copper ore was dangerous, and some bronze production processes created highly toxic arsenic fumes. Many smiths became crippled as a result of their work, which may be why the smiths portrayed in the myths from ancient societies, such as the Greek god Hephaestus, are often described as deformed or hunchbacked. The Egyptians used convict labor at their bronze foundries, just as the Romans and other cultures later relied on slaves to mine hazardous materials. The Romans, for example, recognized the flame-retardant properties of asbestos but also realized exposure to its dust caused lung damage. Slaves worked the Roman asbestos mines.

In Europe, Asia, and Africa, the use of iron spread much more quickly than the use of bronze, as once the secrets to smelting the metal were known, bog iron proved much easier to obtain than copper. Small ironworks became common in societies in southern Africa in the regions now occupied by the nations of Zimbabwe, Mozambique, and Zambia as well as throughout Europe and Asia. Still, although metalsmiths in the ancient world learned to work with iron, they were unable to raise the temperature of the metal high enough to melt it for casting. The harder a metal, generally the higher its melting point. Gold melts at a comparatively low temperature so metalsmiths learned early to cast gold ornaments. Iron requires much higher temperatures. All the iron used in ancient societies was wrought iron forged by repeatedly heating, being beaten with a hammer to shape it, and then cooled.

ADDITIONAL RESOURCES

DeCamp, L. Sprague. *The Ancient Engineers.* New York: Ballantine, 1960.

Hodges, Henry. *Technology in the Ancient World.* New York: Barnes and Noble Books, 1992.

Pacey, Arnold. *Technology in World Civilization.* Cambridge, Mass.: MIT Press, 1990.

SEE ALSO: Africa, East and South; Chavín de Huántar; China; Copper Belt; Egypt, Prepharaonic; Great Wall of China; Greece, Classical; Indus River civilization; Maya; Olmecs; Persia; Pyramids and the Sphinx; Rome, Imperial; Shi Huangdi; Stonehenge; Sumerians; Weapons and warfare.

—*Nancy Farm Mannikko*

TRADE AND COMMERCE

For many centuries, agriculture was the primary means of living for early civilizations. The earliest civilizations had little contact with one another, and trade and commerce were limited. Ultimately, these independent civilizations developed specialties that took advantage of their natural resources or the technical skills of their people, and eventually, the various civilizations began to exchange ideas, skills, and commodities.

Exchanges of commodities were facilitated by trade routes. Initially, these trade routes were quite short, often from one village to the next. Whether over water or land, trade routes reflected the conditions and attitudes of the times. A road, for example, had to interact closely and carefully with the terrain and communities through which it passed, with changing vehicle technology, and with the various aptitudes and frailties of the individual drivers and riders. Harbors had to be located in places to which consumers or merchants want to have merchandise shipped. Eventually, municipalities with popular harbors discovered that a tax could be imposed on ships entering the harbor, so taxes and tariffs came into being.

The existence of trade routes and the related commerce led first to increased barter between cultures, then to the need for monetary exchange, and later to the development of large businesses (caravans and fleets) that were devoted to international trade. These large businesses, in turn, led to the need for greater accountability. The entire profession of accounting developed along with the expansion of trade on the various trade routes. For example, a small business with a single owner did not need an elaborate accounting system; however, a large caravan, ship, or fleet, probably financed by someone other than the traveler, had to be able to provide a proper accounting of all monies invested and profits earned. Some of the accounting documents from trade caravans and voyages—in the form of clay, papyrus, and paper—have survived to the present day. It is through those accounting records that historians have been able to learn the details of the early trade routes.

Many archaeologists believe that the entire concept of writing developed around 8000 B.C.E. along with accounting and trade. There was no need for writing until the problem arose of dealing with merchants situated long distances away. This led to a need for an internal control system so that a consignor could notify a consignee of what merchandise had been placed aboard a ship or on a caravan. These documents, originally in the form of baked clay, ultimately evolved into writing as notations for goods became standardized. These earliest clay symbols of trade goods were tokens, or counters, and the later form that started in about 3100 B.C.E. were clay tablets. It is this later form that is most often associated with writing, but the earlier tokens were used for similar purposes.

The spread of the Arabic numbering system was also a result of trade routes. The Romans used what is known today as Roman numerals, but these were somewhat limiting for trade purposes because they could not be added or subtracted in a columnar manner. Therefore, Arabic numerals quickly replaced the Roman numerals once they were introduced by traders into Europe. Arabic numerals actually originated in India, but the trade route passed through Arabia, so the Europeans thought that the new numbering system came from Arabia, and the name stuck.

THE TIGRIS-EUPHRATES VALLEY

From their beginnings more than 7,000 years ago, the Chaldean-Babylonian, Assyrian, and Sumerian civilizations produced some of the earliest surviving business records. Various types of small industries and service businesses and extensive trade soon developed both within and outside the Mesopotamian valley. Banks existed in ancient Sumer and Babylonia, and the concept of credit was well known. The cities of Babylon and Nineveh were known as the queens of commerce. Formal legal codes made the recording of business transactions mandatory. The best known legal code, that of Hammurabi (r. 1792-1750 B.C.E.), required agents selling goods for a merchant to give the merchant a sealed memorandum listing prices. If this was not done, the agreement was unenforceable. Therefore, even the smallest of transactions were put in writing. As a result, Babylonians became obsessive bookkeepers. The scribe, the predecessor of today's accountant, was an indispensable part of society.

Babylonian scribes were also sent to distant parts of the kingdom to collect taxes for the royal treasury. The taxes were usually paid in the form of cattle, cereals, or other commodities. The same scribes then saw to it that the tax payments were sold or used by the royal family. There are also examples of royal audits of the scribes' work.

EARLY CHINESE COMMERCE

Governments contributed to the success of early Chinese commerce through the development of financial administration and accountability. During the Xia (c. 2100-1600 B.C.E.) and Shang (1600-1066 B.C.E.) Dynasties, money was being coined, and a centralized banking system was in use. A bureau of currency and produce exchange acted as a sort of buffer in the commodity markets to provide loans and purchase unsalable goods. These unsalable goods were stored in government granaries until needed for relief purposes. By the time of the Zhou Dynasty (1066-256 B.C.E.), the Chinese systems of budgeting and audit were the best in the world.

TRADE ROUTES

Early trade routes, often nothing more than walking trails, were short in length, connecting one tribe or clan to another. Eventually, as donkeys and camels were domesticated, the trade routes lengthened. Virtually all civilizations had trade routes of some type. In some places, such as North America, beasts of burden were not available, thus limiting the length of trade routes and the extent of trade.

One of the earliest civilizations to develop primarily because of a trade route (rather than agriculture) was on the Greek island of Crete in about 2600 B.C.E. The people of Crete, known as Minoans, traded actively with peoples in the Middle East, Sicily, and continental Greece. Crete was ideally located in the middle of an important sea route. Because of trade, the culture of Greece gradually spread to other lands.

The earliest major trade routes were developed by seafaring peoples. As early as 2750 B.C.E., the Egyptians were sailing their papyrus boats in search of spices, precious stones, and other valuables. Starting in the seventh century B.C.E., Phoenician merchant seamen were searching the Mediterranean Sea, the Atlantic Ocean, and the African coast for opportunities to increase their vast economic empire. Through both military victories and trading expeditions, the ancient Greeks expanded trade to the British Isles and India.

When Mycenaean society broke up around 1100 B.C.E., the commercial routes that had linked mainland Greece with the rest of the Mediterranean were cut. After a period of prolonged recovery, the Greeks began colonizing the shore regions of the Mediterranean and Black Seas. Greeks founded settlements in such diverse areas as present-day France, India, Italy, Libya, Portugal, and Turkey. This colonization activity (especially from 750-550 B.C.E.) was propelled by a need for more living space for a rapidly expanding population and the need for new markets. The colonies were able to supply Greece with wheat, meat, dried fish, hides, wool, timber, and basic metals in exchange for mainland finished products such as olive oil and wine.

The Greeks also traded with the peoples of the Scandinavian countries, as evidenced by the Greek coinage found in pre-Viking sites in Norway, Sweden, Finland, and Denmark. Although Greek coinage has been found in far-flung locations, it is actually Greek pottery that serves as the best evidence of the movements of the ancient Greeks and the distribution of their trade around the Mediterranean and Black Sea basins. Central and northern Italian Etruscan cemeteries have been particularly informative as their tombs have produced thousands of Greek vases. Alternatively, Etruscan goods have rarely been unearthed at Greek sites, which means that Etruria must have traded lump iron, lead, and bronze in exchange for the Greek pottery. Initially, Corinth dominated the pottery trade, but by 525 B.C.E., Athens had established a monopoly in luxury pottery–particularly Attic Black Figures. By 300 B.C.E., Greek manufactured goods were freely circulating to North Africa, Spain, the Rhone Valley, the Balkans, and as far east as India and as far north as Sweden.

Merchants of the Roman Empire played an important role in expanding the empire's realm. Roman merchants carried on trade with what was then all of the known (Western) world. After the fall of the Western Roman Empire, roads were completed and extended across the Alps and into Spain, France, and Germany. Water routes also played a major role in European trading. Early merchants shipped goods on the Seine, Danube, Volga, Don, and Rhine Rivers. Seaports such as Bordeaux and Nantes on the Atlantic coast developed to trade French wine, grain, and honey to Britain, which offered metals for trading. Spain offered oil and lead to complete the Atlantic trading. The Atlantic seaports also offered a haven for the occasional Scandinavian ship packed with ivory trade goods. These European routes continued to be important through medieval times.

Another trade route that traversed Europe was sometimes known as the Amber Road. Extending from amber's source at the Baltic Sea at Jutland, due south to the Alps, over the Brenner Pass into Italy, or east along the Danube River, the Amber Road served as a path over which semiprecious amber, often used in jewelry, was shipped. Despite the name of the route, amber was usually only a secondary trade item, falling behind tin, silver, and marble, until demand rose under the influence of the Greeks. Even before land routes, amber was a common trade commodity. For example, the Phoenicians had traded amber with Britain and on the western coast of Spain.

AFRICAN TRADE

Europe was linked to African trade via the Saharan trade routes. The Saharan trade extended from the sub-Saharan West African kingdoms across the Sahara desert and on to Europe. In fact, the lifeblood of the Ghana empire, located between the upper Niger and Senegal Rivers, just below the Sahara, was trade. Merchants carrying foodstuffs to Ghana would trade them for locally produced goods such as cotton cloth, metal ornaments, leather goods, and the most important commodity of all, gold. Koumbi was the trade center and capital of the Ghana empire. Even though gold was in great supply, there was an inadequacy of salt. The present-day regions of Morocco and Algeria, however, had plenty of salt resources. Not surprisingly, a gold-salt trade developed, and the Arab desert merchants flourished. That trade route extended from the northern city of Sidjilmassa (near the present-day Moroccan-Algerian border), through the salt-rich village of Taghaza, through the Sahara and finally to the gold region of the Ghana empire near the Senegal River. The king of Ghana not only profited from trading but also by means of taxes imposed on traders who used his trade routes. Later, in the Middle Ages, a second major gold-salt route passed through Tunis, Cairo, and ended in Egypt's interior.

Merchants transported more than commodities along the routes across the Sahara. Islam reached West Africa through the Arab merchants on the Saharan caravan routes. During the Ghana empire, Arab merchants brought the Qur'ān and the written Arabic language to the traditionally oral cultures in West Africa. Some West African rulers, who understood the importance of trade to their region, converted to Islam to curry favor with the Arab traders.

For many years, Timbuktu, a city in Mali at a bed in the Niger River, was the center of sub-Saharan African trade. Salt was mined in the desert and carried to Timbuktu for transport on the river to distant locales. The city's wealth eventually made it a great religious and educational site, but it began to decline with the coming of the Portuguese. Actually, Timbuktu is an anomaly in sub-Saharan Africa in that it is one of the few sites of major trade. The people south of the Sahara rarely had any contact with the rest of the world. Even the few rivers that flow from sub-Saharan Africa could not be used as trade routes because of the many high waterfalls along the way. Also, the sub-Saharan Africans seemed to have a fear of venturing out into the ocean, so large seaports did not develop. Therefore, much of Africa, like North America, never developed extensive trade

These Phoenician traders and their camels carry bundles of goods across the sands. Until 535 B.C.E. when Phoenicia became part of the Persian Empire, it was known for trading items such as cedar, purple-dyed cloth, and glass. (North Wind Picture Archives)

routes. Village-to-village was the extent of most routes.

The Egyptians were the real trade merchants of ancient Africa. The most important extensive trade route, and the earliest, was the Nile River, which was navigable throughout the length of the country. Similarly, the nearby Red Sea gave access to other parts of Africa and the Far East, and the Mediterranean Sea gave the Egyptians access to countries in and around that area. The Egyptians imported timber from Syria and Lebanon; copper came from Cyprus, and tin from Asia and Europe. Other items were imported from Crete and Greece. In return, Egypt exported yarn, fine linen cloth, glass bottles, vases, and paper. Most records of the Greek and Roman empires that have survived to the present day are written on Egyptian paper. Egyptian science and technology were also exported, primarily to Europe. Egyptian inventions that went to Europe include the potter's wheel, the lock, weaver's looms, pulleys, pumps, bellows, siphons, and sluice gates.

THE SPICE TRADE

The trading of spices and herbs has ancient origins and was of great cultural and economic significance. Spices such as cinnamon and ginger have been traded for thousands of years. Cinnamon has been an important trade commodity in the Middle East since at least 2000 B.C.E. Even earlier, southern Arabia was a trading center for frankincense, myrrh, and other resins and gums. Although there were overland routes, it was the sea trade that was the most important in the spice trade. Arabians were making long sea voyages long before the common era, and the Chinese traded throughout the Spice Islands (East Indies). Ceylon (now Sri Lanka) was a major trading point.

Eventually, India partially displaced the Arab spice trade with Europe. By 80 B.C.E., Alexandria, Egypt, was the greatest commercial center in the world, primarily because of its role as a middleman in the spice trade between India and Europe. The spice trade led to the development of major trading cities in Europe. The Indian spice trade

with Europe dwindled by 600 C.E., whereas the Arab trade endured through the Middle Ages.

Alexandria was not the first trading center in Egypt. As early as 1400 B.C.E., the entire Nile River valley was a trading center. Goods such as gold, clothing, jewels, ivory, leopard skins, giraffe tails, and wood floated down the Nile then were transferred to caravans that traversed the desert regions in all directions. At this time, the Egyptians used donkeys for the transport of goods; horses were brought to Egypt sometime between 1539 and 1295 B.C.E. The domesticated camel was not used as a pack animal in Egypt until after 500 B.C.E.

It should be noted that some trade routes of the spice trade and many other trade routes were used by military regimes on their way to the Crusades. Similarly, the Persian Royal Road, stretching 1,700 miles (2,735 kilometers) from Susa, the ancient capital of Persia, to the Aegean Sea was used by Alexander the Great in his invasion and conquest of the Persian Empire.

THE FRANKINCENSE TRAIL

One of the least well-known trading routes is called the Frankincense Trail. For 2,400 years (from about 2000 B.C.E. to 400 C.E.), large caravans snaked across the southern tip of the Arabian peninsula bearing the precious, fragrant resin from spindly frankincense trees, which grow only in the present-day countries of Oman and Yemen. Frankincense burns well because of its natural oil content and also was used for medicinal purposes. The Frankincense Trail led from Qana (Bir 'Ali) in southern Arabia to Gaza in Palestine, running inland roughly parallel to the Red Sea and covering a total distance of more than 2,000 miles (3,200 kilometers). Myrrh was a similar product, and both were considered as valuable as gold. Supposedly not a temple or wealthy home in Babylon, Egypt, Greece, Jerusalem, or Rome did not require these precious resins. The Romans reportedly kept the prices of frankincense at a high level by using large amounts in cremations.

Those frankincense trade routes and the fortified cities that guarded them have long since disappeared beneath the sands of Oman and Yemen. However, detailed radar topographic maps of the region taken by the space shuttle reveal faint traces of camel caravan trails. Combining this technology with Islamic, biblical, and classical references to the trade caravans led to the discovery of several major sites worthy of excavation. The mysteries of the Frankincense Trail may soon be uncovered with planned excavations at such sites as the recently discovered lost city of Ubar in Yemen, a frankincense hub mentioned in the Bible. Other forts may also be found because the ancient Roman historian Pliny the Elder recorded that there were eight fortresses on the Frankincense Trail. Pliny also stated that control of the frankincense trade had made the south Arabians the richest people on earth. Although the frankincense trade soon began to decline, business was sufficient to maintain the wealth of the southern Arabians until at least 600 C.E.

SILK ROAD

The eastern and western sides of the Asian continent are connected by a series of trade routes known as the Silk Road. The western portion developed earlier than the eastern part because of the development of Persia and Syria as trading centers. Also, the western portion had terrain that was easier to negotiate than did the eastern portion of the continent. In addition, the warring Chinese states kept trade from prospering until about 200 B.C.E. It was a search for military alliances that contributed to the development of the Silk Road in about 138 B.C.E.

The term "Silk Road" is misleading in that there is no single route. The area across Central Asia developed several branches that passed through various oases. Branches led south to India and a northern route led to the Caspian and Black Seas and ended at Byzantium (now Istanbul). Because the northern route was considered more dangerous and expensive to traverse, much of the silk trade traveled by the middle route, which passed through the Persian Gulf and Euphrates Valley and ended in such cities as Damascus. Silk was not the only merchandise carried

on the route. Many other commodities were also traded, including ivory, gold, and exotic plants and animals. However, it was silk that seemed the most exotic to Europeans, and that name was applied to the route.

The development of the Silk Road caused problems for the Han rulers of China because of the need for policing the road. Bandits soon learned of the rich merchants plying their trade along the road, and many areas in Central Asia provided easy terrain to assist in the plunder of the caravans. As a result, caravans needed their own defense forces, which added to the cost of the goods being shipped. Portions of the Great Wall of China were reportedly built to protect sections of the Silk Road from plunderers.

The high cost of doing business along the Silk Road and most other trade routes meant that a single merchant was unable to afford to finance not only inventory but also the cost of outfitting and protecting the caravan. As a result, the concept of business partnerships developed. Multiple owners could more easily finance large caravans than could a single merchant. The existence of multiple owners increased the need for accountability. As a result, scribes and other early accountants traveled with the caravans to ensure that all revenues were properly recorded for the benefit of the partners hundreds of miles away.

Few merchants actually traversed the entire Silk Road from east to west. Instead, most simply covered part of the journey and then sold their wares after traveling perhaps less than a couple hundred miles. As a result, goods moved slowly across Asia because they changed hands many times. The various settlements along the road reflected the trade passing through the region. As a result, silk and other exotic commodities from distant areas were common, even in small villages.

Interestingly, many scholars believe that silk and other commodities were not the most important things carried along the Silk Road. Religion, in the form of Buddhism, followed the same route from India to eastern China. Buddhist artwork followed as early as the second century C.E. By the seventh century, the importance of the Silk Road diminished because of the development of the Sea Silk Route (sometimes called the southern silk route). The Sea Silk Route and most other sea routes were generally superior to land routes because land travel was more time-consuming and dangerous because of attacks from bandits and nomadic tribes. Although piracy could be a problem on the seas, it was less of a problem than bandits. Ultimately, the Silk Road became more important for communication purposes than for trade purposes. The Sea Silk Route led from China around the southern tip of India, up the Red Sea, and then overland to the Nile and northern Egypt.

Although the Silk Road was arguably the most important Asian trade route, there were also many others of national and regional significance, including the Ambassador's Road, the Burma Road, the Royal Road, the Lower Royal Road, the King's Highway (which started in Egypt), the Eurasian Steppe Route, and various Russian river routes. By the year 200 C.E., there were also routes from India to western Indonesia and other spots in Southeast Asia.

SEA ROUTES TO POLYNESIA

Around 2500 B.C.E., Southeast Asians began to migrate throughout the Pacific. Over the next three thousand years, they had colonized every habitable island in a huge triangle bound by Hawaii on the north, New Zealand on the southwest, and Easter Island to the east. Sturdy 100-foot-long (30-meter) outrigger canoes were apparently used to carry people and trading items across rough seas from island to island.

The maritime skills of the ancient natives of South America also led to trade opportunities with Pacific Islanders. Coconuts were among the first trade goods that crossed portions of the Pacific. Coconut palms originated in South America but are widely known on various Pacific Islands, such as Cocos Island, which is about 300 miles (480 kilometers) off the coast of Costa Rica. Cocos Island is directly on the sea route that would connect Guatemala with Ecuador and Peru, and trade with this island was probably a by-product of sea trade between these countries. The ancient Peruvians

built buoyant seaworthy rafts of balsa wood. The secret of the success of such rafts was their ability to rise with any threatening sea, thus staying on top of the dangerous water that might have broken most other small craft. Estimates are that such craft could sail for 4,000 miles (6,440 kilometers) or more (based on the recreation in 1947 by anthropologist Thor Heyerdahl).

TRADE ROUTES IN THE AMERICAS

Trade routes in the Americas were rare and usually short. The lack of beasts of burden in North America meant that trade goods had to be carried by humans. Therefore, most trade was between villages fairly close together. There were some exceptions to this generalization, such as the Turquoise Road of the Southwestern United States. Turquoise mined at a huge underground mine near present-day Santa Fe, New Mexico, was the basis of a large civilization that grew as an extensive complex of towns sometime after 600 C.E. Major trade took place with customers in Mexico over the Turquoise Road, which stretched over the Sierra Madres and extended into the central valley of Mexico. This trade made the Anasazi civilization a wealthy one. The turquoise was valued both as a personal gem and for religious purposes.

Still farther south, in southern Mexico, the Maya civilization had extensive trade routes, not only within their own region but also to outside locales as well. In southern Mexico, the two oceans are quite close together, so some of the Maya trade routes connected the Atlantic to the Pacific coast. The Maya originated about 1000 B.C.E. and reached their peak between 600 and 900 C.E. The various trade routes developed over this entire span. Maya society consisted of many independent states, each with a rural farming community and large urban sites built around ceremonial centers. Therefore, the trade routes were essentially links among the various states.

TRADE AND CIVILIZATION

The development of trade and commerce and the associated trade routes did much to advance the state of civilization in the ancient world. Many business practices traversed the same roads over which commodities passed, and some of those practices have continued to the present day. Similarly, conquering armies and the spread of religions also traveled the same routes.

ADDITIONAL RESOURCES

Boulnois, Luce. *The Silk Road*. Translated by Dennis Chamberlain. New York: Dutton, 1966.

Charlesworth, M. P. *Trade Routes and Commerce of the Roman Empire*. 2d ed. Cambridge, England: Cambridge University Press, 1926.

Chu, Daniel, and Elliot Skinner. *A Glorious Age in Africa: The Story of Three Great African Empires*. Trenton, N.J.: Africa World Press, 1990.

Durant, Will, and Ariel Durant. *The Story of Civilization*. 11 vols. New York: Simon & Schuster, 1935-1975.

Heyerdahl, Thor. *Sea Routes to Polynesia*. Chicago: Rand McNally, 1968.

Hopkirk, Peter. *Foreign Devils on the Silk Road*. New York: Oxford University Press, 1980.

Kranz, Rachel. *Across Asia by Land*. New York: Facts on File, 1991.

Natkiel, Richard, and Anthony Preston. *Atlas of Maritime History*. New York: Facts on File, 1986.

Parkins, Helen, and Christopher Smith, eds. *Trade, Traders, and the Ancient City*. New York: Routledge, 1998.

SEE ALSO: Africa, East and South; Africa, North; Arabia; Babylonia; Buddhism; China; Crete; Egypt, Pharaonic; Etruscans; Ghana; Great Wall of China; Greece, Classical; Greece, Mycenaean; Hammurabi's code; Han Dynasty; Hawaii; India; Islam; Maya; Phoenicia; Polynesia; Shang Dynasty; Silk Road; Southwest peoples; Sumerians; Zhou Dynasty.

—*Dale L. Flesher*

WAR AND WEAPONS

The history of war is essentially the history of humankind. While pre-Neolithic peoples probably did not spend much time analyzing war as an activity, they were certainly not a stranger to it. The bows and arrows, clubs, and other crude weapons they used for hunting animals could be, as cave art has shown, just as easily used for fighting other people. To be sure, the probable spontaneous nature of the fighting that occurred could hardly be called war—at least in the sense that historians use that term. However, as agriculture and the herding of domesticated animals began to compete with hunting and gathering as a means of obtaining sustenance, the necessity to acquire and protect property gave rise not only to permanent settlements and eventually to states but also to a more organized and definitive kind of warfare. The following is an examination of the development of war and weapons among selected civilizations that flourished between circa 2000 B.C.E. and 700 C.E.

as well as among some groups of primitive people who remained virtually pre-Neolithic until more recent times.

EGYPT

The early Egyptians were united into a state about 3100 B.C.E. by the warrior-ruler Menes, who, in the absence of a standing army, used a militia from which troops were called up as needed to defend the frontiers or to move out in campaigns to gain control of more territory. The Egyptians went to war armed with spears, bows, and battle axes as their primary weapons. Disdaining body armor in the beginning, they wielded a heavy shield of wood and bull hide. After 1500 B.C.E., the sword, along with the dagger, also became an important weapon. Armor and coats of mail were also adopted at this time.

From 1800 to 1600 B.C.E., the Egyptians were invaded by the Hyksos, from whom they copied a new style of two-wheeled chariot made of wood and open at the back. Boasting no seat, it had barely enough room for the charioteer and a combatant armed with either arrows, a spear, or a javelin. The spoked wheels were made of wood and moved freely on their axle, providing much more maneuverability than the earlier four-wheeled chariots used by the Sumerians. The speed of this vehicle, in terms of shock and of getting into battle quickly, was to change warfare dramatically.

The whole operation demanded considerable training for the horses, the charioteer, and the combatant, along with facilities for maintenance. Indeed, a kind of hierarchical camaraderie sprang up among charioteers, similar to that of the aviators of World War I, regardless of which side they fought on. The Egyptians used this form of the chariot to great advantage in expanding their empire to the eastern Mediterranean and into parts of Mesopotamia and Asia Minor.

ASSYRIA

As the Assyrians settled in northeastern Mesopotamia along the Tigris River with no natural barriers to protect them, the constant attacks from the Hittites and numerous other invaders made war pervasive in their culture. A strong, fierce people who worshiped a strong, fierce god, Ashur, Assyrians developed a military system under Tiglath-pileser I (r. c. 1115-1077 B.C.E.) based on a well-organized and trained standing army that would be unmatched until the advent of the legions of Rome. Resplendent in their conical helmets of bronze and well equipped with weapons of iron, the Assyrian army's masses of spearmen, slingmen, archers on horseback, and charioteers well versed in the use of the new two-wheeled light chariot all fought with a strikingly brutal coordination yet unseen in the ancient world. Following tactics of terror, they gave no quarter, often killing not only enemy soldiers but also great numbers of civilians in captured territories. The words of the English poet Lord Byron in his poem "The Destruction of Sennacherib" are apt: "The Assyrian came down like a wolf on the fold, / And his cohorts were gleaming in purple and gold."

Assyrian battle tactics consisted of archers firing their arrows into their enemies' formations, followed by mass chariot charges. As the situation warranted, well-trained cavalry—Assyria was the first to use cavalry in any significant way—often played a significant role in the chariot charge. Finally, large masses of spearmen advanced relentlessly in a final mopping up of what was usually by this time a bloodied and disorganized enemy force.

Although they were not the first to use siege techniques against the almost impregnable walled cities of Asia Minor, the Assyrians improved upon them dramatically, employing powerful battering rams that swung from massive frames to demolish gates and walls, along with immense movable towers from which archers could fire their arrows into the city and from which drawbridges could be lowered against breached walls to allow spearmen to enter.

Assyria was the first great military power of the Iron Age and the first nation truly based on war. Its conquests included Egypt, Syria, Palestine, the eastern part of present-day Turkey, and parts of Armenia. The empire began to disintegrate about 625 B.C.E., and with the capture and destruction of the capital Nineveh by the Medians and the Babylonians in 612 B.C.E., Assyria came to an end.

GREECE

The beginning of Greek history is generally considered to have begun with Homer's *Iliad* (c. 800 B.C.E.; English translation, 1616), the legendary story of the fall of Troy. The favorite epic of the Greeks, it served as a kind of handbook on how an individual could gain glory in war by fighting with courage and skill. The Greek people, an amalgam of various migrant groups, turned to seafaring and colonizing in an effort to make up for poor farming conditions, both of which gave them a cosmopolitan background and an understanding of other people that stood them in good stead militarily.

Of the several city-states into which Greece developed, Sparta in many ways stands out as a parallel to Assyria. Spartan society was based on the inevitability of war, with the army and the state being essentially one. At the age of seven, boys of all classes were taken from their homes and put into barracks for highly disciplined military training that was both harsh and exhaustive.

The result was a professional army that with its red coats, oiled hair, and polished weapons was a most frightening sight to any enemy. By 600 B.C.E., Sparta was the strongest city-state in Greece. Although the Spartans fought with the Athenians against the Persians, the growing rivalry between the two eventually resulted in the Peloponnesian War (431-404 B.C.E.), in which Sparta defeated Athens.

Instead of the expensive chariots and cavalry that could not function well on much of Greek terrain, the phalanx became the dominant fighting force. This well-trained and disciplined infantry militia, made up primarily from the middle and upper classes, was armed with spears in the right hand and shields in the left and fought as a tightly massed formation with practically no maneuverability. Battles between phalanxes required at least a semblance of level ground and were really great shoving matches in which one major effort usually forced one side to give way and leave the field in defeat. The fact that the shield was carried in the left hand caused the whole phalanx to move to the right, as soldiers sought protection from their comrades' shields. The strongest individuals were put on the right flank to counter this shifting.

Over the centuries, the use of ships for war as well as for commerce was common among those living along the Mediterranean and Aegean Seas. The Greeks, however, particularly the Athenians, developed naval warfare to a high degree with the use of the trireme—a long, narrow craft using three levels of oarsmen as well as some sails. Although boarding an enemy vessel in battle was practiced occasionally, the basic Athenian tactic was to ram the opponent with the trireme's deadly metal beak. The Athenians also used amphibious-landing tactics in their attack against Sicily in 415 B.C.E. When Athens and Sparta clashed in the Peloponnesian War, however, it was Athens' naval and military disaster at Syracuse that provided

victory for Sparta. The Athenian trireme, nevertheless, was copied widely during this and later periods by various groups vying for military advantage on the sea.

PERSIA

The rise of the Persian Empire was, if nothing else, swift. Uniting some of the remnants of the fallen Assyrian Empire, Cyrus the Great, a Persian prince, moved on a path of conquest that eventually gained control of Media, Lydia, Babylon, and Chaldea. Killed in battle against the Masagetae in 530 B.C.E., Cyrus was succeeded by his son Cambyses II, who added Egypt to the Persian Empire. At Cambyses' death, Darius the Great assumed power. After putting down some internal conflicts, Darius consolidated his empire and began plans to bring the Greek city-states under Persian control.

The Persian Empire, well-organized and deftly controlled, was the largest yet seen in the world and the most permanent—indeed an empire ready for the military genius of Darius.

The political system was based on some twenty provinces, each governed by an able and loyal official and each boasting a military garrison commanded by a general who reported directly to the king.

Like the army of Assyria, that of Persia was based on chariots, foot archers, and cavalry, the bow being the most important weapon. The goal was to disorient the enemy with the arrows from swarms of foot archers in the front and cavalry on the flanks and to follow with the main charge of the chariots. As the Romans were to do later, the Persians required military service of conquered people, thus making their forces multinational.

From 499 to 449 B.C.E., the Persians tried to bring Greece to heel in the Greco-Persian Wars. Following a number of invasions by the Persians, the Greeks, particularly the Athenians and the Spartans, managed to unite long enough to hold back the Persians and ultimately to defeat them on both land and sea at the Second Battle of Salamis (in Cyprus) in 450 B.C.E. A peace treaty was arranged in 449 B.C.E.

MACEDONIA

The Macedonians from northern Greece were generally thought of by the rest of Greece as an inferior people. Under Philip II, however, they became an innovative and dominant military power. With Philip's assassination in 336 B.C.E., his son Alexander the Great, destined to become one of the world's great military leaders, assumed power at the age of twenty and soon had control over all Greece.

Because numerous Greeks in various places still lived under Persian rule, many in Greece wanted to go to war once again against Persia. Alexander, with great confidence in his capabilities and those of his army, led an allied Greek force into Asia Minor and defeated the Persians at Granicus (334 B.C.E.) and at Issus the next year. A year later, he was in Egypt, where he founded the city of Alexandria. From there, he moved to Mesopotamia to overthrow the Persian Empire of Darius III (331 B.C.E.). His thirst for power and conquest led him through Asia to northern India (326 B.C.E.), but the weather, the terrain, and particularly the Gedrosian Desert proved too much for an army that was more interested in going home than in any further conquests. War was in Alexander's blood, and without it, he was lost in depression and alcohol, dying from a fever in 323 B.C.E. Whatever his end, his accomplishments speak for themselves.

Alexander's generalship was based on flexibility in both leadership and organization. Featuring the formidable and highly mobile base of a phalanx that could charge on the run and the speed and shock of cavalry, Alexander's army on numerous occasions was able to seize opportunities and surprise the enemy. His oblique order of attack in which his troops would fall back in one place in order to hit the enemy with superior forces in another and then to roll them up in a flanking movement became a hallmark in military theory. He followed a strict logistical system of movement and attack in which nothing was overlooked. Organized for speed, his army marched an average of 10 to 15 miles (16 to 24 kilometers) per day, with each soldier carrying 80 pounds (36 kilograms) of weight.

Like his father, Alexander was a pioneer in siege warfare, using new lighter versions of catapults and ballistae that could be carried by pack trains and expeditiously set up as needed.

INDIA

About 2000 B.C.E., Aryan invaders and Indo-European people came into the Indus Valley, which was populated by the dark-skinned Dravidians. There was enough mixture between the dominant Aryans and the Dravidians to produce a new Aryan Hindu culture that eventually settled throughout the Indus and Upper Ganges valleys.

Though little is known regarding the military practices of the Hindus before 600 B.C.E., two works of classical literature provide some idea of the conduct of warfare: the *Rigveda* (also known as *Ṛgveda*, c. 1500-1000 B.C.E.; English translation, 1896-1897) and the *Mahābhārata* (400 B.C.E.-400 C.E., present form by c. 400 C.E.; *The Mahabharata of Krishna-Dwaipayana Vyasa*, 1887-1896). For example, Arjuna, the primary warrior of the *Bhagavadgītā* (c. 200 B.C.E.-200 C.E.; *The Bhagavad Gita*, 1785), refuses to kill until he is instructed in his duty by the god Krishna to "arise, O son of Kunti, intent on battle." Although the Hindu tribes were acquainted with most metals, footmen armed with bows made up the great majority of the early Hindu armies. Cavalry and chariots were used, but because horses were scarce, they were used primarily by the kings and nobles. The warriors enjoyed considerable prestige and were a leading class.

By about 600 B.C.E., the area between the Himalayas and the Nerbudda River was divided into sixteen more-or-less independent states. Although little is known of this semi-mythical period, it evidently was a time of numerous wars. Two constant factors, however, in all of Indian history—and certainly in military history—are geography and climate, both of which have dictated over the centuries the success or failure of invasions. Two successful invasions that occurred within approximately twenty years of each other were that of Cyrus the Great of Persia in 537 B.C.E. and that of Darius the Great of Persia from 517 B.C.E. to 509

B.C.E. Cyrus probably reached the Indus, and Darius succeeded in conquering the western bank of the Indus and part of the northwestern Punjab.

The Hindu military system of this period used the usual chariots (of various sizes), archers, and javelin throwers. The most important innovation in the makeup of Hindu armies, however, was the elephant. By 400 B.C.E., elephants had become the mainstay of offensive warfare. Replete with armor and carrying a driver and several archers and javelin throwers, these pachyderms were a sight to behold. Moreover, they were trained to perform a large variety of movements, including lying down, charging, and stamping, and whatever else might be deemed necessary in battle. Despite all this training, elephants were not totally reliable, and the driver was armed with a kind of spike to drive into the elephant's head should it get out of control. As usual, an offensive weapon brings on a defensive one, and special arrows were developed to be used against elephants.

Even with chariots and elephants, Hindu armies consisted largely of foot soldiers with bows that had not been changed in more than two thousand years. Eventually, the sword came more into play as a companion weapon to the bow. Shields were carried by all except the archers, who needed both hands free to shoot their arrows. Although the best horses were reserved to pull the chariots, some cavalry units were used.

In the spring of 326 B.C.E. Alexander the Great invaded central India and faced Porus, the leading monarch of the Punjab. Porus had about one hundred elephants with his army and was confident that Alexander's horses would not face such beasts. Alexander, however, had his infantry harass the elephants, so much so that some of them turned and stampeded through their own lines, causing intense confusion. Though the Hindus fought valiantly, the Macedonians won the day, and Porus was captured—at least to some degree a victim of his own elephants.

In circa 323 B.C.E., Chandragupta Maurya came to power. With a strong administrative and military mind, he organized an efficient government and a large military establishment of some 600,000 infantry, 30,000 cavalry, and 9,000 elephants. Chariots were also still in use and remained so for another one thousand years. Elephants were used into the nineteenth century C.E., some two thousand years after the disappearance of the Mauryan Empire.

CHINA

Before becoming a unified state in the third century B.C.E., China was marked by numerous, often overlapping dynasties. During the Shang Dynasty (1600-1066 B.C.E.) some central authority was established, supported by a small standing army that could be reinforced militia fashion from the supporters of minor rulers. Infantry from the lower classes and chariots from the upper classes formed the basic structure of this force.

The highly decorated chariots, fashioned after those of the Egyptians, served as symbols of rank and power. Divided into squads of five, they each carried a driver, an archer, and a warrior with a dagger-ax, and each was supported by a group of infantry, armed with halberds, spears, and bows with bronze-tipped arrows. Leather armor, bronze helmets, and large shields of wood and leather provided protection. Because horses were expensive and saddles and stirrups did not yet exist, there was no use of cavalry.

Defeating the Shang in battle at Muye in 1028 B.C.E., the Zhou created a ruling dynasty covering a large area from the midlands east to the sea and north to what is now Manchuria. The Zhou maintained large numbers of forces, including their own and those of the conquered Shang, to control their sprawling dominions. Chariots pulled by four horses were widely used in mass chariot battles with invaders from the steppes. As time passed, however, infantry surpassed the chariot in importance, probably because of the maintenance expense of the chariot and of its lack of maneuverability in rough terrain. Both weapons and armor slowly evolved to match the needs of the Zhou armies, including development of the sword as an addition to the dagger-ax.

By 722 B.C.E., the Zhou Dynasty was losing control of much of its domain to internal fighting as each state sought more power. By 481 B.C.E., the size of armies of the warring states had increased up to 4,000 chariots and 10,000 men in some battles. When the Qin were fighting the Zhou in 403 B.C.E., the total combatants reached 1 million or more. This period also saw considerable emphasis on fortification of cities, followed by powerful siege engines to break through those fortifications. Armies continued to consist of masses of infantry and, for the first time, cavalry, with chariots playing a lesser role.

Following the defeat of the Zhou, King Zheng (later first emperor Shi Huangdi) of the Qin Dynasty created the first real unified empire in China in 221 B.C.E. A consummate politician and general, Zheng increased the use of cavalry in his armies as he fought the nomads from Mongolia. Although the Qin Dynasty was short-lived, ending in 206 B.C.E., from it came the empire that was to last more than two thousand years.

ROME

Rome began as a small city-state and ended as an empire in control of vast areas of Europe, North Africa, and Asia Minor, an area containing more than 60 million people. From the beginning, Rome was a warrior state recognizing that to create and maintain an empire, a nation needed a strong and effective military. All Roman citizens between the ages of seventeen and forty-six owed sixteen years of military service to the state. Moreover, no Roman could run for political office until he had been on at least ten military campaigns. In short, the military and social cultures of Rome were closely related and highly disciplined and organized. When Rome went to war, officers (aristocrats) and common soldiers fought side by side with a ferocity seldom, if ever, matched in military history.

The legion was the base of the army. Made up of 10 cohorts of 600 men each, its total manpower was 6,000. Cohorts were made up of 6 maniples of 200 men each. The primary weapon was a heavy javelin with a small, barbed head that would stick in an enemy's shield, making the shield essentially useless, and the gladius, a short sword. Tactically, following skirmishing and missile harassment, the

Ancient warriors, like this Roman general, often wore helmets and armor and carried shields and spears. (Library of Congress)

legion would move to within 20 yards (18 meters) of the enemy, from which position the first two ranks would hurl their javelins. The next line of eight ranks, with a 6-foot (1.8-meter) interval between each man, then charged with shield and gladius. Whenever these ranks had trouble, reserve ranks would move up through the intervals provided, resulting in a continuous moving of lines during a battle. For protection, the legionnaires wore brass helmets with a leather brow and cheek plates, body armor of chain mail, and a 4-by-2-foot (120-by-60-centimeter) curved shield constructed from layers of wood and leather bound with iron that might occasionally be held over their heads in a tortoiselike fashion. Undergirding the above tactics and weapons was the superior organization, discipline, and training that each legionnaire went through.

Of all the enemies that the Roman legions faced, the Carthaginians provided the most competition as they battled each other over areas of Spain, Sicily, and North Africa. Rome's move into Sicily in 264 B.C.E. brought these two powerful opponents to conflict in the First Punic War (264-247 B.C.E.), which lasted seventeen years before Carthage was forced to make peace. The Second Punic War (218-201 B.C.E.) began when the Carthaginians, led by Hannibal, clashed with Rome over a Greek city in Spain. Hannibal, accompanied by elephants, mounted a daring attack through the Alps that, even though less than half of his army reached Italy, did result in the defeat of a Roman army and the rise of Quintus Fabius Maximus to dictator in Rome. Following a series of battles on both land and sea, Rome prevailed, ending Carthage's role as a power in the Mediterranean.

Though it receives less attention than war on land, naval war played a significant role in the Punic Wars. Each side had a great number of ships involved, sometimes as many as 350 in a single fleet. At a given time, a total from both sides of more than 1,000 ships could be at sea, with close to 300,000 seamen and marines manning them. The classic Greek trireme was replaced with the larger quinquireme. On balance, the Carthaginians were superior to the Romans in seamanship, as well as in the quality of their ships.

On its rise to power following the Punic Wars, Rome stressed domination of its neighbors, using client states as a first line of defense. Between 30

and 90 B.C.E., these states were taken into the empire, and legions were deployed along the perimeter for protection. Between 200 and 400 C.E., Rome began to weaken both internally and externally. The heavy cost of maintaining such a far-flung empire was taking its toll, and the ever-increasing inroads made by the Teutonic barbarians were becoming more and more difficult to control. The traditional Roman legion gave way to heavy cavalry, and the army in general was made up by a larger percentage of barbarians.

NORTH AMERICA

Whatever the actual date that humans reached the New World, any knowledge of their chronological development is scant at best. They left no cave drawings, no great monuments, and no written records. They spoke a plethora of languages, often having to communicate by sign language; and they did not use the wheel or the plow. Although projecting back through time cannot ensure complete accuracy, it seems safe to assume that these Indians did not change much from pre-Neolithic times to the first arrival of Europeans.

For the majority of the Indians of North America—whether of the frozen tundras of the Arctic, the deserts of the Southwest, the plains of the Midlands, or the forests of the East—religion and war were a significant part of their cultures. Although they lacked the sophisticated warfare techniques employed by their contemporaries in Europe, Asia Minor, and Asia, the Indians of North America practiced their own versions of warfare, and many were quite good at it. These Native Americans did not fight wars on a grand scale, but rather primarily battles employing hit-and-run tactics and ambushes, all designed to achieve a fairly specific goal, whether it be gaining or defending territory or stealing women, food, or other material things. Their weapons were primarily bows and arrows, spears, lances, war clubs, stone axes, and rawhide slings, along with primitive shields for protection. Although some of the more settled, agricultural tribes were not particularly warlike, there were others who practiced war frequently and with considerable skill. These latter groups often had warrior societies that celebrated those who proved themselves brave and effective fighters.

Interestingly enough, killing an enemy was not always the highest mark of bravery or skill. Taking coup, that is taking the weapon or some other possession from an enemy or even merely touching him with a stick, was often the goal of warriors. In this way, a warrior could gain the power of his enemy and make it part of his own. Scalping was practiced also, though often not considered as significant as taking coup. For the North American Indian, there was little stimulus to fight to the death, even in the later years in their struggle against the invading Europeans. A captured enemy, however, was frequently tortured and even cannibalized. Like many of the activities of all Indians of the Americas, the preparation for war and the actual carrying out of battle were highly ritualistic and closely related to the religious beliefs of the specific group.

MESOAMERICA

Successors of the Olmecs, whose culture reached its peak about 1000 B.C.E., the Maya began settling in the Yucatán Peninsula and Guatemala about 1000 B.C.E. Advancing from hunting and gathering to a primitive form of agriculture based on the dominant crop maize and the myth of the Maize God, the Maya eventually developed a most remarkable civilization. Tribes and clans, bolstered by a strong warrior spirit, began building cities about 500 B.C.E., some of which would grow to many thousands of inhabitants. Although the Maya may be best remembered for their Long Count calendar and their system of hieroglyphics, the populous city-states that grew throughout their territories were ruled not by stargazers but by aggressive kings who practiced a brutal form of warfare—mostly against each other.

Never really unified into a single kingdom, the cities of the Maya were ruled by kings thought to be semi-divine. Like the feudal lords of later times, they lived in relative luxury and abundance with all the accouterments of royalty. Of all their responsibilities of leadership, none was more important than the defense and extension of their holdings. The ruins of the arch-rival cities of Tikal and Calakmul serve as examples of the constant conflicts among Maya cities, large or small, that eventually played a significant role in the decline of that civilization.

Armies were organized on the clan or vassal basis. Armed with striking, slashing, and piercing weapons such as bows and arrows (sometimes poisoned), clubs, and spears hurled with the help of an atlatl (spear-thrower), the warriors making up these armies were highly individualistic in their military demeanor. As in much primitive warfare, the authority of command was not of primary concern. The resulting battles—really not much more than glorified raids—reflected little if any sense of tactical theory and more often than not were reduced to individual combat such as Homer described in the *Iliad*, in which opponents might be well known to each other. The goal, it seems, was to capture an enemy rather than to slay him, because a prisoner, particularly one of some rank, could be ritualistically tortured and ultimately offered up as a sacrifice to the serpent gods, whose appetite for human blood was apparently never satisfied.

Again, as with most primitive societies, war was closely tied to religion and was carried out with appropriate preparatory ceremonies, complete with dancing and hallucinogenic drinks. It has, for instance, been reported that before going into battle, the king would puncture his penis with a stingray spine, while his queen would draw a string of thorns through her tongue. More gruesome, however, were the rituals faced by the defeated captive, who might be pitted in gladitorial combat against other captives in a traditional game of mythic importance in which two teams would attempt to keep a hard ball from touching the ground. A captive might, alternatively, be drugged and placed on a pedestal of stone surrounded by a group of captor warriors anxious to spill his blood though a graphic display of skill in the use of weapons. Another practice was to behead the captive, displaying his head along with those of other fallen enemy warriors. The Maya were also known to "roll up" their enemies, tie them into a ball, and throw them down steps of stone. Occasionally the enemy's flesh might find its way into a blood stew.

The Maya were thought by early scholars to be primarily a peace-loving people intent on mastering writing, mathematics, and the engineering of magnificent pyramids. Later scholars have recognized that, in addition to these accomplishments, the Maya occupied a culture in which the brutality of warfare was a stark reality.

SUB-SAHARAN AFRICA

Like the Indians of North America, the early inhabitants of sub-Saharan Africa left little for archaeologists to work with in their attempts to piece together a probable picture of the cultural characteristics of this area. Archaeological evidence indicates that the native groups of sub-Saharan Africa were not really in a Neolithic stage of culture until about the sixth century B.C.E. Until that time, they were nomadic hunter-gatherers. In a vast land that was thinly populated, they had no need for organized permanent settlements, nor for anything more than rudimentary military knowledge. Their very isolation, the result of two oceans and a desert, was protection enough. Probably because of the wide availability of iron ore, the Iron Age arrived in the sixth century B.C.E. in West Africa, making possible the production of good-quality spears and hoes.

Any warfare carried out was probably limited to impromptu and spontaneous raiding parties to steal or destroy an enemy's possessions or to capture women and children. Revenge was often a cause for warfare in African culture, but as in most primitive cultures, there were no abstract causes for which warriors were willing to die. Each tribe kept its own place, though occasionally a group of hunters from one tribe might run into a group from another, in which case there might be a battle that would last until one group was beaten or got tired and left. By the first century C.E., high-yield food crops, spreading up from the south, were discovered by the Bantu speakers along the Zambezi-Congo river system. This phenomenon gave rise to a pastoral-farm culture and the emergence of village life that, according to rock paintings and engravings, caused conflicts between this new culture and the hunter-gatherers, as the latter raided the herds and fields of the former.

Like the North American Indians, African males often belonged to warrior societies that assured them of superior cultural status and wore fetishes and various kinds of badges for bravery. Also, like the former, they participated in highly stylized behavior and rituals with drums and dancing before engaging in warfare. War, after all, was exciting and provided an opportunity to break the boredom of everyday life and to feel good that the gods were on their side. As in most primitive societies, during any kind of warfare, the women were often ritually ignored by the men and left to take care of the home front. Young boys, however, constantly practiced with bows and arrows and other weapons as they awaited their chance to become warriors.

The basic weapons used consisted of war clubs of various kinds, sharp spears, small bows and arrows—some tipped with poison strong enough to kill almost instantly—along with bracelets of spikes or blades and circular iron knives, also worn on the wrist. Shields of hides and wood, some highly decorated, provided the necessary protection. The early arrival of the Iron Age in some parts of sub-Saharan Africa (c. sixth century B.C.E.) made possible the production of good quality spears and other metal weapons.

ADDITIONAL RESOURCES

Feest, Christian. *The Art of War.* London: John Calmann and Cooper, 1980.

Ferrill, Arthur. *The Origins of War.* New York: Thames and Hudson, 1985.

Fox, Robin. *Alexander the Great.* New York: Penguin, 1994.

Healy, Mark. *The Ancient Assyrians.* London: Osprey, 1992.

_____. *Armies of the Pharaohs.* London: Osprey, 2000.

Keegan, John. *A History of Warfare.* New York: Vintage Books, 1993.

Peddie, John. *The Roman War Machine.* Conshohocken, Pa.: Combined Books, 1997.

Peers, Chris. *Ancient Chinese Armies*. London: Osprey, 1990.

Turney-High, Harry H. *Primitive War*. Columbia: University of South Carolina Press, 1971.

SEE ALSO: Africa, East and South; Africa, North; Africa, West; Alexander the Great; Assyria; Athens; Atlatl; Babylonia; Ball game, Mesoamerican; *Bhagavadgītā*; Carthage; Chandragupta Maurya; China; Cyrus the Great; Darius the Great; Egypt, Pharaonic; Egypt, Prepharaonic; Fabius Maximus, Quintus; Granicus, Battle of; Greece, Classical; Greece, Mycenaean; Hannibal; Hittites; Homer; Hyksos; India; Indus Valley civilization; Macedonia; *Mahābhārata*; Mauryan Dynasty; Maya; Olmecs; Paleo-Indians in North America; Peloponnesian War; Persia; Philip II; Punic Wars; Qin Dynasty; Rome, Imperial; Rome, Prerepublican; Rome, Republican; Shang Dynasty; Shi Huangdi; Zhou Dynasty.

—*Wilton Eckley*

WOMEN'S LIFE

Women's lives in ancient times reflected the diversity of cultures but shared some common themes. In some cases, transitions from matriarchal to patriarchal systems resulted in a lower social status for women. One problem in historical studies is the balance of documentation, which is weighted heavily in favor of cultures with written traditions as opposed to oral traditions. When written documentation exists, it often makes little mention of women. Therefore, in the study of ancient women, personal narratives are very valuable, and artifacts are especially important. Clues can also be found in myths, legends and folklore.

RELIGION

Artifacts from Eurasia during the Neolithic period suggest that ancient peoples were profoundly concerned with the mysteries of life and death, and the power of childbearing was expressed in sculptures of figures with swollen abdomens, hips, and breasts. These sculptures, which might have been made for religious purposes, support theories that some form of mother goddess is among humanity's most ancient deities. After the emergence of writing, various names for this type of goddess were recorded: Isis in Egypt, Astarte in the Middle East, Kali in India, and Aphrodite/Venus in the Greco-Roman world. In the oral traditions of many Native American and African societies, the supreme deity and source of life is female. Specific representations vary, but the basic powers and attributes of this type of female deity were remarkably consistent throughout many cultures over a very long period of time. Although by the second millennium C.E., mother goddesses had been largely displaced in Europe and the Middle East by the rise of Christianity and Islam, this type of deity is still worshiped in many parts of the world. Despite the prominence of this female deity in the belief systems of many ancient societies, the goddess's power was not necessarily reflected in the status of women in those cultures.

Female deities, in addition to fertility and motherhood, were often associated with the Moon. Male deities were typically linked to the Sun, with the notable exception of Japan, which viewed the Sun goddess Amaterasu as a major deity. In many parts of East Asia, religious systems featured a system of cosmic duality (yin-yang), balancing the female and male principles and associating them with darkness and brightness, respectively.

Other female deities throughout the world were associated with nature spirits, often attached to particular locations. Goddesses in various pantheons included those associated with learning and wisdom, such as Athena in Greece and Saraswati in India. Women often served as priestesses or spirit mediums, serving both female and male deities in ancient societies. Many women were martyred in the early days of Christianity, and some of these became known to later generations as saints. Although the three great monotheistic religions address the supreme being in paternal terms, women who played important roles in these religions are admired as models of virtue. Christians honor Mary (1st century C.E.), the mother of Jesus Christ; Muslims honor Fatima (seventh century C.E.), the daughter of the Prophet Muḥammad; and Jews honor women of faith and strength who appear in the Torah. In China, wives were considered necessary participants in rites honoring their husbands' ancestors, and female shamans were often called upon for rain invocations.

MARRIAGE AND FAMILY LIFE

In the most stratified societies of the ancient world, marriage practices tended to be more formal at the highest levels of society and less formal at the lowest levels. Family relationships among the elite classes were in some cases made more complex by the practice of polygamy, which appeared to varying degrees in the Middle East, West Africa, India, China, and in other ancient cultures. Concubinage was another practice through which women could become associated with wealthy and powerful households, although the official legal status of concubines was lower than that of second or third wives. Arranged marriage was another widespread practice associated with the elite and ruling classes of many nations throughout the ancient world. Marriages could be arranged for political or economic purposes. Most marriages in the ancient world were monogamous, and in patriarchal cultures, there was a strong preference for the birth of sons to carry on the family name.

In some cultures, including many West African societies, the custom of dowry payments was balanced by payments made by the groom's family. These exchanges of money were not viewed as payments for a commodity but as gestures of respect. In the Babylonian laws of Eshnunna (Tall al-Asmar), circa 1770 B.C.E., such payments are included as part of the standard marriage contract. In contrast to "bride price," however, the more widespread practice of dowry payments reinforced preferences for male children, was a great burden on poor families, and contributed to female infanticide in ancient China and other cultures. Among the Maya, the groom was often required to work for the bride's family for a number of years in a kind of dowry agreement.

Property rights of women varied considerably from culture to culture. In ancient Egypt, for example, women could own and inherit property, including land, and property was divided equally among children, while in Mesopotamia, inheritance was patrilineal. Although sons were favored, it was possible for women to inherit property in the Maya culture. Generally, women had more rights in matrilineal societies, such as in Japan before it adopted Chinese-style institutions (c. 700 C.E.). In native cultures of North America, nomadic lifestyles often made the transfer of property less of an issue, but as full participants in the struggle for survival, capable women could claim a relatively equal importance in both matrilineal and patrilineal societies.

Divorce practices also varied considerably from culture to culture, and even within cultures, depending on the time period and geographic location. In ancient Mesoamerican cultures such as the Maya, a simple verbal repudiation by either party could terminate a marriage, and the wife would return to her family with the possibility of remarrying. In many other ancient cultures, however, the divorced women and widows were often marginalized, and initiating divorce was a male prerogative.

In spite of the obvious connection between social stability and protection from violence, rape was not always punished with severity in the ancient world. As in more recent times, it was sometimes carried out in the context of warfare, but even within a society, rape carried certain ambiguities as a crime. For example, in ancient Rome, it was regarded as a property crime against the husband or male relatives rather than a crime against the actual victim. This attitude is illustrated in the story of Lucretia, who upon being raped by a Roman prince, killed herself after asking her male relatives to avenge her.

EDUCATION, LITERATURE, AND THE ARTS

Although often excluded from formal education, women participated in intellectual life since the beginning of writing itself. Enkeduanna, a high-priestess at the Moon god temple of Ur in Sumer and a writer of religious poetry dating to circa 2300 B.C.E., was one of the earliest authors for which documentation is available. In the gradual transition from oral to written traditions, many of the narratives involving women were documented by male scribes. The women who played essential roles in the Hebrew Bible and other classic religious texts are often described in very favorable terms that recognize their intellectual abilities. For example, two women of ancient India, Maitreyi and Gargi, were mentioned as participants in scholarly theological debates in the *Bṛhad-āraṇyaka Upaniṣad* (c. 800 B.C.E.).

One of the most influential authors of ancient times was the Greek poet Sappho, an aristocratic woman who lived on the island of Lesbos during the seventh century B.C.E. Recognized for her greatness throughout the Greco-Roman world, she is still admired today for the quality of her poetry, which was in the lyric form, meant to be sung to the accompaniment of a lyre. By emphasizing love, personal experience, and emotions, she departed from the heroic and devotional themes of her male predecessors. Through consensus among the ancient literati, Sappho and her student Erinna of Telos were honored by inclusion among the nine Terrestrial Muses, earthly reflections of the demi-goddess muses (from which the word "music" is derived), whose role it was to inspire poets. Other women on the list of earthly muses include Myrtis of Anthendon and Corrina of Tanagra, who incorporated local mythologies into their writing, Telesilla of Argos, Praxilla of Sicyon, known for her drinking songs, and three women of later generations: Locris of Italy (fourth century B.C.E.), Anyte of Tegea, and Moero of Byzantium (third century B.C.E.).

Around the same time in India, women's voices were first heard in the written anthologies of Tamil poetry, which expressed the experiences of women of diverse backgrounds. In China, the historian and scholar Ban Zhao (48-116 C.E.) wrote *Nüjie* (first century C.E.; "instructions for daughters") and finished her brother's *Han Shu* (also known as *Qian Han Shu*, completed first century C.E.; *The History of the Former Han Dynasty*, 1938-1955) after he died.

In the performing arts, women were often trained in the arts of dance and music. Musicians in the courts of ancient Egypt were almost exclusively female. Music, dance, and other arts were often conducted by women in the context of religious duties. This was the case with the devadasis of India and many other groups throughout ancient history. Although these groups were not always of high social standing and were associated in some cultures with concubinage, they sometimes provided women with an opportunity for social mobility. Aside from these elite groups serving the church or state in centers of power, women of the agricultural peasantry and of traditional nomadic societies developed, maintained, and transmitted a vast body of songs, dances, and other forms of art to accompany their various activities and to entertain, comfort, and educate themselves and their families. The Hebrew Bible describes women playing hand drums to welcome troops returning from battle and as composers and singers of lamentation songs.

LABOR AND ECONOMICS

One of the most widespread and ancient patterns in the gender-based division of labor was the assignment of weaving to women. In Neolithic times, women were often buried with their weaving spools, and the legends, myths, and proto-histories from around the world are filled with stories that include a woman or female deity weaving. Si Lingchi (c. 2640 B.C.E.), the legendary first empress of China, is credited with the invention of silk-extraction technology. In Greek mythology, it was a weaving contest between the goddess Athena and the talented human woman Arachne that was used both to warn people against pride and to explain the existence of spiders. For the Mesoamerican Maya, whose women wove for both trade and household use, the patroness of weaving was goddess Ix Chel Yac, the daughter of the goddess of pregnancy. In many ancient cultures, weaving was an important outlet for women's artistic creativity.

The degree of physical mobility accorded to the sexes was often related to the nature of the work women were expected to perform. Because women were responsible for caring for infants, hunting was generally assigned to men. Agriculture, however, was usually a shared responsibility, and records of women's participation in agricultural activities are almost as ancient and widespread as accounts of their weaving. As managers of large households, and as partners and advisers to powerful men, women of the mercantile and elite classes in stratified cultures had influence on the economies and financial policies of their villages, cities, and nations.

LEADERSHIP AND POLITICS

Even in strongly patriarchal societies of the ancient world, a married woman was viewed as having a certain degree of authority over the affairs of her household. Women of wealthier families in stratified societies were managers of very large groups of people, including servants and slaves as well as children and grandchildren. In many cases, women derived political power from their marriages to rulers or from other relationships with men. In some cases, women actually ruled from behind the scenes by serving as the most influential and trusted advisers to less competent men or served as powerful regents for male rulers too young to assume their duties.

In some situations, women assumed direct political authority. Legends and archaeological evidence suggest that women leaders were common in matriarchal societies in parts of the world that later became patriarchal, including pre-Buddhist Japan, parts of pre-Muslim Africa, and specific areas of Europe. In many cases, however, resourceful women assumed power by taking advantage of circumstances that made it possible for them to function in positions that were traditionally held by men.

The legends of the Greeks tell of Penthesilea

(c. twelfth century B.C.E.), who led an army of Amazons to Troy but was killed by Achilles. The Amazons appeared in Greek mythology as warrior women who lived apart from men and battled with the Greek heroic figures. They were supposed to have used men only for conceiving children and to have destroyed male babies. It has been theorized that these legends derived from early Greek encounters with nomadic Scythians, whose women sometimes participated in warfare. Tombs in Central Asia have yielded burials of women warriors. Although the Amazons were legendary, the state of Sparta, which invited significant participation by women in political affairs, represented a very real cultural and (at times) military threat to the classical civilization of Athens.

The Hebrew Bible recounts several women leaders of ancient Israel. Although they did not often rule as queens, women in the Near East had been accepted as prophetesses since the eighteenth century B.C.E., according to records from the city of Mari. As the Israelites struggled to maintain their political and cultural identity, they sometimes relied on religious leaders such as the prophetesses Deborah, Noadiah, and Huldah, rather than on the male monarchy. The Bible also recounts an African monarch, the Queen of Sheba (Ethiopia), who visited King Solomon in Jerusalem. The extensive kingdom of the Queen of Sheba, who ruled for fifty years during the tenth century B.C.E., was based in Axum on the western coast of the Red Sea.

In Egypt, the monarchy was also traditionally male, although queens could be very influential. However, two women pharaohs, Hatshepsut of the fifteenth century B.C.E., and Cleopatra VII of the first century B.C.E., ruled Egypt at critical times in its history. Hatshepsut became regent when her husband and half-brother Thutmose II died, and her nephew was underage. She had herself declared pharaoh and reigned for nearly twenty years until her nephew regained the throne. During her rule, she increased Egypt's wealth with trade and diplomacy. Cleopatra VII, the last pharaoh (69-30 B.C.E.), formed personal and political alliances with Julius Caesar and Marc Antony, in or-

Cleopatra VII, shown riding in a boat down the Nile River, was the last Egyptian pharaoh. (Hulton Archive)

der to secure Roman support for Egypt. After her death, Egypt become a Roman province.

Also in the first century B.C.E., a female ruler based in Meroe led a successful struggle to defend her African kingdom against the garrisons of Rome, losing some initial battles but eventually negotiating an agreement that would limit the southern reaches of the Roman Empire to Egypt. The powerful female rulers of Meroe were often described in historical records by their title *kandake*, the Merotic word for queen from which the English woman's name Candace comes.

On the other side of the Roman Empire, another woman leader led a less successful challenge to Roman authority in Britain. After her husband, Prasutagus, king of the Iceni, died in 59 C.E., his widow Boudicca, when trying to assert her prop-erty rights, was flogged by the Romans and her daughters raped. Boudicca then roused the Iceni of Britain and led them through several successful battles. Later, they massacred the Roman inhabitants of London but were eventually defeated. Boudicca and her daughters drank poison to escape capture, and she remains a national symbol of strength.

Also during the first century C.E., the Trung sisters of Vietnam led a temporarily successful armed uprising against Chinese colonialists. Like Boudicca and her daughters, they committed suicide after being defeated militarily and were subsequently remembered as national heroes.

Queen Sondok of Korea ruled from 634 to 647 C.E., after inheriting the throne from her father. As part of the Silla Dynasty, she encouraged the spread of Buddhism and intellectual influence from China, although she benefited from the traditional Korean respect for female shamans and a degree of matrilineal authority that eventually weakened under sustained Confucian influence.

In China during the seventh century C.E., the empress Wu Hou reigned after outliving the two male emperors in whose courts she had served as concubine. Although she came to power through intrigues similar to those of her male counterparts, she was respected as a fair and capable ruler.

In the ancient South American and Mesoamerican kingdoms, women were important in the determination of royal lineage and were often portrayed on stelae. One of the most prominent was the sixth century C.E. woman of Tikal, mother of the Maya ruler Double Bird. The Maya city of Palenque had two women rulers: Kanal-ikal, whose reign began in 583 C.E., and Zak K'uk', who gained power in 612 C.E. In the matrilineal societies of North America, women were often clan leaders who would control the selection and tenure of male chieftains.

MEDICINE, SCIENCE, AND PHILOSOPHY

Throughout the ancient world, including the Americas, women were involved in the practice of medicine and were especially respected for their knowledge of medicinal herbs. In many situations, as for priestesses of the Igbo and Yoruba in West Africa, medical practice was associated with religious offices held by women. Egyptian women physicians were painted on tombs as early as the third millennium B.C.E., and Mesoamerican women healed on the basis of maintaining balance, a system not unlike the East Asian system of balancing yin and yang. In ancient Greece, one of the most famous women physicians was Philista (318-372 B.C.E.), also popular as a medical educator and lecturer.

Because philosophy, natural science, and religion were more unified in ancient times, the contributions of women in these areas often overlap. This is especially true of the women who participated in the Pythagorean school (founded in the sixth century B.C.E.), an intellectual commune of male and female Greek philosopher-mathematicians, located in southern Italy. The students were originally led by Pythagoras, who had studied with the female philosopher Themistoclea. After Pythagoras's death, his wife, Theano, assumed leadership of his school and later wrote about number theory. Another Phythagorean, Perictione, wrote *Harmonia* (fourth-second century B.C.E.; on the harmony of women).

A second famous school uncharacteristically open to women was Plato's Academy, inspired by the teachings of Socrates. In Plato's *Symposion* (388-368 B.C.E.; *Symposium*, 1701), Socrates acknowledges the woman philosopher Diotima as his teacher. Another prominent female philosopher and scientist was Arete of Cyrene, whose father had studied with Socrates and promoted hedonism.

One of the last great woman scientists of ancient times was Hypatia (c. 370-415 C.E.), who taught natural philosophy and mathematics at the university in Alexandria, Egypt. She wrote major treatises on algebra, geometry, and astronomy and is credited with numerous inventions, such as the planisphere and astrolabe. As the leading Neoplatonist philosopher in Alexandria, which was officially Christian, she represented a political threat to the city's powerful bishop and was dragged into the streets by a mob and torn to pieces.

Women were allowed more freedom in East Asia during the flowering of Buddhism in the region, especially from the fourth through seventh centuries C.E. In the city of Kyongju, Korea, during the seventh century C.E., Queen Sondok of the Silla Dynasty built the Tower of the Moon and Stars, considered to be the first observatory in the Far East.

CURRENT VIEWS

Many scholars are reexamining the role of women in the ancient world, looking at the range of attitudes and social structures regarding them, the appearance of prominent women in many fields, and their political influence. Researchers are also turning to the ancient world for clues as to how the role of women has evolved over time.

ADDITIONAL RESOURCES

Cameron, Averil, and Amelie Kuhrt. *Images of Women in Antiquity*. Detroit, Mich.: Wayne State University Press, 1983.

Fantham, Elaine. *Women in the Classical World*. New York: Oxford University Press, 1994.

Foley, Helene P. *Reflections of Women in Antiquity*. New York: Gordon and Breach Science Publishers, 1984.

Lefkowitz, Mary R. U., and Maureen B. Fant. *Women's Life in Greece and Rome: A Source Book in Translation*. Baltimore: Johns Hopkins University Press, 1992.

Pantel, Pauline Schmitt, ed., and Arthur Goldhammer, trans. *From Ancient Goddesses to Christian Saints*. Vol. 1 in *A History of Women in the West*. Cambridge, Mass.: Harvard University Press, 1992.

Pomeroy, Sarah B. *Goddesses, Whores, Wives, and Slaves*. New York: Schocken Books, 1975.

Van Sertima, Ivan, ed. *Black Women in Antiquity*. New Brunswick, N.J.: Transaction, 1988.

Vivante, Bella, ed. *Women's Roles in Ancient Civilizations: A Reference Guide*. Westport, Conn.: Greenwood Press, 1999.

SEE ALSO: Archaic North American culture; Ban Gu; Bible: Hebrew; Boudicca; Britain; Buddhism; China; Christianity; Cleopatra VII; Confucianism; Daily life and customs; Egypt, Pharaonic; Egypt, Prepharaonic; Greece, Classical; Greece, Hellenistic and Roman; Greece, Mycenaean; Hatshepsut; Hypatia; India; Islam; Israel; Japan; Korea; Lucretia; Maya; Medicine and health; Napata and Meroe; Palenque; Plato; Pythagoras; Religion and ritual; Rome, Imperial; Rome, Prerepublican; Rome, Republican; Sappho; Sheba, Queen of; Socrates; Sumerians; Vietnam.

—*Alice Myers*

WRITING SYSTEMS

The evolution of writing systems was one of the most significant cultural phenomena of humankind. Although spoken language was a naturalistic development, the invention of written language resulted purely from people's ingenuity and served as the vehicle of civilization and recorded history.

The history and development of writing is different from the history and development of languages. Language necessarily precedes but does not necessarily lead to written language in any given civilization. For example, many peoples, languages, and civilizations of varying levels of sophistication flourished in ancient North and South America; however, these areas did not develop writing systems before pre-Columbian times. The same is true for parts of ancient Africa.

The development of writing systems coincided with the shift from nomadic to agricultural lifestyles. Roaming hunters and gatherers settled and became farmers, shepherds, and craftspeople.

This led to the need to keep track of business accounts, transactions, and other aspects of daily life. Prehistoric mnemonic devices were no longer adequate to record specific details. The earliest form of true written communication, which avoided ambiguity and provided permanence, began to develop around the fifth millennium B.C.E. Script styles as well as innovations in the writing systems were often a direct reflection of the various writing materials used.

PICTOGRAPHIC/IDEOGRAPHIC/LOGOGRAPHIC WRITING

The earliest writing systems were not phonetic; the symbols used did not directly reflect the speech sounds of the language. Rather, the first writing was pictographic, consisting of simplified drawings of objects and animals. This limited system gradually began to include ideographic signs, which symbolized more abstract concepts relating to the original pictograph. For example, a pictograph of the sun might also come to mean "day" or "light." Eventually, logographic signs were added. These were signs invented to symbolize words but no longer had a direct pictorial connection.

Sumer. The Sumerian farmers living between the Tigris and Euphrates Rivers in southern Mesopotamia are generally credited with the first known instance of writing, toward the end of the fourth millennium B.C.E. The principal writing material was clay, which was compacted and smoothed into a tablet. Bones, sticks, or reeds were carved into a stylus with a triangular tip. The stylus was used to create impressions in the clay, creating a writing script known as cuneiform, from the Latin *cuneus*, or "wedge." The script was rigid and angular as a result of the clay medium. When the writing was complete, the tablet was baked or left to dry in the sun. The Sumerians often used a form of clay envelope. The tablet was covered with a secondary layer of clay on which the same message was written, thus ensuring transmittal in spite of potential damage.

Indus Valley. As early as 2500 B.C.E., the peoples living in this area, located within present-day Pakistan, invented a pictographic writing system called the Indus script. It eventually became purely logographic, in that it used highly evolved symbols that no longer resembled particular objects, and most signs stood for whole words. Only a few samples of stone inscriptions remain, presumably because the principal writing medium was something perishable. The script has not been deciphered.

Crete and Cyprus. The ancient Cretans developed a writing system between the second and third millenniums B.C.E. Their Minoan script started out pictographic and developed into a logographic system. By 1700 B.C.E., two cursive scripts, called Linear A and Linear B, were in existence. They employed characters that were made of lines, rather than pictures, and they were largely phonetic. Only Linear B has been deciphered. About a thousand years later, a syllabic Cypriot script was in existence on the island of Cyprus. Because it represented the Greek language, it could

be deciphered and was instrumental in the decipherment of Linear B.

China. The Chinese began developing their writing system around 2000 B.C.E. It began with pictograms and developed into a logographic system. It was codified by about 1500 B.C.E., and the earliest samples were written with a brush in ink on bone and tortoiseshell. At this time, a single language was in use by all the Chinese peoples. Over the next two thousand years, many dialects developed, often mutually unintelligible. Because Chinese writing remained logographic, all Chinese, regardless of dialect, could read it. People who could not converse verbally could still communicate in writing.

The logographic system also worked well for the Chinese because their language was made up of many homophones, which were distinguished verbally by pitch and context. The script could handle this easily because it used symbols to provide context. In addition, Chinese grammar worked by rearranging whole words, and a logographic system suited it well. The Chinese script used thousands of signs.

Brush and ink were used on a variety of mediums, such as stone and wood tablets, metal, and most commonly, bamboo and silk. Writing was from top to bottom, with columns progressing from left to right. Calligraphy was from early on an artform.

The first paper was systematically produced by the Chinese during the Han Dynasty, about 105 C.E. Paper was made from tree bark, rags, fishnets, and hemp. These fibrous substances were crushed and pressed into a mold. As they dried, they resulted in a thin sheet of paper. The Chinese guarded their papermaking techniques for six hundred years and exported it to the Middle East and the Mediterranean.

ANALYTIC WRITING

Analytic, or transitional, writing systems used ideograms and logograms in combination with phonograms (signs that represent sounds). Sumerian cuneiform began employing pictograms to signify parts or syllables of words. An example would be combining the pictures for "bee" and "leaf" to form the word "belief." This rebus writing was the first crucial step in creating a relationship between sound and symbol. Cuneiform began with an unwieldy two thousand symbols. As it became logosyllabic, this was reduced to six hundred symbols. Cuneiform began to spread throughout Mesopotamia to almost all of the major peoples of the ancient Near East.

Akkad/Babylonia/Assyria. The Akkadians of northern Mesopotamia, the Babylonians, and the Assyrians succeeded each other as the dominant powers in Mesopotamia from 2500 to 700 B.C.E. They adapted cuneiform to fit their Semitic languages and simplified it to an increasingly syllabic system. Throughout this period, the Sumerian language was often transcribed as a parallel text. About 570 signs remained, but 300 were used most frequently.

Cuneiform adaptations. Many other peoples adopted the cuneiform system but invented their own signs to reflect the needs of their languages. The Eblaites and the Hurrians of Syria used cuneiform and wrote in Sumerian, with a small percentage of words in their own languages. In Persia, the Elamites invented a writing system around 2500 B.C.E. but discarded it in favor of cuneiform. They created many of their own signs for their non-Semitic language. Peoples farther west in the Persian Empire invented Old Persian cuneiform script in an attempt to distinguish themselves but abandoned it by 300 B.C.E. and adapted Mesopotamian cuneiform. The Urartians, northwest of Mesopotamia, similarly adapted cuneiform. In Asia Minor, the Hittites invented their own glyphic system around 1500 B.C.E. It came to be used mainly for carving inscriptions on stone monuments. Cuneiform was adopted for ordinary purposes, along with new signs to better translate their three Indo-European languages of Hittite, Palaic, and Luwian.

Mesoamerica. On the other side of the world in Mesoamerica, the development of writing was closely tied to the civilization's advanced astronomical knowledge and its desire to record it. The ancient Olmec civilization left behind only a few clues suggesting that they had some form of writing system, which was probably rudimentary. The first real evidence of writing occurs with the Zapotec civilization in the Oaxaca Valley at the site of Monte Albán, around 500 B.C.E. This writing had many calendrical and noncalendrical glyphs, the latter being logosyllabic. Samples of the Epi-Olmec and Isthmian script of the Izapa civilization in the village of La Mojarra in Veracruz date to the second century C.E. and are also a mixture of logographic and phonetic components. Both remain largely undeciphered. Inscriptions bearing the Nuine script of the Mixteca Baja region of Oaxaca date between 400 and 700 C.E. The script consists of about two hundred primarily pictorial elements.

The Maya civilization arose during the first millennium B.C.E. and flourished for hundreds of years. It covered a vast area that encompasses the present-day countries of Honduras, Belize, El Salvador, Guatemala, the Yucatán Peninsula, and the Mexican states of Tabasco and Chiapas. The Maya had the first fully developed writing system. It is generally believed that the Olmecs influenced their culture and may have been the originators of the calendar and hieroglyphics. The Maya believed that writing was a gift from Itzamna, the lord of the heavens, and this reflects the intertwined relationship between the mystical powers of the heavenly bodies, the calendar, and writing in Maya culture. The earliest writing samples date back to the third century C.E. They used hundreds of glyphic pictograms and ideograms as well as syllabic and phonetic elements. Because of its complexity, the decoding of Maya hieroglyphics has challenged scholars. There are many variant signs for a single sound, the same word could be written several ways, and there were also many homonyms. In addition, glyphs were often melded together in the same fashion as in Chinese writing, making it difficult to identify the individual elements. The discovery of the Dresden codex, which contains thirty-nine leaves with pictures of animals and gods accompanied by their glyphic symbols, was key to the decipherment of Maya writing, although the process is still not complete.

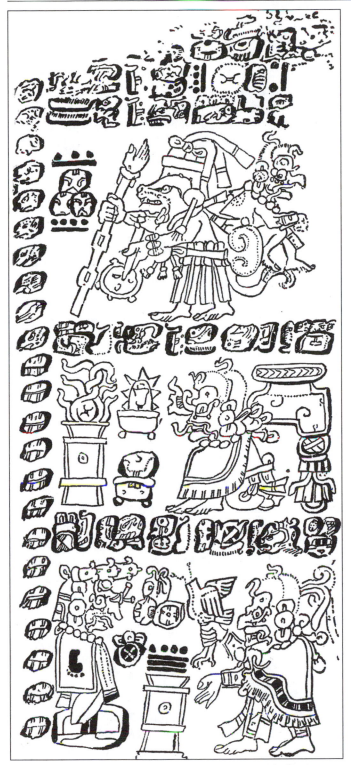

The Dresden codex (plate 25 is shown here) provided important clues to the decipherment of Maya writing. (North Wind Picture Archives)

Writing was from left to right, in columns from top to bottom. Inscriptions were carved on stone stelae, wooden monuments, walls, and lintels, and written on pottery and everyday utensils. Codices were widely used, which were folded books made from bark paper coated with gesso. The Dresden codex is illustrative of the codices produced during the height of the Maya civilization. They had covers made of jaguar skin and were painted with brush or feather pens. Red and black ink was held in conch shells.

The sophisticated civilization of Teotihuacán, which flourished between the start of the common era and 750 C.E., left behind no evidence of a writing system, although a few scattered calendrical hieroglyphs have been found.

Egypt. The Egyptians invented a writing system that rivals Sumerian cuneiform in its antiquity. Recent evidence indicates that it may actually predate cuneiform. During the fourth millennium B.C.E., the Egyptians were building a civilization along the Nile River. They invented hieroglyphics, literally "sacred engraved writing." From the start, it was a very complete writing system in that it could effectively record all aspects of spoken language. It consisted of three types of signs: pictograms, phonograms, and determinatives, clarifying symbols that indicated the category of ideas pictured. Because hieroglyphics were thought to be divinely inspired (a gift from the god Thoth), scribes were considered noble and the majority of the population could not write. Writing was usually right to left, but sometimes went from bottom to top, or in alternating directions on each line, a technique called boustrophedon ("as an ox travels back and forth plowing a field").

Papyrus flourished in the Nile Delta, and it was the principal writing medium. Papyrus stems were cut into several strips that were laid down overlapping to form a layer. A second layer was placed on top at a right angle. This was dried under pressure and then polished. Starch paste was used to stick the sheets together to form a scroll. The writing tool was either a sharpened reed stylus or a brush made by hammering the end of the reed to expose its frayed fiber, which would absorb and hold ink. A flat board was used for smoothing the papyrus and for leaning on to write. It had two wells to hold black and red ink. The scribe unrolled the scroll with one hand, wrote, and rerolled the scroll with the other.

The making of papyrus was time-intensive, and it was in demand throughout the Mediterranean region. It was therefore somewhat expensive. This led to the reusing of papyrus by erasing the original text, resulting in a palimpsest. Limestone and pottery were alternate writing surfaces for less important needs. Wooden tablets painted over with a layer of white plaster were also used. Parchment was very costly and was used only for the most valuable documents.

Hieroglyphics soon came to be used to record history, magic, science, cookery, commerce, law, and literature. Two faster forms of writing developed. A more flowing cursive hieratic script, used by scribes and priests, appeared very early and was used concomitantly with hieroglyphics for three thousand years. Around 650 B.C.E., an even more cursive demotic script appeared as the writing of the people. The discovery of the Rosetta stone (196 B.C.E.) provided the key to the decipherment of Egyptian writing because it portrayed three parallel texts in hieroglyphics, demotic, and Greek.

Hieroglyphic writing had hundreds of signs, with twenty-four symbols representing consonants. However, the Egyptians never took advantage of the potential for phonetic simplification and continued to use redundant combinations of ideograms and phonograms. The fluid use of a reed brush on papyrus may not have provided the incentive for simpler writing. Hieroglyphics were also decorative and appreciated for their stylistic beauty and cryptic nature. The numerous symbols

were perhaps viewed not as a hindrance but as a hallowed and integral part of writing.

Ancient Egyptian civilization began to mix with that of Greece and Rome around the beginning of the common era. The Egyptians adopted the Greek alphabet in the second century C.E. to record their Coptic language. They began to make codex books by sewing along the edge of the papyrus sheets.

PHONETIC WRITING

Truly phonetic writing systems are those in which there is a direct connection between each symbol and a speech sound. A syllabary has a sign for each syllable in a language. Cuneiform never evolved into a true syllabic system. A consonantal script has a sign for all consonants with little emphasis on vowel sounds. An alphabet has a sign for each individual sound.

Kush. The African kingdom of Kush (Napata) flourished in ancient Nubia in the area of present-day Sudan from the ninth century B.C.E. to the fourth century C.E. In the late seventh or early sixth century B.C.E., its capital was moved to Meroe. The Meroites adapted Egyptian hieroglyphics and, by the third century B.C.E., had devised their own primarily alphabetic system, known as Meroitic script. It had both a cursive version for everyday use and a hieroglyphic variant for monuments. It had fifteen consonantal signs and three vowels. The kingdom collapsed around the fourth century C.E., but the script was used through the fifth century C.E. to write various Nubian languages, after which it was gradually replaced by the Greek-based Coptic alphabet, spread by the coming of Christianity. Although the script has been deciphered, the language itself is unknown, and thus the meaning of much of the surviving samples is unknown.

Canaanites. By the beginning of the second millennium B.C.E., several North Semitic scripts were developing among the Canaanite peoples, Semites who had migrated from Arabia west to Palestine. They contained the precursors of an alphabetic system. Semites also occupied the Sinai Peninsula from 1800 to 1400 B.C.E. They used a script consisting of only twenty-seven different signs. It remains undeciphered but was probably alphabetic in nature.

Ugarit. The city of Ugarit, on the northwest coast of Syria, left behind tablets with a script employing only twenty to thirty characters. A fourteenth century B.C.E. inscription was found that supplied sounds in roughly the same sequence as would later appear in the Phoenician alphabet. The characters were similar to cuneiform but bore no resemblance to Mesopotamian cuneiform or any other scripts.

Phoenicia. The Phoenicians were North Semitic sailor merchants based along the Mediterranean coast of Syria. Several tablets from the city of Byblos dating from the eleventh century B.C.E. display a pseudohieroglyphic script that was probably syllabic. It had about eighty characters, a substantial decrease from any preexisting syllabic scripts. By about 1000 B.C.E., the Phoenicians developed the first truly phonetic script. It could be applied to many languages because it was based on sound alone. It consisted of twenty-two consonants but no vowels. It was a fluid script and had simple, clear letterforms, two essential characteristics of a utilitarian and effective script that could be mastered easily by the general population. From the tenth century B.C.E., the Phoenicians colonized westward throughout the Mediterranean region, on the islands of Cyprus, Sicily, and Sardinia, in Italy and Greece, southern Spain, and along the northern coast of Africa, particularly in Carthage. Their script spread with them.

North Africa. The Berber peoples living in North Africa, in the area known as Numidia, were ruled by Phoenicians, Greeks, and Romans during the period between the first millennium B.C.E. and 500 C.E. The Phoenicians established Carthage, and the Greeks established Cyrene. Their scripts disseminated throughout the area. After the Romans conquered Cyrene, there followed a period of turbulence during the second century B.C.E. between Carthage and the Romans, known as the Punic Wars. This gave the Berber peoples an opportunity for a period of independence. During this time, they derived their own consonantal Ber-

ber script from the Semitic models. It remained in use through the third century C.E. and was applied to the various Berber languages. The modern-day Tifinagh script used for the Tuareg language is a descendent of this script. As the Romans extended their rule across North Africa during the first centuries C.E., Christianity was introduced and the Latin script was again used. This lasted until the arrival of Arab culture in the seventh century C.E. and the introduction of Arabic script.

Iberians. Indigenous peoples living in southern Spain and in Portugal, in the area known as the Iberian Peninsula, developed Iberian scripts during the first millennium B.C.E. These scripts were part syllabic and part alphabetic and of unknown origin, although they are probably partly derived from the writing of the Phoenicians and Greeks who colonized there. Celtic peoples who migrated to the area between the eighth and the sixth centuries also used this script.

Aramaic/Hebrew/Arabic. The Aramaic peoples living in Syria had a writing system almost identical to Phoenician. By the first century B.C.E., their scripts replaced Mesopotamian cuneiform and also spread to the Persian Gulf, Afghanistan, India, and Mongolia. Several books of the Old Testament were written in Aramaic. The rest were written in Hebrew. Early Hebrew was a form of proto-alphabetic writing in use during the first millennium B.C.E. in Israel. It gave way to Square Hebrew, which was a derivative of Aramaic. Both of these scripts were used in the writing of the Dead Sea Scrolls. Arabic writing also developed from Aramaic by the sixth century C.E. and coincided with the beginning of the Muslim era. The Qur'ān was transcribed in Arabic script around 650 C.E. Because of the rapid expansion of Islam, the Arabic script also spread through the Byzantine Empire, Africa, Asia Minor, and also eastward to India and China.

Sabaeans. In South Arabia, a civilization of peoples called the South Semites developed a consonantal writing system that differed from the North Semitic scripts. It was in use by the first millennium B.C.E. and consisted of twenty-nine letters. Unlike North Semitic, it did not spread outside of the Arabian peninsula, except for Ethiopia on the African continent.

Ethiopia. Early in the first millennium B.C.E., the Sabaeans began to colonize in Ethiopia and the kingdom of Axum arose. By the fourth century C.E., the Axumites modified the consonantal South Semitic script into an Ethiopic syllabary with vowel indicators to fit their language of Ge'ez, which had developed with the introduction of Christianity. The direction of writing was reversed to run from left to right, which was probably a Greek influence. Ethiopia resisted the onslaught of Islam and retained its culture. The Ethiopic script forms the basis of modern-day Ethiopic writing.

India. By about 800 B.C.E., the Brahmi script was created; it is believed to have developed from the Aramaic scripts. By the fourth century B.C.E., the script was highly structured, largely because of the work of the grammarian Pāṇini. The Kharoṣṭī script also developed during the fifth century B.C.E. Both of these scripts required sophisticated phonological knowledge in order to organize the alphabet to reflect the articulation of the Indian language. The earliest known writing medium was ink on birch bark. Palm leaf manuscripts were prevalent and contributed to the development of a more rounded script because firm straight lines would rip the leaf. Inscriptions were hammered in copper for official records. Cotton and silk began to be used around the fourth century C.E. Between the fourth and sixth centuries C.E., the Gupta script evolved from Brahmi. The Siddhamatrka script developed from Gupta during the sixth century C.E. This was the ancestor of the modern Devanāgarī script, which is used for Sanskrit.

Greeks. With the Dorian invasion of Greece about 1100 B.C.E., the use of the early Linear B script ceased. The earliest use of a new script using the consonantal Phoenician alphabet occurs in 850 B.C.E. This alphabet was somewhat inadequate for the Greek language, which had many vowel sounds compared with the Semitic languages for which it had been used. The Greeks adapted the alphabet by borrowing signs for consonant sounds that did not exist in their language and using them

instead to transcribe their vowels. By 403 B.C.E., Ionic script existed. It had twenty-four signs, with seventeen consonants and seven vowels. This is considered the first complete alphabet. Greek was at first written right to left, as were many of the ancient scripts. This phenomenon is not fully understood. Over time, Greek writing changed direction, first to the transitional boustrophedon phase and eventually left to right. This change may be attributable to the introduction of the split-reed pen, cut from a hollow-stemmed reed in which ink could be stored. It had a hard tip, which may have resisted being pushed backward across the page compared with the soft reed brush. The Greeks produced a great body of literature using their new alphabet.

A large uppercase was used mainly for inscriptions on stone and a cursive variation for writing on papyrus or wax tablets. Wax tablets were convenient for everyday use. They were slates covered with a layer of wax, and writing could be erased by smoothing over the soft wax surface. A cheaper material was "ostraca," clay potshards on which writing was painted. Around the second century B.C.E., shortages in papyrus began to occur. Parchment, made from animal skins, came into use. Preparation techniques were much improved from earlier times. True parchment was of sheepskin, but cattle, goatskin, gazelle, and antelope were also used. Only the hair side was written on. Vellum was the finest form made of calfskin, on which both sides were written.

Romans. The early Romans adopted the Greek alphabet either directly or through the Etruscans. The Etruscans ruled northern Italy until the fourth century B.C.E., when they were driven out by the Romans. The Etruscan script was written in Greek characters, but the language was not similar to any others and has not been decoded. By the third century B.C.E., the Roman Empire had an alphabet of nineteen letters, and the majority of the population was literate.

Several script forms arose. Stone inscription involved detailed preparation and was considered an art. The size of the letters had to be calculated and the text measured out. Guidelines were drawn, and then the letters were painted on. They were then engraved with a chisel, which created thicker and thinner lines as the chisel edge turned. Cursive scripts were developed for writing on papyrus and wax tablets. Parchment came into use and had a smoother, more even writing surface. The quill pen was devised using goose feathers. These materials allowed for finer, smaller writing.

As Christianity began to spread during the fourth century C.E., the codex form of book grew in popularity. This was made of signatures of leaves of parchment, folded and sewn together. Parchment was more flexible than papyrus and was conducive to this development. Monastic scribes developed an uncial script, which was a more rounded bookhand. As the Roman Empire came to an end in 476 C.E., missionaries continued to move north.

Runes. The ancient Germanic peoples of Europe used writing known as Runic script. More than four thousand inscriptions have been found primarily in Sweden, Denmark, Norway, and Germany, some dating back to the second century C.E. The script consisted of twenty-four letters and is of uncertain origin, although some characters bear a relation to the Roman alphabet. Runes were associated with secrecy and mystery and may have first been used in making charms and spells. They were scratched on armor, jewelry, wooden monuments, and tombstones. Therefore, the characters were created mostly from straight lines. It is not known if runes were used widely for secular purposes. A separate runic script called the ogham alphabet was used by the Celts of the British Isles and originated around the fourth century C.E. Runic script was eventually replaced by the Roman alphabet as Christianity spread.

Other Latin scripts. In the early Dark Ages, monasticism took root in Ireland. The monks developed a unique form of writing based on various influences, including the Scandinavian runic script. They modified the Roman uncial scripts into their own Insular script. The Celts also created the first true minuscule (lowercase) family of letters. The uncial scripts ceased being used by the eighth century C.E. Many different miniscule scripts developed as the Old World fell into disorganization. Among these were the Anglo-Saxon script of England, the Merovingian script of the Franks, the Visigothic script of Spain, and the Beneventan script of southern Italy.

ADDITIONAL RESOURCES

Claiborne, Robert. *The Birth of Writing*. New York: Time-Life Books, 1974.

Daniels, Peter T., and William Bright. *The World's Writing Systems*. New York: Oxford University Press, 1996.

Diringer, David. *The Alphabet: A Key to the History of Mankind*. 3d ed. New York: Funk & Wagnalls, 1968.

_____. *Writing*. New York: Praeger, 1962.

Jackson, Donald. *The Story of Writing*. New York: Taplinger, 1981.

Jean, Georges. *Writing: The Story of Alphabets and Scripts*. New York: Harry N. Abrams, 1992.

Robinson, Andrew. *The Story of Writing*. New York: Thames and Hudson, 1995.

Vervliet, Hendrik D. L., ed. *The Book Through Five Thousand Years*. New York: Phaidon, 1972.

Walker, C. B. F. *Cuneiform*. Berkeley: University of California Press, 1987.

SEE ALSO: Africa, North; Akkadians; Arabia; Assyria; Babylonia; Berbers; Cai Lun; Canaanites; Carthage; Celts; China; Crete; Egypt, Pharaonic; Egypt, Prepharaonic; Ethiopia; Etruscans; Germany; Greece, Archaic; Greece, Classical; Greece, Mycenaean; Han Dynasty; Hittites; Indus Valley civilization; Islam; Israel; Judaism; Linear B; Maya; Monte Albán; Napata and Meroe; Olmecs; Pāṇini; Persia; Phoenicia; Rome, Prerepublican; Rosetta stone; Spain; Sumerians; Teotihuacán; Zapotecs.

—Barbara C. Beattie

ENCYCLOPEDIA

— A —

ʿABD AL-MALIK

ALSO KNOWN AS: ʿAbd al-Malik ibn Marwān
BORN: 646-647 C.E.; Medina, Arabia
DIED: October, 705 C.E.; Damascus
RELATED CIVILIZATIONS: Arabia, Umayyad
Dynasty
MAJOR ROLE/POSITION: Caliph

Life. The reign of Caliph ʿAbd al-Malik (ahb-dool-muh-LIHK), fifth ruler of the Umayyad Dynasty (661-751 C.E.), proved pivotal for both the regime and the development of medieval Islamic government. His family elevated him to the caliphate in 685 C.E. as anti-Umayyad revolts threatened to shatter the recently created Muslim empire. An astute and patient strategist, ʿAbd al-Malik pacified Syria, Palestine, and Egypt be-fore regaining Iraq one province at a time. By 690 C.E., ʿAbd al-Malik had isolated his primary opponent, ʿAbd Allāh ibn az-Zubayr of Arabia. His armies finally defeated ʿAbd Allāh Ibn az-Zubayr outside Mecca in late 692 C.E., ending the civil wars.

Caliph ʿAbd al-Malik inaugurated a decade of political consolidations designed to centralize the government. He made Arabic the language of administration, replacing the languages of the defeated Persians and Byzantines, and standardized the tax code. He created the Arab empire's first currency. Militarily, ʿAbd al-Malik laid the groundwork for new territorial expansion after his death. To the west, his forces pacified Tunisia by 698 C.E. and began deep raids into Algeria and Morocco. In the east, Muslim expeditions probed into

Caliph ʿAbd al-Malik, fifth ruler of the Umayyad Dynasty (661-751 C.E.), built the Dome of the Rock mosque, also known as Bab El Silsileh, in Jerusalem. (PhotoDisc)

eastern Persia, Afghanistan, and Turkistan. A patron of culture, 'Abd al-Malik built Jerusalem's Dome of the Rock mosque.

Influence. 'Abd al-Malik ended the 683-692 C.E. civil wars and transformed the Muslim caliphate into a stable, powerful, and unified imperial structure.

ADDITIONAL RESOURCES

The Encyclopaedia of Islam. Prepared by a number of leading orientalists; edited by an editorial committee consisting of H. A. R. Gibb et al. under the patronage of the International Union of Academies. New ed. Leiden, Netherlands: E. J. Brill, 1960-[2000].

Hawting, G. R. *The First Dynasty of Islam: The Umayyad Caliphate* A.D. *661-750*. New York: Routledge, 2000.

Shaban, M. A. *Islamic History,* A.D. *600-750: A New Interpretation*. Cambridge, England: Cambridge University Press, 1973.

SEE ALSO: 'Abd Allāh ibn az-Zubayr; Arabia; Islam; Umayyad Dynasty.

—Weston F. Cook, Jr.

'ABD ALLĀH IBN AL-'ABBĀS

ALSO KNOWN AS: Ibn 'Abbas; al-Ḥibr (the doctor); al-Baḥr (the sea)
BORN: c. 619 C.E.; Mecca, Arabia
DIED: 687/688 C.E.; aṭ-Ṭā'if, Arabia
RELATED CIVILIZATIONS: Islam, Arabia
MAJOR ROLE/POSITION: Scholar, military leader

Life. 'Abd Allāh ibn al-'Abbās (ahb-dool-AH-ihb-uhn-uhl-uhb-BAHS) was cousin and companion to the prophet Muḥammad and ancestor of the 'Abbāsid Dynasty, as well as the first to interpret, or provide an exegesis of, the Qur'ān. His mother Ummu'l-Fadl Lubabe, who had accepted Islam, brought him up Muslim.

He was a counselor to 'Umar ibn al-Khaṭṭāb, 'Uthmān ibn 'Affān, and 'Alī ibn Abī Ṭālib and accompanied the armies sent into Egypt (639-642 C.E.), Ifrīqiya (647 C.E.), Ṭabaristān (650-651 C.E.), and Istanbul (668 C.E.). 'Uthmān, just before his assassination, appointed Ibn 'Abbās to conduct the pilgrimage to Mecca (656 C.E.). He participated in the Battles of Camel (656 C.E.) and Ṣiffīn (657 C.E.). 'Alī appointed him as governor to Basra, but as their relation became severe, he left for Mecca (658-659 C.E.).

After the death in 680 C.E. of Mu'āwiyah I (the first leader of Islam after the legitimate caliphs and founder of the Umayyad Dynasty), he paid homage to his son Yazīd I. He tried to talk Ḥusayn, Muḥammad's grandson, into not going to Al-Kufa, for he believed that its inhabitants were not sincere, and he felt a grave sorrow when he learned of his assassination at Karbalā'. He left Mecca and went to aṭ-Ṭā'if because he was not pleased

that 'Abd Allāh ibn az-Zubayr had made Haremi Sherif his quarter, which resulted in sieges in both 683 and 692 C.E.

Influence. Ibn 'Abbās is renowned for his early interpretation of the Qur'ān and for documenting the story of Muḥammad and his companions. He was a leading transmitter of *hadith*, an authority on *fikh* and *fetwas* (opinion on legal matters), and the source of inspiration for many scholarly studies.

ADDITIONAL RESOURCES

Armstrong, Karen. *The Battle for God*. New York: Alfred A. Knopf, 2000.

The Encyclopaedia of Islam. Prepared by a number of leading orientalists; edited by an editorial committee consisting of H. A. R. Gibb et al. under the patronage of the International Union of Academies. New ed. Leiden, Netherlands: E. J. Brill, 1960-[2000].

Esposito, John, ed. *The Oxford History of Islam*. New York: Oxford University Press, 1999.

Holt, P., ed. *The Cambridge History of Islam*. Cambridge, England: Cambridge University Press, 1980.

Walker, George Benjamin. *Foundations of Islam: The Making of a World Faith*. London: Peter Owen, 1998.

SEE ALSO: 'Abd Allāh ibn az-Zubayr; 'Alī ibn Abī Ṭālib; Arabia; Islam; Muḥammad; Qur'ān; 'Umar ibn al-Khaṭṭāb; Umayyad Dynasty; 'Uthmān ibn 'Affān.

—M. Mehdi Ilhan

ʿABD ALLĀH IBN AZ-ZUBAYR

ALSO KNOWN AS: Ibn az-Zubayr
BORN: 624 C.E.; Medina, Arabia
DIED: October or November, 692 C.E.; Mecca, Arabia
RELATED CIVILIZATIONS: Islam, Arabia
MAJOR ROLE/POSITION: Caliph (nominal), military leader, scholar

Life. ʿAbd Allāh ibn az-Zubayr (ahb-dool-AH-ihb-uhn-uhz-zoo-BIR) was the son of Asthma, Abū Bakr's daughter, and paternal grandson of Safiyya, the prophet Muḥammad's maternal aunt. As the leader of the second generation of Mecca's Islamic families, who chafed under the Umayyads' assumption of the caliphate, he led a rebellion against that ruling dynasty. He participated in many battles during the early spread of Islam, including the Battle of Yarmuk (636 C.E.), the conquest of Egypt (639 C.E.), and the fight against the Byzantines in Ifrīqiya, where he killed exarch Gregorious (649 C.E.). The following year, he took part in the campaign to Khurasan.

He was one of four scholars charged by ʿUthmān ibn ʿAffān with the recension of the Qurʾān. He defended ʿUthmān on the day he was assassinated (656 C.E.) and joined the Battle of Camel (656 C.E.), commanding an infantry of ʿĀʾishah bint Abī Bakr's forces. His father was killed on the battlefield.

After the death in 680 C.E. of Muʿāwiyah I (the first leader of Islam after the legitimate caliphs, and founder of the Umayyad Dynasty), Ibn az-Zubayr refused to pay homage to his son Yazīd I. Instead, the people of Hijaz, Iraq, and some parts of Syria paid him homage.

He declared Mecca as the seat of his caliphate and defended first against the forces sent by Yazīd until his death in 683 C.E. and then, after a brief period of peace, those of ʿAbd al-Malik in 692 C.E. Ḥajjāj ibn Yūsuf, ʿAbd al-Malik's commander, laid siege to the city for seven months and forced Ibn az-Zubayr to fight to his death.

Influence. Although Ibn az-Zubayr's rebellion failed, he is remembered for his fight against the hereditary rule of Umayyad caliphs, for his piety, bravery, oratory skills, and for his part in the first official exegesis of Qurʾān.

ADDITIONAL RESOURCES

The Encyclopaedia of Islam. Prepared by a number of leading orientalists; edited by an editorial committee consisting of H. A. R. Gibb et al. under the patronage of the International Union of Academies. New ed. Leiden, Netherlands: E. J. Brill, 1960-[2000].

Esposito, John, ed. *The Oxford History of Islam.* New York: Oxford University Press, 1999.

Holt, P., ed. *The Cambridge History of Islam.* Cambridge, England: Cambridge University Press, 1980.

Walker, George Benjamin. *Foundations of Islam: The Making of a World Faith.* London: Peter Owen, 1998.

SEE ALSO: ʿAbd al-Malik; ʿĀʾishah bint Abī Bakr; Arabia; Islam; Muḥammad; Qurʾān; ʿUthmān ibn ʿAffān.
—*M. Mehdi Ilhan*

ʿABD ALLĀH IBN SAʿD IBN ABĪ SARḤ

BORN: late seventh century C.E.; place unknown
DIED: 656 or 658 C.E.; Askalon or Ramala (later the West Bank)
RELATED CIVILIZATIONS: Arabia, Egypt
MAJOR ROLE/POSITION: Military conqueror

Life. Two years after the Arab conquest of Egypt by ʿAmr ibn al-ʿĀṣ in 642 C.E., ʿUmar ibn al-Khaṭṭāb, the second caliph of Islam, made the financier ʿAbd Allāh ibn Saʿd ibn Abī Sarḥ (ahb-dool-AH-ihb-uhn-SAH-ihb-uhn-ahb-EE-SAHRK) governor of Upper Egypt in order to increase revenue from the province. In the following year, ʿUthmān ibn ʿAffān, ʿAbd Allāh's foster brother, became caliph, recalled ʿAmr, and appointed ʿAbd Allāh governor over the entire country. The Byzantine recapture of Alexandria late in 645 C.E. persuaded ʿUthmān to send ʿAmr back to Egypt to retake the city. ʿAmr refused a power-sharing arrangement in Egypt following this successful campaign, and left ʿAbd Allāh in full control of the province.

ʿAbd Allāh oversaw the expansion of the province to the west as far as Carthage. In 651-652 C.E., he led a southern military campaign that resulted in a treaty with the Christian kingdom in Nubia. His most successful operations, however, were naval in nature. Together with Muʿāwiyah I, the governor of Syria, ʿAbd Allāh built the first Islamic navy, with which Cyprus and other Mediterranean islands were conquered. The Byzantine fleet was defeated twice by this navy, first near Alexandria in 652 C.E. and then at Dhāt al-Ṣawārī, off the Turkish coast, in 655 C.E. In the latter battle, ʿAbd Allāh was a co-commander.

Influence. ʿAbd Allāh's naval operations helped ensure the growth of Islamic power in the Mediterranean.

ADDITIONAL RESOURCES

Butler, A. *Arab Invasion of Egypt*. Brooklyn, N.Y.: A & B Publishing, 1992.

Fahmy, Aly Mohamed. *Muslim Sea-Power in the Eastern Mediterranean*. London: Dan Bosco, 1950.

SEE ALSO: Saracen conquest; ʿUmar ibn al-Khaṭṭāb; ʿUthmān ibn ʿAffān.

—*Thomas J. Sienkewicz*

ABIPÓN

ALSO KNOWN AS: Callaga
DATE: 6000 B.C.E.-700 C.E.
LOCALE: Andes, Argentina
SIGNIFICANCE: The Abipón were the first group in evidence in Argentina and were known to produce influential women shamans, powerful warriors, and great hunters.

Also called the Callaga, the Abipón (ah-beh-POHN) were nomadic hunter-gatherers who lived along the lower Bermejo River in the Gran Chaco area of north-central Argentina. Their language group was Guaycuruan, and they spoke three dialects, depending on where they lived. They called themselves either Forest People (Nakaigetergehè), Open Country People (Riikahè), or later, Water People (Yaaukanigá).

The Abipón are believed to be the first people to occupy the Gran Chaco area, arriving from the north by approximately 6000 B.C.E. They hunted, fished, and gathered plants in season. They were roaming nomads, crossing the grassy plains in search of rhea, guanaco, peccary, and jaguar. Social organization was based on kinship groups, and differentiation among members was based primarily on gender and age. Women ran the camps, gathered most of the food, and carried on ritual ceremonies while men hunted and fought. Wealthy, powerful women most often acted as the shamans. Men were organized by the shaman-approved war chief. Limited natural resources in their marginal area as well as the simple tools and materials of their culture led them to be widely scattered and simply organized, although they produced fierce warriors and powerful hunters.

Both men and women made and wore ornaments of horn, wood, bone, thread, and metal. They also could be recognized for their shaved heads and plucked eyebrows. High-ranking women had extensive tattoos. The Abipón could climb, swim, and run with the best and were skilled in the use of bola, lance, and bow and arrow. They scalped their enemies of hair, nose, and ear skin, made pipes and whistles from their bones, and drank from their skulls.

After 700 C.E. In 1750, when the Jesuits arrived, the Abipón numbered about five thousand members. Their numbers fell by slaughter, disease, and assimilation, and by about 1912, the Abipón had ceased to exist.

ADDITIONAL RESOURCES

Radin, Paul. *Indians of South America*. New York: Greenwood Press, 1969.

Schobinger, Juan. *The Ancient Americans*. Armonk, N.Y.: M. E. Sharpe, 2000.

Steward, Julian. *Handbook of South American Indians*. 7 vols. New York: Cooper Square Publications, 1963.

SEE ALSO: Andes, central; Andes, south; Archaic South American culture; South America, southern.

—*Michael W. Simpson*

ABRAHA

FLOURISHED: sixth century C.E.
RELATED CIVILIZATIONS: Ethiopia, Arabia
MAJOR ROLE/POSITION: Viceroy of Yemen

Life. Little is known about Abraha's (AHB-rah-hah) early life. In 523 C.E., he participated in the 70,000-person Abyssinian expedition across the Red Sea to avenge the Christian massacre in Najran by Yūsuf As'ar (also known as Dhū Nuwās), the Jewish ruler of Yemen. Following an initial but inconclusive military victory, Abraha replaced his commander, Arya, and became viceroy of Yemen following the death of Yūsuf As'ar in battle in 525 C.E.

Abraha constructed a major cathedral in Ṣan'ā' as a rival pilgrimage site to the pagan Mecca. This building, known in Arabic as al-Qalīs from the Greek *ekklesia* ("church"), was defiled by members of the cult of the Ka'bah in Mecca, probably in 570 or 571 C.E., the year of Muḥammad's birth. Abraha retaliated against Mecca with an expedition that included at least one elephant. Despite Arab wonder at the unfamiliar animal, the expedition failed because of a smallpox epidemic. This year is known as the "year of the elephant."

One of the burstings of the Ma'rib Dam, known in Arabic tradition as the great flood, occurred in 542-543 C.E., during Abraha's reign. This break was at least the second such event, but a more catastrophic one took place between 542 and 570 C.E. and is traditionally associated with the decline in the civilization of South Arabia.

Nothing is known of Abraha's death, but the Abyssinians had lost control of Yemen to the Persians by 575 C.E.

Influence. The Christian culture that Abraha supported in Arabia was replaced by an Islamic culture in the next century.

ADDITIONAL RESOURCE

Smith, G. Rex. *Studies in the Medieval History of the Yemen and South Arabia.* Brookfield, Vt.: Ashgate, 1997.

SEE ALSO: Arabia; Christianity; Islam; Judaism; Muḥammad.

—Thomas J. Sienkewicz

ABŪ BAKR

ALSO KNOWN AS: al-Ṣiddīk, the upright
BORN: 573 C.E.; Mecca
DIED: August 23, 634 C.E.; buried in Medina
RELATED CIVILIZATIONS: Byzantium, Persia
MAJOR ROLE/POSITION: First caliph

Life. A merchant from the tribe of Quraysh, Abū Bakr (ah-bew-BAK-ur) was an early convert to Islam and the father-in-law of Muḥammad. He accompanied the prophet in his flight (*hijrah*) from Mecca to Medina in 622 C.E., helped negotiate vital intertribal alliances in the later 620's C.E., and fought in Muḥammad's military campaigns.

After the prophet's death in 632 C.E., Abū Bakr was elected caliph (*khalīfah*, or successor) by an assembly of leading Muslims. Over the next two years, he defeated rival claimants to his position, crushed secessionist movements, spread Muslim power throughout the Arabian peninsula, and made significant military gains at the expense of the Byzantines and Persians. Shortly before his death in 634 C.E., he chose 'Umar ibn al-Khaṭṭāb as his successor.

Influence. Abū Bakr was renowned among early Muslims for his steadfast support of Muḥammad, his diplomatic skill, his courage in combat, and his personal rectitude. His election to the caliphate established the principle of succession by merit, an important concept in the majority Sunni branch of Islam. Abū Bakr kept the infant Islamic state from dissolving after the death of Muḥammad, expanded its borders, and began the formal process of assembling materials for inclusion in the Muslim sacred book, the Qur'ān.

ADDITIONAL RESOURCES

Donner, F. M. *The Early Islamic Conquests.* Princeton, N.J.: Princeton University Press, 1981.

Kennedy, H. *The Prophet and the Age of the Caliphates*. London: Longman, 1986.

SEE ALSO: Byzantine Empire; Islam; Persia; Qurʾān; ʿUmar ibn al-Khaṭṭāb.

—Michael J. Fontenot

ACCIUS, LUCIUS

BORN: 170 B.C.E.; probably Pisaurum, Umbria, Italy
DIED: c. 86 B.C.E.; place unknown
RELATED CIVILIZATION: Republican Rome
MAJOR ROLE/POSITION: Poet

Life. Lucius Accius (LEW-shee-uhs AK-shee-uhs) was born to manumitted parents and came to Rome at an unknown date. He stated that he presented a play when he was thirty years old; whether the play was his first is uncertain. Accius is reported to have refused to rise in recognition of the rank of Gaius Julius Caesar Strabo, also a writer of tragedy, because of his own superiority in the writing of tragedy. Accius is also said to have had a statue of himself placed in the temple of the Camenae and was ridiculed because the statue was so large in comparison to the rather short poet. Statesman and philosopher Cicero stated that he himself had talked to the old poet.

Influence. Accius wrote in a variety of genres: history, mythography and theology, agriculture, and love.

More than seven hundred lines and more than forty titles of tragedies and *praetextae* (serious Roman historical drama) are assigned to him, representing the Trojan cycle principally, but including the Theban cycle and various other legendary subjects, many of which he introduced to the Roman audience. Although more verses of Accian tragedy have survived than those of any other Roman tragedian, few long passages exist; most are brief quotations preserved by grammarians for some peculiarity of language. Accius was the last major poet of the golden age of Roman drama.

ADDITIONAL RESOURCES
Warmington, E. H. *Remains of Old Latin*. Cambridge, Mass.: Harvard University Press, 1967.
Wender, Dorothea. *Roman Poetry*. Carbondale: Southern Illinois University Press, 1991.

SEE ALSO: Rome, Republican.

—C. Wayne Tucker

ACHAEAN LEAGUE

DATE: fourth century B.C.E.-c. 323 B.C.E. and 280 B.C.E.-146 B.C.E.
LOCALE: Peloponnese in southern Greece
RELATED CIVILIZATIONS: Hellenistic Greece, Republican Rome
SIGNIFICANCE: The Achaean League, a federation of Greek city-states, was the chief military power in Greece in the third and early second centuries B.C.E.

A confederation of Achaean (uh-KEE-uhn) cities, located in the northern Peloponnese, existed during the fourth century B.C.E., but this league was dissolved after the Macedonian conquest. The league was revived in 280 B.C.E., and in 251 B.C.E., it extended membership to Sicyon (Sikyon), a non-Achaean city. Under the leadership of Aratus of Sicyon, the league grew, and by 228 B.C.E., it had expelled the Macedonians from the Peloponnese and become the chief power in southern Greece.

The Achaean League was governed by a federal assembly, but a council and several magistrates handled daily business. The chief league official was an annually elected general who could hold office only in alternate years. Member cities did not give up local autonomy and lived under their own laws.

The resurgence of Sparta forced the Achaean League into alliance with Macedonia in 224 B.C.E., but Achaea joined Rome against Macedonia in 198 B.C.E. Relations with Rome soured, and in 167 B.C.E., the Romans took one thousand Achaeans, including the historian Polybius, to Rome as hostages. In 146 B.C.E., the Romans declared war on and defeated the Achaean

League. The league was dissolved, ending the last vestige of Greek freedom.

ADDITIONAL RESOURCES
Larsen, J. A. O. *Greek Federal States: Their Institutions and History.* Oxford, England: Clarendon Press, 1968.

Walbank, F. W. *The Hellenistic World.* Rev. ed. Cambridge, Mass.: Harvard University Press, 1993.

SEE ALSO: Achaean War; Greece, Hellenistic and Roman; Macedonia; Polybius; Rome, Republican.
—*James P. Sickinger*

ACHAEAN WAR

DATE: 146 B.C.E.
LOCALE: The southern Greek peninsula known as the Peloponnese
RELATED CIVILIZATIONS: Hellenistic Greece, Republican Rome
SIGNIFICANCE: The Achaean War resulted in the defeat of the Achaean League, the last important and independent military force in Hellenistic Greece.

Background. In the second century, the Peloponnese housed two competing powers, Sparta and the Achaean (uh-KEE-uhn) League. After decades of disagreement, their quarreling provoked decisive Roman intervention.

Action. At first, Rome attempted to arbitrate. Responsible for the Republic's foreign affairs, the Roman senate dispatched ambassadors in 147 B.C.E. However, its instructions to detach several cities from the league angered the Achaeans, who at Corinth threatened the ambassadors with violence. Although Rome sent another, more conciliatory embassy, the Achaeans obstructed negotiations and soon afterward declared war on Sparta.

In 146 B.C.E., Quintus Caecilius Metellus Macedonicus and a Roman army marched south from Mace-donia, defeating Achaean troops in central Greece. Caecilius's successor, Lucius Mummius, crushed the league's remaining forces at the isthmus in late summer. After sacking Corinth, Mummius began organizing Greek affairs with the assistance of ten commissioners from Rome.

Consequences. While Corinth was razed to the ground, those communities that had fought against the Republic were attached to the Roman province in Macedonia. Kept under the watchful eye of a Roman governor, the entire Greek peninsula was eventually incorporated into Rome's overseas empire.

ADDITIONAL RESOURCES
Green, Peter. *Alexander to Actium: The Historical Evolution of the Hellenistic Age.* Reprint. Berkeley: University of California Press, 1993.
Gruen, Erich S. "The Origins of the Achaean War." *Journal of Hellenic Studies* 96 (1976): 46-69.

SEE ALSO: Achaean League; Greece, Hellenistic and Roman; Mummius, Lucius; Rome, Republican.
—*Denvy A. Bowman*

ACHAEMENIAN DYNASTY

ALSO KNOWN AS: Achaemenid, Hakhamanishiya (*Persian*)
DATE: 705-330 B.C.E.
LOCALE: Persia (modern Iran)
SIGNIFICANCE: The Achaemenian kings ruled over the Persian Empire, which stretched from Egypt to India.

Achaemenes (c. 705-675 B.C.E.?) is the Greek form of Hakhamanish, the eponymous ancestor of the Achaemenian (ak-ih-MEHN-ee-uhn) Dynasty, who reigned over the Persians. Teispes, his son, fathered both a senior and a junior line of kings. The first line included Cambyses I (r. c. 600-559 B.C.E.); Cyrus the Great (r. 558-530 B.C.E.), who defeated his Median grandfather, Astyages (r. c. 585-550 B.C.E.), conquered Lydia in 546 B.C.E. and captured Babylon in 539 B.C.E., allowing the Jews to return to Palestine; and Cambyses II (r. 529-522 B.C.E.), who murdered his younger brother Smerdis and in 525 B.C.E. conquered Egypt and the Nile Valley down to Nubia but died of an accidental wound in 522 B.C.E.

The junior line of kings took over with Darius the Great (r. 522-486 B.C.E.), who unified the empire, suppressed the Ionian Revolt (499-494 B.C.E.), and lost the Battle of Marathon (490 B.C.E.) to the Greeks. The empire now reached to the Hyphasis (Beas) River in the east, Macedonia and Libya in the west, the Caucasus Mountains and the Aral Sea in the north, and the Persian Gulf and the Arabian desert in the south. Xerxes I (r. 486-465 B.C.E.) launched a massive invasion of Greece, winning at Thermopylae (480 B.C.E.) but suffering defeat at Salamis (480 B.C.E.) and Plataea (479 B.C.E.). Hostilities continued under Artaxerxes I (465-425 B.C.E.) until the Peace of Callias (449).

Darius II (r. 424-405 B.C.E.) gave monetary aid, which enabled the Spartans to defeat the Athenians in their civil war. Artaxerxes II (r. 405-359) was challenged by his brother Cyrus the Younger, who was killed at the Battle of Cunaxa in 401 B.C.E. Artaxerxes III (r. 359-338 B.C.E.) saw the rise of the Macedonian king Philip II, whose son Alexander the Great overran the Persian Empire during the reign of Darius III (r. 336-330 B.C.E.).

Governing the vast empire was accomplished through a system of provinces called satrapies, governed by satraps who were periodically observed by the king's own officials. Examples of Achaemenian architecture survive at Pasargadae (modern Mashad-i-Murghab north of Lake Bakhtegān) and at Persepolis thirty miles (forty-eight kilometers) southwest. Persians maintained their records in three languages, inscriptions appearing in Old Persian, Elamite, and Akkadian. A fourth language, Aramaic, was used for the day-to-day work of government and international correspondence. Many art objects, including sophisticated works in gold, have survived.

This rock carving portrays a victorious Darius III (r. 336-330 B.C.E.). (North Wind Picture Archives)

ADDITIONAL RESOURCES

Cook, J. M. *The Persian Empire*. New York: Schocken, 1983.

Dandamaev, M. A. *A Political History of the Achaemenid Empire*. Leiden: Brill, 1989.

Frye, R. N. *History of Ancient Iran*. Munich: C. H. Beck, 1984.

Gershevitch, I., ed. *The Cambridge History of Iran II: The Median and Achaemenian Periods*. Cambridge, England: Cambridge University Press, 1985.

Yamauchi, E. *Persia and the Bible*. Grand Rapids, Mich.: Baker, 1990.

SEE ALSO: Alexander the Great; Astyages; Babylonia; Cyrus the Great; Darius the Great; Darius III; Greco-Persian Wars; Marathon, Battle of; Persia; Philip II; Plataea, Battle of; Salamis, Battle of; Thermopylae, Battle of; Xerxes I.

—*Edwin Yamauchi*

ACHILLES PAINTER

FLOURISHED: c. 460-c. 430 B.C.E.
RELATED CIVILIZATION: Classical Greece
MAJOR ROLE/POSITION: Artist

Life. Named after the figure of Achilles on an amphora, or wine jar, in the Vatican Museums, the Achilles Painter (uh-KIHL-EEZ PAYN-tuhr) was one of the finest Athenian vase painters of the Classical period. More than 230 vases of various shapes, large and small, have been attributed to him. A pupil of the Berlin Painter, the Achilles Painter worked mainly in the red-figure and white-ground techniques but occasionally in black-figure for Panathenaic amphoras. His most beautiful vases are white-ground *lekythoi*, or oil jugs, decorated in delicate colors on a white background, often with a mistress and maid or two mourners at a tomb.

The drawing style of the Achilles Painter is exceptionally fine, with a beautiful quality of line. His figures tend to be serene and noble, similar to the contemporary sculptures of the Parthenon. The artist favored a variety of figure types, including deities, heroes, and mortals. Once, on a *lekythos* in Lugano, he represented an exquisite scene of two Muses on Mount Helicon.

Apparently the Achilles Painter's vases were prized commodities, for they have turned up not only in Athens and nearby Eretria, but as far afield as Etruria, Sicily, Egypt, and Turkey.

Influence. The Achilles Painter set the standard of excellence for white-ground *lekythoi*. His pupils, such as the Phiale Painter, continued his style into the later fifth century B.C.E.

ADDITIONAL RESOURCES

Beazley, J. D. *Attic Red-Figure Vase-Painters*. Oxford, England: Clarendon Press, 1963.

———. *Paralipomena*. Oxford, England: Clarendon Press, 1971.

Boardman, John. *Athenian Red Figure Vases: The Classical Period*. London: Thames and Hudson, 1989.

Kurtz, Donna Carol. *Athenian White Lekythoi: Patterns and Painters*. Oxford, England: Clarendon Press, 1975.

SEE ALSO: Art and architecture; Greece, Classical.

—*Evelyn E. Bell*

ACHILLES TATIUS

ALSO KNOWN AS: Achilles Statius
FLOURISHED: second century C.E.; Alexandria
RELATED CIVILIZATION: Roman Greece
MAJOR ROLE/POSITION: Novelist

Life. Achilles Tatius (uh-KIHL-EEZ TAY-shee-uhs) was a sophisticated Greek writer from Alexandria, who lived during the second century C.E. Little is known about his life, but papyri show that his novel *Leukippe and Kleitophon* (English translation first published in 1597) was written by the late second century. The *Suda*, a Byzantine lexicon compiled at the end of the tenth century, identifies the author as a native of Alexandria and lists various other writings, now lost.

Leukippe and Kleitophon, a love story replete with adventures—torture, shipwrecks, pirates—is notable for its comic rewriting of romantic motifs, its psychological realism, and its resilient heroine. After a brief introduction, the novel, eight books long, is narrated entirely from the limited first-person perspective of the hero Kleitophon. Kleitophon seeks advice on how to woo, Leukippe runs away to spite her mother, and Kleitophon is unfaithful to his beloved. The novel includes descriptions of Alexandria and the lighthouse on the Pharos island. The *Suda* claims the author ended up a Christian and a bishop, although that is doubtful.

Influence. Achilles Tatius's novel is important not only as an early form of the genre but also for its information on contemporary tastes and attitudes, including learned digressions, a debate on heterosexual versus homosexual love, and a description of a painting of Europa. The novel has been criticized for its explicit sex and praised for its depictions of characters and emotions. It played an important role in the twelfth century Byzantine Greek revival of the novel. In the sixteenth century, translations began appearing in Latin and modern languages. This novel had influence on Elizabethan prose fiction (including the writings of Robert Greene) and in the seventeenth century was reworked by Pierre Du Ryer as a French tragicomedy.

ADDITIONAL RESOURCES

Bartsch, Shadi. *Decoding the Ancient Novel: The Reader and the Role of Description in Heliodorus and Achilles Tatius*. Princeton, N.J.: Princeton University Press, 1989.

Hägg, Tomas. *The Novel in Antiquity*. Berkeley: University of California Press, 1983.

Konstan, David. *Sexual Symmetry: Love in the Ancient Novel and Related Genres*. Princeton, N.J.: Princeton University Press, 1994.

Schmeling, Gareth, ed. *The Novel in the Ancient World*. Leiden: E. J. Brill, 1996.

SEE ALSO: Greece, Hellenistic and Roman; Heliodorus of Emesa; Longus.

—*Joan B. Burton*

ACTE, CLAUDIA

BORN: first century C.E.; Asia Minor
DIED: c. end of first century C.E.; Italy
RELATED CIVILIZATION: Early Imperial Rome
MAJOR ROLE/POSITION: Freedwoman, courtesan of the emperor Nero

Life. Originally from Asia Minor and reputedly, though unlikely, a descendant of the former kings of Pergamum, Claudia Acte was a member of the imperial household during the reign of Claudius, Nero's uncle and predecessor. The Roman historian Tacitus states that she was a freedwoman when she began a liaison with Nero in 55 C.E., while he was still married to Octavia. Up to this point, Nero's mother, Agrippina the Younger, had maintained control over him, but by developing a relationship with Acte, Nero defied his mother's wishes. One person who did approve of Nero's relationship with Acte was his tutor Seneca the Younger, who saw it as a way of freeing Nero from Agrippina's control. Nero reconciled with his mother within a year, however, and by 58 C.E., Poppaea Sabina replaced Acte in his affections.

Acte owned land in both Italy and Sardinia, and records suggest that she became a wealthy woman. Despite having been dismissed by Nero, when the emperor committed suicide in 68 C.E., Acte reportedly obtained his remains and placed them in the tomb of the Domitii, his family tomb.

Influence. Acte's relationship with Nero corresponds to the best year of his reign.

ADDITIONAL RESOURCES

Barrett, Anthony A. *Agrippina: Sex, Power, and Politics in the Early Empire*. New Haven, Conn.: Yale University Press, 1996.

Griffin, Miriam T. *Nero: The End of a Dynasty*. Reprint. London: B. T. Batsford, 1996.

Suetonius. *The Twelve Caesars*. Translated by Robert Graves. London: Viking Press, 2000.

SEE ALSO: Agrippina the Younger; Nero; Poppaea Sabina; Rome, Imperial; Seneca the Younger; Tacitus.

—*T. Davina McClain*

ACTIUM, BATTLE OF

DATE: September 2, 31 B.C.E.
LOCALE: Actium, a promontory at the mouth of the Gulf of Ambracia, on the western coast of Greece
RELATED CIVILIZATIONS: Republican and Imperial Rome, Ptolemaic Egypt
SIGNIFICANCE: Ended the era of the civil wars and made Octavian (later Augustus) master of the Roman world.

Background. After the death of Julius Caesar in 44 B.C.E., the rivals Marc Antony and Octavian were reconciled and formed (with Marcus Aemilius Lepidus) the Second Triumvirate. In 32 B.C.E., the Triumvirate ceased and the two were again enemies. Octavian returned to Rome, gained power, and had war declared on Marc Antony and Cleopatra VII.

Action. Marc Antony was camped at Actium (AK-shee-uhm) with 70,000 infantry and 500 ships. Octavian, advancing from the north with 80,000 infantry and 400 ships, blockaded Antony. Antony drew up his fleet outside the gulf, facing Octavian's fleet to the west, with Cleopatra's more than 60 galleys be-hind him in reserve. Both fleets tried to outflank each other to the north. With the sea battle going against Antony, Cleopatra (perhaps on Antony's orders) broke through the center and suddenly fled with her galleys; Antony fought through to the open sea with a few ships and followed her to Egypt. The battle continued until the rest of Antony's fleet was set on fire. Antony's land forces surrendered a week later.

Consequences. The battle was a decisive victory by Octavian over Antony and Cleopatra, who fled to Egypt, where they were pursued by Octavian.

ADDITIONAL RESOURCES
Carter, J. M., *The Battle of Actium: The Rise and Triumph of Augustus Caesar.* London: Hamish Hamilton, 1970.
Southern, P. *Augustus.* New York: Routledge, 1998.

SEE ALSO: Antony, Marc; Augustus; Cleopatra VII; Egypt, Ptolemaic and Roman; Rome, Imperial; Rome, Republican.

—*Thomas McGeary*

ADENA CULTURE

DATE: 1000 B.C.E.-100 C.E.
LOCALE: Primarily the area that became southern Ohio, also modern Kentucky, Indiana, West Virginia, and possibly Pennsylvania
RELATED CIVILIZATION: Hopewell
SIGNIFICANCE: The Adena culture preceded maize cultivation in eastern North America and influenced the development of the advanced Hopewell culture in the Ohio and Illinois Valleys.

Named for an estate near Chillicothe, Ohio, that has yielded much related archaeological data (including a large burial mound), the Adena (ah-DEHN-ah) were a culture of hunter-gatherers that thrived between 1000 B.C.E. and 100 C.E. They were centered in present-day southern Ohio, but archaeological evidence has also identified Adena peoples in Indiana, West Virginia, Kentucky, and possibly Pennsylvania.

The Adena commonly resided in villages in circular, conical-roofed dwellings made of poles, willows, and bark. They were known to have sometimes lived in rock shelters, natural stone overhangs that served as dry and relatively comfortable homes. Because they existed before the introduction of maize cultivation in eastern North America, their diet was composed of fish, game animals, and wild plants. Artifacts found at Adena sites include stone projectile points, hoes, blades, and similar lithic tools, stone smoking pipes, and plain pottery, as well as beautiful ornaments of mica, copper, and seashell that indicate that the Adena were part of an extensive trade network.

Adena funeral culture was centered around earthen burial mounds, which were enlarged with each new interment. Before the first century C.E., their dead, among whom there were few noticeable distinctions, were buried with utilitarian objects and a few ornaments. After this period, burial customs became more elaborate, and some bodies were interred in log tombs with rich grave goods.

Sometimes referred to as the climax of the Early

Woodland period, the Adena culture was partly emulated by the transitional Hopewell people, an impressive mound-building culture that reached its height in the Ohio and Illinois Valleys between 100 B.C.E. and 200 C.E.

ADDITIONAL RESOURCES
Webb, William S., and R. S. Baby. *The Adena People, No. 2.* Columbus: Ohio Historical Society, 1957.
Webb, William S., and C. E. Snow. *The Adena People.*
Reprint. Knoxville: University of Tennessee Press, 1988.
Woodward, Susan L. *Indian Mounds of the Middle Ohio Valley.* Newark, Ohio: McDonald & Woodward, 1986.

SEE ALSO: Archaic North American culture; Middle Woodland traditions.

—Jeremiah R. Taylor

ADRIANOPLE, BATTLE OF

DATE: August 9, 378 C.E.
LOCALE: Adrianople, Thrace
RELATED CIVILIZATIONS: Visigoths, Imperial Rome
SIGNIFICANCE: Visigoth victory at Adrianople (aydree-uh-NOH-puhl) resulted in the emergence of a new Roman policy toward barbarian peoples.

Background. In 376 C.E., facing pressure from the advancing Huns, the Visigoths obtained permission to cross the Danube into Roman territory. However, they were mistreated by Roman authorities and consequently rose up in revolt in 377 C.E.

Action. The Eastern Roman emperor Valens, not wishing to share the glory of victory with his nephew the Western emperor Gratian, decided to attack before the arrival of Gratian's army. Valens's army of about 25,000 men advanced toward the wagon-ringed encampment of Fritigern's Visigoth army, which numbered about 20,000 men. The Visigoths repelled an initial attack by Roman light cavalry. Roman cavalry on the left wing then attacked but became separated from the main body of Roman infantry in the center. Ostrogoth and Alani cavalry, allies of the Visigoths, drove off the Roman cavalry and outflanked the infantry.

The Roman infantry was quickly surrounded by enemy cavalry and infantry and pressed so tightly together that the soldiers could not use their weapons effectively. About two-thirds of the Roman army, including Valens, perished.

Consequences. The Visigoths moved into Rome's Balkan provinces but were eventually forced back into Thrace. In 382 C.E., they concluded a treaty with Theodosius the Great that permitted them to live as an independent nation within Roman territory.

ADDITIONAL RESOURCES
Marcellinus, Ammianus. *The Later Roman Empire.* Translated by Walter Hamilton. New York: Penguin Classics, 1986.
Williams, Stephen, and Gerard Friell. *Theodosius: The Empire at Bay.* New Haven, Conn.: Yale University Press, 1994.

SEE ALSO: Goths, Gratian; Huns; Rome, Imperial; Theodosius the Great; Valens.

—Thomas I. Crimando

ADVAITA

DATE: concept appears in *Upaniṣads*, compiled c. 1000-c. 200 B.C.E.
LOCALE: India
RELATED CIVILIZATION: India

The earliest expressions of the concept of *advaita* (ahd-VAH-ee-tah) in the Hindu world appeared in the *Upaniṣads* (a large group of documents compiled and composed c. 1000-c. 200 B.C.E.), particularly the *Chāndogya Upaniṣad* (n.d.; English translation in *The Sacred Books of the East: Part 1, the Upanishads,* 1900). It was during the era immediately after the appearance of the *Upaniṣads* that the concept of *advaita* began to replace the former Hindu belief in dualism.

The best-known exponent of *advaita*, however, was Śaṅkara, the Hindu philosopher of the eighth century C.E. who expounded the concept in his commentaries on the *Upaniṣads*, the *Brahmāsūtras* (group of documents and fragments also known as the *Vedānta Sūtras*, compiled between 400 B.C.E. and 200 C.E.), and the *Bhagavadgītā* (c. 200 B.C.E.-200 C.E.; *The Bhagavad Gita*, 1785). The studies of Śaṅkara resulted in the formalization of Advaita Vedānta, one of the six philosophies, or *darsanas*, of which Hinduism consists.

Advaita addresses the Hindu concern with the paradox of the simultaneous existence of the universal and the individual. According to the *advaita* view, the only reality is *brahman*, the primary origin and essence of all things. The multiplicity of the universe as people perceive it, apparently made up of so many entities, including individual persons, is the result of illusion (*māyā*) and ignorance (*avidyā*). A person's individual soul (*ātman*)—the "I" that one perceives in oneself—is actually *brahman*. This is expressed succinctly in the term itself, as *advaita* in Sanskrit means "without a second." The term is most commonly translated, however, into the philosophical term "nondualism." A commonly quoted passage from the *Chandogya Upaniṣad* expresses the idea succinctly: *tat tvam asi*, or "that you are."

According to the Vedānta philosophy, the goal of humankind is to come to realize this truth, and the diverse paths of spiritual study—discipleship with a guru and yoga practice—have this common aim. One's identity with *brahman* is realized with the complete removal of illusion and ignorance, which is effected only by means of rigorous effort. The result of this effort is expressed in the phrase *brahmavid brahmaiva bhavati*, or "one who comes to know *brahman* is *brahman*."

Because it admits of no existence separate from *brahman*, *advaita* precludes the existence of god. Conceptions of a supreme being (*īśvara*) are the illusion of an omniscient and omnipotent divine personality, like the figure of Krishna (*Kṛṣṇa*) in the *Bhagavadgītā*. The individual existence of such a god cannot be real, however, for the same reason that the individual person is not essentially real; that is, *brahman* is indivisible, eternal being (*sat*), pure consciousness (*cit*), pure bliss (*ānanda*). The classic phrase in the *Bṛhadāraṣnyaka Upaniṣad* for this is *neti neti*, or "not this, not this [other]." Illusory conceptions of divinity serve only to focus one's attention and clarify concepts that can lead one to a realization of *brahman*.

ADDITIONAL RESOURCES

Lipner, Julius. *Hindus: Their Religious Beliefs and Practices*. New York: Routledge, 1994.

Sundararajam, K. R., and Bithika Mukerji, eds. *Hindu Spirituality I: Vedas Through Vedanta*. New York: Crossroad, 1997.

Zimmer, Heinrich, with Joseph Campbell, ed. *Philosophies of India*. Princeton, N.J.: Princeton University Press, 1969.

SEE ALSO: *Bhagavadgītā*; Brahmanism; Hinduism; India; *Upaniṣads*; Vedas; Vedism.

—Dennis C. Chowenhill

AEGOSPOTAMI, BATTLE OF

DATE: September, 405 B.C.E.
LOCALE: Aegospotami, in The Chersonese on the shore of the Hellespont (Dardanelles)
RELATED CIVILIZATIONS: Athens, Sparta
SIGNIFICANCE: Sparta captured approximately 170 Athenian ships and executed more than 3,000 Athenian soldiers, thus sealing its victory over Athens in the Peloponnesian War.

Background. In the last stage of the Peloponnesian War (431-404 B.C.E.), Sparta built a fleet, thanks to Persian support, and carried out operations along the coast of Asia Minor, but with only moderate success.

Action. To block the route of grain ships heading from the Black Sea to Athens, Lysander of Sparta entered the Hellespont with the Peloponnesian fleet and seized Lampsacus by force. The Athenian generals stationed their ships on the opposite shore at Aegospotami (ee-guh-SPAH-tuh-mi), but they could not lure Lysander into battle. Then, according to historian Xenophon, Lysander attacked the Athenians while they were searching for food and captured nearly the entire fleet. Only nine ships escaped.

Consequences. After this battle, Sparta besieged Athens by land and by sea. Lacking the resources to rebuild its fleet, Athens could not withstand the siege and was forced to surrender to Sparta in (probably late March) 404 B.C.E. Terms included the destruction of defensive walls and fortifications, reduction of the fleet to twelve ships, surrender of foreign lands, and an alliance with Sparta.

ADDITIONAL RESOURCES

Kagan, Donald. *The Fall of the Athenian Empire.* Ithaca, N.Y.: Cornell University Press, 1987.

Strauss, Barry. "Aegospotami Reexamined." *American Journal of Philology* 104 (1983): 24-35.

SEE ALSO: Lysander of Sparta; Peloponnesian War.

—Andrew Wolpert

ÆLLE

ALSO KNOWN AS: Aella; Aelli
BORN: c. 450 C.E.?; place unknown
DIED: c. 491 C.E.?; place unknown
RELATED CIVILIZATIONS: Saxony, Briton, Imperial Rome
MAJOR ROLE/POSITION: Military leader, founder of South Saxon kingdom

Life. According to entries in the *Anglo-Saxon Chronicle* (assembled 871-899 C.E.), Ælle (AL-uh), in 477 C.E., led three shiploads of his folk—each ship commanded by one of his sons (Cymen, Wlencing, and Cissa)—to what is now Sussex, landed, defeated the Romano-Britons, and after driving them out, set up the kingdom of the South Saxons.

The entry for 485 C.E. has Ælle fighting the Romano-Britons again at the Mearcredesburna (unidentified, perhaps the Alun River), and the final entry for 491 C.E. has him, assisted by his son Cissa, capturing the town of Anderidum (modern Pevensey) and massacring its inhabitants. According to the early eighth century C.E. historian Bede, these victories led to his acclamation as bretwalda, or "ruler of Britain." However, most modern scholars are agreed that the term (originally spelled *brytenwealda*—literally meaning "wide ruler") would originally have signified a very different type of lordship, one related to military prowess, yet with a religious connotation—that is, "forest-spirit" ruler. Given the inability of medieval sources to link Ælle with later Sussex kings, the similarities of his tale to other Indo-European founding "histories," and the anthropomorphizing tendencies of the Indo-Euro-

peans, Ælle and his three sons were undoubtedly the tribal gods of the "South Saxons." Why Bede would have included Ælle as a bretwalda cannot now be determined but undoubtedly relates to the strength of the invasion legends, the sources from which he gathered his material, the Christianizing tendencies of the age, and the political situation of his own time.

Influence. In the end, whether Ælle was a historical personage or a Saxon deity does not matter, as the true influence lay in the South Saxon concept of the *brytenwealda*, the military and religious "overlord," which, in the ninth and tenth centuries C.E., would provide the ideological basis for the kings of Wessex as rulers of all England.

ADDITIONAL RESOURCES

Basset, Steven, ed. *The Origins of Anglo-Saxon Kingdoms.* London: Leicester University, 1989.

John, Eric. *Reassessing Anglo-Saxon England.* New York: Manchester University Press, 1996.

Kirby, D. P. *The Earliest English Kings.* London: Routledge, 1992.

Myres, J. N. L. *The English Settlements.* New York: Clarendon Press, 1986.

Oosten, Jarich G. *The War of the Gods: The Social Code in Indo-European Mythology.* London: Routledge and Kegan Paul, 1985.

Whittock, Martyn J. *The Origins of England, 410-600.* Totowa, N.J.: Barnes & Noble, 1986.

SEE ALSO: Angles, Saxons, Jutes; Britain.

—Jerome S. Arkenberg

AEMILIUS PAULLUS, LUCIUS

BORN: 255 B.C.E.; place unknown
DIED: 216 B.C.E.; place unknown
RELATED CIVILIZATION: Republican Rome
MAJOR ROLE/POSITION: Political/military leader

Life. Lucius Aemilius Paullus (LEW-shee-uhs ih-mihl-ee-AY-uhs PAWL-uhs) was the leader of the Aemilii, one of the leading patrician families in Rome. He was consul in 219 B.C.E., defeating Demetrius of Pharos in the Second Illyrian War. In 218 B.C.E., he took part in the Roman delegation to Carthage that declared war. Paullus and his allies in the senate helped engineer the declaration (though they were unable to force Rome to attack immediately) and governed Roman strategy and tactics during the early course of the war.

Paullus is best known for his role in the Battle of Cannae in 216 B.C.E. As consul, he was one of the commanders of the huge Roman army assembled to crush Hannibal. He commanded part of the infantry and died with them. The fortunes of the Aemilii family fell with Paullus. The number of Aemilii who held political of-fice fell sharply in the years following Cannae. The Fabian family and its strategy of delay dominated Rome and led to Hannibal's eventual defeat.

Influence. Paullus was a powerful political leader in Rome and an outstanding general. If Rome had attacked Hannibal immediately as Paullus had desired, the Second Punic War may have ended much sooner than it did and resulted in many fewer Roman deaths. His son Lucius Aemilius Paullus Macedonicus defeated Perseus at the Battle of Pydna in 168 B.C.E. His daughter married Scipio Africanus.

ADDITIONAL RESOURCES

Plutarch. *Roman Lives.* Translated by Robin Waterfield. New York: Oxford University Press, 1999.
Scullard, H. H. *Roman Politics, 220-150 B.C.* 2d ed. Oxford, England: Clarendon Press, 1973.

SEE ALSO: Cannae, Battle of; Carthage; Hannibal; Punic Wars; Rome, Republican; Scipio Africanus.

—*James O. Smith*

AENEAS

FLOURISHED: c. twelfth to tenth centuries B.C.E.
LOCALE: Troy, Mediterranean, and en route to Italy
RELATED CIVILIZATIONS: Rome, Classical Greece
SIGNIFICANCE: Considered by the Romans to be the semidivine ancestor of their people.

Aeneas (uh-NEE-uhs) was a figure in the myth and literature of ancient Greece and Rome, the son of Anchises and the goddess Aphrodite (Venus), who blinded his father, Anchises, for daring to look at her. He appears in Homer's *Iliad* (c. 800 B.C.E.; English translation, 1616), married to Creusa, daughter of Priam, king of Troy. Aeneas's son, Ascanius, was renamed Iulus by Vergil in his *Aeneid* (c. 29-19 B.C.E.; English translation, 1553) to establish an ancestry for the adoptive Julian family of the emperor Augustus, his patron. He is known for his piety and filial loyalty.

In the *Aeneid*, Aeneas escapes from Troy with the statuettes of his family gods, his father, and his son, leaving Creusa behind. The image of Aeneas carrying his father Anchises on his back during this retreat is often depicted on Greek vases of the sixth century B.C.E. After ten years, Aeneas sailed west, experiencing many of the same adventures as Odysseus. Forced to land at Libya to rebuild his fleet, Aeneas met the founder of Carthage, Dido, and supposedly fell in love with her. Later abandoned by Aeneas, Dido committed suicide, foreshadowing future hostilities between Rome and Carthage.

After successfully visiting the Underworld, Aeneas led his followers to Latium near the Tibur River. There Aeneas embarked on a series of *Iliad*-like battles that ended with his killing his arch-rival suitor, Turnus, and marrying Lavinia, daughter of the local king, Latinus. Aeneas's son starts a settlement near Rome named Alba Longa, where his descendant, Rhea Silvia, is chosen by Mars to give virgin-birth to Romulus, the eponymous founder of Rome, and his twin brother, Remus.

Aeneas's migration toward Italy and accompanying adventures are recorded in more than the *Aeneid*, attesting to a cult of hero-worship for Aeneas as Rome's founder. Historians think it likely that Romans of the third century B.C.E., coming into contact with Greece, found it useful to encourage this connection of an early founder or ancestor of Rome with the legendary Trojan enemy of the Greeks.

ADDITIONAL RESOURCES

Perkell, Christine, ed. *Reading Vergil's Aeneid: An Interpretive Guide*. Norman: University of Oklahoma Press, 1999.
Quinn, Stephanie. *Why Vergil? A Collection of Interpretations*. Wauconda, Ill.: Bolchazy-Carducci, 2000.
Virgil. *The Aeneid*. Translated by Robert Fitzgerald. London: Penguin Books, 1990.

SEE ALSO: Carthage; Dido; Greece, Classical; Homer; Rome, Pre-Republican; Romulus and Remus; Troy; Vergil.

—Bernard F. Barcio

AESCHINES

BORN: 390 B.C.E.; probably Athens, Greece
DIED: c. 315 B.C.E.; possibly Samos, Greece
RELATED CIVILIZATION: Classical Greece
MAJOR ROLE/POSITION: Orator

Life. Originally a civil official and then an actor, Aeschines (EHS-kih-neez) seems to have entered political life at a relatively advanced age. In 348 B.C.E., when Philip II was threatening the Chalcidice, Aeschines was sent as an ambassador to rouse the Greek states against him. He was a member of the *boulē*, or council, in 347/346 B.C.E. and served on embassies to Philip in connection with the Peace of Philocrates, as did Demosthenes, in 346 B.C.E. Aeschines believed that the only peace attainable was a Common Peace, and this, together with his more conservative policy and conciliatory attitude to Philip, clashed with Demosthenes. This was the start of a long personal enmity between Aeschines and Demosthenes, seen in the famous court battles in 343 B.C.E., when Demosthenes prosecuted Aeschines for misconduct on the embassies and narrowly lost, and in 330 B.C.E., when Aeschines prosecuted Ctesiphon, who had proposed a crown in 336 B.C.E. for Demosthenes' great services to the state, and overwhelmingly lost.

Between 343 and 330 B.C.E., Demosthenes' political influence rose; however, Aeschines seems to have played a passive role in politics. He was prominent at a meeting of the Amphictyonic Council in 339 B.C.E., but in persuading that council to vote for a Sacred War on Amphissa, he opened the door for Philip's further involvement in Greece. After the Greeks' defeat at Chaeronea in 338 B.C.E., Aeschines served as ambassador to Philip to discuss peace terms. In 336 B.C.E., he impeached Ctesiphon for making an illegal motion to crown Demosthenes, but the case did not come to court until 330. The impeachment was an attack on Demosthenes; hence, it was Demosthenes who delivered the official defense speech. Misjudging the political situation, not to mention Demosthenes' influence, Aeschines failed to win one-fifth of the votes and went into self-imposed exile. According to tradition, he opened a school of rhetoric on Rhodes and later moved to Samos, where he died.

Only three speeches by Aeschines have survived. They are marred by personal attacks, emotional arguments, and too great a tendency to quote from poetry; he is at his best in the narrative sections of his speeches, where his vocabulary is simple and effective. However, his oratorical ability was enough for him to be included in the canon of the ten Attic orators.

Influence. Aeschines' speeches from the false embassy and Ctesiphon/Demosthenes trials survive, as do those of Demosthenes; although the speeches of both orators are riddled with bias and embellishment, they are vital source material for the history of this period.

ADDITIONAL RESOURCES

Harris, E. *Aeschines and Athenian Politics*. New York: Oxford University Press, 1995.
Kennedy, G. *The Art of Persuasion in Greece*. Princeton, N.J.: Princeton University Press, 1963.

SEE ALSO: Demosthenes; Government and law; Greece, Classical.

—Ian Worthington

AESCHYLUS

BORN: 525/524 B.C.E.; Eleusis, Greece
DIED: 456/455 B.C.E.; Gela, Sicily
RELATED CIVILIZATIONS: Classical Greece, Sicilian Greece
MAJOR ROLE/POSITION: Playwright

Life. Aeschylus (EHS-kuh-lus), son of Euphorion, spent his youth as a soldier—necessarily, as his early life corresponds almost exactly with the Persian invasion of the Greek Peloponnese. He fought bravely at Marathon, Salamis, and Plataea, which may well account for the patriotic and political themes of his plays, although Greece was still a collection of city-states, not a political entity. The war with Persia claimed his brother Cynegeirus at Marathon. Some accounts list Aminias, a hero at Salamis, as another family member. Still, it is certain that Aeschylus felt great pride in his heritage. His own son Euphorion, whose works survive only as fragments, achieved almost as much fame as Aeschylus as a tragedian.

War probably delayed Aeschylus's career as a dramatist until he was about thirty, and his first victory at the Dionysia did not occur until 485 B.C.E. He clearly was prolific and reportedly wrote from seventy-two to ninety plays. The number of prizes he won, thirteen, implies that the judges considered forty-two of his plays first-rate, since a new trilogy plus a satyr play made up each entry. This means that Aeschylus garnered first prize in nearly half or more than half of the contests he entered.

Hieron I, king of Syracuse, offered subventions to the celebrated poets of the day, so Aeschylus was probably at the height of his fame in 470 B.C.E. when he resided at Hieron's court along with the lyric poets Pindar and Simonides. He died at Gela during his second visit to Sicily. Hellenistic legend concocted the tale that Aeschylus died when an eagle dropped a tortoise on his bald head, having mistaken it for a rock on which to crack the shell.

Aeschylus's revived plays appeared in competition against new works, implying that they were considered a standard against which to measure new dramas. Aristophanes, in his comedy the *Batrachoi* (405 B.C.E.; *The Frogs*, 1780) removes Aeschylus from competing with his junior contemporaries Sophocles and Euripides in the celebrated contest of that play, further attesting to his special place.

Influence. Though only seven of his plays are extant, they confirm Aeschylus's role as pioneer of Greek drama. In his works, he does not use a bipartite chorus but has three featured actors portray distinctive characters. The idea of protagonist, antagonist, and supporting actor, not codified until Aristotle's *De poetica* (c. 335-323 B.C.E.; *Poetics*, 1705), in fact begins with Aeschylus. The chorus remains important for deepening, highlighting, or metaphorically embellishing dramatic narrative but never alters or influences action. Aeschylus's successors Sophocles and Euripides further diminished the role of the chorus.

ADDITIONAL RESOURCES

Conacher, D. J. *Aeschylus: The Earlier Plays and Related Studies.* Toronto: University of Toronto Press, 1996.

Herington, John. *Aeschylus.* New Haven, Conn.: Yale University Press, 1986.

Ireland, S. *Aeschylus.* Greece and Rome: New Surveys in the Classics 18. Oxford, England: Clarendon Press, 1986.

McCall, Marsh, Jr., ed. *Aeschylus: A Collection of Critical Essays.* Englewood Cliffs, N.J.: Prentice-Hall, 1972.

Aeschylus. (Library of Congress)

Podlecki, Anthony J. *The Political Background of Aeschylean Tragedy*. Ann Arbor: University of Michigan Press, 1966.

Spatz, Lois. *Aeschylus*. Boston: Twayne, 1982.

SEE ALSO: Aristophanes; Euripides; Greco-Persian Wars; Marathon, Battle of; Performing arts; Pindar; Plataea, Battle of; Salamis, Battle of; Simonides; Sophocles.

—*Robert J. Forman*

AESOP

BORN: probably early sixth century B.C.E.; Thrace, Greece

DIED: probably sixth century B.C.E.; Delphi, Greece

RELATED CIVILIZATION: Archaic Greece

MAJOR ROLE/POSITION: Slave, storyteller

Aesop. (Library of Congress)

Life. Practically nothing is known about Aesop's (EE-sahp) life. He seems to have been born in Thrace, the region of southeastern Europe now divided between Greece and Turkey, and to have spent most of his life as a slave on Samos, an island lying off the coast of Asia Minor. Traditional accounts give his master's name as Xanthus.

Despite his status, Aesop appears to have worked as a kind of personal secretary to his master and to have enjoyed a great deal of freedom. His reputation derived from his skill at telling fables as illustrations of points in argument, possibly even in court. Such stories, which usually dealt with animals or mythological figures and were often quite caustic, were common throughout the ancient world.

Influence. Aesop was apparently so talented at recounting fables that memorable examples became attached to his name, regardless of their origin or date. Thanks to later writers who collected them, these fables have become an integral part of the heritage of Western literature and folklore.

ADDITIONAL RESOURCES

Aesop. *Aesop Without Morals: The Famous Fables, and a Life of Aesop*. Translated, edited, and with an introduction by Lloyd W. Daly. New York: Yoseloff, 1961.

———. *The Complete Fables*. Translated by Olivia and Robert Temple, with an introduction by Robert Temple. New York: Penguin Books, 1998.

SEE ALSO: Greece, Archaic; Languages and literature.

—*Grove Koger*

ÆTHELBERT

ALSO KNOWN AS: Ethelbert
BORN: sixth century C.E.; southern England
DIED: 616 C.E.; southern England
RELATED CIVILIZATIONS: England, Anglo-Saxon
MAJOR ROLE/POSITION: Military leader and statesman

Life. Æthelbert (ATH-uhl-behrkt) became king of Kent in southeast England in 560 C.E. Little is known of the first thirty-seven years of his reign except that he forged a successful political union with other kings in southern England, leading to his status as the "overlord" of the region. The eighth century C.E. historian Bede lists Æthelbert among the seven most powerful and influential English kings.

In 597 C.E., Augustine (later Saint Augustine of Canterbury) arrived in Kent to convert the Anglo-Saxons to Christianity. Æthelbert became the first Anglo-Saxon king to be converted to the faith, and he subsequently prompted other kings to convert. His law code, written between 597 and 616 C.E. and therefore the oldest piece of writing in Old English, reflects his new faith by outlining penalties for crimes against the Christian Church.

Influence. Though various kings reverted to paganism upon his death, Æthelbert, by promoting Christianity, stands as one of the most important figures in Anglo-Saxon history. Starting with its foothold in Kent, the Church began successfully converting the Anglo-Saxons. Æthelbert also influenced the Anglo-Saxon political structure with his law codes because he wrote his codes not singlehandedly but in consultation with his advisers.

Saint Augustine of Canterbury converts Æthelbert, king of Kent, to Christianity. (North Wind Picture Archives)

ADDITIONAL RESOURCES

Blair, Peter Hunter. *An Introduction to Anglo-Saxon England*. 2d ed. Cambridge, England: Cambridge University Press, 1995.
Campbell, James, ed. *The Anglo-Saxons*. New York: Penguin Books, 1982.
Stenton, Frank. *Anglo-Saxon England*. 3d ed. Oxford, England: Clarendon Press, 1971.

SEE ALSO: Angles, Saxons, Jutes; Augustine of Canterbury, Saint; Britain; Christianity.

—Alexander M. Bruce

AETOLIAN LEAGUE

DATE: fifth-first centuries B.C.E.
LOCALE: West-central Greece
RELATED CIVILIZATIONS: Classical and Hellenistic Greece, Macedonia, Roman Republic

Because of the ruggedness of their homeland, the Aetolians long remained on the periphery of Hellenic history. However, their development of a federal state led to aggressive expansion in the third century B.C.E. The Aetolian (eh-TOH-lee-yen) League saved Delphi from Gallic destruction in 279 B.C.E., then drove across central Greece and acquired influence in Thessaly and the western Peloponnese. The Aetolians, hostile to Macedonia's Antigonid kings, became allies of Rome against Philip V and engaged in widespread piracy and brigandage. Aetolia eventually quarreled with the Roman Republic and sought the support of Syria's ruler, Antiochus the Great. War against Rome concluded with a negotiated peace in 189 B.C.E. Although the league survived, its importance and influence withered. By the late first century B.C.E., Aetolia was depopulated.

An annually elected general served as chief magistrate of the Aetolian League. A primary assembly, consisting of all men of military age, decided issues of foreign policy and met at least twice a year, in spring and autumn. A representative council, elected from constituent cities in proportion to population, governed between these meetings, following the direction of an important committee, the *apokletoi*.

ADDITIONAL RESOURCES

Larsen, J. A. O. *Greek Federal States*. London: Oxford University Press, 1968.
Scholten, Joseph B. *The Politics of Plunder: Aitolians and Their Koinon in the Early Hellenistic Era, 279-217* B.C.E. Berkeley: University of California Press, 2000.

SEE ALSO: Antiochus the Great; Delphi; Greece, Classical; Greece, Hellenistic and Roman; Macedonia; Philip V; Rome, Republican.

—*Denvy A. Bowman*

AFANASIEVO CULTURE

DATE: 2500-1100 B.C.E.
LOCALE: Siberia, Kazakhstan, Mongolia, Xinjiang
RELATED CIVILIZATIONS: Kelteminar, Andronovo, Karasuk
SIGNIFICANCE: Afanasievo represented the transition from the Neolithic to the Bronze Age in Siberia and Central Asia.

The Afanasievo (ah-fah-NAH-seh-voh) Neolithic culture of Siberia and Central Asia extended to Mongolia and Xinjiang. People spoke an Indo-European tongue, indicating the eastward migration of Western peoples. The major concentration was associated with metallurgical sites by the Altay Shan and middle reaches of the Yenisey River, especially in the Minusinsk Basin. Metals included copper tools, bronze knives, and bronze, gold, and silver ornaments. The larger axes and pikes were stone.

There were no militant horsemen, although stock breeding of cattle, horses, and sheep was practiced in the later era. Cattle breeding developed in the west, whereas agriculture predominated in the east. Food

gathering and hunting completed the economy. Only in the second millennium was the horse domesticated and used for war chariots.

The largest grave site, dating from the second millennium, is located on the slopes of the Afanasievskaya Mountain near the city of Krasnoyarsk. Grave sites reveal pointed, comb-stamped, decorative pottery, primitively fired in charcoal beds. The later graves contained flat-bottomed pots and egg-shaped dishes like those from Andronovo, suggesting a sedentary and pastoral culture. Inhabitants made censers and bowls similar to those found in Russia. Grave sites, whether earthen mounds or flat, were encircled by stones, suggesting a belief in Sun gods. The burial slabs, like those of Karasuk, depicted masked people and falcons.

ADDITIONAL RESOURCES

Dani, A. H., and V. M. Masson, eds. *The Dawn of Civilization: Earliest Times to 700* B.C. In Vol. 1 of *History of Civilizations of Central Asia*. Paris: UNESCO, 1992.
Davis-Kimball, Jeannine, Vladimir A. Bashilov, and

Leonid T. Yablonsky. *Nomads of the Eurasian Steppes in the Early Iron Age.* Berkeley, Calif.: Zinat Press, 1995.

SEE ALSO: Andronovo culture; Karasuk culture; Kelteminar culture; Mongolia.

—*John D. Windhausen*

AFRASANS

ALSO KNOWN AS: Afroasiatics
DATE: 8000-4000 B.C.E.
LOCALE: Northern Africa and southwestern Asia
SIGNIFICANCE: The Afrasans, who speak languages of the Afrasan (or Afroasiatic) language family, form one of the major groups of peoples in ancient African and Middle Eastern history.

In the eighth millennium B.C.E., numerous Afrasan societies already inhabited nearly all of northeastern and northern Africa as well as the far southwestern tip of Asia. Most of the Afrasans pursued similar livelihoods, and they also shared key common features of culture, inherited from the earlier ancestral Afrasan communities of 13,000-10,000 B.C.E.

In 8000-6000 B.C.E., the Afrasans of the whole northern half of the vast Sahara regions belonged to a culture the archaeologists call the Capsian tradition. The Sahara at that time was wetter in climate than today and had many areas of grassland and steppe environments. The Capsian communities hunted game and collected wild grains as their principal sources of food.

In the far southeastern Sahara, between the Nile and Red Sea, the ancestral Cushitic people of 8000-6000 B.C.E. added a new way of obtaining food. Together with their Nilo-Saharan neighbors to the west, they were the first peoples in the world to domesticate the cow. They collected wild grains just like the Capsians, but they also herded cattle, using them for both meat and milk. The Cushites also domesticated the donkey, a formerly wild animal of the Red Sea hills region of Africa.

Still farther south, in the Ethiopian highlands, lived the Southern Afrasans. They emphasized a different range of plant foods in their diet. The most notable plant for them was the bananalike *enset.* Interestingly, people use the soft inner stem and the bulb of this plant for food but find the fruit unappetizing.

One Afrasan society, the proto-Semites, had moved north out of Africa into far southwestern Asia, at a still uncertain but early period. Originally collectors of wild grains, once they settled in the Levant, they participated, along with neighboring non-Afrasan peoples, in the development of early Middle Eastern agriculture, cultivating wheat and barley and raising goats and sheep.

The period between 6000 and 4000 B.C.E. was a time of great changes for most of the Afrasan peoples. The Capsian societies all adopted the keeping of goats, sheep, and cattle. The southernmost Capsians, the proto-Chadic people, moved far south into the basin of Lake Chad, where they took up Sudanic crops, such as sorghum, from their Nilo-Saharan neighbors. Of the more than one hundred Chadic languages spoken today, Hausa is the most important and best known. In contrast, the Capsian societies of North Africa, ancestral to the Berber peoples of later history, took up the cultivation of the Middle Eastern crops of wheat and barley. The Capsians of the northeastern Sahara, ancestors of the ancient Egyptians, increasingly concentrated along the Nile River, as the climate of the Sahara began to dry out. They, too, took up the farming of Middle Eastern foods, but they soon also adopted from the Nilo-Saharans to the south such Sudanic crops as gourds, castor beans, and watermelons.

In the wetter parts of the Ethiopian highlands, the ancestral Omotic people, a Southern Afrasan society, in the sixth and fifth millennia B.C.E. created a vigorous new agriculture, centered on cultivation of the *enset* plant. Over the same span, the Cushites of the southeastern Sahara spread their cattle-raising way of life southward through the drier portions of the Ethiopian highlands. Still later, in the fourth millennium B.C.E., the southernmost Cushites carried this livelihood still farther south into present-day Kenya and northern Tanzania. The best-known Cushitic peoples of recent times are the Somali and the Oromo of the Horn of Africa.

Interestingly, the early Afrasans followed a henotheistic religion, a kind of belief system unfamiliar to many people. Henotheism is a religion in which each small society possesses its own particular deity. People accept that other communities have different deities but believe in giving their first allegiance to their own society's god. This system of belief persists to the present among some of the Southern Afrasan societies of southwestern Ethiopia. It is also apparent among the earliest Hebrews, a people of the Semitic branch of Afrasan, who originally viewed Yahweh as the deity of just their society. Its earlier existence in predynastic Egypt explains why most of the ancient Egyptian gods started out as the deities of particular nomes (administrative or geographical units of area) before they were incorporated into the national religion.

ADDITIONAL RESOURCES

Bernal, Martin. *Black Athena: The Afroasiatic Roots of Classical Civilization*. London: Vintage, 1991.

Yamauchi, Edwin M. *Africa and Africans in Antiquity*. East Lansing: Michigan State University Press, 2001.

SEE ALSO: Africa, North; Agriculture and animal husbandry; Berbers; Cushites; Ethiopia; Henotheism; Judaism; Nilo-Saharans; Omotic peoples.

—*Christopher Ehret*

AFRICA, EAST AND SOUTH

DATE: 8000 B.C.E.-700 C.E.

LOCALE: *East Africa*, modern Kenya, Uganda, and Tanzania; *South Africa*, modern Zimbabwe, Zambia, and South Africa

SIGNIFICANCE: The migration of Bantu peoples, who brought with them their culture and language, had a lasting effect on East and South Africa.

The ancient history of East and South Africa is complex, involving different peoples interacting with one another and developing specialized economies, technologies, and cultures. Because of the lack of written records, information comes from archaeology and historical linguistics.

East Africa has long been inhabited by Khoisan-speaking hunter-gatherers who developed sophisticated, microlithic tools that were combined into specialized kits by savanna hunters, forest honey gatherers, and lakeside fishers. The first herders and farmers, peoples speaking Southern Cushitic languages, spread slowly from Ethiopia down the Rift Valley, where they raised cattle, sheep, and goats and cultivated sorghum. Later, Sudanic speakers spread south into western Uganda, where they raised cattle, sorghum, and millet.

The first Eastern Bantu speakers edged east from the Congolese rain forest into the highland forests west of Lake Victoria, where they raised yams, oil palms, beans, and groundnuts; they were also fishers and raised goats. They expanded around the lake, displacing many of the earlier populations in the process. Bantu speakers in East Africa were able to combine forest root crops from western Africa with savanna grains and stock from Ethiopia and Sudan in a potent combination that en-abled them to expand explosively throughout the diverse environments of eastern and southern Africa.

Agriculture. From their earliest years, East and South African communities had lived by gathering plant foods and hunting, trapping, and scavenging for meat. Later, people began to make use of domesticated animals and plants. In areas where rainfall was adequate, such as in the east, crops were grown and cattle, sheep, and goats were raised near permanent villages and towns. In the west where the climate was arid, Africans cultivated plants that would withstand such conditions, and nomadic pastoralists, who moved from one location to another, raised domestic livestock.

Linguistic evidence points to northern Botswana as a center of origin for pastoralism in southern Africa. Archaeologists have found sheep bones dating to about 150 B.C.E. that show evidence of sheep being herded extensively in the eastern and western cape provinces. The people in this area herded cattle and sheep and also grew crops, cutting back the vegetation with iron hoes and axes. They gathered wild plant food, engaged in some hunting, and collected shellfish. Villages grew to include hundreds of people, and different groups engaged in trade. For example, salt makers in Mapumalanga traded with the hunter-gatherers who continued to occupy most of the parts of South Africa. By 1000 B.C.E., ceramic-producing and grain-farming complexes were present all over Uganda, in the Serengeti Plains, and in southern Kenya.

Settlements. As the early societies of East Africa became economically specialized, they became culturally and ethnically distinctive, leading to a division between specialized highland farmers such as the Kikuyu

SELECTED SITES IN ANCIENT EASTERN AND SOUTHERN AFRICA

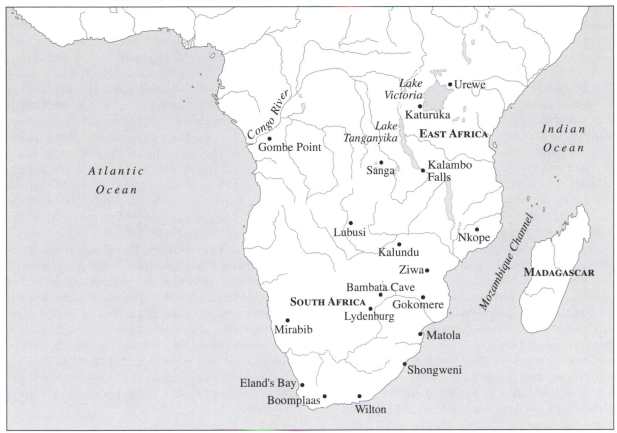

(Gikuyu) or Chaga and forest hunter-gatherers. They divided the varied eastern African environments among themselves while interacting with one another in interdependent regional economies and cultures. Most societies were organized locally, focused on the land they farmed or the stock they herded. They centered on families and kinship groups, the elders who led them, and the age groups that facilitated interaction with other local groups. Other societies, especially those around the Great Lakes, developed centralized chiefdoms or kingdoms.

Early Iron Age settlements in East and South Africa shared common features, many of which continued though the Later Iron Age to modern times. Settlement was normally in villages of round houses with walls of poles and with clay and grass roofs. Villages were scattered within fertile lands, with little concern for establishing defensive positions. Pits were made for burial or for storage. Hunting and food gathering supplemented a mixed agricultural base.

Bantu settled in the wetter areas of the savannas and in the fertile bottomlands of river valleys. Their settlement was facilitated by new food crops such as bananas and tubers introduced from Southeast Asia at the beginning of the common era. The drier savanna lands were left vacant until the Bantu speakers learned food production involving intensive pastoralism and dry-grain agriculture—hardy cereal crops that would grow in all but the driest conditions. Those responsible for the pastoral tradition were Nilotic-speaking peoples, the vanguard of whom began pushing down the natural migration corridor of the Rift Valley by the early centuries of the last millennium B.C.E. from their homeland along the Upper Nile (Sudan). Southern Cushitic speakers and the Eastern Cushites from Ethiopia settled in the Rift Valley and in adjacent highland and plains areas of Kenya and Tanzania. These were some of the earliest settlers in the region.

Toolmaking. Around 8000 B.C.E., the savanna zones of southern Africa and much of eastern Africa underwent modifications in their tool kits and adaptations. Microlithic tools were added, and a particular hunting-gathering subsistence pattern, oriented primarily toward land animals and plants, was developed. The resulting complex, referred to as Wilton industry, is very similar to that of many of the San and similar hunter-gatherers that existed in the savanna and semidesert areas of southern and eastern Africa. Many have concluded that the Wilton and related complexes of southern and eastern Africa represented the prehistoric ancestral pattern of the modern San.

The Bantu speakers absorbed earlier Khoisan populations during their expansion. In the lake area of Eastern Africa, the early Iron Age tradition, distinguished archaeologically by pottery style, was established by 400 B.C.E. The pottery, handmade and fired in an open hearth, was very conservative in form and in decorative technique. At Lydenburg in the Transvaal, sometime between 500 and 700 C.E., clay was molded into head shapes, mostly for ceremonies. The early Iron Age peoples also built tall, cylindrical clay furnaces for the smelting of iron from ore, the basis of the smelter form used into modern times.

Iron. Ironworking first appeared in the western Great Lakes around 800 B.C.E. among Bantu speakers and was established in western Tanzania about 500 B.C.E. Bantu speakers manufactured and used iron for tools and weapons. They cleared the area's forests to obtain charcoal, which opened the land for farming. The early Iron Age tradition spread southward between 300 and 400 C.E. Its limits on the west were the rain forest and desert edge, but to the south, the tradition penetrated to the Indian Ocean coast of South Africa. By the first century C.E., ceramics, grain farming, and ironworking had reached the vicinity of the cape. Three different migrations took place southward from Tanzania: one over Mozambique to Natal and beyond, one over Malawi to Zimbabwe, and one within Zambia. This spread reflects population expansion made possible by the advantages of iron technology and mixed agriculture in areas previously occupied by hunting bands. Although there is debate on the tributaries of dispersion, there is ample evidence that the diffusion of various technologies in eastern and southern Africa was very complicated.

By 500 C.E., ironworking techniques had spread east to the coast and south into southern Africa. Many East African innovations also spread among Western Bantu speakers, facilitating their expansion south into Angola and Namibia.

Language differential. The spread of the East Bantu languages occurred in different circumstances. The ancestral vocabulary shows that Bantu speakers borrowed a whole farming complex, including grain farming and also cattle and sheep herding, from neighbors they met in the Great Lakes area. Foraging and, in most cases, fishing became much less important to them. The farming complex had first taken shape in northeast Africa in the sixth millennium B.C.E. and was established in the Horn of Africa and Kenya before 1000 B.C.E. The beginning of farming among Bantu speakers dates the first dispersal of their languages to later than 3000 B.C.E. Cattle bones have been found near Luanda, indicating that the intrusion of the Mashariki Bantu farming complex into western central Africa had reached the Atlantic before 800 C.E.

South Africa rock art. Engravings found in the rock surfaces in the interior plateau and paintings on the walls of rock shelters in the mountainous regions of southern Africa—for example, the Drakensberg and Cedarberg ranges—date as far back as 25,000 years. Southern African rock art is believed to be the product of medicine people, the shamans. The shamans were involved in the well-being of the band and often worked in a state of trance in rituals involving death and flight, rainmaking, and control of the movement of antelope herds.

ADDITIONAL RESOURCES

Ambrose, Stanley H. "Archaeology and Linguistics in East Africa." In *The Archaeological and Linguistic Reconstruction of African History*, edited by Christopher Ehret and Merrick Posnansky. Berkeley: University of California Press, 1982.

Leakey, Richard E. *Origins Reconsidered: In Search of What Makes Us Human.* New York: Anchor Books, 1992.

Martin, Phyllis M., and Patrick O'Meara. *Africa.* Bloomington: Indiana University Press, 1986.

Oliver, Roland, and Michael Crowder, eds. *The Cambridge Encyclopedia of Africa.* Cambridge, England: Cambridge University Press, 1981.

SEE ALSO: African rock art, southern and eastern; Bantu, Congo Basin; Bantu, Mashariki; Chifumbaze culture; Cushites; Eastern African Microlithic/Khoisan peoples; Khoikhoi; Khoisan; Nilo-Saharans; Nilotes; Rift Valley system.

—*Alex L. Mwakikoti*

AFRICA, NORTH

DATE: 8000 B.C.E.-700 C.E.

LOCALE: Algeria, Egypt, Libya, Morocco, Sudan, Tunisia, and the territory of western Sahara

SIGNIFICANCE: North Africa was a battleground fought over by many empires, the birthplace of one of the world's oldest civilizations, and a cultural and religious mecca.

North Africa was an incubator of successful empires such as Egypt (one of the world's oldest civilizations) and battleground for empires including those of the Greeks, Romans, and Phoenicians. Arabs conquered North Africa in the name of Islam by the end of the seventh century C.E. Arabic remains the official language in Algeria, Egypt, Libya, Morocco, Sudan, and Tunisia, and Islam is the predominant religion of the region. Arabs call the region consisting of Algeria, Morocco, and Tunisia "Maghreb," which means "west" or "land where the Sun sets."

North Africa stretches from the Atlantic Ocean in the west to the Red Sea in the east. It borders the Mediterranean Sea in the north and the Sahel in the south—which, in modern times, is a semidesert area separating North and West Africa. The Nile River is 4,145 miles (6,669 kilometers) long, making it the longest river in the world and the only large river in North Africa.

History. Approximately 18,000 years ago, the Nile was a smaller river with many channels. In less than 500 years (from 12,000 to 11,500 years ago), flooding at the southern headwaters (Lake Victoria) of the Nile transformed the river and valley. More rainwater produced more vegetation, which, in turn, narrowed the river to a single channel. Plants and catfish were scarcer, and the available food supply could not support the population. About 11,000 years ago, the Sahara Desert became a steppe region—a refuge that led to the repopulation of the area. When the climate began to dry out again after 5000-4500 B.C.E., people who lived in the eastern Sahara migrated to the Nile Valley, becoming the forefathers of ancient Egypt.

The widespread use of pottery for cooking and food storage by 7,500 years ago signifies that North Africans were producing food. Some archaeologists hypothesize that pottery accompanied a sedentary lifestyle. It also contributed to population growth by enabling mothers to substitute boiled food for mother's milk, which shortened the period a mother had to breast-feed her babies.

A minor official, Menes (whose name is possibly associated with Narmer), conquered Upper Egypt in the south and Lower Egypt in the north by approximately 3100 B.C.E. Menes established his family as the rulers of a united Egypt. The name given to Menes and his successors was pharaoh, or "great house." The pharaoh was considered to be a god or diety.

About 2,800 years ago, North Africans learned how to fabricate iron from Phoenician sailors and Berber traders. Even before, by 1200 B.C.E., the Berbers, who lived along the Mediterranean coast, were masters of North Africa. The Berbers' military superiority derived from their mastery of fighting on horseback.

The Phoenicians established trading stations along the North African coast. One such colony was Carthage, in present-day Tunisia. Carthage became independent of Phoenicia by 800 B.C.E. By 550 B.C.E., Carthage was an empire united under the leadership of King Mago. In 480 B.C.E., Carthage was defeated by an army of Sicilians and Greeks at the Battle of Himera. Carthage then began developing its expanding North African empire. The Carthaginians and their longtime rivals, the Greeks, fought a series of wars. In 322 B.C.E., the region in the vicinity of Libya was conquered by one of Alexander the Great's Macedonian generals, Ptolemy I Soter. Ptolemy established dynastic control over Egypt. Carthage's long alliance with Rome dates to 510 B.C.E., when Rome had become independent of its Etruscan guardianship. A Roman army invaded North Africa and attacked Carthage in 256 B.C.E. The Carthaginian elephant cavalry and corps crushed the Romans. The first war between Rome and Carthage (called the First Punic War) lasted from 264 B.C.E. to 241 B.C.E. The war ended when a Roman fleet caught a convoy of Carthaginian ships off guard.

The Second Punic War broke out in 218 B.C.E. when the Carthaginian general Hannibal conquered the Greek city of Saguntum on the Catalonian coast. Hannibal then marched his army though the Alps. He destroyed a Roman army at the Battle of Trebia River in December. This victory shocked Rome into abandoning its plans to invade Africa and Spain. Hannibal waged war against the Romans on their own territory. Rome regained military superiority in 207 B.C.E. when a Roman general, Scipio Africanus, invaded Africa in 204 B.C.E. In what some historians consider among the most decisive battles in the ancient world, Scipio defeated the Carthaginian army commanded by Hannibal at Zama. The battle signaled the end of Carthaginian control over North Africa and the ascent of the Roman Empire. Rome sacked Carthage in 146 C.E. By 36 B.C.E., the heir to the assassinated Roman emperor Julius Caesar, Octavian (later the emperor Augustus), controlled all North Africa. The Roman Empire controlled North Africa until the Vandal invasion of the Maghreb in 429 C.E. The first North African emperor of Rome was Lucius Septimius Severus, who reigned from 193 to 211 C.E. He strengthened the empire's Saharan frontiers.

Arabs. Following the death of the Prophet Muḥammad in 632 C.E., Arab-speaking armies invaded Egypt from Palestine in 639 C.E. These Arabs practiced a new religion, Islam, whose adherents believe Muḥammad was the messenger of God. By 642 C.E., Arab armies had conquered Egypt. The first Arab army invaded Tunisia in 647 C.E. Two separate powers opposed the Arab invasion—Byzantium and the Berbers. The conquest of these powers was completed by 710 C.E. Under Islam, North Africa was united by a new religion, a new form of government, and a new code of law.

Agriculture and economics. The domestication of plants and livestock and establishment of towns and villages were the result of adaptation to the semiarid environment of North Africa. The Nile Valley and Delta form a rich agricultural region in which farming had begun by the seventh millennium B.C.E. As the river, which starts almost at the center of the African continent, empties into the Mediterranean, it leaves a rich soil in its wake. The Egyptians trapped water in ponds and then lakes for use in irrigation. Droughts and the drying of the surrounding area caused people to move into the Nile area and rely on grain farming and domesticated animals. Farmers grew wheat and barley and raised domesticated cattle, sheep, and goats. Fishing continued as it had before the practice of agriculture. Catfish spawned on the river were caught for eating; any excess was preserved through sun drying or smoking.

One of the agricultural products was olive oil, which became a major ingredient in the economy of North Africa. Soap, cooking oil, and medicines all contained olive oil. The North Africans also produced wines, and the demand for these wines spurred the production of pottery. The grainfields of North Africa were so productive that the Roman Empire relied on them for food. The Romans, as well as the other states along the Medi-

Reminders of the Roman presence in North Africa can be found in ancient ruins such as this Roman amphitheater in Tunisia. (PhotoDisc)

terranean Sea, traded with North Africa through the many harbors across its northern border, which were probably developed by Phoenician traders.

Language and literature. Ancient North Africans spoke Berber, Egyptian, and also Greek and Latin languages at different eras. The Arab conquerors of North Africa brought with them literary Arabic, which subsequently became a worldwide language.

Religion and ritual. The first Christians probably entered North Africa through coastal cities such as Carthage. The Roman emperor Decius (r. 249-251 C.E.) was the first leader to persecute Christians throughout the empire. Later emperors targeted Church leaders and the economic wealth of the Church for persecution. The rite of baptism, which offered complete forgiveness of sin, played a significant role in the lives of North Africans. Archaeologists have unearthed elaborate rooms or baptisteries dedicated to the ritual that marked the spiritual journey. The emperor Constantine the Great enhanced the power of the Church by giving bishops the power of magistrates and stressing the importance of Sunday as a day of spiritual renewal.

A North African, Saint Augustine, helped shape the history of western Christendom. In works such as *De civitate Dei* (413-427 C.E.; *The City of God*, 1610) and *Confessiones* (397-400 C.E.; *Confessions*, 1620), he analyzed the theological necessity of balancing free will and predestination, original sin and divine grace.

The impact of Christianity was later eclipsed by that of Islam, which entered the area in the 600's C.E. Islam is based on faith, prayer, alms-giving, fasting, and an annual pilgrimage to Mecca. The faith virtually homogenized North Africa. Religious leaders endeavored to create a "pure land" in which the Islamic ideal dominated.

Settlements and social structure. People in North Africa lived in permanent encampments by 8,000 years ago. As the philosopher Aristotle said, people came into cities to live and remained to live the good life. The Phoenicians established the first cities in North Africa early in the last millennium B.C.E.

North Africa played a significant role in the ancient world. It was the home of one of the earliest and longest-lived civilizations (Egypt). It was an incubator for later civilizations and the spread of Islam. Great empires rose and fell during the development of North Africa in the ancient world. Humans continually struggled to enjoy a better quality of life and to adapt to a changing environment.

ADDITIONAL RESOURCES

Brett, Michael, and Elizabeth Fentress. *The Berbers*. Oxford, England: Blackwell Publishers, 1998.

Diamond, Jared. *Guns, Germs, and Steel: The Fates of Human Societies*. New York: W. W. Norton, 1997.

Knox, Paul L., and Sallie A. Marston. *Places and Regions in Global Context: Human Geography*. Upper Saddle River, N.J.: Prentice-Hall, 1998.

Newman, James L. *The Peopling of Africa: A Geographic Interpretation*. New Haven, Conn.: Yale University Press, 1995.

Reader, John. *Africa: A Biography of the Continent*. New York: Vintage Books, 1999.

Rogerson, Barnaby. *A Traveller's History of North Africa: Morocco, Tunisia, Libya, Algeria*. New York: Interlink Books, 1998.

Wenke, Robert J. *Patterns in Prehistory: Humankind's First Three Million Years*. New York: Oxford University Press, 1999.

SEE ALSO: Alexander the Great; Arabia; Augustus; Berbers; Carthage; Christianity; Islam; Egypt, Pharaonic; Egypt, Prepharaonic; Egypt, Ptolemaic and Roman; Greece, Classical; Greece, Hellenistic and Roman; Hannibal; Muḥammad; Phoenicia; Punic Wars; Rome, Imperial; Scipio Africanus; Septimius Severus, Lucius; Vandals.

—*Fred Buchstein*

AFRICA, WEST

DATE: 8000 B.C.E.-700 C.E.

LOCALE: Africa south of the Sahara from Senegal to Cameroon

SIGNIFICANCE: During this period, the peoples of West Africa transformed from Stone Age hunter-gatherers to members of organized political states.

The area of West Africa lies in the continental area west of longitude 20 degrees east between 5 and 20 degrees north latitude. About one-third of West Africa is part of a vast continental platform with an average elevation of about 1,300 feet (400 meters). The major rivers are the Niger, Senegal, Gambia, and Volta. The

SELECTED SITES IN ANCIENT WESTERN AND NORTHERN AFRICA

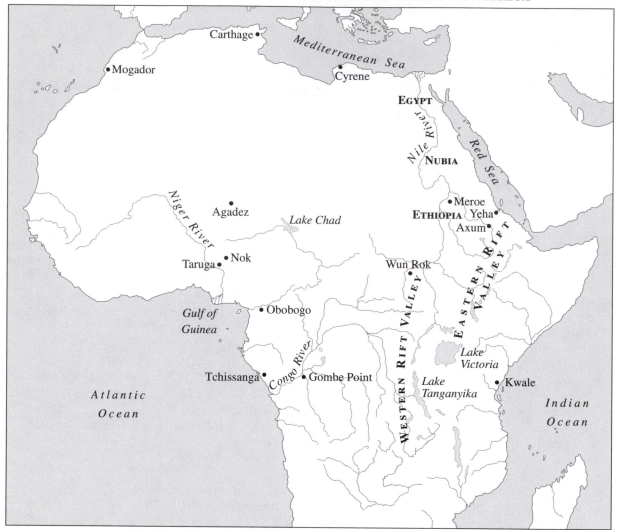

climate is tropical with a rainy and dry season. The shifting weather patterns have changed the ecology of West Africa, causing the Sahara to dry up and often reducing rainfall in the Sahel and savanna areas south of the Sahara.

West Africa contains deserts, savannas, and rain forests. During ancient times, the varied economies of the region were based on agriculture in the coastal and part of the savanna areas. Cattle herding was rare in the coastal areas because of the tsetse fly but was carried out in the savanna areas, where the tsetse fly was absent. The population was concentrated in villages, towns, and cities surrounded by farming areas. Political structures varied from powerful rulers or powerful se-

cret societies to groups in which individuals play a greater part in decision making. Religion was concerned with the control of spiritual forces, and in most West African cultures, the ancestor was an important link with the spirit world. Masks and figures were used as a means to make contact with the spiritual forces. The use of masks can be traced back to about 6000 B.C.E., as shown on rock paintings. Masks were often controlled by secret societies and used to bring fertility, protection, and other benefits to the community. These secret societies often functioned as the social control element in cultures without powerful rulers. In these cases, masks and sometimes figures were used in police and judgment functions.

Early history. Archaeological excavations in Ghana, Nigeria, and Senegal dated about 8000 B.C.E. yielded arrow points, barbs, and knives with blades slotted into shafts. These microliths aided in hunting efforts. During this period, the economy of West Africa was based on hunting and gathering.

Between 8000 and 3000 B.C.E., the Sahara was fertile and supported lush vegetation and animals. Around 8000 B.C.E., engravings of the hippopotamus, buffalo, giraffe, elephant, antelope, and other large animals indicate the people's interest in hunting. By 6000 B.C.E., the ecology was changing, and cattle herding became the way of life. Along with paintings of their herds, the artists depicted ritual dances and the use of masks that are similar to those still used in the West African cultures south of the Sahara. By 2000 B.C.E., the Sahara could no longer support herds of animals, and the people began to move south into the area of West Africa. People in the savanna areas just south of the Sahara continued to be cattle herders.

Many West African peoples have traditions telling of their movement from the north, west, or east into the area they now occupy. The Dogon people in Mali say that there were little red men in the area from which they came. The study of various human remains from sub-Saharan West Africa gives evidence of this migration.

Stone axes are found throughout West Africa. Excavations in forested areas of southeast Guinea, Sierra Leone, Ghana, and Nigeria indicate that ground and polished stone axes were being used at about 5000-4000 B.C.E. This indicates a use of these tools for cutting and clearing forested areas and the possible beginnings of agriculture. Pottery was also found in these excavations.

There is indication that the people living on the plains near the bend of the Niger River began to cultivate red-skin rice, millet, and sorghum from indigenous food plants by 4000 B.C.E. The use of stone axes shows that agriculture was being practiced just as early in the rain forest areas. Millet and sorghum do not grow well in rain forest areas, but the early domestication of a local wild species of yam and the use of oil-palm nuts provided the basic crops. Red-skin rice was brought down and cultivated in the southwest coast areas sometime after 3000 B.C.E.

Northeast of the bend of the Niger River in Mali's Tilemsi Valley, excavations have revealed settlements dated between 2010 and 1670 B.C.E. that produced pottery decorated with roulette and dragged-comb designs. These sites also had anthropomorphic and zoomorphic terra-cotta (fired-clay) figures and clay cylinders.

Later settlements. In the late second millennium B.C.E., the Western Mande, living west of the Joliba River, were in contact with Mediterranean Bronze Age cultures. Around 1000 B.C.E., the Northwestern Mande acquired horses and began state building, which led to the conquest of lands and people. By 500 B.C.E., they had begun to work iron, and the people in the Guinea forest area fled from their southward movement. About 300 C.E., the Soninke established the empire of Ghana (Wagadu) and began to run into conflict with the Berbers in the north. By the third century B.C.E., there is archaeological evidence of the working of iron by the Nok culture in northern Nigeria.

The Nok culture created terra-cotta figures of people and animals in a highly developed technique of hollowed forms with holes for the escape of gases as the pieces were being heated. The creation of large-scale sculptural forms by the Nok culture indicates a highly developed social and religious structure in settled communities by 800 B.C.E. Nok figures have proportions of head to body of one to three and one to four. The enlarged head in relation to the size of the body can be seen in more recent figure sculpture from West Africa, indicating a continuation of stylized proportions over the centuries.

The Nok figures were probably placed in shrines that were destroyed in various floods over a period of time and washed down the river to the tin-mining site where they were discovered. This would account for the fact that many of the pieces are fragments, with the spherical or cylindrical heads being in the best condition after rolling in the river. The tradition of creating terra-cotta sculptures continued until about 875 C.E. Dates ranging from the sixth millenium B.C.E. from Nok sites indicate an early and continuous occupation going back far earlier in time.

A related group of terra-cotta sculptures was discovered at Sokoto, a site not far from Nok. They are primarily head forms with features similar to the Nok pieces and have been dated between 200 B.C.E. and 200 C.E. by thermoluminescence. A third group of pieces, from Katsina in northern Nigeria dating from the same period, depict figures emerging from the tops of globular vessels with bodies barely modeled and having small limbs.

Just south of Lake Chad and north of the area occupied by the Nok people, excavations have revealed the

Sao culture, with pottery dating as early as 550 B.C.E. More highly decorated pottery was produced between 50 and 700 C.E., along with animal and stylized human forms. This indicates a settled community continuing over a long period of time.

Humans were also the subject of art in the southeastern area of Nigeria, where the Bakor clan of the Ejagham were carving stone monuments as symbolic portraits of important clan leaders and other important individuals in the culture.

The stimulus for a stronger political structure was often trade. With a strong leader, trade transactions could be better controlled. The area south of Lake Chad was on an important trade route from east to west south of the Sahara. A little farther to the south of Lake Chad and east of the Nok area is the site that served as the cradle of the Bantu languages between 3000 and 1000 B.C.E. The Bantu languages eventually spread throughout Central Africa.

ADDITIONAL RESOURCES

Church, R. J. Harrison. *West Africa: A Study of the Environment and of Man's Use of It*. New York: Longman, 1980.

Clark, Desmond J. *The Prehistory of Africa*. New York: Praeger, 1970.

Davidson, Basil. *A History of West Africa to the Nineteenth Century*. Garden City, N.Y.: Doubleday, 1966.

De Grunne, Bernard. *The Birth of Art in Black Africa: Nok Statuary on Nigeria*. Luxembourg: Banque Générale du Luxembourg, 1998.

Gillon, Werner. *A Short History of African Art*. New York: Facts On File, 1984.

SEE ALSO: Africa, East and South; Bantu, Congo Basin; Bantu, Mashariki; Ghana; Mande; Niger-Congo; Nok culture.

—*William L. Hommel*

AFRICAN ROCK ART, SOUTHERN AND EASTERN

DATE: c. 23,000 B.C.E.-700 C.E.

LOCALE: Southern Africa and Zimbabwe

RELATED CIVILIZATIONS: East and South Africa

SIGNIFICANCE: These paintings reveal one of the earliest painting traditions and raise questions about ritual function of art in early civilizations.

Images painted on rock slabs found in Apollo II cave in Namibia have been dated between 25,500 and 17,500 B.C.E. Engraved images in stone have been dated to 9000 B.C.E. These images portray animals, religious rituals, and everyday activities of the hunter-gatherers known as the San. Estimates place the number of paintings as up to 20,000, dating from the earliest times to 1800 C.E. Paintings from caves and shelters in Zimbabwe date as early as 12,000 B.C.E. A cave with the most artistically complex paintings was abandoned by 4000 B.C.E.

Most paintings were done where rock overhangs sheltered the painted surface. The pigments are minerals such as iron and manganese oxides. Artists often painted over earlier paintings, indicating that the act of painting was a ritual. People currently living in the area consider the painters to have been shamans and the paintings to be revelations of the spirit world. Dance images relate to experiences that induced trances for the shaman.

These paintings were found in caves in Zimbabwe. (Corbis)

Engraved images were made by abrading the surface within the outline of the figure, simulating the figure's texture.

ADDITIONAL RESOURCES
Garlake, Peter. *The Hunter's Vision: The Prehistoric Art of Zimbabwe*. Seattle: University of Washington Press, 1995.

Lewis-Williams, J. D., and T. A. Dowson. *Rock Paintings of the Natal Drakensberg*. Pietermaritzburg, South Africa: University of Natal Press, 1992.

SEE ALSO: Africa, East and South; Saharan rock art; Tibu.

—William L. Hommel

AGAPETUS, SAINT

ALSO KNOWN AS: Pope Saint Agapitus I
BORN: fifth century C.E.; Rome?
DIED: April 22, 536 C.E.; Constantinople
RELATED CIVILIZATIONS: Imperial Rome, Byzantine Empire
MAJOR ROLE/POSITION: Cleric and pope

Life. Born to the aristocratic Roman priest Gordianus, Agapetus (ag-uh-PEET-uhs) was well educated and became a member of Roman statesman Cassiodorus's circle of Christian intellectuals. He served as a priest of the Roman church of Saints John and Paul and was consecrated bishop of Rome in May, 535 C.E. With Cassiodorus, he planned a Christian academy of theology and literature. During his short but aggressive papacy, he intervened in ecclesiastical affairs in Gaul, Illyria, North Africa, and Constantinople. Agapetus confirmed the Carthaginian church council's decision to bar converted Arians from Holy Orders, and he negated a Marseilles council's condemnation of bishop Contumeliosus for immorality, inserting his own delegates as judges. He also contravened actions of the bishop of Larissa in Illyria.

Ostrogothic king Theodahad sent the pope as a diplomat to Justinian I's court for political reasons, but Agapetus publicly and successfully challenged the Monophysitic beliefs of Patriarch Anthimus I, whom he subsequently excommunicated and Justinian exiled. Agapetus consecrated Justinian's orthodox candidate, Menas, and died shortly thereafter. His body was returned to Rome in a lead coffin.

Influence. Saint Agapetus set further precedents for papal intervention throughout Christendom, but Justinian's wars in Italy limited subsequent popes' ability to exercise broad authority.

ADDITIONAL RESOURCES
Cassiodorus Senator. *Introduction to Divine and Human Reading*. New York: Norton, 1969.
Davis, Raymond. *The Book of Pontiffs*. Liverpool, England: Liverpool University Press, 1989.
Maxwell-Stuart, P. G. *Chronicle of the Popes*. New York: Thames and Hudson, 1997.

SEE ALSO: Arianism; Byzantine Empire; Carthage; Cassiodorus; Christianity; Goths; Rome, Imperial.

—Joseph P. Byrne

AGARISTE

BORN: c. 590 B.C.E.; place unknown
DIED: c. 500 B.C.E.; place unknown
RELATED CIVILIZATION: Archaic Greece
MAJOR ROLE/POSITION: Noblewoman

Life. The only details known about Agariste's (ag-uh-RIS-teh) life concern her wedding to Megacles of Athens. When she reached marriageable age, her father Cleisthenes, tyrant of Sicyon (Sikyon), conducted a yearlong contest to determine who would marry her. Thirteen suitors, the best men of Greece, competed both in the gymnasium and in discussions at dinner until Cleisthenes made his decision. At the end of the year, he threw a banquet, at which he intended to announce his choice of Hippocleides of Athens. As the night wore on, Hippocleides had too much to drink, until he began dancing on a table. Each dance became more outrageous until he stood on his head and rhythmically flailed his legs in the air. At this point, Cleisthenes told Hippocleides that he had danced away his marriage. His response became an Athenian proverb: "It's all the same to Hippocleides." Agariste and Megacles were then married according to the Athenian rites.

The story illustrates the political function of aristocratic marriage in the Archaic period, to foster alliances with important families in other cities. It also contains the earliest historical description of the Athenian marriage rite. Agariste's interest in the proceedings is never mentioned, as her most important functions were to unite the two families through marriage and to bear children for her husband.

Influence. Agariste's primary influence was in the birth of her children, one of whom was Cleisthenes of Athens, a statesman famous for his democratic reforms. Her name became a popular one among her descendants, and her granddaughter Agariste was the mother of Pericles.

ADDITIONAL RESOURCE
Herodotus. *The Histories*. Translated by Robin Waterfield. New York: Oxford University Press, 1998.

SEE ALSO: Athens; Cleisthenes of Athens; Cleisthenes of Sicyon; Daily life, customs, and traditions; Greece, Archaic; Pericles.

—Robert Rousselle

AGATHIAS

ALSO KNOWN AS: Agathias Scholasticus
BORN: c. 532 C.E.; Myrina, Aeolis, Asia Minor
DIED: c. 580 C.E.; Constantinople
RELATED CIVILIZATION: Byzantine Empire
MAJOR ROLE/POSITION: Lawyer, poet, historian

Life. After a period of study in Alexandria, Agathias (ug-GAY-thee-uhs) spent most of his life in Constantinople, where he supported himself by practicing law. Agathias's real love, however, was literature. His poem *Daphniaka* has been lost, but much remains of his *Cycle* (sixth century C.E., preserved in part in *The Greek Anthology*, twelfth century C.E.; English translation, 1848). The *Cycle*, Agathias's collection of contemporary epigrams on erotic, funerary, and other themes, includes epigrams by Agathias as well as by Paul the Silentiary and other prominent men who belonged to Agathias's literary circle. Agathias wrote the preface to the *Cycle* as a panegyric to Justin II in the hope of gaining the emperor's support but failed to win imperial patronage.

Agathias also wrote *Histories* (c. 580 C.E.; *History of the Reign of Justinian*, 1975), a continuation of Procopius's *Polemon* or *De bellis* (550-553 C.E.; *History of the Warres*, 1653, better known as *History of the Wars of Justinian*). Although he intended to continue his narrative up through the 570's C.E., he died before he could complete the work, which covers only the years from 553 to 559 C.E. Like his epigrams, his historical writing imitates the style of classical Greek historians such as Herodotus and Thucydides. Agathias's narrative focuses on wars in Italy and the Caucasus region but includes ethnographic digressions on the Franks and the Persians.

Influence. Agathias's works exemplify the Byzantine devotion to earlier models of classical literature. His works were well received: Much of the *Cycle* was preserved in the *Greek Anthology*, and subsequent secular historians imitated Agathias's practice of beginning their historical narrative where the previous historian had stopped.

ADDITIONAL RESOURCES
Cameron, Alan. *The Greek Anthology*. Oxford, England: Clarendon Press, 1993.
Cameron, Averil. *Agathias*. Oxford, England: Clarendon Press, 1970.

SEE ALSO: Byzantine Empire; Constantinople; Justinian I; Procopius.

—Martha G. Jenks

AGATHON

BORN: c. 445 B.C.E.; place unknown
DIED: c. 400 B.C.E.; Macedonia
RELATED CIVILIZATIONS: Athens, Classical Greece
MAJOR ROLE/POSITION: Tragedian

Life. Although none of Agathon's (AG-uh-thahn) works are extant, he is described by Plato, Aristotle, and Aristophanes as a tragic playwright. Plato's *Symposion* (388-368 B.C.E.; *Symposium*, 1701) depicts a celebration that takes place in Athens after the victory of one of Agathon's plays in 416 B.C.E. Plato portrays Agathon as a gentleman, well versed in the duties of hospitality. In this dialogue, Agathon joins his guests in eulogizing the god Eros. In a speech that Socrates compares to those of the Sophist Gorgias, Agathon initially describes Eros as both the most beautiful and the most virtuous among gods. However, like many of Socrates' interlocutors, after speaking with Socrates, Agathon admits to knowing nothing definite about the topic. In *De poetica* (c. 335-323 B.C.E.; *Poetics*, 1705), Aristotle says that Agathon's tragedies are among the first to be composed of fictitious characters and events. He also attributes to Agathon the inclusion of choral songs that are not connected to the plots of his plays. In Aristophanes' *Thesmophoriazousai* (411 B.C.E.; *Thesmophoriazusae*, 1837), Agathon is comedically depicted as delicate and effeminate. However, in Aristophanes' *Batrachoi* (405 B.C.E.; *The Frogs*, 1780), Dionysus describes him as a decent poet who, in death, is lamented by his friends.

Influence. Because none of his works survives, it is difficult to attribute to Agathon any lasting influence. However, Aristotle's descriptions of his works suggest that he had an impact on the poetry of ancient Greece.

ADDITIONAL RESOURCES
Aristotle. *Poetics*. Translated by S. H. Butcher. New York: Hill & Wang, 1989.
Plato. "Symposium." In *The Dialogues of Plato*. New York: Bantam Classics, 1986.

SEE ALSO: Aristophanes; Aristotle; Athens; Gorgias; Greece, Classical; Plato.

—*Sara MacDonald*

AGAW

ALSO KNOWN AS: Agau; Agew
DATE: 2500 B.C.E.-700 C.E.
LOCALE: Ethiopia
RELATED CIVILIZATION: Cushites, Ethiopia
SIGNIFICANCE: This early Cushitic-speaking group practiced agriculture and animal husbandry.

The Agaw (AH-gah) were the ancient Cushitic-speaking people who lived in the northern and central Ethiopian plateau around the Amhara, Gojjam, and Shoe regions. The ancestral Cushites developed agriculture and animal husbandry about 7000 B.C.E. The Agaw and four other groups—the Beja, Eastern Cushitic, Western Cushitic, and Southern Cushitic—have similar historical, linguistic, or cultural Cushitic background. The Jewish blacks known as the Falasha are believed to have descended from the Agaw, a belief based on their linguistic expression, especially their religious vocabulary.

Sometime after 700 C.E., Agaw languages replaced Omotic tongues in northern and central Ethiopia; Eastern Cushitic languages predominated in most areas around the Rift Valley and the eastern side of the highlands. Agaw languages are still spoken in the mountainous region of Simen northeast of the City of Gonder and in the southeast region of Gonder. The Agaw gradually merged with other groups that presently constitute only a small ethnic minority in modern Ethiopia, but the phonetic reflexes of the proto-Cushitic sounds are still evident in many of the Ethiopian groups, including the Amharic. Other historical evidence suggests that Semitic-speaking Coptic Christian Axumites subdued the Agaw during the ninth and tenth centuries C.E.

ADDITIONAL RESOURCES
Vogel, Joseph A., ed. *Encyclopedia of Precolonial Africa: Archaeology, History, Languages, Cultures,*

and Environments. Walnut Creek, Calif.: AltaMira Press, 1997.

Yakan, Mohamad Z. *Almanac of African Peoples and Nations*. New Brunswick, N.J.: Transaction, 1999.

SEE ALSO: Africa, East and South; Beja; Ethiopia; Rift Valley system.

—*Alex L. Mwakikoti*

AGESILAUS II OF SPARTA

ALSO KNOWN AS: Agesilaos
BORN: c. 444 B.C.E.; Sparta
DIED: c. 360 B.C.E.; Cyrene (in modern Libya)
RELATED CIVILIZATIONS: Classical Greece, Persia
MAJOR ROLE/POSITION: Statesman, military leader

Life. Agesilaus (uh-jehs-uh-LAY-uhs) II of Sparta was the younger son of Archidamus II, a Eurypontid king of Sparta, and his second wife, Eupolia. Because he was not expected to become king, Agesilaus underwent the rigorous Spartan system of military training,

Agesilaus II. (Library of Congress)

known as the *agōgē*. However, he did become a ruler in about 399 B.C.E., when the Spartan general Lysander of Sparta persuaded the Spartans that Agesilaus's nephew, the heir-apparent, was actually the son of the Athenian Alcibiades.

Agesilaus ascended the throne at a time when Sparta and its allies dominated the Greek world following the defeat of Athens in the Peloponnesian War (431-404 B.C.E.). In 396-394 B.C.E., he campaigned successfully against the Persians in Asia Minor in support of the independence of Greek cities there. He was soon recalled home, however, to defend Sparta against an alliance of Athens, Thebes, Corinth, and Argos. Agesilaus defeated the allies at Coronea in 394 B.C.E., and Spartan hegemony over Greece was confirmed in the King's Peace (386 B.C.E.; also known as the Peace of Antalcidas).

Agesilaus spent the next decade and a half warding off several challenges to Sparta's power. Although he was an inspiring battlefield leader, Agesilaus failed to prepare the Spartan army for the military innovations of the fourth century B.C.E. Using a wider and deeper phalanx and an oblique battle line, the Thebans destroyed the Spartan army, led by King Cleombrotus (Sparta had a dual monarchy), at Leuctra (371 B.C.E.). Agesilaus was able to prevent a Theban seizure of Sparta by hard campaigning in 370-369 B.C.E., but Spartan supremacy in Greece was effectively ended. He died while leading a mercenary expedition to Egypt.

Influence. Sparta's inability to maintain its power was mainly caused by the fact that its institutions were unsuited to empire building and by a progressive decline in the numbers of Spartan citizens. Agesilaus contributed to his city's decline by alienating Sparta's allies through frequent interference in their internal affairs.

ADDITIONAL RESOURCES
Hamilton, Charles D. *Agesilaus and the Failure of Spartan Hegemony*. Ithaca, N.Y.: Cornell University Press, 1991.

Plutarch. *The Age of Alexander: Nine Greek Lives.* Translated by Ian Scott-Kilvert. New York: Penguin Books, 1973.

Shipley, D. R. *A Commentary on Plutarch's Life of Agesilaos.* Oxford, England: Clarendon Press, 1997.

SEE ALSO: Archidamus II of Sparta; Athens; Greece, Classical; King's Peace; Leuctra, Battle of; Peloponnesian War; Persia.

—Michael S. Fitzgerald

AGRICOLA, GNAEUS JULIUS

BORN: June 13, 40 C.E.; Forum Julii, Gallia Narbonensis
DIED: August 23, 93 C.E.; place unknown
RELATED CIVILIZATIONS: Britain, Imperial Rome
MAJOR ROLE/POSITION: Governor

Life. Gnaeus (NEE-uhs) Julius Agricola (uh-GRIHK-uh-luh) was the son of an ordinary Roman farmer. He rose through the ranks of Roman administration serving as a quaestor in 64 C.E., praetor in 68 C.E., and legatus praetorius, or governor, in Britain from 78 to 84 C.E. The Roman historian Tacitus, Agricola's son-in-law, wrote a glowing biography of him.

Agricola achieved his greatest success while governor of Britain. He continued the empire's dual goals of Romanizing the province and expanding control over the indigenous tribes. His first battles were fought against the Ordivices, a fierce tribe located in Wales. In the winter campaign of 78 C.E., he crushed them, ending their raids into Roman territory. He established a series of forts that allowed the Romans to control the countryside and maintain peace.

Agricola drove into Scotland by land and sea. In 83 C.E., at the Battle of Mons Graupius, his legions defeated several thousand Caledonians, driving them into the swamps. The victory temporarily ended their raids into England. However, Agricola was unable to conquer the remainder of the island or act on a planned invasion of Ireland. Removed by the emperor Domitian in 84 C.E., possibly because of the governor's growing popularity, Agricola retired, then died in 93 C.E.

Influence. As governor of Britain, he pacified the Welsh population and ended the raids against Roman territory by Scottish tribes. During his tenure, Roman control over Britain solidified.

ADDITIONAL RESOURCES

Salway, Peter. *Roman Britain.* New York: Oxford University Press, 1981.

Tacitus. *The Agricola and the Germania.* London: Penguin Publishing, 1970.

SEE ALSO: Britain; Rome, Imperial; Tacitus.

—Douglas Clouatre

AGRIPPA, MARCUS VIPSANIUS

BORN: 63 B.C.E.; Italy
DIED: March, 12 B.C.E.; Campania, Italy
RELATED CIVILIZATION: Imperial Rome
MAJOR ROLE/POSITION: Colleague of Octavian/ Augustus from 44 B.C.E.

Life. Marcus Vipsanius Agrippa (MAHR-kuhs vihp-SAY-nee-uhs uh-GRIHP-uh) was the ally and right-hand man to Octavian, who later became the first Roman emperor, Augustus—as a military leader, founder of Roman colonies, and civil administrator. His power during the transition from the Republic to the Empire was second only to that of Augustus himself.

Agrippa's main campaigns and offices included Perusia (41-40 B.C.E.), praetor (40), Gaul (39-38), consul (37), Italy-Sicily (37-36), Illyria (35-34), aedile (33), Actium (31-30), and consul II and III (28-27) when Octavian became Augustus *princeps.* He received the ill Augustus's signet ring in 23, which meant Agrippa would have succeeded Augustus had he died. Agrippa held *imperium proconsulare maius* (supreme command) for five years from 23, in the Eastern Empire from 23 to 21; in 18, this power was renewed for another five years, in addition to which Augustus conferred tribunician power on him, making him coregent. He was in the Eastern Empire again from 17 or 16 to 13, where he befriended Herod and treated the Jews benevolently. He was appointed to conquer Pannonia in 12 but upon his return fell ill and died in March. His ashes were interred in Rome's mausoleum of Augustus.

Agrippa's wives were Caecilia Attica (37), Augustus's niece Marcella (28), and Augustus's widowed daughter Julia (21). His children were Vipsania (c. 33, who later married Tiberius), Gaius (20), Julia (19/18), Lucius (17), Agrippina (14, the Elder), and Agrippa Postumus (12). A fragment of Augustus's funeral oration for Agrippa survives in Greek translation.

Influence. Agrippa's merits go far beyond military competence. His consulships helped smooth the transition from the Triumviral period to the Principate. His utilitarian construction projects, including the Pantheon, the Roman baths, and an overhaul of the sewer and water-supply systems, contributed to Octavian's rise and, as Augustus, his glorification of Rome. Finally, through his daughter Agrippina the Elder, he was a grandfather of the emperor Caligula and great-grandfather of the emperor Nero.

ADDITIONAL RESOURCES

Aicher, P. *A Guide to the Aqueducts of Ancient Rome.* Wauconda, Ill.: Bolchazy-Carducci, 1995.

Carter, John M. *The Battle of Actium.* New York: Weybright and Talley, 1970.

Favro, D. *The Urban Image of Augustan Rome.* Cambridge, England: Cambridge University Press, 1996.

Reinhold, M. *Marcus Agrippa.* Geneva, N.Y.: Humphrey, 1933.

Syme, R. *The Augustan Aristocracy.* Oxford: Oxford University Press, 1987.

SEE ALSO: Agrippina the Elder; Agrippina the Younger; Augustus; Caligula; Julia (daughter of Augustus); Nero; Rome, Imperial; Tiberius.

—*Thomas H. Watkins*

AGRIPPINA THE ELDER

ALSO KNOWN AS: Vipsania Agrippina
BORN: c. 14 B.C.E.; place unknown
DIED: October 18, 33 C.E.; island of Pandateria, Tyrrhenian Sea
RELATED CIVILIZATION: Imperial Rome
MAJOR ROLE/POSITION: Aristocrat, political power broker

Life. The first emperor of Rome, Augustus, tried to engineer the succession to power through his daughter Julia. By her second husband, Augustus's colleague Agrippa, Julia was the mother of Gaius (born 20 B.C.E.), Lucius (17), Julia minor (18), Agrippina (14), and Agrippa Postumus (12). On the disgrace of her sister (2 B.C.E.) and the deaths of her brothers by 4 C.E., Agrippina (ag-rih-PI-nuh) was at the center of the struggles over imperial succession. Upon the death of Agrippa in 12 B.C.E., Augustus forced his stepson Tiberius to marry his daughter Julia to serve as a father figure for her children with Agrippa.

Agrippina married Germanicus Julius Caesar, Tiberius's nephew. Upon Augustus's death in 14 C.E., Tiberius came to power. Germanicus and Agrippina had nine children, including Tiberius's successor Caligula (born 12 C.E.) and Agrippina the Younger (born 15 C.E., mother of Nero). The instinctively politi-cal Agrippina ostentatiously courted the favor of the Rhine army in 14-16 and opposed Tiberius's governor of Syria, Piso, and his wife, Plancina, in 17-19. She publicly suspected Tiberius and his mother Livia of responsibility for Germanicus's untimely death in 19 (which modern historians doubt).

When Tiberius's son by his former wife Vipsania, Drusus the Younger, died (possibly at the hands of Sejanus, Tiberius's prefect of the Praetorian Guard) in 23, Agrippina's sons Nero, Drusus III, and Caligula were placed in line for the succession. Sejanus opposed Agrippina in order to further his own agenda and had Nero and Drusus III eliminated; Caligula, however, would remain to succeed Tiberius upon the latter's death in 37. Sejanus also took advantage of the mutual suspicion between Tiberius and Agrippina the Elder to see that she was exiled to Pandateria in 29, and four years later she died there of starvation. A famous portrait of her survives in Rome's Capitoline Museum.

Influence. Since Rome neither had a titled nobility nor allowed women to hold public office, Agrippina was only an aristocrat, not a princess. Her flair for dramatic action, however, accelerated the trend whereby the great ladies of Rome were increasingly prominent in politics, as is readily apparent in the *Annals* (c. 116) of Tacitus.

ADDITIONAL RESOURCES

Barrett, A. A. *Agrippina*. New Haven, Conn.: Yale University Press, 1996.

_____. *Caligula: The Corruption of Power*. New Haven, Conn.: Yale University Press, 1990.

Bauman, R. *Women and Politics in Ancient Rome*. New York: Routledge, 1992.

Syme, R. *The Augustan Aristocracy*. Oxford, England: Oxford University Press, 1986.

SEE ALSO: Agrippa, Marcus Vipsanius; Agrippina the Younger; Augustus; Caligula; Julia (daughter of Augustus); Nero; Tiberius.

—Thomas H. Watkins

AGRIPPINA THE YOUNGER

ALSO KNOWN AS: Agrippina Minor; Julia Agrippina
BORN: November 6, 15 C.E.; Cologne
DIED: March, 59 C.E.; near Naples
RELATED CIVILIZATION: Imperial Rome
MAJOR ROLE/POSITION: Political leader

Life. Agrippina (ag-rih-PI-nuh) the Younger was the great-granddaughter of Augustus and daughter of Nero Claudius Drusus Germanicus (later Germanicus Julius Caesar), leading heir to the principate. Senators opposed to the emperor Tiberius rallied around her family. Tiberius's suspicions led to arrests and assassinations. Germanicus was murdered when Agrippina was three; she last saw her mother when she was thirteen. Two brothers died in prison.

At age thirteen, Agrippina married Gnaeus Domitius Ahenobarbus, to whom she bore a son in 37 C.E.; Ahenobarbus died in 40 C.E. In 39 C.E., her brother Caligula, now emperor, exiled Agrippina on charges of plotting to overthrow him. After Caligula's assassination in 41 C.E., Agrippina returned from exile. In 49 C.E., she married her uncle, the emperor Claudius, who adopted her son, afterward called Nero.

Barred from ruling because of her gender, Agrippina was a powerful influence behind the scenes for the rest of Claudius's reign. She arranged for Nero to become emperor when Claudius died in 54 C.E. (probably poisoned by Agrippina). She virtually ruled Rome for five years until Nero, impatient with her interference, had her murdered. She wrote a memoir, which does not survive.

Influence. Agrippina was the first Roman imperial woman to wield power publicly, even putting her image on coins with Nero. Women of later dynasties followed her example.

ADDITIONAL RESOURCES

Barrett, Anthony A. *Agrippina: Sex, Power, and Politics in the Early Empire*. New Haven, Conn.: Yale University Press, 1996.

Humphrey, J. W. "The Three Daughters of Agrippina Maior." *American Journal of Ancient History* 4 (1979): 125-143.

SEE ALSO: Augustus; Caligula; Claudius; Nero; Rome, Imperial; Tiberius.

—Albert A. Bell, Jr.

AHAB

BORN: c. 900 B.C.E.; Israel
DIED: c. 853 B.C.E.; Ramoth-Gilead, Israel
RELATED CIVILIZATIONS: Israel, Syria, Assyria
MAJOR ROLE/POSITION: King, military leader

Life. Ahab, son of King Omri, reigned as seventh king of the northern kingdom of Israel. After the division of Israel, the northern kingdom had been ruled by at least four dynasties, each terminated by a palace coup. Therefore, Ahab's twenty-two-year reign (c. 874-c. 853 B.C.E.) was something of a feat.

The biblical account, to be found mainly in 1 Kings 16:29-22:50, gives a mixed judgment of him. As a secular leader, he prospered, fortifying his cities and particularly his capital, Samaria. He fought the Syrian king Ben-Hadad I, defeating him twice and securing a trading partnership. The third campaign, undertaken jointly with the king of Judah, Jehoshaphat, ended in death.

Assyrian accounts also document Ahab's participation in the Battle of Karkar (Qarqar) in 853 B.C.E., which temporarily stayed Assyrian advances.

Ahab's marriage to Jezebel, daughter of King Ethbaal of Sidon, may have been a good match politically and commercially, but religiously it was a disaster. Jezebel imported her own priests and shrines and actively persecuted the prophets of Yahweh. Ahab was opposed by Elijah the prophet. Several dramatic encounters ensued, the one on Mount Carmel being the most famous. Ahab's failure to rule justly is illustrated by his seizing of Naboth's vineyard.

Influence. Ahab is condemned in the severest terms by the biblical writer (1 Kings 21:25-6). He weakened the moral and spiritual fiber of the nation. His political and commercial gains were short-lived: A maritime expedition came to grief, and the vassal state of Moab broke away on his death.

ADDITIONAL RESOURCES
Bright, John. *A History of Israel.* Philadelphia: Westminster Press, 1959.
Grant, Michael. *The History of Ancient Israel.* N.Y.: Charles Scribner's Sons, 1984.
Rogerson, J. W. *Chronicle of the Old Testament Kings.* London: Thames and Hudson, 1999.

SEE ALSO: Assyria; Ben-Hadad I; Bible: Jewish; Israel; Phoenicia.

—*David Barratt*

AIDAN, SAINT

BORN: date unknown; Ireland
DIED: August 31, 651 C.E.; Bamburgh, Northumbria, Britain
RELATED CIVILIZATION: Early medieval Britain
MAJOR ROLE/POSITION: Christian monk-bishop

Life. Recognized as a saint, whose feast day is August 31, Aidan was born in Ireland and became a monk at Iona. At the invitation of King Oswald of Northumbria, Aidan left this island off the western coast of Scotland and founded Lindisfarne Abbey in 635 C.E. His diocese as bishop consisted of the whole of Northumbria, but as abbot, he followed the monastic life at Lindisfarne. Convinced that the best ways to spread Christianity were through the conversion of the royalty and the adoption of the religious life, Aidan founded the monasteries of Melrose, Gateshead, and Hartlepool all along the coast bordering the North Sea. He died at the castle of Bamburgh.

Influence. Northumbria was the area in England where three traditions came together to determine the future Christian Church in Britain. Although others introduced the Roman and Gallic forms, Aidan was responsible for the Celtic/Irish method of church organization, which was based on abbatial rather than episcopal supervision. Ironically, although Aidan is credited with teaching the monastic life to Abbess Hilda of Whitby (d. 680 C.E.), it was under her sponsorship that a synod held in 664 C.E. opted for the Roman form with bishops

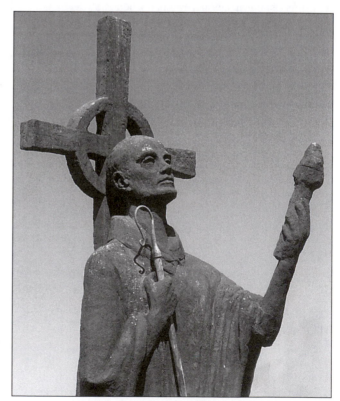

Saint Aidan. (North Wind Picture Archives)

in control. Lindisfarne Abbey became known as an artistic and intellectual center, renowned for its Gospels manuscript, created around 690 C.E.

ADDITIONAL RESOURCES
Blair, Peter. *Roman Britain and Early England: 55* B.C.-A.D. *871*. New York: W. W. Norton, 1963.

Lawrence, C. H. *Medieval Monasticism: Forms of Religious Life in Western Europe in the Middle Ages*. 2d ed. New York: Longman, 1989.

SEE ALSO: Britain; Christianity.

—*John A. Nichols*

AIṄKURURNŪRU

AUTHORSHIP: Ammuvan, Otalantai, Orampoki, Kapilar, and Peyan
DATE: second or third century C.E.
LOCALE: Tamil Nādu
RELATED CIVILIZATION: India (Tamil)
SIGNIFICANCE: This anthology of secular poetry is part of the larger anthology *Eṭṭūtokai*.

Aiṅkururnūru (aheen-KEW-rew-NEW-rew; English translation in *Poets of the Tamil Anthologies*, 1979) is an anthology of five hundred poems written by various poets, probably between about 100 B.C.E. and 250 C.E. The work, which belongs to the Maturait Tamilc Caṅkam (Śaṅgam) literary collection, is divided into five sections of one hundred poems, each of which portrays the five basic situations of love in the five regions (*aintinai*)—*kuriñici* (mountain), *neytal* (seashore), *pālai* (arid), *mullai* (forest), and *marutam* (lowland). Poems of the *Aiṅkururnūru* belong to the *akam* (internal) genre of Caṅkam literature. Ranging in length from three to six lines, these poems describe inner and personal human experiences such as love and its emo-

tional phases. Nature is very significant in Caṅkam secular poetry, and *Aiṅkururnūru* poems portray nature in an objective manner with the use of similes and metaphors. Human emotions, the primary subject of this anthology, provide valuable information about intimate relationships of the people of erstwhile Tamil country.

ADDITIONAL RESOURCES
Jotimuttu, P. *Ainkururnuru: The Short Five Hundred Poems on the Theme of Love in Tamil Literature: An Anthology*. Madras, India: Christian Literature Society, 1984.
Marr, John Ralston. *The Eight Anthologies*. Madras, India: Institute of Asian Studies, 1985.
Ramanujam, A. K. *Poems of Love and War, from the Eight Anthologies and the Ten Songs of Classical Tamil*. New York: Columbia University Press, 1985.

SEE ALSO: Caṅkam; India; *Kalittokai*; *Kuruntokai*; *Paripāṭal*; *Patirruppattu*.

—*Salli Vargis*

AINU

DATE: c. 7500 B.C.E.-700 C.E.
LOCALE: Japanese archipelago
RELATED CIVILIZATION: Japan
SIGNIFICANCE: The Ainu were the indigenous people of the islands that make up the modern nation of Japan.

Archaeologists believe that the Ainu (i-NEW) are descendants of the Jōmon people, who inhabited Japan for thousands of years, beginning more than 10,000 years ago. The origin of the Jōmon culture, however, has been

the source of disagreement among scholars. Various theories, including the Mongoloid theory, the Caucasoid theory, the Oceania race theory, and the old Asian race theory, have been put forward to explain the existence of the Jōmon and ultimately the Ainu. Modern scholars generally accept the theory that the ancestors of the Ainu were southern Mongoloids who settled the Japanese archipelago, including Okinawa, more than 10,000 years ago. As the Jōmon culture, they were the first people to design and use pottery. Jōmon pottery, which has a special cord design, was fashioned before the Jōmon people began farming, a very unusual cultural progression.

Although the Jōmon had lived on the Japanese islands for thousands of years, they were driven off most of Honshū, the main island, by northern Mongoloid people, probably Koreans and maybe Chinese, who migrated onto the archipelago sometime around 1000 B.C.E. According to legend, by 660 B.C.E. when Jimmu became the first emperor of Wa (the original name for Japan, derived from the Chinese), the group known as the Ainu could be found only on the northern Japanese island then called Ainu Moshiri (renamed Hokkaidō in 1889). They also lived on Sakhalin and on the Kuril Islands. The Ainu who had settled on Hokkaidō adopted a sedentary lifestyle and supplemented fishing and hunting with the growing of some agricultural products. However, those who lived on Sakhalin and on the Kurils were nomadic, moving from place to place to capture game or to fish different areas.

The Ainu lived in patrilineal kinship groups. Each group, which usually consisted of eight to ten households, was headed by a chief. The men hunted and fished, and the women grew small plots of grain as part of their household duties. The women also gathered berries, smoked meat, and made clothing from animal skins, fur, and grass.

The Ainu were a deeply religious people. They believed in the existence of two worlds, the world of the human and the world of the spirit. The word *ainu* means "human," or "not spirit," in the Ainu language. Their religion was animistic. They believed in spirit gods who lived in animals such as bears, foxes, and spotted owls. They also believed in nature gods such as fire, wind, and water; plant gods such as aconite, mushroom, and mugwort; and object gods such as boats and pots. These gods, just like the animal spirit gods, all lived in things and helped and protected humans.

The Ainu created rituals, songs, and dances to worship and satisfy the spirit world. The Ainu culture was preliterate, so these rituals, songs, and dances were passed on orally for hundreds of years, creating a rich oral culture. One of the most elaborate Ainu religious ceremonies was the winter ceremony, in which a bear that had been raised for two or three years was killed and its spirit released to the spirit world. The Ainu believed that the spirit of the grateful bear would watch over the group that had released it.

Beyond 700 C.E. In the late eighteenth century, the Japanese government incorporated Hokkaidō into Japan and allowed many Japanese homesteaders to take land away from the Ainu. The Japanese government also insisted that the Ainu learn to speak Japanese.

During much of the twentieth century, many Japanese people regarded the Ainu as an inferior group of people who had encroached on Japanese territory. However, in 1997, a Hokkaidō court ruled that the Ainu were the indigenous people of Japan. Subsequently, a bill was introduced in the Japanese Diet demanding that the Ainu be accorded the civil rights that United Nations documents indicate an indigenous people must have.

ADDITIONAL RESOURCES

Fitzhugh, William W., and Chisato O. Dubrevil, eds. *Ainu: Spirit of a Northern People.* Olympia: University of Washington Press, 2000.

Honda, Katsuichi, David L. Howell, and Kyoko Selden, trans. *Harukor: An Ainu Woman's Tale.* Los Angeles: University of California Press, 2000.

Johnson, D. W. *The Ainu of Northeast Asia.* East Windsor, N.J.: Idzat International, 1999.

Kayano, Shigeru, et al. *Our Land Was a Forest: An Ainu Memoir.* Boulder, Colo.: Westview Press, 1994.

Munro, Neil Gordon. *Ainu Creed and Cult.* London, England: Kegan Paul International, 1996.

SEE ALSO: Japan; Jimmu Tennō; Jōmon.

—*Annita Marie Ward*

'Ā'ishah bint Abī Bakr

ALSO KNOWN AS: Umm al-Mu'mineen; Humairah
BORN: c. 614 C.E.; Mecca, Arabia
DIED: 678 C.E.; Medina, Arabia
RELATED CIVILIZATIONS: Islam, Arabia
MAJOR ROLE/POSITION: Scholar

Life. 'Ā'ishah bint Abī Bakr was the daughter of Abū Bakr, the prophet Muḥammad's closest supporter, and was married to Muḥammad in Medina in 624 C.E. partly to solidify that support. As a child, 'Ā'ishah had played with her friends in her father's courtyard and later in Muḥammad's house. She became his most beloved spouse (she was his third of several, in keeping with the Muslim tradition), and although she had little effect on his religious thought or political acts, he trusted her so completely that, when she was once accused of being unfaithful, he castigated her accusers rather than doubting her. She participated in the Battle of Uhud (625 C.E.) and served at the back lines attending the wounded. She also accompanied the Prophet in his last pilgrimage. The Prophet spent his last days in May, 632 C.E., at her dwelling and died in her arms. She was eighteen and childless.

About a decade later, she became politically active, stirring opposition against the third caliph, ʿUthmān ibn ʿAffān (r. 644-656 C.E.). She also opposed his successor, ʿAlī ibn Abī Ṭālib, during the Battle of Camel (656 C.E.), so called for the camel she rode during the battle.

Two incidents in her life gave her grave sorrow. One was the search for her lost onyx necklace during an expedition with Muḥammad, which made her fall behind the army returning from the Bani al-Mustaliq campaign and thus become subject to the slander of hypocrites; it ended in the revelation of nine verses that safeguard the chastity of all women and men alike who might be subject to slander at any time (Qurʾān XXIV/11-20). The second was the Battle of Camel, which ended in her defeat by her opponent ʿAlī, who nevertheless treated her with respect and sent her back to Medina.

Influence. ʿĀʾishah's command of the Arabic language, poetry, history, genealogy, and the customs of pre-Islamic Arabia made her instrumental in comprehending the sayings of Muḥammad and transmitting them to the next generations. She is considered an important exegete of the Qurʾān.

ADDITIONAL RESOURCES

Abbott, Nabia. *Aishah: The Beloved of Mohammed.* 1942. Reprint. London: Al Saqi, 1985.

Kennedy, Hugh. *The Prophet and the Age of the Caliphates.* London: Longman, 1986.

Spellberg, D. A. *Politics, Gender, and the Islamic Past: The Legacy of ʿĀʾishah bint Abī Bakr.* New York: Columbia University Press, 1994.

SEE ALSO: Abū Bakr; ʿAlī ibn Abī Ṭālib; Arabia; Islam; Muḥammad; Qurʾān; ʿUthmān ibn ʿffān.

—*M. Mehdi Ilhan*

ĀJĪVIKAS

DATE: sixth century B.C.E.-fourteenth century C.E.
LOCALE: India
RELATED CIVILIZATION: India
SIGNIFICANCE: Influenced yogic, tantric, and other philosophies.

The Ājīvikas (ah-JEE-vee-kah-s) were an ascetic and deterministic sect that emerged in India at the same time as Jainism and Buddhism, in the sixth century B.C.E. They were heretical, denying the validity of the Vedas and believing instead that both human fate and the transmigration of souls (rebirths) were completely predetermined by *niyati* (Sanskrit "destiny" or "rule"). There was no cause of depravity or of purity, and therefore, there was no free human will, sin and dharma were nonexistent, and it was impossible to change or improve one's lot.

The Ājīvikas went about completely nude, carrying staffs and begging for their food; they were itinerant bards. Asceticism (including the practice of lying on a bed of thorns, squatting for long periods of time, holding hot stones with bare hands, severing muscles, or amputating parts of the body) and the drinking of cow urine were obligatory; sexual encounters were condoned and often employed for occult purposes. These practices were not purposeful but were considered to be their determined lot.

During the fourth and third centuries B.C.E., the Ājīvikas were accepted and even patronized by rulers of the Mauryan Dynasty such as Aśoka (r. c. 265-238 B.C.E.), but they declined thereafter, although they survived until the 1300's in the region of modern Mysore, where the sect's founder, Gośāla Maskarīputra, was worshiped as a divinity. Although the sect died, Ājīvika rituals became the basis for some tantric and yogic practices.

ADDITIONAL RESOURCES

Basham, A. L. *History and Doctrines of the Ājīvikas.* London: Luzac, 1951.

Walker, Benjamin. *Hindu World: An Encyclopedic Survey of Hinduism*. London: George, Allen and Unwin, 1968.

SEE ALSO: Buddhism; Gošāla Maskarīputra; Jainism; Mauryan Dynasty; Tantras; Vedas.

—Arthur W. Helweg

AKANĀNŪRU

ALSO KNOWN AS: *Nedunthogai*
AUTHORSHIP: Compiled by Uruthirasanman
DATE: second or third century C.E.
LOCALE: Tamil Nādu
RELATED CIVILIZATIONS: Dravidian civilization, India
SIGNIFICANCE: This work presents a collection of longer Tamil love poems in the *akam* (internal) genre.

Believed to be compiled by Uruthirasanman at the instance of King Ukkirapperuvazhuthi, *Akanānūru* (ah-kah-NAH-NEW-rew; English translation in *Poets of the Tamil Anthologies*, 1979) is a collection of four hundred love songs, self-sufficient and independent of each other, in the *akam* (internal) genre. Because of the length of the songs, varying from thirteen to thirty-one lines, *Akanānūru* is also called *Nedunthogai*—the shorter poems of the Caṅ-kam age are called *Kuruntokai*. The four hundred songs are classified as follows: The first 120 are called *Kalirriyanai Nirai* (an array of male elephants), songs 121 to 300 are called *Manimidaipavalam*, and the last hundred songs (301 to 400) are called *Nithilakkovai*. Noted for their vivid descriptions of nature, apt similes and metaphors, and accurate historical allusions, the poems are ascribed to 145 poets. The poems are carefully arranged so that those bearing odd numbers belong to *pālai* (arid) settings; poems bearing numbers 2, 8, 12, 18, 22 . . . relate to the *kuriñici* (mountain) themes, those bearing numbers 4, 14, 24, 34. . . deal with *mullai* (pastoral) settings; those numbered 6, 16, 26, 36 . . . with the *marutam* (river) situations; and those numbers that are multiples of ten relate to *neytal* (seashore) settings. Not only are the poems replete with generous historical allusions to Nandas, Mauryas, Yavanas, and chieftains of Tamil Nādu, but they also display an admirable gift of observation and a keen understanding of human psychology.

ADDITIONAL RESOURCES
Hart, George L. *Poets of the Tamil Anthologies*. Princeton, N.J.: Princeton University Press, 1979.
Nalladi, R. Balakrishna Mudaliyar. *The Golden Anthology of Ancient Tamil Literature*. Madras, India: The South India Saiva Sidhantha Works Publishing Society, 1959.
Zvelebil, Kamil V. *Literary Conventions in Akam Poetry*. Madras, India: Indian Institute of Asian Studies, 1986.

SEE ALSO: Caṅkam; India; *Kuruntokai*.

—Kokila Ravi

AKAPANA PYRAMID

DATE: c. 200 B.C.E.-200 C.E.
LOCALE: Near Lake Titicaca and modern Tiwanaku, Bolivia
RELATED CIVILIZATION: Tiwanaku
SIGNIFICANCE: Stone cutting and linking methods indicate the earliest use of metal tools in the building of large structures in the Western world.

The Akapana (ah-KAH-pah-nuh) pyramid is the largest structure at the Tiwanaku site of pre-Incan ruins in Bolivia. The pyramid is 12 miles (19 kilometers) southeast of Lake Titicaca, at approximately 12,500 feet (3,810 meters) above sea level, in the highest American city of the ancient world. The remaining structure is a truncated, terraced, andesite-faced pyramid 50 feet (15 meters) high, with sides about 200 feet (61 meters) long around the base and exactly oriented toward the cardinal directions. It has seven levels of nearly perfectly joined stone blocks that were once faced with carvings, paintings, and metal plaques.

The stone was quarried 60 miles (97 kilometers) away.

The pyramid appears to represent the cosmogenic myths of the Tiwanaku. Water collected in a square basin at the top of the pyramid and was directed through intricate interior channels so that it poured out of the walls of each level and then ran back into the structure, finally to exit into an underground river returning the water to Lake Titicaca. Besides being an engineering marvel equal to the Great Pyramid at Giza, the Akapana is the sacred mountain at the center of the world, a reflection of the distant Quimsachata range of the Andes. The natural flow of its rainy-season waters is the source of the abundant fertility of the earth and human life. When the waters ran full, the sound of their passage would have made the whole structure vibrate and roar like a huge bell of stone. The true name of Tiwanaku was Taypikhala, which, in the local language means "the stone in the center."

ADDITIONAL RESOURCES

Kolata, Alan. *The Tiwanaku*. Cambridge, England: Blackwell, 1993.

Masuda, S., et al. *Andean Ecology and Civilization*. Tokyo: University of Tokyo Press, 1985.

Moseley, Michael E. *The Incas and Their Ancestors: The Archaeology of Peru*. London: Thames and Hudson, 1992.

SEE ALSO: Andes, central; Andes, south; Archaic South American culture; Tiwanaku.

—*Michael W. Simpson*

AKHENATON

ALSO KNOWN AS: Amenhotep IV; Amenophis IV (*Greek*); Ikhnaton
BORN: c. 1390 B.C.E.; Egypt
DIED: c. 1360 B.C.E.; Akhetaton (modern Amarna), Egypt
RELATED CIVILIZATION: Pharaonic Egypt
MAJOR ROLE/POSITION: Pharaoh

Life. One of the first acts of the pharaoh Amenhotep IV was the construction of a temple to the Aton, or "solar disk," at Thebes. In his fifth regnal year, he changed his name to Akhenaton (ahk-uh-NAHT-uhn), "radiance of the Aton," and moved to Akhetaton, the "horizon of the Aton," modern Amarna. Around year nine, he proscribed the worship of all gods except the Aton. During these years, Akhenaton also promoted the Amarna style of art, which emphasized movement and emotion. He himself was depicted in a startling fashion, with wide hips, spindly arms, and slight breasts. This may reflect his nearness to the Aton, the father and mother of humanity.

Akhenaton's last years are obscure. The Amarna diplomatic archive suggests that local squabbles and the intrigues of the Hittite king Suppiluliumas I eroded Egyptian control over Syria-Palestine. Also alarming was Suppiluliumas I's conquest of Mitanni and the outbreak of a

Akhenaton. (Library of Congress)

plague. The ensuing anxiety is evidenced by the rise of military men such as Ay, Horemheb, and Rameses I.

Influence. Egyptians considered Akhenaton a heretic and tried to forget him. Nonetheless, his ideas affected hymnography and art. Akhenaton was the first monotheist and the first founder of a religion in history. It is important to recognize, however, that he venerated a mute vehicle for light-energy, not an ethical god such as that of Judaism, Christianity, or Islam.

ADDITIONAL RESOURCES

Aldred, Cyril. *Akhenaten: King of Egypt*. London: Thames and Hudson, 1988.

Redford, Donald B. *Akhenaten: The Heretic King*. Princeton, N.J.: Princeton University Press, 1984.

SEE ALSO: Ankhesenamen; Egypt, Pharaonic; Hittites; Mitanni; Nefertiti; Suppiluliumas I.

—*Steven M. Stannish*

AKIBA BEN JOSEPH

ALSO KNOWN AS: Akiva ben Joseph; Aqiba ben Joseph
BORN: c. 40 C.E.; probably near Lydda (modern Lod), Palestine
DIED: c. 135 C.E.; Caesarea, Palestine
RELATED CIVILIZATIONS: Israel, Imperial Rome
MAJOR ROLE/POSITION: Religious scholar, Jewish nationalist

Life. Akiba ben Joseph (ah-KIHV-ah behn JOH-zehf) was born into very humble circumstances and remained an illiterate shepherd well into adulthood. Thereafter, he quickly became known throughout Palestine as one of the foremost religious scholars of his generation. He was chosen by the other rabbis in Palestine to argue before Emperor Hadrian (r. 117-138 C.E.) against the recent imposition of decrees outlawing the Jewish religion and the theological study of Judaism. The deputation was unsuccessful. In 132 C.E., a large-scale Jewish revolt against Roman rule broke out in Palestine. The charismatic leader of the revolt was Bar Kokhba, a man whom Akiba publicly acknowledged to be the long-awaited Jewish messiah who would free Israel from its foreign (Roman) oppressors. Akiba's

blessing of Bar Kokhba caused thousands to join in the three-year revolt against Roman rule. Akiba was imprisoned by the Roman authorities for his refusal to cease preaching and teaching. He was tortured by the Romans and died.

Influence. In addition to his role in the revolt against Roman rule, Akiba was also the leader in systematizing the vast body of legal literature in the Torah. He argued that the Torah can be read both literally and allegorically.

ADDITIONAL RESOURCES

Eusebius of Caesarea. *Ecclesiastical History: Complete and Unabridged*. Translated by Christian Frederic Crusé. Peabody, Mass.: Hendrickson, 1998.

Finkelstein, Louis. *Akiba: Scholar, Saint, and Martyr*. 2d ed. New York: Schocken Books, 1962.

Neusner, Jacob. *A History of the Jews in Babylonia*. Vol. 4. Leiden, Netherlands: E. J. Brill, 1969.

SEE ALSO: Bar Kokhba; Hadrian; Judaism; Rome, Imperial.

—*Victoria Erhart*

AKKADIANS

DATE: c. 2300-2100 B.C.E.
LOCALE: Mesopotamia, Iraq
SIGNIFICANCE: Akkadians built the first Mesopotamian territorial state and introduced innovations in administration and ideology to control and unify the Mesopotamian population.

The Akkadians (a-KAD-ee-uhns) in Mesopotamia in the latter part of the third millennium B.C.E. used a Semitic language called Akkadian. Although their existence in Mesopotamia can be detected from the Early Dynastic period, the culmination of their culture was the Akkadian Dynasty, also called the Dynasty of

Agade or the Sargonic Dynasty. Akkadian culture was absorbed by other ethnic groups who subsequently entered Mesopotamia.

The Akkadian period can be divided into two parts: from the establishment of the dynasty by Sargon through the reigns of his sons Rimush and Manishtusu, and from the golden period achieved by his grandson Naram-Sin to the period of collapse.

The first dynast, Sargon (r. c. 2334-2279 B.C.E.), came from humble origins. His rise to power and military successes served to inspire the "Sargon legend," which partially parallels the later biblical story of the birth of Moses. Sargon built his capital Akkad (Agade; perhaps modern Ishan Mizyad) near Babylon. He campaigned in northern Mesopotamia, Syria, eastern Turkey, and western Iran and then conquered southern Mesopotamia. He tried to replace native local rulers in southern Mesopotamia with his family or Akkadian officials, although this was not always possible. He introduced year names, calling a year by a memorable event, and systems of unified measurements (although this may be the work of his successors). He also appointed one daughter, Enheduanna, as high priestess in the Sumerian city of Ur, to better control the important city. The installation of a princess as high priestess of Ur became a tradition for five hundred years. Enheduanna was also known as a compiler of various hymns and lauded as the first female poet.

Naram-Sin's campaigns to Syria, eastern Turkey, and western Iran are better attested, although his actual control was apparently limited to Mesopotamia proper. He was the first Mesopotamian king to deify himself in art and royal titulary. However, later literary compositions blame the collapse of the dynasty on his sacrilegious destruction of a temple. The real cause of the collapse was probably the dynasty's loose control over conquered territory and pressure from various neighboring ethnic groups, not merely the Gutian invasion, as was formerly believed. In reality, the Akkadian Dynasty was still stable even in the reign of Naram-Sin's successor Shar-kali-sharri, although its territory was probably reduced to Akkad and its environs. Hegemony of southern Mesopotamia was seized by Utu-Hegal of Uruk some decades after Shar-kali-sharri.

ADDITIONAL RESOURCES

Franke, Sabina. "Kings of Akkad." In *Civilizations of Ancient Near East*. Vol. 1. New York: Charles Scribner's Sons, 1995.

Hallo, W. W., and W. K. Simpson. *The Ancient Near East: A History*. 2d ed. New York: Harcourt Brace Jovanovich, 1998.

Kurt, Amélie. *The Ancient Near East c. 3000-330* B.C. London: Routledge, 1995.

SEE ALSO: Assyria; Babylonia; Sargon of Akkad; Sumerians.

—*Atsuko Hattori*

ALANI

DATE: 1-400 C.E.
LOCALE: Southeastern Europe
SIGNIFICANCE: One of the groups in the barbarian invasion of the Roman Empire in the fifth century C.E.

A group of nomadic pastoralists originally occupying the region northeast of the Black Sea, the Alani were first mentioned in Roman literature in the first century C.E. They were the most powerful of the three main divisions of a group known as the Sarmatians, the other two being the Rhoxolani and the Izayges, which moved westward across the Don in the early third century B.C.E. and displaced the Scythians. In Roman sources, the Alani were considered very warlike and were known for their horse-breeding skills. They frequently raided the Parthian Empire and the Caucasian prov-

inces of the Roman Empire until 370 C.E., when they were overwhelmed by the Huns, after which many fled westward. They crossed into Gaul with the Vandals and the Suebi in 406 C.E., and many settled near Orleans and Valence. The remainder of the westward migration continued on into North Africa, where the kingdom was officially titled "the Kingdom of the Vandals and the Alani." Those Alani who remained under Hunnic rule, the "inner clans" known as the Os, are said to be the ancestors of the Ossetians of the Northern Caucasus.

One of the "outer clans" of the Alani, called the Rukhs (also Ros or Rus), lived northwest of the Caucasus and are thought to have given their name to Russia (called "Rus" in medieval times), although they are not ethnically related to the Slavs.

ADDITIONAL RESOURCES

Bachrach, Bernard S. *A History of the Alans in the West: From Their First Appearance in the Sources of Classical Antiquity Through the Early Middle Ages.* Minneapolis: University of Minnesota Press,1973.

Miclczarek, Mariusz. *The Sarmatians.* Oxford, England: Osprey, 2000.

Sulimirski, Tadeusz. *The Sarmatians.* New York: Praeger, 1970.

SEE ALSO: Africa, North; Huns; Parthia; Rome, Imperial; Scythia; Suebi; Vandals.

—*Michael C. Paul*

ALARIC I

BORN: c. 370 C.E.; Feuce Island (later in Romania)
DIED: 410 C.E.; Casentia, Bruttium (later Cosenza, Italy)
RELATED CIVILIZATIONS: Visigoths, Imperial Rome
MAJOR ROLE/POSITION: Statesman, military leader

Life. Born of noble lineage, Alaric I (AL-uh-rihk) served as commander of the Gothic troops in the Roman army. Shortly after the death of Emperor Theodosius the Great in 395 C.E., he left the army and was elected chief of the Visigoths. Claiming that his tribe had not received the subsidies promised by Rome,

Alaric raided the eastern provinces, marching on Constantinople and ravaging Greece. In 397 C.E., Eastern emperor Arcadius placated Alaric by appointing him *magister militum* (master of the soldiers) in Illyricum.

Moving from the East to Italy in 401 C.E., Alaric was defeated by the Roman general Flavius Stilicho in 402, but later (c. 405) became his auxiliary. The expense of Alaric's mercenary forces was unpopular with the Roman aristocracy, and Stilicho's execution under the emperor Honorius (408 C.E.) left Alaric's army unpaid and without provisions. After several sieges of Rome and a brief elevation of a rival emperor, Alaric captured and

Visigothic leader Alaric I relaxes in Athens. (North Wind Picture Archives)

sacked Rome for three days (August 24-26, 410 C.E.) to extract payment by force. This was the first time that Rome had been captured by a foreign army in nearly eight hundred years. Although the Visigoths plundered the city, they treated the inhabitants humanely, respected church property, and burned only a few buildings. After abandoning a plan to invade Africa, the Visigoths marched northward. Alaric died during this journey.

Influence. Alaric's sack of the "eternal city" shocked the entire Mediterranean world. This event prompted the publication of both Saint Augustine's *De civitate Dei* (413-427; *The City of God*, 1610) and Orosius's *Historiarum adversus paganos libri VII* (after 417 C.E.;

Seven Books of History Against the Pagans, 1936), two of the most influential works of late antiquity and the Middle Ages.

ADDITIONAL RESOURCES
Heather, P. J. *The Goths*. Malden, Mass.: Blackwell Publishing, 1997.
_____. *Goths and Romans, 332-489*. New York: Oxford University Press, 1991.

SEE ALSO: Alaric II; Goths; Greece, Hellenistic and Roman; Rome, Imperial; Stilicho, Flavius; Theodosius the Great.

—*A. G. Traver*

ALARIC II

BORN: c. 466 C.E.; place unknown
DIED: 507 C.E.; place unknown
RELATED CIVILIZATIONS: Visigoths, Franks
MAJOR ROLE/POSITION: Visigoth king

Life. Alaric II (AL-uh-rihk) was the son of the Visigoth king Euric and Ragnahild. After Euric died from natural causes, Alaric II became king of the Visigoths on December 28, 484 C.E. The Visigothic kingdom, sometimes referred to as the kingdom of Toulouse, encompassed Spain and southern Gaul. In 502 C.E., Alaric II and the Frankish king Clovis were able to come to terms and end the constant fighting between their kingdoms. In February of 506 C.E., Alaric II issued the *Breviarum Alaricianum* (also known as *Lex Romana Visigothorum*, 506 C.E.; "Alaric's breviary"), which was a Visigothic codification of Roman law based on the *Codex Theodosiusianus* (438 C.E.; *The Theodosian Code*, 1952).

The peace between the Franks and Visigoths was short-lived, and in 507 C.E., the Christian Clovis declared war on the Arian Goths. That summer at Vouillé

near Poitiers, the Frankish army defeated the Visigoths, and Alaric II was killed, ending the Visigothic kingdom.

Influence. Although the death of Alaric II resulted in the destruction of the Visigoth kingdom, his legislation, the *Breviarum Alaricianum*, became the basis for Roman law in the early medieval world.

ADDITIONAL RESOURCES
Heather, P. J. *The Goths*. Malden, Mass.: Blackwell Publishing, 1997.
Jones, A. H. M. *The Later Roman Empire, 284-602*. Norman: University of Oklahoma Press, 1964. Reprint. Baltimore: Johns Hopkins University Press, 1986.
Wolfram, Herwig. *The Roman Empire and Its Germanic Peoples*. Translated by Thomas Dunlap. Berkeley: University of California Press, 1997.

SEE ALSO: Alaric I; Arianism; Christianity; Clovis; Franks; Goths; Rome, Imperial.

—*R. Scott Moore*

ALBOIN

BORN: date and place unknown
DIED: 572 C.E.; Verona, Lombardy, Italy
RELATED CIVILIZATIONS: Langobards, Franks, Byzantine Empire
MAJOR ROLE/POSITION: King of the Langobards

Life. Alboin (AL-bawn) became king of the Langobards circa 565 C.E. His first wife was Clodosuiuntha, daughter of the Frankish king Chlotar I. The Franks and Byzantine Empire were Catholic, but the Langobards had embraced Arianism, which ensured complex diplomatic and military relationships between the powers. In 566 and 567 C.E. with Avar support, Alboin attacked the Gepids led by Cunimund and effectively eliminated them.

In 568 C.E., Alboin left Pannonia and led the Langobards into Italy. They were joined by a group of Saxons hoping to settle in a more prosperous territory, but soon they became unhappy with Lombard domination and decided to return to their homeland, where they were eventually overcome by the Swabians who had settled there. The invasion of Italy was virtually unopposed, and after Pavia was captured, Alboin made it the capital of the new Lombard kingdom. It was this invasion that entangled the Franks in Italian affairs on the instigation of the Byzantine Empire. Alboin was assassinated in 572 C.E. by an agent of his wife, Rosamund, daughter of Cunimund.

Influence. Alboin's invasion of Italy in 568 C.E. established a Lombard kingdom that lasted until the time of Charlemagne.

ADDITIONAL RESOURCES

Christie, Neil. *The Lombards: The Ancient Longobards*. Malder, Mass.: Basil Blackwell, 1998.

Paul the Deacon. *History of the Lombards*. Translated by W. D. Foulke. Philadelphia: University of Pennsylvania Press, 1972.

Tabacco, Giovanni. *The Struggle for Power in Medieval Italy*. Cambridge, England: Cambridge University Press, 1989.

SEE ALSO: Angles, Saxons, Jutes; Arianism; Byzantine Empire; Christianity; Franks; Langobards.

         —Brian Hancock

ALCAEUS OF LESBOS

ALSO KNOWN AS: Alkaios
BORN: c. 625 B.C.E.; Mytilene, Lesbos
DIED: c. 575 B.C.E.; place unknown
RELATED CIVILIZATION: Archaic Greece
MAJOR ROLE/POSITION: Lyric poet, political partisan

Life. Alcaeus of Lesbos (al-SEE-uhs of LEHZ-bahs) was born into an aristocratic family of Mytilene, the most important city-state on the Aegean island of Lesbos. His contemporary, the poetess Sappho, belonged to the same social class in Mytilene. Alcaeus and his brothers were energetically involved in the bitter rivalries that characterized the political affairs of Mytilene during his lifetime, and his poetry is replete with political references and partisan invective.

None of Alcaeus's poems has survived complete. The extant verses and any knowledge of lost poems are derived from a combination of mutilated papyrus copies and quotations and descriptions by later Greek and Roman writers. The poems were lyric, in the strict sense of the word, and monodic: Namely, they were composed to be sung by one person, originally Alcaeus, who accompanied himself on the lyre. Common themes were wine, warfare, politics, and pederastic

love, although some were short hymns to individual Olympian gods. Among the surviving verses are portions of two allegorical poems in which Alcaeus's party is represented as a storm-tossed ship.

Influence. Alcaeus was greatly admired throughout classical antiquity, and the scholars at Alexandria placed him in the canon of nine Greek lyric poets. He exercised a profound influence on the *Odes* (23 B.C.E., 13 B.C.E.; English translation, 1621) of the Roman poet Horace in matters of form, theme, image, and versification.

ADDITIONAL RESOURCES

Burnett, Anne Pippin. *Three Archaic Poets: Archilochus, Alcaeus, Sappho*. London: Bristol Classical Press, 1998.

Lattimore, R., trans. *Greek Lyrics*. Chicago: University of Chicago Press, 1960.

Martin, H. *Alcaeus*. New York: Twayne, 1972.

Walker, Jeffrey. *Rhetoric and Poetics in Antiquity*. New York: Oxford University Press, 2000.

SEE ALSO: Alexandrian library; Greece, Archaic; Languages and literature.

         —Hubert M. Martin, Jr.

ALCIBIADES OF ATHENS

ALSO KNOWN AS: Alkibiades; Son of Clinias
  (Kleinias)
BORN: c. 450 B.C.E.; Athens?, Greece
DIED: 404 B.C.E.; Phyrgia, Asia Minor
RELATED CIVILIZATION: Classical Greece
MAJOR ROLE/POSITION: Statesman, military leader

Life. A controversial, flamboyant general and an ambitious leading politician, Alcibiades (al-suh-BI-uh-

Alcibiades of Athens. (North Wind Picture Archives)

deez) of Athens came from an ancient noble family that had diplomatic relations with Sparta. He received an excellent education and was a favorite pupil of the philosopher Socrates. He was an able speaker, and his physical beauty and charm were renowned.

Alcibiades competed with the demagogues who followed the generation of his uncle Pericles, but Alcibiades' chief opponent was the elder statesman Nicias of Athens. Alcibiades sought to expand Athenian influence, reversing the defensive strategy of the Peloponnesian War (431-404 B.C.E.). He engineered two military expeditions, Mantinea (418 B.C.E.) and Sicily (415 B.C.E.), but both ended in defeat. The Athenians banished Alcibiades following numerous accusations of sacrilege against important cults. He aided Sparta and Persia during this exile but lost their confidence. Upon returning to Athens in 407 B.C.E., he led a successful military campaign but withdrew again after a blunder. At war's end (404 B.C.E.), Alcibiades was murdered under mysterious circumstances.

Influence. A master of intrigue, Alcibiades was known as both a gifted and brilliant leader. Though admired, he was often feared. His personal excesses and recklessness aroused deep suspicions.

ADDITIONAL RESOURCES
Ellis, W. *Alcibiades*. New York: Routledge, 1989.
Forde, S. *Ambition to Rule: Alcibiades and the Politics of Imperialism in Thucydides*. Ithaca, N.Y.: Cornell University Press, 1989.
Gribble, D. *Alcibiades and Athens: A Study in Literary Presentation*. Oxford, England: Clarendon Press, 1999.

SEE ALSO: Mantinea, Battles of; Nicias of Athens; Peloponnesian War; Pericles; Socrates.
—*Christopher Sean Planeaux*

ALCMAN

ALSO KNOWN AS: Alkman
BORN: seventh century B.C.E.; Asia Minor
DIED: early sixth century B.C.E.; Greece
RELATED CIVILIZATION: Archaic Greece
MAJOR ROLE/POSITION: Lyric poet

Life. Traditional accounts claim that Alcman (ALK-muhn) was originally a slave in the Lydian city of Sardis before being sold and taken to Sparta. He earned fame as a choral writer for various public festivals. Of his reported six books of poetry, one work, *Par-*

theneion (n.d.; English translation, 1936), a choral piece that includes both mythical narrative and dialogue for a chorus of young women, survives intact along with various fragments. Alcman's work covered a wide range of topics: marriage, love, religion, nature, and myths.

Influence. A style of lyric meter was named after Alcman by ancients who considered his poetry difficult to understand because of his style and subject matter. Modern scholars cite his works as the earliest example of Greek choral poetry and as examples of the prevailing theme of eros, women as both object and subject of love poetry, and the high culture of archaic Sparta.

ADDITIONAL RESOURCES

Bing, Peter, and Rip Cohen. *Games of Venus*. New York: Routledge, 1991.

Calame, Claude. *The Poetics of Eros in Ancient Greece*. Translated by Janet Lloyd. Princeton, N.J.: Princeton University Press, 1999.

Davenport, Guy. *Archilochos, Sappho, Alkman: Three Lyric Poets of the Late Bronze Age*. Berkeley: University of California Press, 1980.

Robbins, Emmet. "Public Poetry: Alcman." In *The Companion to the Greek Lyric Poets*, edited by Douglas E. Gerber. Leiden, Netherlands: E. J. Brill, 1997.

SEE ALSO: Greece, Archaic; Languages and literature.

—*Tammy Jo Eckhart*

ALESIA, BATTLE OF

DATE: July-October, 52 B.C.E.
LOCALE: Northeast Celtic Gaul (later Alise-Sainte-Reine, France)
RELATED CIVILIZATIONS: Republican Rome, Gauls
SIGNIFICANCE: Caesar's victory gave Rome control over the province of Gaul.

Background. Between 58 and 53 B.C.E., Julius Caesar fought in Gaul (modern France) to enhance his wealth and political standing. In 53 B.C.E., the Gauls finally rallied around a single leader, Vercingetorix. The Gauls attacked Roman-held cities in southern France, provoking Caesar to action.

Gallic leader Vercingetorix, defeated and captured, is brought before Caesar. (North Wind Picture Archives)

Action. Caesar spent the early part of 52 B.C.E. recapturing lost cities, then marched to attack the Gauls, who had retreated to the fortified hill-city of Alesia (uh-LEE-zhuh). The Romans built two parallel walls around Alesia, one to keep Vercingetorix in and the outer wall to defend against relief attacks. In October, a relief force arrived and attacked Caesar's army, while Vercingetorix launched coordinated sallies from Alesia. The Romans beat back both assaults, aided by German cavalry hitting the relief force from the rear. After almost four months in Alesia, the Gauls ran out of food and surrendered.

Consequences. After Alesia, there were no more serious uprisings in Gaul, which meant that Rome could tap into the wealth and resources of Western Europe for another four centuries. Caesar's success prompted a political power struggle with his former ally Pompey the Great. Caesar's victory over him marked the beginning of the end of the Roman Republic and laid the groundwork for the Roman Empire.

ADDITIONAL RESOURCES

Caesar, Julius. *War Commentaries of Caesar.* Translated by Rex Warner. New York: New American Library, 1960.

Meier, Christian. *Caesar.* Translated by David McClintock. New York: HarperCollins, 1995.

O'Reilly, Donald. "Besiegers Besieged." *Military History* 9, no. 6 (February, 1993).

SEE ALSO: Caesar, Julius; Celts; Gauls; Pompey the Great; Rome, Republican; Vercingetorix.

—*Paul K. Davis*

ALEUTIAN TRADITION

DATE: 2000 B.C.E.-700 C.E.
LOCALE: Subarctic, southeastern Alaska
SIGNIFICANCE: This subarctic group depended largely on the sea.

The Aleutian (uh-LEW-shuhn) Islands are part of an archipelago stretching more than 1,300 miles (2,100 kilometers), from the southwestern Alaskan mainland nearly to Kamchatka and Eurasia. The Aleutian tradition has existed since at least 1000 B.C.E. Stone tools have been unearthed that date back to 10,000-6500 B.C.E., characterized as being much thicker than the contemporary Arctic Small Tool or the Northwest Microblade types. Inuit subtraditions from the north and Asia later began to infiltrate and disperse, diverging into the later island societies still evident in the twenty-first century. The Aleutian peoples have their own language and culture, though they are distantly related to the Inuit.

The Aleutian people generally numbered about 15,000 and called themselves the Unangan ("the people"). They depended on the sea for most of their livelihood. Men honored the spirits of the sea mammals and game (sea otters, seals, sea lions, whales, and fish). They hunted while wearing gut-skin shirts highly decorated with glass beads, hair embroidery, yarn, and other materials handcrafted or obtained by trade. At sea in their waterproof sea-lion and seal-skin suits and large boats, or *umiaks*, the men wore conical wooden hats with various sizes of bills that denoted their social positions.

The Aleutians dug down as deep as 6 feet (nearly 2 meters) to build round subterranean lodgings from approximately 500 to 700 square feet (47 to 65 square meters) in size, then covered the radial log roof with earth and grass and entered from above. Heat and light were generated by seal-oil lamps. Each man stood on his roof daily at dawn to "swallow light" and scan the sea for signs. Small villages were located on or between bays, where lookouts, escape routes, and protected landings were easily found. A good salmon stream provided food and water, and the gravel beaches provided the driftwood and whalebone needed to build their *barabara*, or underground houses. Nearby woods provided birds, eggs, plants, and some game (caribou, bear).

Village life was highly structured, based on inherited social ranking from high noble, to commoner, to slave. They practiced bilateral descent, and powerful shamans were consulted regarding illness and hunting taboos. Leaders were chosen from among the elite nobles and chiefs. Living space, as well as burial plots, was allocated by rank. Living in relative isolation from prehistoric times, until the mid-1700's and initial decimating contact with Russian seafarers, less than two thousand Unangan carried on the ancient Aleutian traditions in historic times.

ADDITIONAL RESOURCES
Jones, Dorothy M. *Aleuts in Transition*. Seattle: University of Washington Press, 1976.

Laughlin, William S. *Aleuts: Survivors of the Bering Land Bridge*. New York: Holt, Rinehart & Winston, 1997.

SEE ALSO: American Paleo-Arctic tradition; Archaic tradition, northern; Ipiutak; Kachemak tradition.

—*Michael W. Simpson*

ALEXANDER POLYHISTOR, LUCIUS CORNELIUS

BORN: c. 105 B.C.E.; Miletus, Asia Minor
DIED: c. 35 B.C.E.; Laurentum, near Rome
RELATED CIVILIZATION: Republican Rome
MAJOR ROLE/POSITION: Teacher, writer

Life. Alexander was captured in the Mithradatic Wars and sent to Rome, where he served as a slave in the family of the prominent Cornelius Lentulus. Around 80 B.C.E., he received the name Lucius Cornelius (LEW-shuhs kawr-NEEL-yuhs) when Lucius Cornelius Sulla granted him his freedom and Roman citizenship. Alexander became known as Polyhistor (pahl-ee-HIHST-ur) because he was "widely learned," writing at least twenty-five works. The topics he wrote about attest to the variety of his interests, from the early history of Italy and Rome, to ethnographic and geographical writings about the Jews, Babylonians, Egyptians, and other peoples from the East, to Pythagorean philosophy and the Delphic Oracle.

Unfortunately none of Alexander's works has survived intact, but 145 fragments of varying lengths have been found quoted in later authors. They show that although learned, he was rarely original, and his works frequently reproduced the errors of his sources. Alexander was also a teacher, earning sufficient income to purchase a home in the Roman suburbs, where he perished in a fire around 35 B.C.E.

Influence. Alexander's greatest value is not in what he wrote but in what he transmitted from earlier authors, whom he copied accurately. For example, his *On the Jews*, quoted extensively by Eusebius of Caesarea, preserves portions of the writings of several Hellenistic Jewish authors that might otherwise have been lost entirely.

ADDITIONAL RESOURCES
Gruen, E. S. *Heritage and Hellenism*. Berkeley: University of California Press, 1998.
Rawson, E. *Intellectual Life in the Late Roman Republic*. Baltimore: Johns Hopkins University Press, 1985.

SEE ALSO: Eusebius of Caesarea; Rome, Republican; Sulla, Lucius Cornelius.

—*Robert Rousselle*

ALEXANDER THE GREAT

ALSO KNOWN AS: Alexander III of Macedonia
BORN: 356 B.C.E.; Pella, Macedonia
DIED: June 10 or 13, 323 B.C.E.; Babylon
RELATED CIVILIZATIONS: Macedonia, Greece, Near East, Egypt, Persia, India
MAJOR ROLE/POSITION: King, military leader

Life. Alexander the Great was the son of King Philip II of Macedonia and Olympias, an Epirote princess. From age thirteen to sixteen, he studied under Ar-

istotle, who inspired his interest in science, medicine, philosophy, and literature. At age sixteen, Alexander served as regent for his father, and at age eighteen, he led the decisive cavalry charge at the Battle of Chaeronea. A rift between father and son occurred in 337 B.C.E., but the two were reconciled within a year. Philip was assassinated in 336 B.C.E., and Alexander was acclaimed as king of Macedonia. His swift and forceful actions enabled Alexander to succeed his father as *hēgemōn*, or leader, of the League of Corinth and

Alexander the Great consults the Oracle at Delphi. (Library of Congress)

Babylon, Susa, and Persepolis. Subsequently, he established himself as Persian king. In 327 B.C.E., Alexander invaded India (modern Pakistan) and a year later defeated Porus, the raja of Pauravas, at the Hydaspes (Jhelum) River. Alexander's troops refused to cross the Hyphasis (Beas) River, and he campaigned southward until he reached Ocean (the Arabian Sea) in 325 B.C.E. Alexander returned to Babylon in 323 B.C.E. and died there at the age of thirty-two from poisoning, a mysterious illness, or excessive drinking.

Influence. Alexander's military genius, iron will, and boundless ambition produced an empire touching on three continents and encompassing two million square miles (more than five million square kilometers). His conquests, founding of new cities (seventy according to historian Plutarch), creation of a uniform currency, and circulation of vast amounts of money contributed to the diffusion of Greek culture and helped usher in the Hellenistic era. Alexander has been portrayed as a philosopher in arms, an apostle of Hellenic culture, and a cosmopolitan visionary. He has also been depicted as a ruthless despot, a brutish despoiler, and a narcissistic drunkard. Nonetheless, Alexander continues to be the subject of impassioned debate more than twenty-three hundred years after his death and has thus achieved the everlasting fame he sought.

to command the invasion of the Persian Empire. In 335 B.C.E., Alexander secured Macedonia's northern borders and destroyed the city of Thebes, thus crushing Greek resistance to Macedonian overlordship.

In early 334 B.C.E., Alexander crossed the Hellespont with an invasion force of more than 37,000 men, joined by advance troops in Asia. His first great victory came at the Granicus River in 334 B.C.E., which opened Asia Minor to conquest. In 333 B.C.E., Darius III, the Persian king, met the invaders at Issus, where Alexander outmaneuvered his adversary and forced him to flee from the battlefield. Campaigning in a southwesterly direction, Alexander established his control over the Levant and was recognized as the Egyptian pharaoh in 332 B.C.E. Returning eastward, he defeated a formidable force under Darius III at Gaugamela in 331 B.C.E. Alexander marched south and then east, occupying

ADDITIONAL RESOURCES

Bosworth, A. B. *Conquest and Empire: The Reign of Alexander the Great.* Cambridge, England: Cambridge University Press, 1988.

Hammond, N. G. L., and F. W. Walbank. *A History of Macedonia.* Vol. 3. Oxford, England: Oxford University Press, 1988.

O'Brien, J. M. *Alexander the Great: The Invisible Enemy.* London: Routledge, 1994.

SEE ALSO: Aristotle; Chaeronea, Battle of; Darius III; Egypt, Ptolemaic and Roman; Gaugamela, Battle of; Granicus, Battle of; Greece, Classical; Hydaspes, Battle of; Issus, Battle of; Macedonia; Olympias; Persia; Philip II.

—*John Maxwell O'Brien*

ALEXANDRIAN LIBRARY

DATE: c. 300 B.C.E.-before 700 C.E.
LOCALE: Alexandria, Egypt
RELATED CIVILIZATIONS: Ptolemaic and Roman
    Egypt
SIGNIFICANCE: Greatest collection of Greek literature
    in the ancient world.

Much is in doubt about the Alexandrian library: its founder (Ptolemy I Soter or his son, Ptolemy II Philadelphus); its location (somewhere in the Royal Quarter); its relationship to the Alexandrian museum; the size, nature, and organization of its holdings; and its ultimate fate. The Peripatetic philosopher Demetrius

Phalereus may have been "founding librarian," with Aristotle's library as his model. Subsequent librarians included Zenodotus of Ephesus, Aristophanes of Byzantium, and Aristarchus of Samothrace; all three produced editions of Homer and other poets, demonstrating the library's crucial role in preserving Greek literature for future generations.

Ancient anecdotes highlight dubious collecting methods. Every ship unloading at Alexandria was supposed to be searched, its books seized and copied, and the copies given to the original owners. Other Hellenistic rulers followed the Ptolemies' example in founding libraries, especially the Attalids in Pergamum.

The library may have burned when Julius Caesar set fire to the Egyptian fleet in 48 B.C.E., but the library continued to exist during the Roman period. The bishop of Alexandria led an attack on the Serapeum (temple to Sarapis) in 391 C.E. and presumably destroyed the annex library that had been built there. ʿAmr ibn al-ʿĀṣ, Arab conqueror of Egypt in 642 C.E., is said to have consigned the library's books to Alexandria's baths for fuel, but this story seems to have arisen only in the twelfth century C.E.

ADDITIONAL RESOURCES

Canfora, Luciano. *The Vanished Library.* Berkeley: University of California Press, 1990.

El-Abbadi, Mostafa. *The Life and Fate of the Ancient Library of Alexandria.* 2d ed. Paris: UNESCO, 1992.

Frazer, Peter M. *Ptolemaic Alexandria.* Oxford, England: Clarendon Press, 1972.

SEE ALSO: Apollonius Rhodius; Aristarchus of Samothrace; Caesar, Julius; Demetrius Phalereus; Egypt, Ptolemaic and Roman; Ptolemaic Dynasty; Strabo.

—*T. Keith Dix*

This engraving depicts the Alexandrian library during the time of the Ptolemies. (North Wind Picture Archives)

ALEXANDRIAN PATRIARCHS

DATE: 100-700 C.E.
LOCALE: North Africa
RELATED CIVILIZATIONS: Roman Egypt, Imperial Rome
SIGNIFICANCE: The Alexandrian patriarchs were leaders of the early Christian Church who were involved in the theological controversies of the 400's, 500's, and 600's. As a result of these controversies, the Church divided into two groups: the Monophysites and the Orthodox. The Monophysites eventually emerged as the Coptic Church, the national church of Egypt.

The city of Alexandria became, with Rome and Antioch, one of the main church centers in the late Roman Empire. By 382 C.E., Egypt was a diocese, with Alexandria as its capital. The bishops of Alexandria may actually have been the first church leaders to use the title of archbishop.

The patriarchs of Alexandria—including the great bishops Athanasius and Cyril —were powerful as a result of their vast land holdings, the prestige of Egypt's monastic tradition within the empire, and Egypt's longstanding tradition of centralized authority. By the 300's, all Egypt and much of northern Africa had been brought under the central control of the Alexandrian patriarchs. Such power led the Egyptian churchmen—supported by the population—to seek greater independence from Constantinople, a rival for the role of most important Christian center in the East. Religious controversy over the nature of Christ saw Alexandria bolt from the fold of orthodoxy. At the Council of Chalcedon (451 C.E.), the church rejected Monophysitism, a heresy that held that Christ had one nature, which was divine. The Alexandrian patriarch Dioscorus supported the heresy. Both he and the heresy were condemned at Chalcedon. Afterward, Alexandria's prestige declined within the church, and its church leaders split into two camps: an orthodox minority and the Monophysite majority, which became the Coptic Church. The Arab conquest of Egypt in the 600's marked the end of the patriarch's independence. Constantinople took charge of appointing the Alexandrian patriarchs, who now led a small Christian population in Muslim-ruled Egypt.

ADDITIONAL RESOURCES

Johnson, Maxwell E. *Liturgy in Early Christian Egypt.* Cambridge, England: Grove Books, 1995.

Pearson, B. A., and J. E. Goehring, eds. *The Roots of Egyptian Christianity.* Philadelphia: Fortress Press, 1986.

SEE ALSO: Chalcedon, Council of; Christianity; Constantinople; Egypt, Ptolemaic and Roman; Rome, Imperial.

—*Adriane Ruggiero*

ʿALĪ IBN ABĪ ṬĀLIB

ALSO KNOWN AS: Haydara, the lion
BORN: 600 C.E.; Mecca, Arabia
DIED: 661 C.E.; in Al-Kufa, Iraq
RELATED CIVILIZATIONS: Byzantium, Persia
MAJOR ROLE/POSITION: Fourth caliph

Life. The prophet Muḥammad's first cousin and son-in-law through his marriage to Fāṭima, ʿAlī ibn Abī Ṭālib (a-LEE ihb-uhn AB-i tuh-LIHB) was an early convert to Islam, a close adviser of the Prophet, and an inspiring military leader.

Following Muḥammad's death in 632 C.E., ʿAlī became embroiled in a succession dispute with the first caliph, Abū Bakr. Claiming that the Prophet had selected him as the rightful successor, ʿAlī contested Abū Bakr's election. Disgruntled by his rejection, ʿAlī abstained from politics until his own selection as fourth caliph in 656 C.E.

ʿAlī's caliphate was marred by political discord, sporadic rebellions, and full-scale civil war. Increasingly isolated by political blunders, ʿAlī proved unable to prevent the rise of a rival caliphate headed by Muʿāwiyah I. The issue was resolved in Muʿāwiyah's favor in 661 C.E. when ʿAlī was assassinated.

Influence. ʿAlī's political shortcomings led to the establishment of the Umayyad caliphate centered in Damascus. He also inspired the Shīʿite branch of Islam, which maintains that the true successors (imāms) of

Muḥammad must be tied to him by consanguinity. Most Shīʿites see ʿAlī as an avenue to salvation, and some extremists have deified him.

ADDITIONAL RESOURCES
Chirri, M. J. *The Brother of the Prophet Muḥammad (The Imām ʿAlī).* Qum, Iran: Ansanyan, 1996.

Jafri, J. H. M. *The Origins and Early Development of Shi'i Islam.* London: Longman, 1979.

SEE ALSO: Abū Bakr; Islam; Muḥammad; Umayyad Dynasty.

—*Michael J. Fontenot*

ALLEMANNI

ALSO KNOWN AS: Alamanni; Alemanni
DATE: second-sixth centuries C.E.
LOCALE: Northern Europe, especially around modern Germany
SIGNIFICANCE: In the third century C.E., the Allemanni were among the first Germanic tribes to claim lands from the Roman Empire.

The Allemanni (ah-leh-mah-NEE) tribe (the name means "all men" or "all humankind") were a mixed group of Germanic and non-Germanic people. Although they existed as a group from the second until the very early sixth century C.E., the name (first used in 289 C.E.) is applied differently: Initially, when they were fighting the Romans, the Allemanni were recognized as a large, distinct group, but by the sixth century, the name refers to a much smaller tribe within the greater Gothic forces.

The Allemanni are best known for their confrontations with Rome in the third century C.E. They were among the first Germanic tribes to invade. They broke through the Roman frontier in northern Europe, crossed the Rhine and the Danube rivers, and in 258 C.E. penetrated as far as Milan. Because they lacked a cohesive army, they were driven back by the Romans, but the Romans themselves later withdrew from northern Europe in the fourth and fifth centuries C.E., leaving the land for the Allemanni and other Germanic tribes.

ADDITIONAL RESOURCES
Todd, Malcolm. *The Northern Barbarians: 100 B.C.- A.D. 300.* London: Hutchinson, 1975.
Wolfram, Herwig. *History of the Goths.* Translated by Thomas J. Dunlap. Berkeley: University of California Press, 1988.
_____. *The Roman Empire and Its Germanic Peoples.* Translated by Thomas Dunlap. Berkeley: University of California Press, 1997.

SEE ALSO: Germany; Goths; Merovingian Dynasty; Rome, Imperial.

—*Alexander M. Bruce*

ALTAR DE SACRIFICIOS

DATE: 200-900 C.E.
LOCALE: Confluence of the Río Pasión and Río Usamacinta in the Petén, Guatemala
RELATED CIVILIZATION: Maya
SIGNIFICANCE: Altar de Sacrificios represents the earliest settled and longest occupied lowland Maya city in the Petén region.

Altar de Sacrificios thrived on the commerce that passed along the Río Pasíon and Río Usamacinta during the Classic period (250-900 C.E.). Although its size and architecture did not rival the expansive cities of

Tikal or Yaxchilán, Altar de Sacrificos fully participated in Maya culture including hieroglyphic inscriptions, stelae dedication, and ceremonial warfare. Composed of a plaza group with several formal structures, the site of Altar de Sacrificios is renowned for the Altar Vase, a ceramic masterpiece that depicts funerary rituals associated with the death of a Maya noblewoman.

Although the nearby Mixe-Zoque culture may have influenced the settlement of Altar de Sacrificios, it was established by Maya in Preclassic times (approximately 200 C.E.). Achieving preeminence in the Late Classic period (600-900 C.E.), this city used its advantageous locale to exploit extensive trade networks that transported valuable goods including obsidian, jade, and cacao (chocolate) from long distances.

However, warfare with other Maya cities, combined with overpopulation, drought, and environmental devastation, imposed a great decline on Altar de Sacrificios and other Maya lowland cities. At the end of the Terminal Classic period, outside groups overtook Altar de Sacrificios, and shortly thereafter, the city was abandoned.

ADDITIONAL RESOURCES

Coe, Michael. *The Maya.* New York: Thames and Hudson, 1993.

Henderson, John S. *The World of the Ancient Maya.* 2d ed. Ithaca, N.Y.: Cornell University Press, 1997.

Sharer, Robert. *The Ancient Maya.* Stanford, Calif.: Stanford University Press, 1994.

SEE ALSO: Maya; Tikal.

—*Michelle R. Woodward*

ALWA

ALSO KNOWN AS: Alodia
DATE: c. 400-700 C.E.
LOCALE: Upper Nubia
SIGNIFICANCE: The Christian kingdom of Alwa was the last barrier to Islam in the Sudan in the early sixteenth century C.E.

After the fourth century C.E. collapse of Meroe, three Nubian kingdoms emerged: Nobatia in the north, Makouria, and Alwa in the south. Alwa was located in the fertile valleys of the Blue and White Niles. Boundaries, although undefined, extended from Meroe south to the Gezira and Butana regions and east to the Red Sea. The kingdom occupied most of modern central Sudan. At the crossroads of major trade routes, it was a prosperous multicultural commercial center. The capital, Soba, was located near modern Khartoum.

Pliny the Elder's *Historian naturalis* (77 C.E.; *The Historie of the World*, 1601; better known as *Natural History*) mentions Alwa along with other Meroitic cities. Alwa appears again circa 350 C.E. on Axumite King Ezana's stele, which also describes the aggressive Noba, former subjects of Meroe. Although when coalescence into an independent state took place is unclear, Noba groups later united with others to form the kingdom of Alwa.

Alwa's emergence as a Christian kingdom was recorded in the sixth century *Ecclesiastical History* of John of Ephesus (fragmentary work, part 3 has been translated as *The Third Part of the Ecclesiastical History of John, Bishop of Ephesus*, 1860). It provides some of the first reliable Nubian information since the time of Kush. Missionary activity and conversions were religious and political: Rival rulers adopted rival Christian sects. Longinus converted Alwa to the Monophysite (Coptic) sect in about 580 C.E. The kingdom maintained its independence until the early sixteenth century C.E. After one thousand years, it was the last Christian barrier to Islamic expansion in the Sudan.

ADDITIONAL RESOURCES

Shinnie, P. L. *Ancient Nubia.* New York: Kegan Paul International, 1996.

Zarroug, Mohi el-Din Abdalla. *The Kingdom of Alwa.* Calgary, Alberta: University of Calgary Press, 1991.

SEE ALSO: Axum; Christianity; Ezana; Islam; Makouria; Napata and Meroe; Nobatae; Nubia; Pliny the Elder.

—*Cassandra Lee Tellier*

AMARAVĀTĪ SCHOOL

DATE: c. late second century B.C.E.-225 C.E.
LOCALE: Andhra Pradesh, South India
RELATED CIVILIZATION: Ancient India
SIGNIFICANCE: The earliest south Indian school of art, it flourished for about four hundred years.

The Amaravātī (ah-mar-ah-VAH-tee) school of art flourished under the Sātavāhana Dynasty and was the early phase of the Andhradesha school. Located in the southeastern Deccan region, modern Andhra Pradesh, the school flourished for approximately four hundred years. Production focused on a large complex consisting of the Great Stupa and a number of minor stupas and buildings. Discovered in 1880, the Great Stupa consisted of a large circular mound (192 feet, or 73 meters, in diameter) surrounded by a huge circular railing (*vedika*) with four entrances. The foundation of the Great Stupa dates to the time of Aśoka in the third century B.C.E., but it was enlarged and refurbished under the Sātavāhanas. The Great Stupa has now been destroyed, but those remains that have been recovered consist of upright and crossbeams of the *vedika* and large slabs that probably were used as casing stones for the stupa mound. There are distinctly discernible phases among the fragmentary finds, but the stylistic chronology has not been determined with certainty.

The elegant sculpture of all phases reflects a beautiful regional style that represents human figures with plastic, fluctuating surfaces and minute, lavish detail of seemingly infinite variety. The subject matter, generally consisting of Buddhist aniconic and iconic narrative scenes, indicates a shift from Hīnāyāna to Mahāyāna Buddhism. The earliest sculptural treatment is less densely arranged, but the work became increasingly elaborate in subsequent centuries. Regardless of the period, the sculpture demonstrates a rapt spirituality. One of the greatest of all ancient Buddhist sculptural achievements, the richness of the work reflects a thriving kingdom grown wealthy from trade.

ADDITIONAL RESOURCE

Knox, Robert. *Amaravati: Buddhist Sculpture from the Great Stupa.* London: British Museum Press, 1992.

SEE ALSO: Andhradesha school; Aśoka; Buddhism; Sātavāhanas.

—*Katherine Anne Harper*

AMARU

ALSO KNOWN AS: Amaruka
FLOURISHED: seventh or eighth century C.E.
RELATED CIVILIZATION: India
MAJOR ROLE/POSITION: Poet

Life. Amaru (ah-MAH-rew) was a Sanskrit poet who has been identified as a prominent member in the court of a king named Vikramāditya (c. 95 B.C.E.-78 C.E., not to be confused with the seventh and eighth century Cālukya kings of the same name) who ruled over Ujjain, a city located on the Sipra River in central India and a meeting ground for many nations, including the Greeks. He may, however, have been a contemporary of Kālidāsa (c. 340-c. 400 C.E.), the greatest Sanskrit dramatist, or he may have been the king Amaru (c. 640-700 C.E.), whose dead body was believed to have been occupied by the philosopher Śaṅkara when the king desired to acquaint himself with the arts of love.

Influence. Amaru's *Amaru-śataka* (seventh or eighth century C.E.; *Amarusatakam*, 1984) is some-

times classed as a *kāvya*, a poem in Sanskrit literature with serious intent. Its goal is the creation of a series of emotional word-pictures, often within the compass of a brief stanza, similar to the *Sattasai* (the seven hundred), compiled by Hāla. Amaru's *Amaru-śataka* is considered an important lyrical work that portrays sensuous and erotic love rather than romantic love. Its theme, however, is also interpreted in religious terms as illuminating the passionate quest of the soul for god.

ADDITIONAL RESOURCES

Keith, A. Berriedale. *Classical Sanskrit Literature.* Calcutta: YMCA Publishing House, 1958.
Walker, Benjamin. *Hindu World: An Encyclopedic Survey of Hinduism.* London: George Allen and Unwin, 1968.

SEE ALSO: India; Kālidāsa.

—*Arthur W. Helweg*

AMASIS PAINTER

BORN: c. 555 B.C.E.; place unknown
DIED: c. 525 B.C.E.; place unknown
RELATED CIVILIZATION: Archaic Greece
MAJOR ROLE/POSITION: Painter

Life. "Amasis made me" is a signature found on many sixth century Greek vases. Eight vases so signed were also painted by the same artist, who is known to us today simply as the Amasis (uh-MAY-suhs) Painter. Today 132 vases are attributed to the Amasis Painter. This artist has a distinctive, sharp, flat, and meticulous black figure style. Black figure vase painters left the background of the vase "in reserve" (the natural color of the clay) and painted their subjects in black, with touches of white and red. Additionally, patterns in textiles and hair were incised through the paint to reveal the lighter color beneath. The Amasis Painter's figures are portrayed in silhouette, are muscular but sleek, and represent gods, nobles, and heroes. These elegant scenes exhibit exquisite detailing in hair, dress, and decorative bands of petals and spirals. The Amasis Painter pre-ferred to paint on amphorae, vases with two handles used for storage, and is known for creating designs harmonious with the vases' shape.

Influence. One of the Amasis Painter's most well-known amphorae illustrates Dionysus and the Maenads on the front panel and Athena and Poseidon on its obverse. The Amasis Painter is known for the use of uncommon shapes, variations of standard scenes, and a refined, elegant style, often influencing other Attic painters, among them Exekias.

ADDITIONAL RESOURCES

Boardman, John. *Athenian Black Figure Vases*. Reprint. New York: Thames and Hudson, 1991.
Von Bothmer, Dietrich. *The Amasis Painter and His World: Vase Painting in Sixth-Century* B.C. *Athens*. New York: Thames and Hudson, 1985.

SEE ALSO: Art and architecture; Greece, Archaic.
—*Laura Rinaldi Dufresne*

AMAZONIA

DATE: 8000 B.C.E.-700 C.E.
LOCALE: Flood plains and intermediate uplands of the Amazon River and its major and minor tributaries along the northern third of South America, east of the Andes but including the eastern piedmont
RELATED CIVILIZATIONS: Marajóara, Arawak, Carib
SIGNIFICANCE: The rain forests of Amazonia have been home to a number of native cultures, beginning with hunter-gatherers and including the more sedentary groups who settled on its flood plains.

Amazonia consists of an equatorial and subequatorial region of more than 2 million square miles (5.5 million square kilometers) along the Amazon River and its tributaries. The area contains the largest equatorial and tropical rain forests in the world. Until recently, it was mistakenly believed that the region could not accommodate significant or dense human population because its nutrients are concentrated primarily in the air rather than the soil. However, extensive archaeological data show evidence of longtime human habitation in the region.

Stone tools, cave paintings, and other evidence indicate that the region was consistently inhabited beginning nearly eleven thousand years ago, at the very end of the Pleistocene period. These inhabitants were pre-Amerindian hunter-gatherers. The people of the Early Amazonia period lived along the rivers, some also occupying upland areas. They survived by gathering seeds, palms, and tuberous roots; picking nuts and fruits; fishing; and hunting small aquatic and land animals along with birds and water fowl. They used plants for medicinal and hallucinogenic purposes. Their paintings included fantasized formulaic designs and included zoomorphic and human figures.

About five thousand years ago, human habitation in the area became more complex. More varied and finely made stone tools appeared. The inhabitants of the Middle Amazonia period improved the processing of food and their means of acquiring it, incorporating slash-and-burn agriculture. They cultivated beans and some cereals including maize, rice, and wetland grasses. Villages appeared along the river plains, and the inhabitants made battle instruments that could be used to acquire or defend territory. Red-and-white pottery appeared, and the use of woven fiber materials increased.

Two thousand years ago, considerably greater settlements began to appear. The populations of Late Amazonia were even larger than those of Minoan or Harappān civilizations. Seed crops, fruits, and vegetables were regularly planted, and the gathering and tending of water and land animals further organized. Some of the farming was done on the rich soil of the bottom lands, or *várzea*, along the flood plains, enriched by silting. Requirements for sufficient proteins, carbohydrates, vitamins, and calories were abundantly satisfied. Systematic knowledge of medicinal herbs intensified, incorporating ever greater use of different barks, leaves, seeds, and flowers.

The increase in food production and population resulted in intertribal trade. Pottery became larger, more elaborate, and finely decorated. Intricate art and ritual appeared, evidencing greater metaphorical reasoning. Social organization developed, and people's identities became increasingly defined by labor differentiation. Shamans, or medicine men, had already appeared, and as the elementary hierarchy developed, chiefs emerged to lead tribes. A complex society developed on the island of Marajó, a body of land at the mouth of the Amazon that is larger than Ireland. Marajóara culture flourished for almost nine centuries beginning in 400 C.E. At its height, nearly a million people occupied the island. Their culture is noted for its singularly decorated pottery.

During the Late Amazonia period, the population may have reached fifteen million people, many speaking Tupí-Guaraní languages. Complex social organization occurred from the mouth of the Amazon in Brazil to the middle reaches of the river and into the Ecuadorian and Bolivian Amazon. Sedentary populations along the flood plains practiced root-crop farming, hunted, and fished. In the more remote areas, seminomadic tribes hunted and gathered wild berries, fruits, and nuts, engaging in limited farming. As late as the mid-sixteenth century, explorers observed that villages held tens of thousands of inhabitants. During the ancient period, although the natives' presence altered the forests, no deforestation occurred.

After 700 C.E. The history of ancient Amazonia shows a consistent, progressive development. However, exposure to outsiders, primarily the Spanish and Portuguese in the sixteenth century, decimated the population. Disease swept away village after village; survivors were then wiped out by warfare and slavery. The approximately one million inhabitants who remained formed the basis of the small, isolated Amerindian settlements characteristic of the modern period. Foreigners wrought an immediate and nearly total holocaust on the ancient peoples of Amazonia. As surreptitious as it was sweeping, this devastation was largely unrecognized until the 1980's, when archaeological scholarship began to produce evidence supporting it.

ADDITIONAL RESOURCES

Denevan, W. M. "A Bluff Model of Prehistoric Riverine Settlement in Prehistoric Amazonia." *Annals of the Association of American Geographers* 86, no. 4 (1996): 654-681.

Hemming, J. *Amazon Frontier: The Defeat of the Brazilian Indians*. Cambridge, Mass.: Harvard University Press, 1987.

Pearsall, D. M. "The Origins of Plant Cultivation in South America." In *The Origins of Agriculture: An International Perspective*, edited by C. W. Cowan. Washington, D.C.: Smithsonian Institution Press, 1992.

Roosevelt, A. C. *Moundbuilders of the Amazon: Geophysical Archeology on Marajó Island*. San Diego, Calif.: Academic Press, 1991.

_____. "Secrets of the Forest: An Anthropologist Reappraises the Past—and Future—of Amazonia." *The Sciences* 32, no. 6 (1989): 22-28.

_____, ed. *Amazonian Indians: From Prehistory to the Present, Anthropological Perspectives*. Tucson: University of Arizona Press, 1994.

Smith, N. J. H. *The Amazon River Forest: A Natural History of Plants, Animals, and People*. New York: Oxford University Press, 1999.

SEE ALSO: Archaic South American culture; Brazil, eastern.

—*Edward A. Riedinger*

AMBROSE

BORN: 339 C.E.; Augusta Treverorum, Gaul
DIED: April 4, 397 C.E.; Milan, Italy
RELATED CIVILIZATION: Imperial Rome
MAJOR ROLE/POSITION: Religious figure

Life. Ambrose was the son of the praetorian prefect of Gaul and was raised as a Christian. After being educated in Rome, he began the practice of law. Around 370 C.E., he was appointed governor in northern Italy with headquarters in Milan. When a riot threatened to break out between two contending Christian factions, Ambrose intervened to restore order and found himself the unanimous choice to be bishop. He was consecrated bishop of Milan in 374 C.E.

He achieved a reputation as a pastor of souls and an effective preacher. Ambrose was committed to maintaining the ascendancy of Christianity over pagan opponents. He advocated the removal of the altar of victory from the Roman senate house in 382 C.E.

Ambrose found himself confronting the Christian emperor Theodosius the Great (r. 379-395). Theodosius had ordered the killing of 7,000 people of Thessalonica (modern Thessaloníki) for the murder of several imperial officials. Ambrose excommunicated the emperor and had him do public penance before admitting him back into the Church.

Influence. Ambrose's belief that emperors were subject to the moral law as practiced by the Church had a profound effect on the relations between church and state during the Middle Ages.

ADDITIONAL RESOURCES

Dudden, F. Holmes. *The Life and Times of St. Ambrose.* 2 vols. Oxford, England: Clarendon Press, 1935.
Moorhead, John. *Ambrose: Church and Society in the Late Roman World.* London: Longman, 1999.

Ambrose. (North Wind Picture Archives)

Ramsey, Boniface. *Ambrose.* London: Routledge, 1997.
Williams, Daniel H. *Ambrose of Milan and the End of the Nicene-Arian Conflicts.* Oxford, England: Clarendon Press, 1995.

SEE ALSO: Christianity; Rome, Imperial; Theodosius the Great.

—Leland Edward Wilshire

AMERICAN PALEO-ARCTIC TRADITION

DATE: c. 9000-5000 B.C.E.
LOCALE: Northern North America
RELATED CIVILIZATIONS: Denali complex, Northern Paleo-Indian tradition, Diuktai culture
SIGNIFICANCE: The American Paleo-Arctic tradition represents one of the earliest occupations of humans in North America.

The American Paleo-Arctic tradition is restricted mainly to Alaska and the Yukon Territory, and coastal areas of the Arctic Ocean, and the Bering and Chukchi Seas. The earliest occupation of this area may have occurred around 10,000 B.C.E., but the first substantial occupation dates to 9000 B.C.E. The first definition of this tradition was made by Douglas Anderson, based on an archaeological assemblage from the Onion Portage site in Alaska. Other Alaskan sites, such as Trail Creek caves, the Lower Bench site, Gallagher Flint Station, Anangula Island, and the Ugashik Narrows site, represent the American Paleo-Arctic tradition.

Highly mobile hunters who subsisted primarily on caribou and *Bison antiquus* typify the Paleo-Arctic tradition. These hunters probably lived in groups of twenty-five to fifty people and moved in tandem with the caribou migrations across Alaska and the Yukon Territory. Evidence also suggests that coastal occupations may have occurred seasonally, with an economy focused on marine mammal hunting and fishing, including salmon harvesting, saltwater fishing, and shellfish collecting. This marine resource-focused economy has also been called the Maritime Paleo-Arctic tradition.

Stone tool technology of the Paleo-Arctic tradition is primarily composed of wedge-shaped microblade cores, microblades, blades and blade cores, burins, and gravers. The microblades of the Paleo-Arctic tradition were manufactured by using a core reduction technique very similar to Upper Paleolithic tool traditions. These microblades were then slotted into grooved antler and bone points to form a sophisticated composite projectile point. Blades were probably used for butchering, and the burins and gravers were used to carve bone and wood.

The American Paleo-Arctic tradition has been linked to the Diuktai culture of the Aldun River Valley, Siberia; the Denali complex of interior Alaska; and the Northern Paleo-Indian tradition of the continental United States. The Diuktai culture dates between 33,000 B.C.E. and 9400 B.C.E., and its hallmark is the wedge-shaped core used to manufacture microbades. As for the Denali complex, dating between 8500 B.C.E. and 6000 B.C.E., the stone tool assemblages include bifacial knives and projectile points in addition to the characteristic microblades. The link between the Northern Paleo-Indian and the Paleo-Arctic tradition is that the Northern Paleo-Indian tradition includes fluted projectile points that are associated with sites dating between 10,500 and 7500 B.C.E. In sum, the American Paleo-Arctic tradition is one of the earliest traditions in North America and probably the basis for many later cultures in the New World.

ADDITIONAL RESOURCES

Dixon, E. James. *Bones, Boats, and Bison*. Albuquerque: University of New Mexico Press, 1999.

Fagan, Brian M. *Oxford Companion to Archaeology*. New York: Oxford University Press, 1996.

Jennings, Jesse D. *Prehistoric North America*. Mountain View, Calif.: Mayfield, 1989.

Meltzer, David J. *Search for the First Americans*. Washington, D.C.: Smithsonian Books, 1993.

SEE ALSO: Aleutian tradition; Archaic North American culture; Arctic Small Tool tradition; Maritime Archaic; Microblade tradition, Northwest; Paleo-Indians in North America; Subarctic peoples.

—*Renee Beauchamp Walker*

AMMIANUS MARCELLINUS

BORN: c. 330 C.E.; Antioch, Syria (later Antakya, Turkey)
DIED: c. 395 C.E.; possibly Rome
RELATED CIVILIZATION: Imperial Rome
MAJOR ROLE/POSITION: Army officer, historian

Life. Aside from one letter of the Greek rhetorician Libanius, Ammianus Marcellinus's (am-ee-AY-nuhs mahr-suh-LI-nuhs) life can be recovered only from internal references in his *Res Gestae* (completed c. 391 C.E.; *Compendium of Roman History*, 1896). Probably born into a Greek-speaking family of Antioch's elite, he served as a *protector domesticus* in the Roman army from about 350 C.E. Later he retired to Rome, where he wrote his history. Originally it consisted of thirty-one books covering Roman imperial history from about 96 to 378 C.E., but only the last eighteen books, describing events from late 353 C.E. onward, survive. His history stresses the importance of the foreign and domestic policies of emperors such as Constantius II, Julian the Apostate, Valens, and Valentinian I. The last history of Rome written in Latin by a pagan, Ammianus's *Compendium of Roman History* serves as a window into the Roman Empire immediately before its fall.

Influence. Cited only by the Latin grammarian Priscian in antiquity (for a grammatical point), Ammianus's work started to become important to scholars in the late fifteenth century. Although the first printing of his history occurred in 1474, improved editions were published in the late nineteenth and early twentieth centuries. For the last sixty years, his work has received increased attention as an important source for the fourth century.

ADDITIONAL RESOURCES
Barnes, Timothy David. *Ammianus Marcellinus and the Representation of Historical Reality*. Ithaca, N.Y.: Cornell University Press, 1998.

Matthews, John. *The Roman Empire of Ammianus*. London: Duckworth, 1989.

SEE ALSO: Constantius I-III; Julian the Apostate; Rome, Imperial; Valens; Valentinian I.

—*R. M. Frakes*

AMOS

FLOURISHED: eighth century B.C.E.
RELATED CIVILIZATION: Israel
MAJOR ROLE/POSITION: Religious figure

Life. What is known about Amos (AY-muhs) comes from the biblical book that bears his name. His date of birth, death, and length of prophetic ministry are unknown. Amos lived in the Tekoa area, a village about twelve miles south of Jerusalem. The recorded speeches suggest a ministry in Israel's capital city, Samaria, and at the Bethel temple during the reign of Jeroboam II (r. c. 786-748 B.C.E.).

The book of Amos consists of oracles against the nations, including Israel (1:3-2:16), the moral basis for the prophet's oracle of judgment against Israel (3:1-6:14), and five visions of judgment, followed by a brief epilogue (7:1-9:15). Amos used an array of rhetorical devices to effectively address his audiences. He was fond of assonance, chiasm, disputation, repetition, reversal, rhetorical questions, and sarcasm.

Influence. The enduring social message of Amos was to "Hate evil, love good; maintain justice in the courts" (Amos 5:15). He criticized the evils of immoral sexual behavior, injustice, the amassing of wealth by the powerful rich at the expense of the poor oppressed, and corruption in the court system.

ADDITIONAL RESOURCES
Hasel, Gerhard F. *Understanding the Book of Amos: Basic Issues in Current Interpretations*. Grand Rapids, Mich.: Baker, 1991.
Hayes, John H. *Amos, the Eighth-Century Prophet: His Times and His Preaching*. Nashville: Abingdon Press, 1988.

SEE ALSO: Bible: Jewish; Israel; Judaism.

—*Mark J. Mangano*

ʿAMR IBN AL-ʿĀṢ MOSQUE

DATE: founded 642 C.E.
LOCALE: Cairo, Egypt
RELATED CIVILIZATION: Islamic Egypt
SIGNIFICANCE: This was the first mosque to be built in Egypt after the area was conquered by the Muslims.

ʿAmr ibn al-ʿĀṣ Mosque (am-rewb-nuh-LAHS mahsk) was the first mosque built in Egypt after the Muslim conquest of the country. It was founded on the site where ʿAmr ibn al-ʿĀṣ, the general who led the conquering army, was said to have pitched his tent. It was rebuilt and expanded, reaching its present size in 827 C.E. The most recent renovation was in 1983, at which time extensive archaeological investigation was conducted.

Although the mosque became a very large building, the original building was much smaller, located in the eastern corner of the modern structure. Situated roughly in the center of the central quarter of the Arab city of Al-Fusṭāṭ (which became a suburb of Cairo), its foundation rested on bedrock some ten to twelve feet (roughly three to four meters) above the general level of the surrounding city. It first served as the general mosque for only this quarter of the city but gradually became a congregational mosque, designed to serve the whole community. The original building was built with mud brick walls and palm log columns supporting what was probably a mud-and-thatch roof. In its first rebuilding some thirty-five years after the initial construction, a central court and four minarets were added to the en-larged mosque. The first building and subsequent re-constructions all featured a large columned hall used for prayer.

ADDITIONAL RESOURCES
Ettinghausen, Richard, and Oleg Grabar. *The Art and Architecture of Islam 650-1250*. New Haven, Conn.: Yale University Press, 2001.
Kubiak, Wladyslaw B. *Al-Fusṭāṭ: Its Foundation and Early Urban Development*. Cairo: The American University in Cairo Press, 1987.

SEE ALSO: Egypt, Ptolemaic and Roman; Islam.

—*Sara E. Orel*

ANACREON

ALSO KNOWN AS: Anakreon
BORN: c. 570 B.C.E.; Teos, Iona (later Sighajik, Turkey)
DIED: c. 485 B.C.E.; place unknown
RELATED CIVILIZATIONS: Archaic and Classical Greece
MAJOR ROLE/POSITION: Lyric poet

Life. Anacreon (uh-NAK-ree-uhn) is said to have been among the colonists when the people of Teos escaped the Persians by migrating northward to Thrace. Most of Anacreon's known work, however, is assigned to the period after he left Thrace and settled at Samos, then under the rule of the tyrant Polycrates of Samos. There, in addition to tutoring Polycrates' son in music, he became famous for his love songs and poems. Many of his amorous verses were written to boys. Other poems celebrated wine and carousing. During his stay at Samos, Anacreon steered clear of political themes.

After the fall of Polycrates' tyranny and his dreadful death, Anacreon moved to the court of Pisistratus in Athens. Pisistratus's younger son, Hipparchus, was a patron of the arts and brought both Anacreon and Simonides to Athens to grace the city. Anacreon lived much the same kind of life in Athens as he had in Samos.

Influence. Anacreon's metrical forms were widely copied at least until late Byzantine times. *Anacreontea* (1554 C.E.; *Odes of Anacreon*, 1800), a collection of about sixty short poems on love, wine, and the changing fortunes of life, composed by post-Classical Greek writers but attributed to Anacreon, influenced Renaissance French poetry. His work also influenced poets such as German Johann Wolfgang von Goethe in the eighteenth century.

ADDITIONAL RESOURCES
Bowra, C. M. *Ancient Greek Literature*. New York: Oxford University Press, 1960.
Bowra, C. M., and T. F. Higham. *The Oxford Book of Greek Verse in Translation*. Oxford, England: Clarendon Press, 1948.
Mulroy, David D. *Early Greek Lyric Poetry*. Ann Arbor: University of Michigan Press, 1992.
Podlecki, Anthony J. *The Early Greek Poets and Their Times*. Vancouver: University of British Columbia Press, 1984.

SEE ALSO: Athens; Greece, Archaic; Greece, Classical; Pisistratus; Polycrates of Samos.

—*Robert Jacobs*

ĀNANDA

FLOURISHED: late sixth century B.C.E.; North India
RELATED CIVILIZATION: India
MAJOR ROLE/POSITION: Disciple of the Buddha

Life. Sources for the life of Ānanda (ah-NAHN-dah) are nonexistent. Centuries after the death of the

Buddha, documents were produced containing traditions supporting the historical reality of such a person. These documents portray Ānanda as the Buddha's favorite and "beloved" disciple. He was appointed personal attendant to the great teacher and was charged with bringing him water and his toothbrush, washing his feet, accompanying him abroad, carrying his bowl and cloak, and sweeping his cell. However, he was also regarded as spiritually the youngest and "most backward" disciple. He did not attain Buddhahood until after the Buddha's death. He was a cousin of the Buddha, as was the notorious Devadatta, who opposed the master to the point of plotting his murder. Ānanda persuaded the Buddha to permit women into the order of followers. Attending the Buddha at his death, Ānanda went on to become one of the most prominent members of the Buddhist order.

Influence. Legend has it that a council was held not long after the Buddha's death. Its purpose was to review the Buddha's teachings and establish a canon of scriptures. Ānanda is reputed to have recited from memory all the sermons of the Buddha. Because no person was considered fit to succeed the Buddha as leader of the order, the scriptures were to provide the guide to belief and practice. "Rely on the Law, not the person" remains Ānanda's legacy.

ADDITIONAL RESOURCES

Coomaraswamy, A. *Buddha and the Gospel of Buddhism.* New Hyde Park, N.Y.: University Books, 1964.

Nelson, Walter Henry. *Buddha: His Life and His Teaching.* New York: Putnam, 2000.

Thomas, E. J. *The Life of the Buddha as Legend and History.* London: Routledge, 1927.

SEE ALSO: Buddha; Buddhism; India.

—*John M. Bullard*

ANASAZI

DATE: 100-700 C.E.

LOCALE: American Southwest, present-day Four Corners region of New Mexico, Arizona, Utah, and Colorado

RELATED CIVILIZATIONS: Basketmaker I and II, Puebloans

SIGNIFICANCE: A horticultural people who adapted to an arid environment, the Anasazi are renowned for their great pueblos, large multistoried structures found in cliffs in the American Southwest.

Anasazi (ah-nah-SAH-zee) is a Navajo word meaning "ancestral enemies," so many scholars prefer Ancestral Puebloans or pre-Puebloans to refer to the Native American civilization that thrived in the Four Corners area. The chronology of Anasazi, the Pecos classification, was developed by archaeologists in 1927. Its accuracy is a matter of dispute, but its broad classification of periods in Anasazi history remains in general use.

The first period in which a distinct group that can be identified as Anasazi appeared is called Basketmaker II (there is no Basketmaker I). Basketmaker II people arose from hunter-gatherer groups who inhabited the region. Although they continued to hunt and gather, Basketmaker II people also farmed. Domesticated crops, especially maize, were an important part of their diet. Marking the transition to an agricultural society is difficult, and scholars have given dates ranging from 120 B.C.E. to 400 C.E. for the beginning of Basketmaker II society.

Basketmaker II people lived in villages that consisted of a collection of small houses that were typically constructed in pits and covered with roofs made from branches and mud. Small pits near the houses were used for storage. Because Basketmaker II people still foraged for food, villages were probably occupied for only part of the year, presumably autumn, when crops were harvested.

The next phase in Anasazi culture, Basketmaker III, began around 50 C.E. Scholars point to an increase in rainfall in the American Southwest after 400 C.E. as one potential cause for changes in Anasazi culture. More rainfall meant higher crop yields and the potential for a larger population. Basketmaker III is identified as a period of increased dependence on agriculture, the introduction of new crops including beans and cotton, and the use of pottery. Although they still relied on hunting and gathering to complement their crops, Basketmaker III people were more sedentary than their predecessors. Houses were larger as were storage facilities. In addition, Basketmaker III marked the appearance of the great kiva, or ceremonial room, which was used for religious proceedings. Trade with native peoples to the south probably led to the acquisition of stone tools and the bow and arrow during this period.

After 700 C.E. After 700 C.E., the Anasazi went through a period of intensive development in which they constructed large, complex buildings and an extensive road network whose purpose is still not well understood. In 2000, archaeologists published evidence of cannibalism at Cowboy Wash, an Anasazi homestead in the Four Corners area occupied around 1150 C.E. Its significance has not yet been determined. After 1300 C.E., the Anasazi went into decline, perhaps because of an extended drought. The Pueblos of present-day New Mexico are recognized as the descendants of the Anasazi.

ADDITIONAL RESOURCES

Brody, J. J. *The Anasazi: Ancient Indian People of the American Southwest.* New York: Rizzoli, 1990.

Roberts, David. *In Search of the Old Ones: Exploring the Anasazi World of the Southwest.* New York: Touchstone, 1996.

SEE ALSO: Hohokam culture; Southwest peoples.

—Thomas Clarkin

ANASTASIUS I

BORN: c. 430-440 C.E.; Dyrrhachium, Epirus Vetus (later Durrës, Albania)
DIED: 518 C.E.; Constantinople (Istanbul)
RELATED CIVILIZATIONS: Christian Roman Empire, Byzantine Empire
MAJOR ROLE/POSITION: Courtier, emperor

Life. At the death of the Isaurian emperor Zeno (Tarasicodissa) in 491 C.E., his widow, Ariadne, made her confidential servant (*silentiarius*) Anastasius (an-uh-STAY-zhee-uhs) emperor and married him.

Anastasius protected Constantinople against Bulgar raids from the Danube by rebuilding the western wall, forty miles from the city. He reconquered Theodosiopolis, Martyropolis, and Amida, taken by the Persians in 502 C.E., and forced them in 505 C.E. to accept a seven-year truce. He built the fortress Dara a few miles from Persian Nisibis.

He exiled the Isaurian court clique and asserted imperial authority in the Monophysite-Chalcedonian doctrinal conflicts. The Chalcedonians held that Jesus Christ was both divine and human; the Monophysites held he had a single divine nature. In 511 C.E., he exiled the Chalcedonian patriarch of Constantinople for rebellion, and in 515 C.E., he forced Vitalian, the commander of the barbarian troops in the conflict, into hiding.

Inspectors (*vindices*) watched over the fair assessment of taxes, which were collected in currency commutable only for needed army supplies locally. New copper coins, *folles*, stamped with their progressive base (*nummus*) values (5, 10, 20, 40) speeded business. In 518 C.E., the treasury had a reserve of 320,000 pounds (145,000 kilograms) of gold.

Influence. Because Ariadne, daughter of Emperor Leo I, had married Zeno in 467 C.E. to win the loyalty of the warlike Isaurian mountaineers, Anastasius received a quarter century of inside information when he became emperor. With it, he built a strong Eastern Rome, which encouraged emperors Justin I and Justinian I to reunite the Roman Empire.

ADDITIONAL RESOURCES

Charanis, Peter. *Church and State in the Later Roman Empire: The Religious Policy of Anastasius the First, 491-518.* Madison: University of Wisconsin Press, 1939.

Metcalf, D. M. *The Origins of the Anastasian Currency Reform.* Amsterdam: Hakkert, 1969.

Rosser, John H. *Historical Dictionary of Byzantium.* Lanham, Md.: Scarecrow Press, 2001.

SEE ALSO: Byzantine Empire; Chalcedon, Council of; Constantinople; Justinian I; Leo I (emperor); Monophysitism; Persia.

—Reinhold Schumann

ANATOLIA

DATE: 8000 B.C.E.-700 C.E.

LOCALE: Asia Minor, Turkey

RELATED CIVILIZATIONS: Çatalhüyük, Hittites, Aegean, Phrygia, Lydia, Rome, Byzantine Empire, Seljuqs

SIGNIFICANCE: At the crossroads of Asia and Europe, Anatolia saw the rise of the Hittites and the Aegean civilizations and was the site of countless advances in, and conflicts between, civilizations.

Today known as Asia Minor, Anatolia is a geographical region: the peninsula bound on the north by the Black Sea, on the south by the Taurus Mountains and Mediterranean Sea, and on the west by the Aegean Sea. This central location made Anatolia witness to the interplay of many civilizations from Paleolithic to historic times. This brief review can merely sketch the progression of human development in the region with some weight toward prehistoric times as a background to fuller treatment of the later civilizations provided elsewhere in these pages.

Evidence of the earliest human culture is most likely buried under the alluvium gathered in Anatolian valleys after the sea-level rise at the end of the last Ice Age (c. 10,000 B.C.E.). Archaeologists have found such evidence in Paleolithic cave sites such as Yarimburgaz near modern Istanbul. Agricultural settlements of Neolithic peoples were established between 8000 and 7000 B.C.E. People lived in painted brick houses at Hacilar, near Lake Burdur, during the early end of this period, and one thousand years later, a more sophisticated agricultural and pottery-making society was found there.

By 6200 B.C.E., a highly advanced city, known as Çatalhüyük, thrived on the plains of Anatolia. Discovered in the 1960's, it is the first known city to use irrigation, to domesticate animals, to cultivate crops such as peas and lentils, and to develop a system of commerce. The murals found on some of the elaborate brickwork houses, along with bone and stone tools and clay figurines, tell a story of daily life and religion far more sophisticated than previously thought. During the sixth millennium B.C.E., further advances can be seen at places like Hacilar, Can Hasan, and Mersin, where contiguous mud-brick houses and walls suggest villages organized for military defense.

The forging of iron was first practiced in Anatolia well in excess of 3,500 years ago. Distinct cities from the early and middle Bronze Age, such as the legendary Troy and the trading station at Nesa, have been unearthed. During the third and second millennia B.C.E., with advances in metalworking, wine making, and jewelry making, came regional political organization, social rituals, trade, taxes, and, perhaps most important, writing. Records refer to Assyrian kings who occupied the region during the 1800's and 1700's B.C.E., including Erishum, Sargon I, Puzur-Ashur, and Shamshi-Adad I.

By the seventeenth century B.C.E., the Hittite peoples had infiltrated from the northwest (though controversy about their provenance remains) and had developed into a sophisticated culture. The Hittites spoke several Indo-European dialects, and gradually their language, Nesite, replaced the indigenous central Anatolian language. Their civilization lasted for half a millennium, from the Old Kingdom (c. 1700-c. 1500 B.C.E.) through the New Kingdom (c. 1400-c. 1180 B.C.E.). Documents survive in which the Hittites relate their own history.

By 1100 B.C.E., Aegean peoples from the west and Phrygians from the southern coastal area had settled in Anatolia. These migrations severely altered Anatolia's social and political structures as West and East met in full force. Greeks were establishing settlements on the Mediterranean coast, and the Phrygians greatly influenced the Greek world; the Phyrgian and Greek writing systems are closely related (with some question as to which came first), and the Greeks even record the Phrygian king Midas's marriage to a Greek woman. The Phrygians established a prosperous statehood throughout central and west Anatolia by about 750 B.C.E., with Gordium as the main center. Southeast Anatolia, earlier occupied by descendants of the Hittites called the Luwians, was occupied by Arameans, the state of Urartu in the mid-700's B.C.E., and then the Assyrians from the south. Assyria finally gained the Phyrgians' submission, although thereafter Cimmerians from the Caucasus mountains to the north invaded and destroyed Gordium. By the time of Ashurbanipal (r. 668-627 B.C.E.), the Assyrians were dominant here too, although continually fighting Cimmerians until late in the seventh century B.C.E.

The Lydians entered western Anatolia at about this time, centered on ancient Sardis. They are most renowned for inventing coinage around 650 B.C.E. and had much contact with the Greeks. The Greek historian Herodotus records the Lydians' rise to power in the sixth century and their conflict with the Median civilization from Iran in the east, with whom the Lydians shared much of Anatolia during the mid-sixth century B.C.E. The Medians were replaced by Persians, and in 547-546 B.C.E., Cyrus the Great vanquished the Lydian king Croesus (r. c. 560-546 B.C.E.) and Persia ruled most of Asia Minor. The Ionian Revolt, coming out of Greek Miletus in the west and heralding the Greco-Persian Wars (499-448 B.C.E.), was put down by Darius the Great by 494 B.C.E. Persia's Achaemenian Empire would occupy Anatolia for the next two hundred years, although culturally the Greeks were dominant in the west and the indigenous Luwians survived culturally and linguistically as well.

Eventually, the Greeks defeated Persia, established the Delian League, and during the Peloponnesian Wars (431-404 B.C.E.) pushed Persia back. Alexander the Great had destroyed the Persians' Achaemenian Empire by 333 B.C.E., but after his death, Anatolia was again divided, among the Ptolemies in Egypt and the Seleucids from Syria, and even by Celtic incursions from the north by the early third century B.C.E. Later in this century, the Cappadocians, centered in Pergamum, rose in the west, vying for power with the Seleucids.

The Seleucid threat drew Rome into the conflict.

By 133 B.C.E., the Romans had conquered western Anatolia and by the first century B.C.E. dominated all of Asia Minor, which they reorganized politically into provinces of the Eastern Empire centered on Constantinople (modern Istanbul). The Romans would rule Anatolia for the next six centuries. Intermittent onslaughts by barbarians from Central Asia, the Sāsānians, and ultimately the Muslims ended Roman domination by the mid-sixth century C.E.

ADDITIONAL RESOURCES

Bryce, Trevor. *The Kingdom of the Hittites*. London: Oxford University Press, 1998.
Starr, Chester G. *A History of the Ancient World*. London: Oxford University Press, 1991.

SEE ALSO: Achaemenian Dynasty; Arameans; Ashurbanipal; Assyria; Cimmerians; Croesus; Cyrus the Great; Darius the Great; Greco-Persian Wars; Greece, Classical; Herodotus; Hittites; Islam; Luwians; Lydia; Midas; Persia; Phrygia; Rome, Imperial; Sāsānian Empire; Seleucid Dynasty; Urartu.

—*Lloyd Michael Lohr*

ANDES, CENTRAL

DATE: 8000 B.C.E.-700 C.E.
LOCALE: West Coast of South America, Peru
RELATED CIVILIZATIONS: Chavín, Moche, Nasca, Tiwanaku, Wari
SIGNIFICANCE: The central Andes are the location of one of the six primary civilizations in the world and the site of one of the world's most important agricultural complexes. The Andes have also been an important center of fine arts and crafts.

About 8000 B.C.E., groups of people were fishing and collecting shellfish along the Pacific coast in the central Andes region. During the Paloma phase (6000-3250 B.C.E.), more substantial communities developed, as people became more sophisticated at fishing, hunting, and foraging. Small camps and villages ranged from twenty-five to seventy-five people. During this period, horticulture was developed, but it continued on a small scale until 800 B.C.E. In the highlands, hunting and foraging were replaced by horticulture between 2500 and

1500 B.C.E., and a number of small communities developed at sites such as Huaricoto, Kotosh, La Calgada, and El Paraíso. Stone and masonry architecture developed, and temples were built at ritual centers. Around 2500 B.C.E., potatoes and quinoa were domesticated, as were llamas. However, it was another fifteen hundred years, before agriculture became totally established, after the arrival of maize and beans from Mesoamerica.

The subsequent history of the central Andes is divided into alternating periods of widespread horizon cultures and periods of fragmentation marked by flourishing regional cultures. The first horizon culture was Chavín, which began in the mountains and spread its influence throughout the country. Several regional cultures (Moche, Chimu, and others on the coast and Tiwanaku in the highlands) flourished during the following period.

The first culture of widespread importance in the central Andes emerged in the town of Chavín de Huántar (900 to 200 B.C.E.). The first important stone

SELECTED SITES IN THE CHAVÍN CULTURE AND THE CENTRAL ANDES

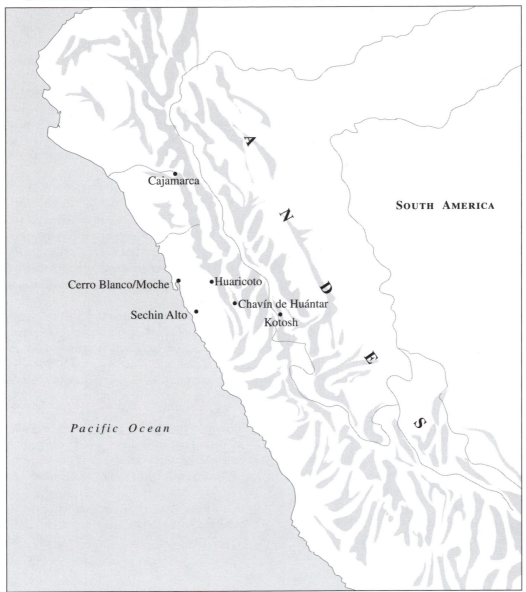

building in the central Andes was built here, and the temple art reflects abstract thought about fantastic beings, the gods of Chavín. From 850 to 460 B.C.E., Chavín was a small agricultural village at a trade crossroads, but it became a major pilgrimage center, oracle, and religious shrine. The objects found in Chavín come from a broad area in northern Peru, indicating widespread trade and travel.

The temple at Chavín is built in the shape of a U, open to the east, the direction of the sunrise. The oldest part of the temple is built around a tall (fifteen-foot- or nearly five-meter-high) stone that resembles a tree trunk and is called El Lanzón. The stone is an *axis mundi*, or world axis, which marks a point of contact between the underworld, the earth, and the heavens. The influence of the Chavín culture seems to have derived from its religious importance and its association with trade. People seem to have traveled from great distances to visit the shrine at Chavín and probably consult its oracle, which was still known in historic times.

There is no evidence of military prowess or conquest on the part of Chavín, so its importance was probably as an ideology and belief system.

The Moche (100 to 700 C.E.) formed one of the most important regional cultures along the northern coast of Peru. The Moche were not city builders, and their towns were primarily ritual centers organized around great *huacas*, or pyramids. However, they built irrigation canals from the foothills of the Andes out into the desert to create agricultural fields. They also produced excellent gold jewelry adorned with precious stones as well as some of the finest ceramics of any early world civilization. Moche pots are made in figurative shapes, such as a seated person, the face of a person, or an animal. They show both common and uncommon scenes, such as house architecture, people with diseases, a jaguar attacking a man, a woman weaving, people making love, and many other activities, including hunting and war scenes.

The demise of the Moche may have been military or environmental, but the strongest indications point to the latter. Moche buildings created late in their civilization show signs of unusual flooding, which suggests a destructive El Niño weather pattern combined with earthquakes. After the flooding, the Moche abandoned their towns and seem to have left the region.

Along the south coast of Peru, the Nasca culture (200 B.C.E.-700 C.E.) built ritual centers around important mounds. Nasca is best known for its line drawings of birds, monkeys, spiders, plants, and even a whale. Hundreds of miles of straight lines were also drawn into the surface of the earth. These large geoglyphs can be seen only from the sky.

The Tiwanaku (200 to 700 C.E.) dominated the area around the southern end of Lake Titicaca, and their influence spread over much of the Andes. The capital city was an important ceremonial center, and its influence spread primarily through ceremony and trade. A number of Chavín-like characteristics can be detected in Tiwanaku, including the iconography of the primary god and architectural design. They practiced metallurgy, working both copper and gold into well-made objects. Their luxury goods also included textiles, ceramics, and wooden sculptures. They seem to have had important trade routes to the coast using caravans of llamas. The economy was based on highland agricultural techniques, cultivating potatoes on elaborate raised earthen platforms in flooded fields.

The Wari (500-700 C.E.) were located in the central valleys of the Andes, and the trade routes from the mountains to the coast passed through their region. They built an important political organization based on an economy of terraced fields on mountainsides and irrigation. The later Inca owed much of their political and ideological systems to the Wari and Tiwanaku people.

ADDITIONAL RESOURCES

Burger, Richard. *Chavín and the Origins of Andean Civilization*. New York: Thames and Hudson, 1992.

Haas, Jonathan, T. Pozorski, and S. Pozorski, eds. *The Origins and Development of the Andean State*. Cambridge, England: Cambridge University Press, 1987.

Moseley, Michael. *The Incas and Their Ancestors*. New York: Thames and Hudson, 1992.

Stone-Miller, Rebecca. *Art of the Andes from Chavín to Inca*. New York: Thames and Hudson, 1995.

SEE ALSO: Andes, South; Archaic South American culture; Chavín de Huántar; Moche culture; Nasca culture; Tiwanaku.

—*Ronald J. Duncan*

ANDES, SOUTH

DATE: 8000 B.C.E.-700 C.E.

LOCALE: Andes, Argentina, Bolivia, Chile, Ecuador, Peru

RELATED CIVILIZATIONS: Pukara, Chavín, Tiwanaku, Paracas, Nasca, Moche

SIGNIFICANCE: The south Andes region was home to some of the most advanced monolithic agricultural civilizations in the Americas.

Although the origin of the first peoples to populate the south Andes is not known for certain, evidence indicates that they may have originated in Eurasia and traveled south through North and Central America or that they might have crossed the Pacific in ancient ships using celestial navigation. In the Tiwanaku cosmogonic myth of Viracocha, the world maker emerged from Lake Titicaca in Bolivia, on the Isle of the Sun, and recreated the world after a time of intense cataclysm and the near extinction of all human beings. Viracocha commanded the Sun, Moon, and stars to return to the heavens and made new people from stones he tossed across the world. Oddly enough, he was said to be a large, bearded, blond man, blue-eyed and pale-skinned. He brought astronomy, writing, metallurgy, agriculture, and other elements of Archaic civilization with him and brought peace wherever he traveled.

Wherever the Paleo-Indians came from, carbon dating at sites in the region indicate that they inhabited the area as early as twelve thousand to twenty-nine thousand years ago, with direct evidence for occupation, at the latest, by 8000 B.C.E. By that time, the megafauna were brought to extinction because of environmental changes or excessive hunting by the early, nomadic hunter-gatherers.

The Archaic Transition, or Preceramic, period began between 8000 and 7000 B.C.E. During this period, the Paleo-Indians shifted to large-scale agriculture, domesticated animals and local plants, and adopted more sedentary lifestyles. By 5000 B.C.E., they had domesticated quinoa, corn, beans, and potatoes. By 2500 B.C.E., they had tamed the camelids of the Andes, the llamas, vicunas, and alpacas. From the end of the Archaic Transition, between 2000 and 1400 B.C.E., and until the rise of the Incas, there were seven major periods, each marked by variations in architecture, use of textiles, and ceramics technology.

Some of the prominent periods and cultures of these later times include the Lower Formative or Initial period from about 2000 to 1000 B.C.E.; the Early Horizon period from 1000 to 300 B.C.E., which saw the rise and fall of the Pukara and Chavín cultures at Sechin Alto and Huántar respectively; the Early Intermediate or Upper Formative from 300 B.C.E. to 100 C.E., when the Paracas and early Tiwanaku cultures arose and built the Paracas necropolis and the extensive ruins near and along the shores of Lake Titicaca; the Florescent or Classic period from 100 to 700 C.E., when the Nasca, Moche, and middle Tiwanaku cultures built their varied monuments on the Isles of the Sun and the Moon at Sipan and Tiwanaku; then the Middle Horizon period (700-1000 C.E.) saw the rise of the Wari and late Tiwanaku at those sites named after them. After 700 C.E. came the Later Intermediate (1000-1400 C.E.) period dominated by the Chimu at Chan-Chan, and the Late Horizon (1400-1538) period when the Inca came to dominate the south Andes from Ecuador to Bolivia.

Most cultures of this region moved from the western coastal lowlands, eastward up the valleys and into the high mountains and altiplano. Originally their subsistence was based on offshore fisheries, but as they moved inland and upcountry they developed large-scale agriculture. Once established in the mountains, they created distinctive raised-bed agriculture systems, made extensive use of domesticated animals, and engaged in agreements with surrounding groups that allowed them to make use of environments outside their home zones. By linking all productive areas together to form a chain of economic "islands," they were able to make or trade for goods from all areas.

Lake Titicaca was the spiritual heart of south Andean civilization. Cities and vast temple complexes arose near the shore. The large, stepped Akapana pyramid, of uncertain age, is one of the more remarkable structures in the area. Others include the Kalasasaya ritual platform, the Underground temple, and the Puma Punku. One of the earliest sites, perhaps as early as 400 B.C.E., is at Pucara. The people who built it began settling in the area around 600 B.C.E. and may, given similarities in their polished polychrome pottery, be the ancestors of those who later built Tiwanaku. Some of the sculptures in the complex have been connected to those of the Chavín culture. The Tiwanaku civilization lasted more than fourteen hundred years and grew to include as many as twenty-five thousand people. The oldest structures were built during the Early Intermediate period. Building continued until the group's decline by the end of the Middle Horizon period. In the local language, Aymara, the place is called Taypikhala, "the central stone," indicating it was viewed as more than a mere physical location; it was the center of the universe, and the symbolic source of all life.

The peoples of this region used complex raised-bed, canal-fed shoreline agricultural systems until an eventual lowering of the water table of the lake led them to abandon the area. During the height of their civilization, the Tiwanaku achieved a truly imperial civilization that included densely populated administrative and religious centers (more than fifty thousand inhabitants in an area a little larger than two square miles, or about six square kilometers), smaller cities on the periphery, and colonial towns that dotted the region.

ADDITIONAL RESOURCES

Kolata, Alan L. *The Tiwanaku*. Cambridge, Mass.: Blackwell, 1993.

_____. *Valley of the Spirits*. New York: John Wiley and Sons, 1996.

Masuda, S., I. Shimada, and C. Morris, eds. *Andean Ecology and Civilization*. Tokyo: University of Tokyo Press, 1985.

Moseley, Michael. *The Maritime Foundations of Andean Civilization*. Menlo Park, Calif.: Cummings, 1975.

Murra, J., N. Wachtel, and J. Revel, eds. *Anthropological History of Andean Polities*. London: Cambridge University Press, 1989.

Richardson, James B., III. *People of the Andes*. Washington, D.C.: Smithsonian Institution Books, 1994.

SEE ALSO: Akapana pyramid; Andes, central; Archaic South American culture; Chavín de Huántar; Huaca de la Luna; Huaca del Sol; Moche culture; Nasca culture; Paleo-Indians in South America; South America, southern; Tiwanaku.

—Michael W. Simpson

ANDHRADESHA SCHOOL

DATE: c. 200 B.C.E.-400 C.E.
LOCALE: Andhra Pradesh, south India
RELATED CIVILIZATION: Ancient India
SIGNIFICANCE: This school of sculpture had a lasting influence on art in south India.

The Andhradesha (AHN-drah-DEH-shah) school of sculpture developed a distinct style that influenced the course of art in south India for centuries. The school was located in modern eastern Andhra Pradesh state along the Krishna River and was supported during the Sātavāhana (c. 200 B.C.E.-225 C.E.) and Ikṣvāku Dynasties (c. 225-350 C.E.). The earliest work in the region actually dates to the time of Aśoka (c. 302-c. 238 B.C.E.) who began construction of the Great Stupa at Amaravatī; granite stone beams with the characteristic Mauryan polish have been recovered at the site.

By the late second to early first century B.C.E. under Sātavāhana rule, a distinctive sculptural tradition emerged as the fragments at Jaggayyapeta and Amaravatī demonstrate. The region's greenish-white limestone (called Palnad marble) was a suitably elegant medium for embellishing the Buddhist monuments that proliferated during the next several centuries. The sculpted decoration of the railing (*vedika*) and casing stones of the Great Stupa and other monuments consisted of dense scenes of figures rendered with a fluid, confident naturalism. The elongated human images are dressed in festoons of precisely rendered ornament.

The members of the later Ikṣvāku Dynasty, although consisting of Hindus particularly devoted to Śiva, were important patrons of Buddhist art. The Ikṣvāku work at Nagarjunakonda emphasizes superb technical proficiency through its complex narrative reliefs with supple figures engaged in lively movements. Other important sites of the Andhradesha school are Goli, Ghantashala, Bhattiprolu, and Gummadidurru.

ADDITIONAL RESOURCES
Knox, Robert. *Amaravati: Buddhist Sculpture from the Great Stupa*. London: British Museum Press, 1992.

Stone, Elizabeth Rosen. *The Buddhist Art of Nagarjunakonda*. Delhi: Motilal Banarsidass, 1994.

SEE ALSO: Amaravatī school; Aśoka; Buddhism; India; Sātavāhanas.

—Katherine Anne Harper

ANDOCIDES

BORN: c. 440 B.C.E.; place unknown
DIED: c. 391 B.C.E.; place unknown
RELATED CIVILIZATIONS: Fifth century Athens, Classical Greece
MAJOR ROLE/POSITION: Orator, politician, merchant

Life. Andocides (an-DAHS-uh-deez) came from an old family known as the Kerykes (Heralds), whose roots were in Eleusis. His life was, in scholar H. J. Rose's description, "one long series of adventures and disgraces." In 415 B.C.E. during the Peloponnesian War (431-404 B.C.E.), he was among those accused of mutilating the herms (statues of Hermes) the night before the Athenian fleet departed for Sicily. He saved his life by turning state's evidence. After punishment by loss of civic rights, he went into exile and became a successful trader. His attempts to regain full citizenship in 411 and 410 B.C.E. failed, but he returned under Athenian general Thrasybulus in 403 B.C.E. and victoriously defended himself against the charge of impiety. Then after a brief time among those envoys negotiating peace during the Corinthian War (395-386 B.C.E.), he went into exile again in 392/391 B.C.E. when their treaty was rejected in Athens and Callistratus began prosecution of the peace team. Nothing further is known about him.

Influence. The surviving orations pertain to Andocides' personal affairs. There is no evidence that he ever wrote for others. Their tone is fresh and eager, and their style is natural, without evidence of seasoned rhetoric. In addition to fragments from four speeches, four speeches are extant, one of which is thought to be a forgery.

ADDITIONAL RESOURCES

Furley, William D. *Andocides and the Hermes: A Study of Crisis in Fifth Century Athenian Religion.* London: Institute of Classical Studies, 1996.

Missiou, Anna. *The Subversive Oratory of Andocides.* Cambridge, England: Cambridge University Press, 1992.

SEE ALSO: Athens; Corinthian War; Greece, Classical; Peloponnesian War.

—Michele Valerie Ronnick

ANDRONOVO CULTURE

DATE: 1750-800 B.C.E.
LOCALE: Kazakhstan, Western Siberia
RELATED CIVILIZATIONS: Kelteminar, Afanasievo, Karasuk
SIGNIFICANCE: Andronovo was the bridge between the Neolithic and Bronze Age civilizations in Western Asia.

Named after a village in the Yenisey Valley near Achinsk, where burials were discovered in 1914 by S. A. Teploukov, Andronovo (ahn-DROH-noh-voh) extended south to the Kopet-Dag and the Pamirs, east to the Altay Shan, and west to the Urals. As Europids, they spoke an Indo-Iranian language. Although they were nomads, irrigation discoveries indicate that many practiced agriculture and raised sheep, cattle, and horses. Wild horses were hunted for food. People lived in earthen huts and made flat-bottomed pottery decorated with triangles and other geometric patterns, including the swastika.

The Fedorovo type maintained earthen burials with bodies in a flexed position and heads turned to the southwest. The Alakul type practiced cremation. Both show evidence of devotion to the Sun god and the god of fire, as noted by horse sacrifices. Burials were faced with stone or wooden slabs, and the valuable artifacts in some graves indicate class differentiation. Burials contained flint arrowheads, copper beads and earrings, and bronze tools and weapons. Andronovo was similar to cultures in southern Russia and the Indo-Iranian world. The custom of burying chariots in graves of rulers was common to Mesopotamia, the late Andronovo steppes, and China. Andronovo probably transmitted this practice to the east. In the later Andronovo era, the greater dependence on the horse strengthened nomadism and a greater reliance on herding than farming.

ADDITIONAL RESOURCES

Dani, A. H., and V. M. Masson, eds. *The Dawn of Civilization: Earliest Times to 700 B.C.* Vol. 1 of *History of Civilizations of Central Asia.* Paris: UNESCO, 1992.

Davis-Kimball, Jeannine, Vladimir A. Bashilov, and Leonid T. Yablonsky. *Nomads of the Eurasian Steppes in the Early Iron Age.* Berkeley, Calif.: Zinat Press, 1995.

SEE ALSO: Afanasievo culture; China; Karasuk culture; Kelteminar culture.

—John D. Windhausen

ANEIRIN

ALSO KNOWN AS: Anerin; Saint Aneirin Gwodryd
BORN: c. 541 C.E.; Scotland
DIED: c. 600 C.E.; Wales
RELATED CIVILIZATIONS: Celtic and Saxon Britain
MAJOR ROLE/POSITION: Bard, monk

Life. Aneirin (uh-NI-rihn) was a younger son of a king of the Northern Pennines. Educated in Llancarfan, Wales, he soon gained a reputation as an accomplished poet, becoming known as Prince Aneirin of the Flowing Verse, Aneirin the Inspired, High King of Bards, and Prince of Poets.

Aneirin is best known for his epic poem, *Y Gododdin* (sixth century C.E.; *The Gododdin*, 1969). This poem is the firsthand account of the Battle of Catraeth, in which the Britons attempted to retake this city from the invading Saxons. *The Gododdin* is also the earliest extant writing in which Arthur and Myrddin (Merlin) are mentioned.

In later life, Aneirin reportedly became a monk, returning to the monastery at Llancarfan. Legend has it that he was martyred there, and many later honored him as a saint.

Influence. *The Gododdin* is generally considered the first British epic poem, and the earliest surviving work to be written in the vernacular. There is some ongoing academic controversy regarding the authenticity of the references to Arthur and Myrddin.

ADDITIONAL RESOURCES

Griffen, Toby D. *Names from the Dawn of British Legend: Taliesin, Anerin, Myrddin/Merlin, Arthur.* Llanerch, Wales: Llanerch, 1994.

Koch, John T. *The Gododdin of Aneirin: Text and Context from Dark Age North Britain.* Andover, Mass.: Celtic Studies Publications, 1997.

Wood, Carol L. *An Overview of Welsh Poetry Before the Norman Conquest.* New York: Edward Mellen Press, 1996.

SEE ALSO: Angles, Saxons, Jutes; Arthur; Britain; Celts.
—*Michael W. Simpson*

ANGLES, SAXONS, JUTES

DATE: c. 400-700 C.E.
LOCALE: England
SIGNIFICANCE: The Anglo-Saxon migrations into England ended Romano-Briton control of the island and gave birth to a distinctively English culture.

Germanic raiders first began to settle on the east coast of Roman Britain late in the third century C.E., usually in temporary camps for marauding. Their enemies and victims, the Romanized Britons, referred to them collectively as Saxons and failed to clear them from the coasts. Some camps turned into permanent settlements, and after the last Roman legion was withdrawn in 410 C.E., leaving a power vacuum, the migration accelerated.

An important escalation occurred in 449 C.E., according to the historian Bede's *Historia ecclesiastica gentis Anglorum* (731/732 C.E.; *A History of the English Church and People*, 1955), when a party of Angles, Saxons, and Jutes arrived at the invitation of Vortigern, a Celtic high king of Christian Roman background. He hired them as mercenaries to protect his land from his neighbors in the north, pagan Scots and Picts. It proved to be a mistake. As soon as the Anglo-Saxons repulsed Vortigern's enemies, they turned on their hosts. They encouraged more migrants to join them from their homelands, and Anglo-Saxons gradually defeated the remaining Briton forces and extended their control of England to approximately the present-day border with Scotland, except for Wales and Cornwall.

The three groups that Bede names came from the areas that are now northwestern Germany and the Netherlands. The Angles settled most of the land north of the Thames River, and the Saxons occupied the land to the south. The Jutes took over Kent and the Isle of Wight. Not all the interactions between the newcomers and the Britons were hostile. Periods of peaceful coexistence, trade, and intermarrying allowed the pagan Anglo-Saxons to absorb a portion of the culture of Britain, but they retained a distinct political organization and culture.

Whatever their origin, the Germanic settlers called themselves "Englisc" and their country "Englalond."

This engraving shows the Anglo-Saxons on the battlefield. (North Wind Picture Archives)

After the arrival of a Roman Catholic mission in 597 C.E., led by Saint Augustine of Canterbury, the Anglo-Saxons gradually converted to Christianity, although some Saxon areas remained pagan until the tenth century C.E. By 700 C.E., seven kingdoms existed, dominated by Mercia in the midlands. Primarily free farmers, the Anglo-Saxons lived under the local control of an earl who was responsible to the king. They developed a distinctive native art and language. A vernacular written literature, based on songs and orally transmitted alliterative poetry, began after Christian missionaries began teaching the Roman alphabet in monasteries and cathedral schools. The literature, which includes the epic *Beowulf* (c. 700-750 C.E.; first printing 1815), emphasized the virtues of loyalty to a lord, unflinching courage, and acceptance of fate.

ADDITIONAL RESOURCES

Hill, David. *An Atlas of Anglo-Saxon England*. Toronto, Canada: University of Toronto Press, 1981.

Laing, Jennifer. *Warriors of the Dark Ages*. Stroud, England: Sutton, 2000.

Laing, Lloyd, and Jennifer Laing. *Anglo-Saxon England*. New York: Charles Scribner's Sons, 1979.

Myres, J. N. L. *The English Settlements*. Oxford, England: Oxford University Press, 1986.

Stenton, F. M. *Anglo-Saxon England*. 3d ed. Oxford, England: Clarendon Press, 1971.

SEE ALSO: Augustine of Canterbury, Saint; Britain; Celts; Germany; Picts; Rome, Imperial.

—*Roger Smith*

ANKHESENAMEN

ALSO KNOWN AS: Ankhesenpaaton
BORN: c. 1371 B.C.E.; Egypt
DIED: c. 1351 B.C.E.; Egypt
RELATED CIVILIZATION: Pharaonic Egypt
MAJOR ROLE/POSITION: Queen

Life. Ankhesenamen (ahn-kehs-uh-NAHM-uhn), or "she lives for [the God] Amon" (originally called Ankhesenpaaton, or "she lives for the Sun disk Aton"), was the third daughter of the heretic pharaoh Akhenaton and the wife of Tutankhamen. She may have also married Tutankhamen's successor, Ay—her cartouche sits beside his on a glass ring in the Berlin Museum. Elsewhere, however, Ay's first wife, Tiy, appears as his consort.

The Hittite annals offer a clue about Ankhesenamen's possible fate. They state that the widowed Egyptian queen Dahammunzu wrote to the Hittite king Suppiluliumas I asking for one of his sons in marriage. The widowed queen, whose name is really a title meaning "the royal wife," has been identified as Ankhesenamen, widow of Tutankhamen. The annals relate that a prince was dispatched to Egypt but that he was murdered en route. In all probability, Ay's supporters eliminated both the groom and the bride to protect his accession.

Influence. Ankhesenamen's correspondence with the Hittite king, a sign of her strong character, may have aimed at salvaging Akhenaton's religion by making an ignorant foreigner king. Unfortunately for his followers, her gambit seems to have sealed the religion's doom.

ADDITIONAL RESOURCES

Desroches-Noblecourt, Christiane. *Tutankhamen: Life and Death of a Pharaoh.* New York: Penguin, 1989.

El Mahdy, Christine. *Tutankhamen.* New York: St. Martin's Press, 1999.

Green, L. "A 'Lost Queen' of Ancient Egypt, King's Daughter, King's Great Wife, Ankhesenamen." *KMT* 1/4 (Winter, 1990-1991): 23-29, 67.

SEE ALSO: Akhenaton; Egypt, Pharaonic; Tutankhamen.

—*Steven M. Stannish*

ANTAE

DATE: 200-300 C.E.
LOCALE: Northeast shores of the Black Sea
SIGNIFICANCE: The Antae represent a very early attempt at unity among Slavic tribes in what became the southern Ukraine.

The Antae (AHN-tah-eh), a loose confederation of tribes in what became the Ukraine and Moldova, were first mentioned by the Roman historian Pliny the Elder in the first century C.E. Pliny provided very little information, however, and later Roman and Germanic writers did not greatly improve the situation. The origins of these people are therefore somewhat obscure.

By the third century C.E., the Antae were the dominant power in the southern Ukraine, an area inhabited by Slavic tribes. They seem to have been Slavs themselves, though there is some dispute about this. They may have been related to, and were certainly influenced by, the Persian-speaking Scythians and the Sarmatians.

The Antae culture was based on family groups, with the father the undisputed leader. They had highly organized agriculture and held the land in common, with tribal groups ruled by a council of family chiefs. The king of the Antae was one of these chiefs.

The Antae rose to prominence by assuming leadership of the surrounding Slavic tribes against numerous invaders. These included the Scythians and Sarmatians and later the Germanic Goths and the Asiatic Huns. As a result, by about the fifth century C.E., the southern Slavs, including the Antae, were influenced by a wide variety of cultures.

ADDITIONAL RESOURCES

Freeze, Gregory L., ed. *Russia: A History.* New York: Oxford University Press, 1997.

Lawrence, John. *A History of Russia.* 7th ed. New York: Meridian, 1993.

SEE ALSO: Goths; Huns; Pliny the Elder; Sarmatians; Scythia; Slavs.

—*Marc Goldstein*

ANTHEMIUS OF TRALLES

BORN: fifth century C.E.; Tralles in Lydia (near Aydin in Turkey)
DIED: before 558 C.E.; possibly Constantinople
RELATED CIVILIZATION: Byzantine Empire
MAJOR ROLE/POSITION: Architect, mathematician

Life. Anthemius of Tralles (an-THEE-mee-uhs of TRAL-eez) was born into a highly educated family. His father, Stephanus, and his two brothers, Dioscorus and Alexander, were physicians; his third brother, Olympius, was a lawyer; and the fourth, Metrodorus, was a professor of literature. Anthemius himself became famous as a skilled *mechanicus*, a profession that can be properly described as an architect with a strong theoretical background in mathematics. According to the contemporary historians Procopius (fl. sixth C.E.) and Agathias (c. 536-c. 580 C.E.), in addition to being a knowledgeable designer and builder, Anthemius was known as a peculiar individual who enjoyed performing bizarre practical jokes.

Anthemius was employed by Emperor Justinian I (r. 527-565 C.E.) to work with Isidoros of Miletus on the rebuilding of the Haghia Sophia church in Constantinople (Istanbul, Turkey). The original building was heavily damaged by fire in 532 C.E. during the Nika Riots. The newly built structure became an architectural wonder celebrated for its monumental dimensions, ellipsoid dome, and masterful interior light effects. Many dramatic reports exist about difficulties encountered during its construction. Reportedly, the emperor himself was concerned about the complexity of the design, and on two occasions, his technical solutions saved the structure from collapsing. The church was completed and dedicated in December 27, 537 C.E. Anthemius is traditionally believed to have died in 534 C.E. before the church's completion; however, this date is disputed. He certainly died before 558 C.E., when the dome crashed after a series of earthquakes. It was later replaced with a modified version of the original design.

Influence. In addition to his architectural work, Anthemius was consulted in regard to issues of irrigation and fortification. He also wrote two partially preserved theoretical studies: *Peri pyreion* (sixth century C.E.; on burning mirrors) and *Peri paradoxon mechanematon* (c. 534; concerning remarkable mechanical devices).

ADDITIONAL RESOURCES

Huxley, G. L. *Anthemius of Tralles: A Study in Later Greek Geometry.* Greek, Roman, and Byzantine Monographs 1. Cambridge, Mass.: Cambridge, 1959.

Mango, Cyril. *The Art of the Byzantine Empire 312-1453: Sources and Documents.* Toronto: University of Toronto Press, 1997.

SEE ALSO: Agathias; Byzantine Empire; Constantinople; Haghia Sophia; Justinian I; Procopius.

—Rozmeri Basic

ANTHONY OF EGYPT, SAINT

ALSO KNOWN AS: Antony; Antonios
BORN: c. 251 C.E.; Coma, near Memphis, Egypt
DIED: probably January 17, 356 C.E.; Mount Kolzim, near the Red Sea, Egypt
RELATED CIVILIZATION: Imperial Rome
MAJOR ROLE/POSITION: Christian ascetic, hermit, saint

Life. A native Copt, Anthony of Egypt grew up in a Christian family environment. Around 270 C.E., after undergoing a self-described religious transformation, Anthony gave away his possessions and devoted himself to a life of asceticism and spiritual contemplation. Placing himself first under the direction of older ascetics in a nearby village, he eventually withdrew to the more remote precincts of an empty mountainside tomb, and then to abandoned ruins in the desert. The holiness and discipline of his life eventually attracted numerous disciples, whom he organized into small communities of hermits, possibly under a "rule," which gave him his traditional epithet of *abbat*, or "father." His spiritual trials with demons, as amply recorded in Saint Athanasius

Saint Anthony of Egypt. (Library of Congress)

of Alexander's biography, furnish a fascinating glimpse into both Anthony's personality and contemporary Christian beliefs.

Despite his devotion to the solitary life, Anthony periodically returned to his roots in the villages of Egypt to counsel his cobelievers, particularly in times of trouble (persecution or heresy problems). Various writings attributed to him survive, including a series of letters, possibly authentic.

Influence. Admired and emulated by contemporaries and later generations of Christian hermits and monastics, Anthony came to symbolize the essence of the Christian ascetic life.

ADDITIONAL RESOURCES

Griggs, C. W. *Early Egyptian Christianity from Its Origins to 451* C.E. Leiden, Netherlands: E. J. Brill, 1990.

Rubenson, S. *The Letters of St. Anthony: Origenist Theology, Monastic Tradition, and the Making of a Saint.* Lund, Sweden: Lund University, 1990.

SEE ALSO: Athanasius of Alexandria, Saint; Christianity; Rome, Imperial.

—*Craig L. Hanson*

ANTIGONID DYNASTY

DATE: 306 to 168 B.C.E.
LOCALE: Macedonia
RELATED CIVILIZATIONS: Eastern Mediterranean, Hellenistic Greece, Roman Republic

After the death of Alexander the Great, his lieutenants proceeded to civil war and a division of the Macedonian empire. A provincial governor, Antigonus I Monophthalmos, the "One-Eyed," acquired Asia Minor and, calling himself king, established the Antigonid (an-TIHG-uh-nihd) Dynasty in 306 B.C.E. He soon perished in battle against a coalition of his enemies. However, his son, Demetrius I Poliorcetes, "Besieger of Cities," survived, only to win and lose Macedonia.

Renewing the dynasty's fortune, Antigonus II Gonatas became king of Macedonia in 276 B.C.E.

and, from Pella, created a secure foundation for the rule of his successors. Although Demetrius II quarreled with Aetolia, Antigonus III Doson established a broad

MAJOR KINGS OF THE ANTIGONID DYNASTY, 306-168 B.C.E.

King	Reign
Antigonus I Monophthalmos	306-301 B.C.E.
Demetrius I Poliorcetes	294-287
Antigonus II Gonatas	276-239
Demetrius II	239-229
Antigonus III Doson	229-221
Philip V	221-179
Perseus	179-168

Hellenic alliance and, as its leader, encouraged cooperation between Greece and Macedonia. Yet Philip V drew that alliance into a dangerous struggle by supporting Hannibal of Carthage against Rome in the Second Punic War (218-201 B.C.E.). After defeating the Carthaginian general, the Romans vanquished Philip at Cynoscephalae in 197 B.C.E. and his son Perseus at Pydna in 168 B.C.E. After abolishing the Antigonid monarchy, Rome established four independent Macedonian republics. Years later, when adventurers claiming descent from Perseus aroused revolt, Rome intervened and reorganized Macedonia as a Roman province.

ADDITIONAL RESOURCES

Billows, Richard A. *Antigonos the One-Eyed and the Creation of the Hellenistic State*. Berkeley: University of California Press, 1990.

Gabbert, Janice J. *Antigonus II Gonatas: A Political Biography*. New York: Routledge, 1997.

SEE ALSO: Alexander the Great; Cynoscephalae, Battle of; Demetrius Poliorcetes; Greece, Hellenistic and Roman; Hannibal; Macedonia; Philip V; Punic Wars; Rome, Republican.

—Denvy A. Bowman

ANTIOCHUS THE GREAT

ALSO KNOWN AS: Antiochus III
BORN: c. 242 B.C.E.; possibly Antioch
DIED: 187 B.C.E.; Elymais, near Susa, Iran
RELATED CIVILIZATION: Hellenistic Greece
MAJOR ROLE/POSITION: King

Life. The youngest son of Seleucus II, Antiochus (an-TI-uh-kuhs) the Great succeeded his assassinated brother Seleucus III in 223 B.C.E. Having put down the revolts of satraps Molon in Media (222-221 B.C.E.) and Achaeus in western Anatolia (220/213 B.C.E.), Antiochus undertook a campaign into the upper satrapies (212/205 B.C.E.) and established control over Commagene, Armenia, Parthia, and Bactria as well as southern Syria, Phoenicia, and Judaea. For his role in restoring and expanding the Seleucid kingdom, he received his title "the Great."

After the Roman defeat of Philip V, Antiochus claimed western Anatolia and Thrace as his ancestral inheritance. Following unsuccessful negotiations, he was defeated by the Romans in the battles at Thermopylae in Greece (191 B.C.E.) and at Magnesia ad Sipylum

in Asia Minor (189 B.C.E.). In accordance with the Peace of Apamea (188 B.C.E.), Antiochus vacated Anatolia to the west of the Taurus Mountains but retained his eastern possessions, which stretched up to central Asia. He died soon afterward, on campaign in Elymais.

Influence. The pinnacle of the Seleucid Dynasty, Antiochus's reign also reflected increasing Roman interference in Greek affairs. He is credited with the separation of military and fiscal administration and the introduction of the royal cult.

ADDITIONAL RESOURCES

Kincaid, C. A. *Successors of Alexander the Great*. Chicago: Argonaut, 1969.

Ma, John. *Antiochus II and the Cities of Western Asia Minor*. New York: Oxford University Press, 1999.

SEE ALSO: Artabanus I-V; Greece, Hellenistic and Roman; Magnesia ad Sipylum, Battle of; Philip V; Rome, Republican; Seleucid Dynasty.

—Sviatoslav Dmitriev

ANTIPATER

BORN: 397 B.C.E.; place unknown
DIED: 319 B.C.E.; Macedonia
RELATED CIVILIZATIONS: Classical and early Hellenistic Greece
MAJOR ROLE/POSITION: General, regent

Life. Antipater (an-TIHP-uht-ur) was one of most able generals of Philip II and Alexander the Great. In 346 B.C.E., he helped negotiate the Peace of Philocrates between Philip and Athens, and in 338 B.C.E. with Alexander, then heir to the Macedonian throne, he returned the bones of the Athenian dead from the Battle of Chaeronea.

Alexander appointed him "regent" of Greece and Macedonia and acting hegemon of the League of Corinth when he left for Persia in 334 B.C.E. As regent, Antipater kept Macedonia united and Greece passive, apart from the war of Agis III of Sparta (331-330 B.C.E.), which he ended with league assistance. In 323 B.C.E., Alexander's death caused a widespread revolt of the Greek states, led by Athens (the Lamian War). Although hard-pressed at first, Antipater ended it in 322 B.C.E. and imposed an oligarchy on Athens. The final years of his life were set against the struggles of Alexander's generals for power. Antipater sided with a group against the Macedonian general Perdiccas, on whose death in 321 B.C.E., Antipater's possession of Macedonia and Greece was confirmed, and he became regent for the young Alexander IV and Philip III. His death in 319 B.C.E. led to further struggles.

Influence. Antipater kept Greece free from revolt and the Macedonian kingdom secure while Alexander was in Persia and further east and also provided him with reinforcements when demanded.

ADDITIONAL RESOURCES

Errington, M. *A History of Macedonia*. Berkeley: University of California Press, 1990.

Heckel, W. *The Marshals of Alexander's Empire*. London: Routledge, 1992.

SEE ALSO: Alexander the Great; Athens; Chaeronea, Battle of; Greece, Classical; Greece, Hellenistic and Roman; Macedonia; Philip II.

—Ian Worthington

ANTIPATER OF IDUMAEA

ALSO KNOWN AS: Antipater II
BORN: date unknown; Idumaea
DIED: 43 B.C.E.; Judaea
RELATED CIVILIZATIONS: Nabataea, Republican Rome
MAJOR ROLE/POSITION: Political ruler

Life. Antipater of Idumaea (an-TIHP-uht-ur of ihj-uh-MEE-uh) was the son of a rich Idumaean, also named Antipater, who had been appointed *strategos* (military governor) of Idumaea by the Hasmonaean ruler of the Holy Land, Alexander Jannaeus (r. 103-76 B.C.E.) when he conquered the region between the Dead Sea and the Gulf of Aqaba. The younger Antipater inherited from his father a fondness for things Roman and perhaps even his political office. Antipater increased his wealth and influence by marrying a woman named Cypros, who was from an illustrious Arabian (probably Nabataean) family. They had four sons: Phasael, Herod (later King Herod the Great), Joseph, and Pheroras.

Antipater pursued policies favorable to the Romans, especially after Pompey the Great's invasion of Palestine in 63 B.C.E. in the wake of a Hasmonaean-caused civil war. In return, Rome favored Antipater. In 47 B.C.E., Julius Caesar appointed Antipater procurator of Judaea and conferred on him Roman citizenship, an honor that devolved to Herod and his sons. Antipater, in turn, gave to Herod and Phasael the tasks of governing Galilee and Jerusalem, respectively, at which time Herod emerged as an increasingly ruthless ruler. Antipater did not live long after these events. In 43 B.C.E., he was murdered by Malichus, a political rival in Judaea.

Influence. Using his inherited wealth and power to capitalize on his own instincts for political opportunity, Antipater cemented relations with the Nabataean kingdom to the east, helped Rome become firmly established in Palestine, and founded the Herodian Dynasty.

ADDITIONAL RESOURCES

Jagersma, Henk. *A History of Israel from Alexander the Great to Bar Kochba*. Philadelphia, Pa.: Fortress Press, 1986.

Richardson, Peter. *Herod: King of the Jews and Friend of the Romans*. Columbia: University of South Carolina, 1996.

SEE ALSO: Caesar, Julius; Herodian Dynasty; Judaea; Pompey the Great; Rome, Republican.

—Andrew C. Skinner

ANTIPHON

BORN: c. 480 B.C.E.; Athens, Greece
DIED: 411 B.C.E.; probably Athens, Greece
RELATED CIVILIZATION: Classical Greece
MAJOR ROLE/POSITION: Orator, speechwriter, politician

Life. Antiphon (AN-tuh-fahn) was born in Athens to an aristocratic family of the deme (local territorial district) of Rhamnus. He became a leading intellectual, writer, and orator. In 411 B.C.E., in the wake of the Sicilian disaster, Antiphon led a coup to replace the democracy with an aristocracy. The revolution failed, and Antiphon was tried and executed for his participation. The historian Thucydides reports that Antiphon's defense speech was the best ever delivered, but unfortunately only a few lines of it survive.

Six speeches Antiphon wrote for others do survive. Three are tetralogies, sets of four speeches each presenting a generic homicide case to demonstrate examples of arguments to be used. In *Against the Stepmother* (430-411 B.C.E.; English translation, 1941), a young man accuses his stepmother of having conspired to poison his father. In *The Murder of Herodes* (430-411

B.C.E.; English translation, 1941), a man defends himself against a charge of murder. In *The Chorus Boy* (430-411 B.C.E.; English translation, 1941), a chorus producer (*chorēgos*) denies having accidentally killed a boy by giving him a potion to improve his voice. More philosophical tracts *Concord* (n.d.; English translation, 1941) and *Truth* (n.d.; English translation, 1941) survive only in fragments. Scholars since antiquity have debated whether a different man named Antiphon wrote them.

Influence. The speeches break ground in using arguments from probability and in developing Attic prose style.

ADDITIONAL RESOURCES
Gagarin, Michael. *Antiphon: The Speeches*. Cambridge, England: Cambridge University Press, 1997.
Gagarin, Michael, and D. M. MacDowell, trans. *Antiphon and Andocides*. Austin: University of Texas Press, 1998.

SEE ALSO: Government and law; Greece, Classical.
—*Wilfred E. Major*

ANTONIA THE ELDER

ALSO KNOWN AS: Antonia Major
BORN: 39 B.C.E.; place unknown
DIED: date and place unknown
RELATED CIVILIZATION: Imperial Rome
MAJOR ROLE/POSITION: Member of the Julio-Claudian royal family

Life. Dynastic marriages transferred legitimacy and were agents of power for the Julio-Claudians. Antonia (an-TOH-nee-uh) the Elder was born out of the union of Marc Antony and Octavia, the sister of Augustus. Their marriage averted civil war, and the hoped-for issue of this dynastic marriage is most likely referred to in Vergil's *Fourth Eclogue* (n.d.; English translation, 1934-1935). Antonia the Elder's life was overshadowed by that of her sister, Antonia the Younger.

Antonia the Elder married Lucius Domitius Ahenobarbus, who was the son of the senator cleared of

Julius Caesar's murder. Antonia and Lucius Domitius Ahenobarbus's son was Gnaeus Domitius Ahenobarbus, who married Agrippina the Younger. Their marriage produced the future emperor Nero, who reigned from 54-68 C.E.

Antonia the Elder is portrayed in bas-relief on the Ara Pacis (13-9 B.C.E.) with her children Domitius and Domitia and husband Domitius Ahenobarbus. This frieze portrays the successors of Augustus.

Influence. Antonia played a role in Roman history as the grandmother of the emperor Nero.

ADDITIONAL RESOURCES
Cary, M., and H. H. Scullard. *A History of Rome: Down to the Reign of Constantine*. 3d ed. New York: St. Martin's Press, 1976.
Hawley, Richard, and Barbara Levick, eds. *Women in Antiquity: New Assessments*. New York: Routledge, 1995.

Wood, Susan E. *Imperial Women: A Study in Public Images, 40* B.C.-A.D. *68.* Mnemosyne Supplementum 194. Leiden, Netherlands: E. J. Brill, 1999.

SEE ALSO: Agrippina the Younger; Antonia the Younger; Antony, Marc; Augustus; Nero; Octavia; Rome, Imperial; Vergil.

—Sally A. Struthers

ANTONIA THE YOUNGER

ALSO KNOWN AS: Antonia Minor
BORN: January 31, 36 B.C.E.; place unknown
DIED: May 1, 37 C.E.; place unknown
RELATED CIVILIZATION: Imperial Rome
MAJOR ROLE/POSITION: Member of Julio-Claudian royal family

Life. Antonia (an-TOH-nee-uh) the Younger was the younger daughter of Marc Antony and Octavia and the niece of the emperor Augustus. In 16 B.C.E., she married Nero Claudius Drusus, the son of Livia Drusilla and brother of the emperor Tiberius. Antonia's children included Nero Claudius Drusus Germanicus (later Germanicus Julius Caesar), the future emperor Claudius, and Livilla. Latin historian Tacitus and biographer Suetonius have provided the most information about Antonia.

Antonia influenced Julio-Claudian politics, mediating between the emperor Tiberius and her son Germanicus, and warning Tiberius of the power of the prefect of the Praetorian Guard, Lucius Aelius Seianus. Seianus had murdered Julius Caesar Drusus (Drusus the Younger), the son of Tiberius, and husband of Antonia's daughter Livilla. In 31 C.E., Antonia reportedly sent a letter warning Tiberius of Seianus's plot against him, which resulted in Seianus's execution.

After Antonia's daughter-in-law, Agrippina the Elder, was banished in 29 C.E., Antonia took in her children Caligula (Gaius Caesar Germanicus) and Drusilla. Once emperor, Caligula granted Antonia the titles of "Augusta" and priestess of the deified Augustus. Eventually she fell out of favor with Caligula and died, allegedly of suicide or poisoning.

Influence. Antonia was the model of a Roman matron. She is depicted in the relief sculpture of the Ara Pacis (13-9 B.C.E.), and Roman coins were minted in her honor during the reign of Claudius.

ADDITIONAL RESOURCES
Cary, M., and H. H. Scullard. *A History of Rome: Down to the Reign of Constantine.* 3d ed. New York: St. Martin's Press, 1976.
Wood, Susan E. *Imperial Women: A Study in Public Images, 40* B.C.-A.D. *68.* Mnemosyne Supplementum 194. Leiden, Netherlands: E. J. Brill, 1999.

SEE ALSO: Agrippina the Elder; Antonia the Elder; Antony, Marc; Augustus; Caligula; Claudius; Livia Drusilla; Octavia; Rome, Imperial; Suetonius; Tacitus; Tiberius.

—Sally A. Struthers

ANTONINUS PIUS

ALSO KNOWN AS: Titus Aurelius Fulvus Boionius Antoninus
BORN: September 19, 86 C.E.; Lanuvium, Latium
DIED: March 7, 161 C.E.; Lorium, Etruria
RELATED CIVILIZATION: Imperial Rome
MAJOR ROLE/POSITION: Emperor

Life. Born to powerful parents and known for his wealth and good character, Antoninus Pius (an-tuh-NI-nuhs PI-uhs) rose quickly through the traditional Ro-

man offices. In 120 C.E., he was elected consul and from 135 to 136 C.E. served as the proconsul in Asia, giving him both provincial and domestic governing experience. However, it was his service to the emperor Hadrian (117-138 C.E.) as a judicial legate in Italy that brought Antoninus to the imperial throne. Adopted by Hadrian to be his son and heir, Antoninus peacefully came to power in 138 C.E., after which he adopted Marcus Aurelius and Lucius Verus as his own successors. His relationship with the Roman senate was such that the senators voted him the title "Pius" in acknowledgment of his good will toward them and toward the traditional gods of the Roman state. This was a relief for the ruling institutions of Rome after years of tension between Hadrian and the senate. The literature from this period and afterward praises Antoninus Pius for a peaceful reign. Though he had to meet the challenges of warfare in Scotland, North Africa, Egypt, and Germany, this emperor successfully negotiated peace with the Parthians and kept the empire financially and politically stable.

Influence. Although the celebration of Rome's nine hundredth anniversary in 148 C.E. took place during a period of strength and peace, the troubles within the Roman Empire and on its borders, so aptly controlled by Antoninus and his successor Marcus Aurelius, would explode into major difficulties by the mid-180's C.E. Antoninus, therefore, oversaw the beginning of the end of the Pax Romana.

ADDITIONAL RESOURCES

Grant, M. *The Antonines: The Roman Empire in Transition*. London: Routledge, 1994.

Hammond, M. *The Antonine Monarchy*. Rome: The American Academy, 1959.

Hüttl, W. *Antoninus Pius*. New York: Arno Press, 1975.

SEE ALSO: Hadrian; Marcus Aurelius; Parthia; Rome, Imperial.

—Kenneth R. Calvert

ANTONY, MARC

ALSO KNOWN AS: Marcus Antonius
BORN: c. 82 B.C.E.; place unknown
DIED: August 30 B.C.E.; Alexandria, Egypt
RELATED CIVILIZATION: Republican Rome
MAJOR ROLE/POSITION: General, statesman

Life. Marc Antony was born into a distinguished but impoverished Roman family. From early in his career, Antony was a partisan of Julius Caesar, through whose influence he attained several important offices. At the time of Caesar's death, Antony was his co-consul and de facto second-in-command, though not his chosen successor. Initially he held out an olive branch to Caesar's assassins but later joined with Octavian (later Augustus) to defeat them at Philippi (42 B.C.E.). This legal but autocratic compact with Octavian and Marcus Aemilius Lepidus, the Second Triumvirate, allowed Antony in effect to rule the eastern half of the empire. During this period, Antony rid himself of his political archenemy, Cicero, whose second Philippic oration is a damning picture of Antony's life and career. The Second Triumvirate even-

Marc Antony visits Egyptian queen Cleopatra VII. (North Wind Picture Archives)

tually broke down, in part because Antony became the consort of Cleopatra VII of Egypt. Octavian's forces defeated those of Antony and Cleopatra in a naval battle at Actium (31 B.C.E.). The two fled and eventually killed themselves to avoid capture and humiliation.

Influence. Later writers portray Antony as a brilliant but dissolute man ultimately destroyed by his weakness of character. Thanks to English playwright William Shakespeare, Antony has become something of a romantic hero.

ADDITIONAL RESOURCES

Huzar, E. G. *Mark Antony: A Biography.* Minneapolis: University of Minnesota Press, 1978.
Pelling, C. "The Triumviral Period." Vol. 10 in *The Cambridge Ancient History.* 2d ed. Cambridge, England: Cambridge University Press, 1996.

SEE ALSO: Augustus; Caesar, Julius; Cicero; Cleopatra VII; Rome, Republican.

—Christopher Nappa

ANYTE OF TEGEA

FLOURISHED: early third century B.C.E.; Tegea, Arcadia, Greece
RELATED CIVILIZATION: Classical Greece
MAJOR ROLE/POSITION: Epigrammatist

Life. Named by Antipater as one of "nine earthly Muses," Anyte (ahn-EE-tay of TEE-jee-uh) was born, lived, and composed epigrams in Tegea in southern mainland Greece. Twenty-one surviving poems have been identified as hers, and three appear falsely attributed. She composed both traditional epigrams as tombstone dedications and epigrams as poems commenting on life. Her subjects included both people and pets and show a strong valuation of domestic life by using "heroic language."

Influence. Her work is perhaps the foundation of the very popular pastoral and animal epigrams of the Hellenistic period, and it was copied by later male writers.

Her style and language has been both praised and criticized by modern scholars, who often cite her as one of only a few women poets of the ancient world whose works survive.

ADDITIONAL RESOURCES

Balmer, Josephine. *Classical Woman Poets.* Newcastle-upon-Tyne, England: Bloodaxe Books, 1996.
Rayor, Diane. *Sappho's Lyre: Archaic Lyric Women Poets of Ancient Greece.* Berkeley: University of California Press, 1991.
Snyder, Jane McIntosh. *The Woman and the Lyre: Women Writers in Classical Greece and Rome.* Carbondale: Southern Illinois University Press, 1989.

SEE ALSO: Greece, Classical; Languages and literature.

—Tammy Jo Eckhart

APEDEMAK

DATE: 600 B.C.E.-350 C.E.
LOCALE: Nubian region of the upper Nile (later Republic of Sudan), northeast Africa
RELATED CIVILIZATIONS: Meroe, Nubia
SIGNIFICANCE: This Nubian god played an important role in the lives of those in Meroe.

Although the Nubian people derived most of their religious ideas and iconography from Egypt, they did have gods of their own that had no Egyptian counterparts. One of these gods, Apedemak, became the most impor-

tant deity of the Nubian region known as the island of Meroe, an area bounded by the Nile and Atabara Rivers. His image is found throughout the region, including the stone reliefs on temples at Naqa, Kawa, Amara, and Musawwarat es-Sufra.

Apedemak is most often represented with the head of a lion and a human body. On a temple pylon at Naqa, he is shown with the body of a serpent. His features and accompanying inscriptions identify him as a war god. In the reliefs at the Lion Temple at Musawwarat es-Sufra, he appears to be wearing leather armor and is carrying a bow and arrow. On another wall, he is shown slaying an enemy in a manner reminiscent of the way pharaohs are often pictured in Egypt. A hymn to Apedemak engraved on the south wall of the Lion Temple hails him as "Lord of Naqa, great god, Lord of Musawwarat es-Sufra, excellent god, the foremost of Nubia; Lion of the south, strong of arm."

ADDITIONAL RESOURCES

Burstein, Stanley M., ed. *Ancient African Civilizations: Kush and Axum*. Princeton, N.J.: Markus Wiener, 1998.

Shinnie, Peter L. *Meroe: A Civilization of the Sudan*. New York: Frederick A. Praeger, 1967.

Taylor, John. *Egypt and Nubia*. London: British Museum Press, 1991.

Zabkar, Louis V. *Apedemak, Lion God of Meroe: A Study in Egyptian-Meroitic Syncretism*. Warminster, England: Aris & Phillips, 1975.

SEE ALSO: Africa, East and South; Napata and Meroe; Nubia.

—Craig E. Lloyd

APOLLODORUS OF ATHENS (ARTIST)

ALSO KNOWN AS: Sciagraphos; Skiagraphos
FLOURISHED: fifth century B.C.E.
RELATED CIVILIZATIONS: Archaic Greece, Republican Rome
MAJOR ROLE/POSITION: Artist

Life. The particulars of the life of Apollodorus (uh-pahl-uh-DOHR-uhs) of Athens are unknown, and none of his work survives. However, he is known to have continued the advances toward realism in art developed by the earlier fifth century B.C.E. painters Micon, Polygnotus, and Agatharcus. Agatharcus, the first to paint a scene for a production of tragedy, wrote a treatise on the use of perspective for creating the illusion of theatrical distance. Apollodorus furthered the illusion of perspective, employing the use of light and shadow to convey spatial relationships, a technique known as chiaroscuro. Apollodorus came to be known as "Sciagraphos," or "Shadow-Painter," from the Greek for "shadow-drawing." Historian Pliny the Elder spoke of him as the first to paint things as they really appear and to give glory to the brush. Yet he seemed to have been surpassed in realism by painter Zeuxis of Heraclea, who added highlights to shading and whose paintings of grapes are said to have deceived birds.

Influence. Apollodorus contributed to realism in painting, a feature that helped form Western taste for most of its history. The general movement toward realism influenced fourth century philosophical discourse, especially that of Plato, who worried over the moral probity of illusion in art, where a two-dimensional medium gives the false impression of three dimensions. In the *Politeia* (388-368 B.C.E.; *Republic*, 1701), Plato's Socrates observes that the painter is several times removed from the pure reality of the idea—even more removed than the craftsperson, who makes a three-dimensional object.

ADDITIONAL RESOURCE

Bruno, V. J. *Form and Color in Greek Painting*. New York: W. W. Norton, 1977.

SEE ALSO: Art and architecture; Greece, Archaic; Plato; Pliny the Elder; Polygnotus; Zeuxis of Heraclea.

—James A. Arieti

APOLLODORUS OF ATHENS (SCHOLAR)

BORN: c. 180 B.C.E.; Athens, Greece
DIED: after 120 B.C.E.; Athens, Greece
RELATED CIVILIZATION: Hellenistic Greece
MAJOR ROLE/POSITION: Scholar, historian

Life. Apollodorus (uh-pahl-uh-DOHR-uhs) of Athens began his studies in his native city but eventually moved to Alexandria, Egypt, where he studied with Aristarchus of Samothrace, head of Alexandria's great library. Apollodorus and other scholars were expelled from Egypt in about 145 B.C.E.; Apollodorus may have gone to Pergamum but later returned to Athens.

Apollodorus was a prolific scholar with diverse interests. All of his works have been lost, but they included treatises on the Greek gods, Athenian comedy, and Homer. He was best known for his *Chronica* (after 120 B.C.E.; "chronicles"), an account of Greek history from the fall of Troy (1184 B.C.E.) to 145/144 B.C.E. Apollodorus later added a chapter covering the period to 120 B.C.E. The *Chronica* provided dates for many historical events, but Apollodorus also touched on the careers of philosophers and poets. Curiously, Apollodorus wrote the *Chronica* in verse, perhaps to make it easier to memorize.

Influence. The *Chronica* of Apollodorus quickly became the standard work on Greek chronology in the ancient world. Apollodorus's reputation as a scholar was so great that works were falsely attributed to him, including the *Library*, an encyclopedic account of Greek mythology that still exists.

ADDITIONAL RESOURCES

Habicht, Christian. *Athens from Alexander to Antony.* Translated by Deborah Lucas Schneider. Cambridge, Mass.: Harvard University Press, 1999.

Mosshammer, Alden A. *The Chronicle of Eusebius and the Greek Chronographic Tradition.* Lewisburg, Pa.: Bucknell University Press, 1979.

SEE ALSO: Aristarchus of Samothrace; Athens; Greece, Hellenistic and Roman; Homer; Languages and literature; Troy.

—James P. Sickinger

APOLLODORUS THE ARCHITECT

ALSO KNOWN AS: Apollodorus of Damascus
FLOURISHED: early second century C.E.; Damascus
RELATED CIVILIZATION: Imperial Rome
MAJOR ROLE/POSITION: Architect, engineer

Life. Apollodorus (uh-pahl-uh-DOHR-uhs) the Architect spent the majority of his career in Rome, where he designed and constructed many imperial buildings under the patronage of the emperor Trajan. Most notable of the structures attributed to Apollodorus are the forum, basilica, library, column, and baths of Trajan. In conjunction with the forum complex, Apollodorus created a vast multistory marketplace wherein he employed, for one of the first times, the cross-vault system of intersecting barrel vaults, which opens up wall space for windows and light. A skilled engineer, Apollodorus assisted Trajan in his campaign to conquer Dacia by designing a half-mile-long (three-quarter-kilometer) timber and masonry bridge for the Roman legions to cross the Danube (the actual bridge design can be seen on the column of Trajan). Apollodorus wrote treatises on both military and civil engineering. The emperor Hadrian, an architect in his own right, quarreled with Apollodorus on several occasions. For Apollodorus's derogatory comments regarding the emperor's architectural designs, Apollodorus was first exiled and later executed.

Influence. Apollodorus set a standard of excellence for the design and engineering of elegant and spacious buildings that has continued to influence architects and architecture through the centuries.

ADDITIONAL RESOURCES

Boardman, John, et al. *The Oxford History of the Classical World.* Oxford, England: Oxford University Press, 1986.

MacDonald, William L. *The Architecture of the Roman Empire.* New Haven, Conn.: Yale University Press, 1982.

Thorpe, Martin. *Roman Architecture.* London: Bristol Classical Press, 1995.

SEE ALSO: Art and architecture; Hadrian; Rome, Imperial; Trajan.

—Sonia Sorrell

APOLLONIUS OF PERGA

BORN: c. 262 B.C.E.; Perga, Asia Minor
DIED: c. 190 B.C.E.; Alexandria, Egypt
RELATED CIVILIZATION: Hellenistic Greece
MAJOR ROLE/POSITION: Mathematician

Life. Little is known about the life of Apollonius of Perga (ap-uh-LOH-nee-uhs of PUR-guh), apart from what is found in the preface to his most well-known work, the *Konica* (n.d.; *Treatise on Conic Sections*, 1896; best known as *Conics*). In the preface, he says that he started planning the work in Alexandria at the request of Naucrates, a geometer about whom nothing else is known. Apollonius hastily put together the eight books of the *Conics* so that they would be ready in time for Naucrates' departure. Apollonius later revised the work. Of the eight books, the first four, which offer a basic introduction to the subject, survive in the Greek original. Books 5-7, which contain extensions of these basic principles, are found only in Arabic translation. The last book has been lost. The only other work of Apollonius to survive is *Logou apotomē* (n.d.; *On Cutting Off a Ratio*, 1987), which exists in Arabic translation.

Influence. In *Conics*, Apollonius described the fundamentals of conic sections in such a systematic manner that it became the standard work on the subject in the ancient and medieval worlds. The work was also known in the Arabic world.

ADDITIONAL RESOURCES

Apollonius of Perga. *Conics: Books I to III*. Translated by R. Catesby Taliaferro. Santa Fe, N.Mex.: Green Lion Press, 1998.

The frontispiece from a Latin translation of the Konica *by Apollonius of Perga.* (Library of Congress)

_____. *Conics: Books V to VII*. Edited and translated by G. J. Toomer. Berlin: Springer-Verlag, 1990.

SEE ALSO: Greece, Hellenistic and Roman; Science.
—*Albert T. Watanabe*

APOLLONIUS OF TYANA

BORN: first century C.E.; Turkey
DIED: 104? C.E.; Asia Minor
RELATED CIVILIZATION: Imperial Rome
MAJOR ROLE/POSITION: Philosopher, religious leader

Life. Apollonius of Tyana (ap-uh-LOH-nee-uhs of TI-uh-nuh) was a first century C.E. neo-Pythagorean who became the focus of a small mystical religious movement in the Roman Empire. Most of the information about him comes from the third century C.E. writer Flavius Philostratus, who was commissioned by Empress Julia Domna to write a biography of Apollonius, most likely in order to counteract the influence of Christianity on Roman civilization. Philostratus depicted Apollonius as Christlike in demeanor, power, and the ability to perform miracles. Shrines and other memorials were erected by some of Apollonius's followers to honor and worship him.

Apollonius promoted the Pythagorean ideal—emphasizing occult wisdom, purity, tolerance, and the achievement of divinity. Many Pythagoreans established communities in which philosophical study, vegetarianism, and sexual abstinence were practiced. Apollonius of Tyana was much influenced by that tradition and believed that he was a reincarnation of Pythagoras. Philostratus portrayed Apollonius as a philosophical saint, comparable to Jesus Christ, who was capable of performing miracles such as the raising of the dead.

Influence. For a brief period of time in the third century C.E., a small religious movement of Apollonius's disciples posed a mild challenge to Christianity. The movement later became one of several minor occult sects.

ADDITIONAL RESOURCES

Mead G. R. S. *Apollonious of Tyana*. Chicago: Ares, 1980.

Philostratus. *The Gospel of Apollonius of Tyana: His Life and Deeds According to Philostratus*. Kila, Mont.: Kessinger, 1999.

_____. *The Life of Apollonious of Tyana*. Cambridge, Mass.: Harvard University Press, 1912.

SEE ALSO: Christianity; Julia Domna; Philostratus, Flavius; Pythagoras; Rome, Imperial.

—*Robert L. Patterson*

APOLLONIUS RHODIUS

ALSO KNOWN AS: Apollonius of Rhodes
BORN: between 295 and 260 B.C.E.; Alexandria or Naucratis, Egypt
DIED: late third century B.C.E.; Alexandria
RELATED CIVILIZATION: Hellenistic Greece
MAJOR ROLE/POSITION: Poet, librarian

Life. The Greek poet Apollonius Rhodius (ap-uh-LOH-nee-uhs ROH-dee-uhs) has traditionally been identified with the island of Rhodes—where he may have withdrawn because of a quarrel with his teacher Callimachus or because his poetry had been poorly received. In any case, Apollonius served as director of the famous library at Alexandria from about 260 to 246 B.C.E.

Apollonius's major work is the *Argonautica* (third century B.C.E.; English translation, 1780), a long poem in four sections describing the adventures of a band of Greek heroes aboard the ship *Argo*. The heroes have been given the quest of seizing the Golden Fleece from King Aeëtes of Colchis on the far shores of the Black Sea. The most famous section of the work describes the passion of King Aeëtes' daughter Medea for the expedition's leader Jason.

Influence. Apollonius's *Argonautica* is the most important classical retelling of the myths involving the Golden Fleece. It has sometimes been compared unfavorably to such epic works as the *Odyssey* (c. 800 B.C.E.; English translation, 1616) of Homer, but it embodies a more psychologically sophisticated treatment of human character.

ADDITIONAL RESOURCES

Apollonius Rhodius. *The Argonautika*. Translated with an introduction, commentary, and glossary by Peter Green. Berkeley: University of California Press, 1997.

Beye, Charles Rowan. *Epic and Romance in the Argonautica of Apollonius*. Carbondale: Southern Illinois University Press, 1982.

Hunter, R. L. *The Argonautica of Apollonius: Literary Studies*. New York: Cambridge University Press, 1993.

SEE ALSO: Alexandrian library; Greece, Hellenistic and Roman; Homer; Languages and literature.

—*Grove Koger*

APPAR

ALSO KNOWN AS: Tirunāvukkarashu; Marunīkkiyār; Vāgīsha
BORN: seventh century C.E.; southeast India
DIED: c. 655 C.E.; place unknown
RELATED CIVILIZATIONS: Pallava and Cālukya Dynasties
MAJOR ROLE/POSITION: Poet-saint

Life. Appar (AH-pahr), a Nāyanār poet-saint, lived during the seventh century C.E. in south India, site of the Śaivite Bhakti Movement. This movement produced numerous poet-saints who were instrumental in leaving a legacy of Śaivite hymns in praise of Śiva for the Tamil-speaking people of India. Of these saints, Appar, born in a wealthy Veḷḷala agriculturist family, left the most endearing hymns that became the basis of Tamil Śaivism. He pursued Jainism, mastered its doctrines, and became head of a monastery at Tiruppādirippuliyūr (Pātālipuram). Disenchanted with Jainism, he turned to the veneration of Śiva, whom he believed cured him of a chronic pain. Brought before the Pallava king Mahendravarman I, Appar's convictions converted the king to Śaivism.

Appar's fame spread throughout south India as he composed and sang simple hymns of self-surrender to Śiva (311 of which are still extant), reflecting hope and courage in facing the future. From the boy-saint Sambandar, he received the name Appar (father), and they became lifelong friends. His hymns are referred to as Devāram ("private worship"), a term used to indicate hymns. His last poetical-hymns petitioned Śiva to relieve him of his earthly journey, a prayer answered circa 655 C.E.

Influence. Appar's hymns became the foundation of Tamil Śaivism. They reflect the quintessence of the Vedas and are sung during religious rituals.

ADDITIONAL RESOURCES
Berry, Thomas. *Religions of India*. Beverly Hills, Calif.: Benziger, 1971.
Pillai, S. Vaiyapuri. *History of Tamil Language and Literature*. Madras, India: New Century Book House, 1956.
Ramachandran, T. N. *Tirumurai the Sixth*. Tamil Nadu, India: Dharmapuram Aadheernam, 1995.

SEE ALSO: Jainism; Mahendravarman I; Pallava Dynasty; Vedas.

—*George J. Hoynacki*

APPIAN

ALSO KNOWN AS: Appianus; Appianos of Alexandria
BORN: c. 95 C.E.; possibly Alexandria
DIED: c. 165; possibly Rome
RELATED CIVILIZATIONS: Roman Greece, Imperial Rome
MAJOR ROLE/POSITION: Historian

Life. What little is known of Appian's (A-pee-uhn) life comes from his own writings and letters of his patron, Marcus Cornelius Fronto. He witnessed a "war" against Jews in Egypt, probably by Emperor Trajan in 116/117, and served as an administrator in Alexandria. After moving to Rome, he acted as a "pleader of cases," using rhetorical skills he probably learned as a child; such a position implies equestrian status. With Fronto's help, he was named procurator by Emperor Antoninus Pius. He is best known for his *Romaica* (n.d.; *History of Rome's Wars*, 1912-1913). Written in Greek and from the point of view of the subject peoples rather than the conquerors, it is organized ethnographically rather than chronologically. As a writer, he depended on earlier sources, several of which are no longer extant. More narrative than analytical in his style, he emphasizes financial and administrative matters more than other Roman historians. Twenty-four books survived into the early Middle Ages, but only nine complete and seven fragmentary ones remain.

Influence. Especially important are his discussions of the Third Punic War (149-146 B.C.E.) and the early first century B.C.E.

ADDITIONAL RESOURCES

Appian. *Appian's Roman History*. Vol. 4. Translated by Horace White. Cambridge, Mass.: Harvard University Press, 1972.

Gowing, Alain M. *The Triumviral Narratives of Appian and Cassius Dio*. Ann Arbor: University of Michigan Press, 1992.

Grant, Michael. *Greek and Roman Historians*. New York: Routledge, 1995.

SEE ALSO: Antoninus Pius; Fronto, Marcus Cornelius; Greece, Roman; Judaism; Punic Wars; Rome, Imperial; Trajan.

—*Joseph P. Byrne*

APPIAN WAY

ALSO KNOWN AS: Via Appia
DATE: 312-244 B.C.E.
LOCALE: From Rome to Brundusium (modern Brindisi)
RELATED CIVILIZATION: Republican Rome
SIGNIFICANCE: The construction of this road was the first major building project that linked Rome with another city.

The Appian (A-pee-uhn) Way was one of two major building projects undertaken in 312 B.C.E. by the censor Appius Claudius Caecus. (The other was the Aqua Appia or the Appian Aqueduct.) The Appian Way began at the Porta Capena on the southeast side of Rome, passed through Tarracina (modern Terracina), and ended at Capua, a total of 132 miles (212 kilometers). Later additions extended the road from Capua through Beneventum (modern Benevento) to Venusia (291 B.C.E.; modern Venosa), then to Tarentum (281 B.C.E.; modern Taranto), and finally to Brundusium (244 B.C.E.; modern Brindisi), thus giving Rome access to most of central Italy and to two major ports on the heel of Italy. Portions of the road are still visible outside Rome and along the original section. Tombs of important figures such as the Scipios and Caecilia Metella as well as some of the milestones still grace the roadside.

That Rome had the ability to create such a structure through the territories to the south is a mark of the power that Rome was beginning to wield through its alliances with and conquests of Sabelline and Samnite towns.

ADDITIONAL RESOURCES

Cornell, T. J. *The Beginnings of Rome: Italy and Rome from the Bronze Age to the Punic Wars, c. 1000-264 B.C.* New York: Routledge, 1995.

Richardson, Lawrence, Jr. *A New Topographical Dictionary of Ancient Rome*. Baltimore: Johns Hopkins University Press, 1992.

SEE ALSO: Claudius Caecus, Appius; Navigation and transportation; Rome, Republican; Trade and commerce.

—*T. Davina McClain*

APULEIUS, LUCIUS

ALSO KNOWN AS: Philosophus Platonicus Apuleius
BORN: c. 125 C.E.; Madaura, Numidia
DIED: after 170 C.E.; place unknown
RELATED CIVILIZATIONS: Hellenistic Greece, Imperial Rome, Egypt
MAJOR ROLE/POSITION: Author, orator

Life. Born into a rich, influential family, Lucius Apuleius (LEW-shee-uhs ap-yuuh-LEE-yuhs) was educated in Carthage and Athens, where he mastered Latin and developed a broad knowledge of Greek poets, prose stylists, and philosophers. He traveled widely in the Mediterranean region, developing an interest in contemporary religious initiation rites (particularly Egyptian). His father, a chief magistrate, helped him gain admission to the town senate.

Falling ill on a journey to Alexandria, he was nursed by a rich widow, Aemilia Pudentilla, whom he married. Unfortunately, Pontianus, heir to Pudentilla's fortune, died suddenly, and Apuleius was accused of murder. He defended himself successfully in a long, brilliant speech, which was later published as the *Apologia* (158-159 C.E.; English translation, 1909). He settled in Carthage, traveling to African towns, lecturing in Latin and philosophy.

Apuleius's greatest work was the lively, highly polished *Metamorphoses* (second century; *The Golden Ass*, 1566), the only classical Latin novel to have survived in its entirety. It has many tales (including one about Cupid and Psyche) within its main tale of the strange and marvelous adventures of Lucius, a young sorcerer's apprentice. Transformed into an ass, Lucius regains his human shape only through the intercession of the goddess Isis.

Influence. Apuleius wrote popularizations of Greek philosophy, but his fame rests on *The Golden Ass*, which is representative of a tradition in classical literature extending from Greek poet Homer to French writer François Rabelais, Spanish novelist Miguel de Cervantes, and Italian writer Giovanni Boccaccio.

ADDITIONAL RESOURCES

Haight, Elizabeth Hazelton. *Apuleius and His Influence.* New York: Cooper Square, 1963.

Harrison, S. J. *Apuleius: A Latin Sophist.* New York: Oxford University Press, 2000.

Tatum, James. *Apuleius and "The Golden Ass."* Ithaca, N.Y.: Cornell University Press, 1979.

SEE ALSO: Carthage; Egypt, Ptolemaic and Roman; Greece, Hellenistic and Roman; Languages and literature.

—Keith Garebian

AQHAT EPIC

AUTHORSHIP: Ugaritic text, author unknown, copied by Ilimilku

DATE: 1400-1300 B.C.E.

LOCALE: Ugarit, extinct city near the Mediterranean coast in modern-day Syria

RELATED CIVILIZATION: Israel

SIGNIFICANCE: Late Bronze Age epic text written in Ugaritic; the Ugaritic texts illuminate the cultural, religious, and mythical traditions of Canaan at a time immediately preceding the Hebrew conquest of Palestine.

Excavations carried out by French archaeologists beginning in 1929 at Tell Ras Shamra in Syria revealed the ancient kingdom of Ugarit. The collection of texts discovered there date primarily to the fourteenth century B.C.E. and were written in a previously unknown alphabetic cuneiform script. Once deciphered, Ugaritic turned out to be a northwest Semitic language closely related to Hebrew and Aramaic. The writings include mythological and ritual texts, letters, and administrative documents. Among the most important for understanding the religion of Canaan in the Late Bronze Age is the Baal myth that details the struggle of the storm and fertility god Baal for supremacy over Yammu the sea god, and Motu the god of death.

The Aqhat epic, unfortunately incomplete, was written on three clay tablets. It features Daniel, a childless patriarch, who was granted offspring by El, the high god. After Aqhat was born, Daniel was given a special bow that he passed on to his son. The goddess Anat, consort of Baal, offered gifts, including immortality, to Aqhat in exchange for the bow, which he rejected. Anat then designed the death of Aqhat, after which the land's vegetation withered. Only after Daniel avenged the death of his son did the land find renewal. The Daniel of this epic seems to be the legendary figure of Daniel mentioned along with Noah and Job in Ezekiel 14:12-20 of the Hebrew Bible.

ADDITIONAL RESOURCES

Aitken, Kenneth T. *The Aqhat Narrative: A Study in the Narrative Structure and Composition of an Ugaritic Tale.* Manchester, England: University of Manchester Press, 1990.

Parker, Simon B., ed. *Ugaritic Narrative Poetry.* Atlanta: Scholars Press, 1997.

SEE ALSO: Bible: Jewish; Canaanites.

—Barry L. Bandstra

ARA PACIS

ALSO KNOWN AS: Altar of Peace
DATE: constructed 13-9 B.C.E.
LOCALE: Rome
RELATED CIVILIZATION: Imperial Rome
SIGNIFICANCE: A monument decreed by the Roman senate and erected as a symbol celebrating the return of Augustus from Gaul and Spain and the Pax Augustae (Peace of Augustus).

Construction of the Ara Pacis (AH-rah pah-CIS) began in 13 B.C.E. with dedication on January 30, 9 B.C.E. Originally located on the Via Flaminia, the structure was moved to a location near the Tiber in the 1930's. On the wings of the altar itself, which was approached by steps, were carved reliefs illustrating a sacrificial procession. Sculpted on the interior panels of a marble screen surrounding the altar are reliefs of garlands, *bucrania* (ox skulls), and sacrificial implements. The lower exterior panels, which depict acanthus scrolls containing birds, lizards, and other animals, and the upper east side reliefs of Earth, two babies, and pastoral scenes represent, allegorically, the prosperity brought about by the Peace of Augustus. A Greek key pattern defines the upper exterior panels, on which various Roman historical and mythological scenes are depicted.

The west side panels illustrate Aeneas sacrificing to the Penates. The procession of the family of Augustus on the south side portrays many prominent persons, including Augustus himself, Marcus Vipsanius Agrippa, Livia, Julia, Germanicus, and the future emperor Gaius Caesar Germanicus (Caligula). The north side panels depict the procession of Roman dignitaries. The screen panels represent three layers of relief in a blend of native Italic and Hellenistic styles.

ADDITIONAL RESOURCES

Castriota, David. *The Ara Pacis Augustae*. Princeton, N.J.: Princeton University Press, 1995.
Conlin, Diane Atnally. *The Artists of the Ara Pacis*. Chapel Hill: University of North Carolina Press, 1997.

SEE ALSO: Art and architecture; Augustus; Rome, Imperial.

—David B. Pettinari

ARABIA

DATE: 8000 B.C.E.-700 C.E.
LOCALE: Arabian Peninsula, West Asia
SIGNIFICANCE: The Arabian Peninsula became the setting for the emergence of the Prophet Muḥammad and the rise of Islam, which, with Christianity and Judaism is one of the major monotheistic traditions of the world.

Muslims refer to the period before the revelation of Islam in 622 C.E. as al-Jāhilīyah ("time of ignorance") because knowledge of this long period is of little value in understanding Islam and the period was characterized by religious ignorance of the one God Allāh. The Arabian Peninsula is the only region in the Middle East that has always been known as a Semitic land and is considered to be the original home of the Semitic peoples.

Arabic tradition speaks of two ethnic groups as the seeds of Arabian origin. The ancient Arabs of South Arabia (uh-RAY-bee-uh) claim descent from the patriarch Yaʾrab ibn Qahtan, from whose name the term "arab" is derived, and northern Arabs claim descent from the patriarch Adnan, a descendant of Ismāʾīl, son of Abraham. Almost every Arabic tribe traces its ancestry to these two patriarchs, although no evidence supports such claims. The vast, largely desert peninsula of Arabia was an absolute monarchy ruled under the title al-Mamlaka al-ʿArabīyah as-Suʿūdīyah ("kingdom of the Arabs of the House of Saud").

The peninsula of Arabia is covered by shifting sand in the south central region of Rub ʿal-Khālī, the Empty Quarter, and by eroded sandstone elsewhere. Three thousand years ago, the Rub ʿal-Khālī was less arid and supported abundant fauna and flora. During the Pleistocene Era, central and northern Arabia was a vast lake system. These lakes eventually dried up and formed riverbeds that run from the southeast to the northwest. The southern and southwestern fringes of the peninsula are more humid, allowing agricultural pursuits. The book of Genesis speaks of this area as the "limit of the known world," and the Roman Empire referred to it as Arabia Felix.

Early history. Unlike Europe, Africa, and Asia, Arabia has only sparse evidence of any Stone Age culture; what exists is limited to northern Arabia and is closely associated with cultures of Asia Minor and Mesopotamia. Only scattered archaeological discoveries point to a Paleolithic or Neolithic presence. Although ancient Mesopotamian cuneiform inscriptions contain numerous references to sites in Arabia such as Magan and Dilmun, and Pharaonic Egyptian records describe trade connections with the Sinai and Red Sea areas, very little direct reference to Arabia is found in them.

The earliest centuries of the first millennium B.C.E. were a time of momentous change represented by the Iron Age in the Middle East and migrations of Semitic Arameans into the Fertile Crescent. Little direct knowledge exists from the era before the emergence of historical kingdoms of Maʿīn and Sabaʾ in South Arabia. The early centuries of Arabic history remain obscure at best. Even the chronology of early southern Arabic history is in question.

South Arabian kingdoms. Greek historical records written during the first centuries in the common era mention the existence of four kingdoms in South Arabia dating from the first millennium B.C.E. These kingdoms derived their considerable wealth from caravan trade with the Mediterranean world and maritime trade in the Indian Ocean and the Red Sea. Collectively known as Himyaritic kingdoms, they included the Sabaeans, Qatabānians, and Minaeans.

As early as the fifteenth century B.C.E., agricultural settlements existed in western South Arabia, and by the tenth century B.C.E., an amalgamation of several Arab tribes gave rise to the kingdom of Sabaʾ, associated with the Queen of Sheba, who visited King Solomon in Israel. The mainstay of South Arabian trade was incense: myrrh from the Hadhramaut and frankincense from Dhafar. The kingdoms of Maʿīn and Qatabān appeared, but Sabaʾ retained its supremacy throughout South Ara-

By the death of Muḥammad, shown fleeing to Medina in this woodcut, Arabia had become united under the banner of Islam. (North Wind Picture Archives)

bia. The cities contained monumental temples and other civic buildings, and an elaborate irrigation system made cultivation possible in the countryside.

The Ḥimyarite rule of Sabaʾ resulted in a four-hundred-year period of unity, but Christian and Judaic rivalry present in South Arabia replaced it with an Abyssinian Christian occupation for ninety-nine years, dominated by Monophysite Coptic, Nestorian, and Arian influences, each disputing the divine and human natures of Christ. In the fourth century C.E., the economic strength and stability of the region were severely compromised by the collapse of the famous Maʾrib Dam, which regulated agricultural wealth and power. The Ḥimyarits emigrated to North Arabia. An alliance with Persia drove out the Abyssinians in 571 C.E., a year that coincided with the birth of the Prophet Muḥammad. Among the distinctive features of the South Arabian kingdoms were their script, alabaster stelae, and large-scale Mediterranean-style bronzes.

Nabataea and Palmyra. Assyrian, biblical, and Persian sources provide occasional references to nomadic peoples of the northern fringes of Arabia. However, classical literature provides detailed information about semisedentarized border states in the Syrian and northern Arabian deserts. These states, Arab in origin, were strongly influenced by hellenized Aramaic culture and generally used Aramaic for their inscriptions. The most important was the Nabataean kingdom, which ruled over an area from the Gulf of Aqaba northward to the Dead Sea, including northern Hejaz. Its capital was at Petra, and it made its first contacts with Republican Rome in 65 B.C.E. Friendly relations were established, and the kingdom served as a buffer state between the Roman East and the vast untamable desert. In 25 B.C.E., Nabataea became the base for the only Roman expedition to penetrate Arabia. Intent on conquering Yemen, the Romans wished to control the southern outlet of the trade route to India. Rome failed and withdrew in an ignominious retreat. In 105 C.E., Rome annexed Nabataea into Provincia Arabia.

A century and a half later, a second Aramaized Arab kingdom, Palmyra, was established in the Syro-Arabian Desert, at the starting point of the western trade route. It became a significant power in the region under its first king, Udhayna, who assisted Rome in its war against Persia. His widow, Zenobia, succeeded him and extended Palmyrene influence as far as Egypt in the south and Asia Minor in the north. In 272 C.E., Rome attacked Palmyra, and Zenobia fled, bringing an end to Palmyrene rule.

The rise of Islam. During the fifth and sixth centuries C.E., the dominant feature of northern and central Arabia was Bedouin tribalism. On the eve of the rise of Islam, the wide-open expanse of desert between South Arabia and the northern fringes was the domain of tribespeople who were constantly engaged in tribal warfare, feuding, raiding, and pagan practices. A few cities did emerge and prosper; Mecca and Medina served as trading posts along the extended caravan routes between South Arabia and the Fertile Crescent. Mecca, located at the crossroads of routes that led south to Yemen, north to the Mediterranean, east to the Persian Gulf, and west to the Red Sea, was occupied and governed by the Quraysh tribe. Prospering from the trade that passed through the city, the Quraysh merchants stressed cooperation, organization, and discipline, those qualities that were absent among other roving tribesmen. These qualities would prove invaluable in administering the vast empire soon to fall under Quraysh sway.

Into this environment, the Prophet of Islam, Muḥammad, was born in 570 C.E. By 632 C.E., when Muḥammad died, Arabia had experienced a total transformation from a land of anarchy to a united state under the banner of Islam. This transformation was due to the charisma and leadership of Muḥammad and to the sacred book of Islam, the Qurʾān, an Arabic standard of revelations of widespread appeal, that could serve as a force to unite petty tribes. This appeal opened the way for Islam to reach far beyond the borders of Arabia after Muḥammad's death under the leadership of Abū Bakr, ʿUmar ibn al-Khaṭṭāb, and ʿUthmān ibn ʿAffān, the first three caliphs. Under the leadership of the Umayyad caliphate (661-751 C.E.), Islam expanded Arabic power and conviction into North Africa, the Indus Valley of India, Afghanistan, and Central Asia. However, internal strife began to rear its head in the far-flung empire. A schism over the rightful succession to the caliphate divided the followers of Islam into two camps, Shīʿite and Sunni. This split has continued to the present.

ADDITIONAL RESOURCES

Hitti, Philip K. *History of the Arabs*. London: Macmillan, 1940.

Hourani, Albert. *A History of the Arab Peoples*. Cambridge, Mass.: Farber, 1991.

Lewis, Bernard. *The Arabs in History*. Oxford, England: Oxford University Press, 1993.

Mansfield, Peter. *The New Arabians*. Chicago: J. G. Ferguson, 1981.

SEE ALSO: Abū Bakr; Islam; Muḥammad; Sheba, Queen of; ʿUmar ibn al-Khaṭṭāb; Umayyad Dynasty; ʿUthmān ibn ʿAffān.

—George J. Hoynacki

ARAKANESE

DATE: c. 3000-2200 B.C.E.-700 C.E.
LOCALE: Myanmar
RELATED CIVILIZATION: Ancient Burma
SIGNIFICANCE: Early inhabitants of eastern region of Myanmar.

The Arakanese are an ancient Burmese ethnic group who inhabit the narrow coastal region east of the Arakan Yoma mountain range. The Arakanese claim a remote ancestry that has been variously dated. One account of the group's antiquity claims that the founding of an

Arakan kingdom occurred in 2666 B.C.E. and continued down through a line of some 227 princes. A second version attributes the founding of the first kingdom of the Rakhine (Arakan) Dynasty to a king named Vāsudeva, who married a local princess and became head of a powerful kingdom. Marayu, the couple's son, conquered Vēsalī (Vaiśālī) and founded his capital at Dinnyawadi on the Thari River in 3000 B.C.E. Both accounts tell of the Rakhine extending their rule over all Myanmar and portions of Bengal and southern China. Although neither history nor archaeology confirms these claims, as many as nine dynasties were located in the region of Dinnyawadi until 326 C.E., when King Mahataing of the Chandra Dynasty moved his capital to Vēsalī. Later Burmese chronicles claim that the Arakanese migrated originally from the Irrawaddy Valley. The Arakanese speech is a form of Burmese with an archaic accent.

Although the earliest inscriptions and coins found in Arakan date from the fourth century C.E., evidence exists of earlier kingdoms in the region. The Arakanese were traditionally Buddhist, and the Mahamuni sculpture, which portrays the temptation of the historical Buddha, has been dated by archaeologists to circa 146 C.E. during the reign of Chandra Suriya, when Buddhism was said to have been introduced to Arakan. Early inscriptions also tell of two missionaries who brought Hinduism into the region and founded shrines at Vēsalī.

After 700 C.E., over the centuries, the Mongols, the Pegus, the Portuguese, and the British have invaded and ruled over the Arakanese.

ADDITIONAL RESOURCES

Eliot, Joshua. *Myanmar (Burma) Handbook*. Bath, England: Footprint Handbooks, 1997.

Gutman, Pamela. *Encyclopedia of Asian History*. Edited by Ainslie T. Embree. New York: Charles Scribner's Sons, 1988.

SEE ALSO: Buddhism; Hinduism; Pyu.

—*Katherine Anne Harper*

ARAMEANS

ALSO KNOWN AS: Aramaeans
DATE: 1100-700 B.C.E.
LOCALE: The Levant, especially Syria, and Mesopotamia
RELATED CIVILIZATIONS: Assyria, Babylonia, Israel
SIGNIFICANCE: The Arameans' use of an alphabetic script to represent both the consonants and vowels of a Semitic language led Aramaic to become the international language of the ancient Middle East by the latter half of the first millennium B.C.E.

The term Aramean (ar-uh-MEE-uhn) designates members of groups related by their use of the Aramaic language. Aramaic is a West Semitic language akin to Hebrew and was used by peoples that inhabited western areas of the ancient Middle East in the first millennium B.C.E., especially Syria and Upper Mesopotamia.

History. Groups designated Aramean made their first appearance in historical documents of the eleventh century B.C.E. The origin of the Arameans remains disputed. Some historians suggest they were pastoral nomads of the Syrian desert fringe who moved into Syria and northern Mesopotamia, eventually extending their influence to southern Mesopotamia as well. Other historians argue the Arameans are continuous with the earlier Amorite and Ahlamu populations of Syria who experienced a resurgence of influence in the late first millennium.

The history of the Arameans is difficult to establish because there are only a few indigenous records, consisting almost entirely of inscriptions. Most information about the Arameans comes from Assyrian historical documents and the Hebrew Bible. From these records, it appears the Arameans never established an empire, instead existing as local states dominated by one or more cities, and some tribes.

Most documentary references to the Arameans are in the context of conflict with the Assyrians or the Israelites. Tiglath-pileser I (r. c. 1115-c. 1077 B.C.E.) recorded his struggles with the Arameans in the upper Euphrates region, who were penetrating Assyrian territories and seizing cities. Aramean power was checked by Assyrian rulers toward the end of the tenth century B.C.E., until Tiglath-pileser III (r. 745-727 B.C.E.) finally dominated the Aramean city-states and incorporated them into Assyrian provinces.

Jewish history has multiple points of Aramean contact. The patriarch Jacob was termed "a wandering Aramean" (Deuteronomy 26:5), and his wives Rachel and Leah and father-in-law Laban were Aramean. When both the Arameans and Israelites expanded into Transjordan beginning in the eleventh century B.C.E., they eventually came into conflict. David of Israel (c. 1030-c. 962 B.C.E.) achieved victory over Hadadezer of Aram, bringing parts of Syria under his influence. The rise of the Aramean state of Aram-Damascus during David's son Solomon's reign began two centuries of intermittent warfare between Aram and the state of Israel, now separated from Judah. Tiglath-pileser III of Assyria put an end to Aram in 732 and Israel in 721 B.C.E.

Language. Early Aramaic is attested only by a few inscriptions on stone. However, its later forms came to dominate Mesopotamia for most of the first millennium B.C.E., to the extent that it became the lingua franca of the ancient Middle East. Aramaic, as attested by surviving writings, was widely used in Babylonia, Persia, Egypt, Palestine, and Asia Minor. It displaced Hebrew as the language of the Jewish community, and portions of the books of Daniel and Ezra of the Hebrew Bible are written in it. The Syriac dialect of Aramaic was used extensively by eastern Christian churches during the Roman and Byzantine periods.

Religion. The early Aramaic inscriptions make reference to deities widely honored in Canaanite religion, indicating that Aramean religion was shaped by its broader surroundings. Equivalent to Canaanite Baal, the Aramean storm-fertility god Hadad was typically the head of an Aramean city-state's pantheon. Other significant deities include the Moon god Sin, the patron god of dynasty Rakib-el, and the Sun god Shamash.

ADDITIONAL RESOURCES

Greenfield, Jonas C. "Aspects of Aramean Religion." In *Ancient Israelite Religion: Essays in Honor of Frank Moore Cross*, edited by Patrick D. Miller, Jr., et al. Philadelphia: Fortress Press, 1987.

Pitard, Wayne T. "The Arameans." In *Peoples of the Old Testament World*, edited by Alfred J. Hoerth et al. Grand Rapids, Mich.: Baker, 1994.

SEE ALSO: Assyria; Canaanites; David; Israel; Solomon; Tiglath-pileser III.

—Barry L. Bandstra

ĀRAṆYAKAS

AUTHORSHIP: Composite; attributed to various legendary sages
DATE: eighth-fifth centuries B.C.E.
LOCALE: India
RELATED CIVILIZATION: India
SIGNIFICANCE: Early Indian ritual texts falling between the earlier *Brāhmaṇas* and the later *Upaniṣads* and closely connected to those texts.

Āraṇyakas (aw-RAHN-yah-kah-s; *The Aitareya Araṇyaka*, 1909) are religious texts of ancient India and were probably originally oral compositions. The term *āraṇyaka*, meaning "relating to the forest" (*āraṇya*), seems to mark these as esoteric texts, ideally to be studied by students living ascetically in the secrecy of a relatively uninhabited area of uncultivated forest. They form the concluding parts or continuations of *Brāh-*

maṇas and like them comment on the ancient ritual but display a development in theological and philosophical thought in comparison with older texts. The interiorization of ritual—a symbolic understanding of older ceremonies as a kind of internal worship—begins to appear in the *Āraṇyakas*. This feature occurs more fully in the later *Upaniṣads*, which can form part of an *āraṇyaka*, or appear as an appendix to one.

The *Āraṇyakas* collected a wide range of materials, written in various styles, including prose lists, lengthier prose discussions, verse citations, explanations in a syntactically simple style, legends, and etymologies. They occasionally supplement the *Brāhmaṇas*, covering ritual material not dealt with in the earlier texts. In content, style, and language (the older Vedic dialect of Sanskrit), *Āraṇyakas* are often hard to distinguish from *Brāhmaṇas* and *Upaniṣads*.

ADDITIONAL RESOURCES

Gonda, Jan. *Vedic Literature (Saṃhitās and Brāhmaṇas)*. Vol. 1 in *A History of Indian Literature*. Wiesbaden, Germany: Harrasowitz, 1975.

Keith, Arthur Berriedale. *The Aitareya Aranyaka*. Delhi, India: Eastern Book Publishers, 1995.

SEE ALSO: *Brāhmaṇas*; Hinduism; India; *Upaniṣads*.

—*Burt Thorp*

ARATUS

ALSO KNOWN AS: Aratus of Soli
BORN: c. 315 B.C.E.; Soli, Cilicia, Asia Minor
DIED: c. 245 B.C.E.; Macedonia
RELATED CIVILIZATIONS: Hellenistic Greece, Rome
MAJOR ROLE/POSITION: Poet

Life. Aratus (uh-RAYT-uhs) was born in Soli in Cilicia, where his portrait appeared on later coins. Ancient accounts associate him with many philosophers and poets, most importantly the Stoics Zeno and Persaeus of Citium. Like Persaeus, he accepted the invitation to join the court of another student of Stoicism, Antigonus II Gonatas, king of Macedonia, probably in 277 or 276 B.C.E. The poet may have worked in Syria and died in Macedonia.

Aratus's *Phaenomena* (n.d.; English translation, 1893), the most important example of Hellenistic didactic poetry, is a rendering in hexameter verse of two prose works, Eudoxus's description of the celestial sphere and a Peripatetic treatise on weather signs. Its affinities to the earlier poems of Hesiod were noted in antiquity, and its emphasis on the predictability of the natural world as evidence of divine providence made it particularly popular within Stoicism and later Christianity. Of the large number of other works attributed to Aratus, only two short epigrams survive.

Influence. *Phaenomena* was praised and echoed by Aratus's contemporaries, Theocritus of Syracuse and Apollonius Rhodius, and by Latin poets including Vergil and Ovid. Several translations into Latin survive in whole or part, as do many late handbooks, often illustrated, that use *Phaenomena* as an introduction to the study of astronomy.

ADDITIONAL RESOURCES

Aratus. *Phaenomena*. Translated by Douglas Kidd. New York: Cambridge University Press, 1997.
Lewis, A. M. "The Popularity of the 'Phainomena' of Aratus: A Re-evaluation." In *Studies in Latin Literature and Roman History*, edited by C. Deroux. 9 vols. Brussels: Latomas, 1979-2000.

SEE ALSO: Christianity; Greece, Hellenistic and Roman; Macedonia; Ovid; Philosophy; Vergil.

—*Mary L. B. Pendergraft*

ARAUSIO, BATTLE OF

DATE: October 6, 105 B.C.E.
LOCALE: Arausio (modern Orange, France)
RELATED CIVILIZATIONS: Republican Rome, Germany, Gaul
SIGNIFICANCE: Rome's defeat in this battle furthered the placement of men from nonconsular families in crucial military commands.

Background. About 120 B.C.E., two Germanic tribes, the Cimbri and Teutones, began to migrate south in search of new homelands, gradually being joined by various Gallic peoples. To halt a potential invasion of Italy, the Romans sent out several armies to Gaul between 113 and 107 B.C.E., but all were defeated.

Action. Quintus Servilius Caepio, consul of 106 B.C.E., managed to recover the Roman garrison at Tolosa (Toulouse), which had been lost in 107 B.C.E. His command was prolonged, but reinforcements were sent out under Gnaeus Mallius, consul of 105 B.C.E. Mallius was Caepio's military superior but social inferior, so Caepio disregarded Mallius's command to combine the camps of their armies. Consequently, when the

Cimbri attacked both camps near Arausio (uh-RAW-zhee-oh), Rome's armies suffered devastating defeats, with casualties of eighty thousand men.

Consequences. As a result of this grave defeat, the command in Gaul was given to Gaius Marius by the Roman people in disregard of the traditional right of the senate to award such appointments. Marius, like Mallius, had been the first in his family to hold the consulship. Owing to his success in the Jugurthine War after being elected consul of 107 B.C.E., Marius was thought by the Roman people to be the most suitable choice to curb the threat of an invasion. Marius did not

disappoint and decisively defeated the Germano-Gallic tribes in 101 B.C.E.

ADDITIONAL RESOURCES

Montagu, John Drogo. *Battles of the Greek and Roman Worlds*. Mechanicsburg, Pa.: Stackpole Books, 2000.

Rivet, A. L. F. *Gallia Narbonensis*. London: B. T. Botsford, 1988.

SEE ALSO: Gauls; Germany; Rome, Republican.

—*Leah Johnson*

ARAWAK

DATE: 300 B.C.E.-700 C.E.
LOCALE: Caribbean and South America
SIGNIFICANCE: The Arawak developed a highly sophisticated economic, political, religious, and social system in the Caribbean although the individual groups shared only a common linguistic heritage.

The Arawak (AR-uh-wahk) were a group of South American Indians whose influence stretched from Florida and the Caribbean to Brazil in South America. They migrated from the eastern slopes of the Andes to the Amazon River into the Orinoco Valley, Venezuela, and Columbia. From there, they went out into the Antilles and perhaps even to the Florida Keys. They were superb navigators of the sea. The name "Arawak" refers to a number of indigenous peoples who spoke a similar language but lacked cultural or racial cohesiveness. This linguistic heritage was shared by the warlike and cannibalistic Carib, who lived in the Lesser Antilles in the Caribbean and in northern South America.

Europeans used the term "Arawak" to describe any Indian people who were not hostile to them; they used the term "Carib" to describe any Indian people who were hostile to them. The correct term for the Arawak would have been Locono, or Lokono. The Locono lived in what became Venezuela and called their homeland Aracauy. The original Arawak came from northern South America and were forced out of the area by hostile tribes. They reached the Greater Antilles around 300 C.E. Because all the tribes in the Caribbean and northern South America had a common linguistic heritage, linguists prefer to call all these Indians Arawak.

The economy of the Arawak centered on fishing, hunting, and agriculture. They grew an adequate amount of corn, cassava, sweet potatoes, and various root vegetables. In the Caribbean, the Arawak used trees, plants, and animals for food and supplies. From trees, they made bowls, chairs, baskets, and agricultural and hunting tools. They also developed a very sophisticated political and social structure. Their leaders were caciques, or kings, who ruled with absolute power. The caciques had numerous privileges such as living in special houses, eating certain foods, and receiving special treatment from the groups below them. In the matrilineal Arawak society, rank was inherited through a female line, which meant that a king was succeeded by his eldest sister's eldest son. The caciques ruled over a stratified society in which slaves (*naborias*) made up the lowest tier. In addition to the slaves and the caciques, there were commoners and nobles (*nitaynos*). The Arawak praised and respected not only their caciques but also their priests and medicine men. The Arawak believed strongly in the power of nature during and after death. They revered local wildlife such as deer, dogs, frogs, turtles, and birds. They believed that the soul survived in the trees, rivers, and the rest of the surrounding environment, and they celebrated the beauty of the stars in the heavens.

After 700 C.E. The Arawak population, once estimated to be as high as three million, fell to a few thousand in the sixteenth century because of takeovers (the Carib and Spaniards), enslavement, disease, and damage to their way of living. Some groups died out; however, by 2000, the number of Arawak in Guyana had topped thirty thousand.

ADDITIONAL RESOURCES

Farabee, William Curtis. *The Central Arawaks.* Oosterhout N.B., Netherlands: Anthropological, 1967.

Olsen, Fred. *On the Trail of the Arawaks.* Norman: University of Oklahoma Press, 1974.

Rogozinski, Jan. *A Brief History of the Caribbean: From the Arawak and the Carib to the Present.* New York: Facts on File, 1992.

SEE ALSO: Amazonia; Caribbean.

—*David Treviño*

ARCHAIC NORTH AMERICAN CULTURE

DATE: c. 8000-2500 B.C.E.
LOCALE: North America
RELATED CIVILIZATIONS: California peoples, Dalton tradition, Eastern peoples, Northwest Microblade tradition, Middle Woodland tradition, Plains peoples, Plateau peoples, Southwest peoples, Subarctic peoples
SIGNIFICANCE: The Archaic culture represents the transition in North America from mobile, foraging societies to more sedentary, horticultural societies.

The Archaic period of North America is characterized by generalized foraging patterns and a mobile lifestyle. The Archaic can be divided into three subperiods: Early, Middle, and Late. The Early Archaic dates from 8000 to 6000 B.C.E. and represents the transition from Pleistocene environmental adaptations to Holocene ecological strategies. Early Archaic sites are typically short-term camps with minimal artifactual remains. The distinguishing characteristic is the presence of large side- and corner-notched projectile points. The Middle Archaic, dating from 6000 to 4000 B.C.E., represents a period of decreasing mobility and the intensive utilization of aquatic resources, particularly in the southeastern United States. Middle Archaic sites in this area often contain large amounts of fish and shellfish remains with lesser amounts of other fauna represented. During the Late Archaic, circa 4000 to 2500 B.C.E., sites were occupied for prolonged periods and contain the remains of early domesticated plants, such as gourds, goosefoot, sumpweed, and sunflowers. Early pottery from Georgia, generally without decoration and fiber-tempered, also dates to the Late, or Terminal, Archaic period. The Archaic period in North America is significant in that it is the foundation of the traditions of later cultures in the area.

ADDITIONAL RESOURCES

Fagan, Brian M. *Ancient North America: The Archaeology of a Continent.* London: Thames and Hudson, 1995.

_____. *Oxford Companion to Archaeology.* New York: Oxford University Press, 1996.

Jennings, Jesse D. *Prehistoric North America.* Mountain View, Calif.: Mayfield, 1989.

SEE ALSO: American Paleo-Arctic tradition; Clovis technological complex; Cochise culture; Dalton; Eastern peoples; Great Basin peoples; Maritime Archaic; Middle Woodland traditions; Old Copper complex; Plains peoples; Plateau peoples; Southwest peoples; Subarctic peoples.

—*Renee Beauchamp Walker*

ARCHAIC SOUTH AMERICAN CULTURE

DATE: 7000-2400 B.C.E.
LOCALE: South American continent
RELATED CIVILIZATIONS: Paijan tradition, Itaparica tradition, Amazonia
SIGNIFICANCE: The Archaic culture in South America represents the varied and numerous archaeological cultures of the continent before the development of substantial cultural and social complexity.

The Archaic period in South America is characterized by peoples who are largely hunters and gatherers. This period is sometimes referred to as Lithic or Preceramic.

The Archaic period follows the Paleo-Indian and can be viewed as a period of adaptive radiation and dispersal following the end of the glacial epoch and the disappearance of large land mammals, such as mastodons and other megafaunal species. Human populations begin to move into new habitats and ecological zones, including the western flanks of the Andes, lands along the Orinoco, Amazon, and Parana Rivers, and the high altiplano that lies between the two cordilleras of the Andes and that runs from northwestern Argentina to southern Colombia. This dispersal reflects population growth as well as an increasingly complex adaptation to local environments.

The diet of these peoples came from broad spectrum hunting and gathering within their environments. The production of lithic (stone) tools was predominantly bifacial, and through time, there was an increasing diversity of projectile point styles throughout the continent, which some have argued represents increasing cultural and ethnic diversification. Examples of these local adaptations include the Paijan tradition of coastal northern Peru, a central and south-central Andean hunting and gathering tradition that focused primarily on wild camelids and deer; the Itaparica tradition of the tropical forests of central Brazil, which focused on deer, tapirs, anteaters, lizards, fish, fruits, and especially palms; and the maritime peoples of southern Patagonia and Tierra del Fuego.

After 5000 B.C.E., substantial increases in population density in much of South America led to the development of more complicated cultures and experiments in increasing the abundance of resources. On the central Peruvian coast, cotton was domesticated, and the nets made from it were used to create large surpluses of marine resources. Camelids were domesticated in the Andean highlands of Peru, Chile, and northwestern Argentina after 4000 B.C.E., and in Amazonia, domesticates such as manioc and palm became important. Peoples in these areas became increasingly sedentary as they became more dependent on these domesticated plants.

By 2400 B.C.E., emergent forms of social complexity appeared. On the Peruvian coast, sites such as El Paraíso and Aspero, each with large mound constructions, reflect some form of social hierarchy. Other areas in which complexity appears by this date include the Lake Titicaca basin, Amazonia, and the coastal region of western Ecuador.

ADDITIONAL RESOURCES

Aldenderfer, Mark. *Montane Foragers: Asana and the South-Central Andean Archaic*. Iowa City: University of Iowa Press, 1998.

Moseley, Michael. *The Maritime Foundations of Andean Civilization*. Menlo Park, Calif.: Cummings, 1975.

Rick, John. *Prehistoric Hunters of the High Andes*. New York: Academic Press, 1980.

Schmitz, Pedro I. "Prehistoric Hunters and Gatherers of Brazil." *Journal of World Prehistory* 3 (1989): 117-158.

SEE ALSO: Amazonia; Andes, central; Andes, south; Brazil, Eastern; Caribbean; Paleo-Indians in South America; South America, southern; South American Intermediate Area.

—*Mark Aldenderfer*

ARCHAIC TRADITION, NORTHERN

DATE: 4000 B.C.E.-100 C.E.
LOCALE: Interior Alaska and the Yukon
RELATED CIVILIZATION: Athapaskan
SIGNIFICANCE: The northern Archaic tradition represents groups of northern subarctic peoples who were primarily hunters and fishers.

This poorly defined cultural group includes assemblages that contain a variety of flaked stone tools indicative of the hunting and lake fishing way of life of northern subarctic peoples. Many of the artifacts found are characteristic of other traditions. Lanceolate bifaces similar to those of the Plano tradition, notched spear points like those found in many places in interior North America, microblades and cores like those of the Northwest Microblade tradition, notched pebble sinkers that have a wide geographic distribution, and numerous end scrapers like those found in many hunting cultures occur in the northern Archaic tradition. It is uncertain whether this amalgamation of technologies is the result of interaction and borrowing between existing cultures or of the mixing of components left during short-term occupations by different seasonally migrant peoples. Specialists disagree on the utility of this grouping.

The term was originally proposed by D. D. Anderson as the successor to assemblages of the American Paleo-Arctic tradition at the Onion Portage site. Two phases, Palisades and Portage, were recognized; neither contained evidence of microblade technology. Northern Athapaskan-speaking peoples occupied this region historically, and it is possible that northern Archaic assemblages were left by their ancestors.

ADDITIONAL RESOURCES

Harris, Cole R., ed. *Historical Atlas of Canada*. Vol. 1. Toronto: University of Toronto Press, 1987.

Helm, June, ed. *Subarctic*. Vol. 6 in *Handbook of North American Indians*. Washington, D.C.: Smithsonian Institution Press, 1981.

SEE ALSO: American Paleo-Arctic tradition; Microblade tradition, Northwest; Subarctic peoples.

—*Roy L. Carlson*

ARCHIDAMIAN WAR

DATE: May, 431-March, 421 B.C.E.
LOCALE: Greece
RELATED CIVILIZATIONS: Athens and Sparta, Classical Greece
SIGNIFICANCE: As part of the Peloponnesian War (431-404 B.C.E.), this conflict contributed to the destruction of the Athenian Empire and helped lead to the endless warfare that would ruin Greece in the fourth century B.C.E.

Background. The growth of Athenian power in the fifty years since the Greco-Persian Wars (499-449 B.C.E.) led to war between the Athenian Empire and Sparta's Peloponnesian League.

Action. The Archidamian War (ahr-kuh-day-MEE-uhn; named after the Spartan king Archidamus II) began as a defensive war on the part of Athens, but when Pericles died of the plague in 429 B.C.E., his plan for sheltering in the Athenian-Piraeus fortress while conducting naval raids on the Peloponnesians died with him. Led on by hawkish demagogues such as Cleon of Athens, the Athenians soon began conducting offensive operations and in 425 B.C.E. established a base at Pylos in the Peloponnese, capturing 120 Spartans in the process. Buoyed by their success, the Athenians re-fused a Spartan peace offer, but a year later, Brasidas of Sparta captured the vital city of Amphipolis. In 422 B.C.E., both Cleon and Brasidas, the main obstacles to peace, were killed in a failed Athenian attempt to recapture Amphipolis, and in March, 421 B.C.E., the ultimately ineffective Peace of Nicias was signed, bringing a temporary halt to hostilities.

Consequences. The war produced dangerous divisions in the democracy and a new aggressive imperialism that would ultimately lead to Athens's defeat in the next two decades.

ADDITIONAL RESOURCES

Kagan, Donald. *The Archidamian War*. Ithaca, N.Y.: Cornell University Press, 1974.

Thucydides. "History of the Peloponnesian War." In *The Landmark Thucydides: A Comprehensive Guide to the Peloponnesian War*, edited by Robert B. Strassler. New York: Free Press, 1996.

SEE ALSO: Archidamus II of Sparta; Athens; Brasidas of Sparta; Cleon of Athens; Greece, Classical; Peloponnesian War; Pericles.

—*Richard M. Berthold*

ARCHIDAMUS II OF SPARTA

ALSO KNOWN AS: Arkhidamos son of Zeuxidamos
BORN: early fifth century B.C.E.; Sparta
DIED: 427 B.C.E.; Sparta
RELATED CIVILIZATION: Classical Greece
MAJOR ROLE/POSITION: King, military leader

Life. A member of the Eurypontid royal line, Archidamus II (ahr-kuh-DAY-muhs) of Sparta probably became king in 469 B.C.E. When a great earthquake leveled the city of Sparta five years later, igniting a revolt by Sparta's helots (state-owned serfs), Archidamus rallied the surviving Spartans and defeated the rebels after a lengthy struggle.

When tensions with Athens mounted in 432 B.C.E., Archidamus unsuccessfully urged a delay in declaring war until Sparta was better prepared. He led the first three invasions of Attica in 431, 430, and 428 B.C.E. during the Peloponnesian War (431-404 B.C.E.), doing considerable damage to the Athenian countryside. This strategy proved ineffective, as he had feared, and he could neither lure the Athenian army into battle nor storm Athens's walls. His unsuccessful assaults of

Oenoe (431 B.C.E.) and Plataea (429 B.C.E.) demonstrated Sparta's lack of skill in siege warfare. His strategy of seeking Persian assistance and preparing a fleet eventually proved successful but failed to achieve anything before, or long after, his death.

Influence. Archidamus preserved Spartan power but failed to defeat Athens, though he showed the way to ultimate success in the Peloponnesian War. His name became attached to the first part of that conflict, called the Archidamian War.

ADDITIONAL RESOURCES

Powell, Anton. *Athens and Sparta*. New York: Routledge, 1996.
Thucydides. *History of the Peloponnesian War*. In *The Landmark Thucydides: A Comprehensive Guide to the Peloponnesian War*, edited by Robert B. Strassler. New York: Free Press, 1996.

SEE ALSO: Archidamian War; Greece, Classical; Peloponnesian War.

—*Scott M. Rusch*

ARCHIDAMUS III OF SPARTA

BORN: c. 400 B.C.E.; Sparta
DIED: 338 B.C.E.; Manduria, Calabria (in modern Italy)
RELATED CIVILIZATIONS: Western Classical Greece, Lucania
MAJOR ROLE/POSITION: King of Sparta

Life. Son of Agesilaus II, Archidamus III (ahr-kuh-DAY-muhs) of Sparta led an unimpressive career in the twilight of Spartan greatness. He commanded the relief force that escorted the defeated Spartans back from Leuctra (371 B.C.E.). He successfully led Spartan forces against Arcadia in 368 and 365 B.C.E. The height of his success was his victory over Arcadia and Argos in the "Tearless Battle," in which he routed the enemy without loss to his own forces. When Epaminondas attacked Sparta in 362 B.C.E., Archidamus led a counterattack that saved the city. The Athenian orator Isocrates wrote two open appeals to him to recapture Messenia, which Sparta

had lost in 369 B.C.E., and to continue the war against Thebes. Archidamus officially ascended the throne only in 359 B.C.E.

During the Third Sacred War (355-346 B.C.E.), Archidamus officially supported the Phocians, who had seized and plundered Apollo's sanctuary at Delphi. In the Peloponnese, he unsuccessfully attacked Megalopolis. At the end of the Sacred War, he attempted to take control of Thermopylae to thwart Philip II of Macedonia but failed.

After the Sacred War, Archidamus served as a mercenary to earn money for Sparta. In 346 B.C.E., he won a small victory in Crete before sailing to Tarentum (Taranto). There he defended the Spartan colony against the Lucanians but was killed in action. Many Greeks felt that he deserved his fate because of his aid to sacrilegious Phocis.

Influence. Archidamus III, though a Spartan king, was insignificant. Like his state, he stood in the shadow of greater events.

ADDITIONAL RESOURCE
Cartlege, Paul. *Agesilaos and the Crisis of Sparta*. Baltimore: Johns Hopkins University Press, 1987.

SEE ALSO: Agesilaus II of Sparta; Epaminondas; Greece, Classical; Isocrates; Leuctra, Battle of; Philip II; Sacred Wars.

—*John Buckler*

ARCHILOCHUS OF PAROS

ALSO KNOWN AS: Archilochos
BORN: seventh century B.C.E.; Paros, Greece
DIED: date and place unknown
RELATED CIVILIZATION: Archaic Greece
MAJOR ROLE/POSITION: Poet

Life. The life of Archilochos of Paros (ahr-KIHL-uh-kuhs of PAR-ahs) is revealed in the few remaining fragments of his poetry and by references to him in the works of later writers. The illegitimate son of Telesicles, he left Paros following the surprising end of his engagement to Neoboule. Her father, Lycambes, first approved of and then forbade the marriage, perhaps because Archilochus publicly revealed his illegitimacy. It is said that the satiric verses that Archilochus wrote in revenge were so powerful that the father and daughter hanged themselves. After he left Paros, Archilochus lived as a mercenary, spending much time in the colonial outpost of Thásos. He died in battle after he had established a new form in poetry, the iambus, in which a short syllable followed by a long one defines the meter.

Influence. Songs of triumph written by Archilochus were sung at the Olympic Games, and he composed elegiac epigrams for social occasions. According to Plutarch, a Greek biographer and historian, Archilochus was a major innovator. The Roman poet Horace claimed to have been the first to introduce Parian (Archolochean) iambuses into Latin. Archilochus is considered a founder of the Western literary tradition.

ADDITIONAL RESOURCES
Burnett, Anne Pippin. *Three Archaic Poets: Archilochus, Alcaeus, Sappho*. London: Bristol Classical Press, 1998.
Rankin, H. D. *Archilochus of Paros*. Park Ridge, N.J.: Noyes, 1977.
Will, Frederic. *Archilochus*. New York: Twayne, 1969.

SEE ALSO: Greece, Archaic; Horace; Languages and literature; Olympic Games; Plutarch.

—*Margaret A. Dodson*

ARCHIMEDES

BORN: c. 287 B.C.E.; Syracuse, Sicily
DIED: 212 B.C.E.; Syracuse, Sicily
RELATED CIVILIZATION: Hellenistic Greece
MAJOR ROLE/POSITION: Mathematician, physicist, inventor

Life. Historians know more about Archimedes (ahr-kuh-MEED-eez) than any other ancient mathematician, although they remain unable to determine the chronology of his discoveries and writings. Archimedes spent most of his life in Syracuse, but he may have also studied with scholars in Alexandria. He certainly continued the development of Euclidean mathematics by establishing numerous theorems in solid geometry.

Archimedes invented a water screw for irrigation and perhaps the compound pulley. He wrote the first proof of the law of the lever, that equal weights at equal distances from the fulcrum will balance. He also proved the basic principle of hydrostatics, that a solid immersed in a fluid is lighter than its true weight by the weight of the fluid displaced. The story that Archimedes discovered an important concept while bathing and ran naked through the streets crying, "Eureka" ("I have found it"), is believed to be no more than popular legend. Although his precise process is unknown, he did determine the volume of a gold crown (suspected to be partly silver) by measuring the amount of water that it displaced.

Archimedes. (Library of Congress)

When the Roman army attacked Syracuse, Archimedes helped defend the city with missile launchers and cranes. One of many possibly fanciful stories about Archimedes relates that he was so focused on a geometrical diagram he had drawn in the dirt that he ignored an approaching Roman soldier, who killed the mathematician with a sword.

Influence. The achievements of Archimedes were not widely known during antiquity. Byzantine and Arab mathematicians exploited his methods in the early Middle Ages. His texts were translated into Latin in the twelfth and fifteenth centuries C.E., making Archimedes the principal influence on European geometers. Finally, Archimedes' skill with the mathematical technique known as the method of exhaustion was a precursor of the principles of integration.

ADDITIONAL RESOURCES

Dijksterhuis, E. J. *Archimedes*. 2d ed. Princeton, N.J.: Princeton University Press, 1987.

Stein, Sherman. *Archimedes: What Did He Do Besides Cry Eureka?* Washington, D.C.: Mathematical Association of America, 1999.

SEE ALSO: Aristarchus of Samos; Eratosthenes of Cyrene; Euclid; Greece, Hellenistic and Roman; Hieron II of Syracuse.

—*Amy Ackerberg-Hastings*

ARCHYTAS OF TARENTUM

ALSO KNOWN AS: Archytus
FLOURISHED: 400-350 B.C.E.; Tarentum, Magna Graecia (later Taranto, Italy)
RELATED CIVILIZATION: Classical Greece
MAJOR ROLE/POSITION: Philosopher and politician

Life. Perhaps a friend of the philosopher Plato, Archytas of Tarentum (ahr-KIT-uhs of tuh-REHN-tuhm) is mentioned in Plato's *Menōn* (388-368 B.C.E.; *Meno*, 1769) as a great ruler of Taras or Tarentum, where he served for seven years. He is mainly known, however, as a scientist and mathematician, the founder of mathematical mechanics. He was a second-generation follower of Pythagoras, who sought to explain all phenomena in terms of numbers. Archytas's achievements in geometry, acoustics, and music theory include solving the problem of doubling the cube, the applica-

tion of proportions to musical harmony, and a resultant theory of pitch intervals in which he posited that pitch is related to the movement of air in response to such stimuli as a stringed instrument. Although some of his conclusions are inaccurate, many are correct.

Influence. Only fragments of Archytas's philosophical works on subjects of mathematical or scientific nature survive. Book 8 of Euclid's *Stoicheia* (compiled c. 300 B.C.E.; *Elements*, 1570) probably borrows from Archytas. Other, nonmathematical fragments have been attributed to him but are more dubious because they are on Platonic themes.

ADDITIONAL RESOURCES

Freeman, Kathleen. *Ancilla to the Pre-Socratic Philosophers*. Cambridge, Mass.: Harvard University Press, 1983.

Tejera, V. *Rewriting the History of Ancient Greek Philosophy.* Westport, Conn.: Greenwood Press, 1997.

SEE ALSO: Euclid; Greece, Classical; Plato; Pythagoras.

—*Tammy Jo Eckhart*

ARCTIC SMALL TOOL TRADITION

DATE: c. 2500-1900 B.C.E.
LOCALE: Alaska, Arctic, and Subarctic Canada
RELATED CIVILIZATIONS: Eskimo-Aleut, Athapaskan
SIGNIFICANCE: The earliest North American cultural tradition for which there is significant archaeological evidence.

The earliest human inhabitants of the Americas for whom any scientific evidence exists are generalized as part of the Arctic Small Tool tradition. The ancient people of the American Arctic and Subarctic areas had no written language before the arrival of the Europeans, and all speculation on prehistoric populations is based on linguistic and archaeological evidence. These ancient people, believed to be the ancestors of the Eskimos, Aleuts, and Athapaskans, apparently migrated from Siberia sometime during the last Ice Age. Estimates of the timing involved vary widely among modern archaeologists.

Evidence of the Small Tool tradition has been found primarily in Alaska and the Yukon Territory, which was largely unexplored by Europeans until modern times.

Apparently, these people used implements made mainly of bone and ivory. Spearheads and harpoons for fishing and for hunting seagoing mammals are commonly found. Making their first appearance in the Americas are bows and arrows, which may have been brought from Siberia or developed very early during the North American period. The Arctic Small Tool tradition emerged into what is known as the Dorset culture sometime around 800 B.C.E.

ADDITIONAL RESOURCES

Friedel, Stuart J. *Prehistory of the Americas.* Cambridge, England: Cambridge University Press, 1987.

Swanson, Earl H., Warwick Bray, and Ian Farrington. *The Ancient Americas.* New York: Peter Bedrick Books, 1989.

SEE ALSO: American Paleo-Arctic tradition; Archaic North American culture; Archaic tradition, northern; Dorset culture; Subarctic peoples.

—*Marc Goldstein*

ARDASHĪR I

FLOURISHED: mid-third century C.E.
RELATED CIVILIZATIONS: Persia, Sāsānian Dynasty
MAJOR ROLE/POSITION: King

Ardashīr I (AHR-duh-shur; r. 224-241 C.E.) was the founder of the Sāsānian Dynasty (224-651 C.E.), which originated in Persis in the third century C.E. According to Persian sources, a Zoroastrian priest at the Anahid temple by the name of Bābak married his daughter to Sāsān, and from this union, Ardashīr was born. Bābak also began to assume political power in Persis (205 C.E.), and when Ardashīr came of age, he began the conquest of Persis and the surrounding areas in the name of his family.

The Parthian king, Artabanus V (r. 213-224 C.E.), was the ruler of the Iranian plateau at the time and saw the aspirations of Ardashīr as a mutiny against his authority. Ardashīr met Artabanus at the Plain of Hormizdagān on April 28, 224 C.E., and was able to defeat and kill the Parthian king. From then on, he is said to have assumed the title "king of kings" and commemorated this event on a rock relief at Naqsh-e Rostam. He then began the conquest of all of the Iranian plateau and fought several campaigns against the Romans in the west.

Because his family had the role of caretaker of the fire temple, it appears that Ardashīr wielded both religious and political power. He was also instrumental in the propagation of Zoroastrianism, which became the state religion. His coins give us some idea about his aspirations and beliefs. The legend on the obverse reads: "Mazda-worshiping majesty Ardashīr, king of kings of Iran whose origin is from the Gods." Before Ardashīr passed away, he made his son Shāpūr I (r. 240-272 C.E.) a coregent and minted a coin with both busts presented together to ensure smooth succession of power. His son became king in 240 C.E., but Ardashīr lived several more years during Shāpūr's rule.

ADDITIONAL RESOURCES

Al-Tabarī. *The History of al-Tabarī, the Sāsānids, the Byzantines, the Lakmids, and Yemen.* Vol. 5. Edited and translated by C. E. Bosworth. New York: State University of New York Press, 1999.

Frye, Richard Nelson. "The Political History of Iran Under the Sāsānians." In Vol. 3 of *The Cambridge History of Iran*, edited by E. Yarshater. Cambridge, England: Cambridge University Press, 1983.

Göbl, Robert. *Sāsānian Numismatics.* Brunswick, Germany: Klinklhardt & Bieman, 1971.

Wiesehöfer, Joseph. *Ancient Persia.* London: I. B. Tauris, 1996.

SEE ALSO: Artabanus I-V; Parthia; Persia; Sāsānian Empire; Shāpūr I; Zoroastrianism.

—*Touraj Daryaee*

ARETAEUS OF CAPPADOCIA

BORN: probably second century C.E.; Cappadocia, Roman Empire
DIED: date and place unknown
RELATED CIVILIZATIONS: Roman Greece, Imperial Rome
MAJOR ROLE/POSITION: Physician

Life. Aretaeus of Cappadocia (ar-uh-TEE-uhs of kap-uh-DOH-shee-uh) is known for his accurate descriptions of many diseases, including angina, arthritis, asthma, bipolar disorder, coeliac disease, depressive disorder, diphtherial ulcers, dysentery, elephantiasis, epilepsy, jaundice, migraine, pleurisy, sciatica, senile dementia, and tetanus. He coined the term "diabetes." His practice was eclectic and relied mostly on gentle methods of therapy and compassion. Among the ancients, his skill in observation was second only to that of the physician Hippocrates. His works, collectively called *Aretaiou Kappadokou ta Sozomena* (n.d.; *The Extant Works of Aretaeus, the Cappadocian*, 1856), were written in the Ionic dialect.

Aretaeus was a follower of the pneumatic school of medicine, for which health or disease was determined by gases in the body. Opposed were the humoral school, which sought a balance of four bodily liquids (humors)—yellow bile, black bile, phlegm, and blood—and the solidic or "methodist" school, which, based on Democritean atomism, believed disease to result from disruption of the solid particles making up the body.

Influence. No additional progress was made in diabetes research until Thomas Willis distinguished between diabetes mellitus and diabetes insipidus in 1679. Many of Aretaeus's clinical descriptions retained their authority into the nineteenth century.

ADDITIONAL RESOURCES

Aretaeus of Cappadocia. *The Extant Works of Aretaeus, the Cappadocian.* Translated by Francis Adams. Reprint. Boston: Longwood Press, 1978.

Gordon, Benjamin Lee. *Medicine Throughout Antiquity.* Philadelphia: Davis, 1949.

Robinson, Victor. *Pathfinders in Medicine.* New York: Medical Life Press, 1929.

SEE ALSO: Hippocrates; Rome, Imperial; Medicine and health.

—*Eric v.d. Luft*

ARGEAD DYNASTY

DATE: c. 700-c. 311 B.C.E.
LOCALE: Macedonia
RELATED CIVILIZATIONS: Greece, Macedonia, Thrace

The Argead (ahr-GEE-uhd) Dynasty represented the ruling house of Macedonia for nearly four hundred years. Although the beginnings of the dynasty can be traced as far back as Karanos (eighth century B.C.E.), it was Perdiccas I (r. c. 670-652 B.C.E.) who led a disparate group of adventurers east from the Haliacmon (Aliákmon) River through northern Greece and became head of the Argeadae Macedones.

By the reign of Amyntas I (r. c. 540-498 B.C.E.), the kingdom of Macedonia stretched into Thrace. In an attempt to assimilate with Greece, Amyntas's son, Alexander I, began the pro-Hellenic policy that would characterize much of the rest of the period. Alexander's son, Perdiccas II, united many of the major Greek cities into a federation with Macedonia.

Perdiccas II's son Archelaus continued his father's pro-Hellenic policy and at the same time created routes through the heavily forested region. In part, this was to allow more rapid movements of his armies, improved with the development of iron and bronze armor and weapons.

It was during the reigns of Philip II (r. 359-336) and his son, Alexander the Great (r. 336-323), that the Greek Empire became a world power, stretching to Egypt and east to India. Following the death of Alexander, the Argead lineage continued for another generation, but the kingdom was divided among Alexander's generals.

ADDITIONAL RESOURCES

Ashley, James. *The Macedonian Empire.* Jefferson, N.C.: McFarland, 1998.

KINGS OF THE ARGEAD DYNASTY, C. 700-311 B.C.E.

King	Reign
Perdiccas I	c. 670-652 B.C.E.
Argaios I	652-621
Philip I	621-588
Aeropos I	588-568
Alketas	568-540
Amyntas I	c. 540-498
Alexander I	before 492-c. 450
Perdiccas II	c. 450-c. 413
Archelaus	c. 413-399
Orestes	399-396
Aeropos II	396-393
Pausanias	393
Amyntas II	393
Amyntas III	393/392-370/369
Argaios II	390
Alexander II	370-368
Ptolemy Alorites	368-365
Perdiccas III	365-359
Philip II	359-336
Alexander the Great	336-323
Philip III Arrhidaeus	323-317
Alexander IV Aegeos	323-311

Hammond, Nicholas, and G. T. Griffith. *A History of Macedonia.* Vols. 1-3. Oxford, England: Clarendon Press, 1979.

SEE ALSO: Alexander the Great; Greece, Archaic; Macedonia; Philip II.

—Richard Adler

ARGISHTI I

BORN: date and place unknown
DIED: c. 756 B.C.E.; Urartu, Asia Minor
RELATED CIVILIZATION: Urartu
MAJOR ROLE/POSITION: King

Life. Nothing is known of the life of Argishti I (ahr-GISH-tee) beyond the events of his reign. His annals were copied as early as 1827 by researcher Friedrich Schulz. In these inscriptions, Argishti I claims to have had at least one military campaign in each year of his rule from 780 to 756 B.C.E. This indicates a relatively long period of expansion in which Urartu was seeking an outlet to the Mediterranean Sea.

Influence. This expansion, which reached the upper and middle Araxes (Araks) River valley, brought the Urartu into contact and conflict with the western reaches of the Assyrian Empire. Other inscriptions celebrate Argishti I's role in building and rebuilding temples and towns within Urartu, including the construction of canals.

ADDITIONAL RESOURCES

Piotrovsky, Boris B. *The Ancient Civilization of Urartu.* Translated by James Hogarth. New York: Cowles, 1969.

Zimansky, Paul E. *Ecology and Empire: The Structure of the Urartian State.* Studies in Ancient Oriental Civilization 41. Chicago: The Oriental Institute, 1985.

_____. "The Kingdom of Urartu in Eastern Anatolia." In *Civilizations of the Ancient Near East*, edited by Jack M. Sasson. New York: Scribner, 1995.

SEE ALSO: Assyria; Sarduri I; Sarduri II; Sarduri III; Urartu.

—*Robert D. Haak*

ARIANISM

DATE: c. 320-c. 400 C.E.
LOCALE: Roman Empire
RELATED CIVILIZATION: Imperial Rome
SIGNIFICANCE: The first major heresy in the Christian Church.

This most important Christian controversy in the fourth century takes its name from Arius (c. 260-336 C.E.), a priest in Alexandria. Around 320 C.E., he began preaching (in a tradition traceable to the Greek Christian Origen) that the Son, while divine, was a creature, different in essence and subordinate to the Father. Arius was excommunicated, although he was not without support. The Council of Nicaea in 325 C.E. condemned Arius and his views, adopting the term *homoousios* (of the same substance) to describe the relationship between the Son and the Father. Constantine the Great ended Arius's exile ten years later, and Arius died shortly after.

The controversy simmered until the full boil of the 350's C.E., when Constantius II sought religious uniformity throughout the empire. Saint Athanasius of Alexandria, the anti-Arian bishop, was forcibly ousted, and bishops East and West signed (sometimes under compulsion) various doctrinal formulas. These formulas are referred to as "Arian," though they cover a spectrum of understandings that contradict the Nicene creed.

Such efforts died with Constantius in 361 C.E., although they were revived briefly under Valens (r. 364-378 C.E.). The Council of Constantinople in 381 C.E. essentially outlawed Arianism (ehr-REE-uhn-ihzm) as heresy and confirmed the Nicene position as standard. However, Arianism was dominant among the Germanic peoples (many of whom had been converted under Constantius). Therefore, as the Goths and Vandals moved west and south, they brought Arian Christianity with them. By the end of the sixth century, however, Arianism had virtually disappeared.

ADDITIONAL RESOURCES

Hanson, R. P. C. *The Search for the Christian Doctrine of God: The Arian Controversy, 318-381.* Edinburgh, Scotland: T & T Clark, 1988.

Rubenstein, Richard E. *When Jesus Became God: The Epic Fight over Christ's Divinity in the Last Days of Rome.* New York: Harcourt Brace, 1999.

Williams, Rowan. *Arius: Heresy and Tradition.* London: Darton, Longman & Todd, 1987.

SEE ALSO: Athanasius of Alexander, Saint; Christianity; Constantine the Great; Constantius I-III; Goths, Ostrogoths, Visigoths; Nicaea, Council of; Origen; Valens; Vandals.

—*Mark Gustafson*

ARISTARCHUS OF SAMOS

BORN: c. 310 B.C.E.; Samos
DIED: c. 230 B.C.E.; Alexandria
RELATED CIVILIZATION: Hellenistic Greece
MAJOR ROLE/POSITION: Mathematician, astronomer

Life. Little is known of the life of Aristarchus of Samos (ar-uh-STAHR-kuhs of sah-MOHS) except that he spent at least some years at the museum in Alexandria. He is known for the first heliocentric (sun-centered) theory of the universe. The scientist Archimedes noted that Aristarchus suggested that the Sun and fixed stars remained still while Earth rotated on its axis and revolved around the Sun.

The only work written by Aristarchus that survived is *On the Sizes and Distances of the Sun and Moon.* In this treatise, Aristarchus made the first truly scientific attempt to estimate the size of the solar system. He calculated that the Sun was eighteen to twenty times farther away from Earth than the Moon, which was actually short by a factor of twenty. Still, Aristarchus's measurement was ignored because he also thought the fixed stars were an enormous distance away compared with the Sun.

Influence. The mathematics required for the theory of a moving Earth was unreasonable according to the observations made by later Greek astronomers. Aristarchus was forgotten until mathematicians began to praise him during the Scientific Revolution in order to convince their contemporaries to accept the heliocentric system of Copernicus.

ADDITIONAL RESOURCES

Gingerich, Owen. "Did Copernicus Owe a Debt to Aristarchus?" *Journal for the History of Astronomy* 16 (1985): 37-42.

Heath, Thomas L. *Aristarchus of Samos: The Ancient Copernicus.* Reprint. Bristol, England: Thoemmes Press, 1993.

Wall, Byron Emerson. "Anatomy of a Precursor: The Historiography of Aristarchus of Samos." *Studies in History and Philosophy of Science* 6 (1975): 201-228.

SEE ALSO: Alexandrian library; Archimedes; Greece, Hellenistic and Roman; Science.

—*Amy Ackerberg-Hastings*

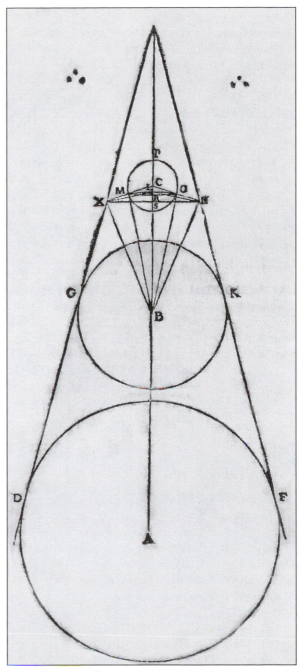

This diagram illustrates Aristarchus's observations and calculations regarding the Sun, Moon, and Earth. He believed that Earth rotated on its axis and revolved around the Sun. (Library of Congress)

ARISTARCHUS OF SAMOTHRACE

BORN: c. 217 B.C.E.; Samothrace
DIED: c. 145 B.C.E.; Cyprus
RELATED CIVILIZATIONS: Hellenistic Greece,
Republican Rome, Egypt
MAJOR ROLE/POSITION: Scholar-librarian

Life. Aristarchus of Samothrace (ar-uh-STAHR-kuhs of sa-MUH-thrays) lived in Alexandria during the reign of Ptolemy VI Philometor (r. 180-145 B.C.E.). He studied under Aristophanes of Byzantium and became the fifth head of the Alexandrian library. He served as a tutor to Philometor's brother, Ptolemy Euergetes II (Ptolemy VIII), and his sons, including Ptolemy VII Neos Philopator, who succeeded his father in 145 B.C.E. Ptolemy Euergetes II had Ptolemy VII murdered in 144 B.C.E. and persecuted the friends of the late king, including Aristarchus. Aristarchus escaped to Cyprus and died shortly afterward.

Aristarchus was most renowned for his Homeric scholarship. He produced two recensions of the Homeric text and commentaries on these editions. Although these works have been lost, parts of Aristarchus's scholarship have been preserved in the scholia of the Venetian codex of Homer's *Iliad* (c. 800 B.C.E.; English translation, 1616). Aristarchus also produced editions and commentaries on other poets and playwrights, including a commentary on Herodotus, the first on a prose writer. In these works, Aristarchus attempted to interpret a writer through the writer's use of language.

Influence. With Aristarchus, Homeric scholarship in Alexandria was regarded as reaching its zenith. Through his followers, his insights were preserved in the scholia. His method of interpreting a writer through the writer's works furnished a model for later scholarship.

ADDITIONAL RESOURCES

Lamberton, Robert, and John J. Keaney, eds. *Homer's Ancient Readers: The Hermeneutics of Greek Epic's Earliest Exegetes*. Princeton, N.J.: Princeton University Press, 1992.
Pfeiffer, R. *History of Classical Scholarship*. Oxford, England: Oxford University Press, 1968.

SEE ALSO: Alexandrian library; Greece, Hellenistic and Roman; Egypt, Ptolemaic and Roman; Homer; Ptolemaic Dynasty; Rome, Republican.

—*Albert T. Watanabe*

ARISTIDES

ALSO KNOWN AS: Publius Aelius Aristides
Theodorus
BORN: 117 C.E.; Hadriani in Mysia (later
northwestern Turkey)
DIED: c. 181 C.E.; Mysia
RELATED CIVILIZATION: Imperial Rome
MAJOR ROLE/POSITION: Sophist

Life. Aristides (ar-uh-STID-eez) was a famous speaker and writer of the Second Sophistic, a period under the Roman Empire when people could attain wealth and high office because of their rhetorical accomplishments. Much of his work survives, including scores of speech texts, hymns that he wrote to pagan deities, and a record of 130 of his dreams over a twenty-five-year period (translated as *Sacred Tales*, 1968). Born into a wealthy, culturally Greek family enfranchised as Roman citizens and well educated in rhetoric, he fell ill on his first speaking tour to Egypt in 142 C.E. Several years of invalidism followed, some of which he spent trying to restore his health by living in the temple of Asclepius (god of healing) at Pergamum. The *Sacred Tales* record instructions received from Asclepius in dreams. After about 147 C.E., he had a successful career speaking, writing, and teaching rhetoric; he also fought legal battles to avoid performing various civic offices. He suffered smallpox in 165 C.E., appealed to the emperor for help for the city of Smyrna after its destruction by an earthquake in 177 C.E., and died at the age of sixty-three.

Influence. Aristides' works were used in teaching as models of rhetorical excellence for hundreds of years. He is also of interest to medical historians because of his unusually detailed record of illness and treatment.

ADDITIONAL RESOURCES
Behr, C. A., trans. *Aristides*. 2 vols. Cambridge, Mass.: Harvard University Press, 1973.
Russell, D. *Antonine Literature*. Oxford, England: Clarendon Press, 1990.

SEE ALSO: Philosophy; Rome, Imperial; Second Sophistic.

—Janet B. Davis

ARISTIDES OF ATHENS

ALSO KNOWN AS: Aristides the Just
BORN: late sixth century B.C.E.; place unknown
DIED: c. 467 B.C.E.; place unknown
RELATED CIVILIZATIONS: Classical Greece, Persia
MAJOR ROLE/POSITION: Statesman, general, admiral

Life. Aristides (ar-uh-STID-eez) of Athens commanded his tribal contingent when the Athenians defeated the Persians at the Battle of Marathon (490 B.C.E.), and he served as archon in 489 B.C.E. In 482 B.C.E., political rivalry led to his ostracism. However, he returned to Athens in 480 B.C.E. under the general recall of ostracized citizens at the time of Xerxes I's invasion of Greece, and he led the Athenian forces that fought as part of the Greek army that defeated the Persians at the Battle of Plataea (479 B.C.E.).

The next year, when the Spartan Pausanias led a naval expedition eastward against the Persians, Aristides was in command of the supporting Athenian fleet. After Pausanias fell from favor, Aristides, who enjoyed the confidence of the allied Greeks, was instrumental in founding (477 B.C.E.) the Delian League, a confederacy whose purpose was to continue the war against Persia under Athenian leadership.

Influence. Aristides' influence was both moral and political. His reputation for integrity provided a paradigm for later generations, and the Delian League became the instrument by which Athens established its maritime empire.

ADDITIONAL RESOURCES
Herodotus. *The Histories*. Translated by Robin Waterfield. New York: Oxford University Press, 1998.
Plutarch. *The Rise and Fall of Athens: Nine Greek Lives by Plutarch*. Translated by Ian Scott-Kilvert. London: Penguin, 1960.

SEE ALSO: Athens; Greece, Classical; Marathon, Battle of; Pausanias of Sparta; Persia; Plataea, Battle of; Xerxes.

—Hubert M. Martin, Jr.

ARISTIDES OF MILETUS

BORN: c. late second century B.C.E.; place unknown
DIED: c. early first century B.C.E.; place unknown
RELATED CIVILIZATIONS: Hellenistic Greece, Republican Rome
MAJOR ROLE/POSITION: Author

Life. Nothing is known about Aristides of Miletus's (ar-uh-STID-eez of mi-LEE-tuhs) life except that his name is associated with the *Milesian Tales*, a collection of Greek short stories, often erotic or obscene in nature. Whether he is the actual author or only the compiler of these tales, of which only a single fragment remains, is uncertain. The historian Plutarch reports that a copy of Aristides' book was found among the effects of a Roman officer following the Battle of Carrhae in 53 B.C.E. The *Milesian Tales* was translated into Latin by Cornelius Sisenna. Ten fragments of this Latin translation survive. Some of these tales may include the story of "The Widow of Ephesus" told in Petronius Arbiter's *Satyricon* (c. 60 C.E.; *The Satyricon*, 1694) and the story of the ass, which is the main plot of Lucius Apuleius's *Metamorphoses* (second century C.E.; *The Golden Ass*, 1566).

Influence. Aristides' *Milesian Tales* may represent the beginning of the Greco-Roman short story genre and had a significant effect on the development of the ancient novel, especially in Rome, where the term "Milesian tale" came to mean any erotic story. Aristides' work influenced not only Latin novels such as Petronius Aribiter's *Satyricon* and Lucius Apuleius's *Metamorphoses* but also later works such as Boccaccio's *Decameron: Precipe Galetto* (1349-1351 C.E.; *The Decameron*, 1620).

ADDITIONAL RESOURCES
Trenkner, Sophie. *The Greek Novella in the Classical Period*. New York: Garland, 1987.
Walsh, P. G. *The Roman Novel*. London: Bristol Classical, 1995.

SEE ALSO: Apuleius, Lucius; Carrhae, Battle of; Greece, Hellenistic and Roman; Petronius Arbiter; Plutarch; Rome, Republican.

—*Thomas J. Sienkewicz*

ARISTOPHANES

BORN: c. 450 B.C.E.; Athens, Greece
DIED: c. 385 B.C.E.; Athens, Greece
RELATED CIVILIZATION: Classical Greece
MAJOR ROLE/POSITION: Comic poet

Life. Born the son of Philippus into a privileged family in the heyday of Classical Athens, Aristophanes (ar-uh-STAHF-uh-neez) wrote comedies and entered them in the competitions held at the annual Dionysia and Lenaea festivals. His *Daitales* (427 B.C.E.; *Banqueters*, now lost) won second prize in 427 B.C.E. and there followed a career of more than forty plays in as many years. Of his personal life, little is known; he had three sons and held no significant political office.

Aristophanes is the best known of a group of poets who produced what is termed Old Comedy. This was a carnivalesque form, with its origins in rituals of fertility and verbal abuse. Its defining features were grotesque costumes, obscene language, and fantastic plots. It made fun of individuals, institutions, and issues of the day. Each play centered on a formal debate, an *agōn*, where a matter of topical interest was argued.

Eleven of Aristophanes' plays survive. They include *Nephelai* (423 B.C.E.; *The Clouds*, 1708), which pokes fun at Socrates and the new educational techniques of the Sophists, and *Batrachoi* (405 B.C.E.; *The Frogs*, 1780), in which Dionysus holds a contest to see if Aeschylus or Euripides is the better tragedian. For much of Aristophanes' career, Athens was at war with Sparta, and several of his plays deal with the question of war versus peace. In the *Lysistratē* (411 B.C.E.; English translation, 1837), the women of Athens seize power in order to end the war, and *Ornithes* (414 B.C.E.; *The Birds*, 1824) describes the construction of a new utopian city in the sky, Cloudcuckooland, as an escape

from war-weary Athens. From *Eirēnē* (421 B.C.E.; *Peace*, 1837), it is clear that Aristophanes was opposed to the continuation of the war after the abortive Peace of Nicias in 421 B.C.E. and that he was out of sympathy with the radical democrats in the city. His plays appear to voice cautionary, even conservative, views and have been seen as a kind of "unofficial opposition" to the policies of prowar leaders such as Cleon of Athens.

Aristophanes. (Library of Congress)

In his last play, *Ploutos* (388 B.C.E.; *Plutus*, 1651), Aristophanes begins the turn toward descriptions of ordinary lives and family relationships that defines his successors in new comedy. Old Comedy was the unique product of a specific cultural setting, the radical democracy of the late fifth century in Athens, and was never recreated.

Influence. Although recognized as the sole surviving representative of Old Comedy, Aristophanes has not been central to the Classical tradition or to the later development of comedy. Traces of influence can, however, be detected in the Roman satirist Juvenal, Greek satirist Lucian, English playwright Ben Jonson, and French dramatist Jean Racine, as well as in some of the more topical and satirical modern television programs.

ADDITIONAL RESOURCES

Cartledge, P. *Aristophanes and His Theater of the Absurd*. London: Bristol Classical Press, 1999.

Dover, K. J. *Aristophanic Comedy*. Berkeley: University of California Press, 1972.

Henderson, J., trans. *Aristophanes*. Cambridge, Mass.: Harvard University Press, 1998.

MacDowell, *Aristophanes and Athens: An Introduction to the Plays*. New York: Oxford University Press, 1995.

Russo, C. F. *Aristophanes: An Author for the Stage*. New York: Routledge, 1997.

SEE ALSO: Aeschylus; Cleon of Athens; Euripides; Greece, Classical; Languages and literature; Performing arts; Socrates.

—David H. J. Larmour

ARISTOTLE

BORN: 384 B.C.E.; Stagirus, Chalcidice, Greece
DIED: 322 B.C.E.; Chalcis, Euboea, Greece
RELATED CIVILIZATIONS: Hellenistic Greece, Macedonia
MAJOR ROLE/POSITION: Philosopher

Life. Aristotle was the son of Nicomachus, the court physician for the royal Macedonian household of King Amyntas II. He originally studied medicine, but at the age of seventeen, he went to Athens and entered Plato's Academy. At the time, Plato's Academy was a place for extensive study of all knowledge. This broad education is reflected in the eclectic nature of Aristotle's writing. Aristotle remained at the Academy until Plato's death in 347 B.C.E. He then went to Asia Minor to the court of King Hermias of Assos. There Aristotle most likely gave lectures to former disciples of Plato.

In 338 B.C.E., he returned to Macedonia and tutored the son of King Philip II, Alexander the Great. After leaving Macedonia, Aristotle returned to his native town of Stagirus and pursued scientific research. In 334 B.C.E., Aristotle returned to Athens and founded his own school, the Lyceum. For the next eleven years Aristotle taught two distinct groups of people. In the mornings, he conducted technical and advanced discourse on logic, philosophy, and science with his students. In the afternoons, he held sessions for the general public on rhetoric, politics, and ethics and discussed

Aristotle. (Library of Congress)

popular issues. Aristotle also created a library with an extensive collection of manuscripts, maps, and museum objects, which he used in his teaching. This library became the model for later state libraries at Alexandria and Pergamum.

Following the death of Alexander the Great in 323 B.C.E., Athens became the center of anti-Macedonian feelings, and Aristotle's connections to Macedonia made him suspect. Aristotle was charged with impiety, the same charge that had been brought against Socrates. This charge was based on a hymn Aristotle had written on Hermias. Unlike Socrates, however, Aristotle left Athens, saying he would not let the Athenians sin twice against philosophy. He went to Chalcis (Khalkís), on Euboea, a stronghold of Macedonian influence, where he died in 322 B.C.E.

Influence. Aristotle's writings covered almost every field of knowledge. He wrote six treatises on logic. He also wrote on natural science, zoology, psychology, basic philosophy, ethics, political science, oratory, and poetry. Aristotle developed a systematic and pluralistic concept about the nature of science. He believed that there was not a single unified science; rather, the totality of knowledge was divided into independent disciplines. He identified theology, mathematics, and the natural sciences as theoretical, ethics and politics as practical, and poetics and rhetoric as productive. In addition, he felt that there was no single set of concepts capable of giving structure to all these disciplines, no single method that the disciplines must follow, and no single standard of scientific rigor. The breadth of Aristotle's influence is unmatched in the history of human thought, and many of his works remain relevant to issues in the contemporary era.

ADDITIONAL RESOURCES

Barnes, Jonathan. *Aristotle and His Philosophy.* Chapel Hill: University of North Carolina Press, 1982.

_____, ed. *The Cambridge Companion to Aristotle.* Cambridge, England: Cambridge University Press, 1995.

Bostock, David. *Aristotle's Ethics.* Oxford, England: Oxford University Press, 2000.

SEE ALSO: Alexander the Great; Greece, Hellenistic and Roman; Macedonia; Philosophy, Plato.

—*William V. Moore*

ARKAMANI

ALSO KNOWN AS: Arqamani; Ergamenes
FLOURISHED: 248-220 B.C.E.
RELATED CIVILIZATIONS: Meroe, Nubia
MAJOR ROLE/POSITION: Meroitic king

Life. Arkamani (ar-ka-MAH-nee) was one of a long line of rulers in the independent Nubian kingdom of Meroe, which existed some six hundred years. His name, like those of many Meroitic kings and queens, is compounded with the name of the major Egyptian god Amun. Although there were periods of strained relations between Meroe and Egypt, Arkamani ruled from 248 to 220 B.C.E., during a time of peace, as evidenced by his collaboration with Ptolemy IV Philopator in the construction of temples at Philae and Dakka. The location of the temple at Dakka indicates that Meroitic power under Arkamani had extended as far north as the First Cataract of the Nile. Arkamani was said to have had some Greek education. He is the only Meroitic king mentioned by name in classical literature, in which he is referred to as Ergamenes. A group of pyramids at Meroe forms what is known as the North Cemetery, the main royal burial ground. Arkamani is one of the earliest kings to be buried there.

Influence. The Greek historian Diodorus Siculus wrote that a tradition among the Meroites required their rulers to obey the priests of Amun even if ordered to commit suicide. This arrangement was said to have ended when Arkamani ordered the priests to be killed so that he could rule in his own way.

ADDITIONAL RESOURCES

Burstein, Stanley M., ed. *Ancient African Civilizations: Kush and Axum.* Princeton, N.J.: Markus Wiener, 1998.

Shinnie, Peter L. *Meroe: A Civilization of the Sudan.* New York: Frederick A. Praeger, 1967.

Taylor, John. *Egypt and Nubia.* London: British Museum Press, 1991.

SEE ALSO: Africa, East and South; Egypt, Ptolemaic and Roman; Napata and Meroe; Nubia.

—*Craig E. Lloyd*

ARMENIA

DATE: c. 2000 B.C.E.-653 C.E.

LOCALE: Asia Minor, Caucasus (modern Turkey and Armenia)

RELATED CIVILIZATIONS: Assyria, Greece, Persia, Rome

SIGNIFICANCE: Long a bone of contention among and "buffer state" between surrounding countries, particularly Rome and Persia, Armenia was arguably the first country to adopt Christianity.

Ancient Armenia extended considerably to the south and west of the modern country, including much of what is now Turkey east of the Euphrates. The earliest known inhabitants were related culturally to the neighboring Hittites, who spoke an Indo-European language, but the language spoken in this area by these people belonged to the Caucasian group. As a result of an invasion by peoples coming from either the north or the west no earlier than the eighth century B.C.E., an early form of the present Armenian language, also Indo-European, was imposed. From about 830 to 640 B.C.E., the kingdom of Urartu, the same word as "Ararat" (the mountain where Noah's ark landed according to the Book of Genesis), occupied the territory of the later Armenian kingdom. Much of the extant evidence is from Assyrian sources, indicating hostility between the kingdom and Assyria.

The word "Armenia" first appears in an inscription of the Persian king Darius the Great dating from 521 B.C.E. Under Assyrian and then Persian rule, the area provided horses and cavalrymen to the ruling group. The Persians restored partial independence to Armenia under two Armenian dynasties: Tirabazus in the north and Erwant or Orontes in the south. This political system continued under Alexander the Great and his successors in Asia, the Seleucids. After the Seleucid king Antiochus the Great was defeated by Rome in 189 B.C.E., complete political independence returned, although the country was not united for almost a century. Greek influence, attested by inscriptions, became extremely strong under the Seleucids and afterward in the north as well as the south. Greek poetry was studied, and Greek plays were read and may have been performed.

In about 98 B.C.E., the Parthian dynasty of Persia, Armenia's eastern neighbor, set up Tigranes the Great as king in return for territory. Tigranes united Armenia in 95 B.C.E. and then conquered much of the area between the eastern shore of the Mediterranean and central Persia, giving internal independence to Greek cities that supported him and generally favoring Greek culture. He established Tigranocerta (modern Silvan) as his capital in southern Armenia, populating it in part with Greeks exiled from cities that had opposed him unsuccessfully, and called himself by the Persian title "king of kings." In 69 B.C.E., Tigranes, owing to his alliance with Mithradates VI Eupator, king of Pontus, found himself at war with Rome. Three years later, after surrendering to the Roman general Pompey the Great, he lost his territory other than Armenia proper and became a vassal of Rome.

Under the descendants of Tigranes and the members of a later dynasty founded by Tiridates I in about 51 C.E., Armenia was fought over repeatedly by Rome and the Parthian and later Sāsānian Dynasties of Persia. Generally it was nominally a Roman protectorate while in fact sympathizing with Persia. During the war of 114-117 C.E., Armenia was temporarily annexed by Rome. Areas to the south, known as "lesser Armenia," were held by a variety of kingdoms allied to Rome during the century beginning in 60 B.C.E., later becoming part of the Roman province of Cappadocia.

For about a century, beginning in the early third century C.E., Persian influence was strong and Zoroastrianism was the prevailing religion. However, circa 300 C.E., Saint Gregory, known as "the Illuminator" (240-332 C.E.), believed to have been a Parthian chief's son sent to Roman Cappadocia to be educated, converted King Tiridates III (r. c. 287 to 330 C.E.) to the Christian religion ten years before the conversion of the Roman emperor Constantine the Great. The Greek Christians had consecrated Gregory as vicar-general of Armenia, but not long afterward, an independent Armenian church, still in existence and using Armenian exclusively in its services, was established. In the opinion of modern scholars, much of Armenia had already been converted to Christianity in the forms of Nestorianism and other heresies, before Gregory's time.

The new religious situation meant alliance with Rome after Constantine's conversion, and strife with still-Zoroastrian Persia. Wars with Persia greatly weakened Armenia politically. Circa 387 C.E., Rome and Persia divided Armenia into spheres of influence, the divided country reverting to semi-independence. Culturally, Armenia continued to flourish with the invention of an Armenian alphabet by Saint Mesrop in about

400 C.E. and the development of a national literature, at first mostly religious. Since about 500 C.E., the Armenian church has been Monophysite, denying that Christ has two natures, one divine, one human. In this respect, the Armenian church resembles the Copts of Egypt and the Ethiopian church, differing from nearly all other branches of Christianity.

Most of the first Armenian Christian clergy were converted pagan priests; the hereditary nature of the priesthood is a pagan survival. Armenian priests wear hoods shaped like the peak of Mount Ararat.

In 451 C.E., a "holy war" between Armenia and Persia resulted in failure to conquer the latter country. In 653 C.E., the Muslim Arabs conquered the country, gradually becoming the majority of the population of the area now part of Turkey, although Armenians continue to live there. At an uncertain date, an Armenian diaspora, consisting mostly of merchants, began to spread through the eastern Mediterranean region.

ADDITIONAL RESOURCES

Colledge, M. A. R. *The Parthians*. New York: Praeger, 1967.

Hovannisian, Richard G. *The Armenian People from Ancient to Modern Times*. New York: St. Martin's Press, 1997.

Luttwak, E. N. *The Grand Strategy of the Roman Empire from the First Century* A.D. *to the Third*. Baltimore: Johns Hopkins University Press, 1976.

Sherwin-White, A. M. *Roman Foreign Policy in the East*. Oxford, England: Clarendon Press, 1984.

SEE ALSO: Antiochus the Great; Assyria; Christianity; Darius the Great; Greece, Hellenistic and Roman; Hittites; Mithradates VI Eupator; Parthia; Persia; Pompey the Great; Rome, Republican; Sāsānian Empire; Seleucid Dynasty; Tigranes the Great; Urartu; Zoroastrianism.

—Stephen A. Stertz

ARMINIUS

ALSO KNOWN AS: Armin; Hermann
BORN: c. 17 B.C.E.; place unknown
DIED: 19 C.E.; place unknown
RELATED CIVILIZATIONS: Germany, Imperial Rome
MAJOR ROLE/POSITION: Military leader

Life. Arminius of the Germanic Cheruscan tribe came in contact with the Romans who had occupied and ruled ancient Gaul, the area known today as France. He served in the Roman army in Gaul from 4 to 6 C.E., rising to the rank of military tribune under emperor Augustus and receiving Roman citizenship.

In 9 C.E., to stop Germanic raids into Gaul, the Romans decided to extend the empire into territories east of the Rhine inhabited by Germanic tribes. Arminius, well versed in Roman military tactics, organized an alliance of several Germanic tribes and met three legions led by the Roman governor Publius Quinctilius Varus in the Battle of Teutoburg Forest. Arminius lured the heavily armored Roman legions and their huge baggage into the dense forests of Germany, where they became immobilized in the swampy terrain and were easy prey for the German warriors, who used guerrilla tactics. About 20,000 Roman soldiers were slaughtered in the fight; Varus and many of his officers committed sui-

cide. The defeat of the professional Roman army by barbarians shattered Roman belief in its invincibility and superiority.

Influence. The devastating Roman defeat at Teutoburg Forest ended Rome's attempts to colonize German territories east of the Rhine and north of the Danube.

During the romantic nationalism in the nineteenth century, historians used the German version of Arminius's name, and he entered the history books of that period as Hermann the Cheruscan, Germany's first national hero. He became the national symbol of Germanic military prowess, signifying that Germans had never been a conquered or enslaved people.

ADDITIONAL RESOURCES

Herwig, Holger H. *Hammer or Anvil?* Lexington, Mass.: D. C. Heath, 1994.

Holborn, Hajo. *A History of Modern Germany*. Princeton, N.J.: Princeton University Press, 1982.

SEE ALSO: Gauls; Germany; Quinctilius Varus, Publius; Rome, Imperial; Teutoburg Forest, Battle of.

—Herbert Luft

The Germanic leader Arminius is depicted after his victory over the Romans in the Battle of Teutoburg Forest. (North Wind Picture Archives)

ARRIA THE ELDER

ALSO KNOWN AS: Arria Major
BORN: c. 1 C.E.; place unknown
DIED: 42 C.E.; place unknown
RELATED CIVILIZATION: Imperial Rome
MAJOR ROLE/POSITION: Senator's wife, heroine

Life. Arria (AR-ree-uh) the Elder was the wife of Caecina Paetus. When her husband was condemned to death for his part in the conspiracy of Lucus Arruntius Camillus Scribonianus by Claudius in 42 C.E., she showed him how to die by stabbing herself, then handing the dagger to him with the words "Paete, *non dolet*" (Paetus, it does not hurt). According to the letters of Pliny the Younger, she denounced Scribonianus's wife, Vinicia, who had volunteered evidence of the revolt. Historian Dio Cassius gives similar details, but says that Arria's intimacy with Valeria Mes-

sallina could have earned her a post of honor.

She was the first of a line of heroic women. Her daughter, Arria the Younger, married Publius Clodius Thrasea Paetus, a practitioner of Stoicism and a senator renowned for moral rectitude. In 66 C.E., she tried to die with her condemned husband but was persuaded to stay alive for the sake of their daughter, Fannia, Arria's granddaughter. Fannia later married Helvidius Priscus, a serious student of Stoicism whose criticism of the Flavian emperors led to his exile by 75 C.E. and subsequent execution.

Influence. Arria's life has drawn the interest of a number of writers, including French writer Michel Eyquem de Montaigne, British writers Joseph Addison and Hester Lynch Piozzi (Mrs. Thrale), and German writers Friedrich Maximilian von Klinger, Adolf von Wilbrandt, and Johann Heinrich Merck.

ADDITIONAL RESOURCES
Howell, Peter. *A Commentary on Book One of the Epigrams of Martial*. London: Athlone, 1980.
Syme, Ronald. *Roman Papers VII*. Edited by Anthony Birley. Oxford, England: Clarendon Press, 1991.

SEE ALSO: Claudius; Dio Cassius; Messallina, Valeria; Pliny the Younger; Rome, Imperial.

—*Michele Valerie Ronnick*

ARRIAN

ALSO KNOWN AS: Flavius Arrianus
BORN: c. 89 C.E.; Nicomedia, Bithia (later İzmit, Turkey)
DIED: c. 155 C.E.; place unknown
RELATED CIVILIZATIONS: Imperial Rome, Roman Greece
MAJOR ROLE/POSITION: Administrator, historian, soldier

Life. The great wealth of Arrian's (AR-ree-uhn) family allowed him to follow interests in literature, rhetoric, and philosophy as well as in hunting and generalship. As a youth, he studied Stoicism under the charismatic teacher Epictetus and recorded Epictetus's classroom lectures as he imagined Xenophon recorded Socrates' words. Under Hadrian, he became a Roman senator and governor of Cappadocia. There he defeated the Alani, who had invaded in 135 C.E. In 145/146 C.E., he was archon in Athens.

A man of action, he took time, however, to write up accounts of interests and exploits. Extant are *The Anabasis of Alexander* (translation 1971), *On India* (translation 1976), *On Hunting* (translation 1964), *Circumnavigation of the Black Sea* (translation 1805), *Taktika* (c. 136-137; *Tactics*, 1994), *Battle Formation*

Against the Alans (translation 1973), and *Enchiridion* (n.d.; known as the *Manual of Epictetus*, 1916). Four of the eight books of Arrian's collection of Epictetus's *Discourses* (translation 1916) have survived as well as portions of *Parthica* (fragments, translation 1994), and *Events After Alexander* (fragments, translation 1989). The lost works include *Dion, Timoleon, Tillorobus, Bithyniaca, On the Alans, On the Nature of Comets,* and *On Infantry Exercises.*

Influence. Arrian was well acclaimed during his lifetime. He preserved Epictetus's teachings and left the most accurate and accessible of all the histories of Alexander the Great. He strove to achieve a notable prose style and to use as much detail as possible.

ADDITIONAL RESOURCES
Grant, Michael, ed. *Readings in the Classical Historians*. New York: Scribner's, 1992.
Stadter, Philip. *Arrian of Nicomedia*. Chapel Hill: University of North Carolina Press, 1980.

SEE ALSO: Alani; Alexander the Great; Epictetus; Greece, Roman; Hadrian; Rome, Imperial.

—*Michele Valerie Ronnick*

ARSACID DYNASTY

DATE: c. 247 B.C.E.-224 C.E.
LOCALE: Parthia, present Turkmenistan and Iran with Iraq
RELATED CIVILIZATIONS: Seleucid Dynasty, Republican and Imperial Rome, Greco-Bactrian Kushan
SIGNIFICANCE: The Arsacids were the heirs of the Seleucids in Iran and prime enemy of the Romans. Parthian culture and art influenced the Near East.

The name of the first ruler Arsaces became the hallmark of the Arsacid (AHR-sah-seed) Dynasty on its coins. The Romans called the group Parthians after their homeland in ancient Parthia, later Khorāsān. The Parthians slowly expanded over the Iranian plateau and Mesopotamia, replacing the Seleucids. After the disastrous defeat of the Romans at Carrhae in 53 B.C.E., the Parthians and Romans fought many battles for possession of northern Mesopotamia and Armenia.

Parthian costumes, especially trousers based on their nomadic background, became the style in the Near East as did their art. Because the dynasty's rulers all used the name or title Arsaces on their coins, it is difficult to identify them. Individuals can be recognized only by outstanding features or headdress. The Parthian kingdom had a feudal aspect with many nobles or vassal kings, who at times contended for supreme power. Members of the Arsacid family, however, maintained appanages in various parts of the realm.

Until the beginning of the common era, the Arsacid rulers used Greek on their coins, at times with the legend *philhellene*, probably to conciliate the Hellenized population of the cities they conquered, such as Seleucia on the Tigris. In the last two centuries of their rule, the word "Parthian" can be found written in an Aramaic alphabet on the group's coins as well as in inscriptions.

Under Trajan and later Lucius Septimius Severus, the Parthian capital Ctesiphon, near Seleucia, was sacked, and disputes among Parthian contenders for the throne weakened the dynasty. The last king, Artabanus V, was defeated by Ardashīr I, a vassal from the southern province of Persis (modern Fārs), who, in 224 C.E., founded the Sāsānian Empire. Only in Armenia did Arsacids continue to rule.

ADDITIONAL RESOURCES

Colledge, M. A. R. *Parthian Art*. London: Thames and Hudson, 1977.

Debevoise, N. C. *A Political History of Parthia*. Chicago: University of Chicago Press, 1938.

Frye, Richard N. *History of Ancient Iran*. Munich: C. H. Beck, 1984.

Wolski, J. "L'Empire des Arsacides." *Acta Iranica* 32 (1993).

SEE ALSO: Ardashīr; Carrhae, Battle of; Mithradates I; Mithradates II; Parthia; Rome, Imperial; Rome, Republican; Sāsānian Empire; Seleucid Dynasty; Septimius Severus, Lucius; Trajan.

—*Richard N. Frye*

ARTABANUS I-V

DATE: c. 211 B.C.E.-224 C.E.
RELATED CIVILIZATION: Parthia
MAJOR ROLE/POSITION: Parthian kings

The name Artabanus (ahr-tuh-BAY-nuhs) is shared by five Parthian kings. Artabanus I (also known as Arsaces II; r. 211-191 B.C.E.) succeeded Arsaces, the first Parthian king. In 209 B.C.E., Seleucid king Antiochus the Great attacked Artabanus and took Hecatompylos, the Parthian capital. Artabanus fled, and the Seleucid and Parthian conflict was ended by a compromise treaty. Artabanus retained his position as king, but after 206 B.C.E., Parthia lost much territory to Euthydemus, king of Bactria.

Artabanus II (r. 128-124 B.C.E.), who succeeded Mithradates I, continued the expansionist policies of his predecessor until the entire Iranian Plateau and the Tigris-Euphrates valley were under the control of the Parthians. The Parthian Empire, however, was troubled by attacks from the nomadic Sakas, or Scythians, in the east.

Artabanus III (r. c. 10-38 C.E.) was supported by the Parthian nobility against Vonones, who had been installed on the throne by the Romans. Artabanus defeated Vonones around 10 C.E. and began to centralize his power and quell local dynastic revolts within the empire. Artabanus angered Rome by placing his son on the Armenian throne (c. 34 C.E.), so in 35 C.E., Rome placed Tiridates III on the Parthian throne. Artabanus regained his throne, fled again, then regained it not long before dying.

Artabanus IV (r. 79-80/81 C.E.), the son of Vologases IV, was killed while fighting against his brother Pacorus II for the throne of Parthia.

Artabanus V (r. 213-224 C.E.), the last Parthian king, came to the throne after he had defeated his brother Vologases V in 213 C.E. In 216 C.E., the Roman emperor Caracalla attacked the Parthians, but the following year, he was killed by Macrinus, his successor. Because Macrinus did not accept Artabanus's demands for peace, a major battle took place at Nisibis, which resulted in Roman defeat in 218 C.E.

By this time, a local Persian prince by the name of Ardashīr I (r. 224-241 C.E.), the son of Bābak, had made conquest in Persis (province of Fārs) and was becoming powerful. At first, Artabanus sent governors to defeat

Ardashīr, but all were unsuccessful. Consequently, he himself faced Ardashīr in battle at the plain of Hormizdagān in 224 C.E. and was killed. This brought an end to the power of the Parthian Dynasty in the Iranian plateau and gave rise to the Sāsānian Empire.

ADDITIONAL RESOURCES

Bivar, A. D. H. "The Political History of Iran Under the Arsacids." In *The Cambridge History of Iran*, edited by Ehsan Yarshater. Vol. 3. Cambridge, England: Cambridge University Press, 1983.

Debevoise, N. C. *A Political History of Parthia*. Chicago: University of Chicago Press, 1938.

SEE ALSO: Antiochus the Great; Ardashīr I; Caracalla; Mithradates I; Parthia; Rome, Imperial; Sāsānian Empire.

—Touraj Daryaee

ARTAVASDES II OF ARMENIA

ALSO KNOWN AS: Artavasd
BORN: first century B.C.E.; Armenia
DIED: c. 32 B.C.E.; Egypt
RELATED CIVILIZATIONS: Armenia, Parthia, Republican Rome
MAJOR ROLE/POSITION: King of Armenia

Life. Little is known about either the life or reign (55-34 B.C.E.) of Artavasdes (ahrt-uh-VAS-deez) II of Armenia. He was the son and successor of Tigranes the Great of Armenia. Though he was not first in line to the throne, Artavasdes was chosen to succeed Tigranes after two of his older brothers were reportedly executed for separately conspiring to usurp their father.

Artavasdes was continually embroiled in the struggles of Rome and Parthia for dominance in the Near East. Marc Anthony's disastrous campaign against Parthia in 36 B.C.E. was lost as soon as Artavasdes withdrew his military support of the Romans. The resulting loss of face in Rome and the decay of his troops' morale were blows from which Marc Antony never recovered. Artavasdes, however, paid the ultimate price for his battlefield reversal. Marc Antony captured Artavasdes and his family, then marched them to Egypt, where they were paraded before Marc Antony's lover and ally, Cleopatra VII, along with the booty taken from Armenia. The execution of Artavasdes is recorded on coins minted by Marc Antony.

Influence. The reign of Artavasdes reveals the precarious position Armenia held between the Western imperial power of Rome and the Eastern imperial power of Parthia. His downfall was secured by a misstep along the tightrope he walked between the two empires.

ADDITIONAL RESOURCES

Bournoutian, George. *A History of the Armenian People*. Costa Mesa, Calif.: Mazda, 1993.

Khorenats'i, Moses. *History of the Armenians*. Translated by Robert W. Thomson. Cambridge, Mass.: Harvard University Press, 1978.

Strabo. *The Geography of Strabo*. Translated by Horace Leonard Jones. Reprint. Cambridge, Mass.: Harvard University Press, 1982.

SEE ALSO: Antony, Marc; Armenia; Cleopatra VII; Parthia; Rome, Republican; Tigranes the Great.

—Melissa Hovsepian

ARTEMIS, TEMPLE OF, AT EPHESUS

DATE: c. 700 B.C.E.-262 C.E.
LOCALE: Ancient city of Ephesus, near modern Selcuk, Turkey
RELATED CIVILIZATIONS: Classical, Hellenistic, and Roman Greece
SIGNIFICANCE: This temple for the goddess Artemis is one of the Seven Wonders of the World.

Considered one of the Seven Wonders of the World, the temple of Artemis at Ephesus (AHRT-ih-muhs at e-FUH-suhs) no longer stands. The foundation of the temple dates back to the seventh century, but it is best known for the great marble structure that was built between 560 and 550 B.C.E. sponsored by King Croesus of Lydia and designed by the architect Chersiphron.

This engraving shows the temple of Artemis at Ephesus as it might have looked in ancient times. (North Wind Picture Archives)

The temple was dedicated to Artemis, goddess of the hunt, whose presence at the temple was believed by the citizens of Ephesus to provide them with wealth and protection. It was the second largest temple in the ancient Greek world, and tourists, pilgrims, and devotees paid homage by coming from far and wide. Legend has it that a man named Herostratus, in an attempt to immortalize his name, burned the temple to ground on the night Alexander the Great was born in 356 B.C.E.

A new temple, larger and more impressive than the first, was built on the same spot. The high terraced base of the temple was rectangular, measuring 380 by 180 feet (115 by 55 meters), with 127 Ionic columns 62 feet (19 meters) high. The architects were Paeonius and Demetrius. The temple suffered at the hands of the Goths in 262 C.E. and was abandoned with the coming of Christianity to the Roman Empire.

ADDITIONAL RESOURCES

Clayton, Peter A., and Martin J. Price. *The Seven Wonders of the Ancient World.* New York: Routledge, 1988.

Seval, Mehlika. *Let's Visit Ephesus.* Istanbul: Minyatur, 1998.

SEE ALSO: Art and architecture; Croesus; Greece, Classical; Greece, Hellenistic; Greece, Roman; Paeonius.

—John A. Nichols

ARTEMISIA I

FLOURISHED: early fifth century B.C.E.
RELATED CIVILIZATION: Persia
MAJOR ROLE/POSITION: Queen of Halicarnassus

Life. Artemisia I (ahrt-uh-MIHZ-ee-uh) came to the throne of Halicarnassus upon the death of her husband. Her city-state was under the suzerainty of the Persian Empire. When Xerxes I invaded Greece in 480 B.C.E., Artemisia contributed five ships that she commanded because of her "spirit of adventure and manly courage," according to the historian Herodotus.

Artemisia distinguished herself in the campaign's first major action, off the coast of Euboea. No details are given of Artemisia's skill during this first encounter, but no one contradicted her when she alluded to it later in conference with Xerxes. In that conference, Artemisia contradicted all Xerxes' other advisers, telling him not to attack the Greek fleet. Xerxes admired her courageous stand but conceded to the majority and ordered his fleet to advance to Salamis, off the coast from Athens.

The narrow waters off Salamis negated the superior numbers of the Persian fleet, and the smaller and more maneuverable Greek ships soon gained the upper hand. Chased by an Athenian ship, Artemisia rammed an allied ship. This convinced her pursuers that she was Greek or had changed sides, so they turned away. Xerxes, watching the battle, assumed the ship she rammed was Greek. Seeing her "success" in the midst of his fleet's defeat, he is said to have remarked, "My men have turned into women, my women into men."

Influence. Artemisia had limited impact, but had her advice been followed before Salamis, all Greek and European history may have been changed.

ADDITIONAL RESOURCE
Herodotus. *The Histories*. Translated by Robin Waterfield. New York: Oxford University Press, 1998.

SEE ALSO: Artemisia II; Greece, Classical; Persia; Salamis, Battle of; Xerxes I.
—*Paul K. Davis*

ARTEMISIA II

BORN: date and place unknown
DIED: c. 350 B.C.E.; Halicarnassus, Turkey
RELATED CIVILIZATIONS: Classical Greece, Persia
MAJOR ROLE/POSITION: Persian ruler

Life. Named after her more famous predecessor who fought against the Greeks for the Persians at the Battle of Salamis in 480 B.C.E., Artemisia II (ahrt-uh-MIHZ-ee-uh) was the wife and also the sister of Mausolus. For twenty-four years (377-353 B.C.E.), they jointly ruled a small section of the Persian Empire along the Aegean Sea in southwestern Turkey. From the capital in Halicarnassus, they extended their territory over other cities and conquered the island of Rhodes. Although Persian, the couple admired the Greek culture and did their best to promote it in the cities under their rule. A revolt by the Rhodians occurred on the death of Mausolus in 353 B.C.E., and a fleet of ships was sent to capture the city of Halicarnassus. Learning of the attack, Artemisia commanded her navy to anchor in a secret location, and when the time was right, they attacked and defeated the rebellion.

Influence. Artemisia ordered the construction of an Ionic-style tomb for her husband's ashes. The greatest Greek artists were commissioned to create the tomb, which when complete was considered one of the Seven Wonders of the World. Artemisia never lived to see the finished tomb, dying only three years after her husband. She also was entombed in the structure. The magnificence of the completed tomb resulted in the coinage of the word "mausoleum" after Mausolus, Artemisia's husband.

ADDITIONAL RESOURCES
Boardman, John, et al. *Greece and the Hellenistic World*. Oxford, England: Oxford University Press, 1988.
Hornblower, S. *Mausolus*. Oxford, England: Oxford University Press, 1982.

SEE ALSO: Artemisia I; Greece, Classical; Mausolus; Persia; Salamis, Battle of.
—*John A. Nichols*

ARTHUR

FLOURISHED: sixth century C.E.; Britain
RELATED CIVILIZATIONS: Britain, Anglo-Saxon
MAJOR ROLE/POSITION: Military leader

Life. As Roman influence waned in Britain, Arthur assumed leadership of the Britons as they struggled against the Irish, the Picts, and the Saxons. Because of the lack of contemporary historians, most knowledge of Arthur comes from Geoffrey of Monmouth, whose twelfth century C.E. *History of the Kings of England* gives an extensive account of Arthur's life and was based on older Welsh sources. Many of Geoffrey's details are fanciful and untrustworthy, but the core of his story is believable (if largely unverifiable).

Arthur decisively defeated the Saxons at Badon Hill (near modern Bath) in his twelfth great battle in 493

C.E., then campaigned against the Picts and Irish. At Camlaan in 514 C.E., Arthur was mortally wounded in a battle with Mordred, his nephew, and withdrew to Aballava ("Avalon") near Hadrian's Wall, to die. In 1190 C.E., monks in Glastonbury opened a tomb that supposedly contained the remains of Arthur and his second wife.

Influence. Arthur failed to prevent the Saxons from overrunning Britain, but his life became a powerful legend that inspired countless works of art, including poems, plays, operas, and novels.

ADDITIONAL RESOURCES

Alcock, Leslie. *Arthur's Britain*. Baltimore: Penguin, 1982.

Holmes, Michael. *King Arthur: A Military History*. New York: Barnes & Noble, 1998.

Thorpe, Lewis, trans. *Geoffrey of Monmouth: History of the Kings of England*. Baltimore: Penguin, 1966.

Turner, P. F. J. *The Real King Arthur*. Anchorage, Alaska: SKS, 1993.

SEE ALSO: Angles, Saxons, Jutes; Britain; Picts.

—*John R. Phillips*

ĀRYABHAṬA

ALSO KNOWN AS: Āryabhaṭa the Elder
BORN: 476 C.E.; Kusumapura (later Patna), India
DIED: 550 C.E.; India
RELATED CIVILIZATIONS: India, Arabia
MAJOR ROLE/POSITION: Scientist, mathematician

Life. In 499 C.E., Āryabhaṭa (AWR-yah-BHAH-tah) summarized the existing knowledge of mathematics and astronomy in his famous work *Āryabhaṭīya* (499 C.E.; *The Aryabhatiya*, 1927). Written in Sanskrit verse, the work covers arithmetic, algebra, plane and spherical trigonometry, as well as astronomy. Āryabhaṭa includes correct methods for determining square and cube roots, summing power series, solving the quadratic equation, and solving indeterminate equations by the application of continued fractions. One of the first mathematicians known to use algebra, Āryabhaṭa made an accurate approximation for pi (3.1416) and compiled tables for the trigonometric sine function.

Influence. Because of his novel mathematical methods and insights into astronomy, Āryabhaṭa gained many disciples and greatly influenced the evolution of ideas in mathematics and science. His method of solving equations using continued fractions is essentially the modern method.

ADDITIONAL RESOURCES

Burton, David M. *The History of Mathematics*. Boston: WCB McGraw-Hill, 1999.

Walker, Christopher, ed. *Astronomy Before the Telescope*. New York: St. Martin's Press, 1997.

SEE ALSO: Arabia; India.

—*Alvin K. Benson*

ASAṄGA

ALSO KNOWN AS: Āryasaṅga
BORN: fourth century C.E.; Puruṣapura, India
DIED: fourth century C.E.; place unknown
RELATED CIVILIZATIONS: Gupta Dynasty, India
MAJOR ROLE/POSITION: Buddhist philosopher

Life. Asaṅga (ah-SAHN-gah), the eldest of three Brahman brothers, was the son of the court priest of Puruṣapura (Peshāwar), the capital of Gandhāra in northwest India. A Sarvāstivāda Hīnāyānist, he became dissatisfied with its teaching and became a disciple of Maitreyanātha (270-c. 350 C.E.), the founder of the Mahāyānist Yogācara or Vijñanavāda school. He induced his brother Vasubandhu to espouse Yogācara, and both emerged as important fathers of the Mahāyānist school.

Asaṅga lived in Ayodhyā, where he systematized Maitreyanātha's teachings into Yogācara philosophy and witnessed the emergence of Mahāyāna as a prominent school. Yogācara, or Vijñanavāda, Buddhist metaphysical idealism, stresses that only thought exists and that the external world is an illusion. The only reality is *śūnyatā*, or emptiness, which is without origin or decay and beyond all description and is pure consciousness and the essence of phenomena. Only through meditation (*yogācara*) are wisdom (*bodhi*) and conscious union with absolute reality realized. Around 700 C.E., Yogācara was referred to as Mantrayāna for its incorporation of mantras and magic circles into the meditative regimen.

Asaṅga's most influential works are *Mahāyāna-saṃgraha* (fourth century C.E.; *The Summary of the Great Vehicle*, 1992), a treatise on the Sambhoga-kāya or Enjoyment Body of Buddha; *Yogācara-bhūmi-shāstra* (fourth century C.E.), the foundation text of Yogācara; and *Mahāyānasūtralankāra* (fourth century C.E.; *Mahayanasutralankara of Asanga*, 1989), an obscure treatise on Mahāyāna philosophy.

Influence. Asaṅga spread Buddhism throughout much of civilized Asia into areas in which people had known nothing of the doctrine.

ADDITIONAL RESOURCES

Asanga. *The Summary of the Great Vehicle*. Translated by John P. Keenan. Berkeley, Calif.: Numata Center for Buddhist Translation and Research, 1992.

Herman, A. L. *An Introduction to Buddhist Thought*. New York: University Press of America, 1983.

Thomas, Edward J. *The History of Buddhist Thought*. London: Routledge and Kegan Paul, 1951.

Williams, Paul. *Buddhist Thought: A Complete Introduction to the Indian Tradition*. New York: Routledge, 2000.

SEE ALSO: Buddhism; India; Vasubandhu.

—*George J. Hoynacki*

ASHURBANIPAL

ALSO KNOWN AS: Ashur-bani-apli
BORN: c. 685 B.C.E.; Nineveh, Assyria
DIED: c. 627 B.C.E.; Nineveh, Assyria
RELATED CIVILIZATIONS: Iraq, Assyria
MAJOR ROLE/POSITION: King of Assyria

Life. Ashurbanipal (ahsh-oor-BAYN-ee-pahl), son of Esarhaddon, was enthroned in 668 B.C.E., superseding his older brother Shamashshumukin, who was given Babylonia and made subject to Ashurbanipal as coregent by Esarhaddon's decision.

Ashurbanipal spent the first part of his reign restoring the borders that had existed during the reign of Sennacherib. As a result, Assyria reached from Thebes in Egypt to Elam (western Iran). Ashurbanipal built a palace in Nineveh decorated with reliefs depicting his campaigns and court life. A literate man, he built the first extensive library, collecting copies of Sumerian and Akkadian texts.

Ashurbanipal's embittered brother rebelled against him in 652 B.C.E. After a four-year siege, Ashurbanipal conquered Babylonia and his brother's ally Elam. Although Ashurbanipal was succeeded by his sons, Assyria virtually collapsed after his death and was soon liquidated by the Babylonians and the Medes in 612 B.C.E.

Influence. Ashurbanipal's palace reliefs and library are one of the greatest sources of information about the

Ashurbanipal. (Library of Congress)

Assyrian military, administration, and court life as well as the languages, literature, and science of the ancient Near East.

ADDITIONAL RESOURCES
Curtis, J. E., and J. E. Reade. *Art and Empire: Treasures from Assyria in the British Museum*. London: British Museum Press, 1995.

Pritchard, James, ed. *Ancient Near Eastern Texts Relating to the Old Testament*. 3d ed. Princeton, N.J.: Princeton University Press, 1969.

SEE ALSO: Assyria; Babylonia; Esarhaddon.
—*Atsuko Hattori*

ASHVAGHOSA

ALSO KNOWN AS: Aśvaghoṣa
BORN: c. 80 C.E.; Ayodhyā, India
DIED: c. 150 C.E.; Peshāwar
RELATED CIVILIZATIONS: Kushān Empire, India
MAJOR ROLE/POSITION: Buddhist scholar and poet

Life. Ashvaghosa (AHSH-vah-GOH-sah), poet, musician, dramatist, scholar, philosopher, and religionist, flourished in India during the second century C.E., when the Kushān Dynasty of Kaniṣka paved the path for Indian civilization to extend to Central and Eastern Asia. Events of his life are sketchy, but he resided in the court of Kaniṣka at Peshāwar. Born a Brahman, he became a Sarvāstivādin but championed the Mahāyānist doctrine of the saving power of the buddhas. Regarded as the first exegete of Mahāyāna, he contributed to its spread outside India and participated in the Fourth Buddhist Council convened to settle codification of Buddhist scripture. However, the council had the effect of splitting Buddhism into Hināyāna and Mahāyāna schools.

Distinguished in Sanskrit epic, dramatic, and lyric poetry, his works, *Buddhacarita* (first or second century C.E.; *Buddhacharitam*, 1911), a masterful epic life of the Buddha ; *Saundarānanda* (first or second century C.E.; *The Saundarananda of Asvaghosa*, 1928), an account of the conversion of his half brother Nanda; and *Mahāyāna-śraddhotoāda* (first or second century C.E.), a treatise of Mahāyāna doctrine, are ranked with works of Vālmīki and Kālidāsa. Other works ascribed to him are doubtful. His literary style is characterized by simplicity in diction and clarity in meaning. His dramatic plays successfully Indianized Greek drama.

Influence. Ashvaghosa was one of the greatest Buddhist and Sanskrit poets, and his works are read far and wide throughout Mahāyāna Asia.

ADDITIONAL RESOURCES
Basham, A. L. *The Wonder That Was India*. New York: Grove Press, 1959.

Winternitz, M. *A History of Indian Literature*. 2 vols. Reprint. New York: Russell and Russell, 1971.

SEE ALSO: Buddhism; India; Kālidāsa; Kaniṣka; Kushān Dynasty; Vālmīki.
—*George J. Hoynacki*

AŚOKA

ALSO KNOWN AS: Ashoka
BORN: c. 302 B.C.E.; probably near Pāṭaliputra, Magadha, India
DIED: c. 238 B.C.E.; place unknown
RELATED CIVILIZATION: India
MAJOR ROLE/POSITION: Emperor of India

Life. Revered in India and Asia as one of the greatest rulers in history, Aśoka (ah-SHOH-kah) Maurya was the grandson of Chandragupta Maurya, who, circa 321 B.C.E., founded the first dynasty to unify most of the subcontinent of India. The Mauryan Dynasty gave India an efficient administration, social stability, internal peace, and prosperity. The Mauryas emphasized service to the people and the preservation of wildlife, fostered trade and manufacturing, and were concerned with protecting territorial boundaries. A vast array of civil servants and army personnel carried out a multitude of functions in this complex society.

Aśoka (r. c. 269-238 B.C.E.) was not the heir apparent, and Buddhist chronicles speak of a bloody fratricidal conflict following the death of his father. In the manner of most successful rulers, after coming to the throne, Aśoka consolidated his empire. He encountered resistance in Kalinga (modern Orissa) and waged and won a battle there in 261-260 B.C.E. This conflict was a turning point in his life. Instead of enjoying his victory, he felt sickened by the grief, misery, and death he had caused to hundreds of thousands of people. After undergoing a lengthy period of personal introspection, he apparently converted to Buddhism, renounced violence, and thereafter devoted himself to the welfare of his subjects.

He propagated the principle of dharma, or the law of the universe, and taught people about the virtues of compassion, truth, tolerance, nonviolence, and mutual responsibility. Calling himself the father of his people, Aśoka propounded this philosophy and his thoughts on rock and pillar edicts scattered throughout his vast empire. He urged Indians to eat as little meat as possible and passed laws to protect many species of birds and animals. He emphasized the importance of a uniform, efficient, and fair legal system, abolished unduly cruel punishment, and pardoned prisoners on special days but retained capital punishment for heinous crimes. He lavishly endowed Buddhist monasteries and educational centers. The emperor funded numerous charities to care for the sick, the aged, and orphans. Hospitals were built for human beings and animals, and herb gardens were grown to supply medicines. Domestic and foreign travelers found the vast highways of India shaded by leafy trees; fruit orchards provided them with food and wells with water. Waystations were built for their comfort.

Having found personal peace in the gentle teachings of Buddhism, Aśoka spread this message by sending ambassadors and missionaries to Ceylon, Macedonia, Syria, and Egypt. Missionaries from India are said to have reached China and Japan with this message and converted thousands to the principles of Buddhism.

Influence. Having one of the largest and most effective armies in the ancient world, Aśoka could have become a great military conqueror, expanded the Indian Empire, and left a legacy of death and destruction. Instead, he eschewed violence and turned India toward conquest of the spirit; this is why his reign is regarded as one of the most significant in Indian history. When India gained independence from British rule in 1947, the new government adopted the pillar of Aśoka as its national emblem, in honor of the greatest of its rulers.

ADDITIONAL RESOURCES

Thapar, R. *A History of India.* London: Penguin, 1990.

Wolpert S. *A New History of India.* New York: Oxford University Press, 2000.

SEE ALSO: Buddhism; Chandragupta Maurya; India; Mauryan Dynasty.

—Ranee K. L. Panjabi

ASPASIA OF MILETUS

BORN: c. 475 B.C.E.; Miletus, Asia Minor
DIED: after 428 B.C.E.; probably Athens, Greece
RELATED CIVILIZATIONS: Classical Greece, Athens
MAJOR ROLE/POSITION: Rhetorician

Life. Aspasia of Miletus (as-PAY-shee-uh of mi-LEE-tuhs) appears to have been well educated in rhetoric before arriving at Athens (c. 445 B.C.E.), where her exceptional intellect and beauty caught the attention of Pericles, a foremost Athenian statesman. After divorcing his wife, Pericles lived openly with Aspasia, and their home became a meeting place for the most famous thinkers and writers of the classical era. Ancient sources refer to Aspasia's ability to discuss rhetoric, philosophy, and politics. Socrates and Plato were said to comment that Aspasia was one of the most intelligent persons of their day. A strong woman in a patriarchal society, Aspasia drew the barbs of critics who accused her of unduly influencing Pericles and inciting Athenian hostilities against other city-states. Contemporary comedies depicted Aspasia and Pericles in unflattering terms and were probably inspired more by political mo-

Aspasia of Miletus. (Library of Congress)

tives than actual fact. After the death of Pericles (429 B.C.E.), Aspasia continued to exert considerable influence over the intellectual life of Athens.

Influence. In a culture in which women were secluded and denied an education, Aspasia was able to make her intellectual abilities known. Her achievements, mentioned by respected Greek and Roman writers, give insight into an otherwise silent Athenian female population.

ADDITIONAL RESOURCES

Henry, Madeleine M. *Prisoner of History: Aspasia of Miletus and Her Biographical Tradition.* Oxford, England: Oxford University Press, 1995.

Powell, Anton. *The Greek World.* London: Routledge, 1995.

SEE ALSO: Greece, Classical; Pericles; Plato; Socrates.

—Sonia Sorrell

ASSYRIA

DATE: c. 2300-612 B.C.E.

LOCALE: Northern Iraq

SIGNIFICANCE: The Assyrians became one of the primary beneficiaries and caretakers of Sumero-Akkadian civilization and created a powerful military state that dominated the entire ancient Near East.

The earliest mention of Assyria is found in third millennium B.C.E. texts from Mesopotamia. Apparently Assyria consisted of a number of autonomous city-states, including Ashur (Assur), Nineveh, and Arbela (Arbīl). Assyria was probably under control of the Akkadian and Third Ur Dynasties (c. 2300-2000 B.C.E.) and regained its independence at the outset of the second millennium B.C.E. At this point, the city of Ashur established a trade colony at Kanish in east-central Anatolia that lasted for more than a century (c. 1900-1750 B.C.E.). Near the end of this period, the Assyrian city-states endured an intrusion from the Amorites, a west Semitic people from Syria who established a number of dynasties in the region. The most notable of the kings was

Shamshi-Adad I (r. c. 1814-1782 B.C.E.), who was able to carve out a large state in the Assyrian heartland. Soon thereafter, the Assyrian city-states lapsed into obscurity and later were under control of the Mitanni Empire (1600-1350 B.C.E.).

Assyria became an independent unified state during the reign of Ashur-uballit I (r. c. 1363-1330 B.C.E.), who established Assyria as one of the major powers of the Near East. During the next 150 years, Assyria dominated its southern neighbor, Babylonia, expanded into the territory of its western neighbor, Mitanni, and was on an equal basis with Egypt and the Hittites, the two greatest powers in the region. However, after the reign of Tukulti-Ninurta I (r. c.1244-1208 B.C.E.), Assyria lapsed into obscurity, partly because of the pressure from Aramean tribes to the west. By the time of Tiglath-pileser I (r. c. 1115-1077 B.C.E.), Assyria began to reestablish its power base. This king fought campaigns in the north and west, where he came into contact with Aramean tribes that were controlling outgoing trade routes. However, the Assyrians had overextended themselves and were weakened until the reign of

Ashur-Dan (r. c. 934-912 B.C.E.) and Adad-nirari II (r. c. 911-891 B.C.E.), both of whom campaigned extensively against the Arameans, pushing the tribes farther west.

The establishment of Assyrian imperial power took place under Ashurnasirpal II (r. c. 883-859 B.C.E.), who established Calah (Nimrud) as his new capital and launched major campaigns in virtually every direction. He successfully subdued the Aramean and Phoenician states to the west. His successor, Shalmaneser III (r. 858-824 B.C.E.), met a powerful western coalition (which included Ahab of Israel) in 853 B.C.E., but the action was indecisive. However, internal rebellion weakened his reign, and Assyria once again became unstable.

Tiglath-pileser III (r. 745-727 B.C.E.) laid the foundations for Assyria's massive empire of the eighth and seventh centuries B.C.E. He most likely came to the throne as a usurper when Assyria was in danger of being conquered by the kingdom of Urartu (in modern Armenia). This Assyrian king was able to drive Urartu from formerly Assyrian-held territories and even invaded Urartu itself. Tiglath-pileser also invaded Syro-Palestine and defeated and made vassals of many of the

Aramean, neo-Hittite, and Phoenician cities, such as Damascus, Tyre, and Byblos. In a later campaign (734 B.C.E.), he conquered Phoenicia and Philistia, creating a trading center to link Assyria to Egypt. He laid siege to and conquered the city of Damascus in 732 B.C.E., thus ending the Aramean state centered there.

Another usurper, Sargon II (r. 721-705 B.C.E.), seized the throne of Assyria when his predecessor, Shalmaneser V, was killed in a palace revolution. Vassal states in Syro-Palestine rebelled against Assyria because of its internal problems. Sargon quickly met and defeated a coalition that included the cities of Damascus, Hamath (Hamāh), Samaria, and Arpad at Karkar (Qarqar) in 720 B.C.E. He subsequently marched through Palestine and claimed to have defeated an Egyptian army near the Egyptian border. In the wake of this campaign, Sargon deposed numerous rulers and deported much of the local population from this area. He also successfully completed the siege of the Israelite capital of Samaria, which had been started by Shalmaneser, and campaigned in eastern Turkey against Midas of Phrygia and against Urartu (located in Armenia), successfully weakening both of these states and creating a peaceful frontier.

ASSYRIA AND BABYLONIA, 600-500 B.C.E.

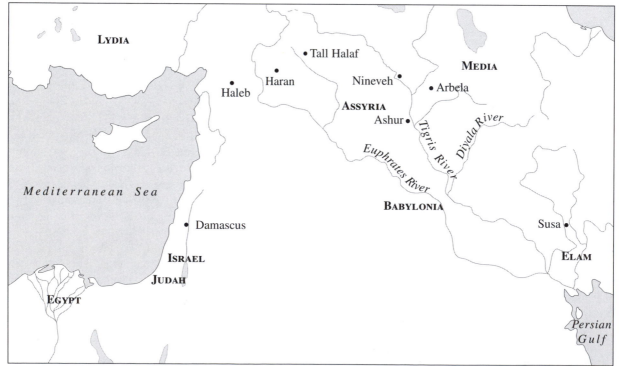

Like his predecessors, Sargon II continued to have problems with Assyria's southern neighbor, Babylon. In 721 B.C.E., Merodachbaladan, a Chaldean, seized the Babylonian throne during the succession problem in Assyria and held it until Sargon deposed him in 710 B.C.E. Sargon died in battle in 705 B.C.E. while campaigning in the north. Because the death of the king in battle was considered an evil omen, Sargon's successor Sennacherib (r. 705-681 B.C.E.) had to endure a major revolt throughout the empire.

Sennacherib invaded Syro-Palestine in 701 B.C.E., claiming to have caged Hezekiah, the king of Judah, in Jerusalem like a bird. However, the Assyrians may have been diverted from capturing Jerusalem by an Egyptian/ Ethiopian army led by Tirhakah to the south. Sennacherib demanded harsh terms from Judah. All fortified cities and outlying areas (including some cities in Philistia and Phoenicia) were seized, Hezekiah's treasury was emptied, and some of his daughters were sent as concubines to Nineveh, Sennacherib's capital.

Even more serious was Sennacherib's Babylonian dilemma. Assyria's neighbor to the south had been its tributary for the last fifty years. Merodachbaladan, the Chaldean chieftain of Babylon, also rebelled against Assyria at Sennacherib's accession; however, the revolt culminated in Babylon's utter destruction by the Assyrians in 689 B.C.E. The next two Assyrian kings, Esarhaddon (r. 680-669 B.C.E.) and Ashurbanipal (r. 668-627 B.C.E.), succeeded in conquering Egypt but were able to keep hold of it for only about fifteen years (c. 673-658 B.C.E.). It appeared that Assyria was at the height of its empire, but a massive civil war (652-648 B.C.E.) crippled the state, and collapse was swift. Assyria was attacked and destroyed by a coalition of Medes and Chaldeans (616-612 B.C.E.), resulting in the destruction of every major Assyrian city, including Nineveh. Assyria never again became a major power.

Socioeconomic structure. The core of Assyrian society was the tribe and family, and the goal of the Assyrian man was the protection and propagation of both. Class structure was associated with wealth, power, and social standing. The king was at the top and under him were various classes of nobles, lesser officials, skilled laborers, and unskilled laborers, including freemen and slaves (both debt slaves and prisoners of war).

The basis for the Assyrian economy was agriculture, animal husbandry, and trade. Because Assyria was at the crossroads of trade routes from Central Asia to Anatolia, the inhabitants were heavily involved with foreign trade, especially because so many resources had to be imported into their own territory.

Although all land in theory belonged to the king, the representative of the god Ashur on earth, in practice, the state had direct control over only a small amount of territory. The remainder of land was controlled by wealthy families, temple institutions, and private individuals. Often, private individuals were given use of state-controlled land in return for performing either civil or military service. As time went on, many of these individuals paid a fee in order to be exempt from this service. The economic organization of the Assyrian state existed to enrich the Assyrian heartland, and little emphasis was placed on the economic productivity of outlying conquered territories as long as they continued to contribute their annual tribute. However, because of the large number of service exemptions being granted, the heartland became a nonproductive entity, and greater demands were made on outlying territories for supplies and manpower. The Assyrians gradually destroyed the economies of these areas in order to support an artificial economy in central Assyria.

Law. The highest legal power in Assyria was the god Ashur, who delegated authority to the king, the chief justice of the land. Most legal disputes, however, were settled at lower levels. Though an important legal document known as the Middle Assyrian Laws has survived, it was not strictly a code but rather a literary text. In the few records of legal disputes in Assyria, these laws are never cited, but the lawyers did cite Assyrian custom and precedent. Many legal texts have survived. These were mostly transactions between two or more parties that included the names of witnesses, the name of the scribe who recorded the transaction, and the date when it took place. Researchers have found four types of transactions: sales (usually the transfer of property), contracts (loans and promissory notes), receipts, and court records. Court records were apparently rare, as most cases were settled by private agreement. Murder, however, was a special legal case because it involved a blood feud, or vendetta.

Religion. Like many religions of the ancient Near East, the Assyrian religion was polytheistic. The Assyrians had inherited the polytheistic traditions of early Mesopotamia but appeared to have a smaller corpus of deities. The king of the gods was Ashur, who ruled and controlled the land of Assyria and had supreme power over other deities. Other deities, such as Ishtar (goddess of love and war), Ninurta (warfare and hunting), Shamash (Sun), Adad (storm), and Sin

(Moon), had individual cults centered on a temple complex, a temple tower (ziggurat), priests, and a large supporting staff. The cults involved the performance of regular and seasonal rituals and the presentation of offerings. The Assyrian pantheon also contained minor deities, demons, and angelic messengers who played a more important role in the life of the individual. The king was considered the chief priest of the religious cults and therefore was normally present at ceremonies, especially the celebration of the New Year, during which the king's right to rule for another year was reaffirmed by Ashur.

Legacy. The Assyrian Empire was the largest in world history up to that time, and later empires (Persia, Macedonia, and Rome) strove to emulate the Assyrians. Furthermore, the Assyrians, like their Babylonian counterparts to the south, took an active role in preserving Mesopotamian civilization by the creation of massive libraries (such as the libraries of Ashurbanipal at Nineveh) that housed many traditional and canonical texts, some of which had been composed two thousand years earlier.

ADDITIONAL RESOURCES

Driver, G. R., and J. Miles. *The Assyrian Laws.* 1935. Reprint. Darmstadt, Germany: Scientia Verlag Aalen, 1975.

Grayson, A. K. *The Royal Inscriptions of Mesopotamia: The Assyrian Periods.* Vols. 1-2. Toronto: University of Toronto Press, 1987-1990.

Larsen, M. T. *The Old Assyrian City-State and Its Colonies.* Copenhagen: Akademisk Forlag, 1976.

Oates, D. *Studies in the Ancient History of Northern Iraq.* London: Oxford University Press, 1968.

Saggs, H. W. F. *Everyday Life in Babylonia and Assyria.* New York: Dorset, 1987.

_____. *The Might That Was Assyria.* London: Sidgwick & Jackson, 1984.

Van Driel, G. *The Cult of Assur.* Assen, Netherlands: Van Gorcum, 1969.

SEE ALSO: Ahab; Ashurbanipal; Babylonia; Egypt, Pharaonic; Esarhaddon; Hittites; Midas; Mitanni; Sammu-ramat; Sargon II; Sennacherib; Tiglath-pileser II; Urartu.

—*Mark W. Chavalas*

ASTYAGES

ALSO KNOWN AS: Arshtivaiga (Old Persian); Ishtumegu (Akkadian)
FLOURISHED: sixth century B.C.E.
RELATED CIVILIZATIONS: Media, Persia
MAJOR ROLE/POSITION: King

Life. Astyages (as-TI-uh-jeez), the son of Cyaxares, was the Median king who reigned from 585 to 550 B.C.E. His capital was located at Ecbatana (modern Hamadān). He was married to a Lydian princess, as part of a peace treaty ending hostilities between the Medes and the Lydians in 585 B.C.E. Their daughter Mandana married a Persian, Cambyses I, and gave birth to Cyrus the Great.

The Chaldean Chronicle of Nabonidus of Babylonia reports that the Median soldiers rebelled against Astyages. According to the historian Herodotus, Cyrus defeated Astyages, thus establishing the ascendancy of the Persians over the Medes, but spared the life of his grandfather.

Influence. Astyages was the last great Median king.

ADDITIONAL RESOURCES

Dandamaev, M. A. *A Political History of the Achaemenid Empire.* Leiden, Netherlands: E. J. Brill, 1989.

Frye, Richard N. *History of Ancient Iran.* Munich: C. H. Beck, 1984.

Gershevitch, I., ed. *The Cambridge History of Iran II: The Median and Achaemenian Periods.* Cambridge, England: Cambridge University Press, 1985.

Yamauchi, E. *Persia and the Bible.* Grand Rapids, Mich.: Baker, 1990.

SEE ALSO: Achaemenian Dynasty; Cyaxares; Herodotus; Persia.

—*Edwin Yamauchi*

ĀŚVALĀYANA

FLOURISHED: c. 400 B.C.E.
LOCALE: India
RELATED CIVILIZATION: Vedic India
MAJOR ROLE/POSITION: Writer

Life. Āśvalāyana (AWSH-vah-LAH-yah-nah), a sage Vedic teacher, is associated with writing two of the *Śrauta Sūtras*, or functional manuals for priests conducting ritual sacrifice relating to the *Rigveda* (also known as *Ṛgveda*, c. 1500-1000 B.C.E.; English translation, 1896-1897). The two texts bear his name, the *Āśvalāyana Śrauta Sūtra* (c. 400 B.C.E.; English translation, 1958) and the *Āśvalāyana Gṛhya Sūtra* (c. 400 B.C.E.; English translation, 1958). He was a student of Śaunāka, who composed the first *Kalpa Sūtra* (fourth century B.C.E. or earlier; English translation, 1958) and other important texts. It is reported that when Āśvalāyana composed one of his works and announced it to his teacher, the latter destroyed his own treatise and proclaimed that Āśvalāyana's *sūtra* was superior and should be adopted by the students of that Vedic Śākhā (school). There can be no doubt that Āśvalāyana was greatly indebted to his teacher because he wrote at the end of the *Āśvalāyana Gṛhya Sūtra* the words *namaḥ Śaunākaya*, or salutation to Śaunāka.

Influence. Āśvalāyana's works provided a guide for performing household or domestic rites. He gives succinct accounts of the sacrifices without introducing any philosophical speculations or doctrinal materials. The texts, produced in succinct and straightforward prose as opposed to verse, provide systematic descriptions of the necessary domestic rites that facilitated Vedic life. All the ceremonies were performed with the help of the *gṛhya* (sacred household) fire. He methodically described setting up the fire, the marriage rites, rites relating to the conception and bearing of children, ceremonies for blessing the child throughout various stages of life, the duties of the student while staying in the teacher's house, ceremonies for various vows, and ceremonies connected with cattle welfare, agricultural operations, and house building. He also includes rites for expiating neglect of duties and special sacrifices for fulfillment of desires.

ADDITIONAL RESOURCES

Gonda, Jan. *The Ritual Sutras*. Wiesbaden, Germany: Otto Harrassowitz, 1977.

Gopal, Ram. *India of Vedic Kalpasutras*. Delhi, India: Motilal Banarsidass, 1983.

SEE ALSO: Hinduism; *Sūtras*; Vedas.

—*Katherine Anne Harper*

ATHANASIUS OF ALEXANDRIA, SAINT

BORN: c. 293 C.E.; Alexandria, Egypt
DIED: May 2, 373 C.E.; Alexandria, Egypt
RELATED CIVILIZATIONS: Egypt, Imperial Rome
MAJOR ROLE/POSITION: Religious figure,
    Alexandrian patriarch

Life. As a deacon, Athanasius (ath-uh-NAY-zhee-uhs) of Alexandria attended the Council of Nicaea, summoned in 325 C.E. by the emperor Constantine the Great, over Arianism. The council condemned Arius, who argued that the Son of God did not share the divinity of God the Father. The council declared instead that the Son and the Father were of the same essence or *homoousios*, a term enshrined in the Nicene Creed. Arians, however, worked to overturn the decisions of Nicaea for decades.

Athanasius became bishop of Alexandria in 328 C.E. and spent the next forty-five years combating Arianism, even when it received imperial support. For his efforts and for accusations of violence against his opponents in Egypt, he was exiled from Alexandria five times, for a total of fifteen years. His principal works include *Vita S. Antonii* (c. 357 C.E.; *The Life of Anthony*, 1697) the authorship of which is disputed, *De incarnatione Verbi Dei* (before 325 C.E.; *On the Incarnation of the Word of God*, 1880), and *Contra Arianos* (350 C.E.; *An Apology Against the Arians*, 1873). The cornerstone of Athanasius's theology is the necessity of the Son's full divinity for human salvation; God became human so that people can partake of the nature of God.

Influence. Athanasius's long career and his survival of repeated exile and attempted arrest demonstrated the

Saint Athanasius of Alexandria. (Library of Congress)

power of bishops in the new Christian empire created by Constantine. His championing of *homoousios* assured the defeat of Arianism and the ultimate triumph of the Nicene Creed. His *Life of Anthony* became a model for subsequent hagiography and exercised a powerful influence on Christian asceticism and the growth of monasticism.

ADDITIONAL RESOURCES

Athanasius. *The Life of Antony and the Letter to Marcellinus.* Translated by R. C. Gregg. New York: Paulist Press, 1980.

_____. *Select Works and Letters.* Translated by A. Robinson. Vol. 4 in *A Select Library of Nicene and Post-Nicene Fathers of the Christian Church,* edited by P. Schaff and H. Wace. 1891. Reprint. Grand Rapids, Mich.: Eerdmans, 1980.

Barnes, T. D. *Athanasius and Constantius: Theology and Politics in the Constantinian Empire.* Cambridge, Mass.: Harvard University Press, 1993.

Brakke, D. *Athanasius and the Politics of Asceticism.* Oxford, England: Clarendon, 1995.

Hanson, R. P. C. *The Search for the Christian Doctrine of God: The Arian Controversy, 318-381.* Edinburgh, Scotland: T&T Clark, 1988.

SEE ALSO: Alexandrian patriarchs; Arianism; Christianity; Constantine the Great; Egypt, Ptolemaic and Roman; Nicaea, Council of; Rome, Imperial.

—Timothy M. Teeter

ATHENS

DATE: 3000 B.C.E.-700 C.E.

LOCALE: Southern Greece, in Attica

RELATED CIVILIZATIONS: Mycenaean, Archaic, Classical, Hellenistic, and Roman Greece

SIGNIFICANCE: Site of the earliest democracy of Western civilization, Athens was the cultural center of Greek civilization from the classical through the Roman periods.

The city of Athens developed around the Acropolis, a rocky hill rising from the central plain of Attica about five miles (eight kilometers) from the Saronic Gulf. Traces of habitation first appear in the late Neolithic period (c. 3000 B.C.E.), and Athens became an important center in the late Bronze Age (1600-1100 B.C.E.). A

Mycenaean palace stood on the Acropolis, which was girded by massive fortifications. These remains lend some support to the tradition that in this period the hero Theseus united all of Attica under Athenian leadership.

Although Athens escaped the destruction endured elsewhere in Greece in the twelfth century B.C.E., the city still entered the Dark Ages of Greece (c. 1000-800 B.C.E.), a period of poverty and depopulation. Athens recovered earlier than other parts of Greece, but it failed to join the colonizing movement of the eighth and seventh centuries B.C.E., when Greek cities sent out colonies to deal with growing populations. One theory holds that Athens suffered a sharp decline in population because of a severe drought around 700 B.C.E.

During the Dark Ages the Athenians replaced their king with officials called archons. By 700 B.C.E., nine archons were elected each year, and they governed Athens with the council of the Areopagus. Around 630 B.C.E., Athenian nobleman Cylon tried unsuccessfully to seize power and make himself tyrant. The failed coup created intense infighting and perhaps led to the legislation of Draco (c. 621 B.C.E.). Later generations remembered Draco's laws as "written in blood" because of their severity.

By 600 B.C.E., Athens faced a severe economic crisis as farmers were falling into debt, and nonaristocrats resented the excesses of aristocratic government. The reforms of Solon (c. 594 B.C.E.) addressed this crisis by canceling debts, promoting trade, and reforming Athenian government. Citizens could appeal the decisions of aristocratic judges, and nonaristocrats gained some access to political office. These reforms were only partly successful, and in about 560 B.C.E., Pisistratus became tyrant. Under his reign and that of his sons, Athens enjoyed increasing prosperity. Pisistratus reorganized religious festivals, built the first large stone temples on the Acropolis, and started a temple to Olympian Zeus. New public buildings and a fountain house were erected in the marketplace, and Athenian pottery dominated foreign markets.

Democratic reforms. The overthrow of the tyranny in 510 B.C.E. was followed by the democratic reforms of Cleisthenes in 508 B.C.E., who sought to break aristocratic control of government. Cleisthenes created ten regionally based tribes and established a council of five hundred citizens, fifty from each tribe, to prepare business for the assembly. He also instituted the practice of ostracism, by which the Athenians could exile potentially dangerous citizens for ten years.

After these reforms, Athens reached its military, political, and cultural zenith. The Athenians defeated the Persians at Marathon in 490 B.C.E., and a decade later, the Athenian navy helped overcome the Persians at Salamis (480 B.C.E.). Athens, however, was sacked. When the Athenians returned in 479 B.C.E., they fortified the city but left their temples in ruins as symbols of Persian impiety. After peace was formally concluded with Persia in 448 B.C.E., Pericles proposed rebuilding the city's temples. This building project began in 447 B.C.E., and over the next forty years, brilliant marble buildings, including the Parthenon, Propylaea, and Erechtheum, rose on the Acropolis and throughout Athens. Meanwhile, Greek artists and intellectuals flocked to the city. Itinerant teachers called Sophists taught anyone who could afford their fees. The historian Herodotus visited Athens while composing his history of the Greco-

The Acropolis of Athens. (PhotoDisc)

OSTRACISM

According to Aristotle, Cleisthenes of Athens introduced the practice of ostracism (*ostrakophoria*) during a reform of the Athenian constitution around 508 B.C.E. It was first used in 487 B.C.E., to ostracize Hipparchus, son of Charmus, and fell out of use after the ostracism of Hyperbolus c. 417 B.C.E. Prominent men who were ostracized include Aristides of Athens, Themistocles, Cimon, and Thucydides, son of Melesias.

In midwinter, Athenians gathered to decide whether to hold a vote on ostracism. At this vote, citizens would write the name of another citizen who they judged to be threatening the stability of the state. When enough votes were gathered, the person was ostracized. He had to leave within ten days and remain away for ten years, although he retained his property and his citizenship.

Persian Wars. The tragedians Aeschylus, Sophocles, and Euripides and the comic poet Aristophanes produced plays that laid the foundation for Western drama.

The advance of democracy. The fifth century B.C.E. also saw the blossoming of democracy. In 462 B.C.E., Athenian Ephialtes deprived the Areopagus of its remaining political powers. Pericles later instituted pay for jury service and public office, thereby enabling poor citizens to participate fully in public affairs. Ironically, the advance of democracy at Athens was accompanied by Athenian imperialism abroad. In 478 B.C.E., the Athenians founded the Delian League, an alliance of Greek cities to fight the Persians. This league, however, pursued Athenian interests, and the Athenians continued to collect funds from their allies even after war with Persia was over. These funds helped finance Pericles' building program.

Athenian democracy was overthrown after the Peloponnesian War (431-404 B.C.E.). Although democratic government was soon restored, the Athenians never regained their former power. Still, the fourth century was not entirely one of decline. Despite the execution of Socrates in 399 B.C.E., philosophy flourished. Plato established a school in the Academy, a gymnasium just outside the city. His student Aristotle set up another school known as the Lyceum. Oratory was perfected by Isocrates, Aeschines, and Demosthenes. Spurred by the speeches of Demosthenes, the Athenians made one final stand against Philip II of Macedonia. Although Philip defeated the Athenians at Chaeronea (338 B.C.E.), Athens was spared destruction.

Athens remained a cultural center during the Hellenistic and Roman periods. Hellenistic kings adorned the city with new buildings, and several philosophical schools developed, most notably the Stoic and Epicurean. The Athenians initially enjoyed good relations with Rome, but when they joined Mithradates VI Eupator in a war against Rome, Lucius Cornelius Sulla sacked the city (86 B.C.E.). Still, Athens continued to attract patrons, and the city prospered under the Roman Empire. In the second century C.E., the emperor Hadrian initiated a building program and finished the temple of Olympian Zeus, and Athens again became a center of learning.

Athens was sacked in 267 C.E. by the Herulians, a Germanic tribe. The city was rebuilt on a smaller scale, but rhetoric and philosophy continued to be taught. After the emperor Justinian I closed the philosophical schools in 529 B.C.E., Athens lost this last link with its glorious past and quickly sank into obscurity.

ADDITIONAL RESOURCES

Camp, John M. *The Athenian Agora: Excavations in the Heart of Classical Athens.* London: Thames and Hudson, 1986.

Frantz, Alison. *Late Antiquity,* A.D. *267-700.* Vol. 24 in *The Athenian Agora.* Princeton, N.J.: American School of Classical Studies at Athens, 1988.

Habicht, Christian. *Athens from Alexander to Antony.* Translated by Deborah Lucas Schneider. Cambridge, Mass.: Harvard University Press, 1999.

Hurwit, Jeffrey M. *The Athenian Acropolis: History, Mythology, and Archaeology from the Neolithic Era to the Present.* Cambridge, England: Cambridge University Press, 1999

Meier, Christian. *Athens: A Portrait of the City in Its Golden Age.* Translated by Robert and Rita Kimber. New York: Metropolitan Books, 1998.

SEE ALSO: Aeschines; Aeschylus; Aristophanes; Aristotle; Chaeronea, Battle of; Cleisthenes of Athens; Demosthenes; Draco; Ephialtes of Athens; Euripides; Greco-Persian Wars; Greece, Archaic; Greece, Classical; Greece, Hellenistic and Roman; Greece, Mycenaean; Hadrian; Herodotus; Isocrates; Justinian I; Marathon, Battle of; Mithradates VI Eupator; Parthenon; Peloponnesian War; Pericles; Philip II; Philosophy; Pisistratus; Plato; Salamis, Battle of; Socrates; Solon; Sophocles; Sulla, Lucius Cornelius.

—James P. Sickinger

ATLATL

DATE: 1200-300 B.C.E.
LOCALE: Veracruz and Tabasco
RELATED CIVILIZATIONS: Olmec, Maya, Teotihuacán
SIGNIFICANCE: This ancient hunting tool was transformed into a weapon of war by the Olmecs of ancient Mesoamerica.

The atlatl (AHT-lah-tel), or Olmec spear-thrower, first appeared some thirty thousand years ago in the Old World and was subsequently introduced to the New World by the earliest Native Americans. In Mesoamerica, atlatls are documented at 4000 B.C.E. in the Tehuacán Valley. Later Olmec monuments (1200-300 B.C.E.) depict the atlatl as a weapon of warriors and the elite. Although this is the earliest known depiction of the atlatl as a weapon, it does not preclude the possibility that the atlatl was used in early tribal warfare. Use of the atlatl was generally limited to central Mexican and northern Mesoamerican contexts where jungle vegetation was not a deterrent to the effective use of the spear-thrower. Subsequently adopted by the Maya during the Middle Classic (300-600 C.E.) period, the atlatl was not used as a weapon of war until the advent of Gulf coast and central Mexican influence in the Maya lowlands. In ancient Teotihuacán (100-750 C.E.), the atlatl was the weapon of choice, and so influenced the nature of highland warfare that battles were often depicted by symbols representing a "rain of darts." Significantly, the antiquity of this instrument undoubtedly lent itself to the atlatl's embodiment as the goggle-eyed face of Tlaloc—the all-important Teotihuacán deity of rain and warfare.

ADDITIONAL RESOURCES

Hassig, Ross. *Aztec Warfare: Imperial Expansion and Political Control*. Norman: University of Oklahoma Press, 1988.

_____. *War and Society in Ancient Mesoamerica*. Berkeley: University of California Press, 1992.

SEE ALSO: Maya; Olmecs; Teotihuacán.

—*Ruben G. Mendoza*

ATOSSA

FLOURISHED: sixth century B.C.E.
RELATED CIVILIZATION: Persia
MAJOR ROLE/POSITION: Queen

Life. Atossa (uh-TAHS-uh) was the daughter of Cyrus the Great. After Cyrus's death, she married her brother Cambyses II, who became the "king of kings." This union was part of the Persian practice of next-of-kin marriage (*xwedodah*), which kept the royal blood pure. After Cambyses died in Egypt, Atossa entered the harem of the usurper, Gaumata (Smerdis), who briefly ruled the Persian Empire. Darius the Great quickly dethroned him and took power. He was from a collateral line of the Achaemenians and not directly descended from Cyrus, so he married Atossa and Artystone in an attempt to legitimize himself in the eyes of the Persian nobility by having children with daughters of Cyrus the Great.

Atossa had four sons by Darius. The eldest son was Xerxes I, who became heir to the throne. Although he was not the eldest among the sons of Darius, it appears that by this time, Atossa had sufficient power in the court and the harem to influence the king to choose this son as the next king. When Xerxes came to the throne, Atossa became the queen mother and became even more influential in the court. She also gave birth to Mandane, who lost three of her sons at the Battle of Salamis against the Greeks. In Aeschylus's *Persai* (472 B.C.E.; *The Persians*, 1777), Atossa plays a prominent role. She is addressed by Cyrus, who is represented as a god-king in this Greek tragedy.

Influence. Although the Greek sources attest her importance in the Persian court and describe her as strong and influential, she is omitted from the Royal Achaemenian Persian inscriptions by Darius. This omission has been explained as Darius's reluctance to remind people of his usurpation of power and that he had to rely on Atossa as the daughter of the founder of the Persian Empire for legitimacy.

ADDITIONAL RESOURCES

Brosius, M. *Women in Ancient Persia, 559-331* B.C. New York: Clarendon Press, 1996.

Wiesehöfer, J. *Ancient Persia*. New York: Tauris, 1996.

SEE ALSO: Achaemenian Dynasty; Cyrus the Great; Darius the Great; Persia; Salamis, Battle of; Xerxes I.

—*Touraj Daryaee*

ATRAHASIS EPIC

AUTHORSHIP: unknown
DATE: c. 1900-1800 B.C.E.
LOCALE: Babylonia
RELATED CIVILIZATION: Babylonia
SIGNIFICANCE: Part of the epic tradition of Mesopotamia, this work features a religious flood story.

The Atrahasis epic is based on an earlier Sumerian flood story. In the epic, the god Enlil determines to destroy humankind because his sleep was disturbed by the noisiness brought on by overpopulation. After various measures prove unsuccessful, Enlil decides to send a massive flood. The lower god Ea selects Atrahasis to survive the flood, thus preventing Enlil from destroying all humankind. Atrahasis is instructed to build a ship that will be loaded with his family, animals, sufficient food, and craftspeople. The Mesopotamian worldview is typified in the reason for the flood, a practical problem eliciting a response from Enlil that trivializes humankind. This poem anticipates the epic of Gilgamesh, in which no reason is given for the flood or for the selection of Utnapishtim as survivor. In contrast, the biblical account of a flood accords Noah a moral worthiness that allows him to survive the flood.

ADDITIONAL RESOURCES

Laessoe, J. "The Atrahasis Epic: A Babylonian History of Mankind." *Bibliotheca Orientalis* 12 (1956): 90-102.

Lambert, W. G., and A. R. Millard, eds. *Atra-hasis: The Babylonian Story of the Flood with the Sumerian Flood Story by M. Civil*. Oxford, England: Clarendon Press, 1969.

Saggs, H. W. F. *Babylonians*. Berkeley: University of California Press, 2000.

SEE ALSO: Babylonia; Christianity; Sumerians.

—*Johnathon R. Ziskind*

ATTALID DYNASTY

DATE: c. 282-133 B.C.E.
LOCALE: Ancient Pergamum, west central Anatolia, Turkey
RELATED CIVILIZATIONS: Hellenistic Greece, Republican Rome, Persia
SIGNIFICANCE: Under the Attalids, Pergamum became a powerful city-state and a center of Hellenistic civilization.

Philetaerus (c. 343-263 B.C.E.), founder of the Attalid Dynasty, named it after his father. A remarkable group of rulers (except for its last member), the Attalids changed Pergamum from a minor hill fortress into an influential and powerful city-state as well as a major center of Hellenistic civilization. With Roman support, Philetaerus freed himself (c. 282 B.C.E.) from the influence of rival powers in the area. With the treasure he had accumulated, he began the policy of the beautification of Pergamum continued by his successors. Efficient use of Pergamene resources as well as heavy taxation kept the treasury filled. The Attalids became known for their fabulous wealth. Eumenes I (r. 263-241 B.C.E.), nephew and successor of Philetaerus, continued the consolidation of power but could not rid Pergamum of the burdensome tribute exacted by the savage neighboring Gauls (Celts).

Relief from the oppressors was achieved in 236 B.C.E. by his cousin and successor, Attalus I (269-197 B.C.E.; r. 241-197 B.C.E.), "the Savior," first to be designated king. An excellent general and astute diplomat, Attalus conquered much of Asia Minor. Pergamum became the strongest military and economic power in the area. Because an important harbor, the nearby coastal city of Ephesus, was under its control,

KINGS OF THE ATTALID DYNASTY, C. 282-133 B.C.E.

King	Reign
Philetaerus	c. 282-263 B.C.E.
Eumenes I	263-241
Attalus I	241-197
Eumenes II	197-158
Attalus II	158-138
Attalus III	138-133

Pergamum also ranked as a maritime power. Eumenes II (r. 197-158 B.C.E.), eldest son of Attalus I, brought Pergamum to the zenith of its power and influence. He wanted his city to be successor to the golden age of Athens, and Pergamum became one of the principal conduits through which Greek culture and tradition passed into the Roman civilization. Pergamum became a major manufacturer and exporter of parchment, the scraped skins of calves and sheep to which the city gave its name, fine fabrics, pitch, and art objects. Artists flocked to the city and achieved a distinctive Pergamene style. The Pergamum library was second in size and excellence only to that of Alexandria, Egypt.

The great artistic achievement of Eumenes II was the construction of the Great Altar of Zeus (180-175 B.C.E.), one of the few top-level Hellenistic architectural and sculptural works. The altar's eye-level frieze is filled with greater than life-size writhing and sinuous figures depicting the mythological battle between the gods and the giants but actually commemorating the battle with and victory over the Gauls.

Attalus II (r. 158-138 B.C.E.), second son of Attalus I, loyally supported and continued the policies of his brother, but by increasing dependence on Rome, he ultimately made Pergamum a pawn of Roman policy. Attalus III (r. 138-133 B.C.E.), "the Benefactor," successor of Attalus II, son of Eumenes II and last of the Attalids, was noted chiefly for his "Testament" ceding Pergamum to Rome.

ADDITIONAL RESOURCES

Fleming, William. "Pergamon." In *Arts and Ideas*. New York: Holt, Rinehart and Winston, 1997.

Hansen, Esther Violet. *The Attalids of Pergamon*. 2d ed. Ithaca, N.Y.: Cornell University Press, 1971.

SEE ALSO: Eumenes II; Gauls; Greece, Hellenistic and Roman; Rome, Republican; Persia; Zeus at Pergamum, Great Altar of.

—*Nis Petersen*

ATTICUS, TITUS POMPONIUS

BORN: 109 B.C.E.; Rome
DIED: 32 B.C.E.; Rome
RELATED CIVILIZATION: Republican Rome
MAJOR ROLE/POSITION: Entrepreneur, patron of letters

Life. Born into the wealthy business (equestrian) class, Titus Pomponius Atticus (TI-tuhs pahm-POH-nee-uhs AT-uh-kuhs) is best known for his friendship with Cicero. Atticus was educated at Rome with Cicero, but in 85 B.C.E., he left for Athens to protect the fortune inherited from his father (and later, from an uncle) from the impending civil war between Lucius Cornelius Cinna and Lucius Cornelius Sulla. He lived in Athens and Epirus until the mid-60's B.C.E., earning the respect and adulation of the citizens of Athens for his many benefactions and acquiring the name Atticus. He came to Rome to help Cicero in his bid for the consulate (62 B.C.E.) and remained for the next year to lend equestrian support to Cicero's projects. He remained Cicero's closest friend, financial adviser, and literary executor for the next twenty years.

Atticus had the ability to maintain strong friendships with important men who were older than himself and political foes of one another. Therefore, he counted as friends Sulla, Quintus Hortensius Hortalus, Pompey the Great, Brutus, Marc Antony, and Octavian. His friendships enabled him to weather civil wars, whichever side had the upper hand. His daughter married Marcus Vipsanius Agrippa, and his granddaughter married the future emperor Tiberius. Atticus lived a long and enjoyable life but committed suicide when he contracted an incurable sickness in 32 B.C.E.

Atticus wrote a monograph on Cicero's consulate (60 B.C.E.), an important yearly history of Rome, the *Liber Annalis* (47 B.C.E.), several family histories of

Rome's prominent families, and a book showing portraits of Rome's greatest men with poetic epitaphs under each image (39 B.C.E.?). All his writings are lost.

ADDITIONAL RESOURCES

Horsfall, Nicholas. *Cornelius Nepos: A Selection, Including the Lives of Cato and Atticus.* Oxford, England: Clarendon Press, 1989.

Shackleton Bailey, D. R. *Cicero's Letters to Atticus.* 7 vols. Cambridge, England: Cambridge University Press, 1999.

SEE ALSO: Agrippa, Marcus Vipsanius; Antony, Marc; Athens; Brutus; Cicero; Octavian; Pompey the Great; Rome, Republican; Sulla, Lucius Cornelius; Tiberius.

—*Robert W. Cape, Jr.*

ATTILA

ALSO KNOWN AS: Attila the Hun
BORN: c. 406 C.E.; Pannonia?
DIED: 453 C.E.; probably Jazberin
RELATED CIVILIZATION: Imperial Rome
MAJOR ROLE/POSITION: Military leader

Life. Son and nephew of chiefs, Attila was born around 406 C.E. after the Huns migrated from Turkestan to the Hungarian plain. His rise to power began in 434 C.E., when he ruled jointly with his brother Bleda. He attained sole control in 445 C.E., when Bleda was murdered, probably on Attila's order. Attila plundered the Eastern Roman Empire in 441 C.E., then moved west and crossed the Rhine River. By forcing elements of the Visigoths, Franks, and Vandals to submit, Attila hastened their settlement within the Western Empire.

In spring, 451 C.E., Attila attacked Gaul until stopped at Châlons by a Roman-German army under Flavius Aetius. Marching into Italy in spring, 452 C.E., he assaulted Aquileia, Milan, and Pavia. A delegation of prominent Romans including Pope Leo I persuaded him not to attack Rome. Attila died of a hemorrhage on his wedding night in 453 C.E., but his burial place has never been found. His successors were annihilated by a Germanic coalition at Nedao in 454 C.E. Subsequently, the Huns vanished from history.

Influence. Attila extended Hunnic rule from the Caspian to the Rhine, hastening a demographic shift of Germans into the Roman Empire. His regime was too large for the limited capabilities of his successors, and it soon dissolved. Legends of Attila survived in Europe, including the story of Etzel (Attila) of the *Nibelungenlied* (c. 1200; English translation, 1848).

ADDITIONAL RESOURCES

Gordon, C. D. *The Age of Attila.* New York: Dorset Press, 1992.

Attila leads the Huns in an attack. (Library of Congress)

Thompson, E. A. *The Huns.* Oxford, England: Blackwell, 1996.

SEE ALSO: Châlons, Battle of; Franks; Gauls; Goths, Ostrogoths, Visigoths; Huns; Leo I, Saint; Rome, Imperial; Vandals.

—*William E. Watson*

AUGUSTINE, SAINT

ALSO KNOWN AS: Aurelius Augustinus
BORN: November 13, 354 C.E.; Tagaste (later Souk-Ahras), Numidia (later Algeria)
DIED: August 28, 430 C.E.; Hippo Regius (later Annaba), Numidia
RELATED CIVILIZATIONS: North Africa, Imperial Rome
MAJOR ROLE/POSITION: Religious leader, philosopher

Life. Augustine was the son of Patricius, a Roman official, and his Christian wife, Monica. He was commonly known as Aurelius Augustinus, but there is no proof this name was given him either at birth or baptism. He had at least one brother, Navigius, and a sister, Perpetua (who became a nun). Except for the five years he taught in Italy, Augustine spent his entire life in North Africa. Following a classical education at a Tagaste grammar school, Augustine attended the Madauros academy. Fond of the Latin language and literature, he never knew or liked Greek. The patronage of a local noble, Romanianus, allowed Augustine to go to the University of Carthage. There in 371 C.E., his mistress gave birth to their son, Adeodatus.

After reading Cicero's *Hortensius* (now lost), Augustine embraced the life of a philosopher. In 373-374 C.E., he taught grammar at Tagaste, and until 383 C.E., he lectured on rhetoric in Carthage. Next he went to Italy, teaching rhetoric in Rome and Milan. Successively, Augustine accepted and rejected various philosophies. For a while, he was a Manichaean, then affirmed the Skepticism of the New Academy. In a memorable work, *Contra academicos* (386 C.E.; *Against the Academicians*, 1957), Augustine repudiated Skepticism and took up Neoplatonism, which profoundly affected his character and career.

In Milan, Augustine was influenced by the preaching of Bishop Ambrose and the prayers of his mother. Following a dramatic conversion, Augustine and Adeodatus were baptized on Easter, April 25, 387 C.E. Returning to Africa, in 388 C.E., Augustine divested himself of his wealth, living a life of poverty and celibacy. He retained only his home, which became a monastery. By popular demand, against his will, he was made deacon and then priest in Hippo in 391 C.E. Five years later, Augustine became bishop of Hippo, a city of 30,000 largely non-Christian inhabitants. Until his death, Augustine expounded and extended the Catholic faith as prelate, preacher, apologist, philosopher, theologian, and author.

Augustine left behind a large body of surviving writing, including one hundred books and treatises, two hundred letters, and more than five hundred sermons. His major works include *De Trinitate* (399-419 C.E.; *On*

Saint Augustine. (Library of Congress)

the Trinity, 1948), an exposition of the Christian doctrine of God; *Confessiones* (c. 397-401 C.E.; *Confessions*, 1912), an adventure in autobiography that amounted to "one long extended prayer"; and *De civitate Dei* (413-427 C.E.; *The City of God*, 1610), composed after the Fall of Rome to refute the accusation that Christians caused it. As bishop, Augustine promoted orthodoxy by refuting Donatism (the belief that sacraments are valid only if performed by "worthy" priests) and Pelagianism (the teaching that humans, being inherently good, "merit" grace). As the last great Christian mind of antiquity and the first of the Middle Ages, Augustine was a bridge between the classical world and the Catholic centuries.

Influence. Regarded as "the greatest of all the Doctors of the Church," Augustine profoundly influenced all subsequent Western theology, especially Saint Thomas Aquinas, Martin Luther, John Calvin, and Karl Barth, as well as Occidental philosophy, from Anselm to René Descartes.

ADDITIONAL RESOURCES
Brown, Peter. *Augustine of Hippo*. Rev. ed. Berkeley: University of California Press, 2000.
Burke, Vernon J. *Wisdom from St. Augustine*. South Bend, Ind.: University of Notre Dame Press, 1984.
Chadwick, Henry. *Augustine*. New York: Oxford University Press, 1986.
Kirwan, C. *Augustine*. Reprint. London: Routledge, 1991.

SEE ALSO: Africa, North; Ambrose; Christianity; Cicero; Philosophy; Rome, Imperial.

—*C. George Fry*

AUGUSTINE OF CANTERBURY, SAINT

BORN: sixth century C.E.; possibly Rome
DIED: May 26, 604/605 C.E.; Canterbury, Kent, England
RELATED CIVILIZATIONS: England, Rome
MAJOR ROLE/POSITION: Bishop, missionary

Life. In 596 C.E., Pope Gregory the Great sent the Italian monk Augustine to England to convert the Anglo-Saxons. The pagan overlord of the Anglo-Saxons, Æthelbert I of Kent, whose wife Bertha was a Christian Frank, allowed Augustine and his companion monks complete freedom to preach Christianity. He also provided them with provisions and gave them the old Roman-British church of Saint Martin. By 601 C.E., Æthelbert had become a Christian.

According to a letter written by Gregory the Great, on Christmas Day in 597 C.E., Augustine's mission baptized 10,000 Anglo-Saxons in the Thames. Although this number is probably inflated, it attests the mission's success. Augustine built a small cathedral and the monastery of Saints Peter and Paul outside the walls of Canterbury. In 601 C.E., Gregory constituted Augustine metropolitan of twelve bishoprics to be established in the south, but only the sees of Canterbury, London, and Rochester were founded during Augustine's lifetime.

Gregory decided that the Briton, or Welsh, bishops should be subject to Augustine, but the Britons refused to give up their ancient Christian traditions in order to conform to the practices of the Roman Church, to bow to the authority of their enemies' missionary, or to aid in the conversion of the Anglo-Saxons.

After almost ten years of missionary work among the Anglo-Saxons, Augustine died and was buried in the monastery of Saints Peter and Paul.

Influence. Saint Augustine of Canterbury brought Latin Christianity and Latin civilization to Anglo-Saxon England.

ADDITIONAL RESOURCES
Deanesly, Margaret. *Augustine of Canterbury*. 2d ed. Southampton, England: Saint Austin Press, 1997.
Farmer, David Hugh, ed. *Butler's Lives of the Saints: May*. Rev. ed. Collegeville, Minn.: Liturgical Press, 1996.

SEE ALSO: Angles, Saxons, Jutes; Britain; Christianity; Franks; Gregory the Great; Paul, Saint.

—*Alison Taufer*

AUGUSTUS

ALSO KNOWN AS: Octavian; Gaius Julius Caesar
  Octavianus; Caesar Augustus; né: Gaius Octavius
BORN: September 23, 63 B.C.E.; Rome
DIED: August 19, 14 C.E.; Nola
RELATED CIVILIZATIONS: Republican Rome,
  Imperial Rome
MAJOR ROLE/POSITION: *Princeps* of Rome

Life. Lacking a son of his own, Julius Caesar
adopted his sister's grandson Gaius Octavius, who on
accepting the will in 44 C.E., became Gaius Julius
Caesar Octavianus. His life thereafter can be divided
into three phases.

In 44-30 B.C.E., Octavian mercilessly eliminated all
rivals in his pursuit of power. Relying on Caesar's veterans, he allied with Marc Antony and Marcus Aemilius Lepidus in the Second Triumvirate (43 B.C.E.). They
proscribed their enemies and defeated Caesar's assassins at Philippi in 42 B.C.E. Octavian steadily won control of the West. Relations with Antony deteriorated
into a war (32 B.C.E.) that Octavian portrayed as a cru-
sade to save the Roman way of life from Cleopatra VII.
He won decisively at Actium (September 2, 31 B.C.E.)
and drove Antony and Cleopatra to Egypt; they committed suicide as Octavian closed in (30 B.C.E.).

Octavian recreated his image and ostensibly restored the traditional state. In 27 B.C.E., he "resigned"
his powers to the Roman senate but was "persuaded" to
continue as consul and retain the governorship of
Spain, Gaul, and Syria. This created the distinction between imperial and senatorial provinces. He also became "Augustus"—the "Revered" or "Exalted"—by
which he is customarily known, and *princeps*, first man
in the state. In 23 B.C.E., he resigned the consulship but
received compensation in supreme military command
and tribunician power (annually renewed).

The third period, from 23 B.C.E. to his death in 14
C.E., was a time of consolidation. He became *pontifex
maximus* (chief priest, 12 B.C.E.) and *pater patriae* (father of the state, 2 B.C.E.). Architectural projects, notably the forum of Augustus and rebuilding of numerous
temples, made Rome the leading city of the empire.
Legislation encouraged family life. A host of writers
flourished; the poet Vergil's hero Aeneas is a precursor of Augustus. Extensive campaigns fixed imperial
boundaries along the Rhine and Danube Rivers; disaster in the Battle of Teutoburg Forest (9 C.E.) ended expansion east of the Rhine.

Influence. To state that Augustus deceived Romans
into accepting imperial rule hidden as a fake restoration
of the Roman Republic misses his political subtlety. He
combined an outward restoration of the ancestral *res
publica* with an unprecedented accumulation of powers. By avoiding Caesar's tyrannical dictatorship and
emphasizing the civilian tribunician power rather than
military *imperium*, he was *princeps* in a way no one had
ever been. Augustus became the model for all "good"
emperors and the founder of the principate.

ADDITIONAL RESOURCES
Favro, Diane. *The Urban Image of Augustan Rome.*
  Cambridge, England: Cambridge University Press,
  1996.
Galinsky, Karl. *Augustan Culture.* Princeton, N.J.:
  Princeton University Press, 1996.
Gurval, R. A. *Actium and Augustus: The Politics and
  Emotions of the Civil War.* Ann Arbor: University of
  Michigan Press, 1995.
Lacey, W. K. *Augustus and the Principate: The Evolu-
  tion of the System.* Leeds, England: Cairns, 1996.
Raaflaub, K., and M. Toher. *Between Republic and Em-*

Augustus. (Hulton Archive)

pire: Interpretations of Augustus and His Principate. Berkeley: University of California Press, 1990.

Syme, R. *The Roman Revolution.* Reprint. New York: Oxford University Press, 1987.

SEE ALSO: Actium, Battle of; Antony, Marc; Caesar, Julius; Cleopatra VII; Philippi, Battle of; Rome, Imperial; Rome, Republican; Teutoburg Forest, Battle of; Vergil.

—*Thomas H. Watkins*

AURELIANUS, LUCIUS DOMITIUS

ALSO KNOWN AS: Aurelian
BORN: c. 215 C.E.; place unknown
DIED: 275 C.E.; near Byzantium (later Istanbul, Turkey)
RELATED CIVILIZATION: Imperial Rome
MAJOR ROLE/POSITION: Emperor

Life. Lucius Domitius Aurelianus (LEW-shee-uhs doh-MIHSH-ee-uhs aw-ree-lee-AY-nuhs) was born to a peasant family on the frontier but rose rapidly in the Roman army to become a general of the cavalry. When Emperor Claudius II died of plague in 270 C.E., Aurelianus was chosen to succeed to the throne.

When Aurelianus took command, the Eastern provinces had broken away from Rome under the leadership of Zenobia of Palmyra. Gaul, Spain, and Britain had also been an independent empire since 259 C.E. The central portion of the empire was suffering constant attack by barbarians.

Aurelianus quickly and decisively restored the unity and security of the empire. He defeated the barbarians, fortified Rome, conquered Zenobia of Palmyra, and ar-

ranged the surrender of the Gallic emperor, all within five years. In 275 C.E., he was treacherously murdered by a group of officers when his secretary, who was about to be prosecuted for corruption, told them they were to be executed.

Influence. Known to his soldiers as "hand to the sword" (*manu ad ferrum*), Aurelianus was the supreme man of action who came along when only such a person would serve. He saved the Roman Empire from destruction, setting the groundwork for its survival for the next few centuries. The walls he built around the city of Rome were its principal defense for many centuries and are still visible.

ADDITIONAL RESOURCES

Gibbon, Edward. *Decline and Fall of the Roman Empire.* New York: Modern Library, 1995.

Watson, Alaric. *Aurelian and the Third Century.* London: Routledge, 1999.

SEE ALSO: Gauls; Rome, Imperial; Zenobia.

—*David Langdon Nelson*

AUSONIUS, DECIMUS MAGNUS

BORN: c. 310 C.E.; Burdigala, Gaul (later Bordeaux, France)
DIED: c. 395 C.E.; Burdigala, Gaul
RELATED CIVILIZATION: Imperial Rome
MAJOR ROLE/POSITION: Poet

Life. Decimus Magnus Ausonius (DEHS-ih-muhs MAG-nuhs aw-SOH-nee-uhs) taught grammar and rhetoric for thirty years in his native Burdigala until appointed tutor of the future emperor Gratian, after whose accession in 375 C.E. he rose to the consulate. When Ausonius's influence began to wane, he withdrew to Burdigala, where his last years were devoted to literary pursuits. He produced much donnish and declamatory

verse; its pagan erudition is unaffected by a Laodicean Christianity, and the political and social issues of the troubled times never impinge on its timeless artificiality. His poetry, which combines technical proficiency with a remarkable engrossment on the part of the poet in himself and his own surroundings, is also marked by a special partiality for the compilation of lists embracing such disparate topics as Latin monosyllables, Burdigala professors, warriors from the Trojan War, his own relatives, and the fish in the Moselle.

Influence. The formal elegance of Ausonian verse ensured its influence on medieval and Renaissance poets, though the former were to some extent deterred by the author's unsuccessful attempt to dissuade his former pupil Saint Paulinus of Nola from embracing the ascetic life.

ADDITIONAL RESOURCES
Green, R. P. H., ed. *The Works of Ausonius*. New York: Clarendon Press, 1991.

Sivan, H. *Ausonius of Bordeaux: Genesis of a Gallic Aristocracy*. New York: Routledge, 1993.

SEE ALSO: Gratian; Languages and literature; Paulinus, Saint; Rome, Imperial.

—Neil Adkin

AUSTRALIA, TASMANIA, NEW ZEALAND

DATE: 8000 B.C.E.-700 C.E.
LOCALE: South Pacific
SIGNIFICANCE: These islands are the site of some of the earliest civilizations outside of Eurasia.

The first peoples to arrive in the largest islands in the South Pacific came originally from Eurasia and traveled by sea south along the Australonesian archipelago, reaching Australia by about 40,000 years ago. Tasmania was isolated from the rest of Australia during the last great rise in ocean levels, about 12,000-6000 B.C.E. New Zealand was reached by ocean much later, perhaps as recently as 1000 C.E., and populated by a seagoing Polynesian people, the Maori, whose origins and culture remain distinct. Animal remains indicate an abrupt disappearance of certain species of birds about 50,000 years B.C.E., coinciding with the probable arrival of the first wave of human immigrants to the unpopulated continent, from the western lands and across the shallow seas.

By the period from 8000 to approximately 5000 B.C.E., human populations—with their tribal technologies, distinctions, distributions, language variations, and common knowledge—had stabilized and were associated with specific locales. These cultures had differentiated and adapted to areas from tropical coastal lowlands to high desert plateaus. During this late Holocene period, Aboriginal populations moved into the interior of the continent to explore desert environments. The evidence indicates that changes in toolmaking increased the efficiency of harvesting of local resources and gave human populations time to explore and exploit marginal environments.

Early populations of hunter-gatherers did not engage in agriculture and were completely dependent on their knowledge of their surroundings and their ability to sustain their yearly yields of local resources as their nomadic bands moved from place to place. These Aboriginal people apparently believed that by keeping the balance and maintaining the blueprint for creation—in the form of behavior, rituals, and ceremonies left by the Dreamtime people, who gave them to humans as instructions for sustaining the environment in all its complex dimensions—they ensured that human beings would continue. Variations in culture were mostly related to the demands of the different environments, and a great degree of cultural continuity is evident in the tools, beliefs, and social and economic forms across what was, before the oceans rose in the last episode of glacial subsidence, isolating Tasmania, a single continent referred to as Sahul.

Around 2000 B.C.E., flaked stone tools appeared, coincidental with the arrival in Australia of a type of wild dog, the dingo. From 1000 to 500 B.C.E., populations increased as these new tools allowed more efficient exploitation of the previously unused marginal environments, and trade between isolated groups became more widespread.

Though disputed to some degree, it is generally agreed that the Aboriginal peoples are of a single type, or perhaps two peoples, who originated in different areas of Indonesia and China and came onto the islands at separate times. There is striking uniformity among the many distinct groups that came to populate what are among the world's largest islands.

Languages, cultural practices, and uses. More than two hundred various languages were spoken among groups referred to as tribes by Europeans. There were as many as five hundred distinctive tribal groups defined by their territorial ranges and named accordingly. Various groups were defined by the set of mythic cycles used in their songs, which were shared at large gatherings at various places from season to season. Their oral tradition was not poetic but includes chants, some several hundred verses long, recited to the accompaniment of clapping sticks, clubs, boomerangs, or other percussive instruments, as well as the didgeridoo, depending on the norms of the areal cultures.

AUSTRALIA AND THE SOUTH PACIFIC

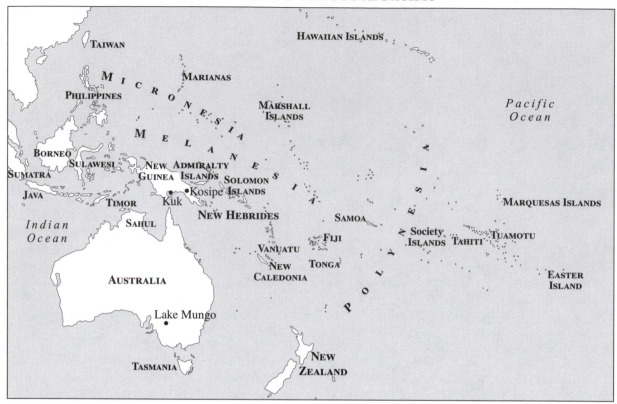

Visual arts were highly developed. As the Aboriginal peoples went naked almost universally, they wore elaborate headdresses and painted and pierced their bodies. They also created complex incised wood carvings, rock and cave paintings, ceremonial hardwood poles, and various fetishes.

Housing types varied depending on weather. In the southern deserts, bough shelters and windbreaks were used in the cooler season, although most of the time people simply slept out in the open. Dogs and fires kept the people warm. In the north, bark shelters were constructed during the monsoon season, or the people retreated to caves or built stilt houses to get above the pests and floods.

Tools had to be, for the most part, portable. Fire kits, boomerangs, and spears thrown with the atlatl are examples of things carried in the Aboriginal peoples' tool kits. Some tools were made on site from available materials, and some were part of sites returned to repeatedly. Tool types evolved in identifiable ways across the islands. The Aboriginal peoples made dugout canoes with stone adzes, as well as bark canoes and rafts rigged with

pandanus sails, harkening back to their ancestors' seagoing origins. They carried things in plaited baskets and wooden dishes, made kangaroo skins into water bags, and drank from skulls in the south. Women also carried kits of stone tools including files made of sharkskin, bone needles, wedges, and digging sticks that could be easily used as weapons. Small bands and family groups were the rule, and they had to be self-sufficient.

Cultural uses and practices have remained fairly consistent over tens of thousands of years and into historic times. Changes in the way people lived originated primarily during periods of climatic change or large-scale geological incidents such as changes in ocean levels. Aboriginal people have proven immensely adaptable.

Aboriginal society. The Aboriginal peoples believed that life came from the Dreaming, a fully integrated world, alive and theirs to sustain by ritual and other appropriate forms of ceremonial and kinship behavior. Timeless truths from the original spiritual beings were enacted in their daily life. If the people followed the original pattern given to their ancestors and handed down from one generation to the next, the world would remain in balance and they would survive. Dances and other forms of sacred ritual dominated daily life, apart from hunting by the men (which could be used as a way to gain spiritual knowledge) and food gathering by the women, and thus daily life was for these Aboriginal peoples an expression of the life of the Dreaming. Everything emerged from it and returned to it in continuous cycle, keeping the world in balance and giving the people a sense of involvement in and control over their surroundings. Life and death were contained in what was given to each generation.

Children were weaned by the age of two to three years. Children learned primarily by imitating adults and older relatives. Girls were taught to provide food and would join their husband's household upon marriage. Kinship shaped all social relationships. Some people, such as in-laws, one learned to avoid, and some, such as elders, one respected. Totemic beliefs, close-knit clans, extended family bands, and social moieties each played a part in the greater community and landscape. Each person could identify himself or herself by birth group, hearth group, or estate group. The spiritual beings of the Dreaming were evident in every shrub, waterhole, and creature.

Boys were initiated between the ages of six and twelve, depending on the group. They were "reborn" as adults, to be guardians of spirit, fertility, and sacred space across time. They depended on their vast, complex, and intricate social and oral traditions for survival. Initiation into adulthood might include circumcision, urethral subincision, body piercing, tooth pulling, genital bloodletting, plucking, or otherwise removing body hair.

Marriage was mostly arranged, and infant betrothal was common. Other forms of negotiating a marriage included contracting, compensatory trades of family members for reciprocal mates from other groups, elopement, and bride capture. Polygyny was acceptable to varying degrees, and depending on the group, men could, in some instances, have from two to twenty-five wives. Divorce was known but not that common. Usually women left the men or were given away to fulfill reciprocal obligations. Women and children were treated well and not abused, although they were made somewhat subservient by social convention.

There were no chiefdoms or other evident political entities or structures, with rare exception. Likewise, the Aboriginal groups lacked class distinctions and were egalitarian in nature. Age and sex were the major determinants of social status. Most conflicts arose over un-explained deaths, arguments over spiritual matters, and fights over women. Shame was the means of social control, and in arguments, elders dealt with the principals and handed out sanctions to settle conflicts. Kinship claims held precedence over all others, and most authority was based on them. Unselfish giving and sharing, free association, exchange and trade, and devotion to the life of community were the most common values. Tools, weapons, red ochre, mind-altering plants, and pearl shell were traded across the continent. Environmental relationships and limitations tended to preclude the development of political structure.

Beliefs tended to be animistic and totemic, directed toward maintaining balance between the Dreaming, the people, and the environment. The creative beings provided the plan, changeless as the law of the Dreamtime. Self-disciplined, autonomous, and proud, the people needed only to participate in the eternal recreation of those original patterns of Dreaming, accessible through nature, trance, and dream. Beliefs drew the people together, and their totemic ties held them in place in their individual and communal relationships with all of creation. All things were thus defined by their relationships to all others. Men, women, and children, though somewhat circumscribed by their social conditioning and roles, all had a place in the sacred life of the world and played their part in the life of the community and its rituals, ceremonies, initiations, and social gatherings.

Social obligations and networks were mirrored in the extensive trade relationships that gradually developed within and between regions. Gift exchanges were the most common form of reinforcing social bonds and redistributing goods geographically. Some members of certain groups would travel hundreds of miles just to engage in social exchange networks. As they were nomadic and traveled light, Aboriginal peoples were not able to accumulate objects that might interfere with their necessary movement within their territories. The economy was based on the local environmental resources; if there were surpluses of objects of value, they were traded or given away to solidify social ties, incur and dispatch debts, and meet other obligations. This supported the continental diffusion of shared cultural characteristics.

Over long stretches of geological time stretching back more than 40,000 years, the peoples of Sahul, which became the continental islands of Indonesia, Papua, and Australia, and Tasmania, developed and stabilized, remaining fully responsive to the demands of the environment as expressed in the beauty and laws of the Dreamtime, adaptable enough to survive the rigors and demands of their place in the historic period after 1000 C.E.

ADDITIONAL RESOURCES
Flood, J. *Archaeology of the Dreamtime*. Sydney: Collins, 1983.

Rouse, I. *Migrations in Prehistory*. New Haven, Conn.: Yale University Press, 1986.
Tindale, N. V. *The Aboriginal Tribes of Australia*. Berkeley: University of California Press, 1974.

SEE ALSO: Djanggawul cycle; Dreaming.

—*Michael W. Simpson*

AVESTA

AUTHORSHIP: Zoroaster and Zoroastrian priests
DATE: 1000-600 B.C.E.
LOCALE: Central Asia, Persia
RELATED CIVILIZATION: Persia

The *Avesta* (AH-vuh-stah) is a collection of hymns that make up the sacred Zoroastrian scripture. The surviving part of the *Avesta* is divided into five sections that differ in content and structure. These are the Yasna, Yasht, Wispered, Vendidad, and Khorde Avesta. The oldest section of the *Avesta* was composed by the Prophet Zoroaster, who lived somewhere in eastern Persia or Central Asia sometime between 1000 and 600 B.C.E. Zoroaster's hymns are known as the *Gathas*, embedded in the Yasna liturgy, which proclaims Ahura Mazda as the supreme deity. The *Gathas* and various other hymns are known as the Old Avestan texts because of dialectal differences within the *Avesta*. All other parts are known as the Younger Avesta.

The Yashts invocations are a series of hymns that concern themselves with other Aryan deities such as Wahram and Mitra. This section of the *Avesta* provides the mythical history of the Iranian people in which several dynasties such as the Peshdadids and Kayanids and feats of their kings and heroes are mentioned. The other

major part of the *Avesta* is the Vendidad "antidemonic law," which deals with issues of purity and pollution, ritual, and prescriptions in such matters as how to dispose of the dead, treatment of women during their menstruation, and treating the sick.

The *Avesta* was written down and codified in the Sāsānian period in the Avestan script (224-651 C.E.). Commentaries, or Zand, also were written. There were probably different interpretations of the *Avesta* in the Sāsānian period, which gave rise to schism and division among the priests.

ADDITIONAL RESOURCES
Darmesteter, James. *The Zend-Avesta*. In *Sacred Books of the East*, edited by F. Max Müller. Oxford, England: Oxford University Press, 1882. Reprint. Delhi: Motilal Banarsidass, 1993.
Insler, Stanley. *The Gathas of Zarathustra*. Leiden, Netherlands: E. J. Brill, 1978.
Kellens, Jean. "Avesta." In *Encyclopaedia Iranica*. London: Routledge and Kegan Paul, 1989.

SEE ALSO: Persia; Zoroaster; Zoroastrianism.

—*Touraj Daryaee*

AVITUS, EPARCHIUS

BORN: c. 395 C.E.; Gaul
DIED: 457 C.E.; place unknown
RELATED CIVILIZATION: Imperial Rome
MAJOR ROLE/POSITION: General, administrator

Life. Eparchius Avitus (uh-PAHR-kee-uhs uh-VIT-uhs) was born into a senatorial family in the Auvergne in Gaul. He had a distinguished civil and military ca-

reer, serving both as a general and, in the late 430's C.E., as praetorian prefect of Gaul. In 455 C.E., he was appointed master of soldiers by the emperor Petronius Maximus. After Maximus's murder during the Vandals' sack of Rome in 455 C.E., Avitus was proclaimed emperor with the support of the Visigothic king Theoderic II (r. 453-466 C.E.). He was duly recognized by the senate of Rome and his reign commenced well enough. The Vandal raiding parties returned to Africa, and Theoderic was sent to Spain to fight the Suebi. On January 1, 456 C.E., Avitus entered the consulate, and his son-in-law Sidonius Apollinaris, a famous Latin writer, delivered a panegyric in his honor.

In the spring, Avitus sent the barbarian general Ricimer against the Vandals, who were defeated twice. Meanwhile, Avitus was blamed for a food shortage at Rome. To save money, he dismissed his Gothic bodyguard, which left him defenseless against a revolt led by the generals Majorian and Ricimer. In October, 456 C.E., he was decisively defeated at Piacenza. He was stripped of his imperial dignity and forcibly consecrated bishop of the city. In early 457 C.E., Avitus attempted to return to Gaul but died on the journey.

Influence. Avitus's brief reign provided the last opportunity for creating a coalition between Romans and barbarians and revitalizing the Western Roman Empire. His failure indicates that the forces of fragmentation, such as the self-interest of Italian senators and barbarian generals and kings, were too strong.

ADDITIONAL RESOURCES

Mathisen, Ralph W. "Avitus, Italy and the East in A.D. 455-456." *Byzantion* 51 (1981): 232-247.

_____. "The Third Regnal Year of Eparchius Avitus." *Classical Philology* 80 (1985): 326-335.

SEE ALSO: Rome, Imperial; Vandals.

—*Ralph W. Mathisen*

AXUM

ALSO KNOWN AS: Aksum
DATE: 1-700 C.E.
LOCALE: Tigray province, northern Ethiopia
RELATED CIVILIZATION: Ethiopia
SIGNIFICANCE: The city of Axum grew rich and powerful between the first and third centuries C.E. Its port was the center of Red Sea coastal trade for many centuries, and by 330 C.E., Ethiopia had become a Christian-led kingdom, which continued to prosper over the next four centuries.

History. Axum (AHK-sewm) rose during the first century C.E. as the Roman Empire stimulated an extensive network of international trade to satisfy its rampant consumerism. Ethiopian traditions link Axum to the wealthy Queen of Sheba, who visited King Solomon of Israel and bore him a son named Menelik I. According to legend, Menelik left Israel, taking with him the Ark of the Covenant, and became Axum's first emperor. However, archaeologists find no evidence of urban life at Axum before the first century. Developments from 100 to 300 C.E. can be gleaned mainly from coin and monument inscriptions and from references to trade in Greco-Roman documents. However, it is evident that Axum gained control over much of Ethiopia by establishing an absolute monarchy supported by a well-organized army.

By the third century under King Ezana (r. c. 320-c. 350 C.E.), Axum succeeded in destroying the kingdom of Meroe, a powerful iron-producing rival that had been the center of Kushitic civilization. Consequently, Axum eliminated its rival for the position of main supplier of African goods to the Roman world. In 330 C.E., Ezana declared Axum to be a Christian kingdom. The decision was influenced by the Byzantine missionary Saint Frumentius, who became first bishop of the Abyssinian Church. However, the decision to facilitate trade relations with Byzantine Egypt was also a major factor. Ezana's conversion, conquests, and building program caused him to be regarded as the Constantine of Ethiopia. He was also the first king anywhere to use the cross on the coinage of the realm.

During the sixth century, King Kaleb led his forces into south Arabia, extending Axumite control to Yemen. Axum became a place of refuge for early believers of Islam, offering refuge for persecuted followers such as Muhammad's wife. This was a favor that the followers of Islam remembered. With the success of Islam and the establishment of a new trading center at Baghdad by the Abbāsids (750 C.E.), Axum's position in world trade had waned. However, Ethiopia continued to exist as a Christian kingdom, immune to attempts at conversion. Legends about a wealthy and powerful Christian kingdom in Africa persisted during the European Middle Ages (the myth of "Prester" John) and eventually served as a subsidiary stimulus for Portuguese exploration of Africa in the fifteenth century. Axum still exists as a city, important for its traditional role as the birthplace of Ethiopian religion, culture, and political unity.

Government. Axum was an absolute monarchy

ruled by a "king of kings" whose main function was to ensure the smooth operation of a tribute system. The king appointed local rulers who could be counted on to collect taxes from both towns and rural areas in an empire numbering approximately 500,000 people. The central bureaucracy appears to have been large, using ambassadors, messengers, interpreters, numerous clerks, and tax officials. In the event of child-kings, women could act as regents.

War and weapons. Axum's army was organized into regiments, all with unique names. Soldiers carried round shields and fought with two types of spears, one having a short and the other a long blade. The king served as war leader. Axum also had a navy to protect merchant shipping from piracy. Warfare was not a prevalent theme in society and was used to guarantee continued payment of tribute. There was little concern about defense as evidenced by the fact that towns were not fortified.

Trade. Axum exported ivory, skins and hides, woven fabrics, brass, copper, glass crystal, gold, frankincense, and myrrh (a resin widely used in ancient medicines and burials). It imported wine, olive oil, metal goods, and textiles. Fine pottery was produced for the wealthy classes and may also have been exported. Axumite coins were widely used in trade and have been found as far away as India and China.

Language and literature. The language of Axum was Ge'ez (Ethiopic), a Semitic language emanating from south Arabia that was written in cursive form. Ge'ez is still used in traditional Ethiopian church ritual. Greek was the official language and was used on inscriptions and coins. Axum is thought to have had a rich literature. Unfortunately, none of it has survived the ravages of time.

Social structure. Very little information exists on stratification, although Axum was known to have skilled craftspeople and a large wealthy class of merchants. Although allusions to slaves, particularly in the export trade, exist, slavery does not appear to have been a major institution in society.

Technology and agriculture. South Arabian hydraulic engineering techniques were used to ensure a reliable water supply. An excellent irrigation system made Axum self-sufficient in food. The rich lands to the south were particularly important in providing staple crops such as wheat and barley. Axum had one of the most advanced coinage systems in the ancient world. It was trimetallic, with gold inlay on both bronze and silver coins.

Religion. Until the coming of Christianity, Axum worshiped polytheistic south Arabian gods associated with the Sun, Moon, and stars. The most important symbols were the disk and the crescent. Ezana's conversion to Monophysite Christianity around 333 C.E. made Axum the first official Christian state in the world. The Abyssinian Church, formed by the Axum Christians, is still in existence. Its most important center is the Cathedral of Mary of Zion in Axum, which claims to have the original Ark of the Covenant hidden in its recesses, under guard by Coptic monks.

Architecture and burial. The most unusual structures are thin, solid stone pillars (stelae), the largest of which (100 feet, or 30 meters) surpasses even the Egyptian obelisks as the largest in the world. Stelae, usually carved in the form of a multistoried house from a single stone, were used to mark the graves of kings. Elaborate catacombs were also built in great number. Although the major catacombs were looted in early times, many still await excavation. Numerous other stone structures formed palaces and houses. They had no mortar and were held together by mud.

Current views. Archaeological excavation first began in 1906, but the main work, undertaken in the 1970's by the British Institute in East Africa, revealed a major civilization of the ancient and early medieval world. Scholars still debate whether Axum was a south Arabian transplant on African soil, a local African phenomenon, an area linked in unknown ways to Egypt and the Sudan, or a synthetic mingling of many elements.

ADDITIONAL RESOURCES

Burstein, Stanley M., ed. *Ancient African Civilizations: Kush and Axum.* Princeton, N.J.: Markus Wiener, 1998.

Kobishchanov, Yuri M. *Axum.* Translated by L. Kapitanoff. University Park: Pennsylvania State University Press, 1979.

Munro-Hay, Stuart. *Aksum: An African Civilization of Late Antiquity.* Edinburgh, Scotland: Edinburgh University Press, 1991.

Phillipson, David W. *Ancient Ethiopia: Aksum, Its Antecedents and Successors.* London: British Museum Press, 1998.

SEE ALSO: Africa, East and South; Byzantine Empire; Christianity; Ethiopia; Ezana; Islam; Israel; Napata and Meroe; Sheba, Queen of; Solomon.

—*Irwin Halfond*

— B —

BABYLONIA

DATE: 1900-1500 B.C.E.
LOCALE: The Fertile Crescent, the region between the Tigris and the Euphrates Rivers, in southeastern Mesopotamia
SIGNIFICANCE: Babylonia was the site of an empire that developed a formal law code, made strides in medicine and mathematics, and used a system of writing that produced an epic poem.

Babylonia covers the stretch of land between the Tigris and Euphrates Rivers, both of which originate in the Armenian highlands and flow into the Persian Gulf. In early times, the southern section of Babylonia was known as Sumer and the northern section as Akkad. Following the unification of Sumer and Akkad by Amorite kings who set up their capital at Babylon in the late eighteenth century B.C.E., the entire region of the Euphrates Valley came to be called Babylonia.

History. The earliest human occupation of the area seems to have occurred in Sumer, perhaps around 5000 B.C.E. The region, inhabited by people who may have been the ancestors of the Sumerians, exhibited the characteristic features of Mesopotamian civilizations—cities, temples, a rudimentary system of writing, and metalwork—during the Protoliterate Era (c. 3500-3100 B.C.E.). The Early Dynastic Period, the first civilized era, began in 3100 B.C.E. under the Sumerians, who remained dominant in the region to about 2350 B.C.E. During the period of Sumerian hegemony, Babylonia consisted of independent city-states ruled by kings who often fought one another over land and water rights. Over time, the victors began to incorporate the territories of the conquered enemy into their own.

In about 2334 B.C.E., a Semitic conqueror from the north called Sargon created a full-fledged empire and established his capital in the northern city of Akkad. The region of Babylonia came to be known as Akkad, the seat of the Sargonid Empire until about 2200 B.C.E. Though Sargon of Akkad set up inscriptions in Sumerian and in Old Akkadian (his native tongue) boasting of imperial conquests of the outlying territories, nothing is known definitely about his achievements that earned him the sobriquet of "True King."

About 2100 B.C.E., a Sumerian revival occurred under the leadership of the kings of the Third Ur Dynasty who came from a mixed race of Sumerians and Semites. In the reign of the monarch Ur-Namma (r. c. 2112-2095 B.C.E.), Sumer-Akkad extended its sway over the Assyrians of the upper Euphrates region, the Elamites, and some cities on the middle Euphrates. Ur-Namma is known as the promulgator of a law code, perhaps the earliest of its kind in the world.

About 2000 B.C.E., the Third Ur Dynasty collapsed under attacks from two directions: the Elamites from the east and the Amorites from the west. The Elamites sacked Ur, and the Amorites occupied Babylonia, conquering most of Mesopotamia by 1900 B.C.E. After a period of disunity during which the lower Euphrates Valley was divided into three kingdoms—the Amorite in the north, the Elamite in the south, and a middle kingdom called Isin and ruled by a semi-Sumerian government—the Amorites, led by their sixth king in Babylon, Hammurabi (r. 1792-1750 B.C.E.), unified lower Mesopotamia by subduing Isin and wresting the city of Larsa from the Elamites. Under the Amorites, Babylonia became a great empire, and its capital city Babylon became a political and commercial center. Hammurabi created a code of law and encouraged science and learning.

Following Hammurabi's long reign, Babylonia lost its political momentum, and the empire disintegrated. The Old Babylonian kingdom could neither master the techniques of imperial government nor protect itself from the geographical hazards of the region—its openness. The city-state of Mari on the middle Euphrates seceded twenty years after Hammurabi's death. A series of political disturbances to the south of Babylon, including a revolt in Larsa, resulted eventually (about eighty years later) in the loss of direct control of the profitable gulf trade and some of the rich areas in the extreme south, in particular the date-groves and the fishing areas of the marshes, with the establishment of the Sealand Dynasty.

Meanwhile, Indo-European-speaking tribes, which had long ago left their homes in north-central Europe, were now invading the area. However, Babylonia maintained its political entity until its sacking in 1595 B.C.E. by Mursilis I, the king of the Hittites. In about 1550 B.C.E., the Kassites from the Armenian mountains established themselves in Babylonia and ruled the land until about 1200 B.C.E. By this time, however, the center of political gravity had shifted to the north, where the Hittites and the Assyrians were to develop a powerful empire.

Government and law. The Sumerian kings (*lugal*) ruled through the *ensi*, the city-prince or the governor, assisted by the assembly of elders (*ukkin*). From the Third Ur Dynasty, the city-princes suffered a decline and were finally eliminated by Hammurabi. The kings exercised a sort of patriarchal despotism, dispensing justice and protecting the weak and the meek. Hammurabi prohibited the Babylonian practice of cultic divination of the king. His successors, however, continued to refer to him as "Hammurabi-ili" ("Hammurabi is my god").

In the third millennium B.C.E., the administration of state and temple probably coincided. Although office-holders with numerous titles existed, it is hard to define their functions precisely. Higher or lower state officials were often called on to oversee public works or to serve as officers and soldiers in times of war. The earliest Sumerian documents refer to the *sukal* or *sukkallu*, who often functioned as ministers but also as lower-ranking officers. As administrative officials of all ranks and types had to learn the art of writing, they were often simply referred to as *dubsar*, or scribe.

Hammurabi's surviving correspondence shows his unremitting zeal in supervising the bureaucracy and its various activities, including maintaining canals, defending the land, and dispensing justice. Most famous of all is Hammurabi's law code carved on a basalt stele 7.3 feet (2.25 meters) high. Its 282 sections represent the king's idea of justice and punishment for crimes.

These ruins in Iraq, photographed in 1950, are part of the remains of the city of Babylon. (Hulton Archive)

War and weapons. The Sumerians used the phalanx for hand-to-hand combat. The Akkadians preferred a well-organized battle rank called *sidru*. About fifty-four hundred men were in perennial service to the king, and they often served as cadres for the formation of larger units. The infantry consisted of lancers, shield bearers, and archers and formed the core of the armies, which often included engineers for constructing roads and bridges. Chariots drawn by onagers (Asian wild asses) were used in battle. Siege warfare developed early on as a special category of warfare.

Society. Hammurabi's laws distinguished three social groups: *awilum* ("man," or a free citizen), *muskenum* ("dependent," a royal retainer or a palace dependent), and *wardum* ("slave"). However, no hierarchical relation between *awilum* and *muskenum* could be inferred. The law viewed women essentially as property in regard to marriage rights. However, Hammurabi's code refers to the daughters of high-ranking officials, the *naditu* of the city of Sipar, who were dedicated to the god Shamash, lived with their servants in the cloister, invested their dowry in profitable businesses, and could will their wealth to their preferred successors.

Economy. The government-sponsored canals expanded the amount of arable land. Ancient documents describe many small plots of land owned and worked by families or individuals. As time passed, the plots tended to be concentrated in large estates owned by nobles and palace officials. The small landholders were gradually crowded out, and many of them ended up as renters and sharecroppers on lands their forebears had once owned.

Trade was controlled by individuals, families, and partnerships. Prosperous merchants with large amounts of capital became moneylenders (*tamkarum*) and collected interest on their loans. Hammurabi's code regulated economic and business matters such as contracts, irrigation procedures, debts, and maximum wages. The wealthy merchants financed other traders, whom they supplied with silver or trade goods and with whom they shared the profits of a trading venture. By the middle of the Old Babylonian period, the traders in the big cities of Babylonia formed loose corporations supervised by the central government.

Medicine and mathematics. The oldest medical text in Babylonia is a Third Ur Dynasty pharmacopoeia, written in Sumerian. It contains a dozen medical prescriptions that reveal a familiarity with elaborate chemical operations and procedures. The Babylonians attributed numerous diseases to evil powers, and numerous medical texts describe treatment by the exorcists (*ashipu*).

Babylonian mathematics was based on the Sumerian sexagesimal system of notation. During the Old Babylonian period, a complex mathematical system developed, and many texts describe various algebraic operations and provide tables for multiplying and dividing and for calculating squares and square roots, cubes and cube roots, reciprocals, and exponential functions.

Religion. The Sumerians worshiped numerous deities, including craft gods, local civic gods, and gods with various specialized functions, although apparently a core of major deities were recognized as national gods throughout the region. The city of Nippur, located near the borders of Sumer and Akkad, was the great religious center for Babylonia. There the chief deity was Enlil, the creator of heaven and earth and the god who directed the activities of the other gods. Major Sumerian deities were connected with astral bodies, something that may have prompted the study of both astronomy and astrology. Samash, the Sun god, was the source of law and Sin or Nanna, the Moon goddess, of wisdom and astronomy. Anu, the sky god, was once the chief deity at Uruk; he later shed some of his attributes, which were taken over by his son Enlil and subsequently by Marduk. Other gods included a god of earth and the underworld ocean, Enki (or Ea), and a god of pestilence, Nergal. Innana (later called Ishtar) was the goddess of love, war, and fertility, and her consort was a young god called Tammuz (or Dumuzi), who died in summer and was reborn with the autumn rains. The gods were visualized in human shape and were represented in statues. In some temples (ziggurats), statues of rulers shared the sanctum with those of gods.

Architecture and sculpture. Lacking ready sources of wood and stone, the Babylonians used sun-dried bricks for building homes and temples. Temples were built on high platforms because of the dangers from the ubiquitous and uncontrollable floods. Painted stucco and colored glazed bricks were used for architectural decoration. Lack of stone also affected Sumerian sculpture, which could never compare with the massive creations of the Egyptians. Nevertheless, Babylonian craftspeople achieved excellence in metal and clay works. The remains of the royal graves from the First Dynasty of Ur, dating from 2500 B.C.E., provide eloquent testimony to Sumerian craftsmanship in gold, silver, bronze, and lapis lazuli.

Myths. Sumerian priests wrote myths to explain how things came to be and why things are as they are.

Among these myths were a creation story, a story of Innana's stealing civilization from Enki and bringing it to humans, and a flood story, the *enuma elish* ("when on high"), that may have influenced the one in the Old Testament.

Writing system and literature. Writing in Babylonia was done in wedge-shaped (cuneiform) characters etched on clay tablets by a stylus with a triangular-shaped point. In the Old Babylonian period, Sumerian dialogical and didactic texts (*adaman-dug-ga*, or "man against man") were used as school texts. Didactic literature developed during the second millennium B.C.E. as a result of rising concern with moral and ethical problems. A little later, philosophical literature developed, emphasizing the assumption that the universe was ruled by the gods, who punished those who neglected them and rewarded those who served them dutifully. The theme of the righteous sufferer who could never distinguish between good and bad because of the remoteness of the gods was reflected in a class of writings known *ludlul bel nemeqi* ("I will praise the lord of wisdom"). The Babylonians looked for no rewards in the afterlife and longed for immortality. This theme is expressed in the Gilgamesh epic, one of the great achievements of the Old Babylonian period. In later ages, the grace and magnitude of this epic, based on the ancient Sumerian ballads, earned it a favorable comparison with Homer's *Iliad* (c. 800 B.C.E.; English translation, 1616) and *Odyssey* (c. 800 B.C.E.; English translation, 1616).

Current views. After the pioneering researches of Heinrich Zimmern, Bruno Meissner, François Thureau-Dangin, and James Pritchard, specialists have come a long way in modifying much of the thinking about Babylon, thanks in part to the field activities of the State Organization of Antiquities and Heritage at Babylon and of the archaeologists from many countries now working in Iraq. The proliferation of research makes it increasingly difficult to write a general commentary on the history and culture of Babylonia.

ADDITIONAL RESOURCES

Kuhrt, Amelie. *The Ancient Near East, c. 3000-330* B.C. 2 vols. London: Routledge, 1995.

Oates, Joan. *Babylon*. Rev. ed. New York: Thames and Hudson, 1986.

Pritchard, James B., ed. *The Ancient Near East: An Anthology in Texts and Pictures*. Translated by William F. Albright. 2 vols. Princeton, N.J.: Princeton University Press, 1973.

Saggs, H. W. F. *Babylonians*. Berkeley: University of California Press, 2000.

Snell, Daniel C. *Life in the Ancient Near East 3100-332* B.C.E. New Haven, Conn.: Yale University Press, 1997.

Starr, Chester G. *A History of the Ancient World*. 4th ed. New York: Oxford University Press, 1991.

Von Soden, Wolfram. *The Ancient Orient: An Introduction to the Study of the Ancient Near East*. Translated by Donald G. Schley. Grand Rapids, Mich.: Wm. B. Eerdmans, 1994.

SEE ALSO: Akkadian Dynasty; Fertile Crescent; Gilgamesh epic; Hammurabi's code; Hittites; Kassites; Sargon of Akkad; Sumerians; Ur-Namma.

—*Narasingha P. Sil*

BACCHYLIDES

ALSO KNOWN AS: Bakchylides
BORN: c. 520 B.C.E.; Iulis, Island of Ceos
DIED: c. 450 B.C.E.; place unknown
RELATED CIVILIZATION: Classical Greece
MAJOR ROLE/POSITION: Choral lyric poet

Life. Bacchylides (buh-KIHL-uh-deez) was the nephew of Simonides of Ceos. Like his contemporary Pindar, he composed odes to be sung to musical accompaniment of lyres and pipes (reed instruments) and to be danced by choruses. Of his nine books of poems collected in the Hellenistic period, a papyrus discovered in 1896 has preserved substantial portions of fourteen epinician (victory) odes and six dithyrambs. Two recipients of his victory odes, Hieron I of Syracuse and Pytheas of Aegina, were also celebrated by Pindar. His odes, like Pindar's, contain aphoristic reflections, mythological vignettes, advice, prayers, and praise of achievement, but his style is considerably simpler and less difficult to translate than Pindar's.

His dithyrambs feature mythological narratives such as Menelaus's mission to Troy to recover Helen, Deianira's destruction of her husband Heracles, Theseus's voyage to confront the Minotaur, while one presents a dramatic dialogue between the chorus and Aegeus, king of Athens.

Influence. Because only a few short fragments of his poetry were known before the papyrus was published, Bacchylides' influence was negligible. Furthermore, he was overshadowed by Pindar, to whom antiquity judged him inferior.

ADDITIONAL RESOURCES

Burnett, A. P. *The Art of Bacchylides*. Cambridge, Mass.: Harvard University Press, 1985.

Campbell, D. A. *Greek Lyric*. Cambridge, Mass.: Harvard University Press, 1992.

Maehler, H. *Die Lieder des Bakchylides*. Vol. 1. Leiden, Netherlands: E. J. Brill, 1982.

SEE ALSO: Greece, Classical; Hieron I of Syracuse; Pindar; Languages and literature; Simonides.

—William H. Race

BACTRIA

DATE: c. fifth century-120 B.C.E.

LOCALE: Central Asia between the Hisar and Hindu Kush Mountains, present-day Uzbekistan, Tajikistan, and Afghanistan

RELATED CIVILIZATIONS: Persia, India, Hellenistic Greece

SIGNIFICANCE: Hellenistic culture spread from this satrapy of the Achaemenian Empire to Inner Asia and India with conquests of Bactrian kings.

Bactria (BAK-tree-uh) was a rich agricultural area watered by irrigation canals from the mountains by the beginning of the first millennium B.C.E., and archaeology has uncovered many sites that were inhabited in ancient times. The history of Bactria, however, begins with its incorporation into the Achaemenian Empire of the Persians.

Bactria, the most important province and center of Achaemenian control in Central Asia, was conquered by Cyrus the Great about 540 B.C.E., and its satrap supported his son Darius the Great in the latter's seizure of the throne about 522 B.C.E. Alexander the Great engaged in much fighting in Central Asia and had established many garrisons in Bactria by 327 B.C.E. when he left for India. More Greeks and Macedonians were settled in Bactria than elsewhere in Alexander's empire because the local inhabitants were prone to revolt and trade routes from Greece to the east had to be maintained.

From 307 B.C.E. when Seleucus I became heir to the Asian portion of Alexander's empire until about 245 B.C.E., Bactria remained subject to his successors. The Seleucids established additional colonies in Bactria, several of which have been excavated. The site that has provided most information about this period of history is Ay Khanum in northern Afghanistan on the Kokcha

River, probably founded by Antiochus I Soter, son of Seleucus I. It was a fully Greek city with an agora (marketplace), gymnasium, theater, and other features of Hellenistic cities. The capital of Bactria was at Bactra (present-day Balkh), which has not been excavated.

About 245 B.C.E., Diodotus I, the Greek governor of Bactria, revolted against Seleucid rule and established the Greco-Bactrian kingdom, striking his own coinage, considered the finest in antiquity for the lifelike features of the rulers. Most of what is known about the rulers of this kingdom comes from their many coins. About 230 B.C.E., a rebel called Euthydemus seized power in Bactria, but about 208 B.C.E., the Seleucid ruler Antiochus the Great defeated him and laid siege to Bactra. Peace was made, and Euthydemus retained his kingdom, succeeded by his son Demetrius. The latter crossed the Hindu Kush Mountains and conquered parts of northwest India. During his absence, Eucratides (c. 170 B.C.E.) apparently seized power of Bactria from Demetrius, either I or II, for the coins are uncertain sources, and only their different styles suggest another ruler with the same name.

The Bactrian kingdom had apparently become divided about the beginning of the second century B.C.E., and various rulers struck coins that cannot be localized and only approximately dated by legends and artistic features. In general, coins with only Greek legends and minted in the Attic weight system are assigned to rulers north of the Hindu Kush Mountains, and coins with both Greek and Indian legends with an Indian weight system are assigned to those Greeks who ruled south of the mountain range. The Parthians encroached on Bactrian domains in the west, and areas north of the Hisar range probably became independent of Greek rule by the second century B.C.E.

The most famous of later Greco-Bactrian rulers was

Menander, who ruled in northwest India (r. c. 155-135 B.C.E.). He is probably to be identified with the king Milinda of a Buddhist book in the Pāli language, the *Milinda-pañha* (first or second century C.E., some material added later, date uncertain; *The Questions of King Milinda*, 1890-1894). The plethora of names on the coins—Antimachus, Agathocles, Pantaleon, Strato, and others—suggest a division of the Bactrian realms into many small kingdoms, as well as the founding of many cities. Greek colonists from the west, however, must have been few after the Parthians expanded their rule over the Iranian plateau by the beginning of the second century.

The extent of Greco-Bactrian possessions in India is unknown, but allusions in a Sanskrit grammar to Greeks besieging towns in the Ganges River valley indicate that they at least raided far into the subcontinent, perhaps in compensation for land lost to the Parthians in what has become southern Afghanistan.

Archaeology has yielded few remains of the Bactrian Greeks, but the inscriptions and art objects that remain compare favorably with those of Greece itself. There is no evidence of major conflicts between the Greeks and the local population, but the site of Ay Khanum suggests that Bactrians left no traces of their occupation in the city until after the nomadic invasions. In time, however, syncretistic tendencies of the Hellenistic world brought local features into the art and architecture of the Greek settlements in Bactria. Local deities were identified with those of the Greeks, and natural features, such as the Oxus River (later Amu Dar'ya River) were deified. This leads to the conclusion that at first the Greeks remained separate from the local population, but assimilation gradually proceeded until the foreigners were absorbed.

About 130 B.C.E., the Greco-Bactrian domains to the north of the Hindu Kush Mountains were overrun by nomads from Central Asia. These were the Sakas, or Scythians as the Greeks called them, and they were followed by other nomads. The last Greek ruler who struck coins in Bactria was called Hermaeus, but apparently copies of his coinage continued to be struck after his reign. Other Greeks continued to rule in India for at least half a century until they too were replaced by Sakas and later the Kushāns. One tribe of the latter gave their name to Bactria, for when the Arabs came to this land at the end of the seventh century C.E. it was called Tokharistan.

ADDITIONAL RESOURCES

Narain, A. K. *The Indo-Greeks*. Oxford, England: Oxford University Press, 1957.

Tarn, W. W. *The Greeks in Bactria and India*. 2d ed. Cambridge, England: Cambridge University Press, 1952.

SEE ALSO: Achaemenian Dynasty; Alexander the Great; Antiochus the Great; Cyrus the Great; Darius the Great; Greece, Hellenistic and Roman; Kushān Dynasty; Menander (Greco-Bactrian king); Parthia; Scythia; Seleucid Dynasty; Seleucus I.

—*Richard N. Frye*

BALL GAME, MESOAMERICAN

DATE: c. 500 B.C.E.-700 C.E.

LOCALE: Mesoamerica

RELATED CIVILIZATIONS: Aztec, Maya, Olmec, Toltec

SIGNIFICANCE: This popular Mesoamerican phenomenon had social, political, and religious import.

The Mesoamerican ball game, played with a solid rubber ball, originated with the pre-Classic Olmec civilization and continued to be played in ancient times. Spanish priests banned it after the Conquest (1521). An integral feature of Mesoamerican culture, it was found at sites ranging from Central America to southern Arizona.

Mesoamerican ball courts were masonry structures that contained a paved playing area, side walls with platforms for spectators, and temples. Many courts were shaped like a capital I and varied in size. The largest, found at the Maya site of Chichén Itzá, measures 150 meters (490 feet) in length.

The object was to score goals in a contest between either single opponents or full teams on each side. Players wore protective equipment to avoid injuries from the ball and hard court floor. In early form, the game was part of a religious cult and a universally shared Mesoamerican ideology. The action symbolized important concepts such as the cycle of death and rebirth in nature and the order of the cosmos in which sky deities battled. In later times, it was played more as a spectator sport but retained ritual connotations. Finally, the game had a powerful role in Mesoamerican trade and politics.

ADDITIONAL RESOURCES

Cohodas, Marvin. "The Symbolism and Ritual Function of the Middle Classic Ball Game in Mesoamer-ica." *American Indian Quarterly* 2, no. 2 (Summer, 1975): 99-130.

Scarborough, Vernon L., and David R. Wilcox, eds. *The Mesoamerican Ballgame*. Tucson: University of Arizona Press, 1991.

SEE ALSO: Chichén Itzá; Maya; Olmecs.

—*David A. Crain*

BAN GU

ALSO KNOWN AS: *Wade-Giles* Pan Ku; Ban Mengjian
BORN: 32 C.E.; Shanxi, China
DIED: 92 C.E.; Shanxi, China
RELATED CIVILIZATIONS: China, Han Dynasty
MAJOR ROLE/POSITION: Historian

Life. Ban Gu's (BAHN-gew) father, historian Ban Biao, wrote a supplement to historian Sima Qian's *Shiji* (first century B.C.E.; *Records of the Grand Historian of China*, 1960, rev. ed. 1993) and began work on a history of the Western Han Dynasty (206 B.C.E.-23 C.E.). When he was sixteen, Ban Gu went to the capital city of Luoyang to study at the Imperial College. At age twenty-three, after his father died, he returned to his hometown and became a historian, collecting the materials on which his father had been working.

Five years later, Ban Gu was falsely accused of having distorted the nation's history and went to prison. His brother Ban Chao wrote to the emperor. After the emperor read the draft of Ban Gu's work, he appreciated its value. Ban Gu was freed and encouraged to continue his work. After working on it for more than twenty years, Ban Gu nearly completed *Han Shu* (also known as *Qian Han Shu*, completed first century C.E.; *The History of the Former Han Dynasty*, 1938-1955). He was arrested on suspicion of being involved in a rebellion attempt in 92 C.E. and died in prison the same year. After his death, his younger sister Ban Zhao resumed writing the history.

Influence. Ban Gu's influence is mainly through *The History of the Former Han Dynasty*, the first Chinese historical record of a single dynasty. Compared with *Records of the Grand Historian of China*, which was a more general work, it preserved more comprehensive and exact historical materials, detailing the society, culture, natural life, and geography of the Western Han Dynasty. The style and format were followed by later historians in China's feudal dynasties.

ADDITIONAL RESOURCES

Hulsewé, A. F. P. *China in Central Asia: The Early Stage, 125* B.C.-A.D. *23*. Leiden, Netherlands: Brill, 1979.

Loewe, Michael. *A Biographical Dictionary of the Qin, Former Han and Xin Periods, 221* B.C.-A.D. *24*. Boston: Brill, 2000.

Pan Ku. *The History of the Former Han Dynasty*. Baltimore: Waverly Press, 1938-1955.

Van der Sprenkel, Otto P. N. *Berkelbach: Pan Piao, Pan Ku, and the Han History*. Canberra: Australian National University, 1964.

SEE ALSO: China; Han Dynasty; Sima Qian.

—*Lihua Liu*

BĀṆA

ALSO KNOWN AS: Bāṇabhaṭṭa
FLOURISHED: seventh century C.E.; India
RELATED CIVILIZATIONS: Harṣa Empire, India
MAJOR ROLE/POSITION: Poet

Life. Bāṇa (BAW-nah) lost his mother early in childhood. He was nurtured by his father, who died when Bāṇa was fourteen. His youth was spent in a self-indulgent manner with artists, ascetics, and low-caste friends. Although a Brahman and a Pāshupata devotee, he scorned caste rules and transcended the bounds of orthodoxy. After receiving a summons from Harṣa (r. 606-647 C.E.), king of Thāneswar and Kanauj, he gained the patronage of the court.

His experience at court produced the *Harṣacarita* (seventh century C.E.; *The Harsa-carita*, 1897), an idealized account of King Harṣa's deeds and reign. Written in Sanskrit, it is a romance rather than history, a narrative poem that displays descriptive and poetic talent. *Kādambarī* (seventh century C.E.; *The Kadambari of Banabhatta*, 1920), a peerless narrative, is replete with images of love, pathos, sympathy, and fidelity in the Moon god's pursuit of the maiden Kādambarī. Bāṇa died before its completion, but his son, Bhūshaṇabhaṭṭa, completed the work. *Caṇḍīshataka*, 102 stanzas in honor of Śiva's consort, serves as a prayer, but is of little importance compared with his great romances.

Bāṇa, a humane poet, sided with the poor, ignored caste rules, and condemned *satī*, the immolation of a widow on her husband's funeral pyre. His language and style are flowery, but his outlook is twentieth century.

Influence. Bāṇa remains the most respected prose writer in India. He set the standard for literature. His *Kādambarī* is the crowning jewel of its genre.

ADDITIONAL RESOURCES

Bāṇabhaṭṭa. *Kādambarī*. Translated by Gwendolyn Layne. New York: Garland, 1991.

Basham, A. L. *The Wonder That Was India*. New York: Grove Press, 1959.

SEE ALSO: Harṣa; India.

—*George J. Hoynacki*

BANPOCUN CULTURE

ALSO KNOWN AS: *Wade-Giles* Pan-p'o-ts'un
DATE: c. 6000-4000 B.C.E.
LOCALE: Shaanxi, China
RELATED CIVILIZATION: Neolithic China
SIGNIFICANCE: The most extensively excavated Neolithic settlement site in China.

Banpocun (BAHN-poh-tsewn), discovered in 1953, is a Neolithic village site in Shaanxi, northwest China. The village covers about seven hectares (about seventeen acres) and has roughly a hundred houses. Each house had timber beams that rested on stone bases; floors and interior walls were plastered with clay and straw. In the center of the village, there was a large rectangular building with a platform. It could have been a communal assembly hall or a clan house.

The principal crop cultivated at Banpocun was millet. Chestnuts, hazelnuts, and pine nuts supplemented the grain diet. Major agriculture tools were bone hoes, axes, knives, and digging sticks. Animal bones uncovered include a variety of domesticated animals such as pigs, dogs, cattle, sheep, and goats. Fish hooks and deer

bones suggest that hunting and fishing also contributed to the subsistence existence.

The most abundant form of art produced by Neolithic cultures is pottery. More than 500,000 pieces of pottery have been unearthed at Banpocun. These pottery items include pots, vessels, bowls, and jars. Most of them were hand formed into a distinctive red ware. Although cooking pots tend to be coarse and gritty, water vessels and serving bowls are made of a finer clay. Chinese archaeologists believe that the occupation at Banpocun was long and continuous.

ADDITIONAL RESOURCES

Wenqing, Wang. *Ten Major Museums of Shaanxi*. Hong Kong: Polyspring, 1994.

Yü, Wei-ch'ao. *A Journey into China's Antiquity*. Beijing, China: Morning Glory Publishers, 1997.

SEE ALSO: China; Liangzhu culture; Longshan culture; Yangshao culture.

—*Hong Xiao*

BANTU, CONGO BASIN

DATE: 3000 B.C.E.-700 C.E.
LOCALE: Area covered by the Congo River,
including Cameroon, Central African Republic,
Gabon, Congo (Zaire), and Zimbabwe
SIGNIFICANCE: The Congo Basin was one area into
which the Bantu speakers migrated, expanded, and
settled.

The Congo Basin covers a large area of modern Cameroon in West Africa, south to Central Africa, and to Congo proper (Zaire) and part of Zimbabwe. The word *bantu* refers to people as well as to a family of about six hundred languages spoken by millions of Africans in the subcontinent south of the line from the southern Nigeria-Cameroon border in the west to southern Somalia in the east. All the Bantu (BAHN-tew) languages stem from a single ancestral language otherwise labeled as proto-Bantu. It is widely accepted that the cradle of the Bantu language and people is the Nigeria-Cameroon area. From there, the Bantu migrated to the Congo Basin and spread south and east along the Congo River tributaries, eventually reaching both coasts. Later, some began to migrate toward southern Africa, while others moved back through the forest in the direction from which their ancestors had come.

Linguists trace the geographical spread through the linguistic convergence in Bantu grammar and vocabulary. According to one theory, the ultimate source of the Bantu people was in central Benue Valley in eastern Nigeria. Migration then took Bantu speakers southward and eastward into the Congo Basin and ultimately across the continent. Another theory is that their origins were in the north, perhaps central Cameroon or the Central African Republic. From there a major center was established in the Luba country of northern Shaba, Zaire, in an area of light woodland. Gradually, areas of higher rainfall were colonized as the Bantu speakers spread south and east of the equatorial forest.

Bantu differences. From the 1970's to the 1990's, linguists established marked linguistic differences of the Bantu using a technique called lexicostatistics, which uses a mass comparison of the most basic vocabulary in the present-day languages. They noticed three distinctive dispersal branches of Bantus: the original, West Bantu, and Mashariki Bantu. The original Bantu language spread from western Cameroon to the northwest of the Great Lakes and southwestward as far as the Ogowe Delta. The ancestral West Bantu language

spread from northern Gabon southward as far as northern Namibia and eastward into the inner Zaire Basin, into the west of the Lulu River, and into Angola. The third branch, ancestral Mashariki Bantu, spread to the Great Lakes eastward toward the Indian Ocean and southward into South Africa.

Archaeological evidence for the latter part of the first millennium B.C.E. points to expansion by Iron Age invaders cultivating sorghum and millet at the expense of indigenous Late Stone Age hunter-gatherers. By the fifth century C.E., Bantu speakers had brought the Iron Age as far south as Swaziland and later into northern Namibia. Archaeologists generally agree that the ancestors of such Bantu speakers as the Kalanga, Karanga, and Venda achieved a peak of material cultural development in the tenth century and built the elegant structures, terraces, pits, and fortresses, including the Zimbabwe ruins, that appear across Zimbabwe into Botswana and at Mapungubwe in the Transversal. Other centralized states with impressive size and technological expertise were the kingdom of Congo, Luba, and the Lozi in Central Africa.

Foods, culture, and forces of expansion. Congo Basin Bantu were hunters, gatherers, and cultivators; they initially formed small villages, usually organized loosely around clan, descent, or lineage groups. Other groups introduced several varieties of food production and iron technology to Bantu speakers in subequatorial Africa. They also acquainted Bantu-speaking societies with patrilineal kinship organizations, which were adopted by many Bantu speakers.

The Bantu speakers embarked on a journey away from their Nigeria-Cameroon homeland, traveling south and southeast, and in the course of the first millennium C.E., they fanned out and established themselves as the dominant people of the southern third of the African continent. Their African yams and oil palms grew well in the close, wet climate of the Congo Basin. Other Bantu settled the savannas east and south of the rain forest, where they raised Sudanic crops such as sorghum and bulrush millet.

In the vicinity of the mouth of Zambezi River, the Bantu found food plants of southeast Asia, notably the banana, Asian yam, and cocoyam. One theory suggests that these plants were brought by Indonesian mariners who had blown across the Indian Ocean on the monsoons and established settlements on the East African coast in the third century C.E. The bananas and yams thrived in hot, moist climates where the Sudanic sorghum and millet did not do well. This allowed the Bantu in the area of the great lakes in Tanzania, Kenya, and Uganda and also in the Congo Basin to create still more productive agricultures.

Political governance. The Bantu speakers lived in relatively stable villages, composed of a few "houses" headed by leaders, whose family members, friends, and servants constituted each house. A group of four or five villages, forming a district, collaborated with each other in economic, matrimonial, medical, religious, and defense matters. Each house also forged cross-alliances with several houses in other villages to constitute clans.

It is important to note that as early as 3000 B.C.E., root-crop agriculture existed at Shum Laka in western Cameroon. In 1500 B.C.E., villages existed in southern Cameroon and in the Gabon Estuary. By 500 B.C.E., Bantus were present on the coast of the Congo and in the western part of the inner Zaire Basin and later in the lower Zaire area. Ironworking appeared in southern Cameroon and Gabon by the fourth century B.C.E., but for several centuries, metalworking, farming, and foraging communities continued to live side by side without apparently borrowing much from each other.

ADDITIONAL RESOURCES

Bobb, F. Scott. *Historical Dictionary of Zaire*. Metuchen, N.J.: Scarecrow Press, 1988.

Forbath, Peter. *The River Congo: Discovery, Exploration, and Exploitation of the World's Most Dramatic River*. New York: Harper & Row, 1977.

Shaw, Thurstan, et al., eds. *The Archaeology of Africa: Food, Metals, and Towns*. London: Routledge, 1993.

SEE ALSO: Africa, East and South; Bantu, Mashariki.
—*Alex L. Mwakikoti*

BANTU, MASHARIKI

DATE: 1000 B.C.E.-700 C.E.
LOCALE: East Africa, present-day Kenya, Uganda, and Tanzania
SIGNIFICANCE: Mashariki Bantu language and people were early settlers of East Africa.

Mashariki (mah-shah-REE-kee) is a Swahili word that means "east," and *bantu* (BAHN-tew) means "people." The Bantu speakers make up a major part of the population of nearly all Africa south of 5 degrees north latitude. They belong to about three hundred groups, each with its own language or dialect. Every Bantu group considers itself a separate cultural and political unit, and each has its own name and history. Groups vary in size from a few hundred members to several million individuals. Large groups in East Africa include the Swahili, whose language is spoken throughout eastern Africa, and the Kikuyu (Gikuyu) in Kenya.

The first Bantu came from the present Nigeria-Cameroon borderlands. Their growing population caused them to move to new lands. These people were farmers who knew how to make iron tools and weapons, knowledge that they brought to much of Africa. As early as 900 B.C.E., these ironworkers were associated with a type of pottery called Urewe ware that had penetrated into the Great Lakes area of East Africa. The sites represent the earliest evidence of iron technology in East Africa. Bantu agriculturists carried their iron technology with them as they ranged farther from the forest margins and deeper into various parts of the southern subcontinent.

The Mashariki Bantu migration was soon confronted with other peoples. The earlier inhabitants of East Africa were several different groups of food-gatherers, including some who spoke the Khoisan language. Southern Cushitic speakers from Ethiopia and the Eastern Cushites from the same area settled in the Rift Valley and in adjacent highland and plains areas of Kenya and Tanzania. Also the central Sudanic speakers came into Uganda, west of the Rift Valley. In each of these regions, the Mashariki societies expanded gradually wider and wider, progressively assimilating the earlier peoples into their societies.

The Mashariki Bantu ancestral vocabulary also shows that social structures had become different from those of the earlier Bantu dispersal. The speakers developed exogamous descent groups whose membership was better defined than that of the houses. The basic groups did not come directly from family and other ties that successful leaders had managed to create. Leaders rose in already constituted and not necessarily residential communities, and some were organized based on grouping males by age. In other places, leadership shifted to religious specialists, especially rainmakers.

Some Mashariki Bantu speakers settled in southeast Zaire and Zambia and carried their grain-based farming complex westward into the savannas and woodlands to the Atlantic Ocean. These fused with the West Bantu speakers who had preceded them there, providing strong influence.

ADDITIONAL RESOURCES

Ehret, Christopher. *An African Classical Age: Eastern and Southern Africa in World History, 1000 B.C. to A.D. 400*. Charlottesville: University Press of Virginia, 1998.

Hombert, Jean Marie, ed. *Bantu Historical Linguistics: Theoretical and Empirical Perspective*. Cambridge, England: Cambridge University Press, 1999.

SEE ALSO: Africa, East and South; Bantu, Congo Basin.

—*Alex L. Mwakikoti*

BAR KOKHBA

ALSO KNOWN AS: Simeon ben Kosiba
BORN: date and place unknown
DIED: 135 C.E.; Bethar
RELATED CIVILIZATIONS: Israel, Imperial Rome
MAJOR ROLE/POSITION: Jewish revolutionary

Life. Nothing is known about Simeon ben Kosiba (later Bar Kokhba) except his role in leading the Second Jewish Revolt against Rome. A courageous and ruthless general, he united Jews from the Tenth and Fifth legions to recapture the Judaean countryside. Simeon was offended by the Roman emperor Hadrian's plan to rebuild Jerusalem (destroyed in 70 C.E.) as a pagan city called Aelia Capitolina and agitated by a ban against the Jewish ritual of circumcision. His success lasted for three and a half years (132-135 C.E.).

Simeon minted coins depicting the destroyed Jerusalem temple and various symbols of the temple cult. Inscriptions reading "year one of the redemption of Israel" or "for the freedom of Jerusalem" demonstrate that his ultimate goal was the recapture of Jerusalem and the rebuilding of the temple. Coin legends also mention Simeon and his official title nasi, or prince. Fifteen letters written in Simeon's own hand discovered in 1960 in the Cave of Letters near the Dead Sea reveal the desperate last days of the revolt. Successful for a time, the revolt was the single blot on Hadrian's record.

Influence. Rabbi Akiba ben Joseph conferred on Simeon the messianic title Bar Kokhba (bahr kawk-BAH), or "son of the star." Simeon provided a last ray of hope for Jewish independence before nearly two thousand years of exile.

ADDITIONAL RESOURCES

Aberbach, Moses, and David Aberbach. *The Roman-Jewish Wars and Hebrew Cultural Nationalism*. New York: St. Martin's Press, 2000.

Yadin, Yigael. *Bar-Kokhba*. London: Weidenfeld & Nicolson, 1971.

Yadin, Yigael, and Jonas Greenfield, eds. *The Documents from the Bar Kokhba Period in the Cave of Letters*. Jerusalem: Israel Exploration Society, 1989.

SEE ALSO: Akiba ben Joseph; Hadrian; Israel; Jerusalem, temple of; Judaism; Rome, Imperial.

—*Fred Strickert*

BASIL OF CAPPADOCIA, SAINT

ALSO KNOWN AS: Basil of Caesarea; Basil the Great
BORN: c. 329 C.E.; Caesarea Mazaca, Cappadocia (eastern Asia Minor)
DIED: January 1, 379 C.E.; Caesarea Mazaca, Cappadocia
RELATED CIVILIZATION: Imperial Rome
MAJOR ROLE/POSITION: Religious figure

Life. Basil of Cappadocia (BAZ-uhl of ka-puh-DOH-shuh) was born into a wealthy and spiritually minded family. His received the best education available at the time, in Caesarea Mazaca, Constantinople, and Athens. At Caesarea Mazaca, he met his lifetime friend, Gregory of Nazianzus, whose work complemented his own. After completing his education, Basil practiced law and taught rhetoric. However, after a trip to study monastic life, especially that of Saint Pachomius of Egypt, he gave up his law practice, gave his wealth to the poor, and established a monastery in Pontus, a province north of Cappadocia. Basil's love of nature formed the basis of his spiritual meditations and became his philosophy of life.

In 365 C.E., Basil was called back to Caesarea Mazaca as a presbyter and, in 370 C.E., became bishop of Caesarea and archbishop of Cappadocia. With his friend Gregory of Nazianzus and his brother Gregory of Nyssa, Basil took a major role in defending the deity of Christ against Arianism. He later undertook benevolence work, including the founding of a hospital for lepers, perhaps the first in the Christian Church.

Influence. The best known of Basil's writings is his *Hexaëmeron* (fourth century C.E.; *The Treatise on the*

Holy Spirit, the Nine Homilies on the Hexameron, and the Letters, 1895), a book of homilies that influenced such leaders as Saints Ambrose and Jerome. His defense of the poor, especially from fiscal claims by civil authorities, won Basil the title of "the great" during his lifetime.

ADDITIONAL RESOURCES

Meredith, Anthony. *The Cappadocians.* Crestwood, N.Y.: St. Vladimir's Seminary Press, 1995.

Pelikan, Jaroslav. *Christianity and Classic Culture.* New Haven, Conn.: Yale University Press, 1993.

SEE ALSO: Ambrose; Arianism; Christianity; Gregory of Nazianzus; Jerome, Saint; Pachomius, Saint; Rome, Imperial.

—Glenn L. Swygart

BATHSHEBA

ALSO KNOWN AS: Bathshua; Bethsabee
FLOURISHED: tenth century B.C.E.
RELATED CIVILIZATION: Israel
MAJOR ROLE/POSITION: Monarch

Life. Bathsheba (bath-SHEE-buh), whose name meant "daughter of abundance," was the child of Eliam, one of King David's advisers, and the wife of Uriah the Hittite. While Uriah battled David's foes at Rabbah, the king summoned and impregnated Bathsheba. Subsequently, David conspired to murder Uriah and married Bathsheba. Bathsheba's first son died, but she eventually bore David four sons, including Solomon. Years later, the court prophet Nathan advised Bathsheba to persuade the dying David to name Solomon, rather than the royal scion Adonijah, as his heir. After David's death, Bathsheba transmitted a request from Adonijah that resulted in King Solomon's putting his half brother to death.

Influence. Bathsheba's ambiguous character and motives have led interpreters to portray her variously as David's innocent victim, a coconspirator in political marriage, or merely (in literary terms) as an agent, lack-

ing the status of a full-fledged character. The author of the biblical book Chronicles remembers her as Bathshua ("daughter of error"), a name that may indicate that historian's judgment. Bathsheba succeeded in securing the throne for Solomon and seems thereby to have ensured her own power and status over the kingdom.

ADDITIONAL RESOURCES

Berlin, Adele. *Poetics and Interpretation of Biblical Narrative.* Winona Lake, Ind.: Eisenbrauns, 1994.

Exum, J. Cheryl. "Bathsheba Plotted, Shot, and Painted." *Semeia* 17 (1996): 47.

Garsiel, Moshe. "The Story of David and Bathsheba." *The Catholic Biblical Quarterly* 17 (March, 1993): 244-262.

Nicol, George. "The Alleged Rape of Bathsheba." *Journal for the Study of the Old Testament* 73 (April, 1997): 43-54.

SEE ALSO: Bible: Jewish; David; Israel; Solomon.

—Walter C. Bouzard, Jr.

BaTwa

ALSO KNOWN AS: Twa; Negrillos; Pygmies (now regarded as pejorative)
DATE: 8000 B.C.E.-700 C.E.
LOCALE: South and Central Africa
SIGNIFICANCE: This South and Central African forest cultural group includes the major subgroup of Mbuti, located in the Ituri forest of Congo.

The BaTwa (bah-TWAH), formerly known as Pygmies, are regarded as one of the major surviving autochthonic groups in Central and South Africa. They have been known from ancient times, making appearances in Greek literature and Egyptian documents. The BaTwa are distinguished from their neighbors by their short stature (usually ranging from 4 feet to 4 feet, 8 inches, or 1.2 to 1.4 meters, in height). Some anthropologists believe that the BaTwa's shortness is an adaptation to life as hunter-gatherers in the forests of equatorial Africa, as their culture is. Mbuti culture, for instance, demonstrates the degree to which the BaTwa have adapted to different forest environments. They have developed different weapons for hunting and different techniques of food-gathering to suit the species, climate, and habitat in which they search for sustenance.

The BaTwa probably moved into Central Africa with the expansion of rain forests into the area at the end of the last major glaciation in Europe, around 10,000 B.C.E. Anthropologists generally believe that the BaTwa formed isolated family groups of around twenty people and developed distinctive languages and culture. This may be part of the reason that they so readily abandoned their own languages in exchange for those of their neighbors when farming and fishing West Bantu speakers moved into the area in the last millennium B.C.E.

The fact that the BaTwa largely adopted the language and culture of their Bantu neighbors reflects the importance of the Bantu settlements to the aboriginal population. Villages gave the BaTwa a focus for activities that otherwise, because of the constraints of the hunter-gatherer lifestyle, would have remained scattered throughout the forest.

These same Bantu speakers developed an extremely equivocal attitude toward their BaTwa neighbors. Most stories handed down by Bantu migrants about the original settlement period depict the BaTwa as teachers, guides, and judges. The original inhabitants of the land, the BaTwa were credited with teaching the Bantu some of the most basic precepts of their civilization: forbidding incest, making fire, using metals, healing, teaching migrants how to manage and navigate through the forest environment, and even standing as witnesses to the transfer of land. Among some West Bantu societies, BaTwa were also used as the models for nature spirit idols.

At the same time, many West Bantu societies regarded the BaTwa as less than human. They refused the BaTwa the right to marry Bantu women, considering them uncivilized and little better than the animals they hunted. However, by the time the Bantu speakers had settled, the BaTwa had abandoned many elements of their own culture, including their own languages, for those of the newcomers. Many BaTwa eventually found themselves held as virtual serfs of their sedentary West Bantu neighbors.

The modern BaTwa continue to survive in the forests and villages of Central Africa. Their numbers are estimated at around 200,000 individuals, with the Mbuti of the Ituri forest (80,000 individuals) making up the largest single group.

ADDITIONAL RESOURCE
Vansina, Jan. *Paths in the Rainforests: Toward a History of Political Tradition in Equatorial Africa.* Madison: University of Wisconsin Press, 1990.

SEE ALSO: Africa, East and South; Bantu, Congo Basin; Bantu, Mashariki.

—Kenneth R. Shepherd

BEAKER PEOPLE

DATE: c. 2300-1800 B.C.E.
LOCALE: Western Europe
RELATED CIVILIZATIONS: Battle-Ax people, Unetician culture
SIGNIFICANCE: The Beaker people were the first to introduce metallurgical technology into Europe.

The Beaker people lived in Western Europe, from Iberia into France (especially Brittany and the Rhone Valley), Britain, Ireland, the Low Countries, and the North German Plain, extending eastward to the Vistula and Danube River Valleys. Sometimes called Bell-Beaker folk, the Beaker people are distinguished by the geometrically decorated bell-shaped drinking vessels (beakers) that have been discovered in their burial places. Unlike the Neolithic peoples who preceded them, the Beaker people interred their dead in individual graves, in a fetal position, cradling a beaker.

Also included in Beaker graves were jewelry items in gold, silver, and copper and some arrowheads and stone wrist-protectors, indicating that archery was a valued skill (though this does not necessarily prove the existence of a warrior aristocracy, as some scholars have previously surmised). The most significant finds, however, are the tanged daggers made from copper, the first example of practical metalworking in Europe. The Beaker people may well have developed this technology in Spain, with its abundant copper lodes.

The Beaker culture and people themselves seem to have spread rapidly north and east and, in Central Europe, apparently intermingled with the Battle Ax people. This amalgamation seems to have brought about the formation of the Unetician culture.

ADDITIONAL RESOURCES

Cunliffe, Barry. *The Oxford Illustrated History of Prehistoric Europe.* Oxford, England: Oxford University Press, 2001.
Piggott, Stuart. *Ancient Europe: From the Beginnings of Agriculture to Classical Antiquity.* Chicago: Aldine, 1968.
Werick, Robert. *The Monument Builders.* New York: Time-Life, 1973.

SEE ALSO: Neolithic Age Europe.

—*Raymond Pierre Hylton*

BEJA

ALSO KNOWN AS: Medjay
DATE: 3000 B.C.E.-700 C.E.
LOCALE: Northern Nubia (later Republic of Sudan), northeast Africa
RELATED CIVILIZATIONS: Blemmyes, Ballana culture
SIGNIFICANCE: One of the nomadic groups that eventually came to control much of Nubia.

These ancient people of the Red Sea Hills region of the Sudan, who still exist as a group, have been known as the Beja (bay-ZHAH) since medieval times. They are usually identified with the Blemmyes, a nomadic tribe descended from the Medjay. The Medjay are often mentioned in Egyptian writing as desert raiders. They were organized into three chiefdoms: Aushek and a divided Webetsepet. Some time between 3000 and 2500 B.C.E., gold was discovered in the hills inhabited by these people. The pharaohs of Egypt established garrisoned mines there, which were worked by slave labor. Although the Beja people were often at odds with Egypt, it is also recorded that their warrior skills led them into the service of the pharaohs as soldiers and police.

In time, the Beja began to use camels, which enabled them to cover greater distances more swiftly. Their raids on Egyptian border outposts prompted the Ptolomaic emperor Diocletian to move the Roman frontier back to Aswan in 289 C.E. Archaeologists group the Blemmyes (Beja) and another nomadic people, the Nobatae, into what is known as the Ballana culture, named after an important royal cemetery.

ADDITIONAL RESOURCES

Adams, William L. *Nubia: Corridor to Africa.* London: Penguin Books, 1977.

O'Connor, David. *Ancient Nubia: Egypt's Rival in Africa*. Philadelphia: The University Museum, University of Pennsylvania, 1993.

Paul, Andrew. *The History of the Beja Tribes of the Sudan*. Cambridge, England: Cambridge University Press, 1954.

Trigger, Bruce G. *History and Settlement in Lower Nubia*. New Haven, Conn.: Yale University Press, 1965.

SEE ALSO: Africa, East and South; Diocletian; Egypt, Pharaonic; Egypt, Prepharaonic; Napata and Meroe; Nobatae; Nubia.

—*Craig E. Lloyd*

BELISARIUS

BORN: c. 505 C.E.; Germania, Illyria
DIED: 565 C.E.; place unknown
RELATED CIVILIZATION: Byzantine Empire
MAJOR ROLE/POSITION: General

Life. Born in Illyria, the present-day Dalmatian coast of Croatia, Belisarius (behl-ih-SAR-ee-uhs) achieved his first command under the emperor Justinian I and distinguished himself in battle against the Sāsānians of Persia in 530 C.E., when he defeated an army that outnumbered his own. Two years later,

Belisarius. (Library of Congress)

Belisarius was instrumental in putting down the Nika Riots when he led the imperial lifeguards in the slaughter of an alleged 30,000 rebels.

The following year, Justinian sent Belisarius to North Africa, where he conquered the Vandal kingdom there in one year. Belisarius then campaigned in Sicily and Italy, capturing the king of the Ostrogoths at Ravenna in 540 C.E. In 541-542 C.E., he returned east to campaign against the Persians, returning to Italy in 543 C.E. and remaining there until 548 C.E., when he was removed through court intrigues and replaced by the eunuch Narses, also a very capable general. Recalled in 558 C.E. to repel a threatened Bulgarian invasion, Belisarius was briefly imprisoned in 562 C.E. He spent the last three years of his life in retirement.

Influence. Through Belisarius's campaigns, the Byzantine Empire was able to briefly reestablish its control over Italy, Sicily, much of North Africa, and the Middle Eastern provinces of the Roman Empire. These campaigns bankrupted and exhausted Constantinople, and the Byzantine Empire was unable to hold these lands or withstand the Arab invasion a half century later.

ADDITIONAL RESOURCES

Boss, Roy. *Justinian's Wars: Belisarius, Narses, and the Reconquest of the West*. Stockport, England: Montvert, 1993.

Oman, Charles W. *The Art of War in the Middle Ages, A.D. 378-1515*. Rev. ed. Ithaca, N.Y.: Cornell University Press, 1953.

Procopius. *History of the Wars, Secret History, and Buildings*. Edited and translated by Averil Cameron. New York: Twayne, 1967.

SEE ALSO: Africa, North; Byzantine Empire; Constantinople; Goths; Justinian I; Narses (Byzantine military leader); Persia; Sāsānian Empire; Vandals.

—*Michael C. Paul*

BEN-HADAD I

ALSO KNOWN AS: Benadad
BORN: date and place unknown
DIED: c. 841 B.C.E.; place unknown
RELATED CIVILIZATIONS: Aram-Damascus, Israel, Judah, Syria
MAJOR ROLE/POSITION: King of Aram-Damascus

Life. Ben-Hadad I (behn-HAY-dad), the son of Tab-Rimmon and grandson of Hezion, is known only from the Hebrew Bible (1 Kings 15:16-22, 2 Chronicles 16:1-6) in connection with a border dispute between Baasha of Israel and Asa of Judah. In response to Baasha's attack against Judah (c. 895 B.C.E.), Asa bribed Ben-Hadad with a substantial gift of silver and gold, urging him to break his treaty with Baasha and to invade Israel from the north. Ben-Hadad agreed and sent his army against some of the important Israelite towns north of the Sea of Galilee. Archaeological excavations at Dan and Hazor have uncovered significant destruction layers that may be attributed to this attack. In the face of this new threat, Baasha was forced to withdraw from his campaign against Judah.

Influence. Ben-Hadad's attack on Israel illustrates the complex nature of Syro-Palestinian politics at the beginning of the ninth century B.C.E.

ADDITIONAL RESOURCE
Pitard, Wayne T. *Ancient Damascus*. Winona Lake, Ind.: Eisenbrauns, 1987.

SEE ALSO: Bible: Jewish; Israel.

—Stephen J. Andrews

BENEDICT BISCOP, SAINT

BORN: c. 628 C.E.; Northumbria, Britain
DIED: January 12, 689/690 C.E.; Northumbria, Britain
RELATED CIVILIZATION: Early medieval Europe
MAJOR ROLE/POSITION: Christian monk

Life. Born into a noble family, Benedict Biscop (BEHN-uh-dihkt BIHSH-ahp) was given lands by the king equal to that of thane (free-retainer) status before his conversion at twenty-five years of age to the religious life. He spent two years on an island off the southern coast of France at the abbey of Lerins and more time in Rome before returning to Britain in 669 C.E. He was part of a missionary team led by the Greek monk Theodore of Tarsus, who became the archbishop of Canterbury for twenty-one years. After spending two years at the abbey of Saints Peter and Paul in Canterbury, Biscop went to Northumbria and founded the monasteries of Monkwearmouth in 674 and Jarrow in 682 C.E.

Influence. In order to provide his monasteries with the learning required to live the monastic life, Biscop made frequent trips back to Rome to secure books to fill the libraries of his two abbeys. Not only did he obtain works by Christian authors, but he secured manuscripts by classical Latin writers as well. Jarrow's most famous monk was Bede, whose *Historia ecclesiastica gentis Anglorum* (731/732 C.E.; *A History of the English Church and People*, 1955) was possible only because of the library and monastery of Jarrow founded by Benedict Biscop.

ADDITIONAL RESOURCES
Blair, Peter. *Roman Britain and Early England: 55 B.C.-A.D. 871*. New York: W. W. Norton, 1963.
Thomas, Charles. *Celtic Britain*. New York: Thames and Hudson, 1997.
Whitelock, Dorothy. *The Beginnings of English Society*. Baltimore: Penguin Books, 1966.

SEE ALSO: Britain; Christianity.

—John A. Nichols

BENEDICT OF NURSIA, SAINT

BORN: c. 480 C.E.; Nursia, kingdom of the
Langobards
DIED: c. 547 C.E.; place unknown
RELATED CIVILIZATION: Early medieval Italy
MAJOR ROLE/POSITION: Religious figure

Life. Born into a wealthy family, Benedict of Nursia
(BEHN-uh-dihkt of NUR-shee-uh) was sent to Rome
to receive his education. Shocked by the city's de-
bauchery, he fled to the solitude of the countryside,
where he became a hermit. He lived for three years in a
cave. News of his religious aptitude spread rapidly and
inspired others to join him in his spiritual quests. After
organizing these followers into twelve communities
under his religious direction, Benedict founded the hilltop monastery of Monte Cassino, where he served as
abbot until his death. Between 535 and 545 C.E., Benedict compiled a monastic rule to guide the daily lives of
his monks, the *Rule of St. Benedict* (c. 540 C.E.; English
translation, 1909). Drawing on earlier rules, particularly the Rule of the Master, as well as providing personal expertise, Benedict's rule consisted of a prologue
and seventy-three short chapters. In addition to stressing obedience, humility, and manual labor, it offered
guidelines on diverse topics such as eating, drinking,
and sleeping that are noteworthy for advocating moder-
ation. Published around 593 C.E., Pope Gregory the
Great's book on the life of Saint Benedict, *Dialogues*
(c. 593 C.E.; *Dialogues of Gregory*, 1942), contributed
to his veneration.

Influence. Considered the father of Western monasticism, Benedict of Nursia compiled the most influential monastic rule in European history. In 1964, the
Catholic Church proclaimed Benedict the patron saint
of Europe. The Benedictine Rule is still used by Catholic monks and nuns.

ADDITIONAL RESOURCES
Boardman, Phillip C. "Rule of St. Benedict." In *En-
during Legacies: Ancient and Medieval Cultures.*
Boston: Pearson, 2000.
Lawrence, C. H. *Medieval Monasticism: Forms of Reli-
gious Life in Western Europe in the Middle Ages.*
London: Longman, 1989.

SEE ALSO: Christianity; Gregory the Great.
—*Shelley Amiste Wolbrink*

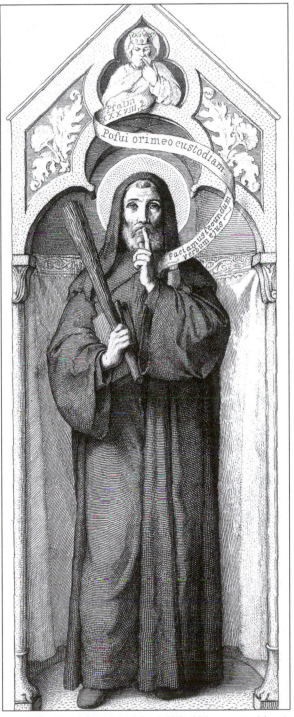

Saint Benedict of Nursia. (North Wind Picture Archives)

BERBERS

DATE: 3000 B.C.E.-700 C.E.
LOCALE: North Africa
SIGNIFICANCE: North African indigenous culture, includes subgroups Kabyle, Riffians, Shluh, and Tuareg.

The Berbers are the descendants of the ancient inhabitants of North Africa from Egypt westward. They have been known since classical times; the name "Berber" is Greek in derivation, coming from the same root as the English word "barbarian." The western tribes usually call themselves *amazigh*, meaning "free man." They have inhabited North Africa and the Sahara Desert since at least 2000 B.C.E., and their origins are a matter of some speculation. By around 1000 B.C.E., Berber clans were spread all across North Africa, where they farmed and raised livestock. Some Berber groups still practice nomadic herding or small-scale farming in the rural areas of several northern and western African states.

Rock paintings that survive in the desert suggest that some of the Berbers between 1000 and 100 B.C.E. used light horse-drawn chariots. It has been speculated that they may have used these chariots to transport trade goods, linking sub-Saharan Africa with the Mediterranean world, but some archaeologists believe that the chariots depicted in the paintings were too flimsy to carry a significant amount of cargo. Phoenician settlements along the coast of North Africa such as Carthage took advantage of the Berber trade, exchanging manufactures such as pottery, glass, iron, and bronze for local North African products such as leather and ivory. Their position as middlemen gave several Berber clans power and status, and several small independent kingdoms were founded on the wealth of this trade. Other Berber societies attached themselves to the Phoenicians, adopting parts of their culture and technology.

The fall of Carthage at the end of the Punic Wars brought the Berbers into the Roman world. Rome had allied itself with some of these Berber kingdoms during the second century B.C.E. and shared Carthaginian territory with them following the Third Punic War. Roman colonists arriving in the area through the second century C.E. slowly merged with the dominant Berber culture, and their combined efforts made the Maghreb a major element of the Roman economy. The emperor Lucius Septimius Severus (r. 193-211 C.E.), who had family roots in North Africa, may have had some Berber ancestry. Many urban Berbers converted to Christianity along with the rest of the Roman world during the same period, and unrest among the Berbers contributed to the collapse of the Western Roman Empire. When the Vandals entered North Africa in 429 C.E., they captured the Roman settlements, but Berbers in the rural areas maintained their traditional culture and language.

Many Berbers adopted Islam as it spread across North Africa in the eighth century C.E., and Berber traders, particularly Tuareg, were probably responsible for introducing the religion into Saharan Africa. A Berber dynasty is credited with establishing the great West African Islamic religious center of Timbuktu sometime before the eleventh century C.E.

ADDITIONAL RESOURCES

Montaigne, Robert. *The Berbers: Their Social and Political Organisation.* Translated with an introduction by David Seddon. London: Frank Cass, 1973.

Phillipson, David W. *African Archaeology.* 2d ed. Cambridge, England: Cambridge University Press, 1993.

SEE ALSO: Africa, North; Carthage; Christianity; Garamantes; Islam; Phoenicia; Punic Wars; Rome, Imperial; Saharan rock art; Septimius Severus, Lucius; Vandals; Znaga.

—*Kenneth R. Shepherd*

BHAGAVADGĪTĀ

AUTHORSHIP: Unknown
DATE: c. 200 B.C.E.-c. 200 C.E.
LOCALE: India
SIGNIFICANCE: Early scriptures on which some Hindu beliefs are based.

The *Bhagavadgītā* (BAH-gah-vahd-GEE-taw; Sanskrit "Song of God"; *The Bhagavad Gita*, 1785) is a philosophhical interlude by an unknown writer comprising the twenty-fifth to the forty-second chapters of the Bhīhmaparva section of the *Mahābhārata* (400 B.C.E.-400 C.E., present form by c. 400 C.E.; *The Mahabharata of Krishna-Dwaipayana Vyasa*, 1887-1896). It consists of seven hundred Sanskrit verses divided into 118 chapters. It is not considered part of the *śruti*, or revealed class of writings, but is part of the *smriti*, or traditional works. It is considered the greatest, most beautiful, and most popular of the Hindu scriptures.

The *Bhagavadgītā* is written in the form of a dialogue that takes place just before the great Battle of Kurukshetra between the Pāṇḍayas and the Kauravas. As the opposing sides are drawing up for battle, the great warrior Prince Arjuna bids his charioteer Krishna (Kṛṣṇa), an earthly incarnation of the god Vishnu (Viṣṇu), to drive to an open space to view the contending forces. Seeing the noble youths and warriors on both sides, Arjuna is struck with remorse at the projected death of his kinsmen as he attempts to gain his kingdom in a just but cruel war—he desired neither fame nor pleasure nor empire. He seeks Krishna's guidance. Krishna's reply constitutes the text of the *Bhagavadgītā* and is considered by many Hindus to be the actual utterances of the supreme deity.

Krishna's reply falls into three parts. The first advocates the pursuit of yoga and sets forth the advantages of self-mortification and asceticism. It emphasizes the need to annihilate the self and the virtue of seeing god in everything. The second part elaborates the pantheistic doctrines of Vedānt, and Krishna reveals himself in all his glory as the supreme deity. The third part expounds the principles of *purusha*, *prakriti*, *buddhi*, and *ahamkāra*, the five subtle and gross senses, and other categories of Sāṁkhya philosophy

Commentators vary widely as to the ultimate teaching of the *Bhagavadgītā*. Some see pantheism as the chief philosophy and the need to discriminate between the self (*ātman*) and the nonself (*prakriti*). Others see devotion to dharma, especially caste duties, as central. Yet others regard the primary message as the doctrine of *Brahmavidya*, that is, the knowledge of Brahmā accompanied by asceticism. Most commentators, however, regard the doctrine of *bhakti*, or devotion, as the chief glory of the *Bhagavadgītā*. It must be kept in mind, however, that the *Bhagavadgītā* itself recognizes the possibility of its multiple interpretations when it states that, "Some by meditation, others by knowledge, others by imitation, action or worship pass beyond death."

ADDITIONAL RESOURCES

Aurobindo, Ghose. *Essays on the Gita, Second Series.* Calcutta: Arya Publishing House, 1945.

Bazaz, Prem Nath. *The Role of Bhagavad Gita in Indian History.* New Delhi: Sterling Publishers, 1975.

Feuerstein, Georg. *Introduction to the Bhagavad-gita: Its Philosophy and Cultural Setting.* London: Rider, 1974.

Hawley, Jack. *Bhagavad Gita: A Walkthrough for Westerners.* New York: New World Library, 2001.

Mitchell, Stephen, trans. *Bhagavad Gita: A New Translation.* New York: Crown Publishers, 2000.

Radhakrishnan, S., ed. *Bhagavadgita.* London: George, Allen and Unwin, 1948.

SEE ALSO: *Advaita*; Hinduism; India; *Mahābhārata*; *Upaniṣads*.

—*Arthur W. Helweg*

BHARATA MUNI

FLOURISHED: c. third century C.E.
RELATED CIVILIZATION: Indo-Aryan civilization
MAJOR ROLE/POSITION: Writer

Legend has it that when the gods asked Brahmā to create a Veda that could be understood by commoners, he created the Panchamaveda (fifth Veda) called *Nātyaveda*. Drawing *pathya* (words) from the *Rigveda* (also known as *Ṛgveda*, c. 1500-1000 B.C.E.; English translation, 1896-1897), *abhinaya* (gesture) from the *Yajurveda*, *geet* (music and chant) from *Sāmaveda*, and *rasa* (sentiment and emotional element) from *Atharvaveda*, he synthesized *Nātyaveda*. After creating *Nātyaveda*, Brahmā asked sage Bharata Muni (BAH-rah-tah MEW-nee) to popularize this Veda on earth.

Sage Bharata wrote *Nātya-śāstra* (between 200 and 300 C.E.; *The Nātyashāstra*, 1950), a great comprehensive work on the science and technique of Indian drama, dance, and music. Enchanted by Bharata Muni's first play, Śiva himself, the lord of cosmic dance, sent his disciple Tandu to teach Bharata the authentic principles of dance, which Bharata included in the chapter "Tandava Lakshana." Bharata Muni evolved ten basic postures of the body, nine of the neck, thirty-six of the hand, and thirteen poses of the head—postures that required the disciplined use of the entire body and all of its expressions. Various schools of dance have elaborated on these principal postures, each of which blossoms into an exactingly coordinated repertoire of associated hand, facial, eye, foot, and total body movements synchronized to the rhythm of intricate instrumental and vocal music to communicate a complex story.

ADDITIONAL RESOURCES

Pande, Anupa. *The Natyasastra Tradition and Ancient Indian Society*. Jodhpur, India: Kusumangali Prakshan, 1993.

Pandey, Sudhakar, and V. N. Jha. *Glimpses of Ancient Indian Poetics from Bharata to Jagannatha*. Delhi, India: Sri Satguru, 1992.

SEE ALSO: India; Nātya-śāstra; Vedas; Vedism.

—Kokila Ravi

BHĀRAVI

FLOURISHED: c. 634 C.E.
RELATED CIVILIZATION: India
MAJOR ROLE/POSITION: Author

Life. Bhāravi (BAW-rah-vee) is the author of *Kirātārjunīya* (seventh century C.E.; *Bharavi's Poem Kiratarjuniya*, 1912), one of six of the most famous Sanskrit *mahākāvyas* (short epics) ever written. Bhāravi's *mahākāvya* is based on an episode in the *Mahābhārata* (400 B.C.E.-400 C.E., present form by c. 400 C.E.; *The Mahabharata of Krishna-Dwaipayana Vyasa*, 1887-1896) in which the hero Arjuna, while worshiping Lord Śiva, is provoked into a fight by a *kirāta*, or mountaineer, who is out hunting. In actuality, the hunter is a disguised Lord Śiva, who is testing the valor of his devotee. When Arjuna discovers the true identity of his invincible adversary, he falls down and worships him. Lord Śiva is satisfied with Arjuna's bravery, skill, and piety and presents him with a *pāśupata*, a magical weapon for use against his enemies.

Influence. Bhāravi's *kāvya* contains brilliant descriptions of natural scenery while being marred by artificiality and verbal tricks that quickly become tiresome. Some lines give the same sense and sound whether read forward or backward, and certain couplets can be read four different ways with four different meanings, while some stanzas have only certain syllables and sounds. Yet Bhāravi's work sets forth a felicity of expression and mastery of verse that remain unequaled among *kāvya* writers, and his story of Arjuna and the "mountain man" is highly regarded in Indian literature.

ADDITIONAL RESOURCES

Chandrasekharan, K., and B. H. S. Sastri. *Sanskrit Literature*. Bombay, India: International Book House, 1951.

Gangopadhyaya, Mrinalkanti. *Bharavi*. New Delhi, India: Sahitya Akademi, 1991.

Har, Saktipada. *Bharavi and "Kiratarjuniyam": A Crit-

ical Study. Calcutta, India: Sanskrit Pustak Bhandar, 1983.

Majumdar, Ramesh Chandra, Achut Dattatraya Pusalkar, and Asoke Majumdar. *The Vedic Age.* Bombay, India: Bharatiya Vidya Bhaban, 1951.

Roodbergen, J. A. F., ed. *Mallin-atha's Ghant-apatha on the Kir-at-arjun-iya.* Leiden, Netherlands: E. J. Brill, 1984.

SEE ALSO: Hinduism; India.

—*Arthur W. Helweg*

BHARTṚHARI

BORN: c. 450 C.E.; Ujjain, Mālwa, India
DIED: c. 500 C.E.; Ujjain, Mālwa, India
RELATED CIVILIZATIONS: Gupta Empire, India
MAJOR ROLE/POSITION: Grammarian, philosopher, poet

Life. Accounts of Bhartṛhari's (BAHR-tree-HAH-ree) life vary. The chief sources for details are the dramatic work by Harihara, *Bhartṛharinirveda* (n.d.; *The Bhartṛharinirveda of Harihara,* 1904), and the journals and notebooks kept by Chinese Buddhist scholars who studied in northern India during the Gupta Empire (fourth to sixth century C.E.). Most accounts concur that Bhartṛhari was native to Ujjain, Mālwa state, where he also died. He was born into nobility, perhaps the elder brother of King Vikramāditya or a king himself. Bhartṛhari studied under the grammarian Vasurāta and may have worked in the court of Maitraka, king of Valabhī, in the state of Gujarāt. In accordance with Hindu practice, Bhartṛhari eventually renounced his material wealth to live as an ascetic, or *sannayāsin,* in a cave near Ujjain, in order to devote himself to his studies.

The works attributed to Bhartṛhari, all fifth century C.E., are the *Srṇgāraśataka,* the *Nītiśataka* and the *Vairāgyaśataka* (translated together as *The Nitisataka*

and Vairagyasataka of Bhartrhari, 1902), a collection of poems entitled *Bhattī kāvya,* and his grammar study, for which he is best known, the *Vākyapadīya* (*The Vakyapadiay of Bhartrhari,* 1977). In his grammar, Bhartṛhari drew from yoga and other Hindu philosophies to assert that words (*sphoṭa*) bear both universal, spiritual meaning and spiritual powers linking humans to *brahman.*

Influence. Living during the golden age of Indian culture, Bhartṛhari became, along with the poet Kālidāsa and the philosopher Diṅnāga, a major representative of Sanskrit culture. By articulating the spiritual power of language and the Vedas, he helped to assure the continuation of Brahmanical ideals.

ADDITIONAL RESOURCES
Coward, H. G. *Bhartrhari.* Boston: Twayne, 1976.
Sundararajam, K. R., and B. Mukerju, eds. *Hindu Spirituality I: Vedas Through Vedanta.* New York: Crossroads, 1997.

SEE ALSO: Brahmanism; Gupta emperors; Hinduism; India; Kālidāsa; Vedas; Vedism.

—*Dennis C. Chowenhill*

BHĀSA

FLOURISHED: second or third century C.E.
RELATED CIVILIZATION: India
MAJOR ROLE/POSITION: Dramatist

Life. Bhāsa (BAW-sa) is best known in south India and is the earliest known dramatist in Sanskrit. He is

referred to by the great Sanskrit dramatist Kālidāsa (c. 340-c. 400 C.E.) and other poets. His *Bāla-carita* (second or third century C.E.; English translation, 1930-1931) focuses on the feats of young Krishna (Kṛṣṇa) slaying the tyrant Karnsa. *Svapna-vāsava-datta* (second or third century C.E.; English translation, 1930-

1931) displays Bhāsa's skill in characterization. His *Cārudatta* (second or third century C.E.; English translation, 1930-1931) survives only as a fragment; the dramatist Śūdraka borrowed much from it.

Influence. Bhāsa's plays display a flagrant disregard for the conventions of Indian drama. His display of killings on stage was new and flouted tradition. In *Pratimā-nāṭaka* (second or third century C.E., English translation, 1930-1931), King Daśaratha laments over the exile of his son Rāma and is shown dying in state; presenting death scenes was contrary to the conventions of Indian drama. After the king dies, his statue is placed in the temple and the widowed queens bring offerings of flowers; exhibiting royal effigies and paying them divine honors was not common in India. These influences can be seen in the dramaturgy of Kālidāsa, who sought to refine them.

ADDITIONAL RESOURCES

Bhattacharyya, Biswanath. *A Critical Survey of Bhāsa's Mahabharatan Dramas.* Calcutta, India: Sanskrit Pustak Bhandar, 1991.

Ganapatisastri, Mahamahopadhyaya T., ed. *Bhāsa's Plays: A Critical Study.* Delhi, India: Bharatiya Vidya Prakashan, 1985.

Gopalakrishnan, Sudha. *From the Comic to the Comedic: The Traditions of Comedy of Bhāsa and Shakespeare.* New Delhi, India: Sharada, 1993.

Majumdar, R. C., ed. *The Age of Imperial Unity.* 2d ed. Bombay, India: Bharatiya Vidya Bhavan, 1953.

Unni, N. P. *Some New Perspectives in Bhasa Studies.* Dharwad, India: Prasaranga, Karnatak University, 1992.

SEE ALSO: India; Kālidāsa.

—Arthur W. Helweg

BHAVABHŪTI

FLOURISHED: 700 C.E.
RELATED CIVILIZATION: India
MAJOR ROLE/POSITION: Dramatist, poet

Life. Bhavabhūti (BUH-vah-BEW-tee) was born in Vidarbha (modern Berar), in central India, of the Brahman caste. He lived in the court of the Yaśovarman, king of Kanauj, a famous city located on the Ganges River at the rishi hermitage, and was given the title Śrikaṇṭha ("Splendid Voice," or "Throat of Experience"). He was second only to the Sanskrit dramatist Kālidāsa (c. 340-c. 400 C.E.). Bhavabhūti's plays depict the grandiose and sublime rather than the simple and commonplace. Replete with learning, logic, metaphysics, and passion, his plays are noted for their suspensefulness and characterization, and his plots are considered superior to Kālidāsa's.

Influence. Bhavabhūti's seven-act *Mahāvīracarita* (c. 700 C.E.; *Maha-vira-charita*, 1871) depicts the fortunes of Rāma's early life as depicted in the *Rāmāyaṇa* (c. 500 B.C.E., some material added later; English translation, 1870-1889) and focuses on the martial and stirring. *Uttararāmacarita* (c. 700 C.E.; *Uttararama-caritam*, 1921) deals with Rāma's later life. His ten-act

Mālatī-mādhava (c. 700 C.E.; *The Malati Madhava of Mahkavi Bhava Bhuti*, 1954) is a powerful romantic drama in which the theme of love is delicately and purely handled, perhaps the best example of the *prakarana*, or drama of domestic life. It is also noteworthy because it relates the practice of human sacrifice among the Aghoris and worshipers of Durgā.

ADDITIONAL RESOURCES

Acharya, P. B. *The Tragicomedies of Shakespeare, Kalidasa, and Bhavabhuti.* New Delhi, India: Meharchand Lachhmandas, 1978.

Borooah, Anundoram. *Bhavabhuti and His Place in Sanskrit Literature.* Gauhati, India: Publication Board, Assam, 1971.

Devi, Akshaya Kumari. *A History of Sanskrit Literature.* Calcutta, India: Vijaya Krishna Brothers, 1940.

Harshë, R. G. *Observations on the Life and Works of Bhavabhüti.* Translated by Jang Bahadur Khanna. Delhi, India: Meharchand Lachhmandas, 1974.

SEE ALSO: India; Kālidāsa; Rāmāyaṇa.

—Arthur W. Helweg

BIBLE: JEWISH

AUTHORSHIP: Compiled by rabbinic authorities
DATE: compilation complete by end of the first
century C.E.
LOCALE: Israel/Roman Palestine
RELATED CIVILIZATIONS: Canaan, Egypt,
Mesopotamia, Greece, Israel
SIGNIFICANCE: This collection of religious literature
of ancient Israel was accepted as normative in both
the rabbinic and Christian traditions and has influ-
enced Islam.

The Jewish Bible is an anthology of religious texts from
ancient Israel. These books were written during the first
millennium, although precise dating of individual books
is difficult. By the fifth century B.C.E., early Judaism began to emerge from the religion of ancient Israel, and it
regarded the religious literature of ancient Israel as holy
scriptures inspired by God and, therefore, normative
for belief and practice.

Among those who considered themselves heirs of
the religious traditions of ancient Israel, there was some
disagreement to the precise number of books that were
accepted as authoritative. The Samaritans and the Sadducees accepted only the five books of Moses as Scripture, but the Pharisees accepted prophetic, poetic, and
sapient works as well. Eventually, the wider collection
of the Pharisaic tradition became widely accepted, as
attested by the first century apocryphal work 4 Esdras
(14:44-46), which gives twenty-four as the number of
books in the Jewish Bible.

The Jewish Bible has a tripartite shape: Torah,
Prophets, and Writings. The Torah contains the Five
Books of Moses known as Genesis, Exodus, Leviticus,
Numbers, and Deuteronomy. Early Judaism gave these
books a preeminent place as its fundamental documents. The second division of the Jewish Bible contains eight books known as the Prophets: Joshua,
Judges, Samuel, Kings, Isaiah, Jeremiah, Ezekiel, and
the Twelve Minor Prophets (considered as one book).
The purpose of this collection is to provide object les-
sons regarding the obligation to live according to the
Torah. The final division, containing eleven books, is
the most diverse, containing narratives, poetry, wisdom
texts, and an apocalypse: Psalms, Proverbs, Job, Song
of Solomon, Ruth, Lamentations, Ecclesiastes, Esther,
Daniel, Ezra-Nehemiah, and Chronicles.

These twenty-four books reflect the customs and id-
ioms of several cultural eras from the Bronze Age to the

Hellenistic period. Still, this diverse anthology does
have several unifying principles. The most important of
these is its concept of God. The Jewish Bible is a mono-

THE JEWISH BIBLE

Torah
Genesis
Exodus
Leviticus
Numbers
Deuteronomy

Prophets (Neviʾim)
Joshua
Judges
First Samuel
Second Samuel
First Kings
Second Kings
Isaiah
Jeremiah
Ezekiel
Hosea
Joel
Amos
Obadiah
Jonah
Micah
Nahum
Habakkuk
Zephaniah
Haggai
Zechariah
Malachi

Writings (Ketuvim)
Psalms
Proverbs
Job
The Song of Songs
Ruth
Lamentations
Ecclesiastes
Esther
Daniel
Ezra
Nehemiah
First Chronicles
Second Chronicles

theistic collection that reflects a continual struggle against the polytheisms of the surrounding cultures. Another such principle is its concept of people as beings called to live in a relationship of love and obedience to the one God who is the source of life and all good. The Jewish Bible provides believers in the one God with an identity and values. These values transcend the boundaries of Judaism and have given shape to both Christianity and Islam.

ADDITIONAL RESOURCES
Birch, Bruce C., ed. *A Theological Introduction to the Old Testament*. Nashville, Tenn.: Abingdon, 1999.
Levenson, Jon D. *Sinai and Zion: An Entry into the Jewish Bible*. Minneapolis, Minn.: Winston, 1985.

SEE ALSO: Bible: New Testament; Canaanites; Ezekiel; Isaiah; Israel; Jeremiah; Judaism; Moses; Samuel; Solomon.

—Leslie J. Hoppe

BIBLE: NEW TESTAMENT

AUTHORSHIP: Compiled by early Church fathers
DATE: composed c. 50-c. 150 C.E.
LOCALE: Roman Empire
RELATED CIVILIZATIONS: Imperial Rome, Greece, Egypt, Israel
SIGNIFICANCE: The central document of Christianity, the New Testament shaped the values of Western civilization. No other book has been translated into so many languages or has survived in so many printed editions and manuscripts.

The Christian Bible is a collection of shorter books. The word "bible" literally means "little books." The first three-quarters, known as the Old Testament, are books of law, prophecy, and literature that were originally written in Hebrew. The final quarter, the New Testament, contains books first written in the Greek that was used throughout the Roman Empire.

The New Testament is more accurately described as a "new covenant" because it refers to an agreement between two parties, human and divine, rather than the legacy of a single party. The Hebrew scriptures describe the covenants that God made with Noah, Abraham, and Moses —covenants symbolized by the rainbow, the circumcision, and the Sabbath. They also include Jeremiah's prophecy of a new covenant written on the hearts of believers rather than on tablets of stone. The Greek scriptures, which refer constantly to the Hebrew, tell of a new covenant that Jesus Christ establishes with those who accept his message—a covenant symbolized by the Lord's supper, the Christian communion.

The gospel, or "good news," was first transmitted by word of mouth. The earliest complete texts in the New Testament are letters that Paul wrote to the churches he established in Greece and Asia Minor. Only after the first generation of Christians was dying off, and especially after the destruction of Jerusalem in 70 C.E., did the surviving accounts of Jesus Christ's life take their present shape.

THE BOOKS OF THE NEW TESTAMENT

The Gospel According to Matthew
The Gospel According to Mark
The Gospel According to Luke
The Gospel According to John
The Acts of the Apostles
The Letter of Paul to the Romans
The First Letter of Paul to the Corinthians
The Second Letter of Paul to the Corinthians
The Letter of Paul to the Galatians
The Letter of Paul to the Ephesians
The Letter of Paul to the Philippians
The Letter of Paul to the Colossians
The First Letter of Paul to the Thessalonians
The Second Letter of Paul to the Thessalonians
The First Letter of Paul to Timothy
The Second Letter of Paul to Timothy
The Letter of Paul to Titus
The Letter of Paul to Philemon
The Letter to the Hebrews
The Letter of James
The First Letter of Peter
The Second Letter of Peter
The First Letter of John
The Second Letter of John
The Third Letter of John
The Letter of Jude
The Revelation to John

Many lives of Jesus were written during the next century, but four had special authority. One bishop remarked that four was a good number, corresponding to the four quarters of the earth. Traditionally, Matthew wrote in Antioch (east), Mark in Egypt (south), Luke in Rome (west), and John in Ephesus (north).

The first three gospels are said to be "synoptic" because they can be "seen together": They present the same teachings and the same events. For this reason, scholars think there were books of sayings that apostles or "envoys" took on their travels. However, each gospel reflects the temperament of a different community. Matthew's has more Jewish people, for example, while Luke's has more gentiles. John's community is especially interested in the mystery of the divine person.

The twenty-one letters in the New Testament may be associated with the various communities. As Paul is connected to Luke, who also wrote the story of the apostles' acts, Peter is traditionally associated with Mark, and James and Jude share Matthew's interest in Jewish customs. Three letters are attributed to John,

as is an apocalypse or vision of the last judgment.

When Christianity became the state religion, the Roman emperor Constantine the Great ordered copies of the New Testament to be made in quantity. These were not scrolls, like the Hebrew Torah, but books with pages. The oldest surviving copies of the New Testament were probably compiled at this time.

ADDITIONAL RESOURCES

Mack, Burton L. *Who Wrote the New Testament? The Making of the Christian Myth*. San Francisco: Harper, 1995.

Metzger, Bruce M. *The Making of the New Testament: Its Transmission, Corruption, and Restoration*. New York: Oxford University Press, 1992.

SEE ALSO: Bible: Jewish; Byzantine Empire; Christianity; Constantine the Great; Jesus Christ; Moses; Paul, Saint; Peter, Saint; Rome, Imperial.

—*Thomas Willard*

BLACK POTTERY CULTURE

DATE: c. 2000-1000 B.C.E.

LOCALE: Centered along the eastern seaboards of China, beginning in the province of Shandong, spreading toward Henan, southern Hebei, and northern Jiangsu Provinces

RELATED CIVILIZATION: Neolithic China

SIGNIFICANCE: This culture exhibited many of the practices of the Shang Dynasty, and its people may be the direct ancestors of the Shang.

The Black Pottery culture has long been synonymous with the Longshan culture, which is generally believed to be later than the Yangshao culture. Through recent finds, the Longshan culture has been determined to have coexisted with the Yangshao culture. The classic Shandong Longshan (or Black Pottery culture) is actually one of the late phases of the Longshan culture.

Villages of the Black Pottery culture were surrounded by protective walls of pounded earth 20 feet (6 meters) high and 30 to 45 feet (9 to 14 meters) thick. Although the Black Pottery culture was once thought to be restricted to Shandong Province, it extended as far south as northern Jiangsu Province. The Black Pottery culture is characterized by the predominance of thin,

highly burnished black wares. The thin black pottery, often thrown on a potter's wheel, was made for rituals. Many of the pottery shapes were repeated in later bronzes.

Within this culture, a new practice appeared: scapulimancy, the method of prognostication by applying heat to the scapulae (shoulder bones) of deer and cattle or the shells of tortoises. Shamans answered questions by interpreting the cracks that appeared. The use of pounded earth for protective walls, the shapes of the black pottery, and the practice of scapulimancy were all cultural elements that persisted in the following Bronze Age.

ADDITIONAL RESOURCES

Rawson, Jessica. *Ancient China: Art and Archaeology*. London: Duckworth, 1980.

Shangraw, Clarence F. *Origins of Chinese Ceramics*. New York: China Institute in America, 1978.

Sylvester, Diane. *India and China*. Torrance, Calif.: Frank Schaffer, 1997.

SEE ALSO: China; Longshan culture; Yangshao culture.

—*Juliana Y. Yuan*

BODHIDHARMA

ALSO KNOWN AS: *Pinyin* Damo; *Japanese* Daruma
BORN: fifth century C.E.; southern India
DIED: sixth century C.E.; place unknown
RELATED CIVILIZATIONS: India, China, Japan
MAJOR ROLE/POSITION: Religious figure

Life. Despite uncertainty about his birth and death dates, Bodhidharma (BOHD-hee-DAHR-mah) is revered as the twenty-eighth patriarch of Buddhism and the first of Zen Buddhism. Probably between 470 and 527 C.E., Bodhidharma brought from India to China a form of Buddhism that employed sitting meditation and is known as Zen (Japanese), *dhyāna* (Sanskrit), or *chan* (Chinese).

Whether Bodhidharma's teaching was written down and which (if any) surviving texts are his remain controversial. He promoted transmission of Buddhist doctrine directly from mind to mind, through an illumination apart from, or in spite of, the use of words: "At every moment, where language can't go, that's your mind."

Legends about his life abound: He cut off his eyelids and sat wall-gazing for nine years until his legs withered away. He died from poisoning, returned to India, or maybe went on to Japan.

Influence. As the founder of Zen Buddhism, Bodhidharma enormously influenced cultural as well as religious life in the Far East. In Japan, the Bodhidharma's religious zeal is remembered through a popular legless doll called Daruma, which when placed on its side, rolls back upright. His legend has also exerted influence in the West. Modern popular tradition holds that Bodhidharma taught Shaolin priests a style of fist fighting (*chuanfa*) and thus was a seminal figure in the martial-arts tradition. This often-repeated story seems to lack solid foundation.

ADDITIONAL RESOURCES

Broughton, Jeffrey. *The Bodhidharma Anthology.* Berkeley: University of California Press, 1999.
Cook, Harry. "Bodhidharma and the Shaolin Temple." In *The Way of the Warrior.* Prudhoe, England: Warriors Dreams Publications, 1999.
Dumoulin, Heinrich. *Zen Enlightenment.* New York: Weatherhill, 1993.
Pine, Red. *The Zen Teaching of Bodhidharma.* San Francisco: North Point Press, 1989.

SEE ALSO: Buddhism; China; Japan.

—Edward Johnson

BOETHIUS

ALSO KNOWN AS: Anicius Manlius Severinus Boethius
BORN: c. 480 C.E.; Rome, Italy
DIED: c. 524 C.E.; Pavia, Italy
RELATED CIVILIZATION: Imperial Rome
MAJOR ROLE/POSITION: Adviser to King Theoderic the Great, philosopher

Life. There is not much reliable information on the life of Boethius (boh-EE-thee-uhs). His classical education was solid, and he spoke both Latin and Greek. He intended to translate the complete works of Plato and Aristotle into Latin but did not live long enough to complete this project. He may have served as the Roman consul around 510 C.E., and it is certain that he worked for the Ostrogothic king Theoderic the Great,

who had invaded and occupied Rome. For reasons that are not clear, Theoderic condemned Boethius to death, and Boethius was executed in 524 C.E. Before his death, in his prison cell, Boethius wrote his extremely eloquent book *De consolatione philosophiae* (523; *The Consolation of Philosophy*, late ninth century). In this very influential work, he explained that pagan philosophy as reinterpreted by Christian theologians can help the unjustly accused to prepare themselves for a holy death.

Influence. Throughout the Middle Ages, *The Consolation of Philosophy* remained one of the most admired works from the early Christian era because it showed how Christian belief was perfectly compatible with the moral teachings of pagan philosophers such as Plato and Aristotle.

ADDITIONAL RESOURCES

Astell, Ann W. *Job, Boethius, and Epic Truth*. Ithaca, N.Y.: Cornell University Press, 1994.

O'Day, Gerard. *The Poetry of Boethius*. London: Duckworth, 1991.

SEE ALSO: Aristotle; Christianity; Goths, Ostrogoths, Visigoths; Philosophy; Plato; Rome, Imperial; Theoderic the Great.

—Edmund J. Campion

BOOK OF THE DEAD

ALSO KNOWN AS: *Book of Going Forth by Day, Coming into Day*

AUTHORSHIP: multiple

DATE: *Coffin Texts* and *Pyramid Texts* (c. 2700-c. 2200 B.C.E.) were probably compiled and edited into what is known as *Book of the Dead* in the sixteenth century B.C.E.

LOCALE: Egyptian New Kingdom

RELATED CIVILIZATION: Pharaonic Egypt

SIGNIFICANCE: Series of mortuary spells to be used by the deceased during the journey into the afterlife.

The *Book of the Dead* is the most famous of several Egyptian works dealing with the afterlife. It was first called *Book of the Dead* as an alternative to the literal translation of the ancient title, *Book of Going Forth by Day, Coming into Day*, by Richard Lepsius, who translated a Ptolemaic text with 165 chapters into English in 1842. Transcribed on papyri, it lists a collection of spells, or chapters, for use by the deceased. Different "editions" vary in content and length, with texts dating back to the Old Kingdom and found on pyramid walls. Many spells were written out in cursive hieroglyphs, but some papyri from the Greco-Roman period used demotic script. Alternately, vignettes summarized the spell, with brief texts interspacing the illustrations. In such cases, the text was written horizontally rather than in the customary vertical manner. Although gaining fa-

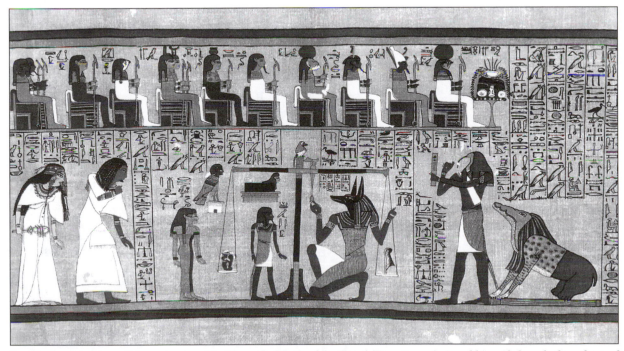

In this reproduction of the papyrus of Ani from the Book of the Dead, *Egyptians Ani and his wife bow before the god Anubis, who balances the scales of justice while Thoth (standing) notes his decision and Amerit the Devourer sits and watches.* (Hulton Archive)

vor beginning in the Eighteenth Dynasty, the *Book of the Dead* fell into disuse by the Twenty-second Dynasty yet experienced a brief revival in the Twenty-sixth Dynasty. As a means to protect and assist the dead in their journey into eternity, it became an essential item in many tombs, which explains why so many copies are available for study.

ADDITIONAL RESOURCES
Andrews, Carol, ed. *The Ancient Egyptian Book of the Dead.* Austin: University of Texas Press, 1990.
Hornung, Erik. *The Ancient Egyptian Books of the Afterlife.* Ithaca, N.Y.: Cornell University Press, 1999.

SEE ALSO: Egypt, Pharaonic; Religion and ritual.
—*Guillaume de Syon*

BOUDICCA

ALSO KNOWN AS: Boadicea
BORN: first century C.E.; Britain
DIED: 60 C.E.; central Britain
RELATED CIVILIZATIONS: Britain, Imperial Rome
MAJOR ROLE/POSITION: Military leader

Life. Little is known about Boudicca's (bew-DIHK-uh) early life. Her husband, Prasutagus, who ruled the Iceni as a client king of the Romans, died in 59 C.E. In his will, he attempted to ensure the welfare of his wife and two teenage daughters by bequeathing half of his

Boudicca and her daughters ride into battle on a chariot, with their supporters behind them. (North Wind Picture Archives)

estate to the emperor Nero. However, greedy local Roman officials reached for more. When Boudicca bravely objected, she was flogged and her daughters raped. Roused to the defense of their queen, the Iceni attacked the Roman garrison at Camulodunum (modern Colchester), annihilated the defenders, and burned and looted the town. Boudicca and her forces then did the same at Londinium (London) and Verulamium (St. Albans).

The Roman governor Gaius Suetonius Paulinus met the rebels in a well-chosen spot somewhere to the northwest of London. Boudicca rode into battle with her daughters on a chariot and shouted encouragement to her supporters. The Britons attacked with wild shouts and trumpet blasts while the Romans waited in orderly ranks. Although outnumbered, the Romans won because of their superior discipline and position. Following the rout, Boudicca drank poison to avoid the humiliation of being paraded—and worse—in Rome and was buried in a magnificent tomb that has never been found.

Influence. Although Boudicca's rebellion failed, it persuaded the Romans to pursue a more diplomatic policy in the pacification of the island. In death, Boudicca has remained a symbol of freedom and independence for the British people.

ADDITIONAL RESOURCES

Ireland, S. *Roman Britain: A Sourcebook*. London: Routledge, 1996.

Webster, Graham. *Boudica*. Totowa, N.J.: Rowman and Littlefield, 1978.

SEE ALSO: Britain; Nero; Rome, Imperial.

—Thomas J. Sienkewicz

BOYLSTON STREET WEIR

DATE: c. 3050-1750 B.C.E.

LOCALE: Boston, Massachusetts

RELATED CIVILIZATION: Archaic North American culture

SIGNIFICANCE: This series of fish traps elucidates the role of perishable technology and communal subsistence practices in the adaptation strategies of Middle Holocene, eastern North American hunter-gatherers.

First encountered during subway excavations in Boston in 1913, the Boylston Street weirs were originally interpreted as a large single structure. Subsequent research in the 1930's, 1940's, 1950's, and 1980's, however, demonstrated that the weirs are instead a series of relatively small constructions built over more than a thousand years.

Erected near the Back Bay shore on the Charles River at points near or just below the low tidemark, the weirs are made of vertical stakes (about one to two meters, or three to seven feet, long and less than three centimeters, or about one and one-eighth inch, in diameter) driven into the subtidal sediments in a linear arrangement paralleling the shoreline. The posts were interspersed with bundles of brush that created a wall or enclosure, trapping small fish as the tide receded. The trapped fish were then secured by baskets, dip nets, leisters (pronged spears), or even by hand, providing a reliable source of protein.

These traps could be maintained through minimal effort by small groups, and after repairs were no longer practical, a new weir was constructed. This weir "complex" was abandoned by about 1550 B.C.E., when siltation in the Back Bay area rendered them no longer cost efficient.

ADDITIONAL RESOURCES

Johnson, F., ed. *The Boylston Street Fishweir*. 4 vols. Andover, Mass.: Phillips Academy, 1942.

Levin, Mary Ann, Kenneth E. Sassaman, and Michael S. Nassaney, eds. *The Archaeological Northeast*. Westport, Conn.: Bergin & Garvey, 1999.

SEE ALSO: Archaic North American culture; Eastern peoples.

—J. M. Adovasio

BRĀHMAṆAS

AUTHORSHIP: Composite; attributed to various legendary authors
DATE: eighth-fifth centuries B.C.E.
LOCALE: India
RELATED CIVILIZATION: India
SIGNIFICANCE: The oldest prose texts in Indian literature, they contain ritual speculations and provide a commentary on earlier verse *Saṃhitās*.

The several lengthy prose texts known as *Brāhmaṇas* (BRAH-mah-nah-s), composed in an archaic dialect of Sanskrit, belong to Vedic literature, which Indian thought regards as divinely "revealed" (*śruti*). The term *brāhmaṇa*, meaning "relating to *brahman*" (a word that in this context refers to the Veda), indicates that they were meant to be commentaries on the earlier four Vedas or *Saṃhitās*, which are collections of hymns to various deities. The *Brāhmaṇas* explain the value and efficacy of the ritual ceremonies that make use of the earlier hymns. They do not, however, detail how the rituals are to be performed, a topic dealt with in later texts. Instead, the authors of these texts organize their understanding of ancient forms of worship into intellectual systems.

In the theological concerns of the *Brāhmaṇas*, it is sometimes possible to discern the germ of later philosophical speculation in India that centers on the nature of *brahman*, understood as the fundamental principle or reality of the universe. Occasionally, in the course of ritual explanations, *Brāhmaṇas* also narrate versions of myths and legends, some of which recur in later Indian texts with significant alterations.

ADDITIONAL RESOURCES

Gonda, Jan. *Vedic Literature (Saṃhitās and Brāhmaṇas)*. Vol. 1 in *A History of Indian Literature*. Wiesbaden, Germany: Harrassowitz, 1975.

Tilak, Sunanda Keshar. *Cultural Gleanings from the Brahmana Literature*. New Delhi, India: Yaska Publishers, 1990.

SEE ALSO: India; Vedas; Vedism.

—*Burt Thorp*

BRAHMANISM

DATE: term coined c. 1700 C.E.
LOCALE: India
RELATED CIVILIZATION: India

The eighteenth century term "Brahmanism" (BRAH-muh-nih-zuhm) refers both to orthodox, conservative interpretations of ancient Hindu scriptures, especially the *Upaniṣads* (compiled c. 1000-c. 200 B.C.E.), and to the stratified social system associated with this orthodoxy. The term derives from Brahmā, the name of Hinduism's supreme deity. In the social sense, the term "Brahmanism" also refers to the dominance of the priestly caste, the Brahman, the most favored of the four main hereditary groupings of people within India's traditional caste system.

During the Vedic period (c. 1500-400 B.C.E.), there was an emphasis on ritual and sacrifice. Specific rituals were believed necessary to maintain cosmic harmony and to preserve the social structure that developed after Aryan invaders established military and political control over the subcontinent. These rituals became the responsibility of the Brahman caste. Although the Brahmans were supposedly at the top of the social structure and were regarded as spiritual authorities, real political power was often in the hands of the next highest caste, the Kṣatriya, who were the nobles and warriors. Beneath them were the Vaiśya, who were farmers and merchants, and beneath these were the Śūdras, the peasants. Even lower than the peasants were the Panchamas, or Untouchables, who were without inherited status or caste. Along with the division of labor came an associated system of ritual cleanliness that discouraged social mobility.

As a social system, Brahmanism was supported in later periods by two important religious concepts; reincarnation, which held out the hope of being born into a higher caste if one led an exemplary life, and the concept of dharma, the duties of life. In addition to universal moral codes, dharma also encompassed the fulfillment of obligations according to one's circumstances, which included caste.

Within classical Hindu theology, Brahmā is referred to as "the creator." Although Hinduism is polytheistic, Brahmā is regarded as the supreme being, the source of all reality. Brahmā's dynamic qualities are personified in Śiva, who is associated with cosmic change, and Brahmā's eternal, unchanging qualities are personified in Vishnu, the preserver. These three deities make up the Hindu trinity. This trinity, together with the mother goddess Kali or Durga (the consort of Śiva), constitutes the principal deities of Hinduism. Other important deities are incarnations or descendants of these, and local practices vary greatly. The complexity of the Hindu pantheon can also be found in the social system of traditional Brahmanism as the four main castes were eventually subdivided into thousands of castes.

Even in ancient times, there were significant challenges to Brahmanism, aside from conflicting interpretations of the ancient scriptures from within Hinduism.

The most serious challenge came from Buddhism, which emphasized personal discipline as a path toward enlightenment and liberation from rebirth and rejected caste divisions. Within Hinduism, there was a gradual shift of emphasis, away from the rituals and rigid social hierarchy of Brahmanism, and toward personal religious devotion.

ADDITIONAL RESOURCES

Basham, A. L. *The Wonder That Was India*. New York: Grove Press, 1959.

De Bary, William. *Sources of Indian Tradition*. New York: Columbia University Press, 1966.

Joshi, L. M. *Brahmanism, Buddhism, and Hinduism*. Seattle: Vipassana Research, 1987.

Monier-Williams, Monier. *Religious Life in Ancient India: Vedism, Brahmanism, and Hinduism*. Delhi, India: Sanjay Prakashan, 1990.

SEE ALSO: Buddhism; Hinduism; *Upaniṣads*; Vedas.
—*John E. Myers*

BRASIDAS OF SPARTA

ALSO KNOWN AS: Brasidas, son of Tellis
BORN: date and place unknown
DIED: 422 B.C.E.; Amphipolis, Macedonia
RELATED CIVILIZATION: Classical Greece
MAJOR ROLE/POSITION: Military leader

Life. Brasidas (BRAS-uh-duhs), the finest Spartan general of the Archidamian War (431-421 B.C.E.), first gained notice in 431 B.C.E., when he saved the city of Methone from Athenian assault. In subsequent years, he advised Spartan naval commanders, always advocating aggressive action, and gallantly led an unsuccessful landing attempt on Athenian-held Pylos.

In 424 B.C.E., he rescued the city of Megara from Athenian attack, then marched into Thrace, where he won over various communities, in particular the important Athenian colony of Amphipolis. In 423 B.C.E., he secured two more cities, Mende and Scione, but could not prevent the Athenians from besieging Scione or retaking Mende and other sites. However, when the Athenian leader Cleon went against Amphipolis in 422 B.C.E., Brasidas surprised his army and routed it with heavy losses, killing Cleon but losing his own life as

well. Their deaths allowed the war-weary Athenians and Spartans to end hostilities, at least for the moment.

Influence. Brasidas won Sparta's only genuine successes of the Archidamian War. The loss of Amphipolis grieved the Athenians for generations and resulted in the exile from Athens of the historian Thucydides, keeping him out of the war and allowing him to write much of his *Historia tou Peloponnesiacou polemou* (431-404 B.C.E.; *History of the Peloponnesian War*, 1550).

ADDITIONAL RESOURCES

Powell, Anton. *Athens and Sparta*. New York: Routledge, 1996.

Thucydides. "History of the Peloponnesian War." In *The Landmark Thucydides: A Comprehensive Guide to the Peloponnesian War*, edited by Robert B. Strassler. New York: Free Press, 1996.

SEE ALSO: Archidamian War; Cleon of Athens; Greece, Classical; Peloponnesian War; Thucydides.
—*Scott M. Rusch*

BRAZIL, EASTERN

DATE: 8000 B.C.E.-700 C.E.
LOCALE: Amazon Basin, Brazil, South America
RELATED CIVILIZATIONS: Tupi-Gusrani, Macro-Jes
SIGNIFICANCE: The earliest inhabitants of eastern Brazil may have been non-Asian Paleo-Indians who arrived from Australia, the South Pacific, or even Africa.

Experts agree that all early South American populations most likely differentiated from a single source: non-Asian Paleo-Indians who arrived in eastern Brazil by at least 12,000 years ago. These Paleo-Indians were the source of all later populations in most of the Western Hemisphere. Evidence indicates they are as likely to have come from Africa, Australia, or the South Pacific as from Siberia and Asia.

The same studies indicate the arrival of a second wave of migration from north Asia, during the Early Archaic period, arriving in South America by approximately 7000 B.C.E. This group could have fused with or wiped out the earlier populations. The most ancient sites, such as those at Caverna da Pedra Pintada, near Monte Alegra, Brazil; Belo Horizonte, north of Rio; Lapa Vermelha in Minas Gerais; and Serra Da Capivara in the remote northeast, clearly indicate that established populations of Paleo-Indians were living in the area thousands of years before the arrival of later Mongoloid populations. The Mongoloid mastered big-game hunting in North America and primitive slash-and-burn tropical rain forest agriculture in their migrations into the southern Americas. Estimates continue to be pushed further back in time as cave paintings, such as those of giant armadillos, extinct before the last Ice Age, and other remains suggest the intriguing possibility that the ancestors of later humans might have first arrived in eastern Brazil as much as 50,000 years ago, by sea from Africa or Australia. They would have then migrated northward along the coast.

Early bands of hunter-gatherers eventually developed the first fishing villages and made the oldest known pottery in the Americas, dated between 7500 and 5000 B.C.E. The vegetation and climate of this area are classified as typical closed canopy forests and humid tropical monsoon, respectively, with rainfall averaging upward of 80 inches (203 centimeters) a year. The Paleo-Indians made extensive use of all available resources, including rodents and bats, snakes and other reptiles, tortoises and turtles, large and small fishes, mollusks, amphibians, large and small game, nuts, seeds from leguminous trees, fruits, palms, and whatever else they could find. Some of the plants they used can still be found in remaining pristine tropical forests in the region. They did not use crop plants, nor is there any evidence that they brought plants from cooler climates to the north.

Many cave paintings have been found in the area, indicating the presence of cultures much older than previously expected. Some authorities believe the Amazonian cave dwellers are related to or descended from Clovis technological complex peoples. That theory is highly speculative, especially as it would have required a southward migration rate twice that of accepted models. Whether arriving by sea or land, from whatever direction, the original inhabitants of eastern Brazil were distinct peoples, quite different from the north Asians who came later. Genetic and biological evidence at the molecular level suggests three clearly defined waves of migration, with at least eleven lineal subdivisions, came into the Americas at different times between 10,000 and 7000 B.C.E. All of them, and perhaps other waves not yet discovered, were together responsible for the initial peopling of the Western Hemisphere. Archaeological and anthropological findings continue to uncover many possible points of origin other than those commonly assumed to be the exclusive geographic and cultural sources for the first peoples in South America and eastern Brazil.

The fact that sites predating all others in the Western Hemisphere have been found in the Amazon Basin and across eastern Brazil lends credence to theories indicating that the original inhabitants of South America and eastern Brazil did not necessarily come from the north at all, or all at once, but could have come from across the oceans or could even have migrated from the south, in multiple waves. Such theories are highly speculative, but mounting evidence suggests they may eventually be proved valid.

After 7000 B.C.E., settled cultures gradually developed in the Amazon Basin and eastern Brazil. The Tupi-Guarani are a group of tribal cannibals that lived along the coast and inland south of the Amazon River, all the way to the Andean foothills to the west. They lived in small communal villages. Their environmental practices and uses indicate they primarily combined hunting, fishing, and gathering with some primitive slash-and-burn agriculture focused on the growth of roots and tubers. Remains indicate the Tupi were expert potters, jewelry and weapons makers, and stone workers. They were a warring people, engaging in constant battles with their neighbors the Macro-Jes, a somewhat less developed hunter-gatherer group. Tupi peoples, including the Tupine, Tupinamba, Tupinikin, Tomoio, Tobajara, and Potiguar eventually drove the Macro-Jes out of most of the eastern coastal region.

Environmental conditions in the eastern Brazilian ecosystem remained relatively stable, with minor variations occurring in rainfall, mean average temperature, and elements of the resource base. Over several centuries, the populations increased so much that hundreds of distinct cultural groups developed to occupy the microclimates and various ecological niches such as inland savannahs of the area. However, their lifestyles remained remarkably consistent and constant, relying on skills developed during earlier periods: hunting and fishing; gathering fruits, nuts, and seeds; and slash-and-burn agricultural practices that required each group to move periodically within its territory to new ground once a site's food-growing potential was exhausted. Tens of thousands lived along the coastline, and hundreds of thousands came to occupy interior areas, especially along or near rivers. Settlements in more productive areas were home to as many as eight thousand people.

Some of the major tribal groups of this area of Brazil include the Yanomami, Omagua, Tapajos, Munduruku, Mawe, Mura, Ingarika, Wapixama, Taurepang, Waimiri-Atroarim Nambiqwara, Kreen-Akarore, Kawahib, Urubu-Kaapor, Surui, Cintas Largas, Crao, Guaja, Guajajara, Urubu-Kaapor Krikate, Timbira, Pataxo Ha Ha Hae, and Makuxi. Their lifestyles were similar, and their scant material remains indicate the process of innovation to be slow and unremarkable among them. There are some indications of cannibalism, but as to whether it was used as ritual practice or for survival is not clear. Without environmental changes requiring adaptive response or conflicts with peoples from elsewhere, there was little need to make the kinds of advances seen elsewhere in South America up to 700 C.E.

ADDITIONAL RESOURCES

Fagan, B. *The Great Journey: The Peopling of Ancient America*. New York: Thames and Hudson, 1987.
Sorenson, J. *Pre-Columbian Contact with the Americas Across the Oceans*. Provo, Utah: Research Press, 1990.

SEE ALSO: Amazonia; Archaic South American culture; Paleo-Indians in South America.

—*Michael W. Simpson*

BRITAIN

DATE: 3000 B.C.E. to 700 C.E.
LOCALE: Island off the northwest coast of Europe
SIGNIFICANCE: Although located on the western fringe of the European continent, most of the forces driving European development played out in, or at least impinged on, Britain.

Britain, along with the rest of northern Europe, was covered by the great Arctic ice sheet until the beginning of the postglacial period, which began about 10,000 B.C.E. A land bridge between Europe and Britain remained in existence until about 6500 B.C.E. Neolithic peoples used the land bridge to cross to Britain, and even after the bridge's submergence, early peoples continued to cross from Europe to the island. There is archaeological evidence of trading relations between the

people of Britain and the Continent from the earliest times. The history of Britain in ancient times divides into four periods: the pre-Celtic period, the Celtic period, the Roman period, and the Anglo-Saxon invasion period.

Pre-Celtic. In the pre-Celtic period, Britain was inhabited by Neolithic and Bronze Age peoples apparently of Indo-European origin. Although they at first supported themselves by foraging and the harvest of game, they soon progressed to agriculture, apparently communally organized, from the river or stream bottomlands uphill to the ridges. There is some archaeological evidence that they engaged in dairying.

The earliest peoples used stone tools, but bronze items date back to at least 2000 B.C.E. The tin that is plentiful in Cornwall became a major asset of the early peoples of Britain, combined with the copper that was available in Wales and particularly in Ireland. From the second millennium B.C.E., Britain and the Continent engaged in a brisk trade in raw metals. By the middle of the first millennium B.C.E., a significant metalworking "industry" had developed in Britain.

One of the most striking features that remains of these early, pre-Celtic peoples is the henge stones, gigantic megaliths erected at various sites and unique to the island. The most famous of these is Stonehenge. They appear to have been related to the inhabitants' religious beliefs, which were connected to solar events. They were also used as burial sites, from which increasingly elaborate items have been retrieved. The bodies themselves were mostly cremated and deposited in urns in excavated burial sites, either on hilltops or in the river valleys. The pottery of this early era appears to have been made locally, but by the first millennium B.C.E., pottery was evidently being imported from the Continent.

The early peoples of Britain apparently experienced significant difficulties during the first millennium B.C.E. as the climate grew colder and wetter. Agriculture was forced to draw back from the more exposed areas and concentrate in the river and stream bottomlands. At the higher elevations, the former fields were converted to pastures for herding. This period also saw more social stratification, with wealthier individuals being differentiated from the ordinary people.

The Celtic phase. The mechanism by which Britain became dominated by warlike Celtic peoples of central Europe is in dispute. Severe population pressure beginning around 400 B.C.E. led the Celts to expand in all directions; some of those moving into Gaul went on to Britain. What is not known is whether the Celts invaded Britain as a group or if they gradually infiltrated the island. However they arrived, theirs became the dominant culture in Britain by 200 B.C.E.

The culture of the Celts, whom the Romans encountered when Julius Caesar invaded the island in 55 B.C.E., is closely associated with the La Tène culture of central Europe. Caesar's commentaries provide some solid written information about these Celts. Their war-making proclivities were proverbial, and their culture celebrated the accomplishments of their leading warriors. They enjoyed the fruits of their plunder, taken during successful raids. By the time of Caesar, they had formed themselves into distinct tribal groups, each associated with a leader of the band who was like a king on a smaller scale.

EARLY BRITISH MILK DRINKERS

Tea, not milk, may appear to be the drink of choice in England, but ancient Britons were drinking milk at least by the Iron Age, between 1,500 and 500 B.C.E. Stephanie Dudd and Richard Evershed, researchers from the University of Bristol, analyzed pottery shards from that period and found evidence of fatty acids from milk products. Their discovery marks the first time traces of milk products have actually been found, although other researchers working in Britain unearthed what appear to be ceramic cheese graters dating to 4,500 B.C.E.

The Celts, like the Romans, believed in multiple gods, whom they apparently associated with specific sites. They practiced human sacrifice and dedicated many material items to their favorite deities, often by casting them into water. A great many Celtic artifacts have been recovered from the lakes, streams, and rivers of Britain. Their wise men, known as Druids, were often feared by their enemies as possessing magical powers. According to the Celtic religion, the year was divided into four segments, beginning roughly around November 1, with the following segments beginning on February 1, May 1, and August 1.

Although the family appears to have been the primary organizing unit of Celtic society, more complex associations also existed. During the Celtic period in Britain, many fortifications were built on hilltops, suggesting that society was organized for its communal defense, perhaps because of continuing incursions of new immigrants from Celtic Europe.

However, despite the disruptions, trade with the Continent continued to expand, and archaeological evidence contains an ever-increasing variety of goods. By 200 B.C.E., the Celts of Britain were tied into the Mediterranean trading system, and their warlike proclivities appear to have declined. The society had a distinctive craft segment that made goods, especially metal items (iron, often swords, from about 400 C.E. onward) for trading with peoples in the Mediterranean, who produced pottery, textiles, and luxury items in return.

Roman Britain. Caesar invaded Britain in 55 B.C.E. and again the following year but did not attempt to annex Britain to the Roman Empire. This was left to the emperor Claudius, who sent an army there in 43 C.E. and visited Britain to accept the surrender of the Celtic community at what became Colchester, Essex. Following this victory, Celtic Britain was extensively Romanized. The government was recast along typical Roman lines, new cities were laid out in the preferred rectangular form, and the whole Roman governmental superstructure of prefects and provincial governors was imposed on the island. An urban culture developed in the Roman towns, which were built overwhelmingly of masonry, after the Roman fashion. The countryside retained much of its traditional Celtic culture, though wealthy Romans built villas on the land, and Latin became the prevailing language throughout the island. The Romans carried their military conquest to the tip of Scotland but then drew back into England, building what came to be called Hadrian's Wall across the narrow part of the island. The wall became Rome's defensive perimeter, and the more primitive Celts north of the wall were generally left to their own devices.

Although the Romans had brought their own gods to Britain, these gave way with the conversion of the emperor Constantine the Great in the years immediately following 312 C.E. to the Christianizing of Roman Britain. Britain became part of the Christian administrative structure created by the Roman emperors, though Britain's peripheral location led to a tendency for it to follow its own version of the Christian faith.

Anglo-Saxon Britain. As the Roman Empire was increasingly penetrated by Germanic tribal groups from the beginning of the third century C.E. onward, the maintenance of Roman rule in Britain became precarious. In 407 C.E., the Roman legions stationed in Britain were withdrawn to be used in the defense of Gaul and other parts of the empire, and in 410 C.E., the emperor Honorius advised his subordinates in Britain that he could no longer provide support for the defense of Britain against German attack—attack that had already produced a line of fortresses on the eastern seaboard called the "Saxon shore."

What happened in the fifth century C.E. is a matter of dispute, for there are no good written sources and the archaeological evidence is scattered. However, most likely the Romanized British civilization collapsed in the face of barbarian attack; the architecture of the cities fell into ruins, and the population declined significantly. The Celtic elements withdrew westward in the face of attack from the Germanic tribes landing on the eastern shore, leading to the division of the island's peoples that persists to this day, the easternmost predominantly Germanic, the westernmost predominantly Celtic.

By the sixth century C.E., the Germanic invaders from the western shores of northern Europe, generally described as Saxons, Angles, and Jutes, had created tribal kingdoms that would prevail until the Middle Ages. The urban culture of Roman Britain had vanished and been replaced by a largely agricultural society, though crafts associated with war and farming existed locally. The invading Germanic tribes were pagan, but Christianity returned to Britain with the mission of Saint Augustine of Canterbury in 597 C.E. He landed in Kent and converted the local Germanic ruler, and from that point, Christianity spread throughout the island. However, the country remained divided into tribal kingdoms among which dominance shifted until the late ninth century C.E.

ADDITIONAL RESOURCES

Cunliffe, Barry. *The Ancient Celts*. Oxford, England: Oxford University Press, 1997.

Dyer, James. *Ancient Britain*. London: Batsford, 1990

Salwey, Peter. *The Oxford Illustrated History of Roman Britain*. Oxford, England: Oxford University Press, 1993.

Welch, Martin. *Discovering Anglo-Saxon England*. University Park: Pennsylvania State University Press, 1992.

Williams, Ann. *Kingship and Government in Pre-Conquest England, c. 500-1066*. London: Macmillan, 1999.

SEE ALSO: Angles, Saxons, Jutes; Augustine of Canterbury, Saint; Caesar, Julius; Celts; Christianity; Claudius; Constantine the Great; Germany; Ireland; La Tène culture; Neolithic Age Europe; Rome, Imperial; Stonehenge.

—Nancy M. Gordon

BRUTUS

ALSO KNOWN AS: Marcus Iunius Brutus; Quintus
   Caepio Brutus
BORN: c. 85 B.C.E.; probably Rome
DIED: October 23, 42 B.C.E.; Philippi, Greece
RELATED CIVILIZATION: Republican Rome
MAJOR ROLE/POSITION: Military leader, politician

Life. Among Brutus's ancestors were Lucius Junius
Brutus, who founded the Roman Republic (509 B.C.E.),
and the tyrannicide Gaius Servilius Ahala, who killed
Spurius Maelius in 439 B.C.E. Because his father was
murdered by Pompey the Great during a revolt in 76
B.C.E., Brutus was adopted by his maternal uncle,
Quintus Servilius Caepio, and educated by his mother's
step-brother, Cato the Younger.

Brutus's early political career is unexceptional. He
came into prominence with the Roman civil war of 49-
48 B.C.E. and its consequences. Making his peace with
Pompey the Great, Brutus fought for the Roman Republic at Pharsalus. Captured and spared by Julius
Caesar, he then changed sides. By 47 B.C.E., he was governing the province of Cisalpine Gaul for Caesar. By 44
B.C.E., he was the chief praetor in Rome and had been
designated consul for 41 B.C.E. Disturbed by tyrannical
developments in government, he joined with Cassius in
leading the plot that resulted in the assassination of
Caesar on March 15, 44 B.C.E. Outlawed for this action,
Brutus and Cassius fought against Octavian and Marc
Antony at Philippi and committed suicide in defeat.

Influence. Remembered for his part in Caesar's assassination, Brutus was a role model for later senators.
The assassination itself served as a reminder that the
emperor ignored the senate at his peril. Rome remained
nominally a republic, and the city's republican institutions were highly esteemed.

Brutus. (Library of Congress)

ADDITIONAL RESOURCES
Clarke, M. L. *The Noblest Roman.* London: Thames
   and Hudson, 1981.
Fuller, J. F. C. *Julius Caesar.* Ware, Hertfordshire, En-
   gland: Wordsworth, 1998.
Syme, R. *The Roman Revolution.* Oxford, England:
   Oxford University Press, 1939.

SEE ALSO: Antony, Marc; Augustus; Caesar, Julius;
Cassius; Cato the Younger; Pharsalus, Battle of; Philippi, Battle of; Pompey the Great; Rome, Republican.
                                                    —*Richard Westall*

BUDDHA

ALSO KNOWN AS: Siddhārtha Gautama; Śākyamuni;
   Tathāgata; Bhagwān
BORN: c. 566 B.C.E.; Kapilavastu, Śākya republic,
   Kosala Kingdom (now in India)
DIED: c. 486 B.C.E.; Kuśingara, India
RELATED CIVILIZATION: Upaniṣadic India
MAJOR ROLE/POSITION: Founder of Buddhism

Life. It is difficult to separate fact from legend in
tracing Buddha's life because salient events in his life are
described only in legendary accounts. He was born to
King Śuddhodana Gautama of the Śākya tribe and his
wife, Māyā, who died seven days after his birth. Legend
states that his mother saw a white elephant enter her
womb, became pregnant, and upon birth, her child

stood and proclaimed that he was the "future Buddha."

He was named Siddhārtha ("he who has achieved his goal") and was brought up by her sister Prajapati in absolute luxury. At age twenty-nine, he married Yaśodharā and then had a son named Rāhula ("the Fetter"); however, he spent most of his time brooding over his overprotective luxurious lifestyle and princely duties. In a state of mental anguish, he made three trips out of the palace during which he encountered, respectively, a decrepit old man, a diseased individual, and a corpse. Each time he returned to the palace, brooded over his experiences, and was moved to pity at the sufferings of humans and beast alike.

Realizing that worldly pleasures would not satisfy him, he left his family and princely life, shaved his head, exchanged his clothes with a hunter, and accepted a *śramanic* way of life. Under several gurus, he pursued forms of meditation, which proved unsatisfactory, for he sought pacification of mental anguish, perfect direct knowledge, and attainment of the unconditional realm. He proceeded to Gāyā and practiced severe austerities for six years but abandoned these because he realized that a healthy body was necessary for the pursuit of wisdom.

At age thirty-five, he sat under a banyan tree (the Bodhi tree), where he discovered the path to enlightenment becoming the Tathāgata, the Perfectly Enlightened One, or the Buddha. He realized the Four Noble Truths and the Middle Way, the core of his dharma, which revealed the meaning and source of suffering, the path to its cessation, and the destiny of all living things. Legend describes how nature rejoiced at his success and how his ancestors paid him homage.

He rose, proceeded to Banāras and preached his first sermon at Sārnāth. Soon a community of monks, nuns, and lay people, the Saṅgha, was created, and it became the seed of the Buddhist faith. He continued his mission in north India for forty-five years, gaining important disciples. At the age of eighty, while in Veśālī, he fell seriously ill from eating a mushroom or pork meal. At Kuśinagara, he passed away in Parinirvāṇa, or final disappearance, between two sala trees. Legend again describes how nature marked the moment with earthquakes and thunder. After a six-day wake, he was cremated and a stupa (reliquary) was erected to enshrine his relics.

Influence. As a reformer of India's spiritual life, his teachings, through the missionary zeal of the Saṅgha, resulted in an expansion of his dharma (or "law") throughout Asia for twenty-five hundred years.

Statue of Buddha. (Library of Congress)

ADDITIONAL RESOURCES

Corless, Roger J. *The Vision of Buddhism.* New York: Paragon House, 1989.

Herman, A. L. *An Introduction to Buddhist Thought.* Boston: University Press of America, 1983.

Nelson, Walter Henry. *Buddha: His Life and His Teaching.* New York: Putnam, 2001.

SEE ALSO: Buddhism; India.

—*George J. Hoynacki*

BUDDHISM

DATE: beginning in the sixth or fifth century B.C.E.
LOCALE: South and East Asia
RELATED CIVILIZATIONS: India, China, Japan, Tibet, Korea
SIGNIFICANCE: Buddhism spread from ancient India to become a major world religion and greatly influenced Asian culture.

Buddhism was founded in northeastern India by Siddhārtha Gautama, known as the Buddha, during the sixth or fifth century B.C.E. The religion spread throughout much of Asia, and by the end of antiquity, it had become one of the continent's dominant faiths.

The life of the Buddha. Siddhārtha Gautama, also known as Śākyamuni, was born in the in the kingdom of the Śakyas in northeastern India. The most commonly accepted dates for his life are circa 566 to circa 486 B.C.E. According to tradition, the Brahmans, or priests, at his father's court foretold that the young prince would either become a world-conquering monarch or a buddha, which means "awakened one" or "enlightened one" in Sanskrit. Wishing to keep his son from taking up the life of a holy man, King Śuddhodana attempted to surround the child with luxury and comfort. Nevertheless, as a young man, Siddhārtha saw old age, sickness, and death, which convinced him of the misery of the world. He also saw a wandering holy man and was inspired to leave home to seek wisdom.

For a time, Siddhārtha starved himself and followed a regimen of extreme asceticism and self-mortification. He decided that his self-imposed suffering would not lead him to enlightenment, and he began to live in a more moderate manner. One morning, he sat down under a banyan tree (the Bodhi tree), and according to Buddhist teaching, he vowed not to rise until he had achieved enlightenment. After struggles with the evil spirit Mara, the lord of passion, Siddhārtha realized the truth about existence.

The Buddha, as he had become, meditated on his realization for several weeks and then began to teach others. The full-time disciples of the Buddha became monks and were known as the Saṅgha ("community" or "order"). At the age of eighty, the Buddha became sick and died.

Essential teachings. The essence of Buddha's realization is usually described as the Four Noble Truths. The first truth is that life is suffering. Suffering continues through an endless chain of rebirths. The second

truth is that suffering is caused by desire. The third is that desire can be ended, and the fourth is that right living according to Buddhist precepts (known as the Eightfold Path) is the way to end desire. With the ceasing of desire, beings enter Nirvana, a state of release from existence.

Buddhists from the earliest times onward have been dedicated to the Three Jewels. The first jewel was the Buddha himself. The second was the dharma, or "law," the truth taught by the Buddha. The Saṅgha, or community of monks, was the third.

Buddhism in ancient India. After the death of the Buddha, his teachings began to spread through northeastern India. Two early councils, gatherings of Buddhist monks, began to compose the Buddhist scriptures and to discuss controversies in doctrine. One of these was held immediately after the Buddha's death, and another was held about a century later. At the second, the Council of Vesālī held about 383 B.C.E., Buddhism began to split over issues of doctrine. This split would gradually lead to the development of the two major sects or schools of Buddhism, Theravāda (also called Hīnayāna) and Mahāyāna.

In the fourth century B.C.E., the rulers of the Mauryan Dynasty united much of northern India in a single empire. The Mauryan emperor Aśoka (r. 269-238 B.C.E.) supported the Buddhist teachings and became the ideal of the Buddhist king. During Aśoka's reign, the Third Buddhist Council was convened at Pāṭaliputra in 250 B.C.E. At this third council, monks completed the collection of the writings that made up the basic canon, known as the *Tipiṭaka*, or "Three Baskets," after its three divisions. Participants also made the decision to send missionaries to other lands.

As a result of the Indian origins of Buddhism, ancient Indian languages became the sacred languages for Buddhists of all nationalities. Some Buddhist scriptures were written in Sanskrit, an ancient language used for Hindu religious texts. The *Tipiṭaka* (collected c. 250 B.C.E.; English translation in *Buddhist Scriptures*, 1913) was written in Pāli, a popular language derived from Sanskrit.

Buddhism gradually began to disappear from its native land. Although the religion received some of its support from kings, such as Aśoka, its greatest support came from India's merchant classes. As the trading economies of India declined over the course of the first centuries of the common era, Buddhism gradually lost this basis. Moreover, the new religion had to compete with India's older religion, Hinduism. Hinduism absorbed some elements of Buddhism, recognizing the Buddha as an incarnation of the god Vishnu (Viṣṇu). At the same time, the Brahmans of India opposed Buddhist philosophy and practice and, by about 700 C.E., Indian Buddhism had mostly withered away, only to reappear in modern times.

Buddhism outside India. Although Buddhism ceased to be a major faith in India, it spread to many other lands. The Mauryan Dynasty maintained close ties with Ceylon (modern Sri Lanka), an island kingdom off the southern tip of India. In 251 B.C.E., Aśoka's son Mahinda went to Ceylon as a Buddhist missionary. Buddhism would later spread from Ceylon to the Southeast Asian lands of Burma, Siam (modern Thailand), Laos, and Cambodia.

By about 200 B.C.E., Buddhism had begun to spread to central Asia. The religion apparently entered China about 61 C.E. According to tradition, this occurred because the Chinese emperor Mingdi (r. 58-75 C.E.) had a dream in which he saw a golden figure flying down from heaven; this figure was identified as the Buddha. About 426 C.E., a persecution of Buddhists began in China, but this was short-lived. Between 470 and 527 C.E., the Buddhist missionary Bodhidharma entered China from India and began to preach a meditative form of Buddhism that later became known as Zen. About 518 C.E., Chinese translations of the *Tipiṭaka* began to appear. From China, Buddhism entered Korea and Vietnam in about the fourth century C.E. Some time after 500 C.E., the Japanese began to receive the Buddhist faith from Korea.

About 600 C.E., the people of Tibet began to adopt Buddhism, just as it was dying out in India. Between circa 627 and circa 650 C.E., Tibet proclaimed Tantric Buddhism to be the state religion. Many of the gods of Tibet's old religion, Bonism, were incorporated into the new faith. During the eighth century C.E., the first Tibetan Buddhist monastery was built, and Buddhism began to play a central role in Tibetan culture.

The schools of Buddhism. Disagreement over questions of how salvation is to be achieved appeared in Buddhism almost immediately after the Buddha's death. By the first century of the common era, there were as many as five hundred sects of Buddhism. The major split that emerged during the first half-century of the religion was between Theravāda ("the way of the elders") and Mahāyāna ("the great vehicle") Buddhism. Theravāda is sometimes referred to as Hīnayāna ("the lesser vehicle"). One of the major distinctions between these two schools or sects has to do with the role of the bodhisattva (literally, "enlightened being"). To simplify a complex doctrinal issue, bodhisattvas, in Mahāyāna Buddhism, are individuals who have achieved enlightenment but delay passing over into Nirvana in order to help with the salvation of others. The position of Theravāda Buddhism is that each individual must achieve enlightenment and salvation by his or her own efforts.

For centuries, Theravāda and Mahāyāna orders existed side by side, frequently in rivalry. In 24 B.C.E., the two most important monasteries in Ceylon—one Theravāda and one Mahāyāna—were founded. Gradually, however, Theravāda Buddhism replaced its rival in Ceylon and became the form of Buddhism that took root in Southeast Asia. Mahāyāna Buddhism is often referred to as the northern form of Buddhism because it established itself in China, Japan, and Korea.

A third school of Buddhism, Vajrayāna (the "thunderbolt vehicle"), developed in eastern India from about the fifth to the seventh centuries C.E. and became dominant in Nepal and Tibet. It was the result of the adoption of the magical rites of a fertility cult known as Tantricism. Therefore, Vajrayāna is often referred to as Tantric Buddhism and relies heavily on seemingly magical practices, such as the recitation of names or phrases.

ADDITIONAL RESOURCES

Keay, John. *India: A History.* New York: Atlantic Monthly Press, 2000.

Nelson, Walter H. *Buddha: His Life and Teaching.* Los Angeles: J. P. Tarcher, 2000.

Reat, Noble R. *Buddhism: A History.* Fremont, Calif.: Asian Humanities Press, 1995.

Skilton, Andrew. *A Concise History of Buddhism.* Trumbull, Conn.: Weatherhill, 1997.

SEE ALSO: Aśoka; Buddha; China; Hinduism; India; Japan; Korea; Mauryan Dynasty; Tantras; Tibet.

—Carl L. Bankston III

BUDDHIST CAVE TEMPLES

DATE: c. 400-700 C.E.
LOCALE: North China
RELATED CIVILIZATION: China
SIGNIFICANCE: The Buddhist cave temples of Dunhuang, Yungang, and Longmen trace the early development of Buddhism in China.

Following the tradition of rock-cut Indian Buddhist shrines, the cave temples of China stand as important monuments to the religion's formative years in China. The principal cave-temple sites are Dunhuang, Yungang, and Longmen.

Buddhism was transmitted from India eastward through Central Asia and into China proper along the Silk Road. Located at the eastern end of this trade route was Dunhuang, a desert oasis set on the eastern edge of the Tarim Basin. Here, beginning in the first half of the fifth century C.E., the Magao caves (also called the Caves of the Thousand Buddhas) were carved into the local stone. Dunhuang served as an important pilgrimage site as worshipers came to view the imagery in the caves. Of the more than 1,000 caves that probably existed at Dunhuang, only 492 remain. Inside the caves are paintings and sculptures of unimaginable beauty, preserved through the centuries by the arid desert climate. The walls are covered with elaborate images including incidents from the life of the Buddha, paradise scenes, and countless heavenly beings. Life-size sculptures, made of clay formed over wooden armatures and painted in bright pigments, were the focus of devotion. In addition, Dunhuang also housed a wealth of scroll paintings, textiles, and manuscripts found in a so-called library cave that was sealed sometime in the eleventh century C.E.

The tradition of rock-cut temples continued into north China at Yungang and Longmen. The principal caves at Yungang were produced from about 460 to 494 C.E., a project supported by the Northern Wei Dynasty (386-533 C.E.) rulers, who were devout Buddhists. Of the five principal caves, one is particularly well known for its colossal Buddha measuring 45 feet (17 meters) in height. Although initial work at the site was sponsored by the imperial family, an additional fifty-three caves came to be supported by donors from all levels of society.

When the Wei rulers moved their capital south to Luoyang, work began at Longmen, a site of spectacular large-scale carving, and continued for about four hundred years. More than thirteen hundred caves were produced. Longmen reached its height under the Tang Dynasty rulers (618-907 C.E.) and is exemplified by a group of five figures, with the cosmic Buddha, Vairocana, flanked by heavenly kings. Vairocana stands 44 feet (nearly 17 meters) in height and, as legend states, bears the facial features of Empress Wu, a devout Buddhist who was one of the main patrons of the site.

ADDITIONAL RESOURCES

Caswell, James O. *Written and Unwritten: A New History of the Buddhist Caves at Yungang.* Vancouver: University of British Columbia Press, 1988.

Stein, Aurel. *Serindia: Detailed Report of Exploration of Central Asia and Westernmost China, Carried On and Described Under the Orders of His Majesty's Indian Government.* 5 vols. Oxford, England: Clarendon Press, 1921.

Whitfield, Roderick, and Anne Farrer. *Caves of the Thousand Buddhas: Chinese Art from the Silk Route.* New York: George Braziller, 1990.

SEE ALSO: Buddha; Buddhism; China.

—*Catherine Pagani*

BUDHASVĀMIN

FLOURISHED: c. seventh century C.E.
RELATED CIVILIZATION: North India
MAJOR ROLE/POSITION: Writer

Life. Budhasvāmin (bew-dahs-VAH-meen) was a greatly admired north Indian writer. He wrote the *Bṛhatkathāślokasaṁgraha* (seventh century C.E.; *Budhasvamin's Brhatkathaslokasamgraha*, 1973). The only surviving manuscript of his work was found in Nepal, but there is no evidence that he was Nepalese as some have assumed. Written in the *kāvya* style (poetic form) of Sanskrit, the work as it exists in modern times is a fragmentary collection of tales divided into *sargas* (cantos). It is estimated that originally there may have been 25,000 verses; only 4,539 survive.

In his lively work, Budhasvāmin praises and acknowledges his indebtedness to an earlier writer, Guṇāḍhya, who wrote the lost *Bṛhatkathā* (n.d., original lost; "great story"). Budhasvāmin's faithfulness to the original work cannot be precisely determined, but many of his stories are presumed to be based on the earlier collection. The work consists of fables and stories of romance and adventure. All have well-conceived characters that he describes in clear and restrained terms. In the stories, he exploits the elements of suspense and surprise. A most striking feature of the work is the typically Indian technique of relating stories within stories. Plots and episodes intertwine with one another, and ultimately all weave together to form a single complex tale.

Influence. Budhasvāmin created one of India's most charming collections of ancient tales. He influenced later writers, most notably Somadeva, the eleventh century writer of the *Kathasāritsāgara* (between 1063 and 1082 C.E.; *Ocean of Stories*, 1862).

ADDITIONAL RESOURCES

Keith, A. Berriedale. *A History of Sanskrit Literature*. Oxford, England: Clarendon Press, 1928.

Maten, E. P. *Budhasvamin's Brhatkathaslokasamgraha: A Literary Study of an Ancient Indian Narrative*. Leiden, Netherlands: E. J. Brill, 1973.

SEE ALSO: Guṇāḍhya; India.

—*Katherine Anne Harper*

BYZANTINE EMPIRE

ALSO KNOWN AS: Eastern Roman Empire
DATE: 330-700 C.E.
LOCALE: Turkey and Asia Minor, Greece and other Balkan countries, at one time reaching from Spain to Persia
SIGNIFICANCE: The early Byzantine Empire became a stronghold of Christianity and produced legal codes that became models for Europe and the New World.

"Byzantine" is a term derived from the provincial Greek town of Byzantium, which Constantine the Great, who ruled the Eastern Roman Empire from 324 to 337 C.E., chose as his capital. He greatly expanded and improved this relatively insignificant town, renaming it Constantinople after himself. Strategically located on the Bosphorus, the strait that separates Europe from Asia, Constantinople soon became Europe's largest and most significant city.

History. By 324 C.E., when Constantine the Great became ruler of the Eastern Roman Empire, the Roman Empire was already in decline and nearing collapse. Diocletian, who ruled from 284 to 305 C.E., realized that the Roman Empire as it then existed was unwieldy and had divided it into the eastern and western empires.

When Diocletian died, civil war erupted, pitting east against west. Constantine defeated his western opponents in 313 C.E. and eleven years later became emperor, marking a distinct turning point in European history. Constantine was a devout Christian who resolutely renounced the Romans' pagan gods and swore allegiance to the Christianity that was sweeping the Roman Empire. Only one of the emperors succeeding him was not a Christian.

Constantine chose Byzantium, not Rome, as his capital because he was disenchanted by the paganism he witnessed during two visits to Rome. Founded in 657 B.C.E. by Greek sailors, Byzantium was small and provincial. Constantine enlarged the city, creating new public areas remarkably similar in design to those of Rome and building fortifications for its protection.

The most revered part of Constantinople was the first milestone, the Milion, with its four triumphal arches that formed a square to support a cupola, above which was Christianity's most cherished relic, the True Cross. Constantine made this holy place the center of the world. All distances in his empire were measured from it.

When Constantinople was dedicated on May 11, 330 C.E., after forty days of festivities, Constantine marked the occasion by attending a high mass in the church of Saint Irene. Simultaneous pagan celebrations were held in various temples throughout the area.

The united empire that Constantine had ruled again proved too large and disparate to be controlled as a sin-

BYZANTINE EMPIRE, CIRCA 565 C.E.

FRANKS

LANGOBARDS

Pontus Euxinus

Ravenna

ILLYRICUM THRACE

Trapezius

VISIGOTHS

CORSICA

ITALY

Thessalonika

Constantinople

Nicaea

Rome Brindisi

ASIA MINOR

Antioch

Cordoba

SARDINIA

Smyrna

Carthage SICILY

Athens

RHODES

CYPRUS

GHASSĀNID ARABS

AFRICA

CRETE

Jerusalem

Mediterranean Sea

Alexandria

Tripoli

EGYPT

■ = Domain of empire

gle entity. Theodosius the Great, ruling from 379 to 395 C.E., was the last emperor of a single Roman Empire. On his death, the empire was redivided into east and west. During the following century, the western part of the Roman Empire was unable to withstand the assaults of barbarians from the north. In 476 C.E., after being ruled by a series of ineffective emperors, the Western Empire collapsed.

The Eastern Roman Empire, with its well-placed capital on the Bosphorus, prospered while its western counterpart faded into obscurity. It became wealthy and was ideally situated for trade with the East. When the Germanic Ostrogoths threatened it in 493 C.E., they were persuaded instead to attack the Western Empire, where they established their kingdom. The Eastern Empire defended itself successfully in its frequent conflicts with Persia.

Nevertheless, the Eastern Empire had its problems, many of them resulting from conflicts between its Christian orientation and the Islamic orientation of the Near East, whose religious convictions were at loggerheads with Christianity and whose native cultures were drastically different from those of Greece and Rome, which prevailed in the Byzantine Empire. The General Councils of the Christian Church considered the religious beliefs of Syria and Egypt heretical. A schism grew when the pope declared himself the supreme head of the entire Christian Church, within which opposing factions were creating a split that led to a division into

the Roman Catholic and the Eastern Orthodox Churches.

Justinian I ruled the Eastern Roman Empire from 527 until 565 C.E. Under his rule, assisted by two great generals, Belisarius and Narses, Justinian reconquered the Western Empire, including Italy, southern Spain, and North Africa. He could not, however, control the incursions of Slavs, who crossed the Danube and wreaked havoc wherever they went. Justinian also fought a war with the Persians that resulted in a standoff and a tenuous truce.

Justinian presided over significant building projects, including the churches of Haghia Sophia in Constantinople and San Vitale in Ravenna. Under his rule, many public works were undertaken. His most lasting achievement, however, was his codification of Roman law, which served as a model for the legal systems of much of Europe and subsequently of the New World. Justinian is counted among the greatest of the Byzantine emperors, although his projects imposed such heavy taxation on the Byzantine citizenry that civil unrest ensued.

The Byzantine Empire eventually was at war with Persia, whose armies defeated Syria, Palestine, Egypt, and Asia Minor and twice very nearly captured Constantinople. In 610 C.E., Heraclius came to Constantinople and declared himself emperor. He ruled until 641 C.E., rebuilding the empire during his first decade as emperor. After religiously zealous Arabs attacked the Near East in 633 C.E., the Byzantine Empire lost much that Heraclius had regained. By 641 C.E., it had lost most of what he had won. All North Africa fell before 700 C.E. The empire was in shambles.

Government and law. The Byzantine Empire was governed by emperors who had virtually absolute authority, although they were often under threat of rebellion by the citizenry when taxation reached insupportable levels. Roman law had ancient origins. It and Hellenistic law, which was monarchical, became the law of the Byzantine Empire. It was codified by Justinian I in the first half of the seventh century C.E.

From the time of Constantine, it was popularly assumed that the emperor was God's chosen representative, his earthly regent. Imperial rule was equated with the celestial rule of God. It was presumed that the Roman emperors had a God-given mandate to rule the world. The world's rulers were considered a family or hierarchy of rulers with the Byzantine emperor at its top. Although emperors were theoretically elected by the senate, such elections were for show. In practice, powerful aristocrats or the army decided who would rule the Byzantine Empire.

The emperor was the lawgiver in Byzantium. Changes in the law came through imperial edicts. Legal commissions were sometimes charged with codifying and revising existing laws, but their alterations were subject to imperial approval. Justinian's *Digesta* (533 C.E., also known as *Pandectae*; *The Digest of Justinian*, 1920), with its supplements called the *Novellae*, remained the law of the Byzantine Empire until the ninth century C.E. when Basil I initiated a substantial revision.

War and weapons. Given its geographical situation and its vast extent, the Byzantine Empire maintained both a strong army and a substantial navy, manned by natives as well as by mercenaries. Ready naval, infantry, and cavalry forces were sustained by giving men farms and salaries as recompense for their service in the armed forces. The military obligation of each such soldier or sailor passed on, along with the land, to the eldest son, which helped to sustain a stable army and navy.

Groups of men were stationed in the provinces, living there cultivating the land they had been granted but ever ready for combat. The best troops, however, were stationed in and around Constantinople and at the Long Wall, thirty miles outside the city. The very top echelon of recruits, who formed the imperial guard, were given special privileges and extra remuneration for performing their important and sensitive duties.

The heavy cavalry was the mainstay of the army. It engaged in hand-to-hand combat and supported the infantry. The navy that guarded the empire's huge coastline consisted of large ships with as many as three hundred oarsmen arranged on two levels. These large, somewhat cumbersome ships were supplemented by smaller, more maneuverable ones that were considerably faster than the larger vessels. The navy gained a reputation for its so-called Greek fire, a mix of sulfur, saltpeter, and naphtha, which was shot by catapults into enemy boats.

Language. Latin was the language of the Roman Empire until it began its decline. It was used officially long after most of the citizens of Byzantium could understand it. By Diocletian's time, Greek was increasingly the language of Byzantium, and it remained so for many years. Around 430 C.E., the praetorian prefect of Constantinople wrote his decrees in Greek, the first Roman prefect to do so. Two centuries later, around 640 C.E., Heraclius declared Greek, the language of both the people and the Church, the official language of the Byzantine Empire.

Architecture and city planning. When Constantine the Great transformed sleepy Byzantium into his capital, he essentially created a city laid out in ways reminiscent of Rome. The Long Wall that protected Constantinople to the west was suggestive of China's Great Wall or of Hadrian's Wall in northern England. Justinian was perhaps the greatest builder in the Byzantine Empire, erecting not only such churches as the Haghia Sophia and San Vitale but also building ornate public baths, aqueducts, and public meeting halls. So great was the building program launched by Justinian that it drained from his empire the very resources it would later need to defend itself adequately.

Religion and ritual. Under Constantine, the Christian religion became firmly established in the Byzantine Empire. The First General Council met in Nicaea in 325 C.E. at Constantine's behest. Out of it grew such declarations of faith as the Nicene Creed. Eventually, however, Christianity in Byzantium was to come into conflict with the Islamic beliefs of the Near East, particularly Persia. There was also a significant philosophical conflict within Christian circles, with one group supporting Monophysitism, a doctrine contending that Jesus Christ's only nature was divine, whereas the orthodox belief was that Christ had both a human and a divine nature. These opposing doctrines led to a split between the Roman and Eastern churches that lasted for thirty-five years and was resolved only when Justin I became emperor in 518 C.E. Eventually the Eastern Church split from the Roman Church and has, to the twenty-first century, continued a separate existence.

Economics. Trade and manufacturing in the Byzantine Empire were overseen by guilds that protected manufacturers, merchants, and their customers. Sales of such mundane items as fish and bread were carefully regulated. Even more carefully monitored was the sale of the fine silks and brocades produced throughout much of the empire. The best of these could not be sold outside the empire but were reserved for the imperial family and its retainers.

Imports were also regulated and could enter the country only through specified channels. The Russians had trade agreements with the Byzantines and sold their wares, including furs, honey, wax, and indentured servants, in Byzantium.

One of the most fruitful sources of income came from land taxes levied on farmers, who lived in fear of the tax collector and often faced financial ruin if a crop failed or if some of their herd died. If they fled to avoid paying their taxes, their tax burden became the responsibility of their neighbors. This arrangement led many small farmers to become tenant farmers rather than landowners.

Current views. The adjective "byzantine" is often used today to describe devious behavior marked by intrigue. This connotation suggests that modern views of the Byzantine Empire are somewhat jaded. Certainly most contemporary people look upon the Byzantine era as one that ended badly because it diminished individuals, whose value it demeaned. Byzantium was characterized by a xenophobia based on the notion that outsiders had no individual importance except to the extent that they could advance or retard the purposes of God for his earthly realm.

ADDITIONAL RESOURCES

Brown, Peter Robert Lamont. *Late Antiquity.* Cambridge, Mass.: Harvard University Press, 1998.

Cameron, Averil. *Changing Cultures in Early Byzantium.* Brookfield, Vt.: Variorum, 1996.

Moorhead, John. *Justinian.* New York: Longman, 1994.

Norwich, John Julius. *Byzantium: The Early Centuries.* New York: Alfred A. Knopf, 1989.

Treadgold, Warren. *A History of the Byzantine State and Society.* Stanford, Calif.: Stanford University Press, 1997.

SEE ALSO: Arianism; Belisarius; Christianity; Constantine the Great; Constantinople; Diocletian; Goths; Haghia Sophia; Islam; Justinian I; Justinian's codes; Narses (Byzantine military leader); Nicaea, Council of; Persia; Rome, Imperial; Slavs; Theodosius the Great.

—R. Baird Shuman

— C —

CAESAR, JULIUS

ALSO KNOWN AS: Gaius Julius Caesar
BORN: July 12/13, 100 B.C.E.; Rome
DIED: March 15, 44 B.C.E.; Rome
RELATED CIVILIZATION: Republican Rome
MAJOR ROLE/POSITION: Statesman, military leader

Life. Julius Caesar (JOO-lee-uhs SEE-zuhr) belonged to an old Roman patrician family. Pursuing a political career, he rose to prominence as an opponent of the dictator Lucius Cornelius Sulla. He received military appointments, became an accomplished orator, and was appointed as a *pontifices*, or priest, a position of political significance. Attaching himself to Marcus Licinius Crassus, Rome's richest man, Caesar was elected chief priest, or *pontifex maximus*. He also cultivated Pompey the Great, whose military accomplishments had led to his becoming Rome's most powerful citizen.

Caesar was elected consul, Rome's highest office, for 59 B.C.E. in spite of senate opposition, which also negated measures favored by Pompey and Crassus. The First Triumvirate was the result, with Caesar, Pompey, and Crassus seizing power from the oligarchic senate. Confirming the alliance, Pompey married Caesar's daughter Julia. After a contentious year as consul, Caesar was awarded with the governorship of Cisalpine Gaul and Illyricum, giving him the opportunity for military fame.

For eight years (58-50 B.C.E.), Caesar waged victorious war, brilliantly if at times unjustly, against the two hundred Celtic tribes of Gaul and their fellow Germans. He was an equally talented writer, as evidenced by his *Comentarii de bello Gallico* (52-51 B.C.E.; translated with *Comentarii de bello cinli*, 45 B.C.E., as *Commentaries*, 1609). The triumvirs' relationship was uneasy, but it held together until the deaths of Julia in 54 B.C.E. and Crassus in 53 B.C.E. With his military command concluded, Caesar faced a crisis. Legally, he could not be consul again until 48 B.C.E., and in the interim, he would be at the mercy of his opponents, now including Pompey.

Knowing he was plunging the empire into civil war, Caesar crossed the River Rubicon, the border between Gaul and Italy, on January 10, 49 B.C.E. In 48 B.C.E., at the Battle of Pharsalus, in Greece, Caesar defeated Pompey. The latter fled to Egypt but was put to death by Ptolemy XIII, eager to curry Caesar's favor. A rival faction, led by Ptolemy's sister-bride, Cleopatra VII, sought Caesar's support. Cleopatra soon became Caesar's mistress, entangling him in Egypt's byzantine politics and keeping him in the East until 47 B.C.E.

Caesar defeated Pompey's sons in Spain in 45 B.C.E. In Rome, he instituted massive building projects, issued new coinage, and initiated calendar reform, replacing the lunar with the solar calendar. His veterans were given grants of land, speeding the Romanization process of the provinces. The senate was packed with his supporters. In 46 B.C.E., Caesar was made dictator for ten years and then in February, 44 B.C.E., dictator for life. Caesar's senatorial opponents, longing for the Republic's restoration and fearing his supposed monar-

Julius Caesar. (Hulton Archive)

chical ambitions, murdered him on March 15, 44 B.C.E.

Influence. Although two millennia have passed, Caesar continues to both inspire and repel. His conquest of Gaul brought Western Europe into the orbit of Western civilization. He brought about the fall of the long-waning Roman Republic, but he failed to replace it with an alternative. That was left to his nephew and heir, Octavian, known as Augustus.

ADDITIONAL RESOURCES

Gelzer, Matthias. *Caesar: Politician and Statesman.* Translated by Peter Needham. Cambridge, Mass.: Harvard University Press, 1968.

Grant, Michael. *Caesar.* New York: Barnes & Noble, 1997.

Meier, Christian. *Caesar: A Biography.* Translated by David McClintock. New York: HarperCollins, 1995.

SEE ALSO: Augustus; Cleopatra VII; Crassus, Marcus Licinius; Egypt, Ptolemaic and Roman; Gallic Wars; Gauls; Julia (daughter of Julius Caesar); Pharsalus, Battle of; Pompey the Great; Ptolemaic Dynasty; Rome, Imperial; Rome, Republican; Sulla, Lucius Cornelius; Triumvirate.

—Eugene Larson

CAI LUN

ALSO KNOWN AS: *Wade-Giles* Ts'ai Lun
BORN: 50 C.E.; Chenzhou, China
DIED: 121 C.E.; China
RELATED CIVILIZATIONS: Eastern Han Dynasty, China
MAJOR ROLE/POSITION: Court official

Life. Cai Lun (TSAHI lewn), a eunuch, worked as a court official in the Eastern Han Dynasty. After he invented paper, he was promoted by Emperor Han Hedi and became rich. Later he got involved in palace intrigue and ended his life drinking poison.

Before Cai Lun's invention, people wrote on wooden boards or bamboo strips. Books were bamboo strips bound together with pieces of string and were very cumbersome and bulky. Silk and cotton were also used for writing, but they were too expensive for the common people. Inspired by the process of making silk, Cai Lun created paper in the following way: First, he collected the raw material, which included old fishing nets, raw bark, twigs, leaves, and old clothes. He

mixed these materials together, heated them over a fire, and mashed them to a fibrous pulp. He spread the mashed pulp over thin bamboo racks to dry. When the pulp dried, it became paper. Cai Lun presented his invention to Emperor Han Hedi in about 105 C.E. The emperor rewarded him.

Influence. Paper, the writing material that Cai Lun invented, was inexpensive and simple to make. It soon replaced wooden boards and bamboo strips and spread throughout China and eventually the world.

ADDITIONAL RESOURCES

Chung, Shih-tsu. *Ancient China's Scientists.* Hong Kong: Commercial Press, 1984.

Hart, Michael. *The One Hundred: A Ranking of the Most Influential Persons in History.* Secaucus, N.J.: Carol Publishing Group, 1992.

SEE ALSO: China; Han Dynasty.

—Yiwei Zheng

CAJAMARCA POTTERY

DATE: 300-400 C.E.
LOCALE: Peru, Andes, Cajamarca Basin
RELATED CIVILIZATIONS: Chavín, Wari
SIGNIFICANCE: Cajamarca pottery is among the oldest in Peru.

Cajamarca (kah-hah-MAHR-kah) pottery of the cursive style, so called because of its painted, scroll-like designs suggestive of writing, was made of pale, calcium-rich kaolin clay. This style appears to be free of any outside influences and was made in Andean Peru from as early as 200 B.C.E. until around 1000 C.E. It was painted red or black, against a creme-colored background, sometimes with small animal figures and faces, and formed, for the most part, into shallow bowls with ring bases. The pottery was a popular trade item from the Early Intermediate period to the end of the Middle Horizon period and among peoples to both the north and south. The pottery and Cajamarca, the city that produced it, reached a peak from 300 to 400 C.E.

The ancestors of the people of Cajamarca were hunter-gatherers who later became agriculturalists and potters. The area was settled by successive groups of people: the Huacaloma, Layozn, Combe Mayo, and the Otuzco. These earlier settlements culminated in the Cajamarca culture. Its demise was most likely caused by changes in climate.

ADDITIONAL RESOURCES

Burger, Richard. *Chavín and the Origins of Andean Civilization.* New York: Thames and Hudson, 1992.

Donnan, Christopher B. *Ceramics of Ancient Peru.* Los Angeles: Fowler Museum of Cultural History, University of California, 1992.

SEE ALSO: Andes, South; Chavín de Huántar; South America, southern.

—Michael W. Simpson

CALIFORNIA PEOPLES

DATE: 8000 B.C.E.-700 C.E.

LOCALE: Northern, central, and southern California

RELATED CIVILIZATIONS: Chumash, Kawaiisu, Tubatulabal, Shoshone, Mojave

SIGNIFICANCE: People settled the length and breadth of California over a period of thousands of years, introducing cultural and technological innovations that made the most of the region's ecological diversity.

During the Archaic period (9000-2000 B.C.E.), ancient peoples settled new and ever more diverse subregions within what became California and the American West. The Archaic period represents the transition from a lifestyle that featured the hunting of larger game animals toward one in which agriculture featured more prominently. During this period, although much of the Americas underwent what has been termed a "broad-spectrum revolution" by archaeologist Kent Flannery, in California, the adoption of agriculture and sedentary village life took place more slowly. California peoples very gradually transitioned toward a dependence on the bountiful seeds, acorns, and maritime resources available in that region. This subsistence pattern initially allowed for relatively small settlements consisting primarily of temporary dwellings housing only a few dozen people per site. The California peoples set up temporary base camps, summer or winter encampments, and other forms of shelter intended to take advantage of seasonally available foodstuffs.

By contrast with the Archaic period, the Pacific period (2000 B.C.E.-1500 C.E.) saw the development of a focal economy. California peoples not only broadened the array of plants and animals they used but also focused on resources and tools that allowed them to take full advantage of a small group of seasonally available plants and animals, thus providing for a relatively stable and predictable lifestyle. Pacific period tools and technologies, which generally elaborated on Archaic period antecedents, included basketry; bedrock and wooden mortars; shell beadwork for rings, pendants, earplugs, and nose ornaments; bone and shell fishhooks and barbed points; charmstones; gaming pieces; and bone-tube whistles. Two of the most important adaptations associated with the Pacific period and its economy were the exploitation of acorn crops and the harvesting of shellfish. In addition, riverine resources, such as salmon, were harvested in growing quantities. Complex societies and extensive trading networks emerged among California peoples, particularly among the ancestors of such groups as the Chumash, Kawaiisu, Pomo, Tubatulabal, Mojave, and Shoshone. Village size in these groups expanded exponentially.

The Pacific period saw the emergence of more than six major settlements with populations exceeding one thousand people and about a dozen with populations exceeding five hundred. These settlements demonstrate the evolution of greater social and political complexity and the emergence of social elites. Most scholars believe that the early California peoples' political structures were probably based on kinship. Along with the formation of political structures, the early settlements experienced craft specialization, trade, and population expansion, leading to a growing number of social distinctions, including the rise of village- and tribal-level leaders, traders, medical and religious practitioners, and warriors.

According to researchers Joseph Chartkoff and Kerry Chartkoff, during the Pacific period, people first occupied a number of previously uninhabited regions, including the southern Sierra, the Lower Klamath River, and the coastal region extending from Santa Cruz to Morro Bay. The basketry tradition, rooted in the Archaic period, became a major source of utility ware as well as a hotbed of artistic development during this time of expanded interregional interaction and trade. The newly introduced shell-bead money system in turn contributed to the variety and kind of trade. The bow and arrow, which were largely unknown in much of North America, were introduced to California peoples during the Middle Pacific period (c. 500 B.C.E.-500 C.E.) and were ultimately adopted into their traditions of hunting and warfare. Oceangoing canoes, fish dams, and specialized storage structures indicate the extent to which native peoples had adopted focal economies centered on specific seed crops or riverine or coastal resources. In northern California and the central valleys, settlement types and housing included pit-house structures, ramadas or porchlike structures, granaries, and larger communal dwellings.

The proliferation in the Middle and Late Pacific periods of rock art sites (including both painted polychrome pictographs and pecked-stone petroglyphs), intaglios or large-scale desert-pavement drawings, elaborate feather, shell, and leather costumes, and painted and tattooed body decorations established the indigenous patterns that persisted into the Spanish colonial mission era. About 300,000 people, representing more than one hundred distinctive language groups, occupied California at the time of the initial European contacts in 1539-1540.

ADDITIONAL RESOURCES

Chartkoff, Joseph L., and Kerry Kona Chartkoff. *The Archaeology of California*. Stanford, Calif.: Stanford University Press, 1984.

Heizer, Robert F., ed. *California*. Vol. 8 in *Handbook of North American Indians*. Washington, D.C.: Smithsonian Institution, 1978.

The Indians of California. Alexandria, Va.: Time-Life Books, 1994.

Kroeber, Alfred L. *Handbook of the Indians of California*. 1925. New York: Dover, 1976.

Moratto, Michael J. *California Archaeology*. New York: Academic Press, 1984.

SEE ALSO: Archaic North American culture; Paleo-Indians in North America; Southwest peoples.

—*Ruben G. Mendoza*

CALIGULA

ALSO KNOWN AS: Gaius Caesar Germanicus
BORN: August 31, 12 C.E.; probably Antium (later Anzio), Italy
DIED: January, 41 C.E.; Rome
RELATED CIVILIZATION: Imperial Rome
MAJOR ROLE/POSITION: Leader

Life. Born to Germanicus Julius Caesar, the adopted nephew of Emperor Tiberius, Caligula (kah-LIHG-yew-luh) was fond of wearing military boots, a trait that earned him the nickname "Caligula," literally, "little boots." After Germanicus's death, Tiberius treated Caligula as an adopted son. When Tiberius died, the military assisted Caligula's ascension to the throne. Soon afterward, he became severely ill (or was poisoned) and was, from that point on, insane.

After his illness, Caligula modeled his leadership on the Egyptian pharaohs—instituting an absolute monarchy, marrying his sister, Drusilla, and considering himself a god. Caligula was also known for his eccentricity. He may have even named his horse, Incitatus, a Roman consul.

Keeping the citizenry happy on a steady diet of bread and circuses, Caligula quickly spent Tiberius's fortune. To continue to fund his lifestyle, Caligula taxed the Roman aristocracy into poverty. He then turned to raising taxes on commoners. When this failed to raise enough gold, Caligula installed a brothel and a casino in his palace.

Caligula was also renowned for his cruelty. It was not uncommon for Caligula to force a father to watch his son being tortured. He grew hostile toward the sen-

Caligula. (Library of Congress)

ate and the very Roman army who supported his ascension to the throne. At age twenty-nine, he was assassinated by a group led by Centurion Cassius Charea.

Influence. The archetypal mad ruler, Caligula was truly an emperor, in every sense of the word, of Rome, wielding absolute power over the largest nation of the day.

ADDITIONAL RESOURCE
Barrett, Anthony A. *Caligula: The Corruption of Power.* New Haven, Conn.: Yale University Press, 1990.

SEE ALSO: Agrippina the Elder; Antonia the Younger; Rome, Imperial; Tiberius.

—B. Keith Murphy

CALLICRATES

ALSO KNOWN AS: Kallikrates
FLOURISHED: fifth century B.C.E.
RELATED CIVILIZATION: Classical Greece
MAJOR ROLE/POSITION: Architect

Life. Callicrates (kuh-LIHK-ruh-teez) and Ictinus (Iktinos) were the architects of the Parthenon (temple of Athena Polias) on the Acropolis in Athens, built between 447 and 432 B.C.E. The Parthenon was the first building erected on the Acropolis in Pericles' grand rebuilding plan. Work on the Parthenon was described in a lost book by Ictinus and Carpion. Callicrates is also credited with the plan of the temple of Athena Nike ("Victory") or Athena Asteros ("Without Wings"), authorized by the Athenian senate in 449 B.C.E. and constructed between 427 and 424 B.C.E. This Ionic temple was the fourth and last building constructed in Pericles' rebuilding plan.

The Athenian temple on the Illissus River also appears to have been designed by Callicrates, on the plan of the temple of Athena Nike. A Doric temple built on the island of Delos has also been attributed to Callicrates on the basis of its style and affinities with the Parthenon. This temple was dedicated by the Athenians in 425 B.C.E.

Influence. The classical style of architecture created by Callicrates influenced temple design of the Greeks and Romans and architecture of the Renaissance and beyond.

ADDITIONAL RESOURCES

Biers, William R. *The Archaeology of Greece: An Introduction.* 2d ed. Ithaca, N.Y.: Cornell University Press, 1996.

Dinsmoor, William Bell. *The Architecture of Ancient Greece.* New York: W. W. Norton, 1975.

SEE ALSO: Art and architecture; Greece, Classical; Ictinus; Parthenon.

—*Sally A. Struthers*

CALLIMACHUS OF CYRENE

ALSO KNOWN AS: Kallimachos
BORN: c. 305 B.C.E.; Cyrene, modern Shahhat, Libya
DIED: c. 240 B.C.E.; Alexandria, Egypt
RELATED CIVILIZATIONS: Hellenistic Greece, Egypt
MAJOR ROLE/POSITION: Poet, scholar, librarian

Life. Callimachus (kuh-LIHM-uh-kuhs) of Cyrene was educated in Athens and traveled to Alexandria, where he worked in the Alexandrian library. He cataloged its works, producing a catalog so detailed that it provides a full literary history of the Hellenic world.

Callimachus wrote prose and criticism, but his poetry had the most influence on later generations of writers. The most famous of his works is *Aitiōn* (c. 270 B.C.E.; *Aetia*, 1958), a four-volume elegy retelling a number of Greek legends and myths. The structure of *Aetia*, a series of short episodes connected by a shared theme, influenced the works of most major Greek and Roman poets, including Vergil, Ovid, and Catullus.

Callimachus's estimated eight hundred works of poetry established learnedness, brevity, wit, and polish as hallmarks of Alexandrian poetry.

Influence. Callimachus provided historians with an insight into Hellenic literature with his catalog of the Alexandrian library. His poetry was so influential that only Homer is quoted more frequently by Hellenic grammarians.

ADDITIONAL RESOURCES

Cameron, Alan. *Callimachus and His Critics.* Princeton, N.J.: Princeton University Press, 1995.

Kerkhecker, Arnd. *Callimachus' Book of Iambi.* Oxford, England: Oxford University Press, 1999.

SEE ALSO: Alexandrian library; Catullus; Egypt, Ptolemaic and Roman; Greece, Hellenistic and Roman; Homer; Ovid; Vergil.

—*B. Keith Murphy*

CALPURNIUS SICULUS, TITUS

FLOURISHED: first century C.E.
RELATED CIVILIZATION: Imperial Rome
MAJOR ROLE/POSITION: Poet

Life. All that we know of Titus Calpurnius Siculus's (TI-tuhs kal-PUR-nee-uhs sihk-yuh-luhs) life comes from his poetry and, possibly, his name. His references to a young emperor with artistic pretensions indicate that Calpurnius wrote during the reign of Nero (54-68 C.E.). Possibly, his name, Siculus ("Sicilian"), refers to

Calpurnius's place of origin. Some, however, regard it as alluding to his poetic predecessor, the Greek bucolic poet Theocritus of Syracuse, who was from Sicily; also, Siculus could allude to the Sicilian setting of some of Vergil's *Eclogues* (43-37 B.C.E.; also known as *Bucolics*; English translation, 1575), Calpurnius's direct model within Latin literature.

Calpurnius Siculus is known for seven bucolic or pastoral poems known as *Eclogues* (n.d.; "Ecologues of Calpurnius," in *Minor Latin Poets*, 1982). Number 1 contains a prophecy of a new golden age, number 4 compares the current emperor to Apollo, and number 7 refers to establishment of a new amphitheater by the emperor. Interspersed among these poems, the remainder, numbers 2, 3, 5, and 6, have more general pastoral themes.

Influence. Although Calpurnius's praise of Nero may strike the modern reader as being unexpected or unacceptable, his poetry is nevertheless interesting as providing a glance at how his contemporaries viewed Nero.

ADDITIONAL RESOURCES
Duff, J. Wight, and Arnold M. Duff. *Minor Latin Poets.* Vol. 1. Cambridge, Mass.: Harvard University Press, 1982.
Pearce, James B. *The Eclogues of Calpurnius Siculus, with an Introduction, Commentary, and Vocabulary.* San Antonio, Tex.: Scylax Press, 1990.

SEE ALSO: Nero; Rome, Imperial; Theocritus of Syracuse; Vergil.

—*Edwin D. Floyd*

CAMILLUS, MARCUS FURIUS

BORN: date and place unknown
DIED: 365 B.C.E.; place unknown
RELATED CIVILIZATION: Republican Rome
MAJOR ROLE/POSITION: Military leader

Life. Marcus Furius Camillus (MAHR-kuhs FYOOR-ee-uhs kuh-MIHL-uhs) was the preeminent Roman general of his time. Though the accounts of his life were composed three centuries after his death and therefore contain many romanticized details, it is clear that Camillus was one of the more important agents of Roman expansion of his time. His first great achievement came as dictator in 396 B.C.E., when he defeated Falerii and Capena and captured Veii. He celebrated his victories with a magnificent triumph but was exiled in 391 B.C.E. for either misappropriating the Veiian spoils or committing a sacrilege while celebrating his triumph.

While Camillus was in exile, the Gauls captured Rome in 390 B.C.E. Rome was about to be ransomed by the payment of a large sum of gold, when Camillus arrived with a new army as the gold was being counted out, defeated the Gauls in battle, and recovered the ransom. He became known as the second founder of Rome because he convinced the Romans to rebuild the city rather than move to Veii. In the following years, Camillus continued to serve Rome with victories over many of its neighbors, as Rome quickly resumed its expansionist policy.

Influence. The role of Camillus as a military leader responsible for Roman expansion in the late fifth and early fourth century B.C.E. is secure. However, many of the details of his life and his purported statesmanship as the second founder of Rome reflect the political turmoil and propaganda of the late Republic.

ADDITIONAL RESOURCES
Livy. *The Early History of Rome.* Baltimore: Penguin Books, 1971.
Plutarch. *Plutarch's Lives: The Dryden Translation, Edited With Notes by Arthur Hugh Clough.* New York: Modern Library, 2001.

SEE ALSO: Gauls; Rome, Republican.

—*Robert Rousselle*

CAMPANTAR

FLOURISHED: seventh century C.E.
RELATED CIVILIZATION: India
MAJOR ROLE/POSITION: Poet

Life. Campantar (sham-PAHN-tar) was born to Bhagavathiyar and her husband, Sivapadahirudayar, a devotee of Lord Śiva who prayed for the eradication of Jainism in India. According to legend, as a baby, Campantar was blessed with the "divine milk" of goddess Pārvatī, Śiva's consort, and composed his first tiruppatikam in *Panniru Tirumurai* when he was barely three years old. Explaining Śiva's act of kindness in chaste Tamil verse, the highly sophisticated poem starts with the first consonant of the vedas (*th*) and the first vowel of the vedas (*o*). It also enumerates the five major actions of Śiva: creating, protecting, destroying, hiding, and blessing. The child continued to sing a total of eleven verses. Later, at age seven, when Campantar was blessed with the "sacred thread ceremony" (*upanayanam*, or initiation), he sang the glory of Pañcākṣaram (the five holy syllables) and not the Gāyātri Mantra, which is traditionally taught to the novice. Every major saint in the Saiva Sidhantha tradition has composed a song on the Pañcākṣaram, as it forms the core of the Vedas.

Influence. Campantar undertook five different tours of all the temples in Tamil Nādu and composed the first three Tirumurai, *Tirumuraikkappu*. Known to have

converted the Pāṇḍya king from Jainism to Hinduism, he contributed remarkably to the revival of Hinduism in India by reestablishing the glory of Śiva. At the age of sixteen, on the day his marriage was arranged, unwilling to enter the bondage of matrimony, along with his bride he is known to have attained divine Samadhi.

ADDITIONAL RESOURCE

Peterson, Indira Viswanathan. *Poems to Siva: The Hymns of the Tamil Saints*. Princeton Library of Asian Translations. Princeton, N.J.: Princeton University Press, 1989.

SEE ALSO: Hinduism; India.

—Kokila Ravi

CANAANITES

DATE: 8000-900 B.C.E.
LOCALE: Levant
RELATED CIVILIZATIONS: Ugarit, Israel
SIGNIFICANCE: The Canaanites developed an alphabet.

Canaanites (KAY-nuh-nitz) were the inhabitants of the land of Canaan—a geographical area also called the Levant, the eastern shores of the Mediterranean Sea, from western Greece to western Egypt. The etymology of the name "Canaan" or "Canaanite" is uncertain, but the world is possibly related to either a Semitic word meaning "subdued" or a non-Semitic word meaning "blue cloth" or "purple dye."

References in various written accounts to the Canaanites reveal how others viewed the group. Canaanites were variously described as "thieves," inhabitants of the Central Hill country, inhabitants of the lowlands along the Mediterranean, and inhabitants displaced by others. Different groups, such as the Ugarit people, Ammonites, Moabites, Israelites, and Phoenicians, were considered Canaanites. The Hebrew Bible or Old Testament texts distinguish Israelites from Canaanites. The Ugaritic texts are usually the basis for describing Canaanite culture and religion.

Archaeological evidence for a Canaanite culture indicates a continuous cultural tradition from the Neolithic (8500-3300 B.C.E.) through Iron I (1150-900 B.C.E.) Ages. Canaanites built walled cities with interior houses and temples in the Neolithic and Chalcolithic periods. Burial practices included placing artifacts with the bod-

ies. In the Early Bronze Age, large urban cities formed as trading centers. The potter's wheel was developed, and potters began to use paint and slip on vessels. Faster-moving wheels were created in the Middle Bronze Age. Also, during this period or at the beginning of the Late Bronze Age, an alphabetic writing system appeared. Canaanites built some cities using the header and stretcher technique and constructed temples within walled areas.

During the Bronze Age, Canaanites at Ugarit wrote myths or stories describing religious traditions of the region. El, Baal, Ashera, Anath, and other deities played prominent roles in the Ugaritic pantheon. The realities of life, such as thunder and rain, became part of the mythological traditions. Records of the monarchy, epic stories, and practical aspects of religion (prayers) were written.

The incursion of the Sea Peoples introduced new groups to Canaan. Remains of these groups are found at such sites as Ashdod, Ashkelon, and Tel Miqne. Canaanites along the coast were forced to move to the central hill country. Egypt tried to reassert control over the area but did not have sufficient military strength or economic resources. As a new nation or city-state developed, building occurred at a number of areas, such as Jerusalem, Hazor, Bethel, and Dan. Hebrew Bible texts describe the rise of the nation, although apparently in a sense more idealistic than real.

The material cultural remains from Canaan suggest a strong continuity of culture from the Early Bronze Age through Iron I. Pottery traditions, architectural design and construction, and city design are consistent. Written accounts provide some additional material for the historian. However, the picture that can be constructed from the texts and archaeology is a rather complex one in which different Canaanite groups established city-states playing prominent roles at different times.

ADDITIONAL RESOURCES
Ahlström, G. *Who Were the Israelites?* Winona Lake, Ind: Eisenbrauns, 1986.

Gray, J. *The Legacy of Canaan*. Leiden: E. J. Brill, 1965.
Redford, D. B. *Egypt, Canaan, and Israel in Ancient Times*. Princeton, N.J.: Princeton University Press, 1992.
Tubb, J. *Canaanites*. Norman: University of Oklahoma Press, 1998.

SEE ALSO: Egypt, Prepharaonic; Israel.

—Roger W. Anderson, Jr.

CAŇKAM

DATE: c. 1-500 C.E.; possibly c. 250 B.C.E.-500 C.E.
LOCALE: South India
RELATED CIVILIZATIONS: Pāṇdyan Empire, India
SIGNIFICANCE: Art and literature created by a learned society of poets, artists, and philosophers nurtured by the Caňkams regulated and set the standards for Tamil literature.

Three different Caňkams (SHAN-kams; "literary academies") have existed in south India during different time periods, beginning about 500 B.C.E. The first, Thalai Caňkam, was founded by the Pāṇdyan king Kaisina Vazhudhi at Thenmadurai and nurtured hundreds of poets of exceptional caliber such as Agasthiyar. After a deluge, Kadungon, a Pāṇdyan king, founded Middle Caňkam at Kapadapuram. This academy fostered scholarly poets who created literary works such as *Tolkāppiyam* (c. 250 B.C.E.). After another deluge ravaged the land, King Mudal Thiru Maran persevered and founded the Third Caňkam in Madurai.

Around two thousand poems were composed during the entire Caňkam period by about 473 poets and compiled in eighteen volumes—eight volumes of shorter lyrics (*Eṭṭūtokai*) and ten volumes of longer poems (*Pattuppāṭṭu*). The most important aspect of this literature is the distinction between *akam*, the interior or the inner, and *puram*, the exterior or the outer, which together represent two sides of reality. *Akam* poetry deals with love, whereas *puram* poetry extols the virtues of heroism. In 1901, Pandithurai Thevar convened the fourth Caňkam at Madurai and launched a library, a center for research in Tamil language and literature, a printing press, and a college for Tamil studies.

ADDITIONAL RESOURCES
Hart, George L., III. *Poets of the Tamil Anthologies: Ancient Poems of Love and War*. Princeton, N.J.: Princeton University Press, 1979.
Periakaruppan, Ramasamy. *Traditions and Talent in Cankam Poetry*. Madurai, India: Madurai Publishing House, 1976.
Shama, T. R. S., ed. *Ancient Indian Literature*. New Delhi, India: Sahitya Akademi, 2000.

SEE ALSO: *Aiṅkurnūru*; *Akanānūru*; Cātanār; Iḷaṅkō Aṭikaḷ; *Kalittokai*; *Kuruntokai*; *Naṟṟiṇai*; *Paripāṭal*; *Patirruppattu*; *Tolkāppiyam*.

—Kokila Ravi

CANNAE, BATTLE OF

DATE: August 2, 216 B.C.E.
LOCALE: Cannae, Italy
RELATED CIVILIZATIONS: Republican Rome, Carthage
SIGNIFICANCE: Cannae was the largest defeat ever of an army of the Roman Empire.

Background. During the Second Punic War (218-201 B.C.E.), Hannibal of Carthage led his North African and Spanish army on an invasion of Italy and Rome. Cannae (KA-nee) was a major food and supply depot for the Roman army and was a vital logistical site for both armies.

Action. Some 68,000 infantry and 6,000 cavalry under the Roman leaders Lucius Aemilius Paullus and Gaius Terentius Varro attacked 25,000 infantry and 10,000 cavalry led by Hannibal. Placing his elite African infantry and cavalry on the ends of his defensive line, Hannibal successfully directed a double envelopment. The center soldiers yielded backward, and with strategic timing, the end/flank troops attacked forward, resulting in the Romans being nearly surrounded, compacted in on themselves, and slaughtered. Estimates of casualties are 60,000 Roman and 8,000 Carthaginian.

Consequences. Cannae did not win the war for Carthage, but it kept the war going for several years un-

til Roman armies under Scipio Africanus would eventually defeat Hannibal in 201 B.C.E.

ADDITIONAL RESOURCES

Cattrell, Leonard. *Hannibal, Enemy of Rome.* New York: DaCapo Press, 1992.

Healy, Mark. *Cannae 216 B.C.* Oxford, England: Osprey, 2000.

SEE ALSO: Aemilius Paullus, Lucius; Carthage; Hannibal; Punic Wars; Scipio Africanus.

—*Alan P. Peterson*

Cao Cao

ALSO KNOWN AS: *Wade-Giles* Ts'ao Ts'ao
BORN: 155 C.E.; Boxian, China (modern Anhui Province)
DIED: 220 C.E.; Luoyang, China
RELATED CIVILIZATIONS: Eastern Han Dynasty, Three Kingdoms, China
MAJOR ROLE/POSITION: Military and political leader

Life. Born to a family of government officials, Cao Cao (TSAH-oh TSAH-oh) showed early prowess both in military arts and as a student of ancient Chinese military classics. When the Yellow Turban rebellion broke out in 184 C.E., he distinguished himself as a cavalry officer in its suppression. After pacification, the north China plain was the scene of warfare between the armed forces of various local leaders. Cao Cao survived and flourished in this environment. His major political coup took place in 196 C.E. when he gained control of the Han emperor. Warfare ensued between Cao Cao and rival military leaders who were jealous of and concerned over his ascendancy. His victory at the Battle of Guandu in 200 C.E. solidified his control over north China and the court. After being defeated at the Battle of Chibi, he seized the northwest and the Gansu corridor.

By 208 C.E., the tripartite division of China was in place, and Cao Cao's increasing power implied that a new mandate of heaven (authorization by heaven to rule) was beckoning him; however, unification needed to take place before a new dynasty could be established. Cao Cao's son Cao Pei (186-226 C.E.), who inherited his father's power, obtained the abdication of the last Han emperor in 220 C.E. and established the Wei Dynasty.

Influence. Cao Cao was a famous cavalry leader and battlefield tactician. He is noted for his commentary on the *Sunzi Bingfa* (probably 475-221 B.C.E.; *Sun Tzu: On the Art of War*, 1910).

ADDITIONAL RESOURCES

Huang, Ray. *China: A Macro History.* Armonk, N.Y.: M. E. Sharpe, 1997.

Hucker, Charles O. *China's Imperial Past.* Stanford, Calif.: Stanford University Press, 1979.

Twitchett, Denis, and Michael Loewe, eds. *The Ch'in and Han Empires.* Vol.1 in *The Cambridge History of China.* Cambridge, England: Cambridge University Press, 1986.

SEE ALSO: Cao Zhi; China; Han Dynasty; Three Kingdoms.

—*John W. Killigrew*

CAO ZHI

ALSO KNOWN AS: *Wade-Giles* Ts'ao Chih
BORN: 192 C.E.; place unknown
DIED: 232 C.E.; place unknown
RELATED CIVILIZATIONS: China, Three Kingdoms
MAJOR ROLE/POSITION: Poet

Life. Cao Zhi (TSAH-oh jee) was a son of Cao Cao, king of the Wei at the time of the Three Kingdoms. Once considered the preferred candidate for the Wei throne, Cao Zhi ultimately lost the position to his elder brother, Cao Pei. After Cao Pei became king of the Wei (and later emperor of the Wei Dynasty), Cao Zhi was regarded as a threat to Cao Pei's throne and was deprived of virtually all political involvement. Disappointed at the failure of his political career, Cao Zhi died at the age of forty.

Although Cao Zhi was not a successful politician, he achieved great success in literature, especially in poetry. According to the legend, Cao Pei once demanded that Cao Zhi compose a poem on the theme of their fraternal relationship within the time of seven paces. Cao Zhi met the demand by composing the famous "seven-pace poem" immediately. The poem is as follows: "They were boiling beans on a beanstalk fire. Beans cried out in the pot: 'We [beans and beanstalk] have the same root. Why hurry to burn each other?' "

Influence. Cao Zhi's achievement in poetry was second to none of his time. He is regarded as a major figure in the literary movement of the Jian'an period.

ADDITIONAL RESOURCES
Chen, Shou. *Empresses and Consorts*. Translated by Robert Joe Cutter and William Gordon Crowell. Honolulu: University of Hawaii Press, 1999.
Dunn, Hugh. *Cao Zhi*. Beijing: New World Press, 1983.

SEE ALSO: Cao Cao; China; Three Kingdoms.

—Yiwei Zheng

CAPELLA, MARTIANUS

ALSO KNOWN AS: Martianus Minneus Felix Capella
FLOURISHED: fifth century C.E.; Carthage, North Africa
RELATED CIVILIZATIONS: Imperial Rome, North Africa
MAJOR ROLE/POSITION: Author

Life. Martianus Capella (mahr-shee-AY-nuhs kuh-PEHL-uh) was a Roman after the Fall of Rome and a pagan in a world officially Christian. He wrote at the end of the fifth century C.E. in Carthage, North Africa, then under the control of Vandals. Capella's surviving work, *De nuptiis Philologiae et Mercurii* (n.d.; *Philologia*, 1971), begins with two books (or chapters) devoted to an allegory of the marriage of Philology ("literary study") with the god Mercury and their ascent to heaven. This allegory implicitly promises divine rewards to scholars who similarly devote themselves to study. There follow seven books that treat each of the seven liberal arts: grammar, dialectic, and rhetoric (the three subjects of the medieval *trivium*) together with geometry, arithmetic, astronomy, and music (the four subjects of the medieval *quadrivium*). The work is written in a mixture of prose and verse (the ancient genre of Menippean satire) and contains much curious and arcane lore from earlier authors, many of whose works were later lost.

Influence. Despite Capella's nostalgia for the pagan past, his encyclopedic compendium of ancient learning was destined to become part of the standard curriculum of the Christian Middle Ages.

ADDITIONAL RESOURCES
Shanzer, D. *A Philosophical and Literary Commentary on Martianus Capella's "De nuptiis Philologiae et Mercurii."* Vol. 1. Berkeley: University of California Press, 1986.
Stahl, W. H., and R. W. Johnson. *Martianus Capella and the Seven Liberal Arts*. 2 vols. New York: Columbia University Press, 1971-1977.
Westra, Haijo, and Tanja Kopke, eds. *The Berlin Commentary on Martianus Capella's "De nuptiis Philologiae et Mercurii."* New York: E. J. Brill, 1998.

SEE ALSO: Christianity; Education and training; Languages and literature; Menippus of Gadara; Rome, Imperial.

—Hans-Friedrich Mueller

CARACALLA

ALSO KNOWN AS: Marcus Aurelius Antoninus
BORN: April 4, 188 C.E.; Lugdunum, Gaul (later Lyon, France)
DIED: April 8, 217 C.E.; near Carrhae, Mesopotamia
RELATED CIVILIZATION: Imperial Rome
MAJOR ROLE/POSITION: Emperor

Life. The eldest son of Lucius Septimius Severus, Caracalla (kuh-RAK-uh-luh) earned a reputation as a vicious and unscrupulous fighter. After his father's death, he briefly shared power with his younger brother Publius Septimius Geta before murdering him in 212 C.E. He conducted a purge of Geta's supporters, killing more than twenty thousand of them, and then launched a series of battles against Rome's enemies. To fund these wars, Caracalla expanded the tax-paying population. In 212 C.E., he issued an edict making every free person in the empire a Roman citizen and hence liable to pay taxes.

In the spring of 215 C.E., Caracalla's fury and brutality were on display with his treatment of Alexandria. Caracalla ordered that the city's young men be gathered together, then had them killed. Roman soldiers conducted a murderous rampage throughout the city that lasted several days.

Caracalla's most successful military campaign also proved to be his last. He attacked the Parthians, located in modern Iraq. After a series of victories against Rome's Eastern enemy, Caracalla was struck down by a member of his bodyguard, Julius Martialis, in 217 C.E. The man behind the attack, Macrinus, was proclaimed emperor.

Influence. Caracalla was unable to continue the unifying policies of his father. Although his expansion of Roman citizenship did create more resources for the government, it also diluted the power of Rome itself.

ADDITIONAL RESOURCES
Brauer, George. *The Decadent Emperors*. New York: Barnes & Noble, 1967.
Grant, Michael. *The Severans*. London: Routledge, 1996.

SEE ALSO: Parthia; Rome, Imperial; Severus, Lucius Septimus.

—Douglas Clouatre

CARATACUS

ALSO KNOWN AS: Caractacus
BORN: early first century C.E.; place unknown
DIED: after 51 C.E.; place unknown
RELATED CIVILIZATIONS: Britain, Imperial Rome
MAJOR ROLE/POSITION: Military leader

Life. Son of the British king Cunobelinus, Caratacus (kuh-RAT-uh-kuhs) served as a significant leader of British resistance to the Roman conquest. Early in his career, Caratacus made himself king of the Dobunni, whom he later led against the Roman emperor Claudius during his invasion of Britain in 43 C.E. After suffering defeat, he retreated west to an unconquered tribe, the Silures, leading them in sustained resistance to Roman expansion for eight years. He was defeated by the Roman governor Publius Ostorius Scapula in 51 C.E. Seeking asylum in northern Britain, he fled to Cartimandua, queen of the Brigantes. An ally of Rome, she immediately surrendered him to Scapula. Caratacus was taken to Rome, where he was spared by Claudius and lived out the remainder of his life.

Influence. The defeat of Caratacus marked a significant milestone in the Roman conquest of Britain. In antiquity, he was depicted as brave, virtuous, dignified, and wise—a model of the noble barbarian king.

ADDITIONAL RESOURCES
Braund, David. *Ruling Roman Britain*. New York: Routledge, 1996.
Frere, S. *Britannia: A History of Roman Britain*. New York: Routledge and Kegan Paul, 1987.
Tacitus, Cornelius. *The Annals of Imperial Rome*. Translated by Michael Grant. Rev. ed. New York: Barnes & Noble, 1993.
Webster, G. *Rome Against Caratacus: The Roman Campaigns in Britain, A.D. 48-58*. London: B. T. Batsford, 1981.

SEE ALSO: Britain; Cartimandua; Claudius; Cunobelinus; Rome, Imperial.

—Shawn A. Ross

CARIBBEAN

DATE: 4000 B.C.E.-700 C.E.

LOCALE: Between North and South America, west of the Atlantic Ocean, and east of the Caribbean Sea

RELATED CIVILIZATIONS: Ciboney, Taino, Arawak, Saladoir, Island Carib, Guanahatabey

SIGNIFICANCE: The Caribbean was home to a variety of Indian groups, ranging from the peaceful and relatively advanced Taino to the warlike Island Caribs.

The islands of the West Indies form a Y, with the tail extending from South America. One arm curves northwest through the Greater Antilles toward the Yucatán Peninsula and the other through the Bahamas toward Florida. The islands extend for almost 2,500 miles (4,000 kilometers). The four largest islands, Cuba, Jamaica, Hispaniola, and Puerto Rico, make up the Greater Antilles. Above the Greater Antilles are more than seven hundred small islands and cays known as the Bahamas group. East of Puerto Rico, the Lesser Antilles extend in an arc that runs southeast from the Virgin Islands on the north to Grenada off the coast of South America on the south. None of the islands are far apart, and most are within sight of one another. Native canoeists could have paddled between any of them in calm weather.

Although the origin of the people of the West Indies is uncertain, some authorities say three groups—the Ciboney, Arawak, and Carib—came from South America beginning in the 1300's. Other scholars believe the migration to the islands took place much earlier. According to these scholars, the Casimoiroid Indians came to western Cuba from the Yucatán Peninsula about 4000 B.C.E., and the Ortoiroid came from South America about 2000 B.C.E. The Ortoiroid were displaced by the Saladoir (200 B.C.E. to 600 C.E.), who also came from South America and were the forebears of the Tainos encountered by Christopher Columbus in 1492. A third group, the Island Carib, came from South America sometime after the arrival of the Saladoir and inhabited the islands from Guadeloupe south. These scholars believe that the Arawak did not migrate to the islands but remained on the continent.

The Taino, who inhabited the area from western Cuba through Puerto Rico, had not advanced beyond the Ceramic Age by the time of Columbus. The Taino of Hispaniola were more numerous and advanced, but all Taino had similar cultural traits. Taino homes were clustered around a center plaza where both men and women participated in ceremonies, dances, and ball games. Although the Taino recognized hereditary provincial chiefs and subchiefs in local areas, only the village headmen had power. Each headman ruled his own village and organized the numerous festivals and games held in each village. Religion played an important role in Taino life. They believed that good and evil spirits inhabited humans and natural objects. Shamen used special powers to try to control the spirits, and individuals attempted to capture them in icons or statues called *zenis*. Burial was an essential part of their religion. Because of the climate, the Taino wore few if any clothes and lived in simple shelters. They practiced slash-and-burn agriculture. After burning off a field, they gathered the nutrients released into piles about knee high and three to six feet (one to two meters) across in which the women planted cuttings with a sharp stick. The most important crops were the bitter cassava and yams. In addition to the cultivated crops, the Taino diet included fruits, fish, small animals, birds, insects, and snakes.

The Island Carib society was male-dominated. The government was decentralized; each village was independent, but one war chief was elected for each island. Their homes were grouped around a house where all the men lived. Women could not enter the central house and were excluded from the activities performed there. The men were expert boat builders and handlers and traded with neighboring islands. They hunted, fished, and waged war. Women did all the other work. The division of labor was more rigid than among the other Indians. The Island Caribs were fierce fighters and always won their battles with other natives. They raided villages and took women for wives. They practiced ceremonial cannibalism on their war victims, but human flesh was not a part of the regular diet. Only the Island Carib survived after the Spanish settled the West Indies.

The Ciboney were in western Hispaniola and Cuba when Columbus arrived but became extinct a century after European contact. They lived in caves, offshore islets, and swamp hammocks. The Ciboney were hunter-gatherers, but the Cuba group used shells and the Hispaniola group used stones in forming tools. Another group that lived in western Cuba at the time of Columbus's arrival was the Guanahatabey. They lived in mobile bands and lacked the pottery or agriculture of their neighbors. They were not advanced and were not numerous.

ADDITIONAL RESOURCES

Claypole, William, and John Robottom. *Foundations.* Vol. 1 in *Caribbean Story.* Trinidad: Longman Caribbean, 1981.

Rogozinski, Jan. *A Brief History of the Caribbean from the Arawaks to the Present.* New York: Penguin, 1994.

Rouse, Irving. *The Taino: Rise and Decline of the People Who Greeted Columbus.* New Haven, Conn.: Yale University Press, 1992.

SEE ALSO: Amazonia; Arawak.

—Robert D. Talbott

CARRHAE, BATTLE OF

DATE: June, 53 B.C.E.

LOCALE: Near Carrhae, Mesopotamia (later Haran, Turkey)

RELATED CIVILIZATIONS: Republican Rome, Parthia

SIGNIFICANCE: The Battle of Carrhae revealed the Roman legion's inability to effectively engage or resist the tactics of mounted archers in open terrain.

Background. Following rapprochement in 56 B.C.E. among Rome's First Triumvirate, Marcus Licinius Crassus received the governorship of Syria. Two years later he initiated an unwarranted invasion of the west Asian kingdom of Parthia.

Action. In northwestern Mesopotamia near the town of Carrhae (KAR-ee), the Parthian general Surena, with an army of some 10,000 cavalry, mostly mounted archers, intercepted seven Roman legions under Crassus. The 40,000 Romans, exposed on open terrain, were encircled by the more mobile cavalry and subjected to sustained fire from the Parthian bowmen. All Roman efforts to relieve the situation through offensive action by light infantry failed, and a strong sally by a mixed formation of 6,000 Roman cavalry and foot soldiers ended in complete disaster when the force was surrounded and destroyed. The shattered remnants of the legionary army initiated a withdrawal toward the Euphrates River. During this final retreat, the Romans were exposed to constant daylight attacks by their more elusive opponent, and an effort to negotiate a surrender resulted only in the murder of Crassus. Only 10,000 Romans survived the flight to Syria.

Consequences. The death of Crassus at Carrhae disrupted the delicate balance of power shared among members of the First Triumvirate, thereby accelerating the political forces that eventually led to civil war between the remaining triumvirs, Julius Caesar and Pompey the Great, in 49 B.C.E.

ADDITIONAL RESOURCE

Dodge, Theodore A. *Caesar.* Mechanicsburg, Pa.: Stackpole Books, 1995.

SEE ALSO: Caesar, Julius; Crassus, Marcus Licinius; Parthia; Pompey the Great; Rome, Republican; Triumvirate.

—Donathan Taylor

CARTHAGE

DATE: c. 800 B.C.E.-697 or 698 C.E.

LOCALE: Northern coast of Africa, present-day Tunisia

SIGNIFICANCE: Through trade, Carthage helped integrate the cultures and economies of the ancient Mediterranean world; in its struggle with Greece and Rome, Carthage helped establish the pattern for the development of Western civilization.

Carthage (KAHR-thihj) was a city founded by Phoenicians, a Semitic seafaring people occupying the narrow coastal strip of the eastern Mediterranean, with Tyre their most important city. Best known as traders, they also created a prized purple dye and are associated with the introduction of the alphabet. The Phoenicians traded with cities and settlements as far west as the Strait of Gibraltar. Carthage was at a midway point and

CARTHAGE, CIRCA 800-146 B.C.E.

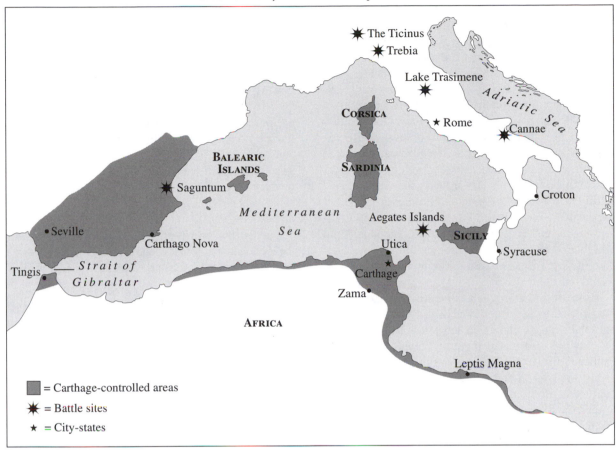

= Carthage-controlled areas

✸ = Battle sites

★ = City-states

served as a way station for obtaining provisions and trading.

History. According to legend, the city was founded by Dido, a princess from Tyre who became its first ruler. Her romance with the Trojan Aeneas, founder of Rome, is fiction ascribed to the Roman poet Vergil. The location of Carthage was ideal; it had a superb natural harbor, a defensible central mound, and a well-watered, fertile hinterland.

Because of a lack of records, little is known of the first four centuries of Carthage's history, only that it soon supplanted Tyre as the leading Phoenician city and for a time was the richest city in the ancient classical world. The centralized mound topped by a formidable citadel became known as the Byrsa. Massive walls encircled the city. Supplementing the natural harbor were two human-made harbors to anchor the Carthaginian naval and commercial ships. As traders, the Carthaginians sailed the Mediterranean in their swift boats

and poured wealth into Carthage. By the fourth century B.C.E., Carthage had created one of the greatest empires of the classical world, stretching west to the Strait of Gibraltar, north to the Ebro close to the Pyrenees, and east across most of Sicily.

The expansion of Carthage inevitably resulted in conflict with Greece and later Rome. The powerful Carthaginian naval fleet protected the home city, and mercenary armies were used for land operations. The complete conquest of Sicily, however, only 171 miles (275 kilometers) off shore eluded them.

The Greek menace was removed through Greek self-destruction in the Peloponnesian War (431-404 B.C.E.). The Roman menace, however, grew increasingly more ominous. Determined to make the Mediterranean a Roman sea (*Mare Nostrum*), Rome neither could nor would tolerate a rival power on its southern borders. Three wars, named "Punic" from the Latin for Phoenician, ensued and resulted in the defeat and finally in the destruction of Phoenician Carthage.

In the First Punic War (264-241 B.C.E.), Carthage lost its monopoly on naval power and control over Sicily. A bloody revolt of the Carthaginian mercenaries, breaking out in 240 B.C.E. and lasting forty months, further drained its resources. The Second Punic War (218-201 B.C.E.) produced a brilliant Carthaginian general, Hannibal, who carried the war into Italy. Only the delaying tactics of the Roman general Fabius saved Rome. A defeat at Zama in 202 B.C.E. sealed Carthage's fate. It lost its entire navy and its possessions outside Africa. Defeats in both wars resulted in heavy indemnities. The Third Punic War (149-146 B.C.E.) occurred because an implacable Rome wished the physical destruction of Carthage itself. The city was stormed, the population slaughtered or removed, and the buildings burned or leveled. Salt was sown into the ruins so no other city would rise there again.

Rule by outsiders. The practical Romans, who ruled Carthage from 44 B.C.E. to 439 C.E., rebuilt the strategic and valuable site of Carthage. The city was resurrected as the new capital of the Roman province of Africa Proconsularis and was soon as rich as its destroyed predecessor. Agriculture was devoted almost exclusively to wheat to feed the Roman proletariat. By the beginning of the millennium, the province delivered to Rome more than 1,750 tons (1.5 million kilograms) a year. Beginning in the second century C.E., Carthage became the seat of a bishopric and a center of Christian learning with Saint Augustine (354-430 C.E.) as its most famous scholar.

In 439 C.E., the Vandal king Gaiseric sacked and conquered Carthage and made it his capital, bringing with him the heretical cult of Arianism. The commercial and cultural life of the city declined precipitously. Vandal misrule caused the Eastern Romans or Byzantines to attempt to reconquer the city, succeeding in 534 B.C.E. under a general named Belisarius. Hopes for a new golden age faded because of religious disputes. The city fell to the Arabs in 697 C.E., and the Arabs plundered and destroyed the city the following year. Its ruins were buried, and its artifacts hauled away.

Religion and ritual. The Carthaginians worshiped two chief gods personifying the male and female elements in nature, Baal-Haman and Tanith. A third god, Melkart, was protector of the city, and a fourth, Eshmun, was god of wealth and

health. A host of lesser gods, many adopted from the Egyptians, were also worshiped. In times of crisis, human sacrifices of infants and children were made to Baal-Haman; those sacrificed were mercifully killed just before being thrown into the flames.

Agriculture and animal husbandry. The Carthaginians made agriculture a science and an industry. Guided by the manuals of the agronomist Mago and the use of irrigation, the phosphate-rich soil around Carthage blossomed into gardens, grain fields, vineyards, and orchards. Carthage was especially noted for its sweet wine and superlative figs. Selective breeding produced superior species of horses, mules, donkeys, sheep, and goats. Wild animals such as elephants were domesticated.

Navigation and transportation. Consistent with their Phoenician heritage, the Carthaginians were excellent sailors and master shipbuilders. Their keel-

The Romans stormed Carthage and destroyed the city during the Punic Wars. (North Wind Picture Archives)

bottomed narrow ships propelled chiefly by oars moved swiftly through the waters. Smaller flat-bottomed boats were used to maneuver in shallow water. Always ready to explore, the Carthaginians sailed through the Strait of Gibraltar and down the African coast as far as modern-day southern Morocco. They sailed north to England and Ireland to procure the tin needed to make bronze.

Trade and commerce. Carthage was devoted to trade, which the Carthaginians preferred to engage in rather than making articles to be traded. For them, nothing profitable could be dishonorable. Their pack mules traversed the deserts; their ships carried goods to and from countless ports. Among the most valued commodities traded were silver, spices, gold, silk, ivory, wild animals, and slaves. The most common trading item was pottery, of which Carthage produced a superior type. The Carthaginians were among the first to use representative money. Leather straps stamped with signs of values were used and accepted throughout their trading areas.

War and weapons. The Carthaginians considered themselves too valuable as traders to be soldiers, so they preferred to hire mercenaries. They much preferred negotiations and bribery to armed conflict. They excelled at naval warfare, and their warships were superb, built with special devices for grappling and for boarding. Removable rams could be used repeatedly rather than staying in the sinking enemy ships. Domesticated elephants were used to frighten or to trample the enemy. The Carthaginians also excelled in fortifications and succeeded in making Carthage almost impregnable. In times of crisis, such as in the final defense of the city, the Carthaginians could be brave fighters.

Women's life. Carthaginian women were veiled and secluded. A sensual people, the Carthaginians expected their women to be beautiful and seductive, adorned with spectacular jewelry and clad in exquisite fabrics. Consistent with the character of the founder of the city,

the women could and did show spirit. In the last hours of Phoenician Carthage, its ruling general pleaded with the Romans for his life, but his wife, denouncing his cowardice, leaped with her sons into the flames of the burning city.

Government and law. It is almost impossible to write of the government of a city whose archives and records have been lost, but from all accounts, Carthage moved from royal absolutism to a republic controlled by an oligarchy of wealth representing maritime interests. The dividing date is given as approximately 395 B.C.E. Citizens elected both a popular assembly with limited powers and a senate. From nominations presented by the senate, the assembly annually chose two *suffetes*, or administrators. Above these bodies and the real ruler of Carthage was a tribunal of 104 judges, who held office for life. Administrators for both Roman and Byzantine Carthage were appointed by the emperors in Rome or in Constantinople.

ADDITIONAL RESOURCES
Durant, Will. "Hannibal Against Rome." In *Caesar and Christ*. New York: Simon and Schuster, 1944.
Lancel, Serge. *Carthage: A History*. Translated by Antonia Nevill. Cambridge, Mass.: Blackwell Publishers, 1995.
Soren, David, Aicha Ben Abed Ben Khader, and Hedi Slim. *Carthage from the Legends of the Aeneid to the Glorious Age of Gold*. New York: Simon and Schuster, 1990.
Warmington, Brian Herbert. *Carthage*. New York: Praeger, 1960.

SEE ALSO: Arabia; Augustine, Saint; Byzantine Empire; Christianity; Fabius; Hannibal; Islam; Phoenicia; Peloponnesian Wars; Punic Wars; Rome, Imperial; Vandals; Vergil; Zama, Battle of.

—*Nis Petersen*

CARTIMANDUA

BORN: first century C.E.; Britain
DIED: after 71 C.E.; Britain
RELATED CIVILIZATIONS: Britain, Imperial Rome
MAJOR ROLE/POSITION: Queen of the Brigantes

Life. In their campaigns in Britain, the Romans encountered, among other Celtic tribes, the Silures in the

west (Wales), and the Brigantes in the north (near modern York). Cartimandua (kahrt-uh-MAN-juh-wuh) ruled the Brigantes from circa 41 to circa 60 C.E. and signed a peace treaty with the Romans in return for their protection. Some of her subjects preferred to resist the Romans and resorted to rebellion in 48 C.E. Meanwhile, Romans under their general Publius Ostorius Scapula routed the Silures in a battle and sent the Welsh leader Caratacus in flight toward Brigantia. Instead of sanctuary, Cartimandua offered him betrayal, and he was taken to Rome in chains. This betrayal further upset the anti-Roman elements in Brigantia, including Cartimandua's husband Venutius, who began to intrigue against her.

Cartimandua formed a liaison with a man called Vellocatus who, along with the Romans, helped her struggle against Venutius, but she was forced to abdicate in 69 C.E. The Brigantes were soon completely subjugated by the Romans.

Influence. Cartimandua's attempts to remain independent ultimately failed, and her self-serving betrayal of Caratacus helped the Romans conquer Britain.

ADDITIONAL RESOURCES

Ireland, S. *Roman Britain: A Sourcebook*. London: Routledge, 1996.

Jackson, Guida M. *Women Who Ruled: A Biographical Encyclopedia*. New York: Barnes & Noble, 1998.

Jones, David E. *Women Warriors: A History*. London: Brassey's, 1997.

Salway, Peter. *The Oxford Illustrated History of Roman Britain*. Oxford, England: Oxford University Press, 1993.

Tacitus, C. *On Imperial Rome*. Translated by Michael Grant. Baltimore: Penguin, 1956.

SEE ALSO: Britain; Caratacus; Celts; Rome, Imperial.
—*John R. Phillips*

CASSANDER

BORN: c. 358 B.C.E.; place unknown
DIED: 297 B.C.E.; place unknown, probably Macedonia
RELATED CIVILIZATIONS: Macedonia, Greece, Asia Minor, Egypt
MAJOR ROLE/POSITION: King of Macedonia

Life. Cassander, who represented his father, Antipater, Alexander the Great's regent, joined Alexander in fighting at Babylon in 324 B.C.E. After Alexander's death in 323 B.C.E, the succession fell to Philip Arridaeus (Alexander's mentally impaired half brother, known as Philip III as regent) and Alexander IV (Alexander's infant son). When Antipater died in 319 B.C.E., Polyperchon became regent while Cassander remained in a subordinate role. Cassander formed an alliance with Antigonus I Monophthalmos against Polyperchon; they invaded Macedonia but were unsuccessful. In 318 B.C.E., Olympias, Alexander the Great's mother, in an attempt to gain power for herself and her grandson Alexander IV, murdered Philip III and forced his wife, Eurydice, to commit suicide. Olympias claimed to rule for her grandson, but Cassander besieged her in Pydna in 316 B.C.E., forced her to surrender, and put her on trial for the murders she had ordered. She was condemned to death and killed by the relatives of her victims. Cassander, now regent, married Alexander the Great's half sister Thessalonice.

In 316 B.C.E., Cassander refounded Thebes, which

Alexander had destroyed earlier. Around 310 B.C.E., he had Alexander IV and his mother murdered but did not assume the throne himself. Around 305 B.C.E., Cassander assumed the title of king. With Antigonus's death in 301 B.C.E., Cassander's title became secure. In 297 B.C.E., he died, leaving the throne to his son Philip IV, who ruled for only four months before dying. Cassander's younger sons Antipater and Alexander V quarreled and lost the kingdom to Demetrius Poliorcetes, the son of Antigonus I Monophthalmos.

Influence. Cassander ended Argead rule in Macedonia and made possible the rise of new and independent Hellenistic kingdoms.

ADDITIONAL RESOURCES

Green, Peter. *Alexander to Actium: The Historical Evolution of the Hellenistic Age*. Reprint. Berkeley: University of California Press, 1993.

Hammond, N. G. L., and F. W. Walbank. *A History of Macedonia*. Vol. 3. Oxford, England: Clarendon Press, 1988.

Will, Édouard. *Cambridge Ancient History*. Vol. 7. Cambridge, England: Cambridge University Press, 1984.

SEE ALSO: Alexander the Great; Antigonid Dynasty; Antipater; Diadochi; Greece, Classical; Greece, Hellenistic and Roman; Macedonia; Olympias.
—*Martin C. J. Miller*

CASSIAN

ALSO KNOWN AS: Saint John Cassian; Johannes Cassianus
BORN: 360 C.E.; Dobruja, Scythia (later in Romania)
DIED: 435 C.E.; Marseille (later in France)
RELATED CIVILIZATIONS: Imperial Rome, medieval Europe
MAJOR ROLE/POSITION: Monk, theologian

Life. Probably of Roman birth, Cassian (KASH-ee-ahn) first settled in a monastery in Bethlehem but later was attracted to the more rigorous religious pursuits of Egyptian monks. Around 399 C.E., he went to Constantinople, where he was ordained a deacon by the patriarch, Saint John Chrysostom. A few years later, after Chrysostom had been deposed, Cassian went to plead his case before the pope. While in Rome, he was ordained a priest. He subsequently founded a convent and a monastery, Saint-Victor, in Marseille around 415 C.E. He remained abbot of the monastery until his death.

Between 419 and 426 C.E., Cassian wrote his monastic work *De institutis coenobiorum* (419-426 C.E.; *The Institutes of the Coenobia*, 1894), a treatise designed to regulate the monastic life. Between 426 and 428 C.E., he wrote his influential *Conlationes* (426-428; *The Conferences*, 1894), dialogues of the desert fathers in Egypt. In 430 C.E., Cassian wrote *De incarnatione comini contra Nestorium* (430 C.E.; *The Incarnation of the Lord*, 1894), a theological treatise directed against the heretic Nestorius and his followers.

On the theological issue of grace, Cassian tried to follow a middle position between those of Saint Augustine and Pelagius. As a result, he was later accused of semi-Pelagianism. This doctrine was formally condemned at the Second Council of Orange in 529 C.E. Because of the charge of semi-Pelagianism, Cassian has never been officially canonized in the West.

Influence. Cassian introduced Western Europe to many of the monastic forms of the East. Saint Benedict of Nursia found inspiration in his *The Conferences* and directed in his Benedictine Rule that it be read daily in monasteries.

ADDITIONAL RESOURCES
Cassian. *John Cassian, "The Conferences."* Translated by Boniface Ramsey. New York: Paulist Press, 1997.
_____. *John Cassian, "The Institutes."* Translated by Boniface Ramsey. New York: Newman Press, 2000.
Chadwick, Owen. *John Cassian*. 2d ed. London: Cambridge University Press, 1968.
Stewart, Columbia. *Cassian the Monk*. Oxford, England: University Press, 1998.

SEE ALSO: Augustine, Saint; Benedict of Nursia, Saint; Christianity; Pelagianism; Rome, Imperial.

—*A. G. Traver*

CASSIODORUS

ALSO KNOWN AS: Flavius Magnus Aurelius Cassiodorus Senator
BORN: c. 490 C.E.; Scyllacium, Calabria, Italy
DIED: c. 585 C.E.; Vivarium, Calabria, Italy
RELATED CIVILIZATIONS: Ostrogoths, Imperial Rome
MAJOR ROLE/POSITION: High-ranking public official, writer

Life. Born to a noble Roman family when Italy was ruled by the invading Ostrogoths, Cassiodorus (kas-ee-uh-DOHR-uhs) quickly rose to high office serving Theoderic the Great and successive Ostrogothic kings. His twelve books of *Variae* (c. 537 C.E.; selected English translation, 1886), intended as models of style, provide examples of letters and documents he composed during his public career. After retiring in his fifties, he pursued religious studies at Constantinople, then returned to found a monastery near his birthplace. He wrote *Institutiones divinarum et saecularium litterarum* (n.d.; *Fundamentals of Divine and Secular Learning*, 1946) for the instruction of the monks. The first book of *Fundamentals of Divine and Secular Learning* guides the study of scripture, and the second outlines the seven liberal arts—grammar, rhetoric, dialectic, arithmetic, music, geometry, and astronomy. He also wrote a history of humankind, a Gothic history, and theological and grammatical works. He died at the monastery he founded.

Influence. Cassiodorus succeeded in his mission to pass on the documents and culture of classical civilization, first by guiding his semiliterate Ostrogothic masters and later by directing his monks to collect and copy ancient manuscripts. His works were principal encyclopedic sources of ancient learning throughout the Middle Ages.

ADDITIONAL RESOURCES

Cassiodorus, Senator. *Variae*. In *Monumenta Germaniae Historica* 12, edited by T. Mommsen. Berlin: Weidmann, 1894.

Mynors, Roger Aubrey Baskerville, ed. *Cassiodori Senatoris Institutiones*. Oxford, England: Clarendon Press, 1963.

O'Donnell, James Joseph. *Cassiodorus*. Berkeley: University of California Press, 1979.

SEE ALSO: Christianity; Education and training; Goths, Ostrogoths, Visigoths; Languages and literature; Rome, Imperial; Theoderic the Great.

—Janet B. Davis

CASSIUS

ALSO KNOWN AS: Gaius Cassius Longinus
BORN: date unknown; probably Rome
DIED: 42 B.C.E.; Philippi, Macedonia (later in Greece)
RELATED CIVILIZATION: Republican Rome
MAJOR ROLE/POSITION: Military leader, politician

Life. Serving as quaestor under Marcus Licinius Crassus in Syria in 53 B.C.E., Cassius participated in the fatal expedition against the Parthians that ended with the defeat of the Roman forces in the vicinity of Carrhae. Cassius led one of the larger remnants of the expeditionary force back to Syria. Over the next two years, in his status as proquaestor, he was to protect the province of Syria from reprisal raids made by the Parthians.

Returning to Rome in 50 B.C.E., Cassius was elected a tribune of the *plebs* (common people) for the following year. In the Roman civil war of 49-48 B.C.E. between Julius Caesar and Pompey the Great, Cassius opted for the side led by Pompey and was put in charge of the Syrian fleet. With this fleet, he harassed the Caesarian fleets in the vicinity of Sicily. Upon learning of the Battle of Pharsalus, he surrendered to Caesar and was pardoned for his part in the civil war. Although Cassius was serving as a praetor in Rome by 44 B.C.E., such honors from Caesar did not suffice. Together with Brutus, Cassius plotted and carried out Caesar's assassination. Driven from Rome, they fought against Octavian (later Augustus) and Marc Antony at the Battle of Philippi. When defeated, they both committed suicide.

Influence. Although unsuccessful in the Battle of Philippi, Cassius and Brutus, by their heroic deaths, provided role models for those opposed to the principate. Their actions demonstrated the necessity of challenging the fiction of a republican government that was effectively a monarchy.

ADDITIONAL RESOURCES

Jiménez, Ramon L. *Caesar Against Rome: The Great Roman Civil War*. Westport, Conn.: Praeger, 2000.

Syme, R. *The Roman Revolution*. Oxford, England: Oxford University Press, 1939.

SEE ALSO: Antony, Marc; Augustus; Brutus; Caesar, Julius; Carrhae, Battle of; Crassus, Marcus Licinius; Parthia; Pharsalus, Battle of; Philippi, Battle of; Pompey the Great; Rome, Republican.

—Richard Westall

CASSIVELLAUNUS

FLOURISHED: first century B.C.E.
RELATED CIVILIZATIONS: Imperial Rome, Britain
MAJOR ROLE/POSITION: Chieftain, soldier

Life. In the middle of the first century B.C.E., Cassivellaunus (kas-uh-vuh-LAW-nuhs) was presumably king, or chieftain, of the Catuvellauni tribe, based north of the Thames in Hertfordshire with a capital at Wheathampstead, or Prae Wood near St. Albans.

In the wake of Julius Caesar's first invasion of southeast England in the late summer of 55 B.C.E. and before his second landing on the shores of Kent in the summer of 54 B.C.E., all the relevant Britons united for the time being and made Cassivellaunus commander in chief.

Defeated in Kent and again on the Thames, Cassivellaunus resorted to guerrilla and scorched-earth tactics, only to have Caesar detach the Trinovantes of Essex, whose king Cassivellaunus had killed and whose exiled prince Mandubracius had already been befriended by Caesar in Gaul. After Mandubracius's restoration, other tribes defected, including the Cenimagni, Segontiaci, Ancalites, Bibroci, and Cassi, who helped the Romans to take Cassivellaunus's capital and make him sue for peace. He agreed to pay tribute and leave the Trinovantes independent, after which Caesar withdrew across the English Channel again, leaving Cassivellaunus alive and the Catuvellauni to dominate southeast England.

Influence. Subversion of his Catuvellauni by the Trinovantes proved the need for unification of the two leading tribes, which took place by merger or conquest early in the next century.

ADDITIONAL RESOURCES

Fere, Sheppard. *Britannia: History of Roman Britain.* London: Routledge, 1987.

Salway, Peter. *The Oxford Illustrated History of Roman Britain.* Oxford, England: Oxford University Press, 1993.

SEE ALSO: Britain; Caesar, Julius; Commius; Rome, Imperial.

—O. Kimball Armayor

CĀTANĀR

ALSO KNOWN AS: Maturai Kulavanikan Cittalaic Cattanar; Kulavanikan Seethalai Sattanar
FLOURISHED: third to fourth centuries C.E.; Maturai, India
RELATED CIVILIZATION: India (Tamil)
MAJOR ROLE/POSITION: Poet

Life. Cātanār (SHAW-tah-nahr), the son of a grain merchant (*kulavanikan*), is considered to be one of the eminent poets of the third Cankam, having contributed at least ten poems in four anthologies including *Akanānūṟu* (second or third century C.E.; English translation in *Poets of the Tamil Anthologies*, 1979). He is the author of *Tiruvaḷḷuvar Malai* (third or fourth century C.E.; poems in honor of Tiruvaḷḷuvar) and the famous Tamil epic *Manimekalai* (third or fourth century C.E.; English translation, 1911), the story of a dancer and courtesan. This epic is a continuation of the story of Kōvalan and Mātavi of *Cilappatikāram* (c. 450 C.E.; *The Śilappadikāram*, 1939) by Iḷaṅkō Aṭikaḷ. Manimekalai, the daughter of Mātavi, is torn between her passion for a princely lover and her spiritual yearnings. Encouraged by her grandmother and mother, Manimekalai runs away from the prince, who pursues her. She attains magical powers, overcomes all dangers, becomes a Buddhist nun, and goes to Pukār (Cōḷa capital). Later, Manimekalai proceeds to Vañci (Cēra capital) to help with famine relief work.

Influence. Cātanār's primary aim was to spread Buddhism in the Tamil country through the use of lively discussions on religion, philosophy, and supernatural elements.

ADDITIONAL RESOURCES

Hikosaka, Shu. *Buddhism in Tamilnadu: A New Perspective.* Madras, India: Institute of Asian Studies, 1989.

Natarajan R. *Manimekalai as an Epic.* Madras, India: Shantha, 1990.

Richman, Paula. *Women, Branch Stories, and Religious Rhetoric in a Tamil Buddhist Text.* Syracuse, N.Y.: Maxwell School of Citizenship and Public Affairs, Syracuse University, 1985.

Subbiah Pillai, K. *The Contributions of the Tamils to Indian Culture.* Madras, India: International Institute of Tamil Studies, 1994.

See also: Buddhism; Caṅkam; Iḷaṅkō Aṭikaḷ; India.

—*Salli Vargis*

CATILINE

Also known as: Lucius Sergius Catilina
Born: c. 108 B.C.E.; place unknown
Died: 62 B.C.E., Pistoria, Italy
Related civilization: Republican Rome
Major role/position: Politician

Life. Born to an old Roman patrician family, Catiline (kat-uhl-IN) was a ruthless politician who strove for power and personal glory at any cost. He was an adherent of the dictator Lucius Cornelius Sulla, reputedly murdering his own brother-in-law in Sulla's proscriptions. He held the regular political offices in Rome and for most of his career was backed by the aristocracy. Prohibited from running for the consulships of 65 and 64 B.C.E., Catiline was defeated by Gaius Antonius Hybrida and the "new man" Cicero for the year 63 B.C.E. After another unsuccessful candidacy, for 62 B.C.E., Catiline organized several disaffected politicians and plotted to overthrow the government and seize power. The plot, known as the Catilinarian Conspiracy, was discovered and denounced by Cicero in the *In Catilinam* (60 B.C.E.; *Orations Against Catiline* in *The Orations*, 1741-1743), delivered to the senate and the people in November and December of 63 B.C.E. The main conspirators were seized in Rome and executed on December 5. Catiline himself raised and led a large army of Sullan veterans who had squandered their pen-

sions, disaffected peasants in the Italian countryside, and perhaps some runaway slaves. Catiline's troops were defeated by the Roman army at Pistoria in January, 62 B.C.E. Catiline died fighting in the front ranks.

Influence. Catiline became an archetype of the evil politician who plotted against the state. He received eternal torment in the underworld in Vergil's *Aeneid* (c. 29-19 B.C.E.; English translation, 1553) and was made the subject of dramas by English playwright Ben Jonson and Norwegian dramatist Henrik Ibsen. All accounts of Catiline are based on the very biased Ciceronian evidence, whether they follow Cicero or react against him. Modern attempts to rehabilitate Catiline and make him a genuine reformer lack convincing evidence for their claims.

ADDITIONAL RESOURCES

MacDonald, C., trans. *Cicero, In Catilinam I-IV, Pro Murena, Pro Sulla, Pro Flacco.* Cambridge, Mass.: Harvard University Press, 1976.

McGushin, Patrick. *Bellum Catilinae: A Commentary.* Lugduni Batavorum: E. J. Brill, 1977.

See also: Cicero; Rome, Republican; Sempronia; Sulla, Lucius Cornelius; Vergil.

—*Robert W. Cape, Jr.*

CATO THE CENSOR

Also known as: Marcus Porcius Cato; Cato the Elder
Born: 234 B.C.E.; Tusculum, Italy
Died: 149 B.C.E.; Rome
Related civilization: Republican Rome
Major role/position: Statesman, orator, historian

Life. One of the most influential statesmen, orators, and Latin prose writers in second century B.C.E. Rome, Cato (KAY-toh) the Censor was born to a plebeian family. He espoused the moral traditions (*mos maiorum*) and conservative values of the hardworking farmers and military men he considered the cornerstone of Roman greatness. As military tribune in the Second Punic War (218-201 B.C.E.), he impressed the patrician Lucius Valerius Flaccus, with whom he began his political career, culminating in the consulship (195 B.C.E.) and censorship (184 B.C.E.), which both men shared. As censor, his harsh attacks against offenders of traditional Roman moral values were remembered for generations and earned him the name *Censorius* ("the Censor"). Cato was an outspoken opponent of the trend toward adopting Greek practices in Rome and continually attacked the Scipio family, the leading philhellenes of the day.

Cato was the first important writer of Latin prose, and he aided the development of Latin poetry by bringing the poet Quintus Ennius to Rome (203 B.C.E.). He wrote the first history of Rome in Latin, the *Origines* (lost work, 168-149 B.C.E.), published at least 150 of his speeches, wrote the treatise *De agricultura* (c. 160 B.C.E.; *On Agriculture*, 1913), and issued other works on military science, law, medicine, and rhetoric, including an encyclopedia for his son. A book of his pithy maxims was compiled after his death.

Influence. After his death, Cato became the archetype of the traditional, conservative Roman statesman, inimical to things Greek; this characterization led to simplistic and unfortunate stereotypes of the early Romans.

ADDITIONAL RESOURCES

Astin, A. E. *Cato the Censor.* Oxford, England: Clarendon Press, 1978.

Rawson, E. *Intellectual Life in the Late Roman Republic.* Baltimore: Johns Hopkins University Press, 1985.

Cato the Censor. (Library of Congress)

SEE ALSO: Cato the Younger; Ennius, Quintus; Punic Wars; Rome, Republican.

—*Robert W. Cape, Jr.*

CATO THE YOUNGER

ALSO KNOWN AS: Cato Uticensis; Marcus Porcius Cato

BORN: 95 B.C.E.; Rome, Italy

DIED: 46 B.C.E.; Utica, Africa

RELATED CIVILIZATION: Republican Rome

MAJOR ROLE/POSITION: Conservative political and military leader

Life. Cato (KAY-toh) the Younger was born the great-grandson of the famous traditionalist, Cato the Censor. The younger Cato was raised a member of the Optimate party, which defended the senatorial oligarchy against the Populares, who sought greater political influence for Rome's lower classes. As Cato advanced in political and military service, he exhibited a strong devotion to Roman duty and senatorial rule. His principles inevitably produced conflicts with the Populares as well as with such men as Marcus Licinius Crassus, Pompey the Great, and Julius Caesar, whom Cato believed were manipulating Rome's political tensions to their advantage.

In 62 B.C.E., Cato supported Cicero against Catiline's conspiracy to take the government by force. As events unfolded, Crassus and Caesar appeared to have supported Catiline. Although Cicero sought a moderate response to this emergency, Cato succeeded in convincing the senate to put the conspirators to death. Eventually, the Triumvirate of Crassus, Pompey, and Caesar was formed and then dissolved because of the competing interests of these dynasts. In the bitter contest between Pompey and Caesar following the death of Crassus, Cato supported Pompey in a desperate attempt to preserve senatorial influence. Caesar defeated his foes at the Battle of Pharsalus in 48 B.C.E., after which Cato fled to Africa with his remaining troops. Following a final military defeat, Cato chose suicide at the city of Utica rather than surrender to Caesar's forces. He thus acquired the title Cato Uticensis after the place of his principled death.

Influence. In later days, both Cicero and Caesar attempted to use Cato as a symbol of either a dedicated republican or a foe of progress. In later centuries, Cato became a symbol of political idealism, making an appearance in Dante's *La divina commedia* (c. 1320; *The Divine Comedy*, 1802) and as a personal hero of U.S. president George Washington.

ADDITIONAL RESOURCES

Fehrle, R. *Cato Uticensis*. Darmstadt, Germany: Wissenschaftliche Buchgessellschaft, 1983.

Richard, C. *The Founders and the Classics*. Cambridge, Mass.: Harvard University Press, 1994.

SEE ALSO: Caesar, Julius; Catiline; Cato the Censor; Cicero; Crassus, Marcus Licinius; Pharsalus, Battle of; Pompey the Great.

—Kenneth R. Calvert

CATULLUS

ALSO KNOWN AS: Gaius Valerius Catullus
BORN: c. 84 B.C.E.; Verona, Cisalpine Gaul
DIED: c. 54 B.C.E.; probably Rome
RELATED CIVILIZATION: Late Republican Rome
MAJOR ROLE/POSITION: Poet

Life. Little information exists on the life of Catullus (kuh-TUHL-uhs), one of the most important lyric poets of his generation, although he seems to have been born into a prominent family. He is generally considered one of the so-called neoteric poets, but he is the only one of these whose work has largely survived. His extant work consists of approximately 116 poems in various meters on a wide variety of topics. Most famous are the Lesbia poems, which describe a love affair with a married Roman woman of the aristocracy. These poems range from expressions of passionate love to bitter outcries of disappointment, jealousy, and rage.

Influence. Catullus is often credited with redefining love, perhaps even creating a notion of "romantic" love, by including within an erotic relationship affection, loyalty, and the kind of mutual respect demanded by other types of social bonds. He thus paved the way for later Roman and European conceptions of love and love poetry. Catullus left his mark on all the major poets of the next several generations, especially the elegists and the Roman poet Martial. His fortunes waned in later antiquity and little was known of him in the Middle Ages as his poems had been lost. They were rediscovered during the Renaissance and have been gathered and translated

Catullus. (Library of Congress)

into English as *Gaius Valerius Catullus: The Complete Poetry, a New Translation with an Introduction* (1957).

ADDITIONAL RESOURCES
Martin, C. *Catullus*. New Haven, Conn.: Yale University Press, 1992.

Wiseman, T. P. *Catullus and His World: A Reappraisal*. Cambridge, England: Cambridge University Press, 1985.

SEE ALSO: Clodia; Martial; Rome, Republican.
—Christopher Nappa

CELSUS

FLOURISHED: c. 178 C.E.
RELATED CIVILIZATION: Imperial Rome
MAJOR ROLE/POSITION: Philosopher, anti-Christian polemicist

Life. All that is left of Celsus (SEHL-suhs) is his influential anti-Christian polemic entitled *Alēthēs Logos* (probably between 175 and 181 C.E.; *On the True Doctrine*, 1987, translated from pieces preserved in the reply written by the Christian writer Origen). Though this work is more emotive than philosophic, it nevertheless suggests an author who was highly educated, particularly in Middle Platonic thought. Portions of this work are reminiscent of philosopher Lucian's satirical portrayal of the charlatan Peregrinus, and the author also exhibits a good knowledge of second century Judaic and Christian perspectives. Celsus probably wrote his polemic during the reign of Marcus Aurelius (r. 161-180 C.E.), a period of military and social troubles that marked the end of the Pax Romana. Indeed, he may have written this polemic for the emperor himself in an effort to encourage persecution of the Christians.

The central theme of this work was that Christians had irrationally abandoned all ancient traditions, creating a novel religion that worshiped a magician and condemned criminal. For Celsus, these cultural rebels represented the worst elements of ignorance and disorder. He understood that Christians had already been divided by heresies and was astounded at their negative attitudes regarding the ancient pagan divinities. Celsus also found hypocritical their apparent disdain for the same Judaic traditions from which they claimed descent. In the end, he wrote to admonish these rebels for their rejection of the traditions that had made Rome strong.

Influence. *On the True Doctrine* may have been written in response to Christian apologetic efforts, particularly one written in the first century C.E. by Saint Justin Martyr. Celsus's work certainly became a focal point of Christian-pagan debate because 90 percent of it was preserved by the Christian writer Origen in his apologetic work, *Kata Kelsou* (248 C.E.; *Origen Against Celsus*, 1660).

ADDITIONAL RESOURCES
Hoffman, R. *Celsus: On the True Doctrine*. Oxford, England: Oxford University Press, 1987.
Origen. *Contra Celsum*. Translated by Henry Chadwick. Cambridge, England: Cambridge University Press, 1965.
Wilken, R. *The Christians as the Romans Saw Them*. New Haven, Conn.: Yale University Press, 1984.

SEE ALSO: Christianity; Justin Martyr, Saint; Lucian; Marcus Aurelius; Rome, Imperial; Origen.
—Kenneth R. Calvert

CELSUS, AULUS CORNELIUS

BORN: c. 25 B.C.E.; possibly near Narbonne on the Mediterranean coast of France
DIED: c. 50 C.E.; probably Rome
RELATED CIVILIZATIONS: Roman Greece, Imperial Rome
MAJOR ROLE/POSITION: Author, scientist, scholar

Life. Nothing is known about the life of Aulus Cornelius Celsus (AW-luhs kohr-NEEL-ee-uhs SEHL-suhs) except that he wrote a number of scientific and scholarly treatises in Latin during the reign of the emperor Tiberius (14–37 C.E.). The subject matter of these works was far-reaching and included rhetoric, law, and philosophy as well as agriculture, military science, and medicine. Except for a few fragments, the only surviving work is his treatise on medicine, *De medicina* (c. 30 C.E.; *The Eight Books of Medicine*, 1830; better known as *De Medicina*, 1935-1938). Whether the scholar

Aulus Cornelius Celsus. (Library of Congress)

Celsus was also a practicing physician is disputed.

Celsus's eight books on medicine are arranged according to types of treatment (such as diet, drugs, and surgery) and include a brief but important history of Greco-Roman medicine. Celsus's descriptions of conditions such as inflammation, insanity, and heart disease are remarkably accurate. Also noteworthy is his emphasis on cleanliness in the treatment of wounds and the use of antiseptics.

Influence. Although Celsus's medical work was not well known in antiquity, its rediscovery by Pope Nicholas V (1397-1455) marked an important stage in the development of modern medicine, and his writing style was often imitated by Renaissance admirers.

ADDITIONAL RESOURCES

Celsus. *Celsus, "De Medicina."* Translated by Walter George Spencer. 1935-1938. Reprint. Cambridge, Mass.: Harvard University Press, 1961.

Hope, Valerie M. *Death and Disease in the Ancient City.* New York: Routledge, 2000.

SEE ALSO: Greece, Hellenistic and Roman; Hippocrates; Medicine and health; Rome, Imperial; Tiberius.

—*Thomas J. Sienkewicz*

CELTS

DATE: 1000 B.C.E.-700 C.E.

LOCALE: Europe and central Asia Minor

SIGNIFICANCE: Celtic peoples dominated much of northern Europe and developed a major civilization with important regional variations.

In the third century B.C.E., at the height of their influence, the peoples identified by language and some aspects of their culture as Celtae or Galli (in Latin; Keltoi or Galatae in Greek) controlled territories that stretched from Ireland to central Asia Minor and from southern Iberia to the Ukraine. Never in any sense united, Celtic peoples developed a distinctive if diverse culture but ultimately fell prey to the inexorable imperialism of Rome and the encroachment of aggressive "barbarians." By the end of the ancient era, Celts dominated only the western fringes of Europe, from Ireland through western and northern Britain to Brittany, all areas still associated with Celtic heritage. Knowledge of

Celtic culture and society is limited to evidence from archaeology, classical writers and sculptors, and linguistics (including personal and place names).

History. Although their ancestors were to be found among the peoples of the Urnfield culture, Celts first emerged as a distinctive culture in the C and D periods of the Hallstatt culture, from about 800 B.C.E. These early Iron Age societies practiced inhumation with rich grave goods and occupied hill forts from which an aristocracy dominated the countryside. The Celtic "heartland," from which later migrations trekked south and eastward, was a broad area surrounding the upper Rhine and Danube Rivers. At the same time, the presence of Celtic peoples in Iberia and the British Isles is clear, though their relation to the heartland is not. Celtic language, customs, and religion may have flowed south and west with trade, for there are no signs of either mass migration or conquest.

As the La Tène culture developed in the fifth century

B.C.E., hill forts were abandoned (or destroyed), sumptuous burials became less common, and there emerged a warrior-aristocracy, whose leaders were buried with their weapons. These changes are apparent across an arc from the Rhone to Transylvania. La Tène cultures are also evident in Bohemia and along the lower Moselle and Marne Rivers. Contact with the Mediterranean world continued along the Rhone corridor (to Greek Massalia) and increased across Alpine passes with the Etruscans and Italian Greeks. The fourth and third centuries B.C.E. saw large-scale migrations of Celts from the upper Rhine-Danube region, especially south and eastward. By at least 400 B.C.E., Celtic tribes had crossed into the Po Valley and, after defeating Etruscan natives, established strong settlements in Milan and probably Brescia, Vicenza, Trent, Bergamo, and Como. Population pressures as well as the attraction of Italian wealth account for the migration and attendant raids, including that on Rome in 390 B.C.E.

A little later, large groups migrated eastward into the Balkans (by 335 B.C.E.) and as far as the northern Black Sea region (after 320 B.C.E.). The collapse of Alexander the Great's empire drew Celts farther south: They raided Delphi in 279 B.C.E. and established a small state in central Asia Minor (Galatia) shortly thereafter.

Rome's expansion in the wake of its victories in the Second Punic War (218-201 B.C.E.) rolled back Celtic power in Iberia (197-133 B.C.E.), northern Italy (from the Celtic defeat at Telamon in 225 to about 190 B.C.E.), and Asia Minor (after the Battle of Magnesia ad Sipylum in 190 B.C.E. to Pompey the Great's seizure of Galatia in 67 B.C.E.). Rome annexed southern Gaul for

CELTIC EUROPE, 60 B.C.E.

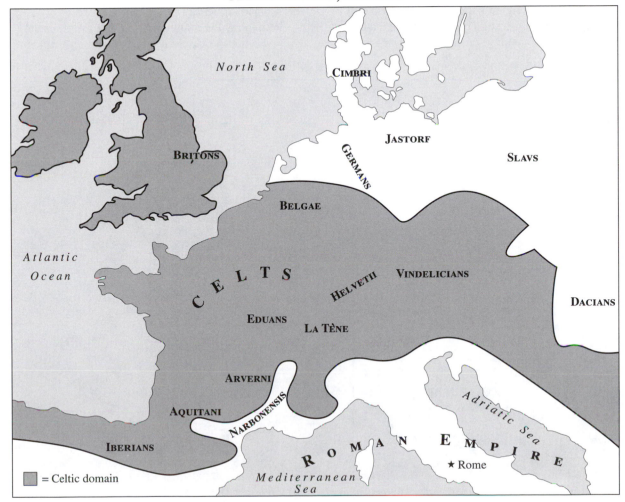

land access to Iberia, and Julius Caesar carried out a systematic invasion of Gaul from 58 B.C.E. until his defeat of Vercingetorix at Alesia in 52 B.C.E. All told, an estimated million Gallic Celts perished, and another million were enslaved. The need for slaves, raw materials, and new markets for Roman goods drove these campaigns and Rome's subsequent invasion of Britain under Emperor Claudius in the 40's C.E. Eastern Celtic peoples were swamped by the aggressive growth of the Dacian state (c. 60 B.C.E.) and expansion of Sarmatian dominance farther east. Remaining Celts in central Europe fell prey to increasingly mobile Germanic tribes, especially the Teutones and Cimbri.

In the wake of Roman disintegration from the fourth century C.E., Celts along the Atlantic fringe grew in boldness. The Irish (Scotti), having never been dominated by Rome, raided Britain and established colonies in Scotland. Welsh Celts settled Brittany. Celts in Roman Gaul and Britain were converted to Christianity in the course of the religion's spread, and the Irish only in the early fifth century C.E. Dynamic representatives of Irish (Celtic) Christianity spread across Britain and Europe from the sixth century C.E., preaching and establishing monasteries.

Society. Wherever found, Celtic societies were stratified and aristocratic. Organization was along tribal or clan lines, with chiefs or kings eventually giving way in Gaul to a broader power structure in which elected councils made most decisions. Julius Caesar noted that the warriors and Druids were the only important people, but to these must be added specialized craftspeople and the bards. Slaves existed, but little is known about them. Likewise, little is known of Celtic law, but Irish Brehon laws were recorded at a late date and may reflect traditional norms. Both late tales and classical authors describe Celtic practices of fosterage and hostage taking. Social status seems to have shifted from a base in material wealth (late Hallstatt) to warrior prowess and success in raiding (as in the Irish Táin). Later, aristocratic potlatch and ritual destruction of valuables developed on the continent and gave way under Roman influence to civic patronage.

Women. Brehon laws suggest that simple monogamy was not the Celtic norm, but women's rights to

Celtic crosses in a cemetery in Clare, Ireland. (Digital Stock)

property were far greater than elsewhere. Widows, for example, received the full estate. As with the Romans, men had power of life and death in families, and marriage itself was a means of social or political bonding. Broader roles for women are inferred from remarks by classical authors. Their participation in warfare can be deduced from Boudicca's leadership of the Iceni and allies and in rulership from Cartimandua's rule over the Brigantes.

Settlements and trade. Small agrarian communities probably exemplify Celtic life, but the nonagrarian classes had other options. Hallstatt hill forts gave way to more open and later enclosed settlements whose surrounding ditches and ramparts are still evident in aerial photographs. Some remain largely intact, as at Dun Aengus in Ireland and Maiden Castle, England. Contact with and influence by classical cultures sometimes refined settlements into true urban spaces, as in Noricum. Trade always played an important part in Celtic life, and settlements often protected sources of raw materials or trade routes. Metals, slaves, furs, amber, and other northern goods were exchanged in Mediterranean entrepôts such as Massalia (Marseilles) for wine, oil, and other luxury goods demanded by the ruling class.

War and weapons. Classical authors agree on the fierce nature of the Celtic warrior. Some tribes fought naked and some displayed body art. Helmets and ring-mail armor were worn by Celts who fought with sword and spear behind a shield, sometimes using a sling or bow. Classical statues depict Celtic warriors and confirm much of what contemporary authors recorded, including use of the distinctive torc or neck ring. Warfare among tribes was often ritualized, with taunting and boasting followed by single combat alone. Like raiding, violence was deeply embedded in Celtic culture. Celts also fought in screaming swarms roused by battle trumpets, relying on an initial charge to carry their victory, and having no tactics in reserve for a sustained fight.

Religion, death, and burial. The fullest information comes from Book 6 of Caesar's *Comentarii de bello Gallico* (51-52 B.C.E. translated together with *Comentarii de bello civili*, 45 B.C.E., as *Commentaries,* 1609) and burial sites. Until Christianization, Celts were polytheistic with an apparent ruling dyad of an earth/fertility/locale goddess and a sky/war/tribe god. Other divinities may be manifestations of these two or a further elaboration of nature cults. The number three was sacred to Celts and is often apparent in statuary and

other ritual elements. As cremation gave way to inhumation in the Hallstatt era, the assumption can be made that a concept of the afterlife either changed or was more clearly articulated. Burial with grave goods certainly implies a material sense of the other world. Excarnation rather than inhumation is evident in Britain. Human sacrifice (drowning, hanging, burning, impaling) is attested to, as is ritual deposition or destruction of valuables. Rituals were overseen by augurs, and by powerful "Druidic" priests, who embodied the cults and proffered the sacrifices. Celtic religion was strongly tied to sacred spaces in nature (*nemeton*): groves, springs, caves, and certain waters such as Lake Neuchâtel and the Thames. Some were built up into formal sanctuaries and many overbuilt by Romans and later Christians.

Druids also oversaw the annual calendar of 354 days with an intercalary month. The first century B.C.E. Coligny bronze calendar lists the "dark" and "light" halves of each month of twenty-nine or thirty days and marks two of the four main feast days: Samhain (November 1), Imbolc (February 1), Beltane (May 1), and Lugnasad (August 1).

Art. Work in all precious metals for decorative, martial, and practical purposes shows a well-developed concept of aesthetic beauty and high level of craftsmanship that would go on to influence medieval art heavily. Totemic animals, vegetal patterns, and geometric—especially curvilinear—forms dominate, with little influence from the classical Mediterranean. Surviving pottery shows clearly derivative patterning and was probably meant for use by the lower classes. Although high-quality metalwork was almost certainly for the warrior or aristocratic classes, specifically religious art seems to be limited to stone sculpture. Coins were struck by Celts from the early third century C.E., and although many were derived from Greco-Roman models, others are clearly Celtic in form. Coins served a very limited function in the barter-based Celtic economy.

Language, writing, and literature. Celtic languages are Indo-European with resemblances to Italic. Linguists recognize five major branches: Hispano-Celtic (Iberia), Gallic, Lepontic (Eastern), Goidelic (Ireland, Scotland, Isle of Man), and Brythonic (Wales, Cornwall, Brittany). Celtic writing is limited to rare inscriptions, of which two bronze tablets in Iberian Celtic—from Botoritta in Spain—and numerous examples in Irish Ogham characters remain. No ancient Celtic literature appears to have been recorded until well into the Middle Ages, though classical authors such as Posidonius remark on the important role of storytellers, poets, and even satirists at warrior feasts. Stories written in Old Irish appear to predate Christian influence (that is, pre-fifth century C.E.); however, the earliest surviving copies date from half a millennium later.

Current views. Virtually every aspect of Celtic life and culture is open to new information and interpretation. Archaeology continues to shed new light as does deeper understanding of classical and Irish texts.

ADDITIONAL RESOURCES

Cunliffe, Barry. *The Ancient Celts*. New York: Oxford University Press, 1997.

Ellis, Peter Beresford. *The Celtic Empire*. Durham, N.C.: Carolina Academic Press, 1990.

_____. *Celtic Women*. Grand Rapids, Mich.: Eerdmans, 1995.

Green, Miranda. *The Celtic World*. New York: Routledge, 1995.

James, Simon. *The World of the Celts*. New York: Thames and Hudson, 1993.

Moscati, Sabatino. *The Celts*. New York: Rizzoli, 1991.

Rankin, H. D. *Celts and the Classical World*. London: Routledge, 1995.

SEE ALSO: Alesia, Battle of; Alexander the Great; Boudicca; Britain; Caesar, Julius; Cartimandua; Christianity; Claudius; Gauls; Halstatt culture; La Tène culture; Magnesia ad Sipylum, Battle of; Punic Wars; Rome, Imperial; Vercingetorix.

—Joseph P. Byrne

CHADIC PEOPLES

DATE: c. 5000 B.C.E.-700 C.E.

LOCALE: Central and West Africa

SIGNIFICANCE: The Chadic peoples were among the precursors to today's speakers of Chadic languages in Nigeria, Niger, Chad, and Cameroon.

Today, the Chadic peoples are those in central, western, and eastern Africa who speak one of the many languages of the Chadic language family, a branch of the Afroasiatic language family. Approximately 26 million people today speak a Chadic language; 22 million of these speak Hausa. Chadic languages use tonal inflection to differentiate meaning in identical words. Chadic languages have been spoken around the Lake Chad region since 5000-4000 B.C.E. Two archaeological sites show Chadic people in settled communities and creating art by the first millennium B.C.E.

Cliff paintings from some nine thousand years ago in the Borkou and Ennedi regions (north-central Chad) depict elephants, rhinoceroses, giraffes, cattle, camels, and harpoon fishing. Lake Chad was then much larger and the region wetter, gradually becoming drier and more desertlike over the next several thousand years. In the fifth century B.C.E., the Greek historian Herodotus described a black population who inhabited caves in the Fezzan area (now a region of desert and oases in southern Libya). Archaeological excavations south of Lake Chad revealed terra-cotta and cast bronze objects associated with a people known as the Sao along the Chari (or Shari) and Lagone Rivers. The period from 550 B.C.E. to 50 C.E. produced decorated pottery vessels. Between 50 and 700 C.E., more finely finished pottery vessels and simplified terra-cotta human and animal figures were made. Head forms created in terra-cotta around 700 C.E. combined human and frog features, symbolizing fertility and the beginning of the rainy season, when the frogs appear. Excavations have revealed tenth century C.E. Sao walled cities and metalworking that suggest the sophistication of their ancient predecessors. The Sao would disappear by the seventeeth century; their modern descendants are probably the Kotoko.

In north-central Nigeria near the village of Nok, terra-cotta sculptures dated between 1000 B.C.E. and 875 C.E. have been excavated. These human and animal heads and figures show a highly developed technical skill with the creation of hollow terra-cotta sculptures. From about 800 B.C.E. to about 200 C.E., the Nok flourished on the Jos Plateau; in addition to sculpting terra-cotta figures, they probably worked tin and iron.

With the expansion of Islam, Arab traders arrived from the north in the seventh century C.E. Soon after, nomads from North Africa who may have been associated with the Toubou arrived and ultimately established, north of Lake Chad, the state of Kanem-Bornu, which reached its height some five hundred years later. The kings of this civilization would become Islamic by the eleventh century.

ADDITIONAL RESOURCES

Connah, G. *Three Thousand Years in Africa.* Cambridge, England: Cambridge University Press, 1981.

Hodges, Carleton, ed. *Papers on the Manding.* Bloomington: University of Indiana Press, 1971.

Koslow, Philip J. *Kanem-Borno: One Thousand Years of Splendor.* New York: Chelsea House, 1994.

Mori, Fabrizio. *The Great Civilisations of the Ancient Sahara: Neolithisation and the Earliest Evidence of Anthropomorphic Religions.* Translated by B. D. Philips. Rome: L'Erma di Bretschneider, 1998.

Nachtigal, Gustav. *Sahara and Sudan: Kawar, Bornu, Kanem, Borku, Ennedi.* Berkeley: Asian Humanities Press, 1979.

SEE ALSO: Africa, West; Nok culture.

—William L. Hommel

CHAERONEA, BATTLE OF

DATE: August 2, 338 B.C.E.
LOCALE: Chaeronea, in Boeotia northwest of Thebes
RELATED CIVILIZATIONS: Classical Greece, Macedonia
SIGNIFICANCE: Macedonia's victory over Greece at Chaeronea (kehr-uh-NEE-uh) effectively ended the era of the Greek city-state.

Background. Philip II of Macedonia (r. 359-336 B.C.E.) modernized the Macedonian army. He taught his factious nobility to serve him loyally, using heavy cavalry, and created a highly professional phalanx of infantry. In the 340's B.C.E., Philip began to penetrate southward through Thessaly while the Greek states were distracted by their perpetual feuds.

Action. War broke out between Macedonia and a united Greece in 340 B.C.E. The decisive battle was probably fought on August 2, 338 B.C.E. Thebans and Boeotians held the Greek right flank, the Athenians the left, and various allies from central Greece and the Peloponnese the center. The Greek phalanx hoped to crush the enemy by its usual straightforward attack.

Philip, a master of innovation, combined use of cavalry and infantry. His right, pretending retreat, lured the Athenians into a charge. The Greek center and left moved obliquely to keep in close ranks. Into this hole the eighteen-year-old crown prince Alexander (later, the Great) led the Macedonian cavalry in wedge formation against the Thebans. Crack units of Macedonian infantry followed. After heroic resistance the Thebans were beaten; the other Greeks, panic-stricken, broke and ran.

Consequences. As a result of this battle, the independent city-states of Greece came under Macedonian control. In 337 B.C.E., Philip organized the Hellenic League with its seat at Corinth. He served as president of the league, and member cities were forbidden to wage war with each other and were forced to follow Philip's foreign policy.

ADDITIONAL RESOURCE

Hammond, N. G. L. *Philip of Macedon.* Baltimore: Johns Hopkins University Press, 1994.

SEE ALSO: Alexander the Great; Greece, Classical; Macedonia; Philip II.

—Thomas J. Sienkewicz

CHALCEDON, COUNCIL OF

DATE: 451 C.E.
LOCALE: Chalcedon (later Kadiköy, Turkey)
RELATED CIVILIZATION: Imperial Rome
SIGNIFICANCE: The council ended a controversy within the Church by ruling that the nature of Jesus Christ was both divine and human.

For more than a century the Christian Church in the East had been torn by theological dissension over Arianism, Apollinarianism, and Nestorianism. As a reaction to Nestorius, who had taught that Jesus Christ was fully human but not fully a deity, Eutyches of Constantinople taught that Jesus was fully God but not fully human. Je-

Bishops met at Chalcedon to resolve questions regarding the nature of Jesus Christ. (Library of Congress)

sus had only one nature, a divine nature, but not a human one. This position was also known as Monophysitism (one nature). This controversy shook the Church in the East, resulting in a call for another council of bishops to settle the matter.

Meeting under both the support and supervision of Emperor Marcian, five hundred or so bishops gathered at Chalcedon (KAL-suh-dahn), just across the Bosphorus from Constantinople. Here the Monophysite opposition, although strongly supported by Alexandria, failed to win a majority of votes. The council accepted a letter from Saint Leo I of Rome that stated that Jesus was fully God, Jesus was fully man, and there was no problem. This did not settle the philosophical issues, but it did state a position that most bishops could accept.

Chalcedonian orthodoxy reworded the Nicene Creed and became the standard position for both the Eastern and Western churches. This remains the standard formula for understanding the person of Christ down to the present for orthodox Christianity. However, the Monophysite churches were so disillusioned by this reversal that they rejected the leadership of the patriarch of Constantinople and, within two centuries, were willing to accept Muslim domination rather than that of Constantinople.

ADDITIONAL RESOURCES

L'Huillier, Peter. *The Church of the Ancient Councils.* Crestwood, N.Y.: St. Vladimir's Seminary Press, 1996.

Noll, Mark A. *Turning Points: Decisive Moments in the History of Christianity.* Grand Rapids, Mich.: Baker Academic, 2000.

SEE ALSO: Arianism; Christianity; Leo I, Saint; Monophysitism; Nestorius; Nicaea, Council of.
—*James B. North*

CHÂLONS, BATTLE OF

ALSO KNOWN AS: Battle of Catalaunian Fields or Mauriac Plain
DATE: July, 451 C.E.
LOCALE: Mauriac Plain, northwest of Troyes
RELATED CIVILIZATION: Imperial Rome
SIGNIFICANCE: The Romans halted the advance of the Huns into Western Europe.

Background. Circa 450 C.E., Attila, king of the Huns, demanded half of the Western Roman Empire. Emperor Valentinian III (425-455 C.E.) refused, and in 451 C.E., Attila and the Hun horde, including the Ostrogoths and Gepids, crossed the Rhine into Gaul. The Western Roman general, Flavius Aetius, cobbled together a ragtag army consisting of the last remnants of the Roman army, Alani auxiliaries, and the independent Visigoths and Franks.

Action. In July, between Troyes and Châlons (shah-LOHN), the armies met. Aetius placed the Visigoths on the left, the Romans on the right, and the Alani in the center, with the Franks in reserve. Attila had the Ostrogoths on the left, the Gepids on the right, and his Huns in the center. Shortly after 5:00 P.M., there commenced "a battle ghastly, confused, ferocious, and unrelenting." The Romans drove off the Gepids, and the Visigoths pushed back the Ostrogoths and then fell upon the flank of the Huns, who retreated to their fortified camp. The following day, neither side was able to resume the battle; 150,000 had been killed. Attila retreated across the Rhine, and the Roman coalition disintegrated.

Consequences. The battle often is portrayed as a victory of "civilization over barbarism," although a victory by the Huns could in fact have resulted in Hun support for the Western Roman throne. As it was, Attila, Aetius, and Valentinian all were soon dead, and the remainder of the Western Empire was cannibalized by its barbarian inhabitants.

ADDITIONAL RESOURCES

Maenchen-Helfen, Otto. *The World of the Huns.* Berkeley: University of California Press, 1973.

Thompson, E. A. *The Huns.* Rev. ed. Peoples of Europe series. Cambridge, Mass.: Blackwell, 1996.

SEE ALSO: Attila; Goths; Huns; Rome, Imperial; Valentinian III.

—Ralph W. Mathisen

CHANDRAGUPTA MAURYA

ALSO KNOWN AS: Candra Gupta; Maurya
BORN: date unknown; India
DIED: c. 286 B.C.E.; Mysore, India
RELATED CIVILIZATIONS: India, Greece, Persia
MAJOR ROLE/POSITION: Emperor

Life. Buddhist tradition claims that Chandragupta Maurya (chuhn-druh-GOOP-tuh MAH-oor-yuh) was of the Mauryan clan and that his family became poor after his father's death in a border clash. Abandoned to a cowherd by callous maternal uncles, he was later sold to a hunter. A Brahman politician and administrator named Kauṭilya then bought and educated him. Legend has it that while sleeping after a meeting with Alexander the Great, he was gently licked by a lion, auguring royal dignity.

On Kauṭilya's advice, Chandragupta gathered a mercenary force and destroyed the Nanda Dynasty, then ruled in the fertile Ganges River Valley (modern Bihār), circa 325 B.C.E. Eliminating all opponents with the help of a secret service, he next took over the Punjab (c. 322 B.C.E.) after Alexander the Great's death. His army of 600,000 helped him assert his dominance from the Himalayas, Kabul, and the Persian borders to the southern tip of India. Using Kauṭilya's tract, the *Arthaśāstra* (300 B.C.E.; *Treatise on the Good,* 1961), Chandragupta governed his empire, taxing the nation's growing commerce, including trade with Greece and Rome.

Chandragupta turned Jain under the influence of a sage who predicted a twelve-year famine. When this tragedy unfolded, the grief-stricken emperor fasted to death at the famous religious site of Belgola in Mysore.

Influence. The founder of the Mauryan Dynasty reigned from around 321 to 297 B.C.E., freeing the country from foreign domination and becoming the first emperor to unify most of India under a single administration.

ADDITIONAL RESOURCES

Bhargava, P. L. *Chandragupta Maurya: A Gem of Indian History.* New Delhi, India: D. K. Printworld, 1996.

Mookerji, Radhakumud. *Chandragupta Maurya and His Times.* 4th ed. Delhi, India: Motilal Banarsidass, 1966.

SEE ALSO: Alexander the Great; Greece; India; Jainism; Kauṭilya; Mauryan Dynasty; Persia.

—Keith Garebian

CHAVÍN DE HUÁNTAR

DATE: 900-200 B.C.E.
LOCALE: Callejon de Huaylas Mountains, Peru
RELATED CIVILIZATION: Chavín
SIGNIFICANCE: The capital city of the Chavín civilization was the center of the Chavín artistic style focusing on the human-feline motif. It had widespread geographic influence throughout Peru, associated with oracles or other religious activities.

Chavín de Huántar (chah-VEEN day WAHN-tahr) was the capital of the Chavín civilization, once considered the earliest Andean civilization, but reevaluated as a significant religious site as evidenced by the widespread copying of its distinctive artistic style focused on the human-feline motif. The Paraíso complex, consisting of Sechín Alto, Huaco Los Reyes, and eight other sites on the north and central coast of Peru actually predate Chavín de Huántar and exhibit earlier evidence of monumental architecture, corporate labor, and high population and are together considered the earliest Andean civilization.

The site of Chavín de Huántar is at 10,227 feet (3,117 meters) in the Callejon de Huaylas of the Andes in Peru. Chavín was excavated by Richard Burger, who found a residential zone in addition to the monumental architecture for which the site is famous. The monumental core of Chavín de Huántar, termed the Castillo (castle), consists of the Old Temple, which is a U-shaped platform facing east, with a circular, sunken plaza. The New Temple, added later, consists of a U-shaped platform facing north, with a square, sunken platform. Fully 25 percent of the platform consists of hidden passageways on two levels. A series of vents and drains is located under the plazas and when these are filled with water, the temple appears to roar like a jaguar, according to Peruvian archaeologist Luis Lumbreras, who has conducted experiments. The central passageways form a cross where a statue called the *Lanzón*, or "smiling god," is located. The *Lanzón* is a human figure carved in low-relief, with the snarling mouth and teeth of a feline. The figure extends to both levels. A hole to the outside may have facilitated its use as an oracle.

Chavín de Huántar was the center of the Early Horizon period (1000 to 300 B.C.E.) art style that spread throughout Peru. It was dominated by the human-feline motif, but raptors, fish, and caymen were also depicted. The style is abstract and two-dimensional. Features of the art style include profile depictions, reversible organization, double-profile heads, bilateral symmetry, a cluttered appearance, and repetitive motifs. The meaning of the iconography is related to the ideology of shamanism, in which a ritual leader is temporarily transformed during a ceremony into a powerful creature and assumes supernatural power. The spread of the Chavín art style is explained by Burger and others as the result of Chavín de Huántar's importance as a pilgrimage and oracle center. The art is an expression of the religion and was used throughout the Andean region wherever suboracles were erected.

ADDITIONAL RESOURCES
Burger, Richard. *Chavín*. New York: Thames and Hudson, 1992.
Moseley, Michael. *The Incas and Their Ancestors*. New York: Thames and Hudson, 1992.

SEE ALSO: Andes, central; Raimondi stone.
—*Heather I. McKillop*

CHICHÉN ITZÁ

DATE: 500's-1000 C.E.
LOCALE: North-central Yucatán state, Mexico
RELATED CIVILIZATIONS: Maya, Toltec
SIGNIFICANCE: Dominated by the Castillo, Temple of the Warriors, El Caracol, and the largest ball court in Mesoamerica, this site exhibits both Maya and Toltec stylistic traits.

Founded by the Itzá Maya in the sixth century C.E., the site of Chichén Itzá (chee-CHEHN eet-SAH) controlled much of the northern lowlands during the Postclassic period and engaged in warfare with other major centers such as Yaxuna and Cobá. The name Chichén Itzá means "the mouth of the well of the Itzá" and is reflective of the site core radiating out from the Cenote of Sacrifice. Offerings to the gods, including jade, gold, pottery, and human sacrifices, were thrown into the *cenote*.

Amazing constructions exhibit images of jaguars, sacrifices, and feathered serpents as well as elaborate stone mosaics. Striking similarities exist between the styles of architecture, art, and iconography of Chichén Itzá and those of the Toltec capital of Tula in Hidalgo. Debates rage as to whether this was reflective of a Maya emulation of the Toltec or a Toltec emulation of the Maya; regardless, it represents a strong interaction between the Maya and cultures of central Mexico.

ADDITIONAL RESOURCES

Coggins, Clemency Chase, and Orrin C. Shane III. "Cenote of Sacrifice: Maya Treasures from the Sacred Well at Chichén Itzá." *Memoirs, Peabody Museum of Archaeology and Ethnography* 10, no. 3 (1992).

Schele, Linda, and Peter Mathews. "Chichén Itza: The Great Ballcourt." In *The Code of Kings*. New York: Charles Scribner's Sons, 1998.

SEE ALSO: Ball game, Mesoamerican; Maya.

—*Jennifer P. Mathews*

The temple of Kukulcan, Maya god of rain, at Chichén Itzá. (PhotoDisc)

CHIFUMBAZE CULTURE

ALSO KNOWN AS: Mwitu
DATE: c. eighth century B.C.E.
LOCALE: East and South Africa
RELATED CIVILIZATION: Bantu speakers
SIGNIFICANCE: The pottery style and iron-smelting traditions characteristic of the East and South African Iron Age were linked with the spread of Bantu speakers throughout the African subcontinent.

The Chifumbaze (chee-fewm-BAH-zay) complex developed in the region west of Lake Victoria. Chifumbaze refers to the early Iron Age industrial complex uncovered in Rwanda, resembling other regional variants of the same time period produced by Bantu speakers. These iron- and pottery-producing Bantu lived in small, dispersed settlements.

Chifumbaze pottery was fired and is characterized by the beveled, fluted rims, narrow cut slits, and stamped bands decorating the exterior. Smiths of the Early Iron Age smelted iron from local ores to produce tools and items for adornment. The introduction of the Chifumbaze tool kit provided farmers with iron technology for field preparation and other economic endeavors, such as hunting and fishing. Tools of this complex include iron axes, hoes, knives, and arrows.

Bantu speakers gained knowledge of iron technology from communities speaking central and eastern Sudanian languages. The technologies were adopted and innovated by Bantu speakers and then diffused out from the western side of Lake Victoria westward into the Congo Basin and southward into southern Africa between approximately 500 B.C.E. and 200 C.E.

ADDITIONAL RESOURCES

Hall, M. *Archaeology Africa*. London: James Currey, 1996.

Phillipson, David W. *African Archaeology*. Cambridge, England: Cambridge University Press, 1993.

Vogel, Joseph A, ed. *Encyclopedia of Precolonial Africa: Archaeology, History, Languages, Cultures, and Environments*. Walnut Creek, Calif.: Altamira Press, 1997.

SEE ALSO: Africa, East and South; Bantu, Congo Basin; Bantu, Mashariki.

—*Catherine Cymone Fourshey*

CHINA

DATE: 8000 B.C.E.-700 C.E.

LOCALE: East Asia

SIGNIFICANCE: A composite of many different peoples inhabiting a vast territory, Ancient China not only was the home of major political states and dynasties but also was the seat of a classical cultural tradition that formed the basis of one of the world's most durable symbols of deeply rooted civilization.

Because of its vast north-to-south and east-to-west expanse, a wide variety of ecological factors contributed to the emergence of early human cultures in China. The existence of several broad phytogeographical zones, with their varying natural and domesticated flora, determined the type of life-sustaining staple crops on which Chinese farmers would become dependant.

Early cultures. Probably as a result of gradually warming post-Ice Age temperatures after about 7500 B.C.E., human populations of the Neolithic era were able to found and develop the earliest cultures in both northern and southern China. Warmer temperatures brought rainfall and extensive vegetation, including forests and grass, to the Liao River Valley. The Liao rises in eastern Manchuria and flows into the Bay of Bohai in northern China. This area would dry out considerably over time, marking the ecological border between nomadic peoples to the north and the southern agrarian groups.

The earliest agricultural pursuits in China involved cultivation of four major seed plants: wheat, millet, rice, and maize. The earliest archaeological sites showing evidence of plant cultivation are millet and rice plantations in the northern and southern regions respectively. Radiocarbon dating of charcoal remains in northern China revealed what may be the oldest evidence of millet cultivation anywhere in the world, going back as far as ten thousand years. People in this area probably combined rudimentary agriculture and hunting and gathering for subsistence. Some sites in northern China have yielded evidence of domestication of both pigs and dogs, while masses of wild animal bones and shells attest to continued hunting and gathering. In central Henan Province between the Yellow and Yangtze River valleys, two signs of early cultural practices were found: a bone flute and pieces of turtle shell bearing rudimentary carved inscriptions.

For many years, archaeologists assumed that the millet-based cultures of northern China developed much earlier than the rice-growing sites to the south. Although early radiocarbon dating proved that rice growing existed in Zhejiang Province (south of modern Shanghai) in the early sixth millennium B.C.E., later finds in the middle Yangtze valley pushed estimates of rice cultures back to the period between 8200 and 7800 B.C.E. At one site, archaeologists found ancient cord-marked pottery, including urns and bowls containing carbonized rice grains whose size and shape suggest domestication of rice, not mere gathering of grains from wild plants.

Archaeologists have relied on differences in human-made implements such as pottery and tools to study regionally distinct prehistoric cultures in China dating to about 5000 B.C.E. The transition from Paleolithic Age chipped and flaked stone implements to Neolithic Age ground and polished stone tools is considered to have been part of the general movement toward agriculturally based cultures. Use of pottery for storing harvests seems also to have been characteristic of early Neolithic cultures.

From the Liao River Basin southward to the coast of China opposite Hainan Island, archaeologists have traced at least seven regional Neolithic cultures between 8500 and 2500 B.C.E. In the north, there was a succession of three interrelated cultures: the Xinglongwa, the Xinle, and the Hongshan. Certain artistic motifs and materials that later became characteristic of more southerly areas of China may have originated here. These include carved jade and the dragon motif. Flat-bottomed pottery vessels evolved into red-patterned bowls and tube shapes by about 5000 B.C.E.

A better-known Neolithic culture was discovered in 1920 in Yangshao, Henan Province, near where the Wei, Jing, Luo, and Fen Rivers join the main northeasterly flow of the Yellow River to the Bay of Bohai. The Yangshao culture was made up of millet-farming communities. A thousand sites from the period between 5000 and 3000 B.C.E. have been excavated. Pottery remains are all reddish in color and are decorated with black or dark brown designs. Their shapes are more diverse than those of Xinle or Hongshan origin and include water bottles and jars. Tripods (*ding*) and ring stands (*dou*) are characteristic of easternmost sites only. Some discoveries suggest a connection between Yangshao art and shamanistic beliefs. For example, on one tomb, a figure, possibly a shaman, is depicted with a dragon on one side and a tiger on the other. Yangshao artistic representations of human figures were typically simple skeletal depictions, but signs of distinction between males and females were included.

The principal rice-growing Neolithic cultures were the Majiabang and Hemudu cultures near the mouth of the Yangtze, the Daxi culture in the central Yangtze River valley, and the somewhat later Dapenkeng culture. The latter ran along the southeast coast of China from points on and opposite Taiwan to the region opposite Hainan Island in the south. All flourished between 5000 and about 2500 B.C.E.

Archaeological investigations of these closely associated cultures show not only cultivation of rice but also dependence on freshwater plants such as water chestnuts and lotus seeds. The Daxi culture zone, with remains of storage facilities and extensive village walls, was perhaps the most advanced in terms of systematic village agricultural organization. The Daxi sites also contain the most extensive examples of Neolithic polished stone tools, including slate sickles. Some distinct pottery shapes, including tall, thin-stemmed stands for flat dishes decorated with black or brown bands were possibly for ceremonial use.

By contrast, Dapenkeng culture seems to have been less developed than the Yangtze communities. Pottery remains are coarse, and decorative effects are limited to cord markings. A main argument underlining the importance of Dapenkeng culture is the probability of linkages between this segment of southern coastal China and areas of linguistically distinct Malayo-Polynesian groupings.

Longshan culture. Discovery in the 1930's of significant archaeological remains in the Shandong and Henan areas provided important clues linking Neolithic cultures to the early Bronze Age Shang civilization. Chinese tradition refers to what archaeologists call the Longshan culture as *wan*

guo, or "ten thousand states." During this period, because of the existence of so many community sites, a pattern of stratified societies emerged, with distinctions between "common" and "privileged" elements. Excavations of graves suggest that a "leader" class took on combined religious, political, and military roles, and that its status was symbolized through association with a variety of increasingly intricate ritual objects.

This period also yielded the first remnants of lacquerware, utilitarian and ritual objects coated with the glossy, resinlike substance drawn from the lacquer tree. Ritual jades ranged from axes to shamanistic objects engraved with depictions of animals. Elements of what would become a structured writing system also appeared for the first time in the Longshan culture.

Apparently religious political elites maintained sep-

HISTORICAL PERIODS OF ANCIENT CHINA

Period	Years
Xia Dynasty	c. 2100-1600 B.C.E.
Shang Dynasty	1600-1066 B.C.E.
Zhou Dynasty	1066 B.C.E.-256 B.C.E.
Western Zhou (1066-771 B.C.E.)	
Eastern Zhou (770-256 B.C.E.)	
Spring and Autumn Period (770-476 B.C.E.)	
Warring States Period (475-221 B.C.E.)	
Qin Dynasty	221-206 B.C.E.
Han Dynasty	206 B.C.E.-220 C.E.
Western Han (206 B.C.E.-23 C.E.)	
Eastern Han (25-220 C.E.)	
Three Kingdoms	220-280
Wei (220-265)	
Shu (221-263)	
Wu (222-280)	
Western Jin	265-316
Eastern Jin	317-420
Southern Dynasties	420-588
Song (420-479)	
Qi (479-502)	
Liang (502-557)	
Chen (557-588)	
Northern Dynasties	386-588
Northern Wei (386-533)	
Eastern Wei (534-549)	
Western Wei (535-557)	
Northern Qi (550-577)	
Northern Zhou (557-588)	
Sui	581-618
Tang	618-907

arate residence complexes in Longshan communities. At some point, groups of elites organized to politically and militarily subject other communities, creating a mixed historical and mythological dawn of dynastic "states" over broader areas associated over time with the geopolitical identity of China. These early communities, called the Xia Dynasty (c. 2100-1600 B.C.E.), are known to the Chinese primarily through heroic epics rather than historical accounts. Historical record keeping, or something approximating it, would not begin until the end of the second millennium B.C.E., during the Shang Dynasty (1600-1066 B.C.E.).

The first traces of the Shang period were found in the late 1930's at the Anyang excavations in northern Henan Province. Excavations at Anyang and in sites along the Huan River uncovered important bronze artifacts, sacrificial burials, and large burial-shaft tombs. Perhaps the most important "new" evidence for the evolutionary progress between Neolithic and Bronze Age cultures came from inscribed oracle bones. These were assumed to be the forerunners of the characters used in the Chinese writing system.

Origins of Chinese writing. A number of theories exist concerning the origins of what would become a very developed system of Chinese writing. One of the earliest sites where archaeologists unearthed pottery and shards covered with marks that may have had symbolic meaning was Banpo, a Yangshao culture site in the Wei River valley. Radiocarbon dating places these near 4773 B.C.E. Markings on burial urns are mainly simple horizontal, vertical, or slanting strokes. Only a few more complex markings were found. These and other discoveries left archaeologists divided as to whether these markings represented only very rudimentary symbolism at the most, or an early form of Chinese characters.

Discoveries from a later Yangshao culture (dated at 4682 B.C.E.) at Jiangzhai in Shandong Province provided further clues as to the origins of characters. Graphlike markings on pottery remnants resemble symbols on later oracle bones from Anyang. It is generally recognized that the Shang culture was the first to devise characters with specific meanings, used primarily in divination practices. Paleographers use the technical term "zodiographs" to describe early Shang characters in which a single inscribed element typically had a single presumed meaning. Tying one character to one word limited such writing considerably. Therefore, specialists looked for progress through two other phases that eventually contributed to more sophisti-

cated use of writing in China, the multivalent and determinative stages. In the former, the practice of "rebus" used essentially identical characters that take on nearly identical or sometimes totally different pronunciation and meaning that emerges only in context. Following this stage, possible ambiguities were lessened by attaching a variety of "determinative" subgraphs to main characters, thus changing both pronunciation and meaning. By the time of the Han Dynasty (206 B.C.E.-220 C.E.), most of the rich classic Chinese literature that had evolved over earlier centuries was recorded in such compound characters. Han lexicologists made clear distinctions between words symbolized by compound characters, or *zi*, and lingering use of single unit zodiographs, or *du ti*.

Major dynasties. From their first capital near what later became Sian in northern China, the Zhou, successors to the loosely structured Shang governing system, held sway over the extensive plains area between Manchuria and the Yangtze. The longevity of the Zhou Dynasty (1066-236 B.C.E.), lasting eight centuries (and longer in some areas), is somewhat misleading. In 1045 B.C.E. during the first long period known as the Western Zhou, Chinese tradition assigned almost cosmic significance to a rather local military conflict between Shang dynastic forces and Wuwang (son of the first Zhou ruler) at Muye. The event was eventually viewed as the mandate of heaven because it ended one form of rule and established another. The third Zhou king, Gongwang, wrote memoirs on early Zhou government. These survive as the *Shujing* (compiled after first century B.C.E.; English translation in *The Chinese Classics*, Vol. 5, Parts 1 and 2, 1872; commonly known as *Classic of History*), perhaps the earliest landmark of classical Chinese literature.

Despite succession struggles after Wuwang's death, Zhou conquests spread rapidly in the central Taihang Mountain area east of the Qin River, a main tributary of the Yellow River. With time, a series of conquests south of the Yellow River and even westward up the Wei River made a third generation of Zhou kings holders of unparalleled political and military force in early Chinese history. A traditional adage associated with their early rulers, who gradually assumed powers that likened them to emperors, was, "Make pliable those distant and make capable those near. Pacify and encourage many countries, large and small." The *Classic of History* credits (whether accurately or not) Muwang (r. 956-918 B.C.E.) with the first systematic code of law to be applied throughout the diverse conquered territories of the Zhou. Muwang's son Gongwang (r. 917-900 B.C.E.) had bronze inscriptions cast proclaiming his responsibility for settling land disputes and generally reforming China's land tenure system.

The second main period of Zhou history is known as the Eastern Zhou (770-256 B.C.E.). By about 800 B.C.E., Zhou imperial authority had been challenged by what became separate states, especially in northern China and on the coastal plains of the Yangtze. Some, such as the Wu and Yue, became almost as important as the presumed imperial state. Two other states, Jin and Qin, intervened at a time when the Zhou rulers were near to losing their hold over their Wei River provinces and helped install Yi Jiu, who took the name Pingwang, in safer territories farther east. Although Pingwang was recognized as the first Eastern Zhou ruler (r. 770-720 B.C.E.), warfare that had begun around 800 B.C.E. never really stopped, making the Eastern dynastic line much less significant than its western predecessors. As the Eastern Zhou entered what Chinese tradition called the Spring and Autumn period (770-476 B.C.E.), "protector" states such as Qin, Qi, and Chu, but particularly Jin, seized on the possibility of expanding their own territorial influence. Qin's ruler Mu Gong, for example, absorbed at least twelve other states in an attempt to extend the influence of his realm back into western territories that had formerly been Zhou.

The complicated period of the Warring States (475-221 B.C.E.) was characterized by a further breaking down of domains that had long since fallen away from Zhou dynastic controls. Qin ascendancy between about 350 and 294 B.C.E. failed to restore the Wei core zone to any identifiable government structure, while alliances encouraging Qin's main rival state Qi created a number of short-lived claims of unified rule. Experts note that, in contrast to earlier concerted Zhou efforts to legislate major institutional controls to support its claims to unified government, rulers in the period of the Warring States depended on sporadic successes by outstanding and able officials to impose taxes or laws. Such "reforms" lasted only as long as the individuals who sponsored them could hold on to power.

Surprisingly, the political fragmentation of the centuries that saw Zhou ascendancy disappear and warring factions rise did not prevent China from experiencing major periods of cultural productivity. Several of the best known classical scholars, including Confucius, who wrote the *Lunyu* (later sixth-early fifth centuries B.C.E.; *The Analects*, 1861); Laozi, the founder of Daoism and the presumed author of the *Dao De Jing*

(possibly sixth century B.C.E., probably compiled late third century B.C.E.; *The Speculations on Metaphysics, Polity, and Morality of "the Old Philosopher, Lau-Tsze,"* 1868; better known as the *Dao De Jing*), and the philosopher Mencius, who wrote *Menzi* (early third century B.C.E.; *The Works of Mencius*, 1861; commonly known as *Menzi*), all lived just before or during these politically troubled centuries. Although Chinese tradition has assigned extremely early origins to major traditional texts such as the *Shujing*, said to have been composed about 3000 B.C.E., most written classics were compiled in book form only after the period of the Warring States. The *Shijing* (traditionally fifth century B.C.E.; *The Book of Songs*, 1937), a collection of more than three hundred poems presumed to be from the Western Zhou period, devoted to extolling heroes from earlier periods, is another example. Compilations drew, of course, on orally transmitted versions that might or might not have reflected the original teachings of ancient masters.

Han and Tang China. By the time of the Han Dynasty (206 B.C.E. to 220 C.E.), many features characteristic of later Chinese periods had taken form. These included state adoption of Confucianism and major territorial expansionist policies, particularly under Emperor Wudi (r. 140 to 87 B.C.E.). Wudi's rule reached as far as Sinkiang and Central Asia in the west, northward to Manchuria and Korea, and southward to Annam (Vietnam).

Another feature of the Han period was the development of state-run civil service examinations to recruit what became an almost elitist body of imperial bureaucrats. A high degree of centralization enabled Han rule to survive a short-lived usurpation of power in 8 C.E. that sought to install a Xin dynastic succession. Return of the Han in 25 C.E. marked the beginning of the Eastern Han period (25-220 C.E.), when the capital moved eastward to Luoyang. Eventual weakening of Han control over such vast territories ended in the division of China for some 350 years into smaller units, beginning with the Three Kingdoms period (220-280 C.E.). Reunification came only under the forceful leadership of Yang Jian, an official from the north who used nomadic cavalry to establish a capital at Chang'an (and later at Anyang) and to bring extensive territory under the sway of the Sui Dynasty (581-618 C.E.). The Sui attempted to broaden support for their religious leadership by patronizing both Buddhism and Daoism. By this date, however, any power hoping to rule inland provinces of China in particular had to cope with possible encroach-

CHINA DURING THE WARRING STATES PERIOD

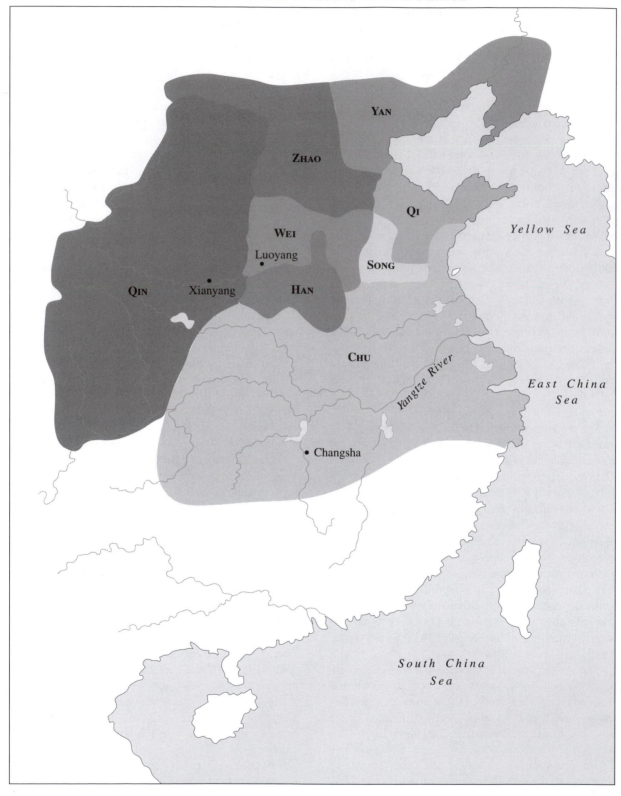

ments by Central Asiatic Turks, some of whom were poised to penetrate the Great Wall. By 615 C.E., the last Sui emperor, Yang Guang, was defeated by Eastern Turks.

The Turks helped a new and long-lived conquering dynasty, that of the Tang (618-907 C.E.), take over many key governing structures established by the Sui (including a major reworking of the Grand Canal to link the Yellow and Yangtze Rivers). The Tang period would mark a return of central imperial control over large reconquered areas (including Korea and Tibet) and a flourishing of state-sponsored artistic creation. Perhaps the most famous remaining examples of Tang painted sculpture are the impressive collections of equestrian statues rediscovered in the mid-twentieth century.

ADDITIONAL RESOURCES

Harper, Donald. *Early Chinese Medical Literature: The Mawangdui Medical Manuscripts*. Vol. 2. London: Kegan Paul, 1997.

Keightley, David N., ed. *The Origins of Chinese Civilization*. Berkeley: University of California Press, 1983.

Loewe, Michael, and Edward L. Shaughnessy, eds. *The Cambridge History of Ancient China from the Origins of Civilization to 221 B.C.E.* Cambridge, England: Cambridge University Press, 1999.

Shaughnessy, Edward L. *Before Confucius: Studies on the Creation of the Chinese Classics*. Albany: State University of New York Press, 1997.

SEE ALSO: Confucianism; Confucius; Daoism; Great Wall of China; Han Dynasty; Laozi; Longshan culture; Mencius; Shang Dynasty; Sui Dynasty; Three Kingdoms; Wudi; Xia Dynasty; Yangshao culture; Yue; Zhou Dynasty; Zhou style.

—*Byron D. Cannon*

CHINCHORRO MUMMIES

DATE: 8000-500 B.C.E.
LOCALE: Atacama Desert, south and central Andes
RELATED CIVILIZATION: South and central Andes
SIGNIFICANCE: The Chinchorro mummies are the oldest found in the Western world and some of the most remarkably well preserved in the world.

The Chinchorro inhabited the Atacama Desert, four hundred miles of South American coastline stretching from Ilo in the southern part of Peru to Antofagasta in northern Chile. The Chinchorro people lived in their extended locale from as early as about 8000 B.C.E. to 500 B.C.E. They lived at the mouths of rivers and subsisted primarily on fishing. Modern peoples would probably know little, if anything, about them were it not for the fame of their well-preserved ancestors, whom they worshiped. During certain yearly celebrations, high-ranking mummies would be brought out in full formal dress to take part in the festivities and visit with family and friends.

The earliest mummy found has been dated to circa 5050 B.C.E. It was discovered in the Camarones Valley, 60 miles (96 kilometers) from Arica, Chile. The art of mummification went through three distinct phases—ash paste, ochre, and mud coverings—over thousands of years, finally disappearing around the first century B.C.E. It was available to all members of society rather than limited to the privileged. The Chinchorro mummies are the oldest known examples of human remains that have been carefully and intentionally mummified. Hundreds of human remains, mummified and otherwise, have been unearthed, opening a wide window on the Andean past.

Mummification developed into a high mortuary art form by 7000 B.C.E. Corpses would be emptied of organs and disassembled. They would be carefully rebuilt using reeds, sticks, clay, bone, and seal skin and preserved by coating the dried skin with a rich black manganese ash paste; later, intense red ochre and clay were used. The bodies may have been dried using hot sand or coals, as evidenced by the scorching of some. The face, body organs and parts, internal and external—including genitalia—were all made of clay, as were elaborate ceremonial helmets and headdresses that were put on top of human-hair wigs up to 24 inches (61 centimeters) long. Their eyes and mouths were often open, suggesting a lifelike appearance. It was believed that the souls of the ancestors would come to inhabit such a mummy if properly cared for and displayed. After many years, or even generations of use, groups of several mummies would be buried together with personal items, mostly pertaining to fishing.

ADDITIONAL RESOURCES

Arriaza, B. *Beyond Death: The Chinchorro Mummies of Ancient Chile*. Washington, D.C.: Smithsonian Institution Press, 1995.

Liitschwager, D., S. Middleton, and H. Pringle. "The Sickness of Mummies." *Discover Magazine*, December 1, 1998.

Wise, Karen. "La ocupacion Chinchorro en villa del mar, Ilo, Peru." *Faceta Arqueologica Andina* 24 (1995): 135-149.

SEE ALSO: Andes, central; Andes, south; Archaic South American culture.

—*Michael W. Simpson*

CHLOTAR I

ALSO KNOWN AS: Lothair
BORN: c. 497 C.E.; northern Gaul
DIED: 561 C.E.; Compiègne, France
RELATED CIVILIZATIONS: Franks, Rome
MAJOR ROLE/POSITION: King of the Franks

Life. As the third surviving son of Clovis and Chlotilde, Chlotar (KLOH-tahr) shared a patrimony with his three brothers upon his father's death in 511 C.E. Given the portion known as the kingdom of Soissons, Chlotar inherited Clovis's power base in northern Gaul.

When the eldest of Chlotilde's sons, Clodomir, was killed in action, Chlotar partitioned his kingdom with his other full brother, Childebert. Chlotar apparently stabbed to death two of his young nephews with his own hand to ensure his claim to their father's throne. He added Childebert's kingdom in 558 C.E., when that king died of "the fever."

Chlotar had seven sons and one daughter by three of his four wives. His youngest child, Chramn, was executed at his command after leading a failed rebellion in alliance with the Bretons.

Influence. Chlotar's place in history is as the Frankish king who, by ruthlessness and longevity, was able to reunite the disparate territories of Clovis under one rule. It was, however, a short-lived enterprise, as Chlotar's lands were divided again among his four surviving sons, Charibert, Guntram, Sigibert, and Chilperic. Nevertheless, Chlotar made a dynamic statement that encouraged the notion that Frankish Gaul should be unified, a lasting and powerful concept for French history.

ADDITIONAL RESOURCES

Thorpe, Lewis, trans. *Gregory of Tours: The History of the Franks*. Harmondsworth, England: Penguin, 1982.

Wood, Ian. *The Merovingian Kingdoms, 450-751*. London: Longman, 1994.

SEE ALSO: Clovis; Franks; Gauls.

—*Burnam W. Reynolds*

CHOLULA

DATE: 200-700 C.E.
LOCALE: 10 miles west of Puebla, Mexico
RELATED CIVILIZATION: Teotihuacán
SIGNIFICANCE: Cholula was a highly important and influential religious city linked to the first urbanized Mesoamerican site, Teotihuacán.

Cholula (choh-LEW-lah) was built in Preclassic times as a satellite city of Teotihuacán. It was a large holy city, containing hundreds of temples and a huge pyramid. The pyramid, which is the largest human-made structure in the Americas, was begun in the Preclassic period and underwent four successive stages of building. The pyramid is lined with corridors and contains frescoes, pottery, bones, and carvings. A residential palace near the pyramid contains long murals of lifelike people shown drinking pulque, an alcoholic beverage made from agave.

Cholula was ruled by one man and six elected nobles. Each noble ruled one of six areas of the city. Excavations show that the area, which functioned as a religious center, had ball courts, dwellings, and well-developed systems of terracing and water control.

The city was part of the Teotihuacán corridor, a trade route from the Preclassic period that monitored movement of materials, products, and people across its various cities. Even after the fall of Teotihuacán in 650 C.E., Cholula remained strong and flourished. It was invaded in about 800 C.E. and subsequently ruled by various groups. It continued to be a large and important city until the Spanish invasion.

ADDITIONAL RESOURCES

Ashwell, Anamaría. *Cholula: La Ciudad Sagrada.* Puebla, Mexico: Volkswagen de México, 1999.

Mountjoy, Joseph B. *Man and Land at Prehispanic Cholula.* Nashville, Tenn.: Vanderbilt University, 1973.

SEE ALSO: Ball game, Mesoamerican; Teotihuacán.
—*Michelle C. K. McKowen*

CHRISTIANITY

DATE: beginning in first century C.E.
LOCALE: Europe, northern Africa, Middle East
RELATED CIVILIZATIONS: Israel, Roman Greece, Imperial Rome
SIGNIFICANCE: Beginning as a small Jewish sect, Christianity grew to become the official religion of the Roman Empire and eventually the dominant religion of European civilization.

Christianity is a religious faith that centers on the person and teachings of Jesus Christ. From the beginning, a great diversity of beliefs existed among various Christian groups, but all groups generally taught that Jesus was divine and that belief in his sacrificial death and resurrection provided a means for the salvation of Christian believers. Most of the earliest Christians appeared disinterested in acquiring political power, and they were organized into local congregations relatively independent of each other. As Christianity grew and expanded, however, the dominant Church was gradually organized into hierarchical structures, and during the fourth century, it began to look to the state to promote its interests and suppress its rivals.

Jesus of Nazareth. The name "Jesus" is the Greek form of a Hebrew name meaning "Jehovah saves," and the Greek word "Christ" means "the anointed one" or "messiah." Most of the information about Jesus's life comes from the four canonical Gospels of the New Testament, although other accounts, such as the Gospel of Thomas, have demonstrated the existence of a variety of early traditions. Jesus was probably born just before the death of King Herod about 4 B.C.E., and following a brief public ministry, he was apparently executed during a Passover celebration, circa 30 C.E. His teachings were essentially Jewish, having much in common with the Pharisee sect. The documents called the Dead Sea Scrolls, discovered between 1947 and 1956, demonstrate that other Jewish movements had ideas that were often similar to those of Jesus and the early Christians.

The complex teachings of Jesus had several aspects. In personal ethics, he taught the value of benevolence toward those in need. Usually endorsing pacifism and nonviolence, he emphasized that a future kingdom would be instituted by divine intervention. Like the Pharisees with whom he debated, he often spoke about rewards in a life following death. Although Jesus was an observant Jew who acknowledged the authoritative nature of Jewish laws (the Torah), he advocated flexibility toward external observances, such as dietary rules and inactivity during the Sabbath. According to the Gospel accounts, he appeared to believe that he and his message were of divine origin, but the Gospels are vague about later controversial issues such as the Trinity and church organization.

Jesus offended and angered orthodox Jews when he insisted that he had the authority to speak in his own name, rejecting many standard doctrines of the religious establishment of the day. The Roman prefect, Pontius Pilate, ordered Jesus to be executed because of fears that his controversial teachings might result in violent conflict among Jews and also because of concern that some Jews believed that Jesus was a promised messiah who would drive the Romans out of Palestine.

The primitive Church. Following the crucifixion, several disciples taught that Jesus had been resurrected and ascended into heaven. At first, most disciples continued to worship in Jewish synagogues on the Sabbath, but gradually they began to constitute a separate religious movement, sometimes meeting on Sundays to commemorate the day of resurrection. Christian teachers reinterpreted and transformed a number of core Jewish beliefs. For instance, rather than practicing animal sacrifice for the forgiveness of sins, some Christians argued that the sacrificial death of the Son of God provided a possibility of salvation for all humans.

Paul, a Hellenized Jew from Asia Minor, is sometimes called "the second founder of Christianity." Following a vision near Damascus, Paul was converted to the new religious movement, and he became convinced that faith in the Christian message provided salvation for both Jews and non-Jews (or Gentiles). He taught, moreover, that Christians did not have to obey all the commands of the Torah and that the ceremony of baptism had replaced the practice of male circumcision. A man of great energy and conviction, Paul converted and baptized a number of Gentiles. About 50 C.E., he traveled to Jerusalem to discuss his ideas with Peter, James, and other leaders of the Jewish Christians. A compromise was worked out so that Gentiles were not required to be circumcised, but they were expected to keep some

of the dietary and sexual rules of the Torah. Before he was beheaded circa 64 C.E., Paul made three long missionary trips, and he explained his doctrines in many epistles, including at least eight that became part of the Christian New Testament.

During the first century, various Christian groups differed greatly in their teachings and rituals. There existed no official list, or canon, of New Testament writings, so that doctrinal beliefs had to be acquired from oral messages and traditions. No centralized organizational structures, moreover, existed to make authoritative decisions concerning orthodox doctrines. Christian teachers often disagreed with each other about the nature of Jesus' divinity, and some Gentile groups entirely rejected the validity of the Hebrew scriptures. Diverse kinds of syncretism with pagan religions emerged. By the second century, a heresy called Gnosticism, teaching salvation through occult knowledge, was wide-

The conversion to Christianity of Constantine the Great, allegedly caused by his vision of a cross lighting up the sky on the day before an important battle, had a major impact on Western civilization. (Library of Congress)

spread, as demonstrated by the Gnostic documents found at Nag Hammadi, Egypt, in 1945.

Orthodoxy and organization. As Christianity expanded, there was a movement to codify recognized doctrines, with a concomitant tendency toward hierarchy and central organization. The adjective "Catholic," meaning general or universal, was widely used to refer to the institutional church of the majority. Major beliefs were summarized in creeds (or professions of faith). In *Adversus haereses* (c. 185; *Against Heresies*, 1872), Bishop Irenaeus argued that the Catholic Church contained the depositary of divine truths, with bishops having the authority to ascertain truthful doctrines because of ordination ceremonies that could be traced back to the original apostles. The ideas of Irenaeus were soon codified into the doctrine of apostolic succession. Likewise, a standard canon of New Testament writings gradually emerged and was officially endorsed by synods of bishops during the fourth century.

In 313 C.E., an imperial edict of toleration legalized Christianity throughout the Roman Empire. Constantine the Great, following his conversion, supported the Christian Church and proscribed many pagan practices. At the time, Saint Athanasius of Alexandria and other orthodox theologians were engaged in a doctrinal conflict with the followers of Arius, who taught that Jesus was not entirely equal with God and had not always existed. To end the dispute, Constantine sponsored an assembly of bishops to meet at Nicaea in 325 C.E., which is considered the first ecumenical council. In addition to producing the Nicene Creed, the council condemned Arianism as a heresy. Those who persisted in the heresy were exiled. About 394 C.E., Theodosius the Great made orthodox Christianity the official religion of the Roman Empire, which often meant the persecution of pagans and Arians.

The development of Christian dogma owed much to the church fathers who lived from the second to the fifth centuries C.E. Because many of them were intellectuals who were trained in Greek philosophy, they often tried to harmonize Christian beliefs with philosophies such as Stoicism and Platonism. The "eight doctors of the church" were especially influential. The four doctors of the Greek Church were Saint Basil of Cappadocia, Gregory of Nazianzus, Saint John Chrysostom, and Saint Athanasius of Alexandria. The four doctors of the Latin Church were Saint Ambrose, Saint Jerome, Saint Augustine, and Pope Gregory the Great.

Christian missionaries were crucially important to the growth of the Christian religion. The activities of Saint Patrick in Ireland and Saint Augustine of Canterbury in England were particularly notable. By converting tribal leaders, missionaries were often able to baptize large groups at one time. Many Christians practiced an ascetic and monastic way of life. Some individuals were quite extreme, such as Saint Simeon Stylites, who sat atop a high pillar for about thirty years. In contrast, monks in organized monasteries combined piety with education and the making of books. About 529 C.E., Saint Benedict of Nursia established an especially influential monastery at Monte Cassino, based on a system of rules providing order and discipline for the daily life of the monks.

The bishop of Rome gradually rose to a position of preeminence in the hierarchy of the church. The title of "pope," which means "father," at first applied to all bishops, but by the fifth century the title was usually limited to the bishop of Rome. Pope Leo I (r. 440-461 C.E.) was especially strong in claiming supreme authority on the theory that the pope was the heir of Peter. Saint Leo helped save Rome from the Huns, and in 451 C.E., he actively helped shape the doctrine of Jesus' divinity at the Council of Chalcedon. Pope Gelasius I (r. 492-496 C.E.) further expanded papal power, adopting the title "vicar of Christ." In times of disorder, powerful popes such as Gregory the Great (r. 590-604 C.E.) became virtual secular rulers in Rome and the surrounding region.

Following the fall of the Western Roman Empire, the tensions and disagreements between the churches of the Greek-speaking East and the Latin-speaking West grew increasingly bitter. During the seventh century, much of the controversy centered on the Monothelite heresy, which taught that the God-man had only "one will." In 680-681 C.E., the Third Council of Constantinople explicitly anathematized Pope Honorius I, who had supported Monothelitism. Roman defenders of papal prerogatives resented the censure. Eleven years later, Rome angered the East when it refused to recognize the ecumenical status of the Fourth Council of Constantinople. Beginning about 725 C.E., the West was horrified by the Eastern practice of iconoclasm, or destruction of religious images. These disagreements contributed to the later schism between Rome and Constantinople.

ADDITIONAL RESOURCES

Chadwick, Owen. *A History of Christianity.* New York: St. Martin's Press, 1995.

Crossan, John. *Jesus: A Revolutionary Biography.* San Francisco: HarperCollins, 1995.

Ehrman, Bart. *After the New Testament: A Reader in Early Christianity*. New York: Oxford University Press, 1998.

Ferguson, Everett. *Backgrounds to Early Christianity*. Grand Rapids, Mich.: Eerdmans, 1994.

McBrien, Richard. *Lives of the Popes*. San Francisco: HarperCollins, 1997.

Urban, Linwood. *A Short History of Christian Thought*. New York: Oxford University Press, 1995.

Vallee, Gerard. *The Shaping of Christianity: The History and Literature of Its Formative Centuries*. Mahwah: Paulist Press, 1999.

SEE ALSO: Ambrose; Arianism; Athanasius of Alexandria, Saint; Augustine, Saint; Saint Augustine of Canterbury, Saint; Basil of Cappadocia, Saint; Bible: Jewish; Bible: New Testament; Chalcedon, Council of; Constantine the Great; Dead Sea Scrolls; Gnosticism; Greece, Hellenistic and Roman; Gregory of Nazianzus; Gregory the Great; Irenaeus, Saint; Israel; Jerome, Saint; Jesus Christ; John Chrysostom, Saint; Judaism; Leo I, Saint; Mary; Monophysitism; Nicaea, Council of; Patrick, Saint; Paul, Saint; Peter, Saint; Rome, Imperial.

—*Thomas T. Lewis*

CHUNQIU

ALSO KNOWN AS: *Wade-Giles* Ch'un-ch'iu
AUTHORSHIP: Anonymous scribes
DATE: fifth century B.C.E.
LOCALE: Pre-Imperial state of Lu
RELATED CIVILIZATION: China
SIGNIFICANCE: The *Chunqiu* was a unique record of events and omens reported to the court of Lu.

The *Chunqiu* (JEWN-chyew; *The Ch'un Ts'ew with the Tso Chuen*, 1872; commonly known as *Spring and Summer Annals*) consists of brief factual entries arranged chronologically, covering the years 722-464 B.C.E. By the fourth century C.E., it was believed to contain the coded historical judgments of Confucius (whose lifetime, 551-479 B.C.E., it overlaps) on people and events, and numerous works have been written to explain this supposed esoteric meaning. Three early commentaries, and in particular the *Zuozhuan* (probably compiled 475-221 B.C.E.; English translation, 1872), with its lively narrative, have almost entirely replaced the text itself in Chinese scholarly usage.

The "judgment" theory of the text has been refuted by scholar George A. Kennedy, which opens the way to treating the *Spring and Summer Annals* as a literal chronicle. This position has been further developed to show that the text reflects a world earlier than and different from that implied by the commentaries, featuring functional cooperation among large and small prebureaucratic states, chivalric rather than mass-army warfare, and a ruler-based rather than a people-based definition of the state. Its value as a source for the history of early China is unexploited but incalculable.

ADDITIONAL RESOURCES
Gardner, Charles S. *Chinese Traditional Historiography*. Cambridge, Mass.: Harvard University Press, 1970.

Kennedy, George A. "Interpretation of the Ch'un-ch'iu." *Journal of Oriental Studies* 62, no. 1 (1942): 40-48.

Legge, James. *The Ch'un Ts'ew with the Tso Chuen*. Oxford, England: Oxford University Press, 1872. Reprint. Taipei: SMC, 1994.

SEE ALSO: China; Confucius.

—*E. Bruce Brooks*

CICERO

ALSO KNOWN AS: Marcus Tullius Cicero
BORN: January 3, 106 B.C.E.; Arpinum, Latium
DIED: December 7, 43 B.C.E.; Formiae, Latium
RELATED CIVILIZATION: Republican Rome
MAJOR ROLE/POSITION: Orator, statesman, philosopher

Life. Sons of a wealthy landowner from Arpinum, Cicero (SIH-suh-roh) and his brother, Quintus Tullius Cicero, were educated to become Roman senators. A junior officer in the Social War (91-87 B.C.E.), Cicero served with young men such as Catiline and Pompey the Great under Pompey's father and Lucius Cornelius

Sulla from 90 to 89 B.C.E. Avoiding civil wars between Sulla and Gaius Marius, he studied law and oratory and married the wealthy, well-born Terentia.

Cicero approved of conservative reforms under the dictatorship of Sulla, but not his excesses. In two early speeches, backed by some of Sulla's supporters, he defended victims of Sulla's regime (80 B.C.E.). Not a strong speaker, he went to Athens, Asia Minor, and Rhodes for further training after Sulla retired (79-77 B.C.E.). He returned much improved, resumed speaking in court, and started up the political ladder. As quaestor (75 B.C.E.), he helped important provincials and Romans in Sicily and obtained needed grain for Rome.

In 70 B.C.E., Cicero brilliantly prosecuted Gaius Verres, a corrupt former governor of Sicily, whom many nobles, including the famous orator Quintus Hortensius Hortalus, defended. He also sought favor with Pompey, who had become a general but was disliked by many nobles. As praetor (66 B.C.E.), Cicero backed the Manilian Law, which gave Pompey command of the Third Mithradatic War. When Marcus Licinius Crassus and Julius Caesar were becoming strong and supported Catiline for consul, Cicero helped block them and was elected consul himself for 63 B.C.E.

After another defeat, Catiline hatched a desperate conspiracy to seize power. Cicero's *In Catilinam* (60 B.C.E.; *Orations Against Catiline* in *The Orations*, 1741-1743) exposed the plot, drove Catiline to death in premature battle, and obtained the execution of other conspirators without trial (63 B.C.E.). Hailed as "father of his country," Cicero glorified himself excessively and alienated even Pompey. When he refused to help the unofficial First Triumvirate of Pompey, Crassus, and Caesar dominate Rome, they supported the violent popular tribune Publius Clodius Pulcher against him. Clodius had Cicero exiled for illegally executing the Catilinarian conspirators (58 B.C.E.) and then attacked Pompey, who supported Cicero's recall (57 B.C.E.). Cicero recovered his confiscated property but divorced Terentia. He then married and soon divorced his young ward Publilia.

Cicero tried to detach Pompey from Crassus and Caesar. They renewed their alliance and forced him to cooperate (56 B.C.E.). Abandoning politics, he tried to reform the Republic through philosophical writings but

Cicero (Library of Congress)

was interrupted by his unwelcome appointment as governor of Cilicia (52 B.C.E.).

After Crassus's death (53 B.C.E.), rivalry between Pompey and Caesar became civil war (49 B.C.E.). Cicero vacillated, joined Pompey, became disillusioned, and accepted Caesar's pardon in 48 B.C.E. The death of his daughter, Tullia, paralyzed him with grief (45 B.C.E.). Although not involved, Cicero welcomed Caesar's assassination (44 B.C.E.). In the *Philippicae* (44-43 B.C.E.; *Philippics*, 1869), he opposed Marc Antony, who allied himself with Caesar's heir, the future Augustus, and had Cicero killed (43 B.C.E.). Nevertheless, Cicero's son, Marcus Tullius Cicero, became consul under Augustus (30 B.C.E.).

Influence. Cicero's surviving speeches, letters, and philosophical works are valuable historical sources for the late Roman Republic. His style and thought have influenced countless orators, writers, thinkers, and statesmen.

ADDITIONAL RESOURCES

Mitchell, Thomas N. *Cicero, the Ascending Years.* New Haven, Conn.: Yale University Press, 1979.

_____. *Cicero, the Senior Statesman.* New Haven,

Conn.: Yale University Press, 1991.

Rawson, Elizabeth. *Cicero, a Portrait.* Ithaca, N.Y.: Cornell University Press, 1983.

SEE ALSO: Antony, Marc; Augustus; Caesar, Julius; Catiline; Clodia; Clodius Pulcher, Publius; Crassus, Marcus Licinius; Mithradatic Wars; Pompey the Great; Rome, Republican; Sulla, Lucius Cornelius; Triumvirate.

—*Allen M. Ward*

CIMMERIANS

DATE: c. 1000-690 B.C.E.

LOCALE: Ukraine

SIGNIFICANCE: The Cimmerians were the first people in recorded history to live in the Russian-Ukrainian area. The Scythians drove them into Asia Minor, where they fought against Phrygia.

Cimmerians (suh-MIHR-ee-ans) were an Indo-European people related to the Thracians. They lived in Ukraine from about 1000 to 690 B.C.E., the oldest historical people in the region. They often raided the cities of Asia Minor. Archaeological evidence indicates that they smelted iron. The Scythians conquered them in the eighth century B.C.E., driving out the leadership in an extended war and absorbing the remainder into their common population. The Greek historian Herodotus writes that in the face of the massive assault of the Scythians, the Cimmerian commoners fled. The Cimmerian aristocracy, unwilling to flee but also unable to fight the Scythians without their followers, fought one

another to the death, and the Scythians entered an uninhabited land.

The fleeing Cimmerians entered Asia Minor pursued by the Scythians. There they fought against the Phrygian king Rusa I and his son and successor Argishti II. They sacked the Phrygian capital at Gordium and captured the environs of Sardis. In the 690's B.C.E., they withdrew to western Asia Minor, where they lived as nomads.

ADDITIONAL RESOURCES

Fasken, William H. *Cimmerians and Scythians.* Haverhill, Mass.: Destiny, 1944.

Kristensen, Anne K. G. *Who Were the Cimmerians, and Where Did They Come From?* Copenhagen: Den Kongelige Danske Videnskabernes Selskab, 1988.

SEE ALSO: Phrygia; Scythia.

—*Frederick B. Chary*

CIMON

BORN: c. 510 B.C.E.; place unknown

DIED: c. 451 B.C.E.; near Citium (modern Larnaca), Cyprus

RELATED CIVILIZATIONS: Athens, Classical Greece

MAJOR ROLE/POSITION: Military leader

Life. Cimon (SI-muhn) was the son of Miltiades the Younger, the hero of the Battle of Marathon (490 B.C.E.), and a Thracian princess. Although Miltiades died in disgrace because of unpaid debts, Cimon restored the

family honor by settling them. His heroic action at the Battle of Salamis (480 B.C.E.) brought him renown, and afterward, he was consistently elected *stratēgos* (general). He was a leader of the conservative party in Athens and stressed the necessity of an alliance with Sparta against the Persians. His handsome stature, successful policies of consolidating the Delian League, and victorious campaigns against Persia maintained his popularity until 461 B.C.E. Then after Sparta humiliated Athens by rejecting the city's help in putting down a revolt of

Cimon. (Library of Congress)

the helots (Spartan serfs), the democratic opposition led by Pericles and Ephialtes of Athens sent him into exile. Pericles later recalled him, and he died on campaign against Persia.

Influence. Cimon was the leading general of Athens and the Delian League from the time of Athenian statesman Themistocles to that of Pericles. Although a leader of the conservative party, he strengthened the position of democratic Athens as the leading city in Greece and successfully fought against the Persians.

ADDITIONAL RESOURCES

Meier, Christian. *Athens: A Portrait of the City in Its Golden Age*. London: John Murray, 1998.

Plutarch. *Plutarch's Lives: The Dryden Translation, Edited with Notes by Arthur Hugh Clough*. New York: Modern Library, 2001.

SEE ALSO: Ephialtes of Athens; Greco-Persian Wars; Greece, Classical; Marathon, Battle of; Miltiades the Younger; Pericles; Salamis, Battle of.

—*Frederick B. Chary*

CINCINNATUS, LUCIUS QUINCTIUS

BORN: early fifth century B.C.E.; place unknown
DIED: after c. 451 B.C.E.; place unknown
RELATED CIVILIZATION: Early Republican Rome
MAJOR ROLE/POSITION: Dictator, military commander, farmer ·

Life. Lucius Quinctius Cincinnatus (LEW-shee-uhs KWIHNK-shee-uhs SIHN-suh-NAT-uhs) is a semi-historical figure who lived in the early Roman Republic. During this period, Rome was engaged in nearly continuous warfare against its Italic neighbors for control of regions around Rome itself. Cincinnatus is the Roman who left his plow to save the Republic.

According to Roman tradition, during a military crisis in 458 B.C.E., Cincinnatus was called from his plow, appointed dictator, and given the command against the Aequi. After saving Rome, he resigned and returned to his farm. He may have been appointed dictator a second time in 439 B.C.E. during a similar crisis. Roman records list him as a consul in 460 B.C.E.

Roman historian Livy (c. 59 B.C.E.-c. 17 C.E.) is the primary ancient source for Cincinnatus, who appears in Books 3 and 4 of Livy's *Ab urbe condita libri* (c. 26 B.C.E.-15 C.E.; *The History of Rome*, 1600). Much of Livy's history consists of "useful and instructive fictions" based on Romans who had lived closer to his time and about whom he had more reliable information. Livy often used his history to glorify Roman virtue and tradition as examples for his contemporaries.

Influence. Consequently, the importance of this story is not its historical accuracy but the traditional Republican virtues displayed by its protagonist, Cincinnatus: courage, selflessness, and dedication to the Republic.

ADDITIONAL RESOURCES

Hornblower, S., and A. Spawforth. eds. *The Oxford Classical Dictionary*. Oxford, England: Oxford University Press, 1996.

Ogilvie, R. M. *A Commentary on Livy, Books 1-5*. Oxford, England: Clarendon Press, 1998.

SEE ALSO: Livy; Rome, Republican.

—*Steve O'Bryan*

CLAUDIAN

ALSO KNOWN AS: Claudius Claudianus
BORN: c. 370 C.E.; Alexandria, Egypt
DIED: c. 404 C.E.; probably Rome
RELATED CIVILIZATION: Imperial Rome
MAJOR ROLE/POSITION: Court poet

Life. Born in Alexandria, Claudian belonged to a fourth and fifth century C.E. group of professional poets of Egyptian background. Having, apparently, attained renown for his Greek poetry in Egypt, he went to Rome about 394 C.E., where he wrote a eulogy on the consuls for 395 C.E., Probinus and Olybrius (sons of the prominent Petronius Probus), of such quality that he drew the attention of the imperial court at Milan. Under the patronage of Stilicho, the emperor Honorius's military commander, Claudian became court poet. His major works include panegyrics on the consulships of Honorius (396, 398, and 404 C.E.), Mallius Theodorus (399 C.E.), and Stilicho (400 C.E.); an epithalamium and some Fescinnine verses celebrating the marriage of Honorius's daughter, Maria (398 C.E.); and invectives against Rufinus (396-397 C.E.) and Eutropius (399 C.E.), Stilicho's rivals in the Eastern Empire (all translated to English in 1922). He also wrote two epics, on the wars with Gildo (*De bello Gildonico*, 398 C.E.; English translation, 1922) and the Goths (*De bellow Getico*, 402 C.E.; English translation, 1922); and unfinished poems on the rape of Proserpina (*De raptu Proserpinae*, n.d.) and on the Gigantomachia (*Gigantomachia*, n.d.). An inscription states that Claudian was rewarded with the title *vir clarissimus* and a bronze statue set up in the forum of Trajan. As Claudian wrote no more poetry after 402 C.E., he is assumed to have died shortly after this date. Though Saint Augustine called Claudian a most perverse pagan, Claudian's poetry is devoid of the usual pantheon of Roman gods (save for his literary work on Proserpina), and his paganism seems to have given no offense to the imperial Christian court.

Influence. Claudian is regarded as the last great poet in the classical tradition. In nine years, he composed some 10,000 verses in polished, flawless Latin hexameters. His style resembles and rivals that of Silver Age Latin poets, especially Publius Papinius Statius and Lucan. His works are important historical sources for his period.

ADDITIONAL RESOURCES

Boyle, A. J., ed. *The Imperial Muse: Ramus Essays on Roman Literature of the Empire, Flavian Epicist to Claudian*. Berwick, Australia: Aureal 1990.

Cameron, Alan. *Claudian: Poetry and Propaganda at the Court of Honorius*. Oxford, England: Clarendon Press, 1970.

Gruzelier, Claire. *De raptu Proserpinae*. Oxford, England: Clarendon Press, 1993.

Hall, John B. *Prolegomena to Claudian*. London: University of London, 1986.

Long, Jacqueline. *Claudian's In Eutropium: Or, How, When, and Why to Slander a Eunuch*. Chapel Hill: University of North Carolina Press, 1996.

SEE ALSO: Augustine, Saint; Egypt, Ptolemaic and Roman; Goths, Visigoths, Ostrogoths; Lucan; Rome, Imperial; Statius, Publius Papinius; Stilicho, Flavius.

—*Judith Lynn Sebesta*

CLAUDIUS

ALSO KNOWN AS: until 41 C.E., Tiberius Claudius Drusus Nero Germanicus; later Tiberius Claudius Caesar Augustus Germanicus
BORN: August 1, 10 B.C.E.; Lugdunum, Gaul (modern Lyon, France)
DIED: October 13, 54 C.E.; Rome, Italy
RELATED CIVILIZATION: Imperial Rome
MAJOR ROLE/POSITION: Roman emperor

Life. Claudius was the son of Drusus (brother of the emperor Tiberius) and Antonia (daughter of Octavia and Marc Antony). Claudius suffered from a disability that caused him to walk with a limp, twitch his head, and stammer when he spoke, possibly cerebral palsy. During his life, he wrote histories of the Etruscans and the Carthaginians, and his own autobiography. No examples of his work have been found.

Claudius became emperor of Rome on January 24, 41 C.E., following the assassination of his nephew Caligula. During Claudius's reign, he expanded the borders of Rome to include regions of Britain and the Mediterranean. In Rome, he built the Aqua Claudia and the Anio Novus aqueducts, and the ill-fated harbor Portus. He gradually eliminated powers held by the Roman senate in order to secure his position.

Claudius was married four times; he divorced his first two wives. The young Valeria Messallina was his third wife; in 48 C.E., she was charged with treason and executed. His fourth wife was his niece Agrippina the Younger; she is rumored to have caused his death by feeding him poisoned mushrooms.

Influence. Through expansion of territory and reduction of senate powers, Claudius shaped a future that would see the emperors of Rome flourish for another four hundred years.

ADDITIONAL RESOURCES

Graves, Robert. *I, Claudius*. New York: Random House, 1934.

Scarre, Chris. *Chronicle of the Roman Emperors*. London: Thames and Hudson, 1995.

SEE ALSO: Agrippina the Younger; Antonia the Younger; Britain; Carthage; Etruscans; Messallina, Valeria; Nero; Rome, Imperial.

—*Kari Naso*

Claudius. (Library of Congress)

CLAUDIUS CAECUS, APPIUS

FLOURISHED: early fourth to late third century B.C.E.
RELATED CIVILIZATION: Republican Rome
MAJOR ROLE/POSITION: Political and military leader

Life. Appius Claudius Caecus (AP-ee-uhs KLAWD-ee-uhs SEE-kuhs), censor in 312 B.C.E. and consul in 307 and 296 B.C.E., is in essence the earliest individual Roman whose life is known to modern historians in any convincing detail. As censor, he commissioned the first paved Roman road from Rome to Capua and the first Roman aqueduct. He reorganized the Roman system of voting districts so that the sons of freedmen were counted in the annual census for the first time. This was probably done so that the unlanded wealthy could be counted as liable to military obligation. Individual Romans had always been liable to military service based on the value of their land. The introduction of the first Roman silver coins about this time and a sudden increase in new building construction suggests a fast-growing economy in nonagricultural sectors. Many former slaves—at this date almost exclusively captured enemy soldiers—had become wealthy in Rome's expanding trade. Appius's reforms may therefore be seen as an attempt to capitalize on this new wealth. The censor of 304 B.C.E., Quintus Fabius Maximus, redistributed these freedmen throughout the noncity voting districts so that their relative predominance in the four city districts would not unduly affect elections.

Influence. Appius enjoyed a great deal of prestige in his day. For example, as an old man, he was carried into the senate house circa 280 B.C.E. to harangue his colleagues against a treaty with King Pyrrhus of Epirus. Because of the high regard in which he was held, some of his speeches in the senate were preserved for hundreds of years.

ADDITIONAL RESOURCE
Cornell, T. J. *The Beginnings of Rome.* London: Routledge, 1994.

SEE ALSO: Fabius Maximus, Quintus; Rome, Republican.

—*Randall S. Howarth*

CLEISTHENES OF ATHENS

BORN: c. 570 B.C.E.; place unknown
DIED: after 507 B.C.E.; place unknown
RELATED CIVILIZATIONS: Athens, Classical Greece
MAJOR ROLE/POSITION: Political leader

Life. Born into Athens' most powerful family, the Alcmaeonids, Cleisthenes (KLIS-thuh-neez) of Athens held the archonship in 525/524 B.C.E., but soon afterward his family was driven into exile by the tyrant Hippias of Athens. Spending lavishly at Delphi to influence the oracle to pressure the Spartans, Cleisthenes convinced King Cleomenes to overthrow the tyranny in 510 B.C.E., but in the ensuing factional struggles, he was outdone by his rival Isagoras, who was elected archon in 508/507 B.C.E. In reaction, Cleisthenes appealed to the people, leading Isagoras to call in Cleomenes, but popular support for Cleisthenes sent Isagoras and the Spartan king packing.

Refashioning Solon's constitution in order to create a less fractious government and enhance his own political position, Cleisthenes then established the basic machinery of the fifth century B.C.E. democracy, creating the ten tribes and the Council of Five Hundred. He also created the institution of ostracism and established contacts with Persia in order to protect the new government from the Spartan threat, which ended with the failed Peloponnesian invasion of 507 B.C.E. Having thus set Athens on the path from an aristocratic tribal state to a true democracy, Cleisthenes disappeared, presumably dying of old age.

Influence. Whatever Cleisthenes' personal motives, the government he created enabled the development of the fifth century B.C.E. democracy and all that would mean to the West.

ADDITIONAL RESOURCES
Aristotle. *The Politics, and the Constitution of Athens.* Rev. ed. Edited by Stephen Everson. New York: Cambridge University Press, 1996.
Burn, A. R. *Persia and the Greeks: The Defense of the West, 546-478 B.C.* Stanford, Calif.: Stanford University Press, 1984.
Herodotus. *The Histories.* Translated by Robin Waterfield. New York: Oxford University Press, 1998.
Hignett, C. *A History of the Athenian Constitution.* Oxford, England: Oxford University Press, 1952.

SEE ALSO: Delphi; Greece, Classical; Hippias of Athens; Solon.

—*Richard M. Berthold*

CLEISTHENES OF SICYON

ALSO KNOWN AS: Kleisthenes of Sikyon
BORN: seventh century B.C.E.; Greece
DIED: c. 570 B.C.E.; Greece
RELATED CIVILIZATION: Archaic Greece
MAJOR ROLE/POSITION: Statesman, military leader

Life. Cleisthenes (KLIS-thuh-neez) was tyrant of Sicyon (SIHS-ee-ahn) from about 600 to 570 B.C.E. At war with Argos, Cleisthenes of Sicyon banned the Homeric epics because of their praise of the Argives, stripped honors from Adrastus, an Argive hero buried in Sicyon, and gave the Sicyonian tribes new names differing from the Dorian names used at Argos.

Cleisthenes took part in the First Sacred War (c. 595 B.C.E.) and won the chariot race at the Pythian Games (582 B.C.E.), after which he dedicated two buildings at

Delphi. The metopes from one of these buildings are among the finest examples of archaic Greek sculpture. After winning the chariot race at Olympia (576? B.C.E.), he invited the best of the Greeks to compete for the hand of his daughter Agariste. After entertaining and testing the suitors for a full year, Cleisthenes chose Megacles of Athens as his son-in-law.

Influence. Cleisthenes' career shows how a tyrant could use religious and cultural propaganda and illustrates a tyrant's concern for magnificence and display. He was the grandfather of Cleisthenes of Athens and an ancestor of Pericles and Alcibiades of Athens.

ADDITIONAL RESOURCES

Griffin, Aubrey. *Sikyon*. Oxford, England: Clarendon Press, 1982.

Ogden, Daniel. "Cleisthenes of Sicyon, Leuster." *Classical Quarterly* 43 (1993) 353-363.

Sealey, Raphael, *A History of the Greek City States*. Berkeley: University of California Press, 1976.

SEE ALSO: Agariste; Alcibiades of Athens; Cleisthenes of Athens; Greece, Archaic; Pericles; Sacred Wars.

—George E. Pesely

CLEMENT OF ALEXANDRIA

ALSO KNOWN AS: Titus Flavius Clemens
BORN: c. 150 C.E.; probably Athens
DIED: c. 215 C.E.; place unknown
RELATED CIVILIZATIONS: Coptics, Imperial Rome
MAJOR ROLE/POSITION: Teacher, writer, philosopher

Life. Clement of Alexandria became a convert to Christianity as an adult. His travels took him through Greece and Palestine. He settled in Alexandria, where he studied under the Greek philosopher Pantaenus, head of a "school of oral instruction." This catechetical school offered instruction in pagan philosophy as well as Christian theology. Clement, who became head of the school (c. 190 C.E.), taught that while the fullest expression of God was found in Jesus Christ, the study of philosophy was an indispensable component of a Christian's training. This is reflected in Clement's repeated references to Jesus Christ as "the Word" (*logos*, or reason), the influence of Plato and the Stoics in his writings, and his teaching that the educated Christian was the "true Gnostic" (*gnosis*, or knowledge).

Clement and his successor Origen taught that an allegorical rather than a literal interpretation of the Scriptures would reveal their true meaning. The persecution of the Christians in 202 C.E. under Emperor Lucius Septimius Severus (r. 193-211) forced Clement to flee to Caesarea in Cappadocia, where he died circa 215 C.E.

Influence. The Coptic Bible used by the Coptic Orthodox Church was translated from the Greek under the direction of Pantaenus and Clement.

ADDITIONAL RESOURCES

Buell, D. *Making Christians: Clement of Alexandria and the Rhetoric of Legitimacy*. Princeton, N.J.: Princeton University Press, 1999.

Karavites, P. *Evil, Freedom, and the Road to Perfection in Clement of Alexandria*. Leiden, Netherlands: E. J. Brill, 1999.

SEE ALSO: Christianity; Origen; Philosophy; Rome, Imperial; Severus, Lucius Septimius.

—Roger S. Evans

CLEMENT I

ALSO KNOWN AS: Clemens Romanus; Clement of Rome; Saint Clement
BORN: date unknown; possibly Rome
DIED: c. 99 C.E.; perhaps in the Crimea
RELATED CIVILIZATION: Imperial Rome
MAJOR ROLE/POSITION: Bishop of Rome

Life. Little is known of Clement I's life except what appears in the writings of other early Christians. Saint Hegesippus (c. 110-180 C.E.), Saint Irenaeus (c. 115-c. 202 C.E.), and Saint Jerome (c. 347-419/20 C.E.) name Clement as the fourth bishop of Rome, which would put his reign from 88 to 97 C.E. Internal evidence from *Epistola ad Corinthios I* (first century C.E.; *The Epistle of St. Clement, Bishop of Rome*, 1899), traditionally attributed to Clement, suggests that these dates are correct. When the author of *The Epistle of St. Clement* speaks of "the suddenly bursting and rapidly succeeding calamities and untoward experiences that have befallen us," he may be referring to the persecution initiated by the emperor Domitian (r. 81-96 C.E.) in 95-96 C.E.

However, no internal evidence indicates who the author of the *The Epistle of St. Clement* actually was. The author does not name himself, and the introduction to the letter simply reads, "The Church of God which sojourns in Rome to the Church of God which sojourns in Corinth."

Influence. It appears the letter eventually gained wide acceptance. Bishop Dionysius of Corinth (fl. c. 170 C.E.) indicates that the Corinthian church often read the letter "formerly sent to us from Clement." Also, Eusebius of Caesarea (c. 260-c. 399 C.E.) says that "this letter was publicly read in the common assembly in many churches."

ADDITIONAL RESOURCES

Bowe, B. *A Church in Crisis*. Minneapolis: Fortress Press, 1988.

Fuellenbach, J. *Ecclesiastical Office and the Primacy of Rome*. Washington, D.C.: Catholic University of America Press, 1980.

Jeffers, James S. *Conflict at Rome*. Minneapolis: Fortress Press, 1991.

Clement I. (Library of Congress)

SEE ALSO: Christianity; Domitian; Eusebius of Caesarea; Irenaeus, Saint; Jerome, Saint; Rome, Imperial.

—*Roger S. Evans*

CLEON OF ATHENS

BORN: date and place unknown
DIED: 422 B.C.E.; Amphipolis, Macedonia
RELATED CIVILIZATION: Classical Greece
MAJOR ROLE/POSITION: Political leader

Life. Cleon of Athens, the first demagogue, was a tanner who made enough money to enter political life by 430 B.C.E. He was perhaps a member of the *boulē*, or council, in 428 B.C.E., and in 427 B.C.E. in the Mytilene debate, he proposed the execution of all male Mytileneans after that town's revolt in 428 B.C.E. He was successful, but the next day, the assembly reversed its decision. In 425 B.C.E., Cleon's criticism of Nicias of Athens's ability to capture besieged Spartans on

Sphacteria led to his extraordinary command, and with Demosthenes' help, he captured the Spartans. When Sparta sued for peace, Cleon blocked the proposals.

Cleon's influence was now paramount in Athens. He was elected *stratēgos* (general) for 424 B.C.E., increased the tribute paid by the Athenian allies and pay for the jurors, and was perhaps responsible for Thucydides' exile for failing to save Amphipolis from Sparta. In 422 B.C.E., as *stratēgos*, he marched to Amphipolis, where he was defeated and killed in battle by a Spartan force. The presentation of Cleon in contemporary sources by Thucydides and Aristophanes is biased, but there is no question that he was an able orator who wanted to increase Athens' power.

Influence. Cleon was the first demagogue in the Athenian democracy and set a trend for the non-noble "new politicians" who followed him, thereby changing the dynamics of Athenian political life.

ADDITIONAL RESOURCES

Kagan, Donald. *The Archidamian War.* Ithaca, N.Y.: Cornell University Press, 1974.

Woodhead, A. G. "Thucydides' Portrait of Cleon." *Mnemosyne* 13 (1960): 289-317.

SEE ALSO: Archidamian War; Aristophanes; Brasidas of Sparta; Greece, Classical; Nicias of Athens; Thucydides.

—Ian Worthington

CLEOPATRA VII

ALSO KNOWN AS: Cleopatra Philopator
BORN: 69 B.C.E.; Alexandria, Egypt
DIED: August 3, 30 B.C.E.; Alexandria, Egypt
RELATED CIVILIZATIONS: Ptolemaic Egypt, Rome
MAJOR ROLE/POSITION: Pharaoh of Upper and Lower Egypt

Life. Cleopatra VII was the third child born to Ptolemy XII Neos Dionysus (Auletes). She was educated in Greek and Egyptian traditions and bred for politics. As a child, she showed not only a remarkable intelligence but also a talent for learning languages. She was the only member of the Ptolemaic line able to speak the common language (Egyptian) of their subjects, a skill that would serve her in uniting Upper and Lower Egypt during her reign as pharaoh (51-30 B.C.E.).

Upon the death of Ptolemy XII in 51 B.C.E., Cleopatra became queen at the age of eighteen. According to Egyptian tradition, she married her brother Ptolemy XIII, then aged ten, to serve as co-ruler with him. This was a marriage in name only, and as the elder of the sovereigns, she was free to rule as she chose.

In 48 B.C.E., Ptolemy XIII's guardians forced Cleopatra from the throne. At about this time, Roman ruler Julius Caesar arrived in Alexandria in pursuit of Pompey the Great. He and Cleopatra met and fell in love. Caesar helped Cleopatra regain her throne, and she became co-ruler with her younger brother, Ptolemy XIV.

In 47 B.C.E., Cleopatra gave birth to Caesar's son. The child, Ptolemy XV Caesar, was called Caesarion by the Egyptians. At Caesar's invitation in 46 B.C.E., Cleopatra went to stay in Rome and took Caesarion and Ptolemy XIV with her. They remained in Rome until Caesar was assassinated in 44 B.C.E.

In 41 B.C.E., Marc Antony invited Cleopatra to Tarsus (Turkey). She and Antony fell in love, had twins, and married in 37 B.C.E. The two had ambitious goals for an Egyptian-Roman alliance. Antony, one of three rulers of Rome, hoped to become sole ruler. Cleopatra hoped to put their children, but es-

Cleopatra VII. (North Wind Picture Archives)

pecially her son Caesarion, in line as future Roman rulers.

Her ambitious plans for Egypt came to ruins in 30 B.C.E. Antony mistakenly thought Cleopatra was dead and killed himself. She committed suicide soon after learning of his suicide. Upon her death, the Ptolemaic line of Egyptian pharaohs ended. Caesarion was executed by the Romans, who feared he would claim to be heir to Caesar and thus Roman ruler.

Influence. Cleopatra's diplomatic acumen and facility for foreign languages allowed her to unite, for a brief time, the Upper and Lower Nile valleys, earning her the title "mistress of two lands." She successfully ruled with her two brothers and with her son, Ptolemy Caesar. Her ability to speak Egyptian, and her concern for the welfare of her subjects, earned her their respect

and admiration. As the last ruler of the Macedonian dynasty in Egypt, Cleopatra kept Egypt out of Roman hands through political and romantic alliances with Julius Caesar and Marc Antony.

ADDITIONAL RESOURCES

Flamarian, Edith. *Cleopatra: The Life and Death of a Pharaoh*. New York: Harry N. Abrams, 1997.

Foss, Michael. *The Search for Cleopatra*. New York: Arcade, 1997.

SEE ALSO: Actium, Battle of; Antony, Marc; Caesar, Julius; Egypt, Ptolemaic Dynasty; Ptolemaic and Roman; Rome, Republican.

—Lisa A. Wroble

CLODIA

BORN: c. 95 B.C.E.; Rome
DIED: after 45 B.C.E.; Rome
RELATED CIVILIZATION: Republican Roman
MAJOR ROLE/POSITION: Lover of Catullus, political influence

Life. Most of Clodia's (KLOHD-ee-uh) life is known only through hostile sources such as Cicero. It is known that she descended from a famous Roman consular family that included Appius Claudius Caecus, censor in 312 B.C.E. Appius was famous because he was instrumental in the peace agreement with Pyrrhus and initiated the construction of aqueducts and the paving of the Appian Way.

Clodia married twice. By 62 B.C.E., she had married her first cousin, Quintus Caecilius Metellus Celer, and after his death, she married Lucius Licinius Lucullus. In 59 B.C.E., Clodia met the twenty-seven-year-old poet Catullus, who wrote a series of love poems celebrating her as Lesbia. However, upon the sudden death of her husband (59 B.C.E.), Clodia left Catullus in favor of Marcus Caelius Rufus, who was even younger than Catullus. After Caelius left Clodia, she sued him in 56 B.C.E. for attempting to poison her and for failure to return a sum of money she had lent him. Cicero willingly took over Rufus's defense against these charges because it gave Cicero the opportunity to attack Clodia's brother, Publius Clodius Pulcher. Clodia's brother had led attacks against Cicero, resulting in Cicero's temporary exile. In his defense speech, Cicero portrays

Clodia as Rome's most famous prostitute, although he as well as his friend Titus Pomponius Atticus had used Clodia as a messenger in their dialogues with Clodius. Furthermore, Atticus gathered information through her about Clodius's plans, which helped Cicero gauge his own political fortunes.

Influence. Clodia is an example of first century B.C.E. Roman women who chose to differ from the model matron propagandized by men. She was well educated and a literary patroness. Through her brother, Clodia played an indirect role in Roman politics. She owned property in Rome and a villa in Baiae on the Bay of Naples. The frequent gatherings there made her easy prey to the character assassination in Cicero's speech and subsequent treatments of her by other writers. She was probably still alive in 45 B.C.E.

ADDITIONAL RESOURCES

Cantarella, Eva. *Pandora's Daughters*. Baltimore: Johns Hopkins University Press, 1987.

Cicero. *Pro Caelio*. Loeb Classical Library 13. Cambridge, Mass.: Harvard University Press, 1970.

Gruen, Erich S. *The Last Generation of the Roman Republic*. Berkeley: University of California Press, 1974.

SEE ALSO: Catullus; Cicero; Claudius Caecus, Appius; Clodius Pulcher, Publius; Licinius Lucullus, Lucius; Rome, Republican.

—Brigitte Hees

CLODIUS PULCHER, PUBLIUS

BORN: c. 92 B.C.E.; place unknown
DIED: January, 52 B.C.E.; Bovillae, Latium, Italy
RELATED CIVILIZATION: Republican Rome
MAJOR ROLE/POSITION: Politician

Life. Publius Clodius Pulcher (PUHB-lee-uhs KLOHD-ee-uhs PUHL-kuhr) is best known as the arch-enemy of Cicero, who testified against him on the charge of profaning the rites of the Bona Dea in 61 B.C.E. After serving as quaestor in Sicily, he had himself adopted into a plebeian *gens*—he was patrician by birth—probably with support from Julius Caesar, in order to seek the office of tribune of the *plebs* (common people), which he then held in 58 B.C.E. Along with other legislation, he sponsored a bill to exile anyone who had executed Roman citizens without trial. This was aimed particularly at Cicero, who was exiled but later recalled. In 52 B.C.E., Clodius stood for the office of praetor, but before the elections could take place, he was murdered by Titus Annius Milo, a strong supporter of Cicero.

Influence. Clodius has often been viewed as a pawn of more powerful figures, namely Caesar, but he has begun to be seen as an independent force in Roman politics. He was the brother of Clodia, who was attacked by Cicero in 56 B.C.E. in the speech *Pro Caelio* (English translation in *The Orations*, 1741-1743) and who was often thought to lie behind the Lesbia of Catullus's poems.

ADDITIONAL RESOURCES

Gruen, E. S. *The Last Generation of the Roman Republic*. Berkeley: University of California Press, 1974.
Tatum, W. J. *The Patrician Tribune: Publius Clodius Pulcher*. Chapel Hill: University of North Carolina Press, 1999.

SEE ALSO: Caesar, Julius; Catullus; Cicero; Clodia; Rome, Republican.

—Christopher Nappa

CLOVIS

ALSO KNOWN AS: Chlodovech; Chlodovic
BORN: c. 466 C.E.; probably Tournai
DIED: November 29, 511 C.E.; Paris
RELATED CIVILIZATIONS: Franks, Gaul, Merovingian Dynasty
MAJOR ROLE/POSITION: Military and political leader

Life. In 481 C.E., Clovis succeeded his father Childeric I as the leader of the Salian Franks. Originally centered at Tournai, Clovis expanded his territory southward and eventually established headquarters in Paris. By defeating Syagrius near Soissons, the Allemanni around the Rhine River, and the Visigoths in the Loire Valley, Clovis increased his domination of Gaul. Upon the urging of his wife, Clotilda, and after praying successfully for victory in battle, Clovis converted to Christianity. Thereafter, Clovis associated closely with the Gallo-Roman bishops, made donations to monasteries and churches, and called for a church council at Orléans. The Lex Salica, a law code combining Germanic and Roman elements, was commissioned during his reign. Upon Clovis's death, the administration of his territorial lands was divided among his four sons.

Clovis. (North Wind Picture Archives)

Influence. The Frankish kingdom established by Clovis continued to expand in the sixth century C.E. until it encompassed much of Gaul. As a result, Clovis has been referred to as the founder of the French monarchy. The alliance of Clovis with orthodox Christianity, rather than Arianism, furthered the development of a Christian Europe.

ADDITIONAL RESOURCES

Geary, Patrick. *Before France and Germany: The Creation and Transformation of the Merovingian World.* New York: Oxford University Press, 1988.

James, E. *The Origins of France from Clovis to the Capetians.* New York: St. Martin's Press, 1982.

Wood, Ian. "Gregory of Tours and Clovis." *Revue belge de philologie et d'histoire* 63 (1985): 249-272.

_____. *The Merovingian Kingdoms, 450-751.* London: Longman, 1994.

SEE ALSO: Allemanni; Arianism; Chlotar I; Christianity; Franks; Gauls; Goths; Merovingian Dynasty.

—*Shelley Amiste Wolbrink*

CLOVIS TECHNOLOGICAL COMPLEX

DATE: 11,500-10,500 B.C.E.
LOCALE: Clovis, New Mexico, North America
RELATED CIVILIZATION: Paleo-Indian tradition
SIGNIFICANCE: The Clovis people, who lived across much of North America, fashioned distinctive tools and weapons from stone, using some of them to hunt megamammals.

The Clovis technological complex was named after a town in New Mexico near Blackwater Draw where James Ridgely Whiteman found distinctive spear points among the bones of Columbian mammoths (*Mammuthus columbi*) in 1929. Edgar Billings Howard later confirmed the association in 1932. Besides New Mexico, Clovis sites have been found across North America, from southern Canada to northern Mexico, and extending west to east from the Pacific to the Atlantic Ocean. Clovis people lived in North America during the late-glacial period, which marks the last gasp of the last Ice Age, a time of regional cooling and ice-margin fluctuations, extremely rapid and widespread environmental change, and megamammal extinctions.

Clovis peoples made distinctive weapons and tools including percussion-produced bifaces with distinctive flutes removed from the base of one or more sides, scrapers, knives, gravers, and burins, as well as blades struck from prepared cores, red ochre, and ground, incised, cut, and flaked bone and ivory. Settlement patterns include the kill and scavenging sites of big and small game animals, high-quality stone procurement and workshop sites, short-term habitations, base camps, caches, and burials. Clovis sites are not dispersed across the landscape; rather, they typically occur on overviews and riparian settings, especially those associated with small tributary streams, springs, and high-quality stone source areas. Clovis flaked-stone artifacts have been reported from sites located more than 620 miles (1,000 kilometers) from their source area. Clovis peoples selected high-quality stones that were tenacious, with aesthetic characteristics such as exquisite coloring, translucency, and smooth texture. Caches contain bifaces in various stages of manufacture and in early states of their usable life; many are more than 8 inches (200 millimeters) in length.

Although the artifact assemblage suggests that Clovis groups did nothing but hunt and process game, the animal remains suggest that the Clovis economy was actually a mixed foraging strategy, with an emphasis on the hunting of megamammals. Clovis groups had access to a wider range of species than was available to subsequent Paleo-Indian populations. Many of the smaller species provided Clovis groups with a source of backup or second-choice foods.

The use of red ochre and rock crystal quartz may be associated with Clovis belief systems. As in the Old World, Upper Paleolithic period, red ochre may be associated with ideological aspects of hunting, reproduction, birth, and death. The presence of finished weapons, utilitarian tools, and beads in association with red ochre mines suggests that these localities were used for ceremonial functions. Burial caches of exquisitely knapped tools made from exotic materials may be indicative of ceremonial activity. Clovis peoples used bone, ivory, and stone as art media. Decorative motifs were angular, subparallel, zigzagged, and crosshatched. Although art is quite scarce, incising and painting were used.

ADDITIONAL RESOURCES

Bradley, B. A. "Paleo-Indian Flaked Stone Technology in the North American High Plains." In *From Kostenki to Clovis: Upper Paleolithic-Paleo-Indian Adaptations*, edited by O. Soffer and N. D. Praslov. Plenum Press: New York, 1993.

Frison, G. C. "Paleoindian Large Mammal Hunters on the Plains of North America." *Proceedings of the National Academy of Science* 95 (1998): 14,576-14,583.

Haynes, C.V. "Contributions of Radiocarbon Dating to the Geochronology of the Peopling of the New World." In *Radiocarbon Dating After Four Decades*, edited by R. E. Taylor, A. Long, and R. S.

Kra. New York: Springer-Verlag, 1992.

_____. "Geoarchaeological and Paleohydrological Evidence for a Clovis-Age Drought in North America and Its Bearing on Extinction." *Quaternary Research* 35 (1991): 438-450.

Taylor, R. E., C. V. Haynes, and M. Stuiver. "Clovis and Folsom Age Estimates: Stratigraphic Context and Radiocarbon Calibration." *Antiquity* 70 (1996): 515-525.

SEE ALSO: Archaic North American culture; Folsom technological complex; Paleo-Indians in North America.

—*Kenneth B. Tankersley*

COBÁ

DATE: c. 100-700 C.E.
LOCALE: Yucatán Peninsula, Mexico
RELATED CIVILIZATION: Maya
SIGNIFICANCE: One of the largest Classic Maya cities, with great pyramids and impressive roads.

Cobá (ko-BAH) is located 12 miles (19 kilometers) from the coast in the northeastern part of Mexico's Yucatán Peninsula. The site lies north of the Maya center of Tulum and is near the center of Quintana Roo province. Human occupation began at Cobá about 100 C.E., and the city reached its zenith of development in the Late Classic period (600-900 C.E.), when its estimated population of forty thousand made it one of the larger cities in all Mesoamerica. Dates recorded on stone markers (stelae) range from 613 to 780 C.E.

At its height, Cobá was a powerful regional city-state whose large population sprawled outward from the core in a 28-square-mile (73-square-kilometer) zone. The central area of the ruins at Cobá consists of major pyramid and palace groupings scattered around two large, shallow lakes. Other satellite ruins are dispersed amid five small lakes. Although most of Cobá's ruins are poorly preserved, the relatively small extent of excavation work to date provides a glimpse of the city's former greatness.

Between 600 and 800 C.E., Cobá was apparently a diversified city composed of residential wards and ceremonial complexes and home to many skilled craftspeople. The site's architectural style indicates a link with Classic Maya centers in the Petén area of Guatemala such as Tikal. The complex known as Group B

The Nohoch Mul (Great Mound) pyramid at Cobá in Quintana Roo province, Mexico. (Corbis)

between Lakes Cobá and Macanxoc was the heart of the city. Group C, about three-quarters of a mile (one and a quarter kilometers) distant, contains the Nohoch Mul (Great Mound) pyramid, which faces a large plaza. This structure, the tallest pre-Columbian building in this region, consists of a base terraced in seven sections, a 35-foot-wide (10-meter-wide) stairway ascending the south side, and a well-preserved temple on the top with roof intact.

This site's well-built raised roads or causeways known as *sacheob* are among its most interesting and distinctive features. Cobá has 45 *sacheob*, a much higher total than any other Maya center. These roads mainly link up ceremonial complexes and important buildings within groupings. The longest is a highway connecting Cobá with the minor site of Yaxuná 62 miles (100 kilometers) distant. This causeway rises to 2 to 8 feet (1.2 to 2.4 meters) above ground when crossing marshy areas and has an average width of 32 feet (9.8 meters). The base is made up of boulders topped with small stones laid in cement. The surface was paved with cement or stucco.

Cobá also figures in the religious lore of the contemporary Yucatec Maya. A famous legend states that bee gods involved in the epic of creation dwell at this site.

After 700 C.E. The city declined toward 900-1000 C.E. and experienced some new construction after 1200 C.E., lasting through most of the Late Postclassic period (1200-1400 C.E.).

ADDITIONAL RESOURCES
Ferguson, William M., and John Q. Royce. *Maya Ruins of Mexico in Color.* Norman: University of Oklahoma Press, 1977.
Folan, William J., et al. *Cobá: A Classic Maya Metropolis.* New York: Academic Press, 1983.
Kelly, Joyce. *An Archaeological Guide to Mexico's Yucatan Peninsula.* Norman: University of Oklahoma Press, 1993.

SEE ALSO: Chichén Itzá; Maya; Tikal.

—*David A. Crain*

COCHISE CULTURE

DATE: 8000-1 B.C.E.
LOCALE: Southern Arizona and New Mexico
RELATED CIVILIZATIONS: Hohokam, Mogollon
SIGNIFICANCE: A gathering culture that lived along the region's scant watercourses and now extinct lakes, the Cochise tradition underlay the Hohokam and Mogollon cultures, which flourished in the first millennium C.E.

Following the basic pattern of Paleo and Archaic peoples in the Southwest, the Cochise (ko-CHEEZ) culture adapted to the demands of the arid southwest by building temporary camps along lakes and streams. The earliest Cochise most likely killed large game such as the mammoth for food, and later peoples relied on vegetation and small animals for sustenance. The Cochise had a sophisticated knowledge of plants for food and medicinal uses, which was passed on to subsequent cultural groups in the Southwest. Because of their reliance on a diet of ground nuts and seeds, the Cochise migrated in the summer and fall to procure these foods.

Archaeologists have divided the Cochise into Sulphur Springs, Chiricahua, and San Pedro periods, named for the archaeological sites where artifacts depicting stages of dietary and technological progress have been found. One example of this development is the specialized milling stones that aided in food preparation, which are associated with the San Pedro period.

The introduction of agriculture, pottery (both introduced from central Mexico), and finally permanent dwellings, in the form of pit houses, altered the Cochise culture, which spawned the cultural flowering of both the Hohokam and the Mogollon peoples.

ADDITIONAL RESOURCES
Dick, Herbert W. *Bat Cave.* Santa Fe, N.Mex.: School of American Research, 1965.
Sayles, E. R. *The Cochise Cultural Sequence in Southeastern Arizona.* Tucson: University of Arizona Press, 1983.

SEE ALSO: Archaic North American culture; Hohokam culture; Mogollon culture.

—*Edward R. Crowther*

COLOSSUS OF RHODES

DATE: constructed 292-280 B.C.E., according to Pliny the Elder

LOCALE: Rhodes city, Island of Rhodes

RELATED CIVILIZATION: Hellenistic Greece

SIGNIFICANCE: This statue was the largest recorded from antiquity and one of the Seven Wonders of the World.

The Colossus (koh-LAW-suhs) was an enormous statue erected by the city of Rhodes to commemorate its successful resistance to Demetrius Poliorcetes' year-long siege of 305-304 B.C.E. The Rhodians financed this statue of their patron deity, the Sun god Helios, from the sale of Poliorcetes' abandoned siege equipment. The appearance of the statue, probably a standing nude male wearing a crown of Sun rays, is known only from ancient sources, mainly Strabo, Pliny the Elder, and Philon of Byzantium. Reportedly, the Rhodian sculptor Chares of Lindos, a pupil of Lysippus, was commissioned to oversee the project. The statue was composed of cast bronze sections over an iron framework and stood some 110 feet (33 meters) tall on a white marble base (compare the Statue of Liberty at 152 feet, or 46 meters). It was steadied by stones placed inside and took twelve years to complete. The Colossus has been popularly depicted from the medieval period onward with its legs spanning the entrance to the Rhodian harbor later known as Mandraki. This reconstruction, however, is not possible, because the distance is more than 1,300 feet (396 meters). The Colossus stood only fifty-six years before it fell, broken at the knees, in an earthquake around 226 B.C.E. The statue lay in ruins until Arabs, invading Rhodes in 654 C.E., sold the remains as scrap metal to a Syrian. Tradition has it that nine hundred camels were needed to transport the fragments.

This engraving depicts the Colossus of Rhodes as it might have appeared. (North Wind Picture Archives)

ADDITIONAL RESOURCES

Clayton, Peter A., and Martin J. Price, eds. Reprint. *The Seven Wonders of the Ancient World.* New York: Routledge, 1998.

Romer, John, and Elizabeth Romer. *The Seven Wonders of the World: A History of the Modern Imagination.* New York: Henry Holt, 1995.

SEE ALSO: Demetrius Poliorcetes; Greece, Hellenistic and Roman; Lysippus; Pliny the Elder; Strabo.

—*Lee Ann Turner*

COLUMBA, SAINT

ALSO KNOWN AS: Columcille
BORN: c. 521 C.E.; Tyrconnell (modern County Donegal, Ireland)
DIED: June 8/9, 597 C.E.; Iona (modern Inner Hebrides, Scotland)
RELATED CIVILIZATIONS: Ireland, Scotland
MAJOR ROLE/POSITION: Religious leader

Life. Saint Columba (koh-LUHM-bah) was educated in the monasteries of Moville, Clonard, and Glasnevin and is credited with the founding of the Irish monasteries of Derry and Durrow. Scholars have been unable to confirm the tradition that a quarrel with Saint Finnian of Moville in 561 C.E. led to Columba's exile after a rebellion against the high king Diarmit and the bloody Battle of Culdrevny, but in 563 C.E., with twelve followers, Columba went to Argyllshire, where Irish invaders from Ulster, "Scots," were maintaining their kingdom of Dalriada with great difficulty against the generally pagan Picts. There on the island of Iona, he founded a monastery from which his followers spread Christianity and the monastic ideal throughout Scotland and northern England.

By ordaining Aidan, king of Dalriada, in 574 C.E. and securing his independence both from the Picts and from the Irish in Ulster, Columba is credited with the establishment of the dynasty that ruled Dalriada and then, for five centuries, all Scotland.

Influence. Columba may be considered the earliest of the founders of the Scottish nation. Because he influenced the establishment of monasteries in Scotland and northern England that spread the monastic ideal to the continent, he must be credited with an inspirational role in the conversion of the peoples of central Europe to Christianity.

ADDITIONAL RESOURCES
Adamnan. *Life of St. Columba*. Translated by Richard Sharpe. New York: Penguin Books, 1995.
Bradley, Ian. *Columba, Pilgrim and Penitent*. Glasgow, Scotland: Wild Goose, 1996.
Simpson, W. Douglas. *The Historical St. Columba*. Edinburgh, Scotland: Oliver and Boyd, 1963.

SEE ALSO: Britain; Ireland; Christianity; Picts.
—*Robert L. Berner*

COLUMELLA

ALSO KNOWN AS: Lucius Junius Moderatus Columella
FLOURISHED: c. 50 C.E.; Gades (later Cádiz, Spain)
RELATED CIVILIZATION: Imperial Rome
MAJOR ROLE/POSITION: Author

Life. Little is known of Columella's (kahl-yuh-MEHL-uh) life except that he was a military tribune with the Sixth Legion, serving probably in Syria. He spent most of his life in Italy, where he intensively farmed four separate tracts of land. His literary endeavors focused on this aspect of his life.

A short work, *De arboribus* (n.d.; on trees, in *Of Husbandry*, 1745), extant in only two books, preceded his major publication, *De agricultura* (also known as *De re rustica*, c. 60-65 C.E.; "on agriculture" in *Of Husbandry*, 1745). This latter work, in twelve books, is the longest and most systematic treatment of Roman agriculture known. His practical experience in Italy, famil-

iarity with agriculture in other parts of the Roman Empire, and extensive knowledge of earlier, particularly Greek, agricultural writers imbue his work with a technical detail far exceeding that of his Roman predecessors. Columella champions the slave-worked, profit-motivated villa operation over all opposing views of farm management. Among the topics he treats are organization of the villa and its workforce, viticulture, animal husbandry, horticulture (written in verse), and duties of the bailiff and his wife.

Influence. Columella's treatise dominated Roman agriculture until superseded by simpler, more practicality-oriented works considered more useful for small farmers of the late empire.

ADDITIONAL RESOURCES
Columella. *De re rustica*. 3 vols. Cambridge, Mass.: Harvard University Press, 1968-1979.

Winterbottom, Michael. "Three Emendations in Columella." *Classical Quarterly* 49, no. 2 (1999): 533-634.

SEE ALSO: Agriculture and animal husbandry; Rome, Imperial.

—Robert I. Curtis

COMMIUS

ALSO KNOWN AS: Comm
FLOURISHED: first century B.C.E.
RELATED CIVILIZATIONS: Republican Rome, England, Gaul
MAJOR ROLE/POSITION: Political/military leader

Life. Commius (KOH-mee-uhs) was a noble of the Atrebates, a Gallic tribe near modem Calais. He allied with Julius Caesar when Caesar invaded Gaul, and in return, was made king of the Atrebates. In 55 B.C.E., when Caesar invaded England, Commius preceded him in an attempt to recruit the Gauls there, but they imprisoned him as soon as he arrived. After Caesar defeated them, they sent Commius to negotiate with him. When Caesar invaded Britain again and defeated Cassivellaunus, Commius was again their negotiator. Commius helped Caesar against the Germans in 53 B.C.E. In return, was made king over the Morini. When Vercingetorix revolted, Commius joined him and was one of the commanders of the force that attempted to relieve Caesar's siege of Alesia. Commius and the Atrebates joined the Gallic revolt in 52 B.C.E.; Commius recruited Germans to the cause. When this revolt was defeated,

Commius fled to Germany. He escaped a Roman assassination attempt with a head wound. After the Atrebates surrendered to Caesar in 51 B.C.E., Commius organized a band of cavalry to raid Roman possessions. Defeated by the Romans, he escaped to Britain, where he finished his life as king of the Atrebates there.

Influence. Commius was an important Gallic noble and served Caesar well for a time. However, after he later opposed Caesar, he was forced to flee his homeland. He appears to have issued some of the first coins in Britain.

ADDITIONAL RESOURCES

Caesar, Julius. *The Gallic War.* Translated by Carolyn Hammond. Oxford, England: Oxford University Press, 1996.

Todd, Malcolm. *Roman Britain.* 3d ed. Oxford, England: Blackwell, 1999.

SEE ALSO: Britain; Caesar, Julius; Cassivellaunus; Gauls; Germany; Rome, Republican; Vercingetorix.

—James O. Smith

CONFUCIANISM

DATE: coined after 479 B.C.E.
LOCALE: China, Mongolia, Korea, Japan, and Vietnam
RELATED CIVILIZATION: China
SIGNIFICANCE: Confucianism (kahn-FEW-shun-ih-zuhm) is the most influential belief system in Asia, reaching more than a quarter of all humankind.

Confucius (551-479 B.C.E.) was a product of the Chinese Warring States period, which despite its social and political upheaval, was one of the most productive periods of Chinese philosophy. Confucius is most accurately described as an itinerant teacher, although he may have held one or more minor political posts. He

sought a role as a government adviser but did not convince the local authorities of his value. Regarding himself as a failure, he returned to his home in what became the province of Shandong and ended his years teaching his disciples. After his death, his disciples began compiling his thought in the *Lunyu* (later sixth-early fifth centuries B.C.E.; *The Analects*, 1861) and amplifying them—and his legend—in a process that may not yet have ended.

Hierarchy and legitimacy. Fundamentally, Confucianism deals with people's social relationships by stressing harmony flowing from five key virtues: benevolence, righteousness, propriety, wisdom, and faithfulness. Confucianism sees the family as a microcosm of the state, in which harmony is based on a hierarchy whose legitimacy is shared by all. If everyone acts according to his or her position in the hierarchy, harmony and peace will exist. This hierarchy rests on several relationships, of which the five most important are emperor-subject, father-son, older brother-younger brother, husband-wife, and friend-friend. Women are subordinate in this hierarchy, but so is everyone else but the emperor. The especially repressive Chinese measures toward women did not develop until footbinding and neo-Confucianism evolved after 1100 C.E. in the Song Dynasty (960-1279). Confucius had relatively little to say about women.

The friend-friend relationship is nominally equal, but even within it, hierarchy based on seniority exists, with the older friend having higher status than the younger. Seniority creates a stable, self-regulating, even backward-looking society. However, society can become so stable as to resist important innovations. In later periods, when contact with the technological West required critical change, China's imperial examinations emphasized the slavish copying of Confucian texts.

That seniority is a basis for hierarchy is no accident, for it is bound up with legitimacy. Confucian legitimacy rests on long-standing historical practice, not reason as in Western philosophy nor revelation as in many religions. Confucius never claimed

This twelfth century drawing depicts Confucius playing the lute. (Library of Congress)

to be a god nor even a prophet. Although his followers and descendants may have erected shrines where they worship in his honor, Confucius made no claim of divinity nor of contact with divinity. Confucius rejected even the common Chinese practices of divination and superstition, finding them beneath the dignity of the educated person. Confucianism, the least religious of all great religions, is unclear about an afterlife or the existence of a supreme being beyond a vague sense of "heaven." This lack of a clear divinity left a void that

Daoism and later Buddhism attempted to fill. Neo-Confucianism ultimately resulted in a syncretic religious practice combining Confucianism, Daoism, and Buddhism.

Confucius also rejected the practice common to Western philosophy of relying on reason, or at least abstract reasoning, to legitimize what he espoused. The reasoning of any one person might fail, but the collective reason of generations of people was unlikely to do so—the thought underlying the Confucian aphorism about "transmitting but not creating." This historical legitimacy helps explain the concern for ancestors and the reverence for the elderly, who are those most likely to next become ancestors. The elderly may be weak physically, but they are at their peak of wisdom.

Good government. The reverence for the old helps explain a worldview different from that of the West. In religious terms, Christianity contains a millenarian streak with the expectation of decline in society that ultimately brings on the second coming of Christ. For secular Westerners who do not follow such a devout Christian view, there is the contrary belief in the ever-improving onward march of history. Neither view is Confucian. Instead, Confucius posits an idealized high standard that he says was reached in China's ancient Shang Dynasty (1600-1066 B.C.E.) or at the founding of the subsequent Zhou Dynasty (1066-256 B.C.E.). The change from the Shang to the Zhou Dynasty was the first of the famous dynastic cycles—the rise, maturation, and fall of a dynasty, leading to a new dynasty that subsequently rose, matured, and fell. Thinking of history in terms of dynastic cycles is an important corrective to the Western view of history as an upward march of progress. It favors the status quo, which sustained China until the Western intrusion in the nineteenth century.

For Confucius, to govern well was to return to that great and glorious past. Yet Confucius was not a blind antiquarian and may be thought of as a closet reformer. His view of China's past is selective and idealized. The Shang believed in sacrifice of humans for entombment with a departed king or lord, and the Zhou humanely substituted clay models and replicas: Confucius rejected both.

There is more than a little subtlety in Confucius's concern with rectification, or finding the proper names for things. Rectifying the title of the emperor means the emperor must be a good emperor—a good person, a gentleman, an exemplar for the people—or the emperor is not really an emperor at all. A century later, Mencius (c. 372-c. 289 B.C.E.), one of Confucius's followers, pushed the argument further, refining the notion of the mandate of heaven—a concept first appearing to justify the overthrow of the Shang Dynasty by the Zhou—into a clearer standard for evaluating emperors. If the emperor did not behave properly, so that the title did not suit him well, heaven might withdraw its mandate. From this, it is just a short step to giving the people the right to rebel. Such a concept is difficult to institutionalize or put into operation, and this cannot be said to have evolved under either Confucius or Mencius.

Confucianism is hierarchical and monarchial. The ideal is to have a great emperor. The emperor, however, is not a tyrant oblivious to the welfare of the people; indeed, should he become such, he risks losing the mandate of heaven. The emperor's goal should be just and proper government. Rule should not be by brute force but by moral example. If the emperor ceases to serve the people and loses the mandate of heaven, this loss may give the people the right to rebel. This clearly shows a fundamental respect for the ordinary citizen in Confucianism, although it does not make Confucius a "democrat" as some have implied. The Confucian goal is to replace the bad emperor with the good, but to have an emperor nonetheless.

Confucius was unclear as to whether people's basic nature was good or bad, and his followers were divided on the question. Mencius thought people were basically good, and Xunzi (c. 298-c. 230 B.C.E.), living in darker times, thought them inherently evil. Confucius turned the concept of *ren* (human kindness or benevolence) into a reciprocal value with this precept: "Do not do unto others what you would not want them to do unto you."

Needing a mandate of heaven creates a certain moralism in politics. Because there is only one emperor, there is only one right view. Dissent is not tolerated. A person occupying the throne can be wrong but only because he is no longer—under Confucian terminology—a real emperor. Such a person is morally wrong, will lose the throne, and will be replaced by a new emperor. This gives a moral cast to politics and removes the option of dissent and debate. These options are wrong in any case because they disrupt the unity and harmony of China. Dissent based on the possibility of more than one right answer also implies equality, which cannot be accepted in such a hierarchical scheme.

Influence of Confucianism. Confucianism became the state-sanctioned belief system in the Han Dynasty (206 B.C.E. to 220 C.E.). It also became the basis for Chinese culture and was used to civilize its neighbors. Gradually the Han incorporated larger and larger areas, spreading Confucianism to the Chinese-dominated societies of Vietnam and Korea. From Korea, where it was adopted through conquer and assimilation, Confucianism spread to Japan. In Japan, it was adopted by choice, initiating the long-enduring Japanese practice of borrowing from China in language, art, architecture, and government. Because Korea had Confucianism imposed on it, the Koreans do not feel the special sense of ownership that the Chinese do, and they depart from its requirements as they see fit. The Japanese feel even less sense of ownership but do not react against Confucianism because it was never imposed on them.

Neither the Japanese nor Koreans have felt the need to have an officialdom based on pure meritocracy as have the Chinese. Confucius invented the notion that those who govern should do so because of merit and not inherited status, setting in motion the creation of the imperial examinations and bureaucracies open only to those who passed these tests. In China, the test taking was open to anyone. In Korea and Japan, only the hereditary nobility were allowed to take the tests that enabled them to become governmental officials.

ADDITIONAL RESOURCES
Fisher, Mary, and Robert Luyster. *Living Religions*. Englewood Cliffs, N.J.: Prentice Hall, 1991.

Heinz, Carolyn Brown. *Asian Cultural Traditions*. Prospect Heights, Ill.: Waveland, 2000.

Mackerras, Colin, ed. *East and Southeast Asia: A Multidisciplinary Survey*. Boulder, Colo.: Lynne Rienner, 1995.

Murphey, Rhoads. *A History of Asia*. New York: Longman, 2000.

Pye, Lucian. *China: An Introduction*. Boston: Little, Brown, 1991.

Soled, Debra E. *China: A Nation in Transition*. Washington, D.C.: Congressional Quarterly Press, 1995.

SEE ALSO: Buddhism; China; Confucius; Daoism; Han Dynasty; Japan; Korea; Mencius; Xunzi.

—*Richard L. Wilson*

CONFUCIUS

ALSO KNOWN AS: Kong Qiu (*Wade-Giles* K'ung Ch'iu); Kongfuzi (*Wade-Giles* K'ung-Fu-Tzu); Kongzi (*Wade-Giles* K'ung-Tzu)
BORN: 551 B.C.E.; Qufu, state of Lu, China
DIED: 479 B.C.E.; Qufu, state of Lu, China
RELATED CIVILIZATIONS: China, East Asia
MAJOR ROLE/POSITION: Private teacher

Life. Confucius (kahn-FEW-shus) was born to a poor family. He was active during the Spring and Autumn (770-476 B.C.E.) and Warring States (475-221 B.C.E.) periods, when China was divided into numerous states and its society was experiencing chaos as traditional rules were being broken. Confucius took restoring order to society as his mission. At one time, he was minister of law (*Si-Ku*) in the state of Lu. He later quit because he saw no hope of realizing his political ambition based on his philosophy. He was a successful teacher, once claiming a following of seventy-two disciples and three thousand students. With his students, he traveled from state to state to look for a ruler who was willing to adopt his political philosophy; he died without realizing his dream.

Confucius's philosophy centers on the concept of *ren*, which has been rendered in English as humanity, benevolence, goodness, kindness, virtue, and love, and essentially involves good human relationships. He advocated that people should foster positive relationships in which they loved and cared about one another. This type of relationship was first of all to be manifested in family relations among parents and children, siblings, and husband and wife; it was also to be manifested in relationships among good friends and among superiors and their subordinates.

When Confucius was asked what he would do first if he were given power to rule a kingdom, he said he would first rectify names by making sure that names and actualities correspond, namely making sure that the father acts like a father, the son like a son, the ruler like a ruler, and a minister like a minister. In achieving this goal, Confucius believed that it was crucial that everyone follow *li*, appropriate behavior guidelines that were usually crystallized in everyday rituals. He also believed in the notion of *xiao* (filial piety); children must obey and revere their parents. Another notion important to Confucius was *yi*, righteousness, which meant that one must do what was right rather than what was profitable. In his political philosophy, he believed that the government should rule by moral virtue instead of by punishment.

Influence. Confucius's influence cannot be overestimated. After his death, his philosophy was promoted by many later rulers as the official ideology of China under the name of Confucianism. His sayings were recorded by his students in a collection called the *Lunyu* (later sixth-early fifth centuries B.C.E.; *The Analects*, 1861). It was the primary text in Chinese schools for more than two thousand years. From the eleventh century to 1911, knowledge in Confucian teachings was the primary criterion for qualification for civil service. Confucius's influence extended beyond Chinese borders to such countries as Korea and Japan. Confucianism remains one of the major living world traditions.

ADDITIONAL RESOURCES
Brooks, E. Bruce, and A. Taeko Brooks. *The Original Analects*. New York: Columbia University Press, 1998.
Confucius. *The Analects*. Translated with an introduction by D. C. Lau. New York: Penguin Books, 1979.
Fingarette, Herbert. *Confucius: The Secular as Sacred.* Prospect Heights, Ill.: Waveland Press, 1998.
Fung, Yu-lan. "Confucius, the First Teacher." In *A Short History of Chinese Philosophy*. New York: The Free Press, 1948.

SEE ALSO: China; *Chunqiu*; Confucianism; Han Dynasty; Japan; Korea.

—*Chenyang Li*

CONSTANS I

ALSO KNOWN AS: Flavius Julius Constans
BORN: c. 323 C.E.; place unknown
DIED: 350 C.E.; Gaul
RELATED CIVILIZATION: Imperial Rome
MAJOR ROLE/POSITION: Emperor of the West

Life. The youngest son of the emperor Constantine the Great and Fausta, Constans I (KAHN-stanz) was proclaimed Caesar in 333 C.E. Upon his father's death in 337 C.E., he became Augustus together with his two older brothers, Constantius II and Constantine II. The three split responsibilities for the empire, with Constans receiving Italy, Africa, and Illyricum (under Constantine II's supervision). When Constantine II invaded Italy in 340 C.E., he was defeated and killed by Constans, who then took over all the Western Empire. During the next decade, he campaigned on the Rhine, visited Britain (the last Roman emperor to do so), and threatened Constantius II with war if he would not allow Saint Athanasius to return from exile to Alexandria. (Constans was a baptized Christian and, unlike his brother, orthodox, that is, in compliance with the Council of Nicaea.) Internal dissatisfaction led to a rebellion in Gaul under the general Magnentius. Constans was killed, leaving Constantius II the only legitimate ruler of the Roman Empire.

Influence. Constans's death left an opening that, after the defeat and death of Magnentius in 353 C.E., was filled by Constantius II. In his effort to unify the empire religiously, Constantius was now free to impose his Arianizing policy as he saw fit, leading to a flurry of ecclesiastical councils in the 350's C.E. and the intensification of the Arian controversy.

ADDITIONAL RESOURCE
Barnes, Timothy D. *Athanasius and Constantius: Theology and Politics in the Constantinian Empire*. Cambridge, Mass.: Harvard University Press, 1993.

SEE ALSO: Arianism; Athanasius of Alexandria, Saint; Britain; Christianity; Constantine the Great; Constantius I-III; Gauls; Nicaea, Council of; Rome, Imperial.

—*Mark Gustafson*

CONSTANTINE THE GREAT

ALSO KNOWN AS: Flavius Valerius Constantinus
BORN: February 17 or 27, c. 272-285 C.E.; Naissus, Moesia (later Nis, Serbia)
DIED: May 22, 337 C.E.; Nicomedia, Bithynia (later İzmit, Turkey)
RELATED CIVILIZATION: Imperial Rome
MAJOR ROLE/POSITION: Roman emperor

Life. Son of the emperor Constantius I and Helena, Constantine (KAHN-stan-teen) the Great spent his youth in Diocletian's court in Nicomedia and showed great promise as a military leader. Upon Constantius's death at York in 306 C.E., Constantine laid claim to his father's portion of the Roman Empire, although he was not officially recognized as a senior Augustus until 312

C.E. During that year, Constantine defeated the usurper Maxentius at the Battle of Milvian Bridge and won control over Italy. Constantine attributed his victory during this campaign to the aid of the Christian god, which led to the emperor's conversion. Constantine finally united all of Rome by defeating his last rival, Valerius Licinianus Licinius, in 324 C.E. As emperor, he relocated the imperial capital from Rome to the city of Byzantium, renaming it Constantinople in 330 C.E. For the next seven years, Constantine continued his patronage of Christianity and shortly before his death in 337 C.E. received baptism from Eusebius, the bishop of Caesarea.

Influence. Through Constantine's patronage, Christianity became an officially recognized religion of the Roman Empire and prospered as it never had before. To Constantine's credit, he managed to strike a difficult balance ruling a religiously divided empire inhabited by both Christians and pagans.

ADDITIONAL RESOURCES

Barnes, Timothy D. *Constantine and Eusebius*. Cambridge, Mass.: Harvard University Press, 1981.

Drake, H. A. *Constantine and the Bishops*. Baltimore: Johns Hopkins University Press, 2000.

SEE ALSO: Christianity; Constantinople; Constantius I-III; Diocletian; Eusebius of Caesarea; Licinius, Valerius Licinianus; Maxentius; Milvian Bridge, Battle of; Rome, Imperial.

—*Byron J. Nakamura*

Constantine the Great. (Hulton Archive)

CONSTANTINOPLE

DATE: April 2, 330-May 29, 1453 C.E.
LOCALE: Southern end of the Bosphorus, in western Turkey, with the main city on the European side of the Strait and suburbs on the Asian side
RELATED CIVILIZATIONS: Imperial Rome, Byzantine Empire
SIGNIFICANCE: Capital city founded by Constantine the Great, capital of the Eastern Roman Empire until its fall to the Ottoman Turks in 1453.

When Constantine the Great became sole ruler of the Roman Empire in 324 C.E., he recognized the importance of the resources of Asia Minor to the survival of the empire. To take advantage of these resources and to respond more quickly to the Germanic tribes threatening the Balkans, Constantine founded a new capital city named Constantinople (kahn-stan-tih-NOH-pul), or "the city of Constantine." This city took advantage of an easily defended peninsula bordered on the north by an estuary and natural harbor known as the Golden Horn and on the south by the Sea of Marmara. The site had previously been occupied by the city of Byzantium, founded as a Greek colony in the seventh century B.C.E.

Constantine enlarged the city to take in four hills instead of the single one that had been part of Byzantium. Within a century, the city limits would be expanded again, and the city within the walls during the reign of Theodosius II (r. 408-450 C.E.) included seven hills, just as had the old capital of Rome. On the First Hill, the one farthest from the city walls, Constantine built his palace and the church known as the "Old Church" (now Haghia Eirene, rebuilt in the reign of Justinian I). His son Constantius II (r. 337-361 C.E.) built the original "Great Church" (Haghia Sophia). Constantine rebuilt the Hippodrome to be the size of the Circus Maximus in Rome and arranged the city's major monuments along a wide avenue ("Mese," or "Center Street"). This avenue ran from the Hippodrome, to the Forum of Constantine, past the later forum of Theodosius, where it split, the northern branch passing the Church of the Holy Apostles, where Constantine and his successors were buried, and the southern branch connecting to the Golden Gate in the Theodosian Walls, where the emperor ceremonially entered the city.

After Constantine and Theodosius II, the emperor whose reign had the greatest impact on the shape of the city was Justinian I (r. 527-565 C.E.). In 532 C.E., a series of riots destroyed large parts of the city and Justinian rebuilt the Church of the Holy Apostles as well as Haghia Eirene and its neighbor, commissioning the city's most famous Byzantine monument, the church of Haghia Sophia.

The seventh century C.E. saw attacks on the Byzantine Empire that reached the Theodosian Walls of Constantinople but were repulsed with the help of the miraculous appearance of the Virgin, according to the Greek defenders of the city. Constantinople remained the capital of the Eastern Roman Empire, protected by the strong Theodosian land walls and sea walls along the two shores, until the walls were breached by a Muslim army in 1453, when the name of the city was changed to Istanbul and it became the capital of the Ottoman Empire.

ADDITIONAL RESOURCES

Freely, John. *Istanbul: The Imperial City.* New York: Penguin Books, 1996.

Mathews, Thomas F. *Byzantium: From Antiquity to the Renaissance.* Upper Saddle River, N.J.: Prentice Hall, 1998.

SEE ALSO: Byzantine Empire; Christianity; Constantine the Great; Constantius I-II; Haghia Sophia; Islam; Justinian I; Rome, Imperial; Theodosius II.

—*Sara E. Orel*

CONSTANTIUS I-III

DATE: c. 250-421 C.E.
RELATED CIVILIZATION: Imperial Rome
MAJOR ROLE/POSITION: Roman emperors

Life. Of Illyrian origin, Constantius I (kahn-STAN-chee-uhs) was a general and the governor of Dalmatia when Diocletian became emperor. In 293 C.E., as part of the new tetrarchy, Constantius I was appointed Caesar for the Western Empire. Based in Gaul, in 296 C.E., he defeated Allectus, the usurper in Britain, and ended the usurper Carausius's control of the English Channel. His part in the Great Persecution of Christians apparently consisted only of destruction of church buildings. In 305 C.E., upon the abdication of Diocletian and Maximian, Constantius I became Augustus of the West. He died in 306 C.E. in York, and his troops proclaimed his son Constantine as Augustus. He was a competent leader, whose Christianity and relation to the previous emperor Claudius II were fictions created by Constantinian panegyrists. His nickname "Chlorus" was assigned even later.

Constantius II (also known as Flavius Julius Constantius) was born in 317 C.E., the son of Constantine the Great and Fausta (and grandson of Constantius I). He was made Caesar in 324 C.E. In 337 C.E., upon the death of Constantine the Great, Constantius became Augustus (along with his brothers Constantine II and Constans I). His domain was the Eastern Empire, where he spent much of the 340's C.E. warring with the Persians on the eastern frontier. In 351 C.E., he came west to defeat the usurper Magnentius at Mursa, becoming sole emperor in 353 C.E. (Constantine II having died in 340 C.E. and Constans I in 350 C.E.). He oversaw military affairs in the West for several years, celebrating a triumph in Rome in 357 C.E. He then returned to campaigning in the East. Julian the Apostate, who had been appointed Caesar in Gaul in 355 C.E., was proclaimed Augustus by his troops in 360 C.E. Constantius was on his way to confront Julian in 361 C.E. when he died in Cilicia. Although an effective ruler over a long period of time, his military and political difficulties were compounded by ecclesiastical conflict. As sole emperor, Constantius attempted to impose doctrinal uniformity on the church by means of an Arianizing formulation. A small but vehement and growing episcopal group opposed his efforts, and his religious policy died with him.

Constantius III, after the demise of Flavius Stilicho in 408 C.E., was the next dominant power at the court of Honorius, the ineffectual emperor of the West. As *magister militum* (master of the soldiers), he quashed the usurpation of Constantine III, recovered Honorius's sister Galla Placidia from the Visigothic king Ataulphus (to whom she had been married), married her himself in 417 C.E., and settled the Visigoths in Aquitania on Roman territory in 418 C.E. In 419 C.E. his son Valentinian III, the future emperor, was born. In 421 C.E., Honorius made Constantius III his fellow Augustus. He died seven months later.

Influence. Of these three, the most important was undoubtedly Constantius II, who skillfully worked within the structure left by Constantine and whose antipagan efforts set the stage for Julian's pagan revival.

ADDITIONAL RESOURCES

Barnes, Timothy D. *Athanasius and Constantius: Theology and Politics in the Constantinian Empire.* Cambridge, Mass.: Harvard University Press, 1993.

_____. *Constantine and Eusebius.* Cambridge, Mass.: Harvard University Press, 1981.

SEE ALSO: Arianism; Britain; Christianity; Constans I; Constantine the Great; Diocletian; Gauls; Goths, Ostrogoths, Visigoths; Julian the Apostate; Maximian; Stilicho, Flavius; Valentinian III.

—*Mark Gustafson*

COPÁN

DATE: 200-900 C.E.
LOCALE: Western Honduras near the Guatemalan border
RELATED CIVILIZATION: Maya
SIGNIFICANCE: Copán served as a regional center of Maya civilization.

Copán (koh-PAHN), the greatest city of the southeastern Mesoamerica, developed as a small regional center with subordinate cities around it. The Copán Valley reached its peak population of about twenty-five thousand people in the eighth century C.E. Copán had ready access to the great cities lying north and east but was not subordinate to the larger cities of Tikal and Palenque.

The earliest settlement, dating back to 1400 B.C.E., was influenced by cultures from Honduras and Central America, but between 900 and 300 B.C.E., Olmec influence from Mexico can be seen. During the Classic stage beginning in 400 C.E., Maya influence dominated. Hieroglyphic writings and monumental architecture were introduced. For four centuries, Copán grew and controlled a large area.

At the end of the Postclassic stage (800-1000 C.E.), the Copán Valley experienced unprecedented growth that caused environmental deterioration. Malnutrition and diseases reduced the population. The government collapsed. The population decline continued until the remaining few drifted away, and the forest reclaimed the valley.

ADDITIONAL RESOURCES

Fash, William L. *Scribes, Warriors, and Kings: The City of Copán and the Ancient Maya.* New York: Thames and Hudson, 1991.

Henderson, John S. *The World of the Ancient Maya.* 2d ed. Ithaca, N.Y.: Cornell University Press, 1997.

Schmidt, Peter, Mercedes de la Garza, and Enrique Nalda, eds. *Maya.* New York: Rizzoli International, 1998.

SEE ALSO: Maya; Olmecs; Palenque; Tikal.

—*Robert D. Talbott*

COPPER BELT

DATE: first millennium B.C.E.
LOCALE: Central Africa, Kitwe, Zambia to Shaba, Democratic Republic of Congo
RELATED CIVILIZATIONS: Chondwe, Kisalian, Kabambian
SIGNIFICANCE: The Central African Copper Belt is the largest and richest region of copper ores in Africa. Copper is an item of prestige, symbolic of ritual and political power.

Soils of the Copper Belt of Zambia attest both oxide and sulfide copper ores. Copper working in the Copper Belt was initiated in the early Iron Age and reached its height in the later Iron Age. Based on the archaeological evidence, the smelting of copper in the Copper Belt coincided with early iron smelting in furnaces and firing of pottery in kilns. The heart of the Copper Belt lies in northern Zambia and extends north into Lubumbashi, Shaba, Democratic Republic of the Congo. Firing of pots on soils containing copper ore may have initiated the earliest copper smelting in the early Iron Age. Oxide ores and furnaces have been dated to as early as 900 B.C.E.

Archaeologists have uncovered ceramics with early Iron Age motifs at Kansanshi, an early copper-smelting site from the fourth century C.E. At Kipushi on the border between Zambia and the Democratic Republic of the Congo, copper slag from the later Iron Age has been dated to the ninth through twelfth centuries C.E. In Kaonde, Zambia, copper was being smelted from 1500 C.E. Many early copper smelting sites may have been destroyed because of twentieth century copper mining in the region.

Chondwe pottery dated from the sixth to the eleventh centuries C.E. is found in village sites along rivers and streams in the Copper Belt. The pottery is characterized by thick rims decorated with lines of alternate-facing triangular impressions forming a chevron in false relief. These sites also attest evidence of iron and copper working.

By the later first millennium C.E., copper was becoming standardized and bars of copper were traded in the Copper Belt. By the early second millennium C.E., copper was molded in the shape of small crosses and was used as a currency of exchange carrying a standard value.

The evidence in oral traditions reveals that the Yeke people of Kolwezi in the northern Copper Belt were master smelters beginning in 1500 C.E. Yeke men and women excavated deep shafts up to about 100 feet (30 meters) long and placed support beams to hold up these tunnels. Yeke copper production is associated with the collection of the stone carbonate of copper, malachite. The technological sophistication of copper excavation and production among the Yeke attests to the importance of copper as an item of value in Copper Belt societies and economies.

ADDITIONAL RESOURCES
Connah, Graham. *African Civilizations: Precolonial Cities and States in Tropical Africa, an Archaeological Perspective.* Reprint. Cambridge, England: Cambridge University Press, 1995.
Hall, M. *Archaeology Africa.* London, England: James Currey, 1996.
Herbert, Eugenia W. *Red Gold of Africa: Copper in Precolonial History and Culture.* Madison: University of Wisconsin Press, 1984.
Phillipson, David W. *African Archaeology.* Cambridge, England: Cambridge University Press, 1993.

SEE ALSO: Africa, East and South; Africa, West.
—*Catherine Cymone Fourshey*

CORBULO, GNAEUS DOMITIUS

BORN: c. 6 C.E.; probably Rome
DIED: 67 C.E.; Greece
RELATED CIVILIZATION: Imperial Rome
MAJOR ROLE/POSITION: Military leader

Life. From a distinguished family (his father was a consul under Caligula, and his stepsister was one of that emperor's wives), Gnaeus Domitius Corbulo (NEE-uhs doh-MIHSH-ee-uhs KAWR-byuh-loh) became a consul in 39 C.E. As governor of Lower Germany (modern Netherlands) in 47 C.E., he defeated an invasion of the Chauci, a German tribe. Forbidden by Claudius to strike back into enemy territory, Corbulo famously complained, "Happy were the Roman generals before me!" Claudius did make him governor of the important province of Asia (later western Turkey). In 54 C.E., Nero appointed him governor of Cappadocia and Galatia (central Turkey) and commander in chief in a war against Parthia. Between 58 and 63 C.E., Corbulo captured Artaxata and Tigranocerta, installed a client king over Armenia, and concluded a favorable peace with the Parthians, placing a pro-Roman candidate on their throne. Sometime during the war, he was made governor of Syria and given overall authority (*imperium maius*) in the Eastern provinces. His military success and noble descent made him a potential threat to the emperor Nero, and in October of 67 C.E., Corbulo was forced to commit suicide.

Influence. Later Romans considered Corbulo a model general. Corbulo wrote an account of his wars, which was used by the historian Tacitus and others.

ADDITIONAL RESOURCES

Griffin, Miriam T., et al. "Domitius Corbulo, Gnaeus." In *The Oxford Classical Dictionary*, edited by Simon Hornblower and Antony Spawforth. 3d ed. Oxford, England: Oxford University Press, 1996.
Schoonover, Draper Tolman. *A Study of Gn. Domitius Corbulo as Found in the "Annals" of Tacitus*. Chicago: University of Chicago Press, 1909.
Wheeler, Everett. "The Chronology of Corbulo in Armenia." *Klio* 79, no. 2 (1997): 383-397.

SEE ALSO: Caligula; Claudius; Nero; Parthia; Rome, Imperial; Tacitus.

—*Jonathan P. Roth*

CORINTHIAN WAR

DATE: 395-386 B.C.E.
LOCALE: Greece
RELATED CIVILIZATIONS: Classical Greece, Persia
SIGNIFICANCE: Unable to achieve victory on their own, the Spartans invited the Persians to intervene.

Background. Both the Persians and Sparta's erstwhile allies became alarmed by the success of the Spartan expedition in Asia Minor led by Agesilaus II of Sparta.

Action. In 395 B.C.E., the Persians bribed politicians in Argos, Corinth, Thebes, and possibly Athens to instigate a war against Sparta, and an anti-Sparta coalition was formed. After the Spartan defeat at the Battle of Haliartus in Boeotia in 395 B.C.E., Agesilaus II was recalled from Asia Minor. In 394 B.C.E., the Spartans won two land battles, but these victories were negated by the defeat at sea to the renegade Athenian general Conon, in command of the Persian fleet, which put an end to Spartan domination of the sea. Desultory fighting around Corinth ensued. In 392 B.C.E., the Spartans, worried about increasing Athenian naval activity, at-

tempted unsuccessfully to make separate peace agreements with Persia and within Greece. Eventually the threat of renewed Athenian imperialism caused the Persians to intervene in support of Sparta and impose the King's Peace (also known as the Peace of Antalcidas) of 386 B.C.E.

Consequences. The King's Peace thwarted the imperial ambitions of Athens, Argos, and Thebes and confirmed Sparta's hegemony of Greece.

ADDITIONAL RESOURCES

Hamilton, Charles D. *Sparta's Bitter Victories*. Ithaca, N.Y.: Cornell University Press, 1979.
Strauss, Barry S. *Athens After the Peloponnesian War*. Ithaca, N.Y.: Cornell University Press, 1986.
Xenophon. *Hellenika*. Translated by Peter Kretz. Warminister, England: Aris & Philips, 1995.

SEE ALSO: Agesilaus II of Sparta; Greece, Classical; King's Peace; Persia.

—*Frances Skoczylas Pownall*